PRAISE FOR TRANSITIONS, 3/E

"*Transitions* is a great text."

Susan Todd, Jefferson College

"The readings are terrific."

Marti Singer, Georgia State University

"The first two chapters of *Transitions* not only provide valuable pedagogical support to instructors, but also singularly sold me on the textbook itself.[...] The new material on critical thinking and argument is excellent."

Rebecca S. Casey, Kennesaw State University

"Clearly, the strength of *Transitions* is the thoughtful apparatus. These suggestions and questions delve into controversial and complex issues, leading students into the most salient issues of our modern world."

Cheryl Battles, Butte Community College

"My overall impression of *Transitions* is that it is *read and studied* by the students. They are eager to discuss the essays, and in the process, learn from each other."

Mary T. Wilson, Angelina College

"The strengths of the text are what they have always been: good, interesting readings; good discussion and writing topics; and the clearest approach to teaching critical reading as part of the writing process that I've found."

Jane M. Kinney, Valdosta State University

"Many of the choices [of reading selections] are outstanding."

Elaine Sherr, Cuesta College

"One of the definite strengths of this edition is the variety and quality of the essays and articles."

Angela Morales, Merced College

"The strengths of this text [are its] high-interest, literate readings; great organization by theme; and fine writing assignments."

Michael Goodman, Golden West College

TRANSITIONS

From Reading to Writing

TRANSITIONS

From Reading to Writing

Third Edition

Barbara Fine Clouse

McGraw-Hill

Boston   Burr Ridge, IL   Dubuque, IA   Madison, WI   New York
San Francisco   St. Louis   Bangkok   Bogotá   Caracas   Kuala Lumpur
Lisbon   London   Madrid   Mexico City   Milan   Montreal   New Delhi
Santiago   Seoul   Singapore   Sydney   Taipei   Toronto

McGraw-Hill Higher Education

*A Division of The **McGraw-Hill** Companies*

TRANSITIONS: FROM READING TO WRITING

Published by McGraw-Hill Companies, Inc. 1221 Avenue of the Americas, New York, NY, 10020. Copyright © 2002, 1998, 1994 by The McGraw-Hill Companies, Inc. All rights reserved. No part of this publication may be reproduced or distributed in any form or by any means, or stored in a database or retrieval system, without the prior written consent of The McGraw-Hill Companies, Inc., including but not limited to, in any network or other electronic storage or transmission, or broadcast for distance learning. Some ancillaries, including electronic and print components, may not be available to customers outside the United States.

This book is printed on acid-free paper.

2 3 4 5 6 7 8 9 0 DOC/DOC 0 9 8 7 6 5 4 3 2

ISBN 0-07-240521-X

Editorial director: *Phillip A. Butcher*
Executive editor: *Sarah Touborg*
Developmental editor II: *Alexis Walker*
Senior marketing manager: *David S. Patterson*
Senior project manager: *Christine A. Vaughan*
Production supervisor: *Rose Hepburn*
Media producer: *Gregg Di Lorenzo*
Freelance design coordinator: *Artemio Ortiz, Jr.*
Photo research coordinator: *Jeremy Cheshareck*
Supplement producer: *Susan Lombardi*
Cover design: *Trudi Gershenov*
Interior design: *Artemio Ortiz Jr.*
Printer: *R. R. Donnelley & Sons Company*
Typeface: *10/12 Sabon*
Compositor: *GAC Indianapolis*

Library of Congress Cataloging-in-Publication Data

Clouse, Barbara Fine.
   Transitions: from reading to writing / Barbara Fine Clouse.—3rd ed.
    p. cm.
   Includes index.
   ISBN 0-07-240521-X (acid-free paper)
   1. College readers. 2. English language—Rhetoric—Problems, exercises, etc. 3. English language—Grammar—Problems, exercises, etc. 4. Report writing–Problems, exercises, etc. I. Title
PE1417.C6315   2002
808'.0427—dc21   2001034265

www.mhhe.com

ABOUT THE AUTHOR

Barbara Clouse is a seasoned writing instructor who has taught all levels of college composition, first at Youngstown State University in northeastern Ohio and then at Slippery Rock University in western Pennsylvania. She has written a number of composition texts for McGraw-Hill including: *The Student Writer: Editor and Critic; Patterns for a Purpose: A Rhetorical Reader; Jumpstart: A Workbook for Writers;* and *Working It Out: A Troubleshooting Guide for Writers.* In addition, she has developed *Cornerstones II: Readings for Writers,* which is a short prose developmental reader that is part of Primis Online, McGraw-Hill's electronic database that allows instructors to build their own textbooks. Barbara's publications also include *Progressions with Readings* and *Conventions and Expectations: A Brief Handbook and Guide to Writing* for Longman. Barbara is a frequent presenter at national and regional conferences, and she often conducts workshops for writing teachers.

McGraw-Hill Titles by Barbara Clouse

Jumpstart! A Workbook for Writers, Second Edition
ISBN: 0-07-230074-4 (2002)

Jumpstart! With Readings: A Workbook for Writers, First Edition
ISBN: 0-07-241470-7 (2002)

Transitions: From Reading to Writing, Third Edition
ISBN: 0-07-240521-X (2002)

Working It Out: A Troubleshooting Guide for Writers, Third Edition
ISBN: 0-07-236748-2 (2001)

The Student Writer: Editor and Critic, Fifth Edition
ISBN: 0-07-043486-7 (2000)

Patterns for a Purpose: A Rhetorical Reader, Second Edition
ISBN: 0-07-011980-5 (1999)

Cornerstones II: Readings for Writers
Build your own text with McGraw-Hill Primis Online!
(www.mhhe.com/primis)

In Loving Memory of Faye Thomas Clouse

CONTENTS

PART 2

Lives In Transition

CHAPTER 3

The Stages of Life: How Do We Grow and Change? 55

CHAPTER 4

Family Ties: What Does Family Mean?

*New to this edition.

PART 4

Culture in Transition

CHAPTER 7

Gender Issues: What Does it Mean to be Male or Female?

PART 6
Viewpoints in Transition: Responding to Multiple Essays

CHAPTER 11

CHAPTER 12

RHETORICAL CONTENTS

PREFACE

In its third edition, *Transitions: From Reading to Writing* retains its emphasis on the connection between reading and writing with

- 61 high-interest readings that are accessible yet substantial
- an unusually generous number of varied writing activities to inspire many kinds of private and public writing—including writing that moves students beyond the writing classroom
- activities that require writing in response to both single and multiple readings

⇒ SUPPORTIVE APPARATUS

The success of previous editions is owed, in part, to the unusually rich and varied apparatus in *Transitions*, apparatus that supports a broad range of students and provides flexibility for instructors.

- Chapters 1 and 2 provide important underpinnings by explaining
  — reading and writing processes
  — essay structure
  — ways to write in response to reading (including journaling, summarizing, sharing a response, and arguing a position)
  — critical thinking strategies
  — how to read textbooks
- Prereading material includes headnote information on the author, a preview of the selection, and a prereading activity.
- Potentially unfamiliar vocabulary and allusions are glossed.

- Three sets of questions follow the readings in Chapters 3–10: one set to check comprehension, one to highlight rhetorical features, and one to provide critical thinking opportunities.
- A writing workshop and writing workshop activity follow each reading in Chapters 3–10 to highlight a rhetorical, stylistic, grammar, or usage point apparent in the reading. These teach "incidentally," by noting features as they occur in the selections and helping students incorporate them into their own writing.

⇒ SUPPORT FOR MULTILINGUAL STUDENTS

Each reading in Chapters 3–10 is followed by a section headed "Language Notes for Multilingual and Other Writers." These sections explain one or more idioms or grammar and usage points apparent in the reading. The emphasis is on providing support for nonnative users of English, but as the heading notes, many native speakers will benefit from this material.

⇒ WRITING ACTIVITIES

Transitions includes an unusually generous number and variety of writing opportunities.

- Each reading is followed by
  — a journal writing assignment
  — a collaborative writing assignment
  — several traditional essay assignments
  — one assignment that requires students to go beyond the writing class, either to gather information or write for a special audience outside the classroom
- Parts 2–5 close with assignments requiring response to multiple selections
- Part 6, which offers two sets of three readings on each of two narrowly focused themes, includes several assignments requiring responses to multiple selections.
- The writing tasks include a mix of experiential and analytic topics for a range of purposes.

⇒ NEW TO THE THIRD EDITION

In response to users and reviewers of previous editions, the following changes were made to update and improve the text:

- Twenty-eight new readings freshen the text and make it more topical. These readings are longer and more challenging than the ones they replace.
- The readings are now organized into thematic units, with two chapters per unit.
- Chapters of timely readings on technology, bioengineered food, and stem cell research have been added.
- Each of the last two chapters now includes three readings on a current controversy. These selections provide additional opportunities for responding to multiple readings, analysis, summary, and synthesis.
- For ease of use, the introductory rhetorical chapters have been combined and reconfigured.
- Chapter 1 now includes material on critical thinking and reading textbooks and an enhanced discussion of argumentation.
- Material on outlining has been added to Chapter 2.
- Exercises have been added to Chapters 1 and 2.
- Headnotes have been enhanced to provide more background information.
- Part-openers now include photographs depicting historical "transitions." Instructors can use these as departure points for writing.

⇒⇒ SUPPLEMENTS

For Instructors

- The *Instructor's Manual* (ISBN 0-07-245638-8) includes helpful tips on using the text in class.
- A *website* accompanying *Transitions, 3/e* (**www.mhhe.com/transitions**) offers instructional aids and additional resources for instructors, including an electronic version of the Instructor's Manual and online resources for writing instructors.
- *PageOut!* helps instructors create graphically pleasing and professional web pages for their courses, in addition to providing classroom management, collaborative learning, and content management tools. PageOut! Is **FREE** to adopters of McGraw-Hill textbooks and learning materials. Learn more at **http:/www.mhhe.com/pageout.**

For Students

- The *website* accompanying *Transitions, 3/e* (**www.mhhe.com/transitions**) offers instructional aids and additional resources for students, including self-correcting exercises with feedback for right and wrong answers, writing activities for additional practice, guides to doing research on the Internet and avoiding plagiarism, and useful web links.

- *AllWrite! 2.0* is an interactive, browser-based grammar and editing tutorial program that provides an online handbook, comprehensive diagnostic pre-tests and post-tests, plus extensive practice exercises in every area. (User's Guide with Password for Online Access: 0-07-244992-6; also available on CD-ROM: 0-07-236207-3)
- *WebWrite!* is an interactive peer-editing program that allows students to post papers, read comments from their peers and instructor, discuss, and edit *online*. To learn more, visit the online demo at **http://www.metatext.com/webwrite.**

Please consult your local McGraw-Hill representative or consult McGraw-Hill's website at **www.mhhe.com/english** for more information on the supplements that accompany *Transitions, 3/e.*

⇉ ACKNOWLEDGMENTS

Like all books, *Transitions* has been a collaborative effort. At McGraw-Hill, I am grateful to sponsoring editor Sarah Touborg, for her continuing support of this project, and developmental editor Alexis Walker, for her guidance during the development process. I also appreciate the hard work of Christine Vaughan who guided the production process.

To the following reviewers, whose sensitive reading and sound advice are reflected everywhere in this edition, I offer my profound appreciation and respect:

Cheryl Battles, Butte Community College; Rebecca S. Casey, Kennesaw State University; Dale Doll, Seward County Community College; John C. Freeman, El Paso Community College; Michael J. Goodman, Golden West College; Joseph M. Hathaway, South Georgia Regional Educational Consortium; Jane M. Kinney, Valdosta State University; Pierre Laroche, Dona Ana Community College; Susan McKee, California State University, Sacramento; Angela Morales, Merced College; Patricia Pallis, Naugatuck Valley Community–Technical College; Elaine Sherr, Cuesta College; Marti Singer, Georgia State University; Susan Todd, Jefferson College; Carol Watt, Lane Community College; and Mary T. Wilson, Angelina College.

And, as always, I thank my husband, Dennis, for his unflagging support, enthusiasm, and interest.

PART 1

The Transition from Reading to Writing

> "There is no doubt in my mind that, should we have been choosing our leaders on the basis of their reading experience and not their political programs, there would be much less grief on earth."
>
> **Joseph Brodsky**

> "I divide all readers into two classes; those who read to remember and those who read to forget."
>
> **William Lyon Phelps**

> "People want to know why I do this, why I write such gross stuff. I like to tell them I have the heart of a small boy—and I keep it in a jar on my desk."
>
> **Stephen King**

> "How do I know what I think until I see what I say?"
>
> **E. M. Forster**

> "The pen is the tongue of the mind."
>
> **Cervantes**

THE TRANSITION FROM READING TO WRITING

Here's something you already know: College students read a great deal. They read textbooks, journal articles, research reports, lab reports, course outlines, e-mail, postings on message boards and listservs, library materials, class handouts, poems, essays, novels, short stories, college catalogs—and that's not even all of it. Here's another thing you already know: College students write a great deal, and often that writing is done in response to their reading. Essays, research papers, journal entries, position papers, response papers, summaries, analyses, syntheses—all of these and more are a routine part of a college student's life.

Now here's something you may *not* know (or may not know as well as you should): There are specific reading and writing strategies to help you handle your reading and writing tasks efficiently and successfully. This chapter and the next will discuss them.

⇨ FACTS ABOUT READING THAT MAY SURPRISE YOU

In this chapter you will learn how to become an active reader. Before you do, consider these points about reading, some of which may surprise you.

- **A text is not just a textbook.** The word *text* refers to anything that is read, so when you come across this word in this chapter, remember that it means more than a book with a title like *Principles of Engineering;* it means any printed words.
- **Readers do not just discover meaning; they help make it.** Many people believe that a text contains specific meanings the writer had in mind and that the reader's job is to discover those meanings. In fact, a writer may intend to communicate a particular message, but as a reader you bring all of your own experience and knowledge to a text, and these influence the meanings you come away with. For example, say that you lost a friend to drug abuse. That experience will be likely to influence your reading of an essay about a college student killed by drugs. You may finish reading that essay with impressions different from those of a student whose life has not been touched by drug abuse. That is, your knowledge and experience will help you make the mean-

⇨

ings you get from the essay. This is normal, so do not hesitate to relate what you read to what you already know or have witnessed or have experienced.

- **There is no single, correct meaning for a text.** Since personal knowledge and experience affect how individuals respond to what they read, a text can have as many meanings as it has readers. Of course, your textbooks present facts, and your job as a reader will be to discover those facts, learn them, and repeat them on tests. However, the *interpretation* of those facts—their significance—may be as individual as the readers. Thus, when you read in a history textbook about Columbus coming to the New World, you must discover and learn the fact that he touched our shores in 1492. But whether his landing was a positive or negative act is something you must weigh and form an opinion about, and your opinion may differ from those of other readers of the same textbook.

- **Trust your reactions.** Now that you realize that a person's response to a text is shaped by experience and knowledge, you should come to respect and trust your personal reactions to what you read. Stop wondering if you have the "right" interpretation and recognize that your own thoughtful responses are "right," regardless of whether or not they match the responses of other readers.

- **Not everything in print is the highest quality.** A great deal of unimpressive writing makes its way into print. So do not believe everything you read, and do not assume you are not smart enough or something is wrong with you if you question the quality of a text. Learn to exercise your own critical judgment, and rely on it when deciding what to accept or reject. Of course, the more experience you gain as a reader, the more sophisticated your judgment will be.

- **It is okay to be uncertain.** If you are unsure about a text's meaning or quality, just say that you don't know, and then explain why you are doubtful. It is okay to reserve judgment about a text while you think things over, and it is also okay to change your mind. A text that forces a reader to think and examine issues is challenging and exciting. Furthermore, you should not hesitate to change your opinion about a text if a new reading based on new experiences and thoughts prompts you to do so.

⇒⇒ READING CRITICALLY

You may think that reading "critically" means reading "to criticize" or "to find fault," but this is not the idea. **Critical reading** requires you to read "thoughtfully" to see connections, separate facts from opinions, and draw conclusions. Unlike the reading you do to relax, it demands more of you than settling into a comfortable chair and letting the words on the page wash over you. The reading you do for your college courses is critical reading, and it requires you to do the following:

- **Separate fact from opinion.** A **fact** can be proven or has been proven, and it holds true for everybody. For example, it is a fact that during Lyndon Johnson's presidency, the Civil Rights Act of 1964 was passed, making it illegal for employers to discriminate when they hire. An **opinion** is a person's judgment, interpretation, or belief. Opinions can vary from person to person. For example, my opinion might be that the Civil Rights Act of 1964 was the most important legislation passed during the Johnson presidency, but your opinion might be that the Voting Rights Act of 1965 was more important. (However, it would be a *fact* that we hold these *opinions*.)

  When opinions appear in print, especially when they are the opinions of respected authorities, you can easily mistake them for undisputed facts. Look for "judgment words" such as *best, worst, most important, least interesting, excellent, unfortunate,* and *valuable.* Such words generally indicate opinion.

  > *fact:* The Golden Gate Bridge was completed during the Depression.
  >
  > *fact:* The Golden Gate bridge is widely viewed as a remarkable feat of engineering.
  >
  > *opinion:* It is surprising that the Golden Gate Bridge was completed during the Depression.
  >
  > *opinion:* The Golden Gate Bridge is the most beautiful suspension bridge in the world.
  >
  > *opinion:* The Golden Gate Bridge could not be built today with public funds.

  Finally, keep in mind that facts can change. Something true today can be disproved tomorrow. After all, people once held as fact that the earth was flat.

- **Make inferences.** An **inference** is a conclusion you draw based on what the author has written. An inference takes you *beyond* the actual reading, but it is always based on the evidence *in* the reading. For example, a newspaper account of an auto accident might include the sentence, "After a high-speed chase, the police arrested the driver suspected of causing the accident. The name of the suspect has not been released." You could reasonably infer from this sentence that the suspect might be a minor because names of minors involved in crimes are not revealed to the press. Or you could infer that the driver could not be identified because he or she had no ID and refused to give a name. Which inference is more valid? Other information in the article might suggest the answer, or you may never be sure.

  Critical readers make *reasonable inferences*—they draw conclusions supported by evidence in the reading—but they avoid jumping to a conclusion.

Jumping to a conclusion means making an *unreasonable* inference—one not supported by evidence in the reading. For example, you would jump to a conclusion if you decided that the police were incompetent because they failed to get the driver's name.

- **Relate the reading to what you already know.** Connect the ideas in a text to what you have experienced, observed, and learned in your classes and other readings. If possible, determine whether the ideas support or contradict what you already know. For example, perhaps you learned about civil disobedience when you read Thoreau's *Walden* in an American literature class. If you now read about the Indian leader Gandhi in a history textbook and discover that he was a practitioner of civil disobedience, you have a reason to connect these two people. If you knew Martin Luther King, Jr. also believed in civil disobedience, you might connect King to Gandhi and Thoreau.

Recognizing Errors in Logic

Critical readers pay attention to the way information is presented, and they evaluate the logic of what they read. In particular, they discount material that has any of the following examples of faulty logic, especially when they are deliberate attempts to mislead the reader.

- **Overgeneralizing.** Practically nothing is true all the time, so be suspicious of statements such as this:

    Teenage girls get pregnant because they want to drop out of school and get married.

    While this may be true in some cases, it certainly is not true in all.
- **Oversimplifying.** Most important issues are complicated, so be wary of explanations or solutions that avoid the complexities.

    Violent television, movies, and song lyrics have turned us into a violent society.

    The causes of violence are many and complex. While violence in the media may play a role, other factors must also be considered.
- **Either-or reasoning.** Because most important issues are complex, more than two alternatives are likely to exist:

    We must distribute condoms in our schools, or the number of sexually transmitted diseases will never be reduced.

    Other alternatives are ignored: teaching abstinence, making condoms available in places other than schools, and stepping up educational efforts, for example.

- **Assuming an earlier event caused a later event.** The fact that one event came before another does not necessarily mean that the first event caused the other, later one.

From the time rap music became popular, juvenile crime has increased. Clearly, this music is a negative influence on our youth.

If a first event always caused a later one, then you could say that washing your car before a rainstorm caused the rain.

- **Referring to experts without naming them.** If the authorities are not clearly identified—"Stanford University researchers" or "doctors at the Centers for Disease Control," for instance—be suspicious:

Studies show that children of working mothers are more confident and self-reliant.

What studies? Where and when were they conducted?

- **Incorrectly indicating that one point follows from another.** This logical flaw is called *non sequitor,* which means "it does not follow."

Dimitri Sarantoupolis is the best candidate for governor because he has the largest campaign fund.

The size of the campaign fund has nothing to do with ability to govern—one point does not logically follow from the other.

- **Playing on popular sentiment.** This is an attempt to win people over solely by appealing to shared values, beliefs, fears, or prejudices in a manner such as this:

If we do not restrict immigration, Americans will lose their jobs to foreigners who are willing to work for less.

This argument plays on the fear of unemployment and ignores reasoned arguments about immigration quotas.

⇉ BECOMING AN ACTIVE READER

To be an **active reader,** you must *interact* with a text to discover what it offers and what you bring to it. This process requires commitment. You must be willing to invest time and energy, and you must be prepared to read a piece more than once, perhaps several times.

The next sections describe strategies for active reading. Try them, and if you have any trouble, consult with your instructor. Keep in mind that you can vary procedures as you need to. Thus, if you are reading something difficult for an important paper you must write, you may find yourself reading several times, marking up the text extensively, and writing an outline of the selection. However, if you are reading an easier piece for your own interest, you will probably read fewer times, underline only a point or two, and skip the outline.

Step 1: Preview the Text

Before reading from start to finish, preview the text for clues about what you are getting into. The following strategies can help you preview:

- *Think about the title and author.* Does the title offer any hints about the selection? Some titles will and some won't. For example, "The Teacher Who Changed My Life" (p. 181) gives you a pretty good idea about what you are in for, but "Hold the Mayonnaise" (p.118) probably leaves you wondering. Do you already know that the writer is a humorist, a liberal, a newspaper columnist, a political figure? Have you read anything by this person before? If you have any previous knowledge of the author, you may get some clues about what to expect from the piece at hand.
- *Read any headings, picture captions, items in bold type, charts, and lists that appear.* These offer valuable clues to content.
- *Read the first paragraph or two.* Often the opening sets the tone of a piece and presents the topic under consideration.
- *Read the first sentence of each paragraph.* Sometimes these let you know what main points the author will make and how ideas are organized.

Step 2: Read the Text in One Sitting

After previewing the text, you will have expectations about the material and some questions about it. Next you should read the text through from start to finish in one sitting. (Of course, if the material is very long, you may need to take some breaks.) This reading will be likely to answer some of your questions and cause you to form others. Also, it will be likely to prove some of your expectations accurate and some inaccurate. Try the following procedures when you read in one sitting:

- *Read through the text to get whatever you can from the material,* and do not worry about anything you do not understand. You can deal with that later.
- *Circle any words you do not understand* so you can look them up later. Similarly, *place a question mark next to any passages that puzzle you,* and you can study those later as well.

Step 3: Read and Study

Now comes the time for concentrated study of the text to discover as much as you can about it. Although labeled "step 3," reading and studying can be steps 3, 4, 5, 6, and so on. That is, you should reread the text as many times as necessary to complete the strategies and learn the information given below.

- *Grab a pen and prepare to mark up the text* (that is, if it is yours). Pastel highlighters can be good for marking passages to remember in a textbook, but they are not the best choice for the read and study stage of active reading. (Pause now and look at the marked text on p. 10 so you have an idea of what a marked-up text can look like.)
- *Check the meanings of words you do not know,* and write the meanings in the margin.
- *If one or two sentences express what you think the thesis (central point) is, underline that thesis or place a T next to it.* Otherwise, write out the thesis.
- *Underline the most important points*—the points you want to remember or the author's most significant ideas. Be careful not to underline too much or nothing will stand out—everything will be underlined.
- *Carry on a conversation with the author* by responding to the text in the margins. If you like a particular passage, draw a star next to it; if you strongly agree, write "yes!"; if you disagree, write "no!"; if you do not understand something, place a question mark there; if you like a particular word choice, underline it. In addition, you can write any other responses that you have—"where's the proof?"; "I've experienced this"; "too emotional"; "reminds me of Gary"; "seems too critical"; "nice image"; "funny"; "ironic"; "point doesn't seem relevant"; example needed"; and so on.
- *In the margins or in a journal entry, answer these questions* (see p. 14 on journals):
    a. Is the author expressing facts, opinions, or both?
    b. Is there enough detail, and is it convincing?
    c. What inferences have you made?
    d. What can you relate to something you already know?
    e. What is the author's tone (serious, sarcastic, humorous, preachy, angry, insulting, etc.)?
    f. What is the author's purpose—to share something with the reader, to inform the reader of something, to persuade the reader to think or act a particular way, and/or to entertain the reader?
    g. Who do you think the author's intended audience is, a particular group of people or the average, general reader?
    h. Does the author rely on reason, emotion, or both?

Step 4: Write for Comprehension and Retention

To improve your comprehension of what you read and to help you remember it, try one or more of the following writing tasks.

1. Write out your personal reactions to the selection. Did you like it? Why or why not? Did you learn anything? If so, what? Were you surprised, angered, depressed, reassured, or saddened when you read? Would you recommend the selection to a friend? Are the ideas important? Why or why not? What were the chief strengths and weaknesses in the piece?
2. Write a summary of the selection. (See p. 14 for how to write a summary.)
3. Write an outline of the selection that covers the most important points. (See p. 32 on outlining.)
4. Write a one- or two-paragraph explanation of how the ideas in the selection relate to what you already know as a result of your course work, personal experience, and observation.
5. Construct an examination that tests understanding of the selection. Then turn around and take the test and check your answers against the reading.
6. Challenge the author by writing an argument against his or her point of view.

⇒⇒ A SAMPLE MARKED TEXT

For an idea of what a text can look like after a reader marks it during active reading, review the selection on the next page.

The Truth About Our Little White Lies

KAREN S. PETERSON

Wonder how the kids would feel about this.

Gail Safeer, a graduate student in suburban Washington, D.C., doesn't let on to people that two of her three children were born during a previous marriage. "I don't correct people when they assume all three are my husband's," she says. "It's nobody's business. It's a little white lie of omission, like not telling somebody her husband is running around. . . . White lies are not daily currency in my life," adds Safeer. "But we all do it."

leaving out

2   Indeed we do. <u>Each of us fibs at least 50 times a day</u>, says psychologist Jerald Jellison of the University of Southern California in Los Angeles, who has spent a decade musing on the truth about our lies. He says <u>we lie most often about the Big Three—age, income and sex—area where our egos and self-images are most vulnerable.</u> To protect them we even lie non-verbally with gestures, silences, inactions and body language. "You can even lie with your emotions," says Jellison. "The smile you don't mean, or the classic nervous laugh. A man asks a woman, 'Your place or mine?' and then chuckles. If she's offended, he can always elaborate on that laugh by saying, 'Can't you take a joke? I was only kidding.'"

Wow! How does he know this? Seems high.

thinking about

Difference between little and big lie not clear.

3   These types of lies are what Jellison calls "little white lies," the kind we throw around as casually as old sneakers but which he claims are our "social justifications." "<u>We lie because it pays,</u>" he says. "We use (lies) <u>to escape punishment for our small errors</u>. . . . Also, our social justifications help us <u>avoid disapproval.</u> 'I gave at the office,' or 'I'm sorry.'"

Some students say they studied less for a test than they really did. Why?

4   Our most common reason for lying is to spare someone else's feelings, says Jellison. "We often tell ourselves that, but usually we're trying to protect our own best interests. I'll feel that if I tell you the truth, you'll get mad." Adds B. L. Kintz, a psychology professor at Western Washington University in Bellingham: "We lie so often, with such regularity and fluency, so automatically and glibly that we're not even aware we're doing it. The little self-serving deceptions, the compliments we don't mean, stretching the point in a social situation—they are part of reality. Lying is simply something that is."

That's OK.

I always know when I lie—I disagree.

smoothly

5   Jellison couldn't agree more. He believes that white lies are the oil for the machinery of daily life. "Society actually functions fairly well on many small deceptions. They contribute the little, civilized rituals that comfort us. . . . The idea that we must always tell the truth is too simplistic," he says. "Is lying 'right' or 'wrong'? is an impossible question to answer."

I wonder how much people lie to me.

! well put

6   Be it right or wrong, we have become so accustomed to lying and being lied to that we only see it as harmful in daily life when we don't realize that it's happening to us. "We take for granted some degree of lying from politicians, government, business, advertising," says psychiatrist Dr. Irving Baran of the USC San Diego Medical School. "We don't get excited about an ad that hypes some product in a way we know isn't true. But the rub comes when we go to someone we need and trust and are deceived. A banker for a loan who says he's got the best interest rate going. A real estate agent who convinces us his is the best package available. An insurance agent pushing an unsound policy. An auto dealer who doesn't tell you the product's safety record. Then our backs go up, and what isn't true—hurts."

Hard, but not impossible. Jellison seems to imply that little white lies are OK. This needs to be discussed more.

Conclusion needed. What is the author's view? Only authorities give main ideas. I'm not even sure about the thesis. Is it "Everyone tells little white lies"?

⇨ READING TEXTBOOKS

To be a successful student, you must read and comprehend textbooks in a variety of disciplines. The following adaptation of the active reading process you have already studied can help you do this.

Step 1: Preview the Text

Page through the material you are required to read and take a look at the following, if they appear:

- Chapter introductions, outlines, goals, or highlights
- Headings
- Boxes, charts, maps, graphs, photographs, and captions
- Words that appear in boldface, italics, or color
- Marginal comments and chapter summaries

Step 2: Read the Text in One Sitting

Aim for one sitting, but if it is a long assignment or your concentration fades, take a brief break. Be sure to circle unfamiliar words and make a list of every question that you have.

Step 3: Read and Study

When you underline (or highlight) main points, be careful not to mark too much. When you study this material for an exam, you do not want to be memorizing the whole textbook. In addition, do the following:

- Try to answer the questions you noted in the previous step.
- Note in the margins or on a separate sheet any remaining questions or new ones that occur to you. Be sure to ask your instructor these questions.
- Try to relate the material to other things you know or are studying in other classes. This helps "set" the information.

Step 4: Write for Comprehension

This step is particularly important when you are reading textbooks because it helps you retain information. Try these strategies:

- Summarize the material. (See p. 14 on summarizing.)
- Outline the material. (See p. 32 on outlining.)
- List the main points and important supporting details.
- Write study questions, and trade them with a classmate. Answer each other's questions.
- Answer any questions that come at the ends of the chapters.

⇒⇒ THE CONNECTION BETWEEN READING AND WRITING

The fact that you are using this book of readings in a writing class tells you that a connection exists between reading and writing. For one thing, reading can supply ideas for writing. For example, if you need a topic for an essay, reading a newspaper article about drive-by shootings may prompt you to write about gun control laws. Even if you already have a topic, reading can help you come up with ideas for developing that topic. For example, say that your social psychology instructor has asked you to write about how prejudice affects day-to-day living. Reading "Just Walk On By" on p. 195 (about how people react to a black man walking down the street) may give you ideas to include. As you read in this book, keep an eye out for ideas for your future pieces. Record these ideas in your journal (discussed on p. 14) so you do not forget them.

Reading can also provide models to emulate. For example, if you read a piece with a particularly engaging introduction, you may want to remember the approach and try it sometime yourself. If you like the way an author handles a conclusion or provides transitions or uses examples, you can make note of these in your journal for future use. Thus, when you read the selections in this book, stay on the lookout for strategies to try.

Reading and writing are connected in other ways as well. Writing is very much a part of the active reading process. As you read, you write in the margins to carry on a conversation with the author, and in your journal you record observations and answers to key questions about content and approach. To help you comprehend and remember what you read, you can write summaries, outlines, answers to questions, explanations, and reactions to the text.

Writing is a crucial part of reading because writing helps you decide what you think a text means and how you react to it. Writing is far more than a way to *record* your thinking—it is a way to *discover* what you think in the first place. When you write, you challenge an author's position, explore ideas, react to an author's view, relate points to your own experience, and in general pursue thought further than you would if you were thinking without writing. So there you have it: reading prompts you to write, and writing prompts you to have new ideas about your reading.

Writing in Response to Reading

You will often write in response to reading as part of your course work. Sometimes you will write to stimulate your thinking about ideas under consideration, as when you write pieces to analyze and to evaluate what you have read. Sometimes you will write to understand and retain what you have read, as when you take notes or write summaries or write pieces relating your reading to other things you have studied. Sometimes you will write to show your instructor what you have learned, as when you answer essay questions. The next sections highlight some of the ways to write in response to your reading.

Keeping a Reading Journal

The reading journal is an important part of active reading because it provides a place to record your responses—likes and dislikes, general impressions, questions, connections to experience and other learning, and inferences. In addition, a reading journal offers a place to

- Record writing ideas
- Experiment with writing styles and approaches
- Record the meanings of new words encountered during your reading

To start a reading journal, purchase a thick spiral notebook. Use it only for your reading, not for shopping lists, class notes, writing letters, or anything unrelated to your reading and writing in response to that reading.

Because the journal is meant for you, do not worry about grammar, spelling, or other matters of correctness. Do not even worry about neatness—as long as you can read it. Date each entry and label it ("Draft," "Response to 'The Truth about Our Little White Lies,'" etc.) Write in ink so the entries won't fade or smudge. Get in the habit of keeping the journal next to you as you read.

Writing a Summary

To write a summary, restate the author's main ideas in your own words. You can write summaries for yourself because they are helpful study aids. In addition, teachers may require them in order to check whether you have read and understood assigned readings. When you write research papers, you may summarize all or part of the research material you encounter. A summary of a brief piece might be only a paragraph, but a summary of a longer piece could run several paragraphs.

When you summarize, remember the following guidelines:

- **Include only the author's main points.** Since you cover only the main points, a summary is shorter than the original.
- **Keep your own ideas out of the summary.** You may be tempted to respond to an idea, but the place for that is in an essay, not in a summary, which must include only the original author's ideas.
- **Do not change the author's meaning in any way.** Your job is to faithfully record what the original author had to say, so you may not alter his or her meaning.
- **Use your own writing style and wording.** Although you may not change the author's meaning in any way, you are required to rework the sentence style and wording so that the summary is in your own distinctive style. If you need help with this, see the discussion of paraphrasing on p. 19–20.
- **Use quotation marks around key words and phrases** (words and phrases that are part of the author's distinctive style). You may use some of the wording

from the original, but if that wording is clearly part of the author's style, place it in quotation marks. If you have trouble wording a sentence or if you want to preserve the author's original phrasing, quote that part. (Do not rely too heavily on quotations.) If you do not use quotation marks around an author's distinctive wording, you will have a problem with **plagiarism.**

- **Use present tense verbs with the author's name.** Write "Peterson says," "Peterson explains," "the author believes," and so forth.

How to Summarize

When you write your summaries, you may find all or part of this procedure helpful:

1. Identify the main points by underlining them in the essay. If you prefer, make a list of the main points.
2. Write an opening sentence that includes the name of the author; the title of the essay; and the purpose, focus, or thesis of the essay. (See the opening sentence of the sample summary that follows for an example.)
3. Write out each main point in your own words, in the same order as the points appear in the essay. To be sure you use your own style, imagine yourself explaining each point to someone, and then write out the point the way you would say it aloud. If you have trouble explaining something in your own words, use the original wording in quotation marks. (Do not simply rearrange word order or you will have a form of plagiarism.)
4. Repeat the author's name from time to time for transition.
5. Check your summary against the original to be sure you have *not* added or altered *meaning* and to be sure that you *have* altered *style*.
6. Revise as needed.

A Sample Summary

The following summary illustrates many of the points made so far. The notes in the margin are numbered to call your attention to some characteristics of the summary.

Summary of "The Truth about Our Little White Lies"

[1] First sentence gives author, title and focus.

In "The Truth about Our Little White Lies," Karen S. Peterson explains[2] why people tell fibs so often, "at least 50 times a day."[1, 3] For the most part, Peterson reports[4] the findings of others, particularly psychologist Jerald Jellison of UCLA,[5] who explains that people most frequently lie to protect their egos,[6] which means they most often lie about age, income, and sex.[6] Jellison notes[5] that people tell lies "casually"[3] to avoid being punished or to avoid disapproval.

[2] Present tense verb

[3] Key word or phrase is quoted.

[4] Author's name is used for transition. Note the present tense verb.

Peterson goes on to note[4] Jellison's belief[5] that people are most likely to lie in order to avoid hurting someone's feelings and protect themselves from the anger that could follow.[6] In fact, Jellison explains[5] that we lie so smoothly and without realizing it in social situations that "white lies are the oil for the machinery of daily life."[7]

Peterson adds[4] that we are so used to lying that we do not see it as a problem unless it happens to us without our knowing it. In other words, we expect lying from politicians, government officials, business people, and advertisers, but do not see a problem until we are lied to by someone we rely on and trust.[6]

[5]It is important to note that Peterson is reporting another person's findings.

[6]This is a main point.

[7]Exact words appear in quotation marks.

Writing a Response

Personal response writing calls on you to share your reaction to a piece in a paragraph or essay and to explain why you have formed that reaction. You can evaluate the quality of a piece, discuss how the piece makes you feel, tell about similar experiences you have had, discuss your level of agreement or disagreement, question ideas, explore possible meanings, and so forth. The ideas for your personal response writing can come from your experience, your observation, classwork, other reading, television viewing, the marginal notes you made during active reading, and/or the entries you made in your reading journal. The following paragraph is an example of a personal response:

Sample of a Personal Response

"The Truth about Our Little White Lies" raises some interesting issues. In particular, I was fascinated by the idea that little white lies are important for keeping things running smoothly on a daily basis. People may not mean it when they say things like "Good to see you" and "Have a nice day," but these pleasantries make human interaction easier. I'm not so sure this is the case, though, for lies told to spare people's feelings. Jellison says we tell these lies to protect ourselves. I agree, but we should probably stop. After all, if a friend wants to know how the new pants look and they look ridiculous, maybe we should find a tactful way to say so to spare the person embarrassment. I wish Peterson had dealt with this issue more. In fact, everything in the piece seems superficial. I would like to read a debate about the morality of little white lies, and I would like to know how Jellison came up with his findings. How does he know that people lie at least 50 times a day and that they most often lie about age, income, and sex? It's hard for me to believe what Jellison reports when I don't know how he got the information. All in all, I find the subject matter of the essay very interesting, but I'm left feeling that so much more should have been said.

Arguing a Position

You will often be asked to evaluate the ideas in what you read and to agree or disagree with them, supplying support for your view. Other times, you may argue the importance or lack of importance of what an author has to say. For ideas, consult the marginal notes and journal entries you made during active reading, and draw on your experience, observation, and personal knowledge. In addition, remember the following:

- **Be sure your thesis is debatable.** You cannot argue *one* position if there is no *other* position.

  not debatable (unsuitable for an argumentative piece):

  Advertisers do not always tell the truth.

  Some high schools have daycare centers so students who are parents do not need to drop out of school.

  debatable (suitable for an argumentative piece):

  While the untruths and half-truths in advertising may be expected, they are far from harmless. In fact, they can cause serious damage.

  Placing daycare centers in high schools is an excellent way to reduce the high school drop out rate among teenage parents.

- **Be sure to back up everything you say.** To convince your reader, you must support all your points with sound evidence. That evidence can come from your own reasoning, experience, observation, class studies, reading, and television viewing.
- **Use sound reasoning.** When you make and support your points, avoid the errors in logic explained on p. 5.
- **Recognize opposing views.** Because you are arguing a *debatable* issue, many reasonable people will disagree with you. If they have a particularly compelling reason for their view, you should acknowledge it and explain why your view is better. Here is an example:

    Some people believe that daycare centers in high school will increase the rate of teen pregnancy. However, if these centers are combined with education about birth control, that fear need not be realized. Furthermore, it is better to risk a slight increase in teen pregnancies than allow young people to drop out of school and face a life of poverty as a result.

    The following is an example of an essay that argues a position.

The Truth about Advertisements

In "The Truth about Our Little White Lies," Karen S. Peterson says that we are "so accustomed to lying and being lied to that we only see it as harmful in daily life when we don't realize that it's happening to us." According to Dr. Irving Baran, the lies we expect include those told by advertisers. Together, these two people are saying that the lies in advertisements are both expected and not harmful. I disagree. While the untruths and half-truths in advertising may be expected, they are far from harmless. In fact, they can cause serious damage.

Consider, for example, the lies told to children in movie advertisements. Ads for movies such as *The Lion King* and *Batman* target children and lure them in. However, *The Lion King* includes the murder of the hero's father, and *Batman* is full of dark, sinister images. Both films are the stuff nightmares are made of. Of course, parents can refuse to take young children to such films, but very often they, too, are misled by the hype. They take their children, thinking the movies are suitable choices. However, the ads lie—the films are not for children—and children are harmed as a result.

Almost all advertisements aimed at women include lies. Make-up, toothpaste, and shampoo ads suggest that women who use certain products will be beautiful; cleaning product ads suggest that using their products leads to fulfillment. Women buy the products, use them, and discover that very little has changed. They've been victimized, and that is harmful. Even more harmful is the untruthful image of women presented in these ads. Thanks to backlighting, airbrushing, and starvation diets, women in ads depict a lie, an impossible standard of feminine beauty, that readers of the ads often aspire to. When women cannot meet the standard, they are harmed by the beating their self-esteem takes. Every time I see an advertisement for Victoria's Secret lingerie, with the impossibly thin models displayed in practically nothing, I fear for young girls who think they should look like that. No wonder eating disorders are so common.

Both genders are harmed by ads that present luxuries as necessities. Cell phones, laptop computers, luxury cars, designer clothing, fragrances, satellite television—the ads for these products lie to us. They bombard us with the notion that we cannot live without these items. So we buy them when we should be spending money on other things, or we feel bad because we cannot buy them. Either way, we are harmed.

Perhaps the most harmful lying in advertising is the lying done to sell cigarettes and alcohol. Although we know that cigarettes are killers, advertisers insist on selling us the lie that they are pleasurable, sexy, and liberating. The ads tell men to light up a Marlboro to become a macho Marlboro man, and they tell women to light up a Virginia Slims to be liberated. How macho and liberated are people with lung cancer? Similarly, although we know that drunk driving and alcoholism have serious consequences, advertisers continue to push the lie that beer, wine, and whiskey are products that will make you popular and give you fun. No mention is made of hangovers, throwing up on curbs, and killing people while driving under the influence.

As Dr. Baran notes, misleading advertising hype does not bother us. But it should. Lying in advertising is not the same as a little white lie. The consequences are just too serious.

Writing Paraphrases and Quotations

You have learned about journal writing, personal response pieces, arguing a position, and summary writing. In all of these written responses to your reading, you will need to mention the author's ideas and/or reproduce the author's words. This means you should learn how to **paraphrase** (restate an author's ideas in different words) and **quote** (restate an author's exact words).

To see how paraphrase and quotation can be used, take another look at the introduction of "The Truth about Advertising." (It includes both a paraphrase and a quotation.

> In "The Truth about Our Little White Lies," Karen S. Peterson says that we are "so accustomed to lying and being lied to that we only see it as harmful in daily life when we don't realize that it's happening to us." According to Dr. Irving Baran, the lies we expect include those told by advertisers. Together, these two people are saying that the lies in advertisements are both expected and not harmful. I disagree. While the untruths and half-truths in advertising may be expected, they are far from harmless. In fact, they can cause serious damage.

Paraphrasing

To paraphrase, state an author's ideas in your own words and in your own sentence style so that the paraphrase reads differently from the original. In this regard, paraphrasing is like summarizing, which is discussed on p. 14. The difference is that you summarize a long passage or an entire piece, but you paraphrase only a short passage. Many of the rules for summarizing also hold true for paraphrasing:

1. Do not change the author's meaning in any way.
2. Do not add meaning not in the original.
3. Use your own style and wording so the paraphrase reads differently from the original.

To help you understand how paraphrasing works, here is an example from "The Truth about Our Little White Lies" on p. 10.

> *original:* Be it right or wrong, we have become so accustomed to lying and being lied to that we only see it as harmful in daily life when we don't realize that it's happening to us.

> *paraphrase:* Peterson notes that lying to others and having others lie to us is something we are used to. In fact, unless we don't know we are being lied to, we see no harm in it.

Quoting

To quote, you reproduce an author's exact words. Typically, you should reserve quoting for times when you are having trouble paraphrasing something or for times when a passage is written so distinctively that you want to preserve the original wording. Otherwise, paraphrasing is a better idea so your writing has its own style. When overused, quotations can bore a reader.

Certain rules must be followed when you quote. For one thing, quotations must be exact. You may not alter wording, spelling, or punctuation. Other rules are given for you here, using examples taken from "The Truth about Our Little White Lies."

1. Place the quoted words in quotation marks, indicate who wrote the words, and punctuate and capitalize correctly, in one of the three following ways:

> *original:* Be it right or wrong, we have become so accustomed to lying and being lied to that we only see it as harmful in daily life when we don't realize that it's happening to us.

> *quotation 1:* Peterson says, "Be it right or wrong, we have become so accustomed to lying and being lied to that we only see it as harmful in daily life when we don't realize that it's happening to us."

> *quotation 2:* Peterson says that "be it right or wrong, we have become so accustomed to lying and being lied to that we only see it as harmful in daily life when we don't realize that it's happening to us."

> *quotation 3:* "Be it right or wrong, we have become so accustomed to lying and being lied to that we only see it as harmful in daily life when we don't realize that it's happening to us," explains Peterson.

2. Use ellipses within brackets to show that something has been omitted.

> *quotation 4:* According to Peterson, "Be it right or wrong, we have become so accustomed to lying and being lied to that we only see it as harmful [. . .] when we don't realize that it's happening to us."

3. Use brackets to add clarifying words.

> *original:* He believes that white lies are the oil for the machinery of daily life.

> *quotation 4:* Peterson notes that "he [Jellison] believes that white lies are the oil for the machinery of daily life."

4. Use single quotation marks where double quotation marks appear in the source.

> *original:* These types of lies are what Jellison calls "little white lies."

> *quotation 5:* "These types of lies are what Jellison calls 'little white lies,'" explains Peterson.

EXERCISES

1. What kind of reading do you do on a regular basis (textbooks, newspapers, e-mail, etc)? Do you consider yourself a good reader? Why or why not? If you were a better reader, would your life as a student improve? Explain.

2. Label each sentence in the following paragraph a fact or opinion. Use an **F** for fact and an **O** for opinion.

¹The Internet is the most exciting research tool available to students. ²However, students must exercise caution. ³While many websites are thoroughly reliable, others are inaccurate, outdated, and biased. ⁴To be responsible researchers, students must be able to tell the difference. ⁵After all, taking information from an unreliable source is one of the worst mistakes a student can make. ⁶To judge the reliability of a site, students can check who put it up and when it was last updated. ⁷If it's hard to tell these things, the site is questionable. ⁸In general, sites ending in *.edu* and *.gov*

are reliable because they are put up by educational or government institutions. [9]Of course, when in doubt, students can always ask the reference librarian. [10]Finally, students should not rely solely on electronic sources. [11]Paper sources are always available and easier to judge for reliability.

3. On the basis of the first sentence of the above paragraph, what inference can you make about the author's view of technology? From the last three sentences, what inference can you make about the author's view of traditional library resources?
4. Select any essay in this book that looks interesting to you and read it using the active reading process. Then in your journal or on a separate sheet, answer these questions:
   a. Did the procedure you followed differ from your usual reading process? Explain.
   b. Did you benefit more than usual from your reading because you read actively? Explain.
5. Write a summary of the essay you read.
6. Assume you must write an argumentative essay based on the piece you read. Compose a suitable thesis.
7. Quote three sentences from the essay, being sure to punctuate and capitalize correctly. Use ellipses within brackets correctly in one quotation; use brackets correctly in another.

CHAPTER 2

THE TRANSITION FROM IDEAS TO ESSAY

Chapter 1 told you about typical college writing tasks. The logical question now is, "What is the best way to handle those writing tasks?" In truth, there is no single answer to that question because different writers function in different ways. Some writers cannot function without making detailed outlines, and other writers prefer to list only the main points before they draft. Some writers spend days rewriting their introductions before moving on, and others do not labor over the introduction until everything else is written. Some writers must spend most of their time thinking of ideas, and others must spend most of their time reworking drafts. Your job, then, is to discover writing procedures that consistently work well for you.

To help you develop your own successful writing process, the rest of this chapter describes the aspects of writing and some procedures you can try in order to complete each part of the process. As you work to develop your own successful process, keep two things in mind. First, your writing process will not move in a straight line from start to finish, from idea generation to proofreading. More likely, you will find yourself doubling back to something before going forward again. For example, while you are revising to improve your draft, you may think of a new idea to include. This means you have doubled back from the revising stage to the idea generation stage.

The second thing to remember is that the best way to improve your writing process is to pay attention to what you do when you write. Be aware of how you get ideas, write a draft, make changes, and so forth, and be aware of how satisfactory the results of these procedures are. Then make changes as you need to in order to improve your process and thus the quality of your writing. For example, if a reader tells you that you do not include enough information to prove your points, then you must improve your procedures for generating ideas and backing them up. Similarly, if a reader tells you that you have too many spelling errors, you must improve the way you look for mistakes. Keep sampling techniques until you are comfortable with what you do and are satisfied with the results.

⇒ IDEA GENERATION

Idea generation (discovering ideas to write about) is the earliest stage of any writing process. During idea generation, you settle on a writing topic and think about what you want to say about that topic. Because idea generation comes so early on, everything done at this stage is preliminary—all the ideas you come up with are subject to change at any time. Your material will be rough, but you will have plenty of time later to improve things.

Rather than wait for inspiration (which, by the way, is overrated because it seldom arrives when you need it), experienced writers go after the ideas they need. Some of the following techniques can help you do the same.

To Discover a Writing Topic

- **Consider your own experiences and observations.** Take some time to reflect on your classes, jobs, hobbies, family members, friends, and reading. These important aspects of your life may offer up valuable ideas for writing.
- **Check the journal entries and marginal notes you made during active reading.** The impressions, observations, questions, points of agreement, and points of disagreement that you noted will point to one or more writing topics. For example, let's say that after you read "The Truth about Our Little White Lies" in Chapter 1, you wrote in your journal that parents sometimes lie to children about difficult issues like death and Santa Claus. This entry could prompt you to write an essay about whether parents should tell children the truth about Santa Claus.
- **Pick a quotation you have strong feelings about** and let your reactions to that quotation form the focus for your essay. For example, in "The Truth about Our Little White Lies," Peterson says that "we have become so accustomed to lying and being lied to that we only see it as harmful in daily life when we don't realize that it's happening to us." If you disagree, believing that all lies are harmful, you can write an essay that defends your view.
- **Examine the subject of a reading from different angles** by answering the following questions:

Can I describe the subject?

Can I compare and/or contrast the subject with something?

Does the subject make me think of something else?

Can I explain why the subject is important or unimportant?

Can I agree or disagree with the author?

Can I relate the subject to my own experience?

Can I explain the causes or effects of something explained in the essay?

Can I give the author's ideas a larger application or relate them to something I have learned in another class?

What interests me about the subject?

- **Write without stopping for ten minutes.** Simply record any and every idea that occurs to you. Do not pause to decide whether your ideas are any good, and do not worry about grammar, spelling, or neatness. Just write without stopping, getting ideas down as they occur to you. If you run out of ideas before time is up, write the alphabet until new ideas strike you. This technique, called **freewriting,** is a way to use writing to stimulate thought. After ten minutes, read your freewriting, looking for anything—no matter how rough—that can be shaped into a writing topic. Here is an example of freewriting done in response to "The Teacher Who Changed My Life" (p. 181). Notice as you read that the writer does not worry about being correct; she just gets her thoughts down the best way she can.

I'm always amazed when I read about incredible teachers like the one in this essay. I mean this teacher reached out and literaly changed the writers life from day one. Where are these teachers because I never had one. My teachers were like jailors and if you did one little thing wrong, wham! It was detention or your parents got called or you got humiliated in front of everybody. I don't mean to rag on all teachers but teachers like Miss Hurd in the essay never made it to my school system. All my teachers wanted us to do was to keep our mouths shut and do as we were told. I think it was amazing that Miss Hurd had a "project" every year who was some student who wouldn't of made it without her. In my neighborhood she would have more projects than she could handle. I don't think they would do the newspaper either. I dont no what they would respond to. Maybe some kind of job that would get them money for their family. Hmm, not a bad idea. If students could earn money when they go to high school, then they would stay there and learn. Like in English class they could earn money tutoring Spanish kids and in social science they could help take the census or something. I wonder if that would work. Get rid of football and cheerleading and the other junk and let kids go to work.
I also think that really good teachers should get more money. Then more people would try harder to be better. Money makes the world go round.

The student's freewriting suggests several topics to write about:

The poor teachers in her schools

Paying students for work in high school

Paying good teachers more money

- **Try mapping.** To map, write the name of a broad subject area in a circle in the center of a piece of paper, like this:

Then think of ideas related to that subject and add them, like this:

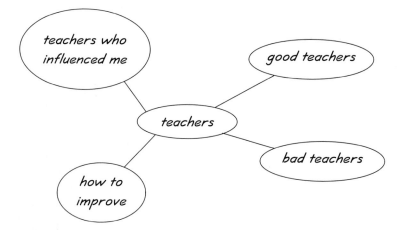

Continue thinking of related ideas and joining them to the appropriate circles until you get something like this:

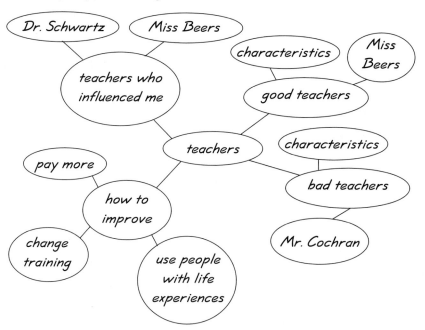

The mapping gives you several possible essay topics, including the characteristics of good teachers, the characteristics of bad teachers, teachers who have influenced the author, and how to improve the quality of teaching. In addition, the mapping brings out some ideas for developing these topics.

- **Consult local and national news media.** Newspapers, television, radio, and news magazines may cover issues you can write about.

To Discover Ideas for Writing about a Topic

- **Check the journal entries and marginal notes you made during active read-ing.** Some of these notations may provide details for developing your topic.
- **Write a discovery draft.** This is not really a first draft; it is a form of prelim-inary writing to help you determine what you know and do not know about a topic. To write a discovery draft, spill out everything you can think of on your topic. Do not agonize over anything; just get things down the best way you can. When you can think of nothing else, go over the draft to decide which ideas are suitable for your next draft—the one that will really be your "first" draft. If you cannot think of much to say in your discovery draft, you may not know enough about your topic, and you should consider changing it or trying other idea generation techniques.
- **List every idea you can think of related to your topic.** Do not pause to eval-uate whether you have good ideas or not—just write whatever occurs to you. When you can think of nothing else, go over your list to decide which ideas to include in your first draft. If you want, you can number the ideas in the order you want to handle them in your draft, and this will give you a **scratch outline.** Here is a sample listing for an essay about how to improve teaching. Notice that all ideas were listed and ones that did not prove usable were crossed out.

    use retired professionals, like accountants and lawyers, as teachers

    improve teacher education programs in colleges

    have experienced teachers train new teachers

    ~~raise public awareness about teachers~~

    require recertification every five years

    have required in-service training

    ~~require psychological testing~~

- **Answer questions about your topic.** You may get ideas for writing about your topic by answering questions such as these:

    What is the most important point I want to make?

    Why is this point important?

    Why is this point true?

    What examples prove this point or illustrate it?

To whom does this point matter? Why?

What is my attitude about this topic?

In addition, you can get ideas by answering the standard journalist's questions: Who? What? When? Where? Why? How?

- **Try mapping.** On p. 25 you learned about mapping to discover a topic. Mapping can also help you come up with ideas once you have that topic. In the center of the page, write your topic with a circle around it. Then as ideas occur to you, join them to the appropriate circles. In addition to helping you think of ideas, mapping has the advantage of showing how your ideas relate to each other. Here is an example of how a mapping might look if you selected a topic from the mapping on p. 26 and then worked to come up with additional ideas:

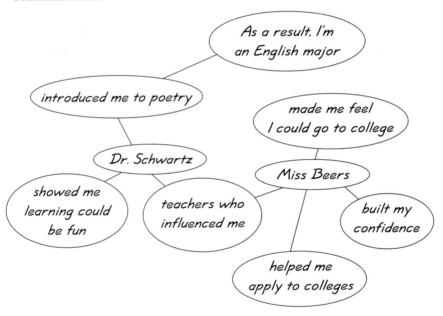

- **Talk to other people about your topic** because they may have suggestions for you. In particular, the students in your writing class may have ideas you can use. Also, if your campus has a writing center, the tutors there can work collaboratively with you to help you come up with ideas.

The Thesis

The **thesis** indicates the essay's central point—its focus. In other words, the thesis lets the reader know what the essay is about. Most often, the thesis is expressed in a sentence or two in the essay, but sometimes it is *implied*. When a thesis is implied, it is not specifically stated. Instead, it is strongly suggested by the information in the essay. When you read the selections in this book, you will often encounter implied thesis statements. However, when you write your own essays, you may find it easier to state your thesis in a specific sentence or two.

A strong thesis often notes the topic under consideration, and the author's view of that topic.

THESIS: Some modern conveniences cause more problems than they solve.

Topic: some modern conveniences

View: They cause problems.

THESIS: State parks are a low-cost alternative to expensive family vacations.

Topic: state parks

View: They offer low-cost family vacations.

THESIS: If funding for the writing center is eliminated, students will suffer.

Topic: eliminating the writing center's funding

View: It will hurt students.

Sometimes a thesis notes the topic, the writer's view, and the main points the essay will cover, as shown here:

THESIS: Used cars are a good buy because they are cheaper to purchase, cheaper to insure, and more profitable to resell.

Topic: used cars

View: They are a good buy.

Points to be covered: the cost to purchase, the cost to insure, and the profit from resale

THESIS: To be the perfect in-law, do not offer advice unless asked, do not visit unless invited, and do not criticize under any circumstances.

Topic: being an in-law

View: what it takes to be a perfect one

Points to be covered: offering advice, visiting, and criticizing

To compose a thesis, study your idea generation material to determine a suitable focus for your writing. Then write a sentence that reflects that focus by noting your topic and view.

The Supporting Details

Most of an essay is made up of the **supporting details,** which are either the ideas that explain the thesis or the evidence that proves that it is true. For a thesis to be properly explained or proven, the supporting details must be *adequate*. That is, the essay must have enough of the right kind of detail so the reader has no trouble appreciating the point made in the thesis.

To appreciate the need for adequate detail, read the following paragraph and then ask yourself whether you are convinced by the evidence.

> Americans have been on a fitness kick since the 1980s, but we remain overweight, in part because we make food a sport or a part of our entertainment. Food should nourish and sustain us; instead, we use it as a way to have a good time. As a result, we feel we must eat in order to enjoy ourselves, and we gain weight as we play. Remember, the purpose of eating is to supply the body with enough fuel to maintain life in a healthy way, not to provide us with recreation.

The paragraph probably left you unconvinced that we use food for sport and entertainment because there are not enough of the right kinds of details. In other words, the supporting details are not *adequate*. To appreciate the difference adequate detail can make, read the following revision.

> Americans have been on a fitness kick since the 1980s, but we remain overweight, in part because we make food a sport or part of our entertainment. The most obvious example of eating for sport is the traditional county fair pie-eating contest. Even though most of us have not participated in this little bit of Americana, we are still guilty of eating for entertainment. For example, we will not watch a movie without popcorn and Raisinettes; we will not go to a ballpark without consuming hotdogs, peanuts, and beer; we will not sit through a Superbowl without ridiculous amounts of chips, dip, submarine sandwiches, and—again—beer. Even our holiday celebrations focus on food: candy at Halloween and Easter, rich gravies and mashed potatoes at Thanksgiving, and fatty hamburgers and hotdogs on Independence Day. Are you going to the beach? Better pack the food. Planning an excursion to the local zoo or amusement park? You'll probably eat cotton candy, caramel apples, and snow cones. Food should nourish and sustain us; instead, we use it as a way to have a good time. As a result, we feel we must eat in order to enjoy ourselves, and we gain weight as we play. Remember, the purpose of eating is to supply the body with enough fuel to maintain life in a healthy way, not to provide us with recreation.

You probably found the revised version, with its adequate supporting details, much more satisfying, because it explains and proves its main point.

In addition to being adequate, supporting details must be *relevant*. This means that all your details should be clearly related to the thesis; you cannot stray into unrelated areas. For example, let's say you have written this thesis:

State parks are a low-cost alternative to expensive family vacations.

As you write about this topic, you cannot discuss the fact that trips to the ocean can also be inexpensive. If you do, you stray from the thesis. To develop adequate, relevant supporting details, you can rely on the idea generation techniques described beginning on p. 27.

Kinds of Supporting Details

To develop a thesis, a writer has many options, including the following: description, narration, exemplification, comparison-contrast, cause-and-effect analysis, process analysis, classification, and definition. Assume, for example, that you have written this thesis:

Students who work while going to college experience many challenges.

Here are eight kinds of supporting details that can help develop this thesis.

1. *Description.* To show how tired the student can get, you can describe what he or she looks like trying to stay awake in an 8:00 A.M. class after working until 2:00 A.M.
2. *Narration (storytelling).* To show how difficult a day can be, you can narrate an account of what goes on in one 24-hour period.
3. *Exemplification (giving examples).* To show that a working student must give up many things for lack of time, you can give examples of parties unattended, invitations refused, and family events missed because of work or school.
4. *Comparison/contrast (showing similarities and differences).* To clarify the nature of the challenges faced by the working student, you can show how his or her life is similar to and different from that of a nonworking student.
5. *Cause-and-effect analysis.* To show how difficult things can be, you can note the stressful effects on the life of the working student and explain how that stress causes the student's family life to suffer.
6. *Process analysis (explaining how something is made or done).* To demonstrate some of the inconvenience associated with working while going to school, you can describe the complicated process of registering for classes to accommodate work schedules and degree requirements.
7. *Classification (sorting by type).* To give an overview of the kinds of challenges working students face, you can group them by type: work

challenges, school challenges, family challenges, challenges to social life, challenges to personal life, and so forth.

8. *Definition.* You can write a definition of "working student" to show how stressed and overworked such a student is.

A single essay will not include all of these strategies; writers choose one or more of them as appropriate for explaining and proving the thesis.

Ordering Supporting Details

The supporting details in an essay must be arranged in some logical order so the reader can easily follow the progression of thought. Three common arrangements are *chronological order* (time order), *spatial order* (arrangement across space), and *progressive order* (order of importance).

1. **Chronological order** is time order: supporting details are arranged in the order they occur or occurred. For chronological order, write out the event that happened first; then write out the event that happened second, and so on, until you get to the last event. Chronological order is often used in narration, when events are written in the order they happened, and in process analysis, when steps in a process are written in the order they are performed.

2. **Spatial order** arranges things according to some pattern across space: near to far, top to bottom, front to back, left to right, inside to outside, and so forth. Spatial order is a useful way to arrange supporting details that describe a place or scene.

3. **Progressive order** arranges details according to their order of importance, starting with the least important detail and moving to the most important. Because progressive order places the most important details at the end of the essay to provide a strong finish, it is useful when your goal is to persuade your reader. Another form of progressive order involves placing your strongest points first and last, with everything else in between. This arrangement gives you the strongest opening and closing.

⇨ OUTLINING

Outlining helps ensure that your supporting details are arranged logically and effectively. How extensively you outline depends on the number and complexity of your ideas. For brief pieces with uncomplicated details, the **scratch outline** may suffice. To write a scratch outline, list the ideas you will include in your draft (or use your idea generation list if you developed one), and number the ideas in the order you plan to write them up. Here is an example using the idea generation list from p. 27:

⁵ use retired professionals, like accountants and lawyers, as teachers

¹ improve teacher education programs in colleges

² have experienced teachers train new teachers

~~raise public awareness about teachers~~

³ require recertification every five years

⁴ have required in-service training

~~require psychological testing~~

The advantage of a scratch outline is that it is quick. The disadvantage is that it is so sketchy, you will be likely to need to develop additional material as you draft.

A more detailed outline is the **informal outline.** To write such an outline, indicate the major points and important subpoints, like this:

major point: *improve teacher education programs in college*

   get students in the classroom sooner

   be honest about the difficulties of teaching

   make the programs more difficult

major point: *have experienced teachers train new teachers*

   new teachers will learn effective techniques sooner

   experienced teachers can point out problems to correct

major point: *require recertification every five years*

   have specific standards that must be met

   unqualified teachers will be rooted out

major point: *have required in-service training*

   keeps teachers aware of latest developments

   allows sharing of successful techniques

   allows discussion of problems

major point: *use retired professionals, like accountants and lawyers, as teachers*

   these people have talent and life experiences to share

   they would be likely to work for less money

The most detailed outline is the **formal outline,** which is useful for longer, more complicated pieces. It uses roman numerals, numbers, and letters to indicate levels of ideas, like this:

preliminary thesis: The quality of teaching would be improved if some key changes were made.

I. Improve teacher education programs in college.
   A. Get students in the classroom sooner.
      1. Begin classroom observations during freshman year.
      2. Let students teach by the end of their sophomore year.
   B. Be honest about the difficulties of teaching.
      1. Emphasize the low pay.
      2. Describe the stress.
   C. Make the programs more difficult.
      1. Raise the required grade point average.
      2. Require rigorous testing before graduation.
         a. Test knowledge of subject matter.
         b. Test knowledge of teaching theory.
         c. Require demonstration of competence in the classroom.
      3. Require evaluation by experienced teachers.
      4. Require evaluation by students.
II. Have experienced teachers train new teachers
   A. New teachers will learn effective techniques sooner.
   B. Experienced teachers can point out problems to correct.
III. Require recertification every five years.
   A. Have specific standards that must be met.
      1. Teachers must demonstrate knowledge in the subject area.
      2. Teachers must demonstrate knowledge of educational theory.
   B. Unqualified teachers will be rooted out.
IV. Have required in-service training.
   A. Make teachers aware of the latest developments.
   B. Allow teachers to share successful techniques.
   C. Allow teachers to discuss problems.
V. Use retired professionals, like accountants and lawyers, as teachers.
   A. They have talent and life experiences to share.
   B. They will work for less money.

Remember that an outline is just a tool. As you draft, you can make any changes, additions, and deletions you find appropriate.

Connecting Ideas with Transitions

Placing supporting details in a logical order is often not enough. Writers must also show how ideas relate to each other by using connecting words and phrases called **transitions**. The following chart shows some common transitions and the relationships they signal.

Transition Chart

Relationship	Transitions	Example
addition	*also, and, too, in addition, further, furthermore*	As far as I am concerned, it is too late to go. <u>Furthermore</u>, the snow is making travel dangerous.
time	*now, then, before, after, earlier, finally, soon, later, next*	The President gave his speech. <u>Then</u> he answered the reporters' questions.
space	*near, next to, alongside, away, inside, to the right, behind*	The car is parked illegally. <u>Next to</u> it is a police cruiser.
emphasis	*indeed, in fact, surely, without a doubt*	The desk is on sale for a reasonable price. <u>Indeed</u>, the price seems too good to be true.
comparison	*similarly, likewise, in the same way, in like manner*	The costumes in the play were breathtaking. <u>Similarly</u>, the sets were well done.
contrast	*however, in contrast, but, still, nevertheless, on the contrary, yet*	Exercise is important for fitness. <u>However</u>, the wrong technique can cause injury.
cause and effect	*since, because, so, as a result, consequently, thus, therefore*	The school levy was defeated. <u>Thus</u>, plans to add a journalism program have been discontinued.
illustration	*for example, for instance, in particular, specifically*	Dr. Liu is a caring teacher. <u>For example</u>, she never ignores a student's question, no matter how long it takes to answer it.
summary or clarification	*In summary, in conclusion, in short, in other words, all in all*	Michael is bright, talented, and handsome. <u>In brief</u>, he has it all.

Connecting Ideas with Repetition

In addition to using transitional words and phrases, writers can connect ideas by repeating words and ideas. Here are some examples.

repeating a word: The Internet has opened up a whole new form of <u>communication</u>. This <u>communication</u> is a source of both problems and benefits.

repeating an idea: <u>Higher interest rates and fewer new housing starts</u> have prompted some real estate analysts to question White House economic policies. According to other analysts, <u>this economic slump</u> should end by spring.

⇛ DRAFTING

Drafting is a first effort at getting your ideas down in paragraph or essay form. First drafts are almost always rough, so do not worry if yours seems to need a great deal of work. A draft is only meant to produce raw material that can be polished later, during revision. When you draft, use your outline as a guide. In addition, the following tips should be helpful.

- **Let your draft be rough.** If you expect this early attempt to be polished, you will become frustrated. Remember, you will have plenty of opportunity to improve things later when you revise.
- **Skip troublesome parts.** Concentrate on what you *can* do and leave the rest for later. If you stop to wrestle with each problem along the way, you may become discouraged. Thus, if you cannot think of a word, leave a blank; check spellings later; leave space to add support if you are not sure how to back up a point. Just keep pushing forward.
- **If you cannot get anything down on paper, return to idea generation.** Perhaps you thought you were ready to draft, but you did not have enough ideas after all. That's okay. Just go back now and generate more ideas. Writers often move back and forth through the writing process.
- **If you have trouble expressing yourself in writing, try writing the way you speak.** Speaking may come more naturally to you than writing. You can always revise later to make your prose more formal, if necessary. As an alternative, speak your "draft" into a tape recorder and then transcribe the tape. Remember, though, that there are differences between spoken and written language, so you will need to revise later to meet the conventions of written English.
- **Write as fast as you can.** You may be more successful getting a draft down if you race through from start to finish, not allowing yourself to stop if you get stuck or when you know something must be revised. Remember, you are only seeking raw material.

In order to draft, you must understand that an essay is built on a structural framework that typically consists of three parts:

- The introduction
- The body paragraphs
- The conclusion

The Introduction

The introduction opens an essay. Usually it is one paragraph, but it can be two or more. The primary purpose of the introduction is to engage the reader's interest. If the opening fails to stimulate the reader's interest, that person may decide not to read on. Perhaps you have had the experience of beginning a magazine article and then flipping to the next article after only a paragraph or so because the opening of the first article did not engage your interest.

To stimulate your reader's interest, many strategies are possible, including the following.

- **Open with some description** to create a picture in your reader's mind. To see how this is done, look at the opening paragraph of "One Man's Kids" on p. 293.
- **Tell a brief story** to spark your reader's interest. For an example of this approach, read the opening paragraph of "Complexion" on p. 63.
- **Establish common ground with your reader** to make that person feel that you share some interests or are on the same side. This approach is illustrated in the opening of "My Grandmother, the Bag Lady" on p. 89.
- **Provide background information** to help your reader understand your thesis, topic, purpose for writing, or some other aspect of the essay. The opening of "Once More to the Lake" (p. 81) provides introductory background information to help the reader understand why the author returned to the lake.
- **Open with an example.** This technique can be effective because in addition to engaging the reader's interest, the example can help prove the truth of the thesis. For an example of this approach, see "Life Is Not Measured by Grade-Point Averages" on p. 399.
- **Open with an interesting quotation.** The key to this approach is to be sure the quotation is genuinely interesting to your reader. Offering the words of a key government official, as they appeared in a local newspaper, can be interesting, but avoid tired expressions such as "Never judge a book by its cover." "Black *and* Latino" on p. 322 is an example of an essay that uses a quotation for an effective opening.
- **Open with a dramatic statement** and you stand a good chance of capturing your reader's interest. Notice how this technique is used in the opening paragraph of "Will Tiny Robots Build Diamonds One Atom at a Time?" on p. 244.
- **Combine approaches.** You need not limit yourself to one technique. For example, you can open with a dramatic statement and then tell a story. Or you

can provide background information and give an example. Use whatever combination of approaches is likely to engage your reader's interest.

In addition to stimulating the reader's interest, the introduction of an essay is likely to present the thesis, particularly when that thesis is stated rather than implied. Notice that this is the case in the sample essay that appears on p. 40. The introduction is reprinted for you here so you can study its parts.

No matter what class I am in, the scene is the same: I look around at a roomful of students poised over their spiral notebooks, pens angled just inches above the lined sheets. Like runners at the starting line tensed and waiting for the gun to signal the start of the race, these students sit at-the-ready, waiting for their teacher to start speaking so they can dutifully scribble down every vital word. Many people would find nothing wrong with this picture of college students eager to take down and to absorb the wisdom the instructor is sure to impart. [However, I see this passiveness as a chronic problem in our educational system.]

> Stimulates reader's interest with description.

> Thesis: The topic is passiveness in education; the view is that it is a problem.

The Body Paragraphs

The supporting details that provide the explanation of or the evidence for the thesis appear in paragraphs after the introduction. These paragraphs are called **body paragraphs**. Typically, each body paragraph focuses on one point that develops or supports the thesis. Often that point is stated in a **topic sentence** that can appear at the beginning, in the middle, or at the end of the body paragraph. Student writers, however, often find it convenient to place the topic sentence at the beginning of the paragraph. To see how a topic sentence and supporting details can make up a body paragraph, study the following body paragraph taken from the sample essay on p. 40.

[A large part of the problem is created in the early years of schooling.] As young children, students are often bursting with unrestrained energy, and part of what our school system does is teach them to restrain it. One of my greatest concerns about my youngest daughter's early education, in fact, was about how in the world my overactive, always busy child could possibly sit still for so many long hours each day. She could not, at first, but after repeated punishments for violations of the "sit still and be quiet" rules, she did indeed learn to sit still and be quiet. Unfortunately, she learned to be too quiet, for she became afraid to ask questions, respond in class,

> Topic sentence indicates paragraph will discuss the fact that the problem (passiveness) begins in the early years of school.

> Supporting details, which are adequate and relevant, develop the topic sentence. They include cause-and-effect analysis and an example.

or interact with other children. Suddenly, instead of an energetic, curious child, I had a shy kid on my hands.

The number of body paragraphs in an essay will depend on how many points are made to support the thesis and how much detail those points are developed with. However, as a general guideline, an essay should have at least two body paragraphs, although most essays will have more.

The Conclusion

After the body paragraphs comes the **conclusion,** the ending of the essay. The conclusion is important because it forms the final impression, which is the most lasting. It must, therefore, be crafted carefully so the reader does not feel let down at the end.

A number of approaches to the conclusion are possible, including these:

- **State the overriding conclusion or idea that can be drawn from the supporting details.** With this approach, you state the idea the supporting details lead to, the conclusion that can be drawn. For example, after explaining many ways the elderly can contribute to society, you could end with the conclusion that any retired person who cannot find anything to do does not have much imagination.
- **Conclude by looking ahead.** With this approach you look beyond the time of the essay and into the future. For example, if you write about your struggle to cope with a learning disability while you are in college, you can conclude by voicing your hopes and fears for the future, after you graduate.
- **Call your readers to action.** If you want your readers to do something, say so in the conclusion. For example, if your essay explains the problems of homelessness, you can conclude by urging your readers to write to Congress.
- **Restate the thesis or another important point** if doing so provides dramatic emphasis. If it does not, avoid this approach because it seems uninspired.
- **Summarize your main points** if doing so will help the reader remember them. If your essay is long, your reader may appreciate a summary. Otherwise, avoid this approach because it seems repetitious.
- **Offer a solution to a problem or an answer to a question** raised in the essay. For example, if your essay explains the effects of teen pregnancy, your conclusion can offer a way to decrease the pregnancy rate among adolescents.
- **Combine approaches** if doing so creates a satisfying ending.

⇉ A SAMPLE ESSAY TO STUDY

The following essay illustrates many of the points made about essay structure. These points are noted in the margins.

Learning to Learn

[1]No matter what class I am in, the scene is the same: I look around at a roomful of students poised over their spiral notebooks, pens angled just inches above the lined sheets. Like runners at the starting line tensed and waiting for the gun to signal the start of the race, these students sit at-the-ready, waiting for their teacher to start speaking so they can dutifully scribble down every vital word. Many people would find nothing wrong with this picture of college students eager to take down and to absorb the wisdom the instructor is sure to impart. However, I see this passiveness as a chronic problem in our educational system.

Paragraph 1 is the introduction. It uses description to create interest. The thesis is the last sentence of paragraph 1. It gives the topic as passiveness in education. The view is that it is a problem.

[2]A large part of the problem is created in the early years of schooling. As young children, students are often bursting with unrestrained energy, and part of what our school system does is teach them to restrain it. One of my greatest concerns about my youngest daughter's early education, in fact, was about how in the world my overactive, always busy child could possibly sit still for so many long hours each day. She could not, at first, but after repeated punishments for violations of the "sit still and be quiet" rules, she did indeed learn to sit still and be quiet. Unfortunately, she learned to be too quiet, for she became afraid to ask questions, respond in class, or interact with other children. Suddenly, instead of an energetic, curious child, I had a shy kid on my hands.

Paragraph 2 is a body paragraph that helps develop the thesis. The topic sentence is the first sentence; it says the paragraph will show that the problem begins in early years. The supporting detail includes an example.

[3]By the time they reach junior high school, most children have learned that the quieter they are, the better they seem to get along in class. The more they challenge and question, the more they are viewed as troublemakers. Furthermore, students learn that the only thing that is valued is correct answers. They learn that if they are right, they are rewarded, and if they are wrong, they are penalized. Thus, they become afraid to try, for fear they will make mistakes that will hurt their grade. This orientation further encourages passiveness. Why should students ask questions, venture answers, test theories, or try out ideas when doing so may mark them as not knowing what they should know? Then there is the fact that if students speak too much, they take up too much of the teacher's time and get labeled as "problems." In fact, when my son was in

Paragraph 3 is a body paragraph. Its first sentence, the topic sentence, notes that the paragraph will deal with junior high school where children learn to be quiet. Notice that the paragraphs are ordered chronologically. The details include cause-and-effect and example.

seventh grade, I was called in for a conference with his English teacher. "The problem," she felt, was that he asked too many questions. In such a climate, students soon learn to sit passively.

[4]By the time students get to college, they have come to believe that their role in their own education is simply to absorb the information given to them. They have learned to take copious notes, memorize facts, and look to their instructors for all the answers. Students now spend considerable time trying to figure out what the instructor wants them to say—not what they themselves think. I have even heard students ask whether or not their grades would be lowered on compositions if their opinions differed from the instructor's. After any kind of assignment is given in any class, students are usually heard asking each other, "What do you think he wants on this?" If an instructor does happen to ask a student what he or she thinks about something, the student becomes so rattled that all he or she can answer is, "I don't know." Of course students don't know. They rarely get the opportunity to think for themselves and so have not even thought about their own ideas. Tests in college further encourage passiveness. They are often multiple choice, true and false, and fill-ins, which call upon students to do nothing more than repeat the facts they have absorbed as a result of their note-taking and memorizing.

In the third body paragraph (paragraph 4), the chronological order continues. The topic sentence comes first and notes that the paragraph will focus on the role students assume in college. The supporting details, which are adequate and relevant, include explanation, cause-and-effect, and example.

[5]So what is the solution? We need to stop restraining students in the early years and rechannel their energies into problem solving, questioning, and hands-on learning activities. We need to encourage students to form and support their own opinions, and we need to encourage teachers to evaluate students on the quality of that support, not on to what extent they agree with the teacher. We need to teach students to use facts to solve problems, not just to repeat them on exams. In short, we must find a way to make students active learners, but to do so we must help students learn how to learn.

The conclusion brings the essay to a satisfying finish by offering a solution to the problem explained in the essay.

⇨ REVISING

Once your draft is down, no matter how rough it is, you have raw material to shape into a form suitable for a reader. When you shape a draft to prepare it for a reader, you are **revising.** To revise, focus on content, organization, and expressing yourself effectively. Save focusing on grammar, spelling, and punctuation for later, when you edit. Remember, revising is more than just changing a word or two; it is a thoroughgoing rethinking and reworking of the draft. Some of the following tips may help you when you revise.

- **Leave your work before you revise.** Pace your writing so you have time to leave your work for a day or so after drafting and before revising. This way, your draft can "cool," and you will stand a better chance of finding problems.
- **Make the easy changes first** to build momentum coming into the more difficult changes. Success breeds success, so after successfully completing easier revisions, you may find harder ones less challenging.
- **Read your draft aloud to listen for problems.** Sometimes we *hear* difficulties that we fail to *see.* However, we have a tendency to read what we *meant* to write rather than what we actually *did* write, so be careful to read exactly what is on the page.
- **If you wrote your draft by hand, type or word-process a fresh copy before revising.** You will notice problems easier in type than in your handwriting.
- **Revise in stages and over a period of days.** Revising is time-consuming and tiring, so be prepared to leave your work whenever you need a break. Also, be prepared to spend several days revising; this task cannot be hurried.
- **Use a checklist,** so you remember what you need to consider. Here is one you may find convenient:

Revising Checklist

1. Be sure your writing has an unmistakable thesis.
2. Be sure all your points are related to your thesis. If something does not relate to the thesis, then it should be eliminated or reworked to be made relevant.
3. Be sure that every point you make is backed up with evidence and/or explanation and/or examples.
4. Be sure your points are in a logical order.
5. Be sure your introduction creates interest.
6. Be sure your conclusion ties things up.
7. Be sure all your points are clear.
8. Eliminate unnecessary words. For example, change "Her hair was red in color" to "Her hair was red."
9. Substitute specific words for vague ones. For example, instead of saying "The dog chased the ball," say "The black labrador chased the tennis ball."

- **Do not edit.** Stick to the revision concerns (content, organization, and effective expression) and avoid dealing specifically with grammar, punctuation, and spelling. Editing too early will distract you from the larger revision issues. It is inefficient to worry about editing details—say, the spelling of a word—since you may eliminate the word as you revise.
- **Trust your instincts.** If you sense something is wrong, assume the feeling is correct and revise the portion in question. Even if you cannot name it, the problem probably exists.
- **Get reader response.** Nothing beats reader reaction for helping a writer decide how to change a draft. Just be sure to use reliable readers, ones who understand the qualities of effective writing and who will not hesitate to offer helpful criticism. Students in your writing class are often reliable readers, as are writing center tutors. Most writers seek the responses of two or more readers and look for agreement. If you want to guide your readers' responses, give them specific questions to answer or ask them to complete a copy of the following form.

Reader Response Form

1. What is the thesis idea?

2. What, if anything, is unrelated to the thesis idea?

3. Which points, if any, are unproven or unexplained?

4. Is anything unclear? If so, what?

5. Are the ideas in a logical order? If not, what problems exist?

6. Does the opening create interest? If so, how? If not, why not?

7. Does the conclusion bring the piece to a satisfying close? If so, how? If not, why not?

8. What do you like best about the essay?

⇉ EDITING

After revising, you can move on to checking grammatical correctness, spelling, punctuation, and capitalization. This is **editing,** and you must not skip it, because readers grow annoyed by writing with errors in it. For example, if you can't spell, the reader won't trust what you have to say, and your whole effort may be doomed. Of course, during editing, ideas may occur to you for revising, and you should respond to them; writers often step back before going forward.

Some of the following tips may help you edit:

- **Leave your work for a day** to clear your head and increase your chances of finding mistakes.
- **Edit more than once.** The first time through, look for any kind of mistake. After that, look for the kinds of mistakes you are in the habit of making.
- **Place a ruler under each line and point to each word and punctuation mark as you go.** This procedure helps you move slowly enough to notice errors. Otherwise, you may go too quickly and overlook mistakes.
- **Read your writing backwards, from last sentence to first sentence.** This procedure can force you to see what is on the page, rather than what you meant to write.
- **Learn the rules.** You cannot be a confident editor without knowing the grammar and usage rules, so each time your instructor or another reader calls an error to your attention, look up and learn the appropriate rule.
- **Have someone read your work out loud to you.** You may *hear* errors you did not see.
- **Trust your instincts.** If something sounds "off," a problem probably exists.
- **Get help.** You can ask a reliable reader, perhaps from your campus writing center, to help you edit. But remember, the responsibility to learn and apply the rules is yours, so use a reliable reader only as backup support.

⇉ PROOFREADING

After editing, depending on what your instructor requires, prepare a clean typed, computer-generated, or neatly written copy of your work for your reader. Before submitting your writing, however, be sure to check for typing or copying errors. This check is **proofreading.** If you find a mistake, make the correction neatly on the page. It is better to submit a paper with a few corrections inked in than a perfectly clean copy with mistakes in it. Of course, if you must make many corrections, rewrite or retype the page. Proofreading must be done slowly to be effective. Think of proofreading as the final quality-control check so that an error-free product is delivered to your reader that you can be proud of. The tips for editing also apply to proofreading.

⇨ A DEMONSTRATION OF THE WRITING PROCESS: AN ESSAY IN PROGRESS

The following pages show how Erika, a student writer, worked through idea generation, outlining, drafting, revising, and editing for an assignment calling for an essay about an issue in the news. For her essay she chose to argue against raising the minimum wage. Examining Erika's material will give you a sense of how the writing process can work.

Erika's List and Scratch Outline

To generate ideas, Erika wrote a list, which produced enough material to get her started. You may need to use a different idea generation technique, or you may need to use a combination of techniques. Remember, each writer must find his or her own best procedures.

List

1 *Most people think raising the min. wage is a good idea.*

3 *Min. wage earners = not usually breadwinners, but teens (econ class)*

4 *Teens will lose their jobs because expenses will go up for employers.*

2 *It creates more problems than it solves.*

People who favor raising min. wage are uneducated.

Unskilled workers don't deserve more money.

6 *Not an incentive to get off welfare.*

5 *Unskilled workers make min. wage & we have shortage of unskilled workers (econ. class)*

Notice that Erika used abbreviations. She wrote whatever occurred to her and did not censor herself.

Ideas are numbered to create the scratch outline

Ideas she decided not to include were crossed out. She also noted in parentheses what she learned in economics class.

Erika's First Draft

Erika felt her listing yielded enough material for a first draft. She wrote her draft without the benefit of an outline. However, you may find that your draft goes more smoothly if you develop an outline to serve as a guide to drafting.

First Draft

A proposal to raise the minimum wage is in the news again. Every time we turn around Congress is proposing bills for an increase in the minimum wage. Republicans are stereotyped as the opposition and the Democrats are stereotyped as the supporters, but do we really need a higher minimum wage? No, a *higher minimum wage wouldn't help the majority of the people earning minimum wage. It would do more harm to these people than it would help.*

Many people who support a raise in the minimum wage do not understand that it will have a negative effect on national unemployment, inflation, and employment opportunities for the unskilled.

The most common misunderstanding is that the average minimum wage earner is the breadwinner supporting the family. Actually, the minimum wage earner is usually a teenager or a second family income, as I learned in my economics class.

If we raise the minimum wage, these teenagers will lose their jobs because employers will think it costs too much to keep them on, which will increase the unemployment rate among teens, which will lead to all kinds of social problems.

Another common misunderstanding is that raising the minimum wage will help the welfare system. Some people think that a higher minimum wage will encourage people to get off welfare and look for a job. While some people might be encouraged to look for work, the unskilled jobs many of them need will no longer exist because they were eliminated to save costs that resulted from the higher minimum wage. New entry-level jobs will not be created because they will be to costly. Thus, the rolls of welfare will not be reduced at all.

Raising the minimum wage does appear on the surface to be a good idea, but it will do more harm than good.

Reader Response to Erika's First Draft

To get suggestions before revising, Erika asked a classmate to answer the questions in the following Reader Response Form.

Reader Response Form

1. What is the thesis idea?
   Raising the minimum wage is not a good idea.

2. What, if anything, is unrelated to the thesis idea?
   Everything seems related to the thesis idea.

3. Which points, if any, are unproven or unexplained?
   It seems like you have excellent ideas to defend your view, but you never really explain them. For example, in paragraph 2 you mention inflation, but you never discuss it. You also say that if teenagers lose their jobs, then there will be social problems as a result. What problems? I think almost everything you say needs more explanation.

---

4. Is anything unclear? If so, what?

   I don't really understand how minimum wage jobs can be eliminated. How will the work get done then?

5. Are the ideas in a logical order? If not, what problems exist?

   yes

6. Does the opening create interest? If so, how? If not, why not?

   The opening isn't bad, but it's not very exciting either. Should the first two paragraphs be joined?

7. Does the conclusion bring the piece to a satisfying finish? If so, how? If not, why not?

   The ending just repeats the thesis. It seems lazy.

8. What do you like best about the essay?

   I think the way the welfare point is developed is strong because it has some detail to it. I also think the points are well thought out. They just need to be explained more. I think I could learn something from this essay.

Erika's Second List

After studying her classmate's response to her draft, Erika decided she needed more ideas, so she did additional listing to focus on developing the points in her draft.

Social Problems That Result When Teenagers Lose Their Jobs

time on their hands leads to getting into trouble

teens turn to crime to get money

teens turn to drugs

teens spend time on the streets

won't get the experience and training needed to move on to better jobs

Unemployment

entry-level jobs for the unskilled will be lost

ranks of the unemployed will grow

ranks of welfare recipients will grow

Erika's Revision

When Erika revised, she considered her reader's response and her additional idea generation material. She did not limit herself to the points her reader made, though. She also made other changes she thought would strengthen the piece.

Revision

Comments

   A proposal to raise the minimum wage is in the news again. Every time we turn around Congress is proposing bills for an increase in the minimum wage. However, raising the minimum wage is not a good idea because it will create a number of serious problems.

Erika reworked her introduction. It is shorter, with a clear thesis. Paragraph 2, which seemed like a thesis, is eliminated.

   Many people think that the minimum wage earner is a breadwinner supporting a family. However, I learned in my economics class that usually the minimum wage earner is a teenager. If we raise the minimum wage, these teenagers will lose their jobs because employers will think it costs too much to keep them on. Then, unemployment will increase among teens, which will lead to all kinds of social problems. Without jobs, teenagers will have too much time on their hands, so they may begin hanging out on the streets, where they may take up drug use. Without jobs, teenagers will also lose a source of income. To get money, some will turn to crime. Also, teens will lose the opportunity to gain work experience and training which can help them move on to better jobs.

In her response to her reader's criticism, Erika developed her point about social problems more.

   Raising the minimum wage will lead to the loss of jobs. Because employers will not be able to pay the extra salaries, they will have to eliminate minimum wage jobs. Since minimum wage jobs are usually unskilled jobs, many unskilled workers will be unable to find work. This will cause the ranks of the unemployed to grow.

Erika adds the point that unemployment will increase.

   With increased unemployment will come an increase in welfare recipients. Some people think that a higher minimum wage will encourage people to get off welfare and look for a job. While some people might be encouraged to look for work, the unskilled jobs many of them need will no longer exist because they were eliminated to save costs that resulted from the higher minimum wage. Thus, the rolls of welfare will not be reduced at all.

Erika revised to show the connection between her points about unemployment and welfare.

Raising the minimum wage may seem like a good idea on the surface, but it will do more harm than good.

Despite reader criticism, Erika did not revise her conclusion.

Teacher Response to Erika's Revision

Erika,

You have an important topic here, and you seem to have given it careful consideration. In fact, a topic this important deserves the strongest possible introduction. Think about reworking yours to be sure you capture your reader's interest. Paragraph 2 is your strongest paragraph because it is well developed and clear. I'm wondering, though, why loss of teenage jobs is such a problem. Can't teens be guided away from the streets, drugs, and crime if they don't work? Can you revise paragraph 3 to make it stronger? Part of that paragraph seems to repeat paragraph 2. Your transition from the discussion of unemployment to welfare is very smooth, but your conclusion needs attention. It seems abrupt. I'm wondering if you can conclude effectively by discussing alternatives to raising the minimum wage.

Erika's Idea Generation

After reading her instructor's comments, Erika decided to try some additional idea generation to develop ideas on alternatives to raising the minimum wage. This time, she tried mapping. Here are the results:

Erika's Final Draft

Erika revised her essay through two more drafts and then carefully edited. The final version appears here.

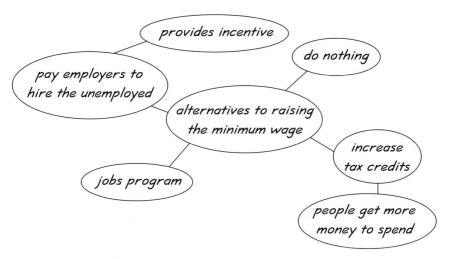

Final Draft

RAISING THE MINIMUM WAGE:
TROUBLE ON THE HORIZON

So you think raising the minimum wage is a good idea, do you? Why not? Everyone else does, including many members of Congress who seem to be proposing bills to increase the wage more often than some people brush their teeth. However, despite public and Congressional support, raising the minimum wage is not a good idea because it will create a number of serious problems.

Many people think that the minimum wage earner is a breadwinner supporting a family. However, I learned in my economics class that usually the minimum wage earner is a teenager. If we raise the minimum wage, these teenagers will lose their jobs because employers will think it costs too much to keep them on. Then, unemployment will increase among teens, which will lead to all kinds of social problems. Without jobs, teenagers will have too much time on their hands, so they may begin hanging out on the streets, where they may take up drug use. Without jobs, teenagers will also lose a source of income. To get money, some will turn to crime. Also, teens will lose the opportunity to gain work experience and training which can help them move on to better jobs.

Some people may think that it is not a big problem if teenagers lose their jobs. They can be guided into other areas to keep them off the streets and away from drugs and crime. However, the money teens make is not always extra income that goes for clothes, CDs, and the hot new tennis shoes. Many families depend on this extra income to make ends meet. Other families expect this money to finance college. Thus, if teenagers lose their minimum wage jobs, some families will face a hardship, and some teenagers will have to give up dreams of college.

Teenagers will not be the only ones who lose jobs if the minimum wage is increased. Many unskilled workers hold minimum wage jobs, and they will be affected. Once the jobs held by unskilled workers become too expensive for employers, these jobs will be

Erika added a title.

The introduction is revised to create reader interest. The thesis remains the same.

Because her teacher considered paragraph 2 to be strong, Erika left this paragraph as it was.

In response to her teacher's question, Erika offers more on why loss of teen jobs is a problem.

At her teacher's suggestion, Erika eliminates repetition from this paragraph and strengthens the detail.

consolidated or eliminated wherever possible, putting more people in the unemployment lines.

With increased unemployment will come an increase in welfare recipients. Some people think that raising the minimum wage will encourage people to get off welfare and look for a job. While some people might be encouraged to look for work, the unskilled jobs many of them need will no longer exist because they were eliminated to save costs that resulted from the higher minimum wage. Thus, the rolls of welfare will not be reduced at all.

Although raising the minimum wage is not a good idea, people who want to do so have some good reasons. They hope to increase the amount of money people have, and they hope to reduce welfare rolls. However, these worthy goals can be achieved in other ways. For example, the government can offer tax credits to those who earn minimum wage. This will give minimum wage earners more money without creating the problems associated with raising the minimum wage. The government could also use job training programs to train those on welfare for jobs that would keep them employed. In addition, the government could pay employers a stipend or offer them a tax break if they hire people who are currently unemployed. Any of these plans would increase the income of people who need the money and help reduce the welfare and unemployment rolls. Thus, raising the minimum wage, which would create problems, is not the best course of action.

At her teacher's suggestion, Erika improved her conclusion by discussing alternatives to raising the minimum wage.

⇒≫ EXERCISES

1. In the following sample thesis statements, underline the topic once and the writer's view of the topic twice.
   a. American culture places too much importance on physical attractiveness.
   b. Because self-publishing on the Internet has become so popular, copyright laws must be reconsidered.
   c. Hate speech, in my opinion, does not deserve Constitutional protection.

d. Although a controversy currently surrounds the use of Ritalin for medicating school children, this drug is a successful treatment for attention deficit hyperactivity disorder.

e. History will prove that Jimmy Carter was one of our most underrated presidents.

2. Using the suggestions beginning on p. 24, identify three topics you might like to write about. If you need help, browse through the readings in this book for ideas.

3. Select one of the three topics you discovered. Using any of the techniques described on pp. 27–28, discover at least five ideas for developing the topic. If one technique does not yield five ideas, try a second one.

4. Study the ideas you generated and compose a suitable thesis statement. Be sure it expresses both your topic and view.

5. Which of the following could help you develop your thesis: description, narration, exemplification, comparison-contrast, cause-and-effect analysis, process analysis, classification, definition?

6. Write an informal outline that could guide your writing of a first draft based on the thesis you composed and ideas you discovered. Does it look as though you have enough material to begin a draft? If not, do some additional idea generation.

7. Write a first draft.

8. Trade drafts with a classmate and complete a Reader Response Form like the one on p. 43.

9. If your instructor requests it, revise and edit your draft for submission.

Lives in Transition

Image provided by EyeWire Inc. 2001

Tony Freeman/PhotoEdit

CHAPTER 3

THE STAGES OF LIFE:
HOW DO WE GROW AND CHANGE?

"We arrive at the various stages of life quite as novices."

Francois de La Rochefoucauld

"In youth we learn; in age we understand."

Marie von Ebner-Eschenbach

"The American ideal is youth—handsome, empty youth."

Henry Miller

"Remember that as a teenager you are at the last stage in your life when you will be happy to hear that the phone is for you."

Fran Lebowitz

The Chase

ANNIE DILLARD

Pittsburgh native Annie Dillard has had a distinguished career. A prolific author of books, essays, literary criticism, and reflections on writing, she won the 1974 Pulitzer Prize for her personal narrative, *A Pilgrim at Tinker Creek*. Dillard is an adjunct professor at Wesleyan University in Connecticut and a contributing editor for *Harper's*. The following selection is from her 1987 autobiography, *An American Childhood*.

Preview.   The thrill of the chase—that's what Dillard writes of in this autobiographical essay. It's the thrill that comes from putting everything you have into a physical activity and never giving up. Perhaps you know that thrill. If you are an athlete, you may have experienced it while racing for the finish line, skiing down a steep slope, or running down court to score a basket. Before reading "The Chase," try to remember when you were 7 years old, and imagine that you have thrown a ball at a stranger's house and broken the window. The owner storms out of the house, clearly very angry, and begins to come after you. What do you do? Why do you do it? How do you feel? Remember, try to answer these questions as the 7-year-old you used to be.

Vocabulary.   If any of the following words from the selection are unfamiliar to you, study their meanings before reading.

crenellated (5)   having notches and indentations like the molding on castle battlements
translucent (6)   clear, allowing light to shine through
mazy (12)   full of confusing turns, like a maze
impelled (14)   moved, forced
labyrinths (15)   mazes
perfunctorily (18)   done as a routine duty and without enthusiasm or interest
dismembered (20)   cut the limbs off

Some boys taught me to play football. This was fine sport. You thought up a new strategy for every play and whispered it to the others. You went out for a pass, fooling everyone. Best, you got to throw yourself mightily at someone's running legs. Either you brought him down or you hit the ground flat out on your chin, with your arms empty before you. It was all or nothing. If you hesitated in fear, you would miss and get hurt: you would take a hard fall while the kid got away, or you would get kicked in the face while the kid got away. But if you flung yourself wholeheartedly at the back of his knees—if you gathered and joined body and soul and pointed them diving fearlessly—then you likely wouldn't get hurt, and you'd stop the ball. Your fate, and your team's score, depended on your concentration and courage. Nothing girls did could compare with it.

2   Boys welcomed me at baseball, too, for I had, through enthusiastic practice, what was weirdly known as a boy's arm. In winter, in the snow, there was neither baseball nor football, so the boys and I threw snowballs at passing cars. I got in trouble throwing snowballs, and have seldom been happier since.

3   On one weekday morning after Christmas, six inches of new snow had just fallen. We were standing up to our boot tops in snow on a front yard on trafficked Reynolds Street, waiting for cars. The cars traveled Reynolds Street slowly and evenly; they were targets all but wrapped in red ribbons, cream puffs. We couldn't miss.

4   I was seven; the boys were eight, nine, and ten. The oldest two Fahey boys were there—Mikey and Peter—polite blond boys who lived near me on Lloyd Street, and who already had four brothers and sisters. My parents approved Mikey and Peter Fahey. Chickie McBride was there, a tough kid, and Billy Paul and Mackie Kean too, from across Reynolds, where the boys grew up dark and furious, grew up skinny, knowing, and skilled. We had all drifted from our houses that morning looking for action, and had found it here on Reynolds Street.

5   It was cloudy but cold. The cars' tires laid behind them on the snowy street a complex trail of beige chunks like crenellated castle walls. I had stepped on some earlier; they squeaked. We could have wished for more traffic. When a car came, we all popped it one. In the intervals between cars we reverted to the natural solitude of children.

6   I started making an iceball—a perfect iceball, from perfectly white snow, perfectly spherical, and squeezed perfectly translucent so no snow remained all the way through. (The Fahey boys and I considered it unfair actually to throw an iceball at somebody, but it had been known to happen.)

7   I had just embarked on the iceball project when we heard tire chains come clanking from afar. A black Buick was moving toward us down the street. We all spread out, banged together some regular snowballs, took aim, and, when the Buick drew nigh, fired.

8   A soft snowball hit the driver's windshield right before the driver's face. It made a smashed star with a hump in the middle.

9   Often, of course, we hit our target, but this time, the only time in all of life, the car pulled over and stopped. Its wide black door opened; a man got out of it, running. He didn't even close the car door.

10   He ran after us, and we ran away from him, up the snowy Reynolds sidewalk. At the corner, I looked back; incredibly, he was still after us. He was in city clothes: a suit and tie, street shoes, Any normal adult would have quit, having sprung us into flight and made his point. This man was gaining on us. He was a thin man, all action. All of a sudden, we were running for our lives.

11   Wordless, we split up. We were on our turf; we could lose ourselves in the neighborhood backyards, everyone for himself. I paused and considered. Everyone had vanished except Mike Fahey, who was just rounding the corner of a yellow brick house. Poor Mikey, I trailed him. The driver of the Buick sensibly picked the two of us to follow. The man apparently had all day.

12   He chased Mikey and me around the yellow house and up a backyard path we knew by heart: under a low tree, up a bank, through a hedge, down some snowy steps, and across the grocery store's delivery driveway. We smashed through a gap in another hedge, entered a scruffy backyard and ran around its back porch and tight between houses to Edgerton Avenue; we ran across Edgerton to an alley and up our own sliding woodpile to the Halls' front yard; he kept coming. We ran up Lloyd Street and wound through mazy backyards toward the steep hilltop at Willard and Lang.

13   He chased us silently, block after block. He chased us silently over picket fences, through thorny hedges, between houses, around garbage cans, and across streets. Every time I glanced back, choking for breath, I expected he would have quit. He must have been as breathless as we were. His jacket strained over his body. It was an immense discovery, pounding into my hot head with every sliding, joyous step, that this ordinary adult evidently knew what I thought only children who trained at football knew: that you have to fling yourself at what you're doing, you have to point yourself, forget yourself, aim, dive.

14   Mikey and I had nowhere to go, in our own neighborhood or out of it, but away from this man who was chasing us. He impelled us forward; we compelled him to follow our route. The air was cold; every breath tore my throat. We kept running, block after block; we kept improvising, backyard after backyard, running a frantic course and choosing it simultaneously, failing always to find small places or hard places to slow him down, and discovering always, exhilarated, dismayed, that only bare speed could save us—for he would never give up, this man—and we were losing speed.

15   He chased us through the backyard labyrinths of ten blocks before he caught us by our jackets. He caught us and we all stopped.

16   We three stood staggering, half blinded, coughing, in an obscure hilltop backyard: a man in his twenties, a boy, a girl. He had released our jackets, our pursuer, our captor, our hero: he knew we weren't going anywhere. We all played by the rules. Mikey and I unzipped our jackets. I pulled off my sopping mittens. Our tracks multiplied in the backyard's new snow. We had been breaking new snow all morning. We didn't look at each other. I was cherishing my excitement. The man's lower pants legs were wet; his cuffs were full of snow, and there was a prow of snow beneath them on his shoes and socks. Some trees bordered the little flat backyard, some messy winter trees. There was no one around: a clearing in a grove, and we the only players.

17   It was a long time before he could speak. I had some difficulty at first recalling why we were there. My lips felt swollen; I couldn't see out of the sides of my eyes; I kept coughing.

18   "You stupid kids," he began perfunctorily.

19   We listened perfunctorily indeed, if we listened at all, for the chewing out was redundant, a mere formality, and beside the point. The point was that he had chased us passionately without giving up, and so he had caught us. Now he came down to earth. I wanted the glory to last forever.

20   But how could the glory have lasted forever? We could have run through every backyard in North America until we got to Panama. But when he trapped us at the lip of the Panama Canal, what precisely could he have done to prolong the drama of the chase and cap its glory? I brooded about this for the next few years. He could only have fried Mikey Fahey and me in boiling oil, say, or dismembered us piecemeal, or staked us to anthills. None of which I really wanted, and none of which any adult was likely to do, even in the spirit of fun. He could only chew us out there in the Panamanian jungle, after months or years of exalting pursuit. He could only begin, "You stupid kids," and continue in his ordinary Pittsburgh accent with his normal righteous anger and the usual common sense.

21   If in that snowy backyard the driver of the black Buick had cut off our heads, Mikey's and mine, I would have died happy, for nothing has required so much of me since as being chased all over Pittsburgh in the middle of the win-ter—running terrified, exhausted—by this sainted, skinny, furious redheaded man who wished to have a word with us. I don't know how he found his way back to his car.

Understanding Content

1. Dillard believed that the adult who chased her knew something that was the special knowledge of children who played football. What did he know?
2. Dillard relishes the memory of the chase so much that she remembers it into adulthood and writes about it. Why does she relish the memory so much?
3. As a child, what was Dillard's opinion of the man who chased her?
4. In a sentence, write out the thesis of "The Chase."

Considering Structure and Technique

1. Dillard opens with a description of playing football. How is this opening related to the chase she later narrates?
2. A master wordsmith, Dillard uses many effective descriptions to create moods and help the reader visualize scene. For example, in paragraph 5, she describes the car's tire tracks as "a complex trail of beige chunks like crenellated castle walls." (See the Writing Workshop on mental images on p. 60 for more on description.) Cite three other examples of effective de-scription.
3. In paragraph 6, Dillard repeats *perfect* and *perfectly*. What is the effect of this repetition?
4. Why is there so little description of the man and the lecture he gave?

Exploring Ideas

1. Using the evidence in the essay for clues, describe the kind of child Dillard was.
2. While she was running, how much danger do you think Dillard believed herself to be in?
3. What is Dillard saying in paragraph 1 about the difference between boys' and girls' activities? Do you agree with her view? Explain.
4. Dillard finds the man's behavior admirable. Do you agree? Explain.

Writing Workshop: Creating Mental Images

Descriptive words help writers create **mental images,** which are pictures in the mind of the reader. For example, in paragraph 8, Dillard writes that the snowball "made a smashed star with a hump in the middle." This description helps the reader form a mental image of the snowball's impact on the windshield. In paragraph 12, Dillard helps the reader form a mental image of a portion of the chase with this description: "We smashed through a gap in another hedge, entered a scruffy backyard and ran around its back porch and tight between houses to Edgerton Avenue." You may think that creating vivid mental images requires lots of descriptive words, but this is not so. You can get the best results by relying on just a few simple, specific words, as Dillard does in the following examples from the essay. (The simple, specific words are underlined as a study aid.)

. . . we heard tire chains come <u>clanking</u> from afar. Paragraph 7

We ran up <u>Lloyd Street</u> and <u>wound</u> through <u>mazy</u> backyards toward the <u>steep</u> hilltop at <u>Willard and Lang</u>. Paragraph 12

I pulled off my <u>sopping</u> mittens. Paragraph 16

For a related lesson, see the workshops on using specific verbs (p. 200).

Writing Workshop Activity

With three or four classmates, write a descriptive sentence to create a mental image of one of the following:

1. The arms of a bodybuilder
2. The way a toddler walks
3. The face of a person who just walked in on his or her own surprise party

Remember to use simple words that are specific. Also, keep in mind that writers usually rewrite their descriptions several times before they are satisfied, so you and your group members should expect to revise repeatedly until you are happy with your sentence.

Language Notes for Multilingual and Other Writers

A number of English idioms refer to movement and/or a person's position in space in relation to another. These idioms are illustrated in "The Chase":

1. *To gain on someone* is to narrow the distance between you.

This man was <u>gaining on us</u>. Paragraph 10

2. *To be on one's turf* is to be positioned on one's home or familiar territory.

We were <u>on our turf</u>; we could lose ourselves in the neighborhood backyards . . . Paragraph 11

3. *To round the corner* is to come around a corner.

Everyone had vanished except Mikey Fahey, who was just <u>rounding the corner</u> of a yellow brick house . . . Paragraph 11

4. *To trail someone* is to follow behind that person.

Poor Mikey, I <u>trailed him</u>. The driver of the Buick sensibly picked the two of us to follow. Paragraph 11

From Reading to Writing

In Your Journal: List your most vivid childhood experiences with adults. Then pick one experience from the list and explain why it is so memorable.

With Some Classmates: In her opening, Dillard suggests that there is a difference between boys' and girls' activities and that boys' activities are better. With some classmates, consider the issue. Are there gender differences in the way children play? Is one gender's play superior to the other's? Cite examples to support your view.

In an Essay

- Retell the story of the chase from the adult's point of view. Like Dillard, use description to create vivid mental images.
- Tell about an encounter with an adult that you had as a child. Be sure the encounter was one that aroused a strong feeling in you or one that revealed something about you or the adult. The previous journal writing may help you with this assignment.

- Tell about a time when you committed yourself completely to a task, activity, or other experience. Discuss the benefits and drawbacks of such total dedication.
- One thing that makes the chase so memorable for Dillard is that an adult behaved in an unexpected way. Tell about a time someone you know acted in an unexpected or improbable way. Also explain the effects of the unexpected behavior.

Beyond the Writing Class: Some educational researchers maintain that boys and girls are treated differently in the classroom. There is no agreement on this issue, however. Some researchers maintain that boys receive preferential treatment, and some maintain that girls do. Observe the way the genders are treated in your own classes, paying attention to such things as which gender is called on more often, which is praised more, which is asked harder questions, and which is given more time to answer. Then write an essay presenting your findings and the conclusions they suggest.

Complexion
RICHARD RODRIGUEZ

San Francisco native Richard Rodriguez is a first-generation Mexican-American who spoke only Spanish until he was 6-years-old. An editor at Pacific News Service and a contributing editor to *Harper's, U.S. News and World Report,* and the "Opinion" section of the *Los Angeles Times,* Rodriguez has also written for the *New York Times, The Wall Street Journal, Mother Jones,* and *The New Republic.* In 1997, Rodriguez received the George Foster Peabody Award, one of television's highest honors, for his NewsHour essays on American Life. The following selection is from his autobiography, *The Hunger of Memory* (1981).

Preview. "Complexion" deals with feeling unattractive as an adolescent. To explore how common it is to feel unattractive as an adolescent and how adolescent feelings of attractiveness or unattractiveness affect people later in life, form a group with three or four classmates. Each of you ask ten people these questions:

1. On a scale of 1 to 10 (10 is the highest), how attractive did you feel in high school?
2. On a scale of 1 to 10, how much do the feelings of attractiveness or unattractiveness that you felt in high school affect you today?
3. What is your age?

Report your group's findings to the rest of the class. As a class, try to draw a conclusion about how much we continue to be affected by the self-concepts we have in high school.

Vocabulary. If any of the following words from the selection are unfamiliar to you, study their meanings before reading.

buoyant (1)   floating
incessantly (2)   nonstop
menial (4)   lowly or fitting for a servant
braceros (7)   Spanish word for Mexican laborers admitted temporarily into the country to do seasonal work, like harvesting crops
taboo (7)   a social restriction
precocious (9)   matured earlier than usual
taunt (9)   tease; insult
pomade (9)   a scented ointment or dressing for the hair
los pobres (10)   the poor ones
effeminate (10)   having feminine characteristics

Complexion. My first conscious experience of sexual excitement concerns my complexion. One summer weekend, when I was around seven years old, I was at a public swimming pool with the whole family. I remember sitting on the damp pavement next to the pool and seeing my mother, in the spectators' bleachers, holding my younger sister on her lap. My mother, I noticed, was watching my father as he stood on a diving board, waving to her. I watched her wave back. Then saw her radiant, bashful, astonishing smile. In that second I sensed that my mother and father had a relationship I knew nothing about. A nervous excitement encircled my stomach as I saw my mother's eyes follow my father's figure curving into the water. A second or two later, he emerged. I heard him call out. Smiling, his voice sounded buoyant, calling me to swim to him. But turning to see him, I caught my mother's eye. I heard her shout over to me. In Spanish she called through the crowd: "Put a towel on over your shoulders." In public, she didn't want to say why. I knew.

2   That incident anticipates the shame and sexual inferiority I was to feel in later years because of my dark complexion. I was to grow up an ugly child. Or one who thought himself ugly. (*Feo.*) One night when I was eleven or twelve years old, I locked myself in the bathroom and carefully regarded my reflection in the mirror over the sink. Without any pleasure I studied my skin. I turned on the faucet. (In my mind I heard the swirling voices of aunts, and even my mother's voice, whispering, whispering incessantly about lemon juice solutions and dark, *feo* children.) With a bar of soap, I fashioned a thick ball of lather. I began soaping my arms. I took my father's straight razor out of the medicine cabinet. Slowly, with steady deliberateness, I put the blade against my flesh, pressed it as close as I could without cutting, and moved it up and down across my skin to see if I could get out, somehow lessen, the dark. All I succeeded in doing, however, was in shaving my arms bare of their hair. For as I noted with disappointment, the dark would not come out. It remained. Trapped. Deep in the cells of my skin.

3   Throughout adolescence, I felt myself mysteriously marked. Nothing else about my appearance would concern me so much as the fact that my complexion was dark. My mother would say how sorry she was that there was not money enough to get braces to straighten my teeth. But I never bothered about my teeth. In three-way mirrors at department stores, I'd see my profile dramatically defined by a long nose, but it was really only the color of my skin that caught my attention.

4   I wasn't afraid that I would become a menial laborer because of my skin. Nor did my complexion make me feel especially vulnerable to racial abuse. (I didn't really consider my dark skin to be a racial characteristic. I would have been only too happy to look as Mexican as my light-skinned older brother.) Simply, I judged myself ugly. And, since the women in my family had been the ones who discovered it in such worried tones, I felt my dark skin made me unattractive to women.

5   Thirteen years old. Fourteen. In a grammar school art class, when the assignment was to draw a self-portrait, I tried and I tried but could not bring myself to shade in the face on the paper to anything like my actual tone. With disgust then I would come face to face with myself in mirrors. With disappointment I located myself in class photographs—my dark face undefined by the camera which had clearly described the white faces of classmates. Or I'd see my dark wrist against my long-sleeved white shirt.

6   I grew divorced from my body. Insecure, overweight, listless. On hot summer days when my rubber-soled shoes soaked up the heat from the sidewalk, I kept my head down. Or walked in the shade. My mother didn't need anymore to tell me to watch out for the sun. I denied myself a sensational life. The normal, extraordinary, animal excitement of feeling my body alive—riding shirtless on a bicycle in the warm wind created by furious self-propelled motion—the sensations that first had excited in me a sense of my maleness, I denied. I was too ashamed of my body. I wanted to forget that I had a body because I had a brown body. I was grateful that none of my classmates ever mentioned the fact.

7   I continued to see the *braceros,* those men I resembled in one way and, in another way, didn't resemble at all. On the watery horizon of a Valley afternoon, I'd see them. And though I feared looking like them, it was with silent envy that I regarded them still. I envied them their physical lives, their freedom to violate the taboo of the sun. Closer to home I would notice the shirtless construction workers, the roofers, the sweating men tarring the street in front of the house. And I'd see the Mexican gardeners. I was unwilling to admit the attraction of their lives. I tried to deny it by looking away. But what was denied became strongly desired.

8   In high school physical education classes, I withdrew, in the regular company of five or six classmates, to a distant corner of a football field where we smoked and talked. Our company was composed of bodies too short or too tall, all graceless and all—except mine—pale. Our conversation was usually witty. (In fact we were intelligent.) If we referred to the athletic contests around us, it was with sarcasm. With savage scorn I'd refer to the "animals" playing football or baseball. It would have been important for me to have joined them. Or for me to have taken off my shirt, to have let the sun burn dark on my skin, and to have run barefoot on the warm wet grass. It would have been very important. Too important. It would have been too telling a gesture—to admit the desire for sensation, the body, my body.

9   Fifteen, sixteen. I was a teenager shy in the presence of girls. Never dated. Barely could talk to a girl without stammering. In high school I went to several dances, but I never managed to ask a girl to dance. So I stopped going. I cannot remember high school years now with the parade of typical images: bright drive-ins or gliding blue shadows of a Junior Prom. At home most weekend nights, I would pass evenings reading. Like those hidden, precocious

adolescents who have no real-life sexual experiences, I read a great deal of romantic fiction. "You won't find it in your books," my brother would playfully taunt me as he prepared to go to a party by freezing the crest of the wave in his hair with sticky pomade. Through my reading, however, I developed a fabulous and sophisticated sexual imagination. At seventeen, I may not have known how to engage a girl in small talk, but I had read *Lady Chatterley's Lover.*

10   It annoyed me to hear my father's teasing: that I would never know what "real work" is; that my hands were so soft. I think I knew it was his way of admitting pleasure and pride in my academic success. But I didn't smile. My mother said she was glad her children were getting their educations and would not be pushed around like *los pobres.* I heard the remark ironically as a reminder of my separation from *los braceros.* At such times I suspected that education was making me effeminate. The odd thing, however, was that I did not judge my classmates so harshly. Nor did I consider my male teachers in high school effeminate. It was only myself I judged against some shadowy, mythical Mexican laborer—dark like me, yet very different.

Understanding Content

1. In your own words, write out the main idea of "Complexion." Which sentence functions as the thesis because it best expresses that main idea?
2. As an adolescent, how did Rodriguez feel about his body?
3. Who caused Rodriguez to feel the way he did about his body?
4. How did the women in Rodriguez's family contribute to the author's self-consciousness?
5. Specifically, how did Rodriguez's feelings about his body affect his life and how he spent his time?

Considering Structure and Technique

1. Writers often use a **topic sentence** to indicate the focus of a particular body paragraph. (See p. 38 for a discussion of topic sentences.) Which of Rodriguez's body paragraphs open with topic sentences? How do those topic sentences help the reader?
2. Rodriguez uses description to create **mental images,** which are pictures formed in the mind. For example, in paragraph 6, he creates a mental image of a hot summer day with the words "my rubber-soled shoes soaked up the heat from the sidewalk." Cite two other descriptions that create mental images. What do such mental images add to the essay? (For a writing workshop on mental images, see p. 60.)
3. The details in "Complexion" are arranged in **chronological** (time) **order.** What words in paragraphs 1, 2, and 3 signal that chronological order? In paragraph 5? In paragraph 8? In paragraph 9?
4. Explain the meaning of *sensational life* in this sentence from paragraph 6: "I denied myself a sensational life."

Exploring Ideas

1. Why do you think Rodriguez was bothered by his dark skin?
2. Why do you think Rodriguez did so much reading? Why do you think he was afraid that his reading and other forms of education might make him more effeminate?
3. Would Rodriguez have been a happy teenager if his skin had been light? Explain your view.
4. Assume you are the guidance counselor in Rodriguez's high school and that Rodriguez tells you about his feelings of inferiority. What advice would you give him?

Writing Workshop: Using Parentheses

Think of material in parentheses as something the author wants to whisper in your ear. Sometimes the whispered information is a side comment or explanation that is less important than the material outside the parentheses, so it is downplayed. But just as a whisper is sometimes saved for important, confidential information, the parentheses can be used for the most important information of all. These examples from "Complexion" illustrate the uses of parentheses:

1. Or one who thought himself ugly. (*Feo.*) Paragraph 2
   The material in parentheses is explanation or definition that is downplayed.

2. (In my mind I heard the swirling voices of aunts, and even my mother's voice, whispering, whispering incessantly about lemon juice solutions and dark, *feo* children.) Paragraph 2
   The material in parentheses is an important revelation that is emphasized as a shared confidence.

Writing Workshop Activity

Examine the two other sets of parentheses in "Complexion." (These are in paragraphs 4 and 8.) Then indicate how these parentheses are used (to downplay or to highlight). Next, look at the parentheses in this paragraph you are reading now and indicate how they are used. When you write from now on, try using parentheses if you want to whisper in your reader's ear. If you feel insecure with this punctuation mark, use it in your journal writing until you feel more comfortable.

Language Notes for Multilingual and Other Writers

In English, prepositions of *place* usually appear before prepositions of *time*. Here is an example from "Complexion":

place   time
[On the watery horizon][of a Valley afternoon], I'd see them. Paragraph 7

From Reading to Writing

In Your Journal: Explain how you felt about yourself as a teenager. Were you self-conscious? Was there something about your physical appearance that you particularly disliked? Also explain whether or not your adolescent view of yourself continues to affect you today. If so, explain how; if not, explain why not.

With Some Classmates: Consider whether or not Rodriguez's adolescent feelings about himself were typical. To support your view, draw on examples taken from observation and personal experience.

In an Essay

- Tell about some aspect of yourself that makes or made you self-conscious. Also discuss what effect this self-consciousness has or had on you. As an alternative, tell about a time you felt self-conscious, being sure to explain why you felt that way.
- In paragraph 1, Rodriguez tells of watching his parents and sensing for the first time that they "had a relationship [he] knew nothing about." Tell about a time when you learned something about one or both of your parents (or someone else close to you). For example, you could tell about the time you first learned that your mother or father had a problem. Also explain how you were affected by the knowledge.
- Things that occur when we are young often influence us into old age. Tell about something in your past that continues to influence you now and that is likely to do so into the future. Try to explain why the effect has been so lasting.
- Explain how society and culture influence our standards of attractiveness. You might consider such things as advertisements, television shows, movie stars, film, the fashion industry, and so forth.

Beyond the Writing Class: Based on what you learned from reading "Complexion" and your own experience and observation, write a report that explains how teachers, administrators, and parents can help teenagers develop strong self-images. Send the report to your local school board.

Graduation

MAYA ANGELOU

In addition to publishing several volumes of poetry, children's books, and five autobiographical volumes, poet laureate Maya Angelou has been a professional dancer and actress. Currently a professor at Wake Forest University, Angelou has also been a coordinator for the Southern Christian Leadership Conference. Raped when she was eight and a mother when she was sixteen, Angelou's life has been filled with adversity and triumph. The following selection is from her autobiographical book, *I Know Why the Caged Bird Sings* (1970).

Preview. In a page or two of your journal, tell about your high school graduation. Was the event what you expected it to be? Did you look forward to it very much? Did it go smoothly? Answer these questions and add any other details you wish to.

Vocabulary. If any of the following words from the selection are unfamiliar to you, study their meanings before reading.

extended family (1)   a couple, their children, and close relatives such as grandparents, aunts, uncles, and cousins; a wide-ranging kinship group
pervaded (3)   spread through the parts of
pique (7)   fabric with a woven design
decipher (9)   make out the meaning of something
trammeled (10)   restrained
purported (17)   claimed
fatalism (20)   the belief that events are governed by fate and cannot be influenced
presentiment (30)   a feeling that something is about to happen
perfunctory (48)   hasty and superficial
elocution (53)   public speaking

The children in Stamps* trembled visibly with anticipation. Some adults were excited too, but to be certain the whole young population had come down with graduation epidemic. Large classes were graduating from both the grammar school and the high school. Even those who were years removed from their own day of glorious release were anxious to help with preparations as a kind of dry run. The junior students who were moving into the vacating

*A town in Arkansas where Angelou and her brother Bailey were raised by their grandmother ("Momma").

classes' chairs were tradition-bound to show their talents for leadership and management. They strutted through the school and around the campus exerting pressure on the lower grades. Their authority was so new that occasionally if they pressed a little too hard it had to be overlooked. After all, next term was coming, and it never hurt a sixth grader to have a play sister in the eighth grade, or a tenth-year student to be able to call a twelfth grader Bubba. So all was endured in a spirit of shared understanding. But the graduating classes themselves were the nobility. Like travelers with exotic destinations on their minds, the graduates were remarkably forgetful. They came to school without their books, or tablets or even pencils. Volunteers fell over themselves to secure replacements for the missing equipment. When accepted, the willing workers might or might not be thanked, and it was of no importance to the pregraduation rites. Even teachers were respectful of the now quiet and aging seniors, and tended to speak to them, if not as equals, as beings only slightly lower than themselves. After tests were returned and grades given, the student body, which acted like an extended family, knew who did well, who excelled, and what piteous ones had failed.

2   Unlike the white high school, Lafayette County Training School distinguished itself by having neither lawn, nor hedges, nor tennis court, nor climbing ivy. Its two buildings (main classrooms, the grade school and home economics) were set on a dirt hill with no fence to limit either its boundaries or those of bordering farms. There was a large expanse to the left of the school which was used alternately as a baseball diamond or a basketball court. Rusty hoops on the swaying poles represented the permanent recreational equipment, although bats and balls could be borrowed from the P.E. teacher if the borrower was qualified and if the diamond wasn't occupied.

3   Over this rocky area relieved by a few shady tall persimmon trees the graduating class walked. The girls often held hands and no longer bothered to speak to the lower students. There was a sadness about them, as if this old world was not their home and they were bound for higher ground. The boys, on the other hand, had become more friendly, more outgoing. A decided change from the closed attitude they projected while studying for finals. Now they seemed not ready to give up the old school, the familiar paths and classrooms. Only a small percentage would be continuing on to college—one of the South's A & M (agricultural and mechanical) schools, which trained Negro youths to be carpenters, farmers, handymen, masons, maids, cooks and baby nurses. Their future rode heavily on their shoulders, and blinded them to the collective joy that had pervaded the lives of the boys and girls in the grammar school graduating class.

4   Parents who could afford it had ordered new shoes and ready-made clothes for themselves from Sears and Roebuck or Montgomery Ward. They also engaged the best seamstresses to make the floating graduating dresses and to cut down secondhand pants which would be pressed to a military slickness for the important event.

5   Oh, it was important, all right. Whitefolks would attend the ceremony, and two or three would speak of God and home, and the Southern way of life, and Mrs. Parsons, the principal's wife, would play the graduation march while the lower-grade graduates paraded down the aisles and took their seats below the platform. The high school seniors would wait in empty classrooms to make their dramatic entrance.

6   In the Store I was the person of the moment. The birthday girl. The center. Bailey had graduated the year before, although to do so he had had to forfeit all pleasures to make up for his time lost in Baton Rouge.

7   My class was wearing butter-yellow pique dresses, and Momma launched out on mine. She smocked the yoke into tiny crisscrossing puckers, then shirred the rest of the bodice. Her dark fingers ducked in and out of the lemony cloth as she embroidered raised daisies around the hem. Before she considered herself finished she had added a crocheted cuff on the puff sleeves, and a pointy crocheted collar.

8   I was going to be lovely. A walking model of all the various styles of fine hand sewing and it didn't worry me that I was only twelve years old and merely graduating from the eighth grade. Besides, many teachers in Arkansas Negro schools had only that diploma and were licensed to impart wisdom.

9   The days had become longer and more noticeable. The faded beige of former times had been replaced with strong and sure colors. I began to see my classmates' clothes, their skin tones, and the dust that waved off pussy willows. Clouds that lazed across the sky were objects of great concern to me. Their shiftier shapes might have held a message that in my new happiness and with a little bit of time I'd soon decipher. During that period I looked at the arch of heaven so religiously my neck kept a steady ache. I had taken to smiling more often, and my jaws hurt from the unaccustomed activity. Between the two physical sore spots, I suppose I could have been uncomfortable, but that was not the case. As a member of the winning team (the graduating class of 1940) I had outdistanced unpleasant sensations by miles. I was headed for the freedom of open fields.

10   Youth and social approval allied themselves with me and we trammeled memories of slights and insults. The wind of our swift passage remodeled my features. Lost tears were pounded to mud and then to dust. Years of withdrawal were brushed aside and left behind, as hanging ropes of parasitic moss.

11   My work alone had awarded me a top place and I was going to be one of the first called in the graduating ceremonies. On the classroom blackboard, as well as on the bulletin board in the auditorium, there were blue stars and white stars and red stars. No absences, no tardinesses, and my academic work was among the best of the year. I could say the preamble to the Constitution even faster than Bailey. We timed ourselves often: WethepeopleoftheUnited-Statesinordertoformamoreperfectunion. . . ." I had memorized the Presidents of the United States from Washington to Roosevelt in chronological as well as alphabetical order.

12   My hair pleased me too. Gradually the black mass had lengthened and thickened, so that it kept at last to its braided pattern, and I didn't have to yank my scalp off when I tried to comb it.

13   Louise and I had rehearsed the exercises until we tired out ourselves. Henry Reed was class valedictorian. He was a small, very black boy with hooded eyes, a long, broad nose and an oddly shaped head. I had admired him for years because each term he and I vied for the best grades in our class. Most often he bested me, but instead of being disappointed I was pleased that we shared top places between us. Like many Southern Black children, he lived with his grandmother, who was as strict as Momma and as kind as she knew how to be. He was courteous, respectful and soft-spoken to elders, but on the playground he chose to play the roughest games. I admired him. Anyone, I reckoned, sufficiently afraid or sufficiently dull could be polite. But to be able to operate at a top level with both adults and children was admirable.

14   His valedictory speech was entitled "To Be or Not to Be." The rigid tenth-grade teacher had helped him to write it. He'd been working on the dramatic stresses for months.

15   The weeks until graduation were filled with heady activities. A group of small children were to be presented in a play about buttercups and daisies and bunny rabbits. They could be heard throughout the building practicing their hops and their little songs that sounded like silver bells. The older girls (non-graduates, of course) were assigned the task of making refreshments for the night's festivities. A tangy scent of ginger, cinnamon, nutmeg and chocolate wafted around the home economics building as the budding cooks made samples for themselves and their teachers.

16   In every corner of the workshop, axes and saws split fresh timber as the woodshop boys made sets and stage scenery. Only the graduates were left out of the general bustle. We were free to sit in the library at the back of the building or look in quite detachedly, naturally, on the measures being taken for our event.

17   Even the minister preached on graduation the Sunday before. His subject was "Let your light so shine that men will see your good works and praise your Father, Who is in Heaven." Although the sermon was purported to be addressed to us, he used the occasion to speak to backsliders, gamblers and general ne'er-do-wells. But since he had called our names at the beginning of the service we were mollified.

18   Among Negroes the tradition was to give presents to children going only from one grade to another. How much more important this was when the person was graduating at the top of the class. Uncle Willie and Momma had sent away for a Mickey Mouse watch like Bailey's. Louise gave me four embroidered handkerchiefs. (I gave her three crocheted doilies.) Mrs. Sneed, the minister's wife, made me an underskirt to wear for graduation, and nearly every customer gave me a nickel or maybe even a dime with the instruction "Keep on moving to higher ground," or some such encouragement.

19 Amazingly the great day finally dawned and I was out of bed before I knew it. I threw open the back door to see it more clearly, but Momma said, "Sister, come away from that door and put your robe on."

20 I hoped the memory of that morning would never leave me. Sunlight was itself still young, and the day had none of the insistence maturity would bring it in a few hours. In my robe and barefoot in the backyard, under cover of going to see about my new beans, I gave myself up to the gentle warmth and thanked God that no matter what evil I had done in my life He had allowed me to live to see this day. Somewhere in my fatalism I had expected to die, accidentally, and never have the chance to walk up the stairs in the auditorium and gracefully receive my hard-earned diploma. Out of God's merciful bosom I had won reprieve.

21 Bailey came out in his robe and gave me a box wrapped in Christmas paper. He said he had saved his money for months to pay for it. It felt like a box of chocolates, but I knew Bailey wouldn't save money to buy candy when we had all we could want under our noses.

22 He was as proud of the gift as I. It was a soft-leather-bound copy of a collection of poems by Edgar Allan Poe, or, as Bailey and I called him, "Eap." I turned to "Annabel Lee" and we walked up and down the garden rows, the cool dirt between our toes, reciting the beautifully sad lines.

23 Momma made a Sunday breakfast although it was only Friday. After we finished the blessing, I opened my eyes to find the watch on my plate. It was a dream of a day. Everything went smoothly and to my credit. I didn't have to be reminded or scolded for anything. Near evening I was too jittery to attend to chores, so Bailey volunteered to do all before his bath.

24 Days before, we had made a sign for the Store and as we turned out the lights Momma hung the cardboard over the doorknob. It read clearly: CLOSED. GRADUATION.

25 My dress fitted perfectly and everyone said that I looked like a sunbeam in it. On the hill, going toward the school, Bailey walked behind with Uncle Willie, who muttered, "Go on, Ju." He wanted him to walk ahead with us because it embarrassed him to have to walk so slowly. Bailey said he'd let the ladies walk together, and the men would bring up the rear. We all laughed, nicely.

26 Little children dashed by out of the dark like fireflies. Their crepe-paper dresses and butterfly wings were not made for running and we heard more than one rip, dryly, and the regretful "uh uh" that followed.

27 The school blazed without gaiety. The windows seemed cold and unfriendly from the lower hill. A sense of ill-fated timing crept over me, and if Momma hadn't reached for my hand I would have drifted back to Bailey and Uncle Willie, and possibly beyond. She made a few slow jokes about my feet getting cold, and tugged me along to the now-strange building.

28 Around the front steps, assurance came back. There were my fellow "greats," the graduating class. Hair brushed back, legs oiled, new dresses and pressed pleats, fresh pocket handkerchiefs and little handbags, all homesewn. Oh, we were up to snuff, all right. I joined my comrades and didn't even see my family go in to find seats in the crowded auditorium.

29   The school band struck up a march and all classes filed in as had been rehearsed. We stood in front of our seats, as assigned, and on a signal from the choir director, we sat. No sooner had this been accomplished than the band started to play the national anthem. We rose again and sang the song, after which we recited the pledge of allegiance. We remained standing for a brief minute before the choir director and the principal signaled to us, rather desperately I thought, to take our seats. The command was so unusual that our carefully rehearsed and smooth-running machine was thrown off. For a full minute we fumbled for our chairs and bumped into each other awkwardly. Habits change or solidify under pressure, so in our state of nervous tension we had been ready to follow our usual assembly pattern: the American National Anthem, then the pledge of allegiance, then the song every Black person I knew called the Negro National Anthem. All done in the same key, with the same passion and most often standing on the same foot.

30   Finding my seat at last, I was overcome with a presentiment of worse things to come. Something unrehearsed, unplanned, was going to happen, and we were going to be made to look bad. I distinctly remember being explicit in the choice of pronoun. It was "we," the graduating class, the unit, that concerned me then.

31   The principal welcomed "parents and friends" and asked the Baptist minister to lead us in prayer. His invocation was brief and punchy, and for a second I thought we were getting back on the high road to right action. When the principal came back to the dais, however, his voice had changed. Sounds always affected me profoundly and the principal's voice was one of my favorites. During assembly it melted and lowed weakly into the audience. It had not been in my plan to listen to him, but my curiosity was piqued and I straightened up to give him my attention.

32   He was talking about Booker T. Washington, our "late great leader," who said we can be as close as the fingers on the hand, etc. . . . Then he said a few vague things about friendship and the friendship of kindly people to those less fortunate than themselves. With that his voice nearly faded, thin, away. Like a river diminishing to a stream and then to a trickle. But he cleared his throat and said, "Our speaker tonight, who is also our friend, came from Texarkana to deliver the commencement address, but due to the irregularity of the train schedule, he's going to, as they say, 'speak and run.'" He said that we understood and wanted the man to know that we were most grateful for the time he was able to give us and then something about how we were willing always to adjust to another's program, and without more ado—"I give you Mr. Edward Donleavy."

33   Not one but two white men came through the door offstage. The shorter one walked to the speaker's platform, and the tall one moved over to the cen-

ter seat and sat down. But that was our principal's seat, and already occupied. The dislodged gentleman bounced around for a long breath or two before the Baptist minister gave him his chair, then with more dignity than the situation deserved, the minister walked off the stage.

34 Donleavy looked at the audience once (on reflection, I'm sure that he wanted only to reassure himself that we were really there), adjusted his glasses and began to read from a sheaf of papers.

35 He was glad "to be here and to see the work going on just as it was in the other schools."

36 At the first "Amen" from the audience I willed the offender to immediate death by choking on the word. But Amen's and Yes, sir's began to fall around the room like rain through a ragged umbrella.

37 He told us of the wonderful changes we children in Stamps had in store. The Central School (naturally, the white school was Central) had already been granted improvements that would be in use in the fall. A well-known artist was coming from Little Rock to teach art to them. They were going to have the newest microscopes and chemistry equipment for their laboratory. Mr. Donleavy didn't leave us long in the dark over who made these improvements available to Central High. Nor were we to be ignored in the general betterment scheme he had in mind.

38 He said that he had pointed out to people at a very high level that one of the first-line football tacklers at Arkansas Agricultural and Mechanical College had graduated from good old Lafayette County Training School. Here fewer Amen's were heard. Those few that did break through lay dully in the air with the heaviness of habit.

39 He went on to praise us. He went on to say how he had bragged that "one of the best basketball players at Fisk sank his first ball right here at Lafayette County Training School."

40 The white kids were going to have a chance to become Galileos and Madame Curies and Edisons and Gauguins, and our boys (the girls weren't even in on it) would try to be Jesse Owenses and Joe Louises.

41 Owens and the Brown Bomber were great heroes in our world, but what school official in the white-goddom of Little Rock had the right to decide that those two men must be our only heroes? Who decided that for Henry Reed to become a scientist he had to work like George Washington Carver, as a bootblack, to buy a lousy microscope? Bailey was obviously always going to be too small to be an athlete, so which concrete angel glued to what country seat had decided that if my brother wanted to become a lawyer he had to first pay penance for his skin by picking cotton and hoeing corn and studying correspondence books at night for twenty years?

42 The man's dead words fell like bricks around the auditorium and too many settled in my belly. Constrained by hard-learned manners I couldn't look behind me, but to my left and right the proud graduating class of 1940 had dropped their heads. Every girl in my row had found something new to do with

her handkerchief. Some folded the tiny squares into love knots, some into triangles, but most were wadding them, then pressing them flat on their yellow laps.

43   On the dais, the ancient tragedy was being replayed. Professor Parsons sat, a sculptor's reject, rigid. His large, heavy body seemed devoid of will or willingness, and his eyes said he was no longer with us. The other teachers examined the flag (which was draped stage right) or their notes, or the window which opened on our now-famous playing diamond.

44   Graduation, the hush-hush magic time of frills and gifts and congratulations and diplomas, was finished for me before my name was called. The accomplishment was nothing. The meticulous maps, drawn in three colors of ink, learning and spelling decasyllabic words, memorizing the whole of *The Rape of Lucrece*—it was nothing. Donleavy had exposed us.

45   We were maids and farmers, handymen and washerwomen, and anything higher that we aspired to was farcical and presumptuous. Then I wished that Gabriel Prosser and Nat Turner had killed all whitefolks in their beds and that Abraham Lincoln had been assassinated before the signing of the Emancipation Proclamation, and that Harriet Tubman had been killed by that blow on her head and Christopher Columbus had drowned in the *Santa Maria*.

46   It was awful to be Negro and have no control over my life. It was brutal to be young and already trained to sit quietly and listen to charges brought against my color with no chance of defense. We should all be dead. I thought I should like to see us all dead, one on top of the other. A pyramid of flesh with the whitefolks on the bottom, as the broad base, then the Indians with their silly tomahawks and teepees and wigwams and treaties, the Negroes with their mops and recipes and cotton sacks and spirituals sticking out of their mouths. The Dutch children should all stumble in their wooden shoes and break their necks. The French should choke to death on the Louisiana Purchase (1803) while silkworms ate all the Chinese with their stupid pigtails. As a species, we were an abomination. All of us.

47   Donleavy was running for election, and assured our parents that if he won we could count on having the only colored paved playing field in that part of Arkansas. Also—he never looked up to acknowledge the grunts of acceptance—also, we were bound to get some new equipment for the home economics building and the workshop.

48   He finished, and since there was no need to give any more than the most perfunctory thank-you's, he nodded to the men on the stage, and the tall white man who was never introduced joined him at the door. They left with the attitude that now they were off to something really important. (The graduation ceremonies at Lafayette County Training School had been a mere preliminary.)

49   The ugliness they left was palpable. An uninvited guest who wouldn't leave. The choir was summoned and sang a modern arrangement of "Onward, Christian Soldiers," with new words pertaining to graduates seeking their place in the world. But it didn't work. Elouise, the daughter of the Baptist minister, recited "Invictus," and I could have cried at the impertinence of "I am the master of my fate: I am the captain of my soul."

50   My name had lost its ring of familiarity and I had to be nudged to go and receive my diploma. All my preparations had fled. I neither marched up to the stage like a conquering Amazon, nor did I look in the audience for Bailey's nod of approval. Marguerite Johnson, I heard the name again, my honors were read, there were noises in the audience of appreciation, and I took my place on the stage as rehearsed.

51   I thought about colors I hated: ecru, puce, lavender, beige and black.

52   There was shuffling and rustling around me, then Henry Reed was giving his valedictory address, "To Be or Not to Be." Hadn't he heard the whitefolks? We couldn't *be,* so the question was a waste of time. Henry's voice came out clear and strong. I feared to look at him. Hadn't he got the message? There was no "nobler in the mind" for Negroes because the world didn't think we had minds, and they let us know it. "Outrageous fortune"? Now, that was a joke. When the ceremony was over I had to tell Henry Reed some things. That is, if I still cared. Not "rub," Henry, "erase." "Ah, there's the erase." Us.

53   Henry had been a good student in elocution. His voice rose on tides of promise and fell on waves of warnings. The English teacher had helped him to create a sermon winging through Hamlet's soliloquy. To be a man, a doer, a builder, a leader, or to be a tool, an unfunny joke, a crusher of funky toadstools. I marveled that Henry could go through with the speech as if we had a choice.

54   I had been listening and silently rebutting each sentence with my eyes closed; then there was a hush, which in an audience warns that something un-planned is happening. I looked up and saw Henry Reed, the conservative, the proper, the A student, turn his back to the audience and turn to us (the proud graduating class of 1940) and sing, nearly speaking,

> Lift ev'ry voice and sing
> Till earth and heaven ring
> Ring with the harmonies of Liberty . . .*

55   It was the poem written by James Weldon Johnson. It was the music composed by J. Rosamond Johnson. It was the Negro National Anthem. Out of habit we were singing it.

56   Our mothers and fathers stood in the dark hall and joined the hymn of encouragement. A kindergarten teacher led the small children onto the stage and the buttercups and daisies and bunny rabbits marked time and tried to follow:

> Stony the road we trod
> Bitter the chastening rod
> Felt in the days when hope, unborn, had died.
> Yet with a steady beat
> Have not our weary feet
> Come to the place for which our fathers sighed?

*"Lift Ev'ry Voice and Sing"—words by James Weldon Johnson and music by J. Rosamond John-son. © Copyrighted: Edward B. Marks Music Corporation. Used by permission.

57   Every child I knew had learned that song with his ABC's and along with "Jesus Loves Me This I Know." But I personally had never heard it before. Never heard the words, despite the thousands of times I had sung them. Never thought they had anything to do with me.

58   On the other hand, the words of Patrick Henry had made such an impression on me that I had been able to stretch myself tall and trembling and say, "I know not what course others may take, but as for me, give me liberty or give me death."

59   And now I heard, really for the first time:

We have come over a way that with tears has been watered,
We have come, treading our path through the blood of the slaughtered.

60   While echoes of the song shivered in the air, Henry Reed bowed his head, said "Thank you," and returned to his place in the line. The tears that slipped down many faces were not wiped away in shame.

61   We were on top again. As always, again. We survived. The depths had been icy and dark, but now a bright sun spoke to our souls. I was no longer simply a member of the proud graduating class of 1940; I was a proud member of the wonderful, beautiful Negro race.

62   Oh, Black known and unknown poets, how often have your auctioned pains sustained us? Who will compute the lonely nights made less lonely by your songs, or the empty pots made less tragic by your tales?

63   If we were a people much given to revealing secrets, we might raise monuments and sacrifice to the memories of our poets, but slavery cured us of that weakness. It may be enough, however, to have it said that we survive in exact relationship to the dedication of our poets (include preachers, musicians and blues singers).

Understanding Content

1. How did Angelou and her family feel about the upcoming graduation? How do you know?
2. What are the first signs of impending trouble at the graduation?
3. How did Angelou react to Donleavy's commencement speech?
4. According to Angelou, why are black poets so important?
5. In paragraph 43, what "ancient tragedy" is Angelou referring to?

Considering Structure and Technique

1. What do paragraphs 1 through 26 contribute to "Graduation"? If these paragraphs were omitted, what would be lost?
2. Angelou includes a great deal of description in "Graduation." What purpose does the description in paragraph 2 serve? The description in paragraph 7? The description in paragraphs 9 and 10?

3. Only one brief paragraph (paragraph 50) is devoted to the moment when Angelou receives her diploma. After all the careful detailing of her anticipation of that moment, why is so little written about it?
4. What elements of contrast are apparent in the selection?
5. How did "Graduation" make you feel? How does Angelou create that feeling?

Exploring Ideas

1. Why does Donleavy's speech have the effect that it does on those who hear it? What does he say that is so hurtful?
2. Do you think that Donleavy was aware that his speech was racially biased? Explain your view.
3. Why did Angelou think that the line from the poem "Invictus" was "impertinent" (paragraph 49)?
4. Why does Angelou "hear" the words of the "Negro National Anthem" for the first time?
5. Why did Henry begin the "Negro National Anthem"? Did his act take courage? Did he do the right thing? Explain your views.

Writing Workshop: Commenting on People, Events, and Scene in Narration

A **narration** tells a story. (The workshop on page 87 discusses narration.) When writers use narration for all or part of an essay, they sometimes comment on the events, scene, or people in the narration in order to point out their significance or in order to help the reader better understand points. For example, in paragraph 13, Angelou comments on the kind of person Henry is; she does this to help the reader understand the traits that helped him take the action he does later in the story. In paragraph 5, the author comments on why an event (graduation) was important so the reader understands its significance. In paragraph 2, Angelou comments on the scene (Lafayette County Training School) to help the reader understand its inferiority.

When you use narration for all or part of an essay, remember to comment on people, events, and scene when you need to communicate important information to your reader.

Writing Workshop Activity

Take another look at "Graduation" and find three additional examples of the author's commenting on people, scene, or events.

Language Notes for Multilingual and Other Students

The following two idioms, which appear in "Graduation," are frequently used in English:

1. A *dry run* is a rehearsal.
   Even those who were years removed from their own day of glorious release were anxious to help with preparations as a kind of <u>dry run</u>. Paragraph 1

2. To be *up to snuff* is to be satisfactory.
   Oh, we were <u>up to snuff</u>, all right. Paragraph 28

From Reading to Writing

In Your Journal: Tell about an important event in your life, one that taught you something you are not likely to forget or one that changed your life in an important way.

With Some Classmates: Consider to what extent racial discrimination exists today. If you wish, you can limit your consideration to one arena: higher education, the workplace, athletics, the entertainment world, and so forth. Use specific examples from the newspapers, magazines, television, radio, your experience, and observation to support your conclusions.

In an Essay:

- When Henry led the auditorium in the "Negro National Anthem," he was a single person taking action to make a difference. Narrate an account of a time you or someone you know did something that made a difference. As appropriate, comment on people, events, and scene.
- Donleavy made his black audience feel that there were limits to what they could achieve. Tell about a time when you were made to feel that your goals were beyond your reach. Explain what happened and how you reacted.
- Maya Angelou's sense of commitment to her race is made clear in "Graduation." Tell about your commitment (or lack of commitment) to a religious, racial, national, or cultural group to which you belong. Explain why you feel the way you do and how your commitment (or lack of it) manifests itself.

Beyond the Writing Class: A number of people who figure prominently in black history are mentioned in "Graduation": Booker T. Washington in paragraph 32, George Washington Carver in paragraph 41, Harriet Tubman, Gabriel Prosser, and Nat Turner in paragraph 45, and James Weldon Johnson in paragraph 55. Go to the library, research the life of one of these people, and write a biographical sketch, being sure to indicate what the individual contributed to black history. Consider submitting the sketch to your campus newspaper during Black History Month.

Once More to the Lake
E. B. WHITE

You may know Elwyn Brooks White as the author of the popular children's book *Charlotte's Web* (1952) or as the author (with William Strunk, Jr.) of the enduring writer's guide, *The Elements of Style* (1959). You may not know that he won the Presidential Medal of Freedom in 1963 for his literary accomplishments, including his "Talk of the Town" column for *The New Yorker*.

Preview.   In "Once More to the Lake," White writes of taking his son to revisit the lake where he spent his summers as a boy. While there, he comes to a startling realization about the passage of time. In a page or two, write about the passage of time. Do you think about aging and ultimately dying? Do you ever look at someone younger and relive an aspect of your past? Does time ever seem to stand still for you? Does time seem to go by quickly or slowly?

Vocabulary.   If any of the following words from the essay are unfamiliar to you, study their meanings before reading.

placidity (1)   quiet and calm
haunts (1)   places visited frequently
gunwale (2)   the upper edge of the side of a ship or boat
primeval (3)   of the earliest times
hellgrammite (5)   a kind of insect larva used for fishing bait
pensively (5)   thoughtfully
petulant (10)   showing sudden irritation
premonitory (12)   suggesting something bad is going to happen
languidly (13)   weakly

One summer, along about 1904, my father rented a camp on a lake in Maine and took us all there for the month of August. We all got ringworm from some kittens and had to rub Pond's Extract on our arms and legs night and morning, and my father rolled over in a canoe with all his clothes on; but outside of that the vacation was a success and from then on none of us ever thought there was any place in the world like that lake in Maine. We returned summer after summer—always on August 1 for one month. I have since become a salt-water man, but sometimes in summer there are days when the restlessness of the tides and the fearful cold of the sea water and the incessant wind that blows across the afternoon and into the evening make me wish for the placidity of a lake in the woods. A few weeks ago this feeling got so strong I bought myself a couple of bass hooks and a spinner and returned to the lake where we used to go, for a week's fishing and to revisit old haunts.

2   I took along my son, who had never had any fresh water up his nose and who had seen lily pads only from train windows. On the journey over to the lake I began to wonder what it would be like. I wondered how time would have marred this unique, this holy spot—the coves and streams, the hills that the sun set behind, the camps and the paths behind the camps. I was sure that the tarred road would have found it out, and I wondered in what other ways it would be desolated. It is strange how much you can remember about places like that once you allow your mind to return into the grooves that lead back. You remember one thing, and that suddenly reminds you of another thing. I guess I remembered clearest of all the early mornings, when the lake was cool and motionless, remembered how the bedroom smelled of the lumber it was made of and of the wet woods whose scent entered through the screen. The partitions in the camp were thin and did not extend clear to the top of the rooms, and as I was always the first up I would dress softly so as not to wake the others, and sneak out into the sweet outdoors and start out in the canoe, keeping close along the shore in the long shadows of the pines. I remembered being very careful never to rub my paddle against the gunwale for fear of disturbing the stillness of the cathedral.

3   The lake had never been what you would call a wild lake. There were cottages sprinkled around the shores, and it was in farming country although the shores of the lake were quite heavily wooded. Some of the cottages were owned by nearby farmers, and you would live at the shore and eat your meals at the farmhouse. That's what our family did. But although it wasn't wild, it was a fairly large and undisturbed lake and there were places in it that, to a child at least, seemed infinitely remote and primeval.

4   I was right about the tar: It led to within half a mile of the shore. But when I got back there, with my boy, and we settled into a camp near a farmhouse and into the kind of summertime I had known, I could tell that it was going to be pretty much the same as it had been before—I knew it, lying in bed the first morning smelling the bedroom and hearing the boy sneak quietly out and go off along the shore in a boat. I began to sustain the illusion that he was I, and therefore, by simple transposition, that I was my father. This sensation persisted, kept cropping up all the time we were there. It was not an entirely new feeling, but in this setting it grew much stronger. I seemed to be living a dual existence. I would be in the middle of some simple act, I would be picking up a bait box or laying down a table fork, or I would be saying something and suddenly it would be not I but my father who was saying the words or making the gesture. It gave me a creepy sensation.

5   We went fishing the first morning. I felt the same damp moss covering the worms in the bait can, and saw the dragonfly alight on the tip of my rod as it hovered a few inches from the surface of the water. It was the arrival of this fly that convinced me beyond any doubt that everything was as it always had been, that the years were a mirage and that there had been no years. The small waves were the same, chucking the rowboat under the chin as we fished at an-

chor, and the boat was the same boat, the same color green and the ribs broken in the same places, and under the floorboards the same fresh water leavings and debris—the dead hellgrammite, the wisps of moss, the rusty discarded fishhook, the dried blood from yesterday's catch. We stared silently at the tips of our rods, at the dragonflies that came and went. I lowered the tip of mine into the water, tentatively, pensively dislodging the fly, which darted two feet away, poised, darted two feet back, and came to rest again a little farther up the rod. There had been no years between the ducking of this dragonfly and the other one—the one that was part of memory. I looked at the boy, who was silently watching his fly, and it was my hands that held his rod, my eyes watching. I felt dizzy and didn't know which rod I was at the end of.

6   We caught two bass, hauling them in briskly as though they were mackerel, pulling them over the side of the boat in a businesslike manner without any landing net, and stunning them with a blow on the back of the head. When we got back for a swim before lunch, the lake was exactly where we had left it, the same number of inches from the dock, and there was only the merest suggestion of a breeze. This seemed an utterly enchanted sea, this lake you could leave to its own devices for a few hours and come back to, and find that it had not stirred, this constant and trustworthy body of water. In the shallows, the dark, water-soaked sticks and twigs, smooth and old, were undulating in clusters on the bottom against the clean ribbed sand, and the track of the mussel was plain. A school of minnows swam by, each minnow with its small individual shadow, doubling the attendance, so clear and sharp in the sunlight. Some of the other campers were in swimming, along the shore, one of them with a cake of soap, and the water felt thin and clear and unsubstantial. Over the years there had been this person with the cake of soap, this cultist, and here he was. There had been no years.

7   Up to the farmhouse to dinner through the teeming dusty field, the road under our sneakers was only a two-track road. The middle track was missing, the one with the marks of the hooves and the splotches of dried, flaky manure. There had always been three tracks to choose from in choosing which track to walk in; now the choice was narrowed down to two. For a moment I missed terribly the middle alternative. But the way led past the tennis court, and something about the way it lay there in the sun reassured me; the tape had loosened along the backline, the alleys were green with plantains and other weeds, and the net (installed in June and removed in September) sagged in the dry noon, and the whole place steamed with midday heat and hunger and emptiness. There was a choice of pie for dessert, and one was blueberry and one was apple, and the waitresses were the same country girls, there having been no passage of time, only the illusion of it as in a dropped curtain—the waitresses were still fifteen; their hair had been washed, that was the only difference—they had been to the movies and seen the pretty girls with the clean hair.

8   Summertime, oh, summertime, pattern of life indelible with fade-proof lake, the wood unshatterable, the pasture with the sweetfern and the juniper

forever and ever, summer without end; this was the background, and the life along the shore was the design, the cottages with their innocent and tranquil design, their tiny docks with the flagpole and the American flag floating against the white clouds in the blue sky, the little paths over the roots of the trees leading from camp to camp and the paths leading back to the outhouses and the can of lime for sprinkling, and at the souvenir counters at the store the miniature birchbark canoes and the postcards that showed things looking a little better than they looked. This was the American family at play, escaping the city heat, wondering whether the newcomers in the camp at the head of the cove were "common" or "nice," wondering whether it was true that the people who drove up for Sunday dinner at the farmhouse were turned away because there wasn't enough chicken.

9   It seemed to me, as I kept remembering all this, that those times and those summers had been infinitely precious and worth saving. There had been jollity and peace and goodness. The arriving (at the beginning of August) had been so big a business in itself, at the railway station the farm wagon drawn up, the first smell of the pine-laden air, the first glimpse of the smiling farmer, and the great importance of the trunks and your father's enormous authority in such matters, and the feel of the wagon under you for the long ten-mile haul, and at the top of the last long hill catching the first view of the lake after eleven months of not seeing this cherished body of water. The shouts and cries of the other campers when they saw you, and the trunks to be unpacked, to give up their rich burden. (Arriving was less exciting nowadays, when you sneaked up in your car and parked it under a tree near the camp and took out the bags and in five minutes it was all over, no fuss, no loud wonderful fuss about trunks.)

10   Peace and goodness and jollity. The only thing that was wrong now, really, was the sound of the place, an unfamiliar nervous sound of the outboard motors. This was the note that jarred, the one thing that would sometimes break the illusion and set the years moving. In those other summertimes all motors were inboard; and when they were at a little distance, the noise they made was a sedative, an ingredient of summer sleep. They were one-cylinder and two-cylinder engines, and some were make-and-break and some were jump-spark, but they all made a sleepy sound across the lake. The one-lungers throbbed and fluttered, and the twin-cylinder ones purred and purred, and that was a quiet sound, too. But now the campers all had outboards. In the daytime, in the hot mornings, these motors made a petulant, irritable sound, at night in the still evening when the afterglow lit the water, they whined about one's ears like mosquitoes. My boy loved our rented outboard, and his great desire was to achieve single-handed mastery over it, and authority, and he soon learned the trick of choking it a little (but not too much), and the adjustment of the needle valve. Watching him I would remember the things you could do with the old one-cylinder engine with the heavy flywheel, how you could have it eating out of your hand if you got really close to it spiritually. Motorboats in those days didn't have clutches, and you would make a landing by shutting off the motor at the proper time and coasting in with a dead rudder. But there was

a way of reversing them, if you learned the trick, by cutting the switch and putting it on again exactly on the final dying revolution of the flywheel, so that it would kick back against compression and begin reversing. Approaching a dock in a strong following breeze, it was difficult to slow up sufficiently by the ordinary coasting method, and if a boy felt he had complete mastery over his motor, he was tempted to keep it running beyond its time and then reverse it a few feet from the dock. It took a cool nerve, because if you threw the switch a twentieth of a second too soon you would catch the flywheel when it still had speed enough to go up past center, and the boat would leap ahead, charging bull-fashion at the dock.

11   We had a good week at the camp. The bass were biting well and the sun shone endlessly, day after day. We would be tired at night and lie down in the accumulated heat of the little bedrooms after the long hot day and the breeze would stir almost imperceptibly outside and the smell of the swamp drift in through the rusty screens. Sleep would come easily and in the morning the red squirrel would be on the roof, tapping out his gay routine. I kept remembering everything, lying in bed in the mornings—the small steamboat that had a long rounded stern like the lip of a Ubangi, and how quietly she ran on the moonlight sails, when the older boys played their mandolins and the girls sang and we ate doughnuts dipped in sugar, and how sweet the music was on the water in the shining night, and what it had felt like to think about girls then. After breakfast we would go up to the store and the things were in the same place—the minnows in a bottle, the plugs and spinners disarranged and pawed over by the youngsters from the boys' camp, the Fig Newtons and the Beeman's gum. Outside, the road was tarred and cars stood in front of the store. Inside, all was just as it had always been, except there was more Coca-Cola and not so much Moxie and root beer and birch beer and sarsaparilla. We would walk out with the bottle of pop apiece and sometimes the pop would backfire up our noses and hurt. We explored the streams, quietly, where the turtles slid off the sunny logs and dug their way into the soft bottom; and we lay on the town wharf and fed worms to the tame bass. Everywhere we went I had trouble making out which was I, the one walking at my side, the one walking in my pants.

12   One afternoon while we were at that lake a thunderstorm came up. It was like the revival of an old melodrama that I had seen long ago with childish awe. The second-act climax of the drama of the electrical disturbance over a lake in America had not changed in any important respect. This was the big scene, still the big scene. The whole thing was so familiar, the first feeling of oppression and heat and a general air around camp of not wanting to go very far away. In midafternoon (it was all the same) a curious darkening of the sky, and a lull in everything that had made life tick; and then the way the boats suddenly swung the other way at their moorings with the coming of a breeze out of the new quarter, and the premonitory rumble. Then the kettle drum, then the snare, then the bass drum and cymbals, then crackling light against the dark, and the gods grinning and licking their chops in the hills. Afterward the calm, the rain steadily rustling in the calm lake, the return of light and hope

and spirits, and the campers running out in joy and relief to go swimming in the rain, their bright cries perpetuating the deathless joke about how they were getting simply drenched, and the children screaming with delight at the new sensation of bathing in the rain, and the joke about getting drenched linking the generations in a strong indestructible chain. And the comedian who waded in carrying an umbrella.

13   When the others went swimming my son said he was going in, too. He pulled his dripping trunks from the line where they had hung all through the shower and wrung them out. Languidly, and with no thought of going in, I watched him, his hard little body, skinny and bare, saw him wince slightly as he pulled up around his vitals the small, soggy, icy garment. As he buckled the swollen belt, suddenly my groin felt the chill of death.

Understanding Content

1. Why do you think White calls the lake a "holy spot" (paragraph 2) and a "cathedral" (paragraph 2)?
2. What is the "dual existence" (paragraph 4) that White often experiences?
3. Paragraphs 5 and 6 present a particular view of time that the author has. Explain what that view of time is.
4. What conclusion does White draw about the passage of time? Where in the essay is that conclusion best expressed?

Considering Structure and Technique

1. White uses a considerable amount of descriptive language in "Once More to the Lake." Cite two examples of description that you particularly like and explain why you like them. To create his description, White appeals to the senses of smell, touch, and sound, in addition to the sense of sight. Cite one example each of description that appeals to smell, touch, and sound. Underline the specific word choice.
2. **Comparison and contrast** shows similarities and differences. In what ways does White compare and contrast?
3. A **metaphor** is a comparison made without using the words *like* or *as*. (For an explanation of metaphors, see p. 121.) What metaphor does the author include in paragraph 2? In paragraph 12? What do these metaphors contribute?
4. White's narration ends with his son deciding to go swimming. Why do you think the author chose not to tell what happened during the rest of their stay at the lake?

Exploring Ideas

1. White has been away from the lake for many years. Why do you think he finally returns after a lengthy absence?

2. A number of times, White mentions that he cannot distinguish himself from his son and that he cannot separate the past from the present. How do you explain this confusion of identities and time?
3. In paragraph 9, White says that his summers at the lake were "infinitely precious and worth saving." Why do you think he feels this way?
4. White is unnerved because the road to the farmhouse has been reduced from three tracks to two tracks. Why do you think he is unnerved by this fact?

Writing Workshop: Using Flashbacks in Narration

Narration is storytelling. (For a discussion of narration, see p. 79). Usually when a story is told, details are arranged in **chronological order,** which means that details are presented in the order they occurred. With chronological order, you write first what happened first, then what happened second, and so on until you get to the last event.

Sometimes, however, writers of narration use a **flashback** technique. In flashback, you interrupt the chronological order to move backward in time. After telling what happened, you return to the point you left when you flashed back. In "Once More to the Lake," White uses a flashback technique in paragraphs 2, 3, 9, 10, and 11. Review those paragraphs now to get a better understanding of flashback in narration.

Writing Workshop Activity

Write a paragraph or two about an experience you had as a child, using chronological order to tell the story. Then rewrite the account to include at least one flashback. Which version of the story do you prefer? Why?

Language Notes for Multilingual and Other Writers

When you are writing in the past tense, you can show that something happened in an even more distant past if you use the past perfect tense, which is formed with *had* and the past participle. In "Once More to the Lake," White often uses the past perfect tense when he is writing in the past tense and wants to tell about something that happened even further back. Notice his use of the past perfect tense here:

          past   past

It <u>seemed</u> to me, as I <u>kept</u> remembering all this, that those times
                      past perfect
and those summers <u>had been</u> infinitely precious and worth saving. There
 past perfect
<u>had been</u> jollity and peace and goodness. The arriving (at the beginning of
       past perfect
August) <u>had been</u> so big a business in itself. . . . Paragraph 9

From Reading to Writing

In Your Journal: In paragraph 12, White narrates what happened when a thunderstorm came up. During that account he notes that "the joke about getting drenched [links] the generations in a strong indestructible chain." In a page or two of your journal, consider what it is that links the generations in your family or the people where you live. Think about events, experiences, circumstances, and anything else you think is significant.

With Some Classmates: With two or three classmates, consider how a young adult reader, a middle-aged reader, and an elderly reader are likely to react to "Once More to the Lake." Discuss how the responses for the three readers are likely to vary and what accounts for the differences.

In an Essay

- In "Once More to the Lake," White recognizes his own mortality. Tell about an event that caused you to recognize or reflect on your own mortality. Explain what happened, how you were affected, and why you were affected that way. If you like, try interrupting the chronology with flashback.
- If you have ever returned to a place after a long absence, tell about the ways the place changed and the ways it stayed the same. For example, you could describe your first trip home after being away at college, a return to the neighborhood you played in as a child, or a visit to your old elementary school.
- White notes, "It is strange how much you can remember about places like [the lake] once you allow your mind to return into the grooves that lead back." Allow your mind "to return into the grooves" and lead you back to a place you had strong feelings about as a child. Describe that place in a way that expresses how you felt about it.

Beyond the Writing Class: Assume you work in your campus's admissions office and you are preparing a brochure to recruit students. Describe some aspect of your campus in a way that will make prospective students want to attend your school. Trade descriptions with a classmate and evaluate how inviting each description is.

My Grandmother, the Bag Lady
PATSY NEAL

Patsy Neal wrote the following essay for the "My Turn" section of a 1985 *Newsweek*. You are likely to be moved by her description of an aged woman fighting to hold on to what is left of her world. Is Neal's grandmother helpless and infirm, or in control of her environment? Try to decide as you read.

Preview.   How do you view old people? Write a list of characteristics that you believe are common to most people in their eighties ("wise," "slow moving," "lonely"—whatever you think). Try to come up with at least ten traits. When your list is complete, join a small group of your classmates to compare traits. Form a master list that contains all the traits that appear on the lists of at least two people in the group. Then share the results with the rest of the class.

Vocabulary.   If any of the following words from the essay are unfamiliar to you, study their meanings before reading.

plight (2)   a difficult and upsetting situation
minutest (3)   smallest
mobile (4)   capable of moving
laboriously (8)   with difficulty
rummaging (10)   searching through
diminished (12)   grown smaller
constrictions (12)   tightenings
invalid (18)   a person too sick or weak to care for himself or herself

Almost all of us have seen pictures of old, homeless ladies, moving about the streets of big cities with everything they own stuffed into a bag or a paper sack.

2   My grandmother is 89 years old, and a few weeks ago I realized with a jolt that she, too, had become one of them. Before I go any further, I had best explain that I did not see my grandmother's picture on TV. I discovered her plight during a face-to-face visit at my mother's house—in a beautiful, comfortable, safe, middle-class environment with good china on the table and turkey and chicken on the stove.

3   My grandmother's condition saddened me beyond words, for an 89-year-old should not have to carry around everything she owns in a bag. It's enough to be 89, without the added burden of packing the last fragments of your existence into a space big enough to accommodate only the minutest of treasures.

4   Becoming a bag lady was not something that happened to her overnight. My grandmother has been in a nursing home these last several years, at first going back to her own home for short visits, then less frequently as she became older and less mobile.

5   No matter how short these visits were, her greatest pleasure came from walking slowly around her home, touching every item lovingly and spending hours browsing through drawers and closets. Then, I did not understand her need to search out all her belongings.

6   As she spent longer days and months at the nursing home, I could not help noticing other things. She began to hide her possessions under the mattress, in her closet, under the cushion of her chair, in every conceivable, reachable space. And she began to think that people were "stealing" from her.

7   **Unsteady.** When a walker became necessary, my mother took the time to make a bag that could be attached to it, so that my grandmother could carry things around while keeping her hands on the walker. I had not paid much attention to this bag until we went to the nursing home to take her home with us for our traditional Christmas Eve sharing of gifts.

8   As we left, my grandmother took her long, unsteady walk down the hallway, balancing herself with her walker, laboriously moving it ahead, one step at a time, until finally we were at the car outside. Once she was safely seated, I picked up her walker to put it in the back. I could barely lift it. Then I noticed that the bag attached to it was bulging. Something clicked, but it still wasn't complete enough to grasp.

9   At home in my mother's house, I was asked to get some photographs from my grandmother's purse. Lifting her pocketbook, I was surprised again at the weight and bulk. I watched as my mother pulled out an alarm clock, a flashlight, a small radio, thread, needles, pieces of sewing, a book and other items that seemed to have no reason for being in a pocketbook.

10   I looked at my grandmother, sitting bent over in her chair, rummaging through the bag on the walker, slowly pulling out one item and then another, and lovingly putting it back. I looked down at her purse with all its disconnected contents and remembered her visits to her home, rummaging through drawers and through closets.

11   "Oh, Lord," I thought with sudden insight. "That walker and that purse are her home now."

12   I began to understand that over the years my grandmother's space for living had diminished like melting butter—from endless fields and miles of freedom as a child and young mother to, with age, the constrictions of a house, then a small room in a nursing home and finally to the tightly clutched handbag and the bag on her walker.

13   When the family sent her to a nursing home, it was the toughest decision it had ever had to make. We all thought she would be secure there; we would

no longer have to worry about whether she had taken her medicine, or left her stove on, or was alone at night.

14   But we hadn't fully understood her needs. Security for my grandmother was not in the warm room at the nursing home, with 24-hours attendants to keep her safe and well fed, nor in the family who visited and took her to visit in their homes. In her mind her security was tied to those things she could call her own—and over the years those possessions had dwindled away like sand dropping through an hourglass: first her car, sold when her eyes became bad and she couldn't drive; then some furnishings she didn't really need. Later it was the dogs she had trouble taking care of. And finally it would be her home when it became evident that she could never leave the nursing home again. But as her space and mobility dwindled, so did her control over her life.

15   **Dignity.** I looked at my grandmother again, sitting so alone before me, hair totally gray, limbs and joints swollen by arthritis, at the hearing aid that could no longer help her hear, and the glasses too thick but so inadequate in helping her to see . . . and yet there was such dignity about her. A dignity I could not understand.

16   The next day, after my grandmother had been taken back to the nursing home and my mother was picking up in her room, she found a small scrap of paper my grandmother had scribbled these words on:

17   "It is 1:30 tonight and I had to get up and go to the bathroom. I cannot go back to sleep. But I looked in on Margaret and she is sleeping *so* good, and Patsy is sleeping too."

18   With that note, I finally understood, and my 89-year-old bag-lady grandmother changed from an almost helpless invalid to a courageous, caring individual still very much in control of her environment.

19   What intense loneliness she must have felt as she scribbled that small note on that small piece of paper with the small bag on her walker and her small purse next to her. Yet she chose to experience it alone rather than wake either of us from much-needed sleep. Out of her own great need, she chose to meet our needs.

20   As I held that tiny note, and cried inside, I wondered if she dreamed of younger years and more treasured possessions and a bigger world when she went back to sleep that night. I certainly hoped so.

Understanding Content

1. In your own words, write a sentence or two to express the main idea of "My Grandmother, the Bag Lady."
2. In paragraph 14, Neal says that her family failed to understand her grandmother's needs. In what way did Neal's family misunderstand what the woman needed?

3. In paragraph 18, Neal says that her grandmother was "still very much in control of her environment." In what ways was she still in control?
4. What did Neal learn when she read the note her grandmother wrote in the middle of the night?

Considering Structure and Technique

1. In paragraphs 1 and 2, Neal compares her grandmother to a homeless woman. What purpose does the comparison serve?
2. What emotion did you feel when you read the essay? How did Neal move you to feel this emotion?
3. Why does Neal repeat the word *small* so often in paragraph 19?
4. A **simile** is a comparison formed with the word *like* or the word *as*. For example, in paragraph 12, Neal uses a simile when she says her grandmother's living space "had diminished like melting butter." She uses another simile in paragraph 14 when she says her grandmother's possessions "dwindled away like sand dropping through an hourglass." What do these similes contribute to the essay?
5. Does the conclusion do a good job of bringing the essay to a satisfying finish? Explain your view.

Exploring Ideas

1. In paragraph 13, Neal says that the decision to place her grandmother in a nursing home was a difficult one. What do you think made the decision so hard?
2. In paragraphs 5, 6, and 10, Neal explains that possessions were very important to her grandmother. Why do you think possessions meant so much to her?
3. Neal's portrait of her grandmother is somber, if not grim, but the admiration the author feels for her grandmother is clear. Do you think Neal's grandmother is admirable? Explain why or why not.
4. Did the family do the right thing when they put Neal's grandmother in a nursing home? Explain why or why not.

Writing Workshop: Writing Titles

Writers often try to capture their readers' attention with intriguing titles. The title "My Grandmother, the Bag Lady" may have aroused your interest because it made you think of homeless older women surviving alone on city streets. Since we do not think of these women as grandmothers, the title makes us curious to read on and learn more. Writers are not required to write clever, attention-getting titles, but you can use this approach to grab the reader's attention early on.

Writing Workshop Activity

Look at the table of contents of this book. Checkmark the essay titles that stimulate your interest. Then pick one of these titles and write an explanation for why it makes you want to read the essay.

Language Notes for the Multilingual and Other Students

In English, you can indicate that something occurs quickly by using the idiom *overnight (over night)*. For example, you can say, "If you use the proper technique you can train your new puppy practically *overnight*," which means you can train your puppy quickly.

To indicate that something does *not* happen quickly, say that it *does not happen overnight*. For example, in "My Grandmother, the Bag Lady," Neal writes:

Becoming a bag lady was <u>not something that happened to her overnight.</u> Paragraph 4

From Reading to Writing

In Your Journal: In paragraph 15, Neal writes a brief but powerful description of her grandmother. Describe one of your friends or relatives. If you like, you can begin the way Neal does: "I looked at _____ again . . ."

With Some Classmates: In paragraph 15, Neal mentions that she cannot understand her grandmother's dignity. Discuss the nature and source of the woman's dignity. Is this kind of dignity common? Explain why or why not, drawing on examples of older people you know.

In an Essay

- Do you feel any differently about the elderly as a result of reading "My Grandmother, the Bag Lady"? Compare and contrast your views of the elderly before and after reading the selection. If you wrote the Preview activity, you can consult it for material that reflects your view of the elderly before reading the essay.
- If you had to fit your possessions in your backpack the way Neal's grandmother kept hers in her bag on the walker, what would you put in your bag? Be sure to explain why you would include those items.
- In paragraph 18, Neal says that she suddenly came to view her grandmother very differently from the way she had viewed her in the past. Have you ever changed your mind about someone? In an essay, tell about an event that

changed your view of someone. Be sure to tell what the event was as well as how you viewed the person both before and after.

• In paragraph 14, Neal explains what security meant for her grandmother, and what it did *not* mean. What is security for you? As an alternative, explain what security is for people of whatever generation you happen to be part of.

Beyond the Writing Class: As the baby boomers age, our society will have more elderly than ever before. Prepare a report that predicts what needs the elderly in your community will have and that explains what can be done to meet one or more of those needs. If you need help coming up with ideas, use the conclusions you have drawn from reading "My Grandmother, the Bag Lady," and interview sociology instructors, nursing home administrators, and members of the medical profession. You can also do some research on the Internet. Try www.aarp.org, the website of the American Association of Retired People.

Can We Stay Young?
JEFFREY KLUGER

Jeffrey Kluger, a senior writer at *Time* magazine, covers science topics, particularly the space program. With astronaut Jim Lovell, he wrote *Lost Moon,* the book that served as the basis for the 1995 movie *Apollo 13.* He has also written for *Discover* magazine, the *New York Times, Gentlemen's Quarterly,* and *The Wall Street Journal.* He is a licensed attorney and an adjunct instructor at New York University. The following selection first appeared in *Time* in 1997.

Preview. In "Can We Stay Young?" Jeffrey Kluger describes the latest research efforts to counteract the aging process and prolong life. It is not out of the question, predicts Kluger, for the average life expectancy to reach 120. If you knew you stood a good chance of living to 120, would you think or behave any differently than you do now? If so, explain how. If not, explain why not.

Vocabulary. If any of the following words from the selection are unfamiliar to you, study their meanings before reading.

teasing out (1)   untangling
demographer (2)   someone who studies the size of human population
centenarian (14)   someone 100 years old or more
pharmacologically (15)   related to drugs and medicine
mortality (17)   rate of death
discernible (17)   identifiable
replications (18)   reproductions
überworms (23)   super worms
peripherally (25)   as a supplement

The rules for aging are quietly being broken. Armed with a growing knowledge of biology, a new breed of longevity specialists is teasing out answers to longer life.

(2)   History shows it's possible. In 1900 the life expectancy for a person born in the United States was 47.3 years. According to U.S. figures, the average life expectancy is now nearly 76, with many Americans living well beyond. Says James Vaupel, a Duke University demographer, "There is no evidence that human life expectancy is anywhere close to its ultimate limit."

(3)   The modern era of aging research began in 1961 when cell biologist Leonard Hayflick made a significant discovery. Troubled by the question of where aging begins, Hayflick, now a professor at the University of California

San Francisco School of Medicine and author of the book *How and Why We Age,* wondered: Did the cells themselves falter, dragging down the whole human organism? Or could cells live on indefinitely were it not for age-related deterioration in the tissues they make up?

4   To find out, Hayflick placed fetal cells in a petri dish. Freed from the responsibility of keeping a larger organism alive, they did the only other thing they knew to do: divide. They doubled their number, and then doubled the doubling. After repeating itself about 50 times, the cycle suddenly stopped. Then the cells did something a lot like aging: they consumed less food, and their membranes deteriorated.

5   Hayflick repeated the experiment, using cells from a 70-year-old. This time the cellular aging began a lot earlier, after 20 or 30 doublings.

6   For gerontologists this was monumental; it meant that somewhere in each cell was an hourglass that gave it only so much time to live and no more. Could this cellular timekeeper be found—and reset?

Energy for Life

7   Scientists who study aging have taken two approaches to achieving this goal. The first is the cellular-damage model of aging.

8   Like all organisms, cells produce waste as they metabolize energy. One of the most troublesome byproducts of this process is a free radical, an ordinary oxygen molecule with an extra electron. The molecule seeks to rectify this electrical imbalance by careening about, trying to bond with other molecules. A lifetime of this can damage cells, leading to a range of disorders from cancer to more general symptoms of aging such as wrinkles and arthritis.

9   In recent years some nutritionists have advocated diets high in fruits and vegetables containing antioxidants—substances that are believed to sop up free radicals and carry them out of the body. But anitoxidants have an uneven record. In some studies they seem to be associated with a dramatic reduction in cancer or other diseases; in other studies, an increase. In either case, few contemporary aging researchers think self-medicating at a salad bar can significantly extend the human life-span.

10   Far more promising might be new research into another byproduct of cellular metabolism: glycosylation—or what cooks call browning. When foods such as turkey, bread and caramel are heated, proteins bind with sugars, causing the surface to darken and turn soft and sticky. In the 1970s biochemists hypothesized that the same reaction might occur in people suffering from diabetes. When sugars and proteins bond, they attract other proteins, which form a sticky, weblike network that could stiffen joints, block arteries and cloud clear tissues such as the lens of the eye, leading to cataracts. Diabetics suffer from all these ailments.

11   But so do the aged. Was it possible that as the cells of nondiabetics metabolize sugars, the same glycosylation might take place, only much slower? Studies seemed to say yes.

12   The gooey glycosylation residue has been given an appropriate acronym: AGE, for advanced glycosylation end products. Investigators at the Picower Institute for Medical Research in Manhasset, New York, are working on a drug, pimagedine, that acts as an AGE solvent by dissolving the connection between AGE and the proteins around it. Essentially it helps unstick what AGE gums up.

No-Fat Centenarians

13   An alternative to changing the way cells process nutrients is to give them less to process in the first place. Studies have shown that rats whose caloric intake is 30 to 40 percent lower than that of a control group tend to live up to 40 percent longer. For a man, that would translate to a spartan diet of just about 1500 calories a day—in exchange for 30 extra years of life.

14   Just how this business of swapping food for time works is not entirely clear, but George Roth, molecular physiologist with the National Institute on Aging in Bethesda, Maryland, has some ideas. When calories are restricted, Roth explains, body temperature drops about 1.8 degrees Fahrenheit. Lower temperature means a less vigorous metabolism, which means less food is processed. "The animals switch from a growth mode to a survival mode," Roth says. "They get fewer calories, so they burn fewer. I think caloric restriction could take us well beyond a life span of 80," he adds. "After all, you rarely see a fat centenarian."

15   In a nation of consumers for whom caloric belt-tightening can mean merely a smaller serving of french fries with their bacon cheeseburgers, it may be more realistic to imitate caloric restriction pharmocologically. "Essentially," explains Roth, "we'd use a pill to trick a cell into thinking less food is coming in."

16   But caloric reduction is essentially maintenance work: little more than patching holes in a sinking ship. What some researchers really want is to get down into the body's engine room—the genes themselves—and rebuild things from the boilers up. Remarkably, it appears there may be a way.

Tip of the Shoelace

17   Hayflick left a question unanswered: why do cells die? In the years following his work, biologists looked for a gene that enforced cellular mortality, but found nothing. One thing that did catch their eyes, however, was a small area at the tip of chromosomes that had no discernible purpose. Dubbed a telomere, it resembled nothing so much as the plastic cuff at the end of a shoelace.

18   Each time a cell divided, the daughter cells it produced had a little less telomere. Finally, when the cell reached its Hayflick's limit of 50 or so replications, the telomere was reduced to a mere nub. Only a few cells were spared telomere loss. Among them were sperm and cancer cells—the cells characterized by their ability to divide not just 50 times but thousands.

19   Working with a single-cell pond organism, molecular biologists Carol Greider and Elizabeth Blackburn, then with the University of California at Berkeley, discovered in 1984 a telomere-preserving enzyme they dubbed telomerase. Five years later, Gregg Morin at Yale University identified the same substance in cancer cells. In the petri dish the agent of eternal life had been found.

20   At Geron Corporation, a biopharmaceutical firm based in Menlo Park, Calif., biologist Calvin Harley is working to find the genes that direct telomerase production, believing he might be able to manipulate them so the regulator for the enzyme can be turned on and off at will.

21   "With a pill or with cell therapy, I think we may be able to treat aging in very specific areas," Harley says.

Superworms

22   Other genes implicated in aging have already been flushed out of hiding. Nematodes in Siegfried Hekimi's genetics lab at McGill University in Montreal have been known to survive up to 75 days. Outside the lab, the tiny, transparent worms barely last nine.

23   Hekimi created his little überworms by breeding long-lived individuals, extending the life-spans of the next generation. He then searched the animals' chromosomes until he found the mutated gene responsible, a gene he dubbed Clock-1.

24   When Hekimi went looking for similar clock genes in people, he found one so similar, he says, "that it's possible the whole clock system works the same way. If we find all of the human clock genes, we can perhaps slow them down just a little, so we can extend life expectancy just a little."

25   The problem is the sheer number of genes involved. Geneticist George Martin at the University of Washington in Seattle believes that even if only a few master-clock genes directly guide aging in humans, up to 7000 more might be peripherally involved. Reengineering even one is an exquisitely complex process. Reengineering all 7000 would be impossible.

26   While the genes involved in the aging process can't yet be manipulated, many researchers are using what they've learned about them to attack disease.

27   Researchers at Geron recently used telomerase RNA to block an enzyme in a cancer culture. Elsewhere investigators are looking into using the AGE drug pimagedine to help clear arteries and improve cardiac health, adding 13.9 years to average national life expectancy.

28   Researchers believe there's no reason many adults won't one day live to see 120. For people dreaming of immortality, that prospect may fall a little short. But four or five additional decades sounds like a splendid first step.

Understanding Content

1. In your own words, write out the thesis of "Can We Stay Young?"

2. What five theories have scientists come up with to explain aging?
3. Which of the five theories seems the most promising?
4. What primary problem prevents researchers from using human clock genes to slow the aging process?
5. What benefits have resulted from the discovery of human clock genes?

Considering Structure and Technique

1. Paragraphs 3–5 present a brief history of the origin of aging research. What purpose does this information serve? Do you find it helpful?
2. **Process analysis** explains how something is made or done. Which paragraphs include process analysis? What processes are explained in these paragraphs?
3. A **metaphor** is a comparison formed without using the words *like* or *as*. (See p. 121 for a workshop on metaphors.) What metaphor is in paragraph 16? What does that metaphor contribute to the essay?
4. What do you think of the essay's title? Is it effective?

Exploring Ideas

1. Does Kluger see increasing longevity as a positive or negative goal for researchers? Do you agree? Explain.
2. Kluger refers to Americans' eating habits. What can you tell about his opinion of the way Americans eat?
3. If you had a million dollars to donate to scientific research, would you donate it to a laboratory working to increase longevity? Why or why not?
4. List two problems and two benefits that would result if the average life span rose to 120.

Writing Workshop: Using the Hyphen

A **hyphen** (-) has several uses, some of which are illustrated in "Can We Stay Young?"

1. The hyphen can join two words to form a single modifier before a noun. For example, *well* can be joined with *known* to create *well-known* politician; *state, of, the,* and *art* can be joined to get *state-of-the-art* computer. In "Can We Stay Young?" this use of the hyphen is illustrated: "*cellular-damage* model" (paragraph 7) and "*master-clock* genes" (paragraph 25). Interestingly, a hyphen is not used when one of the words is an *-ly* adverb, so the correct form is *freshly laundered*, not *freshly-laundered*.
2. The hyphen can join two or more words to form a noun, like this: *sister-in-law* and *editor-in-chief*. This, too, is illustrated in the essay: "the human life-span" (paragraph 9).

3. To prevent misreading, a hyphen is sometimes used to attach a **prefix** (word-beginning) if the last letter of the prefix is the same as the first letter of the base word. This use is illustrated in paragraph 25: "Re-engineering." Usage here is not consistent, so when in doubt, check your dictionary.

Writing Workshop Activity

Find an example of each of the three uses of a hyphen discussed in the previous workshop. You can check your textbooks or newspapers, magazines, and books.

Language Notes for Multilingual and Other Writers

Many English verbs are **phrasal verbs,** which are two- and three-word verbs formed by combining a verb with one or two prepositions. Phrasal verbs are verbs such as *back off, turn on,* and *get away from.* Sometimes the parts of phrasal verbs can be separated, and sometimes they cannot. For example, *fill out* is separable because one can say, "<u>Fill</u> the form <u>out.</u>" *Get along with* is inseparable because *get* cannot be separated from *along with:* Enrico does not <u>get along with</u> Carlotta.

common separable phrasal verbs:

burn up	give back	take out
call up	put off	try on
fill up	shut off	wake up

common inseparable phrasal verbs:

bump into	do without	grow up
come across	give in to	play around

Examples of both separable and inseparable phrasal verbs appear in "Can We Stay Young?"

separable

1. . . . a new breed of longevity specialists is <u>teasing out</u> answers to a longer life. (It is possible to write, "is <u>teasing</u> the answers <u>out.</u>") Paragraph 1

2. What some researchers really want is <u>to get down into</u> the body's engine room. (It is possible to write, "<u>get</u> themselves <u>down into.</u>") Paragraph 16

inseparable

1. Less food is <u>coming in.</u> Paragraph 15

2. Elsewhere investigators are <u>looking into</u> using the AGE drug . . . Paragraph 27

From Reading to Writing

In Your Journal: Paragraph 13 notes that eating less may prolong life. Would you eat a meager diet "in exchange for 30 extra years of life"? Explain why or why not.

With Some Classmates: In his opening sentence, Kluger says, "The rules for aging are quietly being broken." Explain what those rules are and how one or more of them affect us.

In an Essay

- If you could pick the age at which you would die, what age would you pick? Explain why, focusing on the chief benefits and drawbacks of the age you select.
- Describe what you think life would be like if the average life expectancy rose to 120. Focus on the chief benefits and problems that you envision.
- Should there be limits to how long human beings live, or should scientists be allowed to find ways to extend life as much as possible? State and defend your view.

Beyond the Writing Class: People often say that Americans worship youth. Examine the articles and advertisements in several issues of three or four different magazines and explain to what extent they focus on youth. Then pick one issue and speculate about how it would change if the average life expectancy were 120. Present your report to your class.

Predictable Crises of Adulthood
GAIL SHEEHY

Gail Sheehy has written for many popular periodicals, including *the New York Times Magazine, Esquire, McCalls,* and *Rolling Stone.* Her most recent book is *Hillary's Choice* (1999), about Hillary Rodham Clinton. Her books, *Passages* (1976), from which the following selection has been adapted, and its sequel *New Passages* (1995), describe and explain the stages of life.

Preview.   Sheehy believes that most adult Americans go through six stages of life: Pulling up Roots, The Trying Twenties, Catch-30, Rooting and Extending, The Deadline Decade, and Renewal or Resignation. Select two of those stages and predict what you think each one is like.

Vocabulary.   If any of the following words from the selection are unfamiliar to you, study their meanings before reading.

- ✗ **crustacean** (1)   shellfish, like crabs and lobster
- ✗ **sloughed** (1)   plodded through, as if in mud
- ● **plausible** (4)   believable
- ● **impetus** (10)   driving force
- ● **mentor** (14)   tutor or coach
- ● **transient** (18)   passing through with only a brief stay
- ● **wunderkind** (19)   compound of German words that mean one who does something difficult at an early age
- ● **gist** (24)   main point
- ● **visceral** (25)   instinctive, emotional
- ✗ *pro bono* (37)   for free, for charity
- ✗ **crucible** (38)   a severe test
- ● **calcify** (40)   harden

We are not unlike a particularly hardy crustacean. The lobster grows by developing and shedding a series of hard, protective shells. Each time it expands from within, the confining shell must be sloughed off. It is left exposed and vulnerable until, in time, a new covering grows to replace the old.

2   With each passage from one stage of human growth to the next we, too, must shed a protective structure. We are left exposed and vulnerable—but also yeasty and embryonic again, capable of stretching in ways we hadn't known before. These sheddings may take several years or more. Coming out of each passage, though, we enter a longer and more stable period in which we can expect relative tranquility and a sense of equilibrium regained. . . .

3   As we shall see, each person engages the steps of development in his or her own characteristic *step-style*. Some people never complete the whole sequence. And none of us "solves" with one step—by jumping out of the parental home into a job or marriage, for example—the problems in separating from the caregivers of childhood. Nor do we "achieve" autonomy once and for all by converting our dreams into concrete goals, even when we attain those goals. The central issue or tasks of one period are never fully completed, tied up, and cast aside. But when they lose their primacy and the current life structure has served its purpose, we are ready to move on to the next period.

4   Can one catch up? What might look to others like listlessness, contrariness, a maddening refusal to face up to an obvious task may be a person's own unique detour that will bring him out later on the other side. Developmental gains won can later be lost—and rewon. It's plausible, though it can't be proven, that the mastery of one set of tasks fortifies us for the next period and the next set of challenges. But it's important not to think too mechanistically. Machines work by units. The bureaucracy (supposedly) works step by step. Human beings, thank God, have an individual inner dynamic that can never be precisely coded.

5   Although I have indicated the ages when Americans are likely to go through each stage, and the differences between men and women where they are striking, do not take the ages too seriously. The stages are the thing, and most particularly the sequence.

6   Here is the briefest outline of the developmental ladder.

Pulling Up Roots

7   Before 18, the motto is loud and clear: "I have to get away from my parents." But the words are seldom connected to action. Generally still safely part of our families, even if away at school, we feel our autonomy to be subject to erosion from moment to moment.

8   After 18, we begin Pulling Up Roots in earnest. College, military service, and short-term travels are all customary vehicles our society provides for the first round trips between family and a base of one's own. In the attempt to separate our view of the world from our family's view, despite vigorous protestations to the contrary—"I know exactly what I want!"—we cast about for any beliefs we can call our own. And in the process of testing those beliefs we are often drawn to fads, preferably those most mysterious and inaccessible to our parents.

9   Whatever tentative memberships we try out in the world, the fear haunts us that we are really kids who cannot take care of ourselves. We cover that fear with acts of defiance and mimicked confidence. For allies to replace our parents, we turn to our contemporaries. They become conspirators. So long as their perspective meshes with our own, they are able to substitute for the sanctuary of the family. But that doesn't last very long. And the instant they diverge

from the shaky ideals of "our group," they are seen as betrayers. Rebounds to the family are common between the ages of 18 and 22.

10   The tasks of this passage are to locate ourselves in a peer group role, a sex role, an anticipated occupation, an ideology or world view. As a result, we gather the impetus to leave home physically and the identity to *begin* leaving home emotionally.

11   Even as one part of us seeks to be an individual, another part longs to restore the safety and comfort of merging with another. Thus one of the most popular myths of this passage is: We can piggyback our development by attaching to a Stronger One. But people who marry during this time often prolong financial and emotional ties to the family and relatives that impede them from becoming self-sufficient.

12   A stormy passage through the Pulling Up Roots years will probably facilitate the normal progression of the adult life cycle. If one doesn't have an identity crisis at this point, it will erupt during a later transition, when the penalties may be harder to bear.

The Trying Twenties

13   The Trying Twenties confront us with the question of how to take hold in the adult world. Our focus shifts from the interior turmoils of late adolescence—"Who am I?" "What is truth?"—and we become almost totally preoccupied with working out the externals. "How do I put my aspirations into effect?" "What is the best way to start?" "Where do I go?" "Who can help me?" "How did *you* do it?"

14   In this period, which is longer and more stable compared with the passage that leads to it, the tasks are as enormous as they are exhilarating: To shape a Dream, that vision of ourselves which will generate energy, aliveness, and hope. To prepare for a lifework. To find a mentor if possible. And to form the capacity for intimacy, without losing in the process whatever consistency of self we have thus far mustered. The first test structure must be erected around the life we choose to try.

15   Doing what we "should" is the most pervasive theme of the twenties. The "shoulds" are largely defined by family models, the press of the culture, or the prejudices of our peers. If the prevailing cultural instructions are that one should get married and settle down behind one's own door, a nuclear family is born. If instead the peers insist that one should do one's own thing, the 25-year-old is likely to harness himself onto a Harley-Davidson and burn up Route 66 in the commitment to have no commitments.

16   One of the terrifying aspects of the twenties is the inner conviction that the choices we make are irrevocable. It is largely a false fear. Change is quite possible, and some alteration of our original choices is probably inevitable.

17   Two impulses, as always, are at work. One is to build a firm, safe structure for the future by making strong commitments, to "be set." Yet people who

slip into a ready-made form without much self-examination are likely to find themselves *locked in.*

18 The other urge is to explore and experiment, keeping any structure tentative and therefore easily reversible. Taken to the extreme, these are people who skip from one trial job and one limited personal encounter to another, spending their twenties in the *transient* state.

19 Although the choices of our twenties are not irrevocable, they do set in motion a Life Pattern. Some of us follow the lock-in pattern, others the transient pattern, the wunderkind pattern, the caregiver pattern, and there are a number of others. Such patterns strongly influence the particular questions raised for each person during each passage. . . .

20 Buoyed by powerful illusions and belief in the power of the will, we commonly insist in our twenties that what we have chosen to do is the one true course in life. Our backs go up at the merest hint that we are like our parents, that two decades of parental training might be reflected in our current actions and attitudes.

21 "Not me," is the motto, "I'm different."

Catch-30

22 Impatient with devoting ourselves to the "shoulds," a new vitality springs from within as we approach 30. Men and women alike speak of feeling too narrow and restricted. They blame all sorts of things, but what the restrictions boil down to are the outgrowth of career and personal choices of the twenties. They may have been choices perfectly suited to that stage. But now the fit feels different. Some inner aspect that was left out is striving to be taken into account. Important new choices must be made, and commitments altered or deepened. The work involves great change, turmoil, and often crisis—a simultaneous feeling of rock bottom and the urge to bust out.

23 One common response is the tearing up of the life we spent most of our twenties putting together. It may mean striking out on a secondary road toward a new vision or converting a dream of "running for president" into a more realistic goal. The single person feels a push to find a partner. The woman who was previously content at home with children chafes to venture into the world. The childless couple reconsiders children. And almost everyone who is married, especially those married for seven years, feels a discontent.

24 If the discontent doesn't lead to divorce, it will, or should, call for a serious review of the marriage and of each partner's aspirations in their Catch-30 condition. The gist of that condition was expressed by a 29-year-old associate with a Wall Street law firm:

25 "I'm considering leaving the firm. I've been there four years now; I'm getting good feedback, but I have no clients of my own. I feel weak. If I wait much longer, it will be too late, too close to that fateful time of decision on whether or not to become a partner. I'm success-oriented. But the concept of

being 55 years old and stuck in a monotonous job drives me wild. It drives me crazy now, just a little bit. I'd say that 85 percent of the time I thoroughly enjoy my work. But when I get a screwball case, I come away from court saying, 'What am I doing here?' It's a *visceral* reaction that I'm wasting my time. I'm trying to find some way to make a social contribution or a slot in city government. I keep saying, 'There's something more.'"

26   Besides the push to broaden himself professionally, there is a wish to expand his personal life. He wants two or three more children. "The concept of a home has become very meaningful to me, a place to get away from troubles and relax. I love my son in a way I could not have anticipated. I never could live alone."

27   Consumed with the work of making his own critical life-steering decisions, he demonstrates the essential shift at this age: an absolute requirement to be more self-concerned. The self has new value now that his competency has been proved.

28   His wife is struggling with her own age-30 priorities. She wants to go to law school, but he wants more children. If she is going to stay home, she wants him to make more time for the family instead of taking on even wider professional commitments. His view of the bind, of what he would most like from his wife, is this:

29   "I'd like not to be bothered. It sounds cruel, but I'd like not to have to worry about what she's going to do next week. Which is why I've told her several times that I think she should do something. Go back to school and get a degree in social work or geography or whatever. Hopefully that would fulfill her, and then I wouldn't have to worry about her line of problems. I want her to be decisive about herself."

30   The trouble with his advice to his wife is that it comes out of concern with *his* convenience, rather than with *her* development. She quickly picks up on this lack of goodwill: He is trying to dispose of her. At the same time, he refuses her the same latitude to be "selfish" in making an independent decision to broaden her horizons. Both perceive a lack of mutuality. And that is what Catch-30 is all about for the couple.

Rooting and Extending

31   Life becomes less provisional, more rational and orderly in the early thirties. We begin to settle down in the full sense. Most of us begin putting down roots and sending out new shoots. People buy houses and become very earnest about climbing career ladders. Men in particular concern themselves with "making it." Satisfaction with marriage generally does downhill in the thirties (for those who have remained together) compared with the highly valued, vision-supporting marriage of the twenties. This coincides with the couple's reduced social life outside the family and the inturned focus on raising their children.

The Deadline Decade

32   In the middle of the thirties we come upon a crossroads. We have reached the halfway mark. Yet even as we are reaching our prime, we begin to see there is a place where it finishes. Time starts to squeeze.

33   The loss of youth, the faltering of physical powers we have always taken for granted, the fading purpose of stereotyped roles by which we have thus far identified ourselves, the spiritual dilemma of having no absolute answers—any or all of these shocks can give this passage the character of crisis. Such thoughts usher in a decade between 35 and 45 that can be called the Deadline Decade. It is a time of both danger and opportunity. All of us have the chance to rework the narrow identity by which we define ourselves in the first half of life. And those of us who make the most of the opportunity will have a full-out authenticity crisis.

34   To come through this authenticity crisis, we must reexamine our purposes and reevaluate how to spend our resources from now on. "Why am I doing all this? What do I really believe in?" No matter what we have been doing, there will be parts of ourselves that have been supressed and now need to find expression. "Bad" feelings will demand acknowledgment along with the good.

35   It is frightening to step off onto the treacherous footbridge leading to the second half of life. We can't take everything with us on this journey through uncertainty. Along the way, we discover that we are alone. We no longer have to ask permission because we are the providers of our own safety. We must learn to give ourselves permission. We stumble upon feminine or masculine aspects of our natures that up to this time have usually been masked. There is grieving to be done because an old self is dying. By taking in our suppressed and even our unwanted parts, we prepare at the gut level for the reintegration of an identity that is ours and ours alone—not some artificial form put together to please the culture or our mates. It is a hard passage at the beginning. But by disassembling ourselves, we can glimpse the light and gather our parts into a renewal.

36   Women sense this inner crossroads earlier than men do. The time pinch often prompts a woman to stop and take an all-points survey at age 35. Whatever options she has already played out, she feels a "my last chance" urgency to review those options she has set aside and those that aging and biology will close off in the *now foreseeable* future. For all her qualms and confusion about where to start looking for a new future, she usually enjoys an exhilaration of release. Assertiveness begins rising. There are so many firsts ahead.

37   Men, too, feel the time to push in the mid-thirties. Most men respond by pressing down harder on the career accelerator. It's "my last chance" to pull away from the pack. It is no longer enough to be the loyal junior executive, the promising young novelist, the lawyer who does a little *pro bono* work on the side. He wants now to become part of top management, to be recognized as an established writer, or an active politician with his own legislative program. With some chagrin, he discovers that he has been too anxious to please and too vulnerable to criticism. He wants to put together his own ship.

38   During this period of intense concentration on external advancement, it is common for men to be unaware of the more difficult, gut issues that are propelling them forward. The survey that was neglected at 35 becomes a crucible at 40. Whatever rung of achievement he has reached, the man of 40 usually feels stale, restless, burdened, and unappreciated. He worries about his health. He wonders, "Is this all there is?" He may make a series of departures from well-established lifelong base lines, including marriage. More and more men are seeking second careers in midlife. Some become self-destructive. And many men in their forties experience a major shift of emphasis away from pouring all their energies into their own advancement. A more tender, feeling side comes into play. They become interested in developing an ethical self.

Renewal or Resignation

39   Somewhere in the mid-forties, equilibrium is regained. A new stability is achieved, which may be more or less satisfying.

40   If one has refused to budge through the midlife transition, the sense of staleness will calcify into resignation. One by one, the safety and supports will be withdrawn from the person who is standing still. Parents will become children; children will become strangers; a mate will grow away or go away; the career will become just a job—and each of these events will be felt as an abandonment. The crisis will probably emerge again around 50. And although its wallop will be greater, the jolt may be just what is needed to prod the resigned middle-ager toward seeking revitalization.

41   On the other hand . . .

42   If we have confronted ourselves in the middle passage and found a renewal of purpose around which we are eager to build a more authentic life structure, these may well be the best years. Personal happiness takes a sharp turn upward for partners who can now accept the fact: "I cannot expect *anyone* to fully understand me." Parents can be forgiven for the burdens of our childhood. Children can be let go without leaving us in collapsed silence. At 50, there is a new warmth and mellowing. Friends become more important than ever, but so does privacy. Since it is so often proclaimed by people past midlife, the motto of this stage might be "No more bullshit."

Understanding Content

1. A **simile** is a comparison that uses the words *like* or *as,* like this: Grandmother's hands were <u>as gnarled as the roots of a tree</u>. Sheehy uses a simile to compare people to crustaceans. How does she say we are like crustaceans?
2. Sheehy says that, after 18, people are drawn to fads. Why?
3. What is responsible for the turmoil of the thirties?
4. In one or two sentences, define the period Sheehy calls "Catch-30" for a couple.

5. What is likely to happen if a person does not experience a stage of growth or fails to work through issues associated with a stage?

Considering Structure and Technique

1. Sheehy refers to "we" and "us," rather than to "people" or "human beings." Why?
2. Much of Sheehy's detail is arranged in **chronological** (time) **order.** What transitions at the beginning of the following paragraphs help the reader keep track of the time order: paragraphs 7, 14, 32, and 38?
3. Sheehy explains Catch-30 with an extended quotation. Is that technique effective? Why or why not? Do you think she should have used extended quotations to explain any of the other stages? Explain.
4. Sheehy uses a considerable amount of **cause-and-effect** analysis (the explanation of the reasons for an event and the consequences of that event). How does she use cause-and-effect analysis?

Exploring Ideas

1. Sheehy says that a person who does not have an identity crisis while pulling up roots is likely to have one later in life, when the penalties are harsher. Why is a person likely to have the crisis later on? Why are the penalties likely to be harsher?
2. Besides "inevitable," what words do you think Sheehy would use to describe the changes and stages that adults go through?
3. Is Sheehy's analysis true for all Americans or just certain groups? Explain.
4. Do you find Sheehy's analysis and description of the stages of adult life reassuring? Explain.
5. After reading this excerpt from it, are you interested in reading the rest of Sheehy's book *Passages*? Why or why not?

Writing Workshop: Analyzing with Division

Division is the process of identifying and examining the parts of something. For example, you can use division to identify and analyze the various parts of a plan to determine its chances for success, or you can identify and analyze all the components of a tennis serve in an effort to improve your game. In short, division involves separating a whole entity into its parts.

In "Predictable Crises of Adulthood," Sheehy analyzes with division because she takes the years between 18 and 50 (that's the *whole*), and separates them into six stages (those are the *parts*). Division can help you understand a complex subject, by breaking it down into more easily examined parts.

Writing Workshop Activity

To practice analyzing with division, pick one of the following and list its parts. Then select one of those parts and write a description or explanation of it.

- An entertaining horror movie
- An effective lecture
- A top-40 song
- A popular movie star or rock star

Language Notes for Multilingual and Other Writers

Modals are forms of *can, could, may,* and *might*. Modals convey various meanings, some of which are illustrated in "Predictable Crises of Adulthood."

1. *Can* and *could* convey *ability:*

   It's plausible, though it <u>can't</u> be proven . . . Paragraph 4

   "I never <u>could</u> live alone" Paragraph 26

2. *May, might,* and *could have/may have/might have* + past participle convey *possibility.*

   These sheddings <u>may</u> take several years or more. Paragraph 2

   What <u>might</u> look to others like listlessness . . . <u>may</u> be a person's own unique detour . . . Paragraph 4

   "I love my son in a way I <u>could</u> not <u>have anticipated</u>." Paragraph 26

3. *Must* and *have* to convey *obligation.*

   . . . we, too, <u>must</u> shed a protective structure. Paragraph 2

   ". . . then I wouldn't <u>have to</u> worry about her line of problems." Paragraph 29

4. *Will* conveys *intention.*

   A stormy passage through Pulling Up Roots <u>will</u> probably facilitate the normal progression of the adult life cycle. Paragraph 12

5. *Should* conveys *advisability.*

   If the prevailing cultural instructions are that one <u>should</u> get married . . . a nuclear family is born. Paragraph 15

From Reading to Writing

In Your Journal: Have you experienced or observed others experiencing any of the stages that Sheehy describes? If so, tell about what you experienced or witnessed. If not, explain what you *did* experience at one of the ages Sheehy mentions.

With Some Classmates: Sheehy's analysis ends in the mid-forties to fifties. Interview 10 people in their fifties and write a description of the stage after the Renewal or Resignation stage.

In an Essay

- Sheehy says that each stage of adulthood involves some kind of crisis, and how successfully we resolve that crisis determines how successful we are in the next stage. Tell about a time you experienced a crisis and emerged better prepared for what came next.
- Pick one point that Sheehy makes, and agree or disagree with it, using your own experience and observation for evidence.
- Sheehy opens here with, "We are not unlike a particularly hardy crustacean." Write an essay that begins, "We are not unlike _____." (Fill in the blank with something other than "particularly hardy crustacean.") Explain why people are like whatever you designate in the blank.

Beyond the Writing Class. Using division and cause-and-effect analysis, write an essay with the title, "The Predictable Stages of Student Life." If you like, you can limit your focus to the freshman year of college. Submit your essay to your campus newspaper.

CHAPTER 4

FAMILY TIES: WHAT DOES FAMILY MEAN?

"The biological family isn't the only important unit in society; we have needs and longings that our families cannot meet. Indeed, in some cultures, community is more important than the family."

Gloria Steinem

"Happy families are all alike; every unhappy family is unhappy in its own way."

Leo Tolstoy

"Families are about love overcoming emotional torture."

Matt Groening

"Happiness is having a large, loving, caring, close-knit family in another city."

George Burns

Parents Also Have Rights
RONNIE GUNNERSON

In this essay, which originally appeared in *Newsweek*'s "My Turn" column, Ronnie Gunnerson argues that parents should have the right to decide the fate of a pregnant teenager's child. She comes by her opinion through firsthand experience. As you read, ask yourself how much of the author's case is based on logic and how much is based on an appeal to the reader's emotions.

Preview. In your campus library or on the Internet, find out the current rate of pregnancy among unmarried teenagers in the United States. Also discover whether that rate has risen, fallen, or held steady over the last five years.

Vocabulary. If any of the following words from the essay are unfamiliar to you, study their meanings before reading.

besotted (2)   made stupid or foolish
untenable (2, 3)   indefensible
ramifications (3)   consequences
blatantly (9)   offensively obvious
smitten (10)   impressed favorably
malleable (12)   adaptable

What's a parent to do?" is the punch line to many a joke on the perils of raising children. But what a parent does when a teenager gets pregnant is far from a joke; it's a soul-searching, heart-wrenching condition with responses as diverse as the families affected.

2   In an era besotted with concern for both the emotional and social welfare of teenage mothers and their babies, anger seems to be forbidden. Yet how many parents can deny anger when circumstances over which they have no control force them into untenable situations?

3   And untenable they are. What I discovered after my 16-year-old stepdaughter became pregnant shocked me. Parents have no rights. We could neither demand she give the baby up for adoption, nor insist on an abortion. The choice belongs to the teenage mother, who is still a child herself and far from capable of understanding the lifelong ramifications of whatever choice she makes.

4   At the same time, homes for unwed mothers, at least the two we checked in Los Angeles, where we live, will house the teenager at no cost to the family, but they will not admit her unless her parents sign a statement agreeing to pick up both her and her baby from a designated maternity hospital. Parents may

sit out the pregnancy if they so desire, but when all is said and done, they're stuck with both mother and baby whether they like it or not.

5   In essence, then, the pregnant teenager can choose whether or not to have her baby and whether or not to keep it. The parents, who have the legal responsibility for both the teenage mother and her child, have no say in the matter. The costs of a teenage pregnancy are high; yes, the teenager's life is forever changed by her untimely pregnancy and childbirth. But life is forever changed for the rest of her family as well, and I am tired of the do-gooders who haven't walked a yard, let alone a mile, in my shoes shouting their sympathy for the "victimized" teen.

6   What about the victimized parents? Are we supposed to accept the popular notion that we failed this child and that therefore we are to blame for her lack of either scruples or responsibility? Not when we spend endless hours and thousands of dollars in therapy trying to help a girl whose behavior has been rebellious since the age of 13. Not when we have heart-to-heart talks until the wee hours of the morning which we learn are the butt of jokes between her and her friends. And not when we continually trust her only to think afterward that she's repeatedly lied to us about everything there is to lie about.

7   Yes, the teenager is a victim—a victim of illusions fostered by a society that gives her the right to decide whether or not to have an illegitimate baby, no matter what her parents say. Many believe it is feelings of rejection that motivate girls to have babies; they want human beings of their own to love and be loved by. I wouldn't disagree, but another motive may be at work as well: the ultimate rebellion. Parents are forced to cope with feelings more devastating than adolescent confusion. And I'm not talking about the superficial, what-will-the-Joneses-think attitudes. I mean gut-gripping questions that undermine brutally the self-confidence it can take adults years to develop.

8   We can all write off to immaturity mistakes made in adolescence. To what do we attribute our perceived parental failures at 40 or 50? Even as I proclaim our innocence in my stepdaughter's folly, I will carry to my grave, as I know my husband will, the nagging fear that we could have prevented it *if only* we'd been *better* parents.

9   And I will carry forevermore the sad realization that I'm not the compassionate person I'd tried so hard to be and actually thought I was. My reaction to my stepdaughter's pregnancy horrified me. I was consumed with hatred and anger. Any concern I felt for her was overridden by the feeling that I'd been had. I'd befriended this child, housed her and counseled her for years, and what did I get in return? Not knowing her whereabouts that culminated in her getting pregnant with a boy we didn't even know. At first I felt like a fool. When I discovered how blatantly society's rules favor the rule breaker, I felt like a raving maniac.

10   *Resentment and rage:* It took more hours of counseling for me to accept my anger than it did for my stepdaughter to deal with her pregnancy. But then, she had the support of a teenage subculture that reveres motherhood among its

own and a news-media culture that fusses and frets over adolescent mothers. Few ears were willing to hear what my husband and I were feeling. While I can't speak for my husband, I can say that today, a year after the baby's birth, he still turns to ice when his daughter is around. Smitten as he is with his first grandchild, he hasn't forgotten that the joy of the boy's birth was overshadowed by resentment and rage.

11   Fortunately, my stepdaughter recently married a young man who loves her son as his own, although he is not the father. Together, the three of them are a family who, like many a young family, are struggling to make ends meet. Neither my stepdaughter nor her husband has yet finished high school, but they are not a drain on society as many teenage parents are. She and her husband seem to be honest, hard workers, and I really think they will make it. Their story will have a happy ending.

12   My stepdaughter says she can't even understand the person she used to be, and I believe her. Unfortunately, the minds of adults are not quite as malleable as those of constantly changing adolescents. My husband and I haven't forgotten—and I'm not sure we've forgiven—either our daughter or ourselves. We're still writing the ending to our own story, and I believe it's time for society to write an ending of its own. If a pregnant teenager's parents are ultimately responsible for the teenager and her baby, then give those parents the right to decide whether or not the teenager keeps her baby. Taking the decision away from the teen mother would eliminate her power over her parents and could give pause to her reckless pursuit of the "in" thing.

Understanding Content

1. What point is Gunnerson arguing? That is, what is her position?
2. What are Gunnerson's reasons for believing that parents should decide the fate of their teenager's baby?
3. Gunnerson brings up possible objections to her point of view and then counters those objections (weakens them) with points of her own. What objections does she raise and how does she weaken those objections?
4. Gunnerson says that some pregnant teens decide to keep their babies because it is the "in" thing to do (paragraph 12). What does she mean?

Considering Structure and Technique

1. What approach does Gunnerson take to her introduction? Does that introduction engage your interest? Why or why not?
2. What purpose do paragraphs 2 and 3 serve?
3. Gunnerson makes her case by using both logical argument and emotional appeal. Cite an example of each. Which does she rely on more, logic or emotion?
4. What approach does Gunnerson take to her conclusion? Does the conclusion bring the essay to a satisfying end? Explain.

Exploring Ideas

1. "Parents Also Have Rights" first appeared in *Newsweek*. Do you think the emotional appeal in the essay is likely to move the author's intended audience? Explain.
2. Does the fact that the author's daughter married and made a life for herself (although a difficult one) detract from the author's argument? Explain why or why not.
3. In paragraph 6, Gunnerson refers to the parents of pregnant teenagers as "victimized." Why do you think she sees herself and other parents of pregnant teens as victims? Do you think they are victims? Explain.
4. Are you convinced by Gunnerson's arguments? Why or why not?

Writing Workshop: Using Contrast

To emphasize a point or make something vivid, writers can use contrast. For example, in paragraph 1 of "Parents Also Have Rights," Gunnerson contrasts a joke about raising children with the difficulties of raising children, to underscore how hard being a parent can be. In paragraphs 5, 6, and 7, she contrasts teenagers as victims with parents as victims, to emphasize that parents endure more. In paragraph 8, she contrasts the severity of the teenager's mistake with the severity of the parents' mistake, to show that the parents' mistake seems bigger. In paragraph 10, she contrasts the support the pregnant teenager gets with the support the parents get to emphasize that teenagers get more support. Overall, these contrasts serve to show that the parents of the pregnant teenager endure more hardship than the teenager herself.

Writing Workshop Activity

Select one of the following thesis sentences and write a contrast that can help develop that thesis:

- Working students experience more stress than nonworking students.
- Essay tests are more difficult than objective tests.
- Dating practices have changed dramatically in the last 10 years.

Language Notes for Multilingual and Other Writers

A number of frequently used idioms appear in "Parents Also Have Rights":

1. To *walk a mile in someone's shoes* means to experience the same thing someone else is experiencing.

   . . . I am tired of the do-gooders who haven't <u>walked</u> a yard, let alone <u>a mile</u>, in my shoes. . . . Paragraph 5

2. To *keep up with the Joneses* refers to competing socially with one's neighbors or associates by buying what they have or doing what they do.

   And I'm not talking about the superficial, <u>what-will-the-Joneses-think</u> attitudes. Paragraph 7

3. To *be had* refers to being taken advantage of or being made a fool of.

   Any concern I felt for her was overridden by the feeling that <u>I'd been had</u>. Paragraph 9

4. *In* can mean popular or current, as in *in-group, in-crowd, in-restaurant.*

   Taking the decision away from the teen mother would eliminate her power over her parents and could give pause to her reckless pursuit of the "<u>in</u>" thing. Paragraph 12

From Reading to Writing

In Your Journal: Explain whether or not you think Gunnerson's anger is justified. Do you agree that she is a bigger victim than her daughter?

With Some Classmates: Explain why you think the problem of teenage pregnancy exists to the extent that it does. If you wish, you can read a bit about the issue in your campus library or on the Internet before writing your paper.

In an Essay

- If you disagree with Gunnerson's view, write an essay that argues that the pregnant teenager should be allowed to decide the fate of her child. <u>Be sure to raise and counter some of Gunnerson's more compelling points.</u>
- In some school systems, the number of teenage mothers is so high that day-care centers have been placed in the high school so the young mothers can have child care while they work toward their diplomas. What do you think of day-care centers in high schools?
- As one way to address the problems raised by sexually active teenagers, some high schools have begun distributing condoms to students who ask for them. What do you think of this idea?

Beyond the Writing Class: Consider what can be done to deal with the problem of teenage pregnancy and develop a policy aimed specifically at reducing the number of teenage pregnancies. Submit the policy for your local school board to consider.

Hold the Mayonnaise

JULIA ALVAREZ

Julia Alvarez was born in New York City, but her family moved to the Dominican Republic shortly after her birth. When she was 10, her family returned to the United States, fleeing the Dominican Republic because Alvarez's father had participated in an unsuccessful attempt to overthrow the Trujillo dictatorship. Alvarez has taught creative writing and English at a number of schools, but currently she teaches at Middlebury College in Vermont. Winner of numerous writing awards, Alvarez has penned poetry, short stories, and a novel. The following essay first appeared in the *New York Times Magazine* in 1992.

Preview. Divorce and remarriage have changed the shape of the American family. Now, stepparents and stepchildren are a routine part of the mix, presenting new problems, challenges, and joys. In "Hold the Mayonnaise," Alvarez describes her experience joining a family as a stepparent from a different culture. Think about how families have changed as a result of the increased number of stepparents, and list the most important changes that occur to you.

Vocabulary. If any of the following words from the essay are unfamiliar to you, study their meanings before reading.

filial (1)   pertaining to a son or a daughter
Dominicans (2)   people from Santo Domingo
strapping (4)   powerfully built
aficionado (4)   a person devoted to something
condiment (4)   something such as mustard and ketchup that gives extra
    flavor to food
gringa (5)   Spanish for "female foreigner"
tía (7)   Spanish for "aunt"
no comprendo (9)   Spanish for "I do not understand"
lingo (10)   language or speech
usurp (11)   to take by force
Mr. Potato Head (11)   a child's toy with an assortment of plastic noses, eyes,
    ears, and mouths used to make faces on a plastic potato-shaped head
assimilationist (15)   a person who believes that immigrants should conform
    to the ways of the dominant culture

"If I die first and Papi ever gets remarried," Mami would tease when we were kids, "don't you accept a new woman in my house. Make her life impossble, you hear?" My sisters and I nodded obediently and a filial shudder would go through us. We were Catholics, so of course, the only kind of remarriage we could imagine had to involve our mother's death.

2   We were also Dominicans, recently arrived in Jamaica, Queens, in the early 60's, before waves of other Latin Americans began arriving. So, when we imagined who exactly my father might possibly ever think of remarrying, only American women came to mind. It would be bad enough having a *madrastra*, but a "stepmother. . . ."

3   All I could think of was that she would make me eat mayonnaise, a food I identified with the United States and which I detested. Mami understood, of course, that I wasn't used to that kind of food. Even a madrastra, accustomed to our rice and beans and tostones and pollo frito, would understand. But an American stepmother would think it was normal to put mayonnaise on food, and if she were at all strict and a little mean, which all stepmothers, of course, were, she would make me eat potato salad and such. I had plenty of my own reasons to make a potential stepmother's life impossible. When I nodded obediently with my sisters, I was imagining not just something foreign in our house, but in our refrigerator.

4   So it's strange now, almost 35 years later, to find myself a Latina stepmother of my husband's two tall, strapping, blond, mayonnaise-eating daughters. To be honest, neither of them is a real aficionado of the condiment, but it's a fair thing to add to a bowl of tuna fish or diced potatoes. Their American food, I think of it, and when they head to their mother's or off to school, I push the jar back in the refrigerator behind their chocolate pudding and several open cans of Diet Coke.

5   What I can't push as successfully out of sight are my own immigrant childhood fears of having a *gringa* stepmother with foreign tastes in our house. Except now, I am the foreign stepmother in a gringa household. I've wondered what my husband's two daughters think of this stranger in their family. It must be doubly strange for them that I am from another culture.

6   Of course, there are mitigating circumstances—my husband's two daughters were teen-agers when we married, older, more mature, able to understand differences. They had also traveled when they were children with their father, an eye doctor, who worked on short-term international projects with various eye foundations. But still, it's one thing to visit a foreign country, another altogether to find it brought home—a real bear plopped down in a Goldilocks house.

7   Sometimes, a whole extended family of bears. My warm, loud Latino family came up for the wedding: my *tía* from Santo Domingo; three dramatic, enthusiastic sisters and their families; my papi, with a thick accent I could tell the girls found it hard to understand; and my mami, who had her eye trained on my soon-to-be stepdaughters for any sign that they were about to make my life impossible. "How are they behaving themselves?" she asked me, as if they were 7 and 3, not 19 and 16. "They're wonderful girls," I replied, already feeling protective of them.

8   I looked around for the girls in the meadow in front of the house we were building, where we were holding the outdoor wedding ceremony and party. The oldest hung out with a group of her own friends. The younger one whizzed in briefly for the ceremony, then left again before the congratulations started up. There was not much mixing with me and mine. What was there for them to celebrate on a day so full of confusion and effort?

9   On my side, being the newcomer in someone else's territory is a role I'm used to. I can tap into that struggling English speaker, that skinny, dark-haired, olive-skinned girl in a sixth grade of mostly blond and blue-eyed giants. Those tall, freckled boys would push me around in the playground. "Go back to where you came from!" "*No comprendo!*" I'd reply, though of course there was no misunderstanding the fierce looks on their faces.

10   Even now, my first response to a scowl is that old pulling away. (My husband calls it "checking out.") I remember times early on in the marriage when the girls would be with us, and I'd get out of school and drive around doing errands, killing time, until my husband, their father, would be leaving work. I am not proud of my fears, but I understand—as the lingo goes—where they come from.

11   And I understand, more than I'd like to sometimes, my stepdaughters' pain. But with me, they need never fear that I'll usurp a mother's place. No one has ever come up and held their faces and then addressed me, "They look just like you." If anything, strangers to the remarriage are probably playing Mr. Potato Head in their minds, trying to figure out how my foreign features and my husband's fair Nebraskan features got put together into these two tall, blond girls. "My husband's daughters," I kept introducing them.

12   Once, when one of them visited my class and I introduced her as such, two students asked me why. "I'd be so hurt if my stepmom introduced me that way," the young man said. That night I told my stepdaughter what my students had said. She scowled at me and agreed. "It's so weird how you call me Papa's daughter. Like you don't want to be related to me or something."

13   "I didn't want to presume," I explained. "So it's O.K. if I call you my stepdaughter?"

14   "That's what I am," she said. Relieved, I took it for a teensy inch of acceptance. The takings are small in this stepworld, I've discovered. Sort of like being a minority. It feels as if all the goodies have gone somewhere else.

15   Day to day, I guess I follow my papi's advice. When we first came, he would talk to his children about how to make it in our new country. "Just do your work and put in your heart, and they will accept you!" In this age of remaining true to your roots, of keeping your Spanish, of fighting from inside your culture, that assimilationist approach is highly suspect. My Latino students—who don't want to be called Hispanics anymore—would ditch me as faculty adviser if I came up with that play-nice message.

16   But in a stepfamily where everyone is starting a new life together, it isn't bad advice. Like a potluck supper, an American concept my mami never took to. ("Why invite people to your house and then ask them to bring the food?")

You put what you've got together with what everyone else brought and see what comes out of the pot. The luck part is if everyone brings something you like. No potato salad, no deviled eggs, no little party sandwiches with you know what in them.

Understanding Content

1. Mayonnaise figures prominently in Alvarez's essay. It is part of the title and the focus of more than one paragraph. However, mayonnaise is not really the issue here; it is a symbol, a representation of something else. What do you think mayonnaise symbolizes (represents) for Alvarez?
2. What interesting coincidence or **irony** is attached to the fact that Alvarez is the Latina stepmother in a *gringa* household?
3. Why did Alvarez introduce her stepchildren as her husband's daughters?
4. In your own words, explain the advice Alvarez's father gave her, the same advice that Alvarez thinks it is good to follow in a stepfamily. Why do you think her Latina students would rebel at this advice?

Considering Structure and Technique

1. What approach does the author take to her introduction? Does this introduction engage your interest? Why or why not?
2. To some extent, Alvarez develops her supporting details with comparison and contrast. What elements of comparison and contrast appear?
3. Do you think the conclusion of the essay is effective? Why or why not?

Exploring Ideas

1. In paragraph 8, Alvarez says her wedding day was a day "full of confusion and effort." What do you think she means by this?
2. Alvarez describes running errands to kill time until her husband left work and was heading home. Why do you think she did this?
3. Alvarez reaches a point in her distaste for mayonnaise that she can admit it "is a fair thing to add to a bowl of tuna fish or diced potatoes," and she can keep it in the house, although she must "push the jar back in the refrigerator" (paragraph 4). What does this attitude toward mayonnaise signify?
4. For what purpose do you think Alvarez wrote "Hold the Mayonnaise"? What kinds of publications would be interested in reprinting the essay?

Writing Workshop: Writing Metaphors

A **metaphor** is a comparison made without using the words *like* or *as*. Here is a metaphor taken from "Hold the Mayonnaise":

But still, it's one thing to visit a foreign country, another altogether to find it brought home—a real bear plopped down in a Goldilocks house.
Paragraph 6

In this metaphor, the foreign-born stepmother is compared to the bear in "Goldilocks and the Three Bears," and the American-born family is compared to Goldilocks's family. The reversal of the story (where the bear is in Goldilocks's house) represents the confusion of Alvarez's family situation.

Here is another metaphor from the essay:

If anything, strangers to the remarriage are probably playing Mr. Potato Head in their minds, trying to figure out how my foreign features and my husband's fair Nebraskan features got put together into these two tall, blond girls. Paragraph 11

In this metaphor, combining Alvarez's features and her husband's is compared to playing Mr. Potato Head, a game in which plastic facial features are selected and arranged on a plastic potato-shaped head.

Like metaphors, **similes** also compare. But a simile uses the word *like* or *as* in the comparison. For example, the last paragraph compares the stepfamily to a potluck dinner, using the word *like* ("Like a potluck supper").

Writing Workshop Activity

From now on when you read, be on the lookout for metaphors. Each time you notice one that you find particularly interesting, write it out in your journal. To start off, read paragraphs 18 and 20 of "India: A Widow's Devastating Choice" on page 307. What metaphor appears?

Language Notes for Multilingual and Other Writers

Two references in "Hold the Mayonnaise" come from fairy tales. In paragraph 3, Alvarez mentions that all stepmothers are "strict and a little mean." She is not serious, of course, but she is referring to a long tradition of "evil stepmothers" in stories. One of the most familiar evil stepmothers is the one in the fairy tale "Cinderella."

The second fairy tale reference appears in paragraphs 6 and 7. Here Alvarez's references to Goldilocks and the family of bears are taken from the fairy tale "Goldilocks and the Three Bears." In that story, Goldilocks is a stranger and an intruder in the bears' house. Alvarez's use of the reference is explained in this chapter's workshop on metaphors.

From Reading to Writing

In Your Journal: Alvarez associates mayonnaise with white culture and foreign tastes. In your journal, write about a food or foods that have strong associations for you. Explain what those associations are and why they exist for you.

For example, you might explain that lumpy mashed potatoes make you think of your Aunt Bert, who cooked them every Sunday for your family dinner. Then you could go on to tell about the Sunday dinners.

With Some Classmates: Explain how the presence of stepparents and stepchildren has altered the nature of the American family. Your preview activity for this essay may give you ideas. In addition, you may want to interview stepparents and stepchildren.

In an Essay

- In paragraph 9, Alvarez explains, "Being the newcomer in someone else's territory is a role I'm used to." All of us have felt like newcomers or outsiders at times, whether it's been as a new student in a new school, a stranger in a roomful of people who know each other, or a new employee on the job. Tell about an instance when you were a newcomer or an outsider. How did you cope? What were the short-term and long-term effects of being a newcomer or outsider?
- Alvarez says a little but not much about the problems and joys that are part of a family when a stepparent is from a different culture. What do you think some of those problems and joys are? How will dealing with these problems and joys affect the lives of family members?
- Write an essay called "Pass the Mayonnaise" that presents the daughters' points of view on having a stepmother from a different culture.
- In paragraph 14, Alvarez refers to the "stepworld." If you have a stepparent or if you are yourself a stepparent, describe this "stepworld."
- If you are from another country, evaluate the advice Alvarez's father gave her for making it in a new country (see paragraph 15). If you disagree with his advice, give your own.

Beyond the Writing Class: Educators do not agree on how beneficial bilingual education is. Read about bilingual education on the Internet or in your campus library. Also, consider the contrast between the "assimilationist approach" people from other cultures can take to living in the United States and the approach that calls for "remaining true to your roots," referred to in paragraph 15. Then write a paper arguing for or against bilingual education in school districts with a high percentage of students who do not speak English as a first language.

The Transmission of Hope
GEORGE MCKENNA

George McKenna teaches political science at the City College of New York, and he is the coeditor of *Taking Sides: Clashing Views on Controversial Political Issues* (1999). In the following essay, which first appeared in the *Atlantic Monthly*, McKenna recalls his grandfather and the hope he imparted with his generation-connecting stories.

Preview.   McKenna's grandfather was not a saint. He may not even have been virtuous. He did, however, give the young McKenna exactly what he needed—time, attention, and wonderful stories of the past. Write about someone who provided something you needed when you were a child.

Vocabulary.   If any of the following words from the essay are unfamiliar to you, study their meanings before reading.

vole (1)   a small rodent
avid (3)   eager
lurid (3)   sensational or shocking
bandy-legged (4)   bowlegged
*uber*canine (5)   super dog
galley-west (6)   into destruction or confusion
surmised (7)   supposed or suspected
sot (7)   a drunkard
Forrest Gump (8)   character in a popular movie by the same name; Forrest
    Gump stumbled into situations that made him a part of important
    historical events
Upton Sinclair (8)   American author who wrote an exposé of the meat-
    packing industry
The Book of Virtues (12)   a collection of stories about morality
griots (13)   members of an African caste who keep the oral history of the
    village
incredulously (16)   indicating lack of belief
noxious (17)   harmful

When my father died, at the end of 1936, a few months before I was born, my mother moved back into her parents' house, on the southeast side of Chicago. Not long after my birth my mother went to work, and during the day I was cared for by my grandparents, both in their seventies. "I raised him," my grandmother used to say about me in particular, the youngest of four, in later years—which annoyed my mother. Yet Grandmother was at least half right.

She did take care of my physical needs, and she was always there in every season: in the spring, when I was told not to track mud into the house; in the summer, when I was told not to let the back screen door slam; in the fall, when she shooed away my friends and me when we came home from school; and in the snowy Chicago winters, when she complained about mittens dripping on the radiator. Even now I can remember every detail about her, from the black slippers she wore every day, with holes cut to relieve her bunions, to her straight gray hair with little sunset streaks of orange, pinned back in a bun. She was tiny, skinny, wrinkled, and so nearsighted that she squinted under her glasses. Her complexion was ashen, but she was energetic as a little vole, with the quick movements and the stride of someone much younger. She was always in the midst of some crazy project, such as varnishing the linoleum or spraying DDT in the pantry to fight roaches (she stopped that after she passed out one day, smashing dishes in her fall), and she was so busy with these things that she didn't have time to talk. "Get out of the house," she used to say. "Go play in the prairie"—the name we had for the corner sandlot.

2 God knows, Grandma did her best. She minded four children at an age when she should have been able to do what she pleased, and she took the job seriously, at least when it came to me. She dressed me till I was in third grade, rubbed my back every night, talked baby talk to me when I was sick, and slapped and cursed me roundly when I misbehaved. But I don't remember her ever carrying on a sustained conversation with me. That was what my grandfather did.

3 My grandfather was still working in his seventies, as a janitor in a steel-processing mill. His name was Tom Norton. He had been raised on a farm in northern Illinois and had knocked around in various jobs over the years, mainly on paving crews. He had had about two years of education in a country schoolhouse, but he was an avid reader (mainly of Zane Gray, though I once saw among his books a paperback of Faulkner's *Requiem for a Nun* with a lurid cover). He got home late in the afternoon and had to get up at five the next morning, so he ate before the rest of us and went to bed early. But when he was around, he was a delight to me, because he talked to me—talked *with* me—during my childhood years. I remember him coming home from work, up the alley from the streetcar line to our house. "Hi, Grandpa, got any gum?" I used to say. It was a ritual. He would pull out a stick, the wrapping stuck so tight from the heat and sweat of his pocket that I would have to spit out little pieces of tinfoil as I chewed it.

4 Grandpa was a strange sight, especially in the summer, when he wore an overcoat on even the hottest days. He was short and bandy-legged, with a long body and a barrel chest. But the strangest thing about him was his color: he was purple. His skin had turned purple years earlier from a dose of silver nitrate that some quack doctor had prescribed for his ulcer. Silver nitrate is used in the development of black-and-white film, and like film, Grandpa was sensitive to sunlight. He would "develop." In summer, particularly where his skin was exposed, his color was a very dark grayish-purple, but in the unexposed

areas he was more silvery, almost white. I suppose that is why he wore his overcoat in summer.

5   Before he went to bed, my grandfather and I would talk on the steps of the front porch. That, too, was controlled by ritual. "Grandpa," I would say, "let's talk about it," and he would reply, "Well, what's the subject?" "Horses," I would say, or "Dogs," or "Guns," He had a story for every topic. Dogs? He would tell about an *uber*canine he had once owned, a dog so intelligent that even the Albert Payson Terhune collies I used to read about couldn't match him. He had had smart horses, too. "I once had a horse I trained so good he'd back up into the same corner of the yard before he'd do his business. Neat as a pin. And what a riding horse. I could just talk to him and he'd go anywhere. Tell him 'right' or 'left', he'd know. He was almost human."

6   Grandpa had a nice way of telling these tall tales. His big chest cavity gave his voice some depth, and he sounded his *r*s in the wholesome midwestern way. He told his stories slowly, not neglecting any details. Grandpa was a great detail man. When I asked him about guns, he'd tell about going hunting as a boy with a Civil War musket. "First you poured your powder down the muzzle. Then you tamped in the paper. Then the ball. Then more paper. Put the cap on, cock, and get ready to fire." The story had a dramatic coda. "One day I forgot. I put the powder in, tamped the paper, then forgot and put in a *second* charge. Boy, that thing kicked back and sent me galley-west. Coulda blown up and killed me right there." Then there was the story about watching Chicago burn down in 1871. "I looked out over the field and saw them black clouds rising in the sky like mountains." My grandfather was five at the time, and his family's farm was about fifty miles northwest of the city. Could he really have seen those mountainous black clouds? If he did, it *would* have stuck in the mind of a five-year-old. It would have stuck in my mind.

7   Grandpa was not a saintly man. I never thought of him as one even then. He smoked cheap, sulfurous pipe tobacco; he rarely bathed, and angrily resisted my grandmother's demands that he change his shirt. And he drank. He had mellowed in his old age, and I never saw him drunk, though I later surmised that he was a little high when he told me stories. He never missed work because of drink, but in his earlier years he had drunk on the job and drunk even more after work. My mother remembered his coming home late after stopping at the saloon, slumped helplessly in his buggy, careening into the driveway on two wheels as the family mare, who hadn't been fed or watered all day, made a dash for the barn. (Was this the smart horse he had told me about?) My mother, who had seen too much of that and other things over the years, lost all patience with "Pa," as she called him when she bothered to call him anything. Nobody else in the house had much use for him either. To my sister he was all but invisible, and to my brothers he was just a funny old sot, the butt of one-liners—"Hey, Grandpa really drank himself blue in the face, didn't he?" A couple of years ago one of my brothers asked me what the

hell it was that Grandpa and I talked about on the front porch, and I told him some of the stories. "So that was it," he said.

8   If the stories had any truth in them at all, Grandpa was a kind of Forrest Gump, shadowing the great events and men of his time. He watched the Chicago fire at five, hunted with a Civil War musket at twelve, and in his twenties was working as a bellhop at Chicago's Palmer House when Grover Cleveland walked in. "Got so close I coulda punched that silk hat right off his head." (That seemed like such a good idea to me that I missed the sarcasm in my grandmother's reaction: "I'm surprised you didn't, Tom.") He briefly held down a distasteful job as a "knocker" in a Chicago slaughterhouse, hammering the heads of cattle, years before Upton Sinclair arrived on the scene.

9   His best story was also embedded in the events of history. Sometime around the turn of the century Grandpa was working as the boss of a paving gang in Fort Smith, Arkansas, on the Oklahoma border. One day he fired two of his men, Creek Indians from Oklahoma, who then got drunk and barged into the office firing pistols. "I was behind the desk," he said, "on a high stool. They got me in the arm, and over I went. I was under the desk and they coulda just reached over and finished me off. Instead they shot this young fella who was sharpening a lampwick on the other side of the room. He run toward the back door—shouldn't a done that, shoulda just lied down like me and not stirred—and they hit him again, this time in the back. Then they left. I went to him, asked if I could help. Would he take some whiskey? No, he said, he promised his mother he'd never take a drink. He died not long after."

10   Whatever the truth of that story, I am an eyewitness to the fact that *something* had happened to Grandpa's arm. On the front of the forearm was a neat round scar, smaller than a dime, but on the other side was a gigantic mother-of-pearl eruption in his gray flesh. "It was a forty-four," Grandpa boasted.

11   Years later, when I found out about another kind of ugly scar, I marveled again at how Grandpa's life had folded into the contours of American history. It turned out that the Creek Indians, the tribe of the men who had barged into the office with those big-caliber guns, did not come from Oklahoma. They had been moved there, seventy years earlier, because white people wanted their homelands in Georgia and Alabama. During that forced 600-mile trek thousands of them died of hunger, disease, and exposure. The Creeks, though, were very adaptable. After some years they developed crops and farming methods suitable to the new land, and became fairly prosperous. But then a federal law passed in the late 1880s broke up their tribal holdings into individual plots; these turned out to be too small and barren to be farmed profitably. The Creeks were pulled back into poverty. So it is possible that the shooting spree that erupted in the office that afternoon was a reaction to more than a single injury of getting (probably deservedly) sacked. Maybe these two Creeks just added up the whole bill and decided that it was time to start paying people back for what had happened to their grandparents and their parents, what had happened to *them*.

12   But I'll leave the story alone instead of trying to extract any morals from it. Grandpa was a storyteller, not a moralist, and his stories didn't come from *The Book of Virtues*. They had to do with dogs and horses and shooting rattlesnakes and hammering cows on the head. Nietzsche once remarked that if you ask a little boy if he'd like to become "virtuous," he'll stare at you, "but he will open his eyes wide if asked: 'Would you like to become stronger than your friends?'" Grandpa told stories about saloon fights that he and his brother ("I and Jim") had fought against incredible odds, stories that were very satisfying to a slightly undersized boy who had lost just about every fight he hadn't run away from. They were PG-13 stories, rather violent, but their saving grace was the fact that they were *told* to me, right there, face to face, on the front steps, and that I could talk back, ask questions, ask for more details.

13   "Deprive children of stories," the philosopher Alasdair MacIntyre wrote, "and you leave them unscripted, anxious stutterers in their actions as in their words." Alas, many children in today's America are in that predicament. This is one reason why the behavior of such children is as incomprehensible to us as our world—the world passed on to us by our parents and grandparents—must be to them. All societies throughout history seem to have had their griots, their storytellers, who introduced the young into the human community. But in the past generation America has produced a large number of young people who haven't experienced these civilizing rituals.

14   Growing up as I did, fatherless but in a middle-class neighborhood, there was little danger of my becoming a gang member. But I wonder whether in the absence of my grandfather and his stories I would have become one of the "anxious stutterers" MacIntyre referred to.

15   I wish there were some way I could bring a little essence of Grandpa to today's fatherless children. This has to do with hopefulness. In one of his last books the historian Christopher Lasch wrote that hope, unlike optimism, derives not from visions of the future but from memories of the past, memories "in which the experience of order and contentment was so intense that subsequent disillusionments cannot dislodge it." Is there a way of introducing that into the lives of fatherless children? Maybe not. I listened to my grandfather's stories on the front steps of a house that was uncomfortably warm on summer nights and had nothing inside it of immediate interest to a small boy. I listened to the stories and became absorbed, but I listened because there wasn't much of anything else to do. After all, it was the 1940s.

16   The first sign that the decade was over was the disappearance of my mother's elegant washing machine and wringer, which I had liked to watch as it flattened clothes, cartoonlike, into a continuous sheet of wet socks, shirts, and underwear before dumping them into a tub of clear water. Replacing all of that was a gleaming white box—very "modern," I thought, like the new 1950s office buildings. The cockroaches my grandmother had fought so valiantly in the forties also disappeared, after we started shopping at the new supermarket instead of at friendly George Valakas's IGA store. And then, quite suddenly, my grandparents aged. Grandma's mind started wandering, and one day I came home from high school to find her dying of pneumonia. She was lying in my brother's bed, her lips blue, worrying about whether the garbage had been taken out. She died a few nights later, and my mother lit a candle in the dark room and told me to pray. Grandpa lived another two years. When I came into the house one day, he had just collapsed, after telling my sister he felt "lousy." I carried him to bed, but he slipped out of my grip and fell hard into the bed. I was afraid I had killed him, and when the doctor came later and pronounced him dead, I nervously asked him what had caused his death. The doctor stared at me incredulously, "What caused his death? He died of old age."

17   At his wake he didn't look much like himself. They had given his sparse hair a slick comb-over instead of letting it go any which way, which was my grandfather's style. But at least he stayed purple. The undertaker had asked my mother if she wanted anything done about the "flesh tone," but she said to leave it alone so that people would recognize him. So, in the middle of the new decade, they buried the man who had figured so much in my childhood, the purple man who refused to bathe, drank, smoked noxious tobacco, and wore an overcoat in July. He had done me a good turn without realizing it, which is probably the best way.

Understanding Content

1. What was McKenna's grandmother like? Cite evidence from the essay to support your view.
2. Make a list of words and phrases that describe McKenna's grandfather.
3. Why was his grandfather's story-telling important to McKenna?
4. Did McKenna's family share his opinion of his grandfather? Explain.
5. In paragraph 11, McKenna tells about "another kind of ugly scar." What is that scar?

Considering Structure and Technique

1. McKenna uses a great deal of description when writing of his grandparents. For example, in paragraph 1, he writes of his grandmother's "straight gray hair with little sunset streaks of orange, pinned back in a bun." Cite three other examples of description. What does the description contribute?
2. McKenna also uses conversation in the essay. What does that conversation contribute?
3. A number of paragraphs open with a **topic sentence** (a statement of the paragraph's main idea). Cite four paragraphs that begin with topic sentences.

4. Paragraphs 1 and 2 focus on the author's grandmother, yet she is not the primary focus of the essay. Why does McKenna bother to describe his grandmother's appearance and behavior in his opening?
5. What approach does McKenna take to his conclusion? Is the conclusion effective? Explain.

Exploring Ideas

1. In paragraphs 3 and 5, McKenna refers to the rituals that he and his grandfather had. How did the author feel about these rituals? Why did he feel that way?
2. How would you characterize the stories McKenna's grandfather told? For example, were they true or not, merely interesting, important in some way?
3. Why does McKenna offer an explanation for why the Creek Indians barged into his grandfather's office? Is that information relevant to the rest of the essay? Explain.
4. In paragraph 13, McKenna notes the importance of stories for children. Explain what McKenna sees as that importance.
5. Explain the meaning of the essay's title.

Writing Workshop: Capitalizing Titles of Relatives

Capitalize words such as *uncle, aunt, mother, father, grandmother,* and *grandfather* when names can be substituted for these titles.

I asked Sis for a ten-dollar loan.

I told Father about my problem.

In both of these examples, capital letters are used because names could be substituted, like this:

I asked Lorraine for a ten-dollar loan.

I told Frank about my problem.

If the name cannot be substituted for the title, no capital letter is used:

I asked my sister for a ten-dollar loan. We do not usually say, "I asked my Lorraine for a ten-dollar loan."

I told my father about my problem. We do not usually say, "I told my Frank about my problem."

The following sentences from "The Transmission of Hope" illustrate this rule:

When my <u>father</u> died, at the end of 1936, a few months before I was born, my <u>mother</u> moved back into her parent's house. . . . Paragraph 1

Yet <u>Grandma</u> was at least half right. Paragraph 1

"I raised him," my <u>grandmother</u> used to say. . . . Paragraph 1

My <u>grandfather</u> was still working in his seventies. . . . Paragraph 3

"Hey, <u>Grandpa</u> really drank himself blue in the face, didn't he?" Paragraph 7

Writing Workshop Activity

In your journal, write five sentences with titles of relatives appropriately capitalized and five sentences with titles of relatives appropriately not capitalized.

Language Notes for Multilingual and Other Writers

If English is not your first language, a number of expressions in "The Transmission of Hope" may be unfamiliar to you.

1. A *quack* is someone who pretends to have skills, particularly as a doctor.

   His skin had turned purple years earlier from a dose of silver nitrate that some <u>quack</u> doctor had prescribed for his ulcer. Paragraph 4

2. To be the *butt* of something is to be the object of contempt or sarcasm; a *one-liner* is a brief, humorous remark. Thus to be the *butt of a one-liner* is to be marked with scorn as the object of a brief, humorous remark.

   . . . to my brothers he was just a funny old sot, the <u>butt of one-liners</u> . . . Paragaph 7

3. To be *blue in the face* is to be exhausted from excessive effort.

   "Hey, Grandpa really drank himself <u>blue in the face</u>, didn't he?" Paragraph 7

From Reading to Writing

In Your Journal: The author and his grandfather had a number of rituals, including the exchange of gum and story-telling. Tell about a ritual you share or shared with a family member or friend. What does that ritual mean to you?

With Some Classmates: For McKenna, part of the appeal of his grandfather's stories was the fact that they crossed generational lines. How important is it for us to have a sense of the past? Explain.

In an Essay

- Like McKenna, tell about a family member who had a profound effect on you. That effect can be either positive or negative.
- In paragraph 13, McKenna notes that children learn a society's values through stories because stories "introduce the young into the human condition." Explain how this is so, citing one or two stories told to you to illustrate the point.
- In paragraph 15, McKenna writes a brief definition of hopefulness. In an essay, write your own definition of *hope*. As an alternative, write a definition of *optimism*.

Beyond the Writing Class: With increasing frequency, grandparents are being called upon to raise their grandchildren. Investigate this phenomenon, using the Internet and library resources. Note the chief benefits and drawbacks of this family arrangement for either the grandparents or the children.

No Turning Back

POLINGAYSI QOYAWAYMA, AS TOLD TO VADA F. CARLSON

"No Turning Back" is an excerpt from a book by the same name. Polingaysi Qoyawayma told her story to Vada F. Carlson, who wrote the words. This is why Qoyawayma is referred to as "Polingaysi" or "she" (instead of "I"). In the excerpt that follows, Qoyawayma returns to her Hopi village after being away at boarding school and living with and working for a missionary family named Frey. As you read, notice that two events in the narrative are presented together. Ask yourself how they are related.

Preview. Part of "No Turning Back" describes a *rite of passage*, which is a ceremony marking an important event or stage in a person's life. For example, a wedding is a rite of passage marking a marriage. A bar mitzvah is a religious rite of passage, as are a confirmation and a first communion. A commencement ceremony is a rite of passage marking a school graduation. List all the rites of passage in your life and in the lives of your immediate family members. What events or stages do the rites mark?

Vocabulary.   If any of the following words from the selection are unfamiliar to you, study their meanings before reading.

indignation (2)   strong anger or displeasure
contemptuous (3)   scornful
temerity (7)   foolish boldness
chasm (7)   gap
initiation (7, 9)   ceremony of admission
initiatory (8)   granting admission
kiva (10)   a large underground chamber often used for religious ceremonies
G-string (12)   a loin cloth
breech clout (14)   a loin cloth
ruff (14)   a collar made of fur or feathers
reprisals (18)   revenge

In the traditional Hopi pattern, children are advised, instructed, scolded, and sometimes punished, by their maternal uncles. Polingaysi's relations with her mother's brothers had been pleasant, but after she became a member of the Frey household, her old uncle in Moenkopi village began showing disapproval of her. Cousins repeated small remarks he had made about her and she became increasingly aware of his annoyance.

2   One day he sent word for her to come visit him. She went to find him in a state of indignation. He began scolding at once.

3   "You proud and stubborn girl! Why are you straying from the Hopi way of life? Don't you know it is not good for a Hopi to be proud? Haven't I told you a Hopi must not pretend to hold himself above his people? Why do you keep trying to be a white man? You are a Hopi. Go home. Marry in the Hopi way. Have children." His eyes were angry and his mouth contemptuous. "I have said you were Hopi, but you are no longer a true Hopi. You don't know the Hopi way. In a year or so, even if you do go back to Oraibi, you won't know anything. Leave these white people who are leading you away from your own beliefs. Go. Go now."

4   Tears streamed down Polingaysi's cheeks as she listened to the man's bitter words. All her inner confusion, all her painful indecision, swelled in her breast until she could bear it no longer. She lashed back at him.

5   "I won't! I won't go back to the life of a pagan. Never, never again. I've worked for this education you ridicule. At Riverside, I scrubbed miles of dirty floors while I was learning a little about reading and writing and arithmetic. After I learned to sew, I made dresses for others, bending over the sewing machine while the other girls slept, to earn money for my own dresses.

6   "I've worked hard for everything I have. It has not been easy for me to learn this new way of living. Do you think I'll go back to sleeping on the floor and eating out of a single pot? Do you think I want to have a household of children who are always hungry and in rags, as I was in my childhood? No! I don't care what you think of me. I don't care what my Hopi people think. Not any more. I'm going to keep on learning, no matter how much you despise me for it."

7   Trembling violently, she turned on her heel and left his house, amazed at her temerity. How could she have dared talk in those defiant terms to an uncle? It frightened her. She could see the chasm between her two worlds widening; his words had stung like the lashes of the Whipper Kachina on the day of her initiation into the Kachina cult.

8   She had expected those initiatory lashes. Only Hopi children initiated into the Powamua fraternity escape them. She had looked forward to them as an opening of the door to wisdom.

9   As she walked swiftly toward the Frey home on the hillside, smarting under the injustice of her uncle's reproaches, she recalled the day of her initiation.

10   Feeling important and excited, she had walked between her ceremonial "parents" to the kiva, her shoulder blanket clutched close to shield her body from the February chill. The arms of the ladder had seemed to reach out to her, and she had gone into them and down the rungs into the dim warmth of the kiva.

11   Other initiates sat on the plastered stone bench between their sponsors, feet drawn up, simulating young eagles in the nest. Before she joined them she saw the feathers dangling from a peg on the wall, and the beautiful little sand

mosaic beneath them. It was only after she was seated that she saw the larger sandpainting on which she would later stand for whipping.

12   She began to be afraid. The other children also were fearful. Then an old man, naked except for a G-string, came down the ladder and began addressing the initiates. He spoke rapidly and in low tones. Although she listened intently, Polingaysi could not hear all of his words, but she realized that he was telling the ancient history of the Hopis and of their migrations from the beginning.

13   There was an air of expectancy on the part of the older people as the old man left the kiva, and suddenly there was a fearful din at the kiva opening, a sound of running feet, a beating of yucca lashes against the standard.

14   Hearts racing, the candidates for initiation stared at the kiva opening. Two Hu Kachinas, their bodies painted black with white spots, rushed down the ladder carrying armfuls of yucca lashes. They wore nothing except red moccasins, breech clout, mask, and foxskin ruff. The masks were black and bulging-eyed, with horns at each side, white spots on the cheeks, and a white turkey track in the center of each forehead.

15   Crow Mother, Ang-wu-sna-som-ta-qa, which is to say "Man With Crow Wings Tied To," followed, wearing a woman's dress and ceremonial robe with moccasins, and carrying additional pale green yucca lashes for the whippers. Her mask had great black crow wings at each side.

16   At once a little boy was led forward by his sponsors, his naked body trembling. Stepping into the large sandpainting, he raised one hand above his head and covered his genitals with the other. The lashes curled about his body, leaving welts, then his godfather pulled him aside and took the remainder of the whipping for him.

17   When her turn came, Polingaysi was grateful that she was a girl and was allowed to wear her blanket dress. The whipping she received was not painful, but the emotional strain sent her to the bench weeping and weak. It seemed cruel to her that Crow Mother should urge the whippers to strike harder. However, when the whippers whipped each other at the conclusion of the rites, she felt better. Justice had been done.

18   The Powamua chief then dismissed the Kachinas with gifts of breath feathers and cornmeal and began his lecture. The initiates were now at the threshold of knowledge, he told them. They would learn more secrets soon, but must not tell the younger, uninitiated children what had taken place. Telling, they were warned, would bring reprisals from the angry Kachinas.

19   Reaching the Freys' houseyard, Polingaysi looked down into the narrow streets of the old village of Moenkopi, the rock houses huddled on the lower slopes of the sand-dune-bordered wash.

20   "That initiation!" she thought angrily. "What was it but a pagan rite? I must forget it."

21   Not yet calm enough to talk with the Freys about her clash with the old uncle, she went to her room. Turning toward the mirror, she surveyed her solemn reflection unapprovingly.

22   "Maybe I'm not a true Hopi. But what am I? Am I a true anything? Am I sincere? Do I really want to waste my time in trying to bring the gospel to my stubborn, superstition-bound Hopi people? They will only despise me for it."

23   She began taking the pins from her long and heavy black hair, intending to wash it. Suddenly she realized how automatic the gesture had been, how Hopi. Wash the hair. Purify the life stream.

Understanding Content

1. In paragraph 3, the reader learns that Qoyawayma's uncle was furious with her. Why do you think he was so angry? Qoyawayma was equally upset with her uncle. What was her position in the argument?
2. Why is Qoyawayma unwilling to honor her uncle's request and return to her Hopi ways?
3. How did Qoyawayma's view of her Hopi initiation change? What caused this changed view?
4. Overall, what point do you think "No Turning Back" makes?

Considering Structure and Technique

1. What is the special significance of the use of *lashed* in paragraph 4 when Qoyawayma says she "lashed back" at her uncle? What is the special significance of *smarting* in paragraph 9?
2. Why do you think the rite of passage (the whipping) is discussed together with Qoyawayma's argument with her uncle?
3. Exact words are reproduced as quoted material in paragraphs 3, 5, 6, 20, and 22. What does this quoted material contribute to the piece?

Exploring Ideas

1. In paragraph 8, Qoyawayma says that she looked forward to the whipping "as an opening to the door to wisdom." What do you think she means by this? Is there a rite of passage in your culture that symbolizes moving into a period of increased knowledge and understanding?
2. Qoyawayma says in paragraph 17 that when the whippers struck each other, justice was done. Explain the concept of justice referred to here.
3. In your opinion, what do paragraphs 20 through 23 reveal about how Qoyawayma felt after leaving her village?
4. What has Qoyawayma gained, and what has she lost as a result of her conversion to Christianity and her entry into the white world?

Writing Workshop: Using Commas with Introductory Phrases and Clauses

A **clause** is a word group with both a subject and verb, and a **phrase** is a word group that does not have both a subject and a verb. In general, when a phrase or clause comes at the beginning of a sentence, that phrase or clause is followed by a comma, as seen in "No Turning Back."

comma with introductory phrase:	<u>In the traditional Hopi pattern,</u> children are advised, instructed, scolded, and sometimes punished, by their maternal uncles. Paragraph 1
comma with introductory phrase:	<u>Hearts racing,</u> the candidates for initiation stared at the kiva opening. Paragraph 14
comma with introductory phrase:	<u>Reaching the Freys' houseyard,</u> Polingaysi looked down into the narrow streets of the old village of Moenkopi. . . . Paragraph 19
comma with introductory clause:	<u>Although she listened intently,</u> Polingaysi could not hear all of his words. . . . Paragraph 12
comma with introductory clause:	<u>When her turn came,</u> Polingaysi was grateful that she was a girl and was allowed to wear her blanket dress. Paragraph 17
comma with introductory clause:	<u>After I learned to sew,</u> I made dresses for others. . . . Paragraph 5

Writing Workshop Activity

Choose four of the sentence openers from the list below and write sentences using those openers. Be sure to follow introductory phrases and clauses with commas.

Before the rest of the class finished the exam

In the middle of the night

Laughing hysterically

Refreshed by the long nap

Although I see your point

Before I could stop Terry

While you were on vacation

After the instructor passed out the exams

Language Notes for Multilingual and Other Writers

In some languages, the subject of a sentence can appear in an introductory phrase. However, this is not the case in English, so remember that when you begin a sentence with a phrase, the subject of your sentence will not appear in that phrase. Here are some examples from "No Turning Back":

phrase   subject

[In the traditional Hopi pattern,] <u>children</u> are advised, instructed, scolded, and sometimes punished, by their maternal uncles. Paragraph 1

phrase   subject

[At Riverside,] <u>I</u> scrubbed miles of dirty floor while I was learning a little about reading and writing and arithmetic. Paragraph 5

phrase   subject

[Hearts racing,] the <u>candidates for initiation</u> stared at the kiva opening. Paragraph 14

From Reading to Writing

In Your Journal: Qoyawayma experienced a conflict between the world of her family and the world beyond her family. Such conflicts are not unusual. For example, the children of immigrants often feel the conflict between their parents' customs and language and those of their new country. Even if it is less dramatic, you too have probably experienced a conflict between your family's wishes or customs and your own. Choice about mate, dating practices, career plans, school, friends—these and more can put you in conflict with your family. Describe the nature and seriousness of a family conflict that you have experienced.

With Some Classmates: Compare the whipping Qoyawayma endured and her leaving her village after the angry exchange with her uncle. Discuss whether or not both experiences can be seen as a rite of passage and how Qoyawayma was affected by the events.

- When Qoyawayma entered the white world, she gained something and she lost something. She gained a higher standard of living and a faith that was important to her. She lost the goodwill of her uncle and some of her Hopi identity. Tell about a time when you made a change that resulted in both gains and losses. Did you feel the "inner confusion" and "painful indecision" that Qoyawayma felt?
- Using your previous journal writing as a possible source of ideas, tell about a time when, like Qoyawayma, you felt "the chasm between [your] two worlds widening" (paragraph 7). Explain the nature of the conflict, its cause, and its effect on you and your family.

■ If you are from another culture, compare and contrast the ritual for a particular rite of passage in your culture or religion (a wedding, funeral, graduation, and so forth) with a similar one in this country. As an alternative, interview someone from another culture and then compare and contrast the rites of passage.

Beyond the Writing Class: In a cultural anthropology textbook, on the Internet, or in your campus library, look up one of the following life-cycle events: birth, puberty, marriage, death. Find a fairly detailed explanation of one culture's rite of passage for the event you have chosen. (Pick a culture with a rite of passage you are unfamiliar with.) Describe the rite of passage in your own words and go on to explain the purpose it serves. Also note whether any aspects of the rite are similar to aspects of the rites you are familiar with.

Invasion of the Body Snatchers:
Fetal Rights vs. Mothers' Rights
RONNI SANDROFF

Ronni Sandroff wrote the following essay for *Vogue* magazine in 1988. In the piece, she notes an important issue that has arisen with medical science's increased ability to treat unborn children: To what extent can a pregnant woman be forced to submit her body to medical procedures to help the fetus?

Preview. Sandroff presents arguments on both sides of the issue of whether pregnant women should be compelled to endure medical procedures, but you will recognize that the author has a distinct point of view. To gather more opinions on the issue, ask six males and six females the following question and report the answers to the rest of the class: Should the courts order a woman to have a cesarean section that she does not want to have, if failure to have the operation would probably (but not definitely) mean death for the unborn child?

Vocabulary. If any of the following words from the essay are unfamiliar to you, study their meanings before reading.

fundamentalist sect (1)   a religious group that believes every word of the
    Bible is true, exactly as it is written, so there is no room for interpretation
civil libertarians (5)   lawyers and others who work to make sure people are
    not denied the protections afforded by law
critique (6)   criticism
encroachment (7)   intruding on the rights of others
Gallup poll (8)   a survey of public opinion
dissension (9)   strong disagreement
prowess (9)   ability
gestation (9)   the process of carrying a child to birth
indigent (17)   poor
Happy Rockefeller (26)   a member of the wealthy Rockefeller family
mandating (27)   ordering
subside (29)   lessen
prospective (30)   future

The baby and mother were almost certain to die unless a cesarean section was performed. But the mother was part of a small fundamentalist sect that prohibited surgery. And she was surrounded by family members who told her, "You can't have a cesarean section. Even if the baby dies, it's OK."

2   It was not OK with the doctor in charge, Mary Jo O'Sullivan, M.D., professor of obstetrics and gynecology at the University of Miami School of Medicine. "The baby's head was way too large. Without a c-section the only way to get the baby out would be to wait until it died and take it apart, piece by piece. I just couldn't do that. Nor was anyone else at the hospital willing to do it."

3   Dr. O'Sullivan finally took the matter to court, petitioning for the right to override the mother's decision. The court ordered a cesarean, but Dr. O'Sullivan was still uncomfortable about forcing surgery.

4   "To my surprise, when I showed the patient the court order, she seemed relieved that the decision was out of her hands," says Dr. O'Sullivan.

5   The story had a happy ending—mother, baby, and doctor are doing fine—but cases like this are causing alarm among civil libertarians and feminists. "The courts have no business in the delivery room," insists George Annas, professor of Health Law at Boston University School of Public Health. "Competent adults have the right to refuse even lifesaving treatment."

6   And it's irrelevant that, in this case, the mother turned out to be grateful to have the court decide, says Nancy Milliken, M.D., who recently cowrote a critique of cases of court-ordered surgery in the *Journal of the American Medical Association:* "Individuals can't have it both ways. We can't say: we want the right to make our own health decisions and then turn around and expect the doctor to *make us* do what's good for us."

7   Though the number of court-ordered cesareans is small, each one symbolizes a disturbing trend—the encroachment on the rights of the pregnant woman; the view of her as the "jar" or "container" of the next generation. In Wisconsin, for example, a sixteen-year-old pregnant girl was held in detention for her "lack [of] motivation or ability to seek prenatal care." In Michigan and Illinois, courts have permitted the child to sue its mother for damaging it during pregnancy. And, in a number of states, legislation has been introduced to expand the laws on child abuse to cover the fetus. This would permit after-the-fact prosecution of women who do anything during pregnancy (smoke, drink, use drugs, refuse treatment) that damages the offspring.

8   Public support for measures of this kind is surprisingly strong. A recent Gallup poll found that almost half of those surveyed agreed that a woman should be legally liable for damaging her child by drinking or smoking during pregnancy. People were about equally split on whether a woman should be held liable for refusing a cesarean.

9   Doctors are no more in agreement than the general public. The reason for the dissension is that our technological prowess has leapt ahead of our ethical and legal thinking. In the past, obstetricians had one patient: the mother. But new technology has opened up a much greater window on what's going on with the fetus throughout gestation.

10   "We're now taking care of premature infants at twenty-six, twenty-seven, twenty-eight weeks," explain Dr. Milliken. "So we're starting to devise treatments for fetuses as separate patients."

11   But the interests of the fetus are sometimes in conflict with the interests or desires of the mother—if a mother disagrees with medical advice or is reckless about how her actions affect the unborn child. In these cases, who is to defend the "rights" of the fetus?

12   Most experts hold that its physical location makes it impossible for a fetus to have rights: An unborn child cannot be treated without invading the body of its mother and severely affecting her freedom of movement, privacy, and health. Until a baby is born, they argue, it has no more independent rights than any other organ in the mother's body.

13   "On the one hand the interest in fetal rights is new," says Lynn Paltrow, staff counsel for the American Civil Liberties Union Reproductive Freedom Project. "On the other, it is simply a reflection of a historical trend to limit women's rights based on their reproductive ability."

14   Today, the question is whether our new understanding of gestation creates a need for special legislation to protect the interests of the fetus. The legions of infants born deformed, mentally retarded, or addicted to drugs are a burden to society as a whole as well as the individual parents.

15   John A. Robertson, a law professor at the University of Texas at Austin who did some of the earliest ethical work on fetal blood transfusions, believes we can take a stance against prenatal injury of a child who will be carried to term without diminishing a woman's right to abortion: "The rights of the actual offspring to be free of prenatally caused harm, rather than the right of the fetus to complete gestation, is at question."

16   Dr. Milliken, however, believes that the whole concept of fetal rights is unnecessary and has terrific potential for harm: "My impression is that there are very few women who do not undertake tremendous sacrifice for their fetuses."

17   New York City Court Judge Margaret Taylor confesses she never thought about having to intervene in the interests of the fetus until 1980, when doctors at St. Vincent's Hospital petitioned her for a c-section order for a thirty-year-old, indigent woman who had borne nine children. The doctors had found that the umbilical cord was wrapped around the fetus's neck and felt it was in danger of being born brain-damaged.

18   Judge Taylor visited the patient in the hospital to hear her side of the story. "She was a poor woman and women in her neighborhood had not done well after cesarean sections. The hospital was trying to pressure her. I tried to tell her that if she had a brain-damaged child, her whole family would suffer. She said that nature makes these choices. I couldn't convince her. I couldn't see subjecting her to possible death for someone who's not even born yet. It's been held unreasonable to subject an accused criminal to surgery to find a bullet for evidence. If that's unreasonable, this certainly is."

19   Judge Taylor refused to grant the order, then spent "the worst two hours of my life," waiting for the child to be born. To the doctor's, but not the mother's, surprise, the vaginal birth resulted in a healthy baby.

20   Outcomes where the mother's decision proves correct are not rare. In six of eleven cases of requests for court-ordered cesareans, the women went on to successful vaginal births, according to a study by lawyer Janet Gallagher. Many critics accuse doctors of favoring cesarean deliveries because they generate higher fees and reduce the likelihood of malpractice suits.

21   Even when medical decisions are made solely for clinical reasons, they often involve playing the odds—and losing. In the 1950s, doctors urged many women to take diethylstilbestrol (DES) to prevent miscarriages. The resulting daughters have since been found to have a higher risk of cervical cancer. "Now we know that the women who refused treatment were wiser," says Lynn Paltrow. "We have to let decision-making rest with the woman. If someone is going to make a mistake, it has to be her. The real conflict is not over fetal rights, but doctors' rights—they think they should be the ones to decide."

22   A frightening example of what can happen when the fetus's rights are put over the mother's is the case of Pamela Stewart, a poor California woman who was arrested in San Diego months after she bore a severely brain-damaged infant who died about six weeks after birth. The deputy district attorney said Stewart was responsible since "she didn't follow through on medical advice." The charge was based on a California statute that makes it a crime to "willfully omit" necessary support, including medical care, for a child or fetus.

23   Stewart had been through a dangerous pregnancy, marked by placenta previa, a condition that can threaten the life of the mother and fetus. Her doctor told her to seek attention immediately if she started to hemorrhage, but Stewart allegedly bled for several hours before going to the hospital. She also violated medical advice during pregnancy by having sexual intercourse with her husband, smoking marijuana, and taking amphetamines.

24   But Stewart's living conditions were exceedingly difficult. She lived with her two children and husband first in a single hotel room and then with her mother-in-law in a mobile home. Neighbors said the police had been called ten to fifteen times in one year to control the husband's beating of his wife and mother.

25   All of this, plus reports on Stewart's sexual life, were reviewed in great detail in the media, causing public outrage and debate. The charges against her were dismissed in February 1987. The court found that the California child-support statute did not apply, but it left open the future enactment of such a law.

26   A potent argument against forcing women to do what the doctor says is right for their unborn children is that such measures will be used almost exclusively against poor and minority women. As Judge Taylor puts it: "Who would ask a judge to order Happy Rockefeller to have a cesarean?" Fear of prosecution might encourage poor and drug-addicted women to avoid prenatal care altogether.

27   "There's a terrible irony in mandating the mother's actions surrounding birth while not offering money for prenatal care for poor women, or child care, housing, and health care for poor children after birth," Judge Taylor says.

28   Some experts do support prosecution of women who damage their offspring: Let them make their decisions, the argument goes, but hold them responsible for reckless behavior. "When a woman chooses to carry the baby,
rather than abort, society can take the position that she should abide by certain
standards during her pregnancy," says ethicist John Robertson. The standards,
presumably, will be set by medical experts.

29   The turmoil over forced cesareans is likely to subside as physicians and
the public become more accustomed to making decisions amid the wealth of
new knowledge about fetal development. But in the meantime, pregnant
women are being bullied—by everyone from waiters who question a request
for a glass of wine to employers who want to decide if it's in the best interests
of the fetus for mothers not to work during pregnancy.

30   The absurdity of letting future parenthood infringe on an individual's
freedom becomes clearest if we imagine applying it to men. There's some evidence, for example, that fathers who drink heavily during the month of con-
ception have children with lower birth weights, regardless of whether or not
the mother drinks. And it's possible that a father's smoking or drug use also influences the baby's condition at birth. Does this mean we should consider pre-
ventive detention, or sterilization, of men who persist in bad habits? Should we
create a pregnancy police to visit the bedrooms of prospective parents? Insist
that prospective parents be examined and licensed before having a child?

31   The alternative is to rely on education and parental good will and accept
the fact that parents are no more perfect than doctors, judges, and the rest of
society. As law clerk and ethicist Dawn Johnsen puts it: "The state should not
try to transform pregnant women into ideal baby-making machines."

Understanding Content

1. When you read the first four paragraphs of "Invasion of the Body Snatchers," what point of view did you think the author held? Why? Were you
   surprised when you read paragraphs 5 and 6? Why or why not?
2. Why does Dr. Nancy Milliken think it is irrelevant whether or not a
   mother is relieved to have a court decide how her baby is born?
3. Court-ordered procedures for pregnant women were not an issue in the
   past. Why are they an issue now?
4. What is the main dilemma associated with attempts to pass legislation to
   protect the fetus?
5. Does the title give any clue to the essay's content or the author's point of
   view? Explain.

Considering Structure and Technique

1. Which sentence expresses the thesis of the essay?

2. Sandroff uses an example in paragraphs 1 through 5 and another example in paragraphs 17 through 19. What purpose do these examples serve? What purpose does the example in paragraph 21 serve?
3. Does Sandroff present both sides of the issue of fetal protection and remain neutral herself, or does she advance a particular point of view? How do you know?
4. Sandroff frequently cites the words and opinions of experts on both sides of the issue. What purpose does this technique serve?

Exploring Ideas

1. Do you agree with Dr. Milliken's argument in paragraph 16 that the "concept of fetal rights is unnecessary" because so few women do not make sacrifices for their unborn children? Why or why not?
2. If you were a judge, would you have ordered the cesarean section for the women mentioned in the opening paragraphs? Why or why not?
3. Explain why it is ironic to mandate a mother's actions during pregnancy without offering money for prenatal care.
4. Do you agree that one solution is to rely on "education and parental good will" (paragraph 31)? Explain why or why not.

Writing Workshop: Presenting Both Sides of an Issue

In "Invasion of the Body Snatchers," Ronni Sandroff writes to persuade her reader that fetal-protection legislation and court-ordered cesarean sections are inappropriate. When writers want to persuade, they usually present their most convincing arguments and deal with the opposition points only to take some of the power out of these points. In "Invasion of the Body Snatchers," however, Sandroff takes a different approach. She presents the chief arguments on both sides, and then she makes her position clear at the end (although the title and some early sentences do hint at the author's view). If you decide to use Sandroff's approach, present the opposition side first, and then give your side. Close with an explanation of why you take the side that you do. With this organization, you place your views at the end, in the more emphatic position.

Writing Workshop Activity

With two or three classmates, pick a campus issue and make two lists, one that gives reasons to support one side of the issue and a second that gives reasons to support the other side. Then decide which side most group members agree with and write a closing paragraph or two that explains why the group takes the side that it does.

Language Notes for Multilingual and Other Writers

A **participle** is a verb form used as an adjective, so it describes a noun or pronoun. Here are some examples of the use of participles from "Invasion of the Body Snatchers." The participle is underlined and an arrow is drawn to the noun or pronoun described.

1. The **present participle** ends in *-ing*.

   Dr. O'Sullivan finally took the matter to court, <u>petitioning</u> for the right to override the mother's decision. Paragraph 3

   A <u>frightening</u> example of what can happen when the fetus's rights are put over the mother's is the case of Pamela Stewart. . . . Paragraph 22

   "There's a terrible irony in mandating the mother's actions <u>surrounding</u> birth" . . . Paragraph 27

2. The **past participle** ends in *-d, -ed, -n*, or *-t*

   "To my surprise, when I showed the patient the court order, <u>she</u> seemed <u>relieved</u> that the decision was out of her hands. . . ." Paragraph 4

   The turmoil over <u>forced</u> cesareans is likely to subside as physicians and the public become more <u>accustomed</u> to making decisions amid the wealth of new knowledge. . . . Paragraph 29

From Reading to Writing

In Your Journal: If you were a table server at a restaurant and an obviously pregnant woman ordered several alcoholic drinks, would you serve her, knowing that the alcohol could damage her unborn child? What if refusing to serve her would mean loss of your job? Answer these questions in a page or so of your journal.

With Some Classmates: Some of you should write out the arguments in favor of pro-choice legislation, and some should write out the arguments in favor of anti-abortion legislation. Each of you should then incorporate both views in a paper that includes and emphasizes your own point of view.

In an Essay

- Are you for or against court-ordered cesarean sections and legislation requiring certain kinds of prenatal care? Consider the points in "Invasion of the Body Snatchers" and other points that you think of.

- Attack or defend legislation that would allow a child to sue his or her mother for damage or injury sustained during pregnancy, particularly as a result of smoking, drinking, or taking drugs.
- If you do not believe in legislation to require pregnant women to have certain kinds of prenatal care, devise your own plan for ensuring the welfare of unborn children, a plan that considers the inability of the poor to pay for extensive medical care.

Beyond the Writing Class: In paragraph 10, Sandroff quotes Dr. Milliken, who mentions that dramatic kinds of prenatal intervention are now possible. In your campus library, or on the Internet, find out what kinds of prenatal intervention are possible and explain some of the more common and successful interventions.

Stone Soup

BARBARA KINGSOLVER

Born and raised in rural Kentucky, Barbara Kingsolver did not at first imagine herself as a writer because writing did not seem a practical career choice. She has been an archaeologist, copy editor, x-ray technician, house-cleaner, biological researcher, and medical translator. Her many articles have appeared in *The Nation,* the *New York Times,* and many other publications. She has written several novels, short stories, and essays. Kingsolver often writes of the family, as she does in the following essay, which first appeared in *Parenting* in 1995.

Preview.   To Kingsolver, the American family has no one model or ideal form. Instead, she believes that a variety of arrangements resulting from divorce, single parenthood, blended families, and same-sex unions have created a rich array of successful family structures. How would you describe the structure of your family? How do you think society views that structure?

Vocabulary.   If any of the following words from the essay are unfamiliar to you, study their meanings before reading.

contrived (3) created
harbinger (4)   forerunner
imperious (6)   dominant
nuclear family (11)   family group made up of father, mother, and children
caprice (11)   impulsiveness
specious (11)   false
asphyxiation (11)   lack of oxygen
pragmatic (16)   practical
serial monogamy (16)   having more than one spouse, but only one at a time
symmetry (19)   having a shape with balanced proportions
myriad (19)   many
panacea (23)   cure-all
corroborate (23)   confirm
sequestered (23)   isolated
amorphous (24)   shapeless
bell jar (24)   bell-shaped glass used to cover objects or keep gases from
    escaping
Olduvai Gorge (24) a canyon of fossil beds in Tanzania
beleaguered (26)   surrounded by troubles
bouillabaisse (31)   fish soup or stew

In the catalog of family values, where do we rank an occasion like this? A curly-haired boy who wanted to run before he walked, age seven now, a soccer player scoring a winning goal. He turns to the bleachers with his fists in the air and a smile wide as a gap-toothed galaxy. His own cheering section of grown-ups and kids all leap to their feet and hug each other, delirious with love for this boy. He's Andy, my best friend's son. The cheering section includes his mother and her friends, his brother, his father and stepmother, a stepbrother and stepsister, and a grandparent. Lucky is the child with this many relatives on hand to hail a proud accomplishment. I'm there too, witnessing a family fortune. But in spite of myself, defensive words take shape in my head. I am thinking: I dare *anybody* to call this a broken home.

2   Families change, and remain the same. Why are our names for home so slow to catch up to the truth of where we live?

3   When I was a child, I had two parents who loved me without cease. One of them attended every excuse for attention I ever contrived, and the other made it to the ones with higher production values, like piano recitals and appendicitis. So I was a lucky child, too. I played with a set of paper dolls called "The Family of Dolls," four in number, who came with the factory-assigned names of Dad, Mom, Sis, and Junior. I think you know what they looked like, at least before I loved them to death and their heads fell off.

4   Now I've replaced the dolls with a life. I knit my days around my daughter's survival and happiness, and am proud to say her head is still on. But we aren't the Family of Dolls. Maybe you're not, either. And if not, even though you are statistically no oddity, it's probably been suggested to you in a hundred ways that yours isn't exactly a real family, but an imposter family, a harbinger of cultural ruin, a slapdash substitute—something like counterfeit money. Here at the tail end of our century, most of us are up to our ears in the noisy business of trying to support and love a thing called family. But there's a current in the air with ferocious moral force that finds its way even into political campaigns, claiming there is only one right way to do it, the Way It Has Always Been.

5   In the face of a thriving, particolored world, this narrow view is so pickled and absurd I'm astonished that it gets airplay. And I'm astonished that it still stings.

6   Every parent has endured the arrogance of a child-unfriendly grump sitting in judgment, explaining what those kids of ours really need (for example, "a good licking"). If we're polite, we move our crew to another bench in the park. If we're forthright (as I am in my mind, only, for the rest of the day), we fix them with a sweet imperious stare and say, "Come back and let's talk about it after you've changed a thousand diapers."

7   But it's harder somehow to shrug off the Family-of-Dolls Family Values crew when they judge (from their safe distance) that divorced people, blended families, gay families, and single parents are failures. That our children are at risk, and the whole arrangement is messy and embarrassing. A marriage that

ends is not called "finished," it's called *failed*. The children of this family may have been born to a happy union, but now they are called *the children of divorce*.

8   I had no idea how thoroughly these assumptions overlaid my culture until I went through divorce myself. I wrote to a friend: "This might be worse than being widowed. Overnight I've suffered the same losses—companionship, financial and practical support, my identity as a wife and partner, the future I'd taken for granted. I am lonely, grieving, and hard-pressed to take care of my household alone. But instead of bringing casseroles, people are acting like I had a fit and broke up the family china."

9   Once upon a time I held these beliefs about divorce: that everyone who does it could have chosen not to do it. That it's a lazy way out of marital problems. That it selfishly puts personal happiness ahead of family integrity. Now I tremble for my ignorance. It's easy, in fortunate times, to forget about the ambush that could leave your head reeling: serious mental or physical illness, death in the family, abandonment, financial calamity, humiliation, violence, despair.

10   I started out like any child, intent on being the Family of Dolls. I set upon young womanhood believing in most of the doctrines of my generation: I wore my skirts four inches above the knee. I had that Barbie with her zebra-striped swimsuit and a figure unlike anything found in nature. And I understood the Prince Charming Theory of Marriage, a quest for Mr. Right that ends smack dab where you find him. I did not completely understand that another whole story *begins* there, and no fairy tale prepared me for the combination of bad luck and persistent hope that would interrupt my dream and lead me to other arrangements.

Like a cancer diagnosis, a dying marriage is a thing to fight, to deny, and finally, when there's no choice left, to dig in and survive. Casseroles would help. Likewise, I imagine it must be a painful reckoning in adolescence (or later on) to realize true love will never look like the soft-focus fragrance ads because Prince Charming (surprise!) is a princess. Or vice versa. Or has skin the color your parents didn't want you messing with, except in the Crayola box.

11   It's awfully easy to hold in contempt the straw broken home, and that mythical category of persons who toss away nuclear family for the sheer fun of it. Even the legal terms we use have a suggestion of caprice. I resent the phrase "irreconcilable differences," which suggests a stubborn refusal to accept a spouse's little quirks. This is specious. Every happily married couple I know has loads of irreconcilable differences. Negotiating where to set the thermostat is not the point. A nonfunctioning marriage is a slow asphyxiation. It is waking up despised each morning, listening to the pulse of your own loneliness before the radio begins to blare its raucous gospel that you're nothing if you aren't loved. It is sharing your airless house with the threat of suicide or other kinds of violence, while the ghost that whispers, "Leave here and destroy your children," has passed over every door and nailed it shut. Disassembling a mar-

riage in these circumstances is as much *fun* as amputating your own gangrenous leg. You do it, if you can, to save a life—or two, or more.

12   I know of no one who really went looking to hoe the harder row, especially the daunting one of single parenthood. Yet it seems to be the most American of customs to blame the burdened for their destiny. We'd like so desperately to believe in freedom and justice for all, we can hardly name that rogue bad luck, even when he's a close enough snake to bite us. In the wake of my divorce, some friends (even a few close ones) chose to vanish, rather than linger within striking distance of misfortune.

13   But most stuck around, bless their hearts, and if I'm any the wiser for my trials, it's from having learned the worth of steadfast friendship. And also, what not to say. The least helpful question is: "Did you want the divorce, or didn't you?" Did I want to keep that gangrenous leg, or not? How to explain, in a culture that venerates choice: two terrifying options are much worse than none at all. Give me any day the quick hand of cruel fate that will leave me scarred by blameless. As it was, I kept thinking of that wicked third-grade joke in which some boy comes up behind you and grabs your ears, starts in with a prolonged tug, and asks, "Do you want this ear any longer?"

14   Still, the friend who holds your hand and says the wrong thing is made of dearer stuff than the one who stays away. And generally, through all of it, you live. My favorite fictional character, Kate Vaiden (in the novel by Reynolds Price), advises: "Strength just comes in one brand—you stand up at sunrise and meet what they send you and keep your hair combed."

15   Once you've weathered the straits, you get to cross the tricky juncture from casualty to survivor. If you're on your feet at the end of a year or two, and have begun putting together a happy new existence, those friends who were kind enough to feel sorry for you when you needed it must now accept you back to the ranks of the living. If you're truly blessed, they will dance at your second wedding. Everybody else, for heaven's sake, should stop throwing stones.

16   Arguing about whether nontraditional families deserve pity or tolerance is a little like the medieval debate about left-handedness as a mark of the devil. Divorce, remarriage, single parenthood, gay parents, and blended families simply are. They're facts of our time. Some of the reasons listed by sociologists for these family reconstructions are: the idea of marriage as a romantic partnership rather than a pragmatic one; a shift in women's expectations, from servility to self-respect and independence; and longevity (prior to antibiotics no marriage was expected to last many decades—in Colonial days the average couple lived to be married less than twelve years). Add to all this our growing sense of entitlement to happiness and safety from abuse. Most would agree that these are all good things. Yet their result—a culture in which serial monogamy and the consequent reshaping of families are the norm—gets diagnosed as "failing."

17   For many of us, once we have put ourselves Humpty-Dumpty–wise back together again, the main problem with our reorganized family is that other

people think we have a problem. My daughter tells me the only time she's uncomfortable about being the child of divorced parents is when her friends say they feel sorry for her. It's a bizarre sympathy, given that half the kids in her school and nation are in the same boat, pursuing childish happiness with the same energy as their married-parent peers. When anyone asks how *she* feels about it, she spontaneously lists the benefits: our house is in the country and we have a dog, but she can go to her dad's neighborhood for the urban thrills of a pool and sidewalks for roller-skating. What's more, she has three sets of grandparents!

18   Why is it surprising that a child would revel in a widened family and the right to feel at home in more than one house? Isn't it the opposite that should worry us—a child with no home at all, or too few resources to feel safe? The child at risk is the one whose parents are too immature themselves to guide wisely; too diminished by poverty to nurture; too far from opportunity to offer hope. The number of children in the U.S. living in poverty at this moment is almost unfathomably large: twenty percent. There are families among us that need help all right, and by no means are they new on the landscape. The rate at which teenage girls had babies in 1957 (ninety-six per thousand) was twice what it is now. That remarkable statistic is ignored by the religious right— probably because the teen birth rate was cut in half mainly by legalized abortion. In fact, the policy gatekeepers who coined the phrase "family values" have steadfastly ignored the desperation of too-small families, and since 1979 have steadily reduced the amount of financial support available to a single parent. But, this camp's most outspoken attacks seem aimed at the notion of families getting too complex, with add-ons and extras such as a gay parent's partner, or a remarried mother's new husband and his children.

19   To judge a family's value by its tidy symmetry is to purchase a book for its cover. There's no moral authority there. The famous family comprised by Dad, Mom, Sis, and Junior living as an isolated economic unit is not built on historical bedrock. In *The Way We Never Were*, Stephanie Coontz writes, "Whenever people propose that we go back to the traditional family, I always suggest that they pick a ballpark date for the family they have in mind." Colonial families were tidily disciplined, but their members (meaning everyone but infants) labored incessantly and died young. Then the Victorian family adopted a new division of labor, in which women's role was domestic and children were allowed time for study and play, but this was an upper-class construct supported by myriad slaves. Coontz writes, "For every nineteenth-century middle-class family that protected its wife and child within the family circle, there was an Irish or German girl scrubbing floors . . . a Welsh boy mining coal to keep the homebaked goodies warm, a black girl doing the family laundry, a black mother and child picking cotton to be made into clothes for the family, and a Jewish or an Italian daughter in a sweatshop making 'ladies' dresses or artificial flowers for the family to purchase."

20 The abolition of slavery brought slightly more democratic arrangements, in which extended families were harnessed together in cottage industries; at the turn of the century came a steep rise in child labor in mines and sweatshops. Twenty percent of American children lived in orphanages at the time; their parents were not necessarily dead, but couldn't afford to keep them.

21 During the Depression and up to the end of World War II, many millions of U.S. households were more multigenerational than nuclear. Women my grandmother's age were likely to live with a fluid assortment of elderly relatives, in-laws, siblings, and children. In many cases they spent virtually every waking hour working in the company of other women—a companionable scenario in which it would be easier, I imagine, to tolerate an estranged or difficult spouse. I'm reluctant to idealize a life of so much hard work and so little spousal intimacy, but its advantage may have been resilience. A family so large and varied would not easily be brought down by a single blow: it could absorb a death, long illness, an abandonment here or there, and any number of irreconcilable differences.

22 The Family of Dolls came along midcentury as a great American experiment. A booming economy required a mobile labor force and demanded that women surrender jobs to returning soldiers. Families came to be defined by a single breadwinner. They struck out for single-family homes at an earlier age than ever before, and in unprecedented numbers they raised children in suburban isolation. The nuclear family was launched to sink or swim.

23 More than a few sank. Social historians corroborate that the suburban family of the postwar economic boom, which we have recently selected as our definition of "traditional," was no panacea. Twenty-five percent of Americans were poor in the mid-1950s, and as yet there were no food stamps. Sixty percent of the elderly lived on less than $1,000 a year, and most had no medical insurance. In the sequestered suburbs, alcoholism and sexual abuse of children were far more widespread than anyone imagined.

24 Expectations soared, and the economy sagged. It's hard to depend on one other adult for everything, come what may. In the last three decades, that amorphous, adaptable structure we call "family" has been reshaped once more by economic tides. Compared with fifties families, mothers are far more likely now to be employed. We are statistically more likely to divorce, and to live in blended families or other extranuclear arrangements. We are also more likely to plan and space our children, and to rate our marriages as "happy." We are less likely to suffer abuse without recourse or to stare out at our lives through a glaze of prescription tranquilizers. Our aged parents are less likely to be destitute, and we're half as likely to have a teenage daughter turn up a mother herself. All in all, I would say that if "intact" in modern family-values jargon means living quietly desperate in the bell jar, then hip-hip-hooray for "broken." A neat family model constructed to service the Baby Boom economy seems to be returning gradually to a grand, lumpy shape that human families

apparently have tended toward since they first took root in Olduvai Gorge. We're social animals, deeply fond of companionship, and children love best to run in packs. If there is a *normal* for humans, at all, I expect it looks like two or three Families of Dolls, connected variously by kinship and passion, shuffled like cards and strewn over several shoeboxes.

25   The sooner we can let go of the fairy tale of families functioning perfectly in isolation, the better we might embrace the relief of community. Even the admirable parents who've stayed married through thick and thin are very likely, at present, to incorporate other adults into their families—household help and baby-sitters if they can afford them, or neighbors and grandparents if they can't. For single parents, this support is the rock-bottom definition of family. And most parents who have split apart, however painfully, still manage to maintain family continuity for their children, creating in many cases a boisterous phenomenon that Constance Ahrons in her book *The Good Divorce* calls the "binuclear family." Call it what you will—when ex-spouses beat swords into plowshares and jump up and down at a soccer game together, it makes for happy kids.

26   Cinderella, look, who needs her? All those evil stepsisters? That story always seemed like too much cotton-picking fuss over clothes. A childhood tale that fascinated me more was the one called "Stone Soup," and the gist of it is this: Once upon a time, a pair of beleaguered soldiers straggled home to a village empty-handed, in a land ruined by war. They were famished, but the villagers had so little they shouted evil words and slammed their doors. So the soldiers dragged out a big kettle, filled it with water, and put it on a fire to boil. They rolled a clean round stone into the pot, while the villagers peered through their curtains in amazement.

27   "What kind of soup is that?" they hooted.

28   "Stone soup," the soldiers replied. "Everybody can have some when it's done."

29   "Well, thanks," one matron grumbled, coming out with a shriveled carrot. "But it'd be better if you threw this in."

30   And so on, of course, a vegetable at a time, until the whole suspicious village mangaged to feed itself grandly.

31   Any family is a big empty pot, save for what gets thrown in. Each stew turns out different. Generosity, a resolve to turn bad luck into good, and respect for variety—these things will nourish a nation of children. Name-calling and suspicion will not. My soup contains a rock or two of hard times, and maybe yours does too. I expect it's a heck of a bouillabaisse.

Understanding Content

1. In your own words, write out the thesis of Kingsolver's essay.
2. In paragraph 3, Kingsolver says that the reader knows what her "Family of Dolls" looked like. What *did* they look like? What does the "Family of Dolls" represent?

3. Explain Kingsolver's view of divorce.
4. How has Kingsolver's view of divorce changed?
5. When people look to the past and say that family structure used to be better, what do they fail to understand?

Considering Structure and Technique

1. Paragraph 1 describes a scene at a soccer game. Does this paragraph provide an effective opening? Why or why not?
2. Much of Kingsolver's detail comes from personal observation. However, much of her detail comes from other sources as well. What are those sources? Does the fact that Kingsolver's detail comes from a variety of sources make the essay more convincing. Explain.
3. In paragraph 18, Kingsolver uses statistics. What purpose do those statistics serve?
4. Kingsolver relies heavily on rich, descriptive language to create mental images and interesting comparisons. What image appears in paragraph 1? In paragraph 4? What comparison is made in paragraph 4? In paragraph 10?
5. Mention one other mental image or comparison in the essay. What is the effect of the images and comparisons?

Exploring Ideas

1. In paragraph 2, Kingsolver, says, "Families change, and remain the same." What do you think she means?
2. When something occurs that is unexpected, we often call it **ironic**. What is ironic about viewing serial monogamy and current family structures as failures?
3. What is the "raucous gospel" of the radio that Kingsolver refers to in paragraph 11? What larger concept does that "raucous gospel" represent?
4. In paragraph 19, Kingsolver says there is "no moral authority" to the family construction of Dad-Mom-Sis-Junior. Explain what she means.
5. Explain the meaning of the story "Stone Soup" that ends the essay. How does the story relate to the point Kingsolver is making?

Writing Workshop: Using Emotional Appeal

To persuade your reader to think or act a particular way, you can give logical arguments and sound reasons. In addition, you can add to the persuasiveness of your writing by citing authority and data. (See the workshop on p. 230). Yet another persuasive strategy is an appeal to your readers' emotions. Advertisers know how persuasive emotional appeal can be. This is why they say a toothpaste whitens teeth and freshens breath—they know we have an emotional need to look and smell good in addition to an intellectual understanding of the need to prevent tooth decay. Barbara Kingsolver also uses emotional appeal to persuade the reader. She does this three ways:

1. She uses description to create mental images that strike an emotional chord in the reader. For example, in paragraph 1, she creates a heartwarming scene of a "curly-haired boy" with a "smile wide as a gap-toothed galaxy."
2. She encourages readers to feel a connection with her by granting them common emotions and circumstances. For example, in paragraph 6, she brings the reader in by using *we*: "If we're polite, we move our crew to another bench in the park."
3. She invites reader sympathy. In paragraph 8, for example, she says she is "lonely, grieving, and hard-pressed to take care of [her] household chores," which causes readers to feel sympathetic.

Writing Workshop Activity

Reread "Stone Soup" and list the examples of emotional appeal you notice.

Language Notes for Multilingual and Other Writers

If English is not your first language, you may be unfamiliar with these expressions in "Stone Soup."

1. A *hard row to hoe* is a gardening reference that is used to mean "to have a difficult task."

   I know of no one who really went looking <u>to hoe the harder row</u>, especially the daunting one of single parenthood. Paragraph 12

2. *Humpty-Dumpty* is a cartoonlike, egg figure in a children's nursery rhyme: "Humpty-Dumpty sat on a wall/Humpty–Dumpty had a great fall./All the king's horses and all the king's men/Couldn't put Humpty together again." Humpty-Dumpty has come to symbolize fragility.

   . . . once we have put ourselves <u>Humpty-Dumpty</u>–wise back together again, the main problem with our reorganized family is that other people think we have a problem. Paragraph 17

3. *To beat swords into plowshares* is a biblical reference that means "to give up war for peaceful pursuits, such as farming."

   . . .when ex-spouses <u>beat swords into plowshares</u> and jump up and down at a soccer game together, it makes for happy kids. Paragraph 25

4. *Cinderella* is a fairy-tale character who is oppressed by her evil step-mother and stepsisters, but who goes on to happiness, with the intervention of her fairy godmother.

<u>Cinderella</u>, look, who needs her? All those evil stepsisters? Paragraph 26

From Reading to Writing

In Your Journal: Kingsolver makes it clear that family can mean different things to different people. Write your own definitions of *family*.

With Some Classmates: Write an essay that explains the purposes a successful family unit should serve.

In an Essay

- In paragraph 13, Kingsolver says that "two terrifying options are much worse than none at all." Explain what she means and go on to illustrate the truth of this statement with two or more examples.
- In paragraph 18, Kingsolver refers to "family values." Define *family values*.
- Compare and contrast your current family structure or the one you were raised in to the "Family of Dolls" structure mentioned in paragraph 3. Be sure to explain the chief advantages and disadvantages of your particular structure.
- Agree or disagree with a point that Kingsolver makes.

Beyond the Writing Class: In your campus library, find a cultural anthropology textbook and read about family structures in other cultures. Then write an essay that describes several of those structures and the purposes they serve.

On the Brow of the Hill
JUDITH WALLERSTEIN AND SANDRA BLAKESLEE

Judith Wallerstein, who is a research psychologist, runs a well-known center for couseling divorcing families. She also teaches at the University of California at Berkeley. The following selection is the last chapter of *Second Chances* (1990), a book she cowrote with freelance science and medical writer Sandra Blakeslee. In this chapter, Wallerstein discusses the results of her study of the effects of divorce on both children and adults.

Preview. Go to your campus library or on the Internet and check the latest *World Almanac* to discover the current divorce rate in the United States. Also, check whether the rate is up or down from the previous year. Are you surprised by what you have discovered? Why or why not?

Vocabulary If any of the following words from the selection are unfamiliar to you, study their meanings before reading.

sashaying (10) walking or moving easily
continuum (13) a series
mentors (23) counselors or teachers
self-deprecating (24) belittling or undervaluing oneself
disparity (25) lack of similarity
template (27) a pattern
Herculean (35) requiring great strength (like that of Hercules)
maelstrom (41) a powerful, dangerous whirlpool
panacea (56) cure-all
per se (58) of itself

Nearly twenty years have passed since my daughter's friend Karen started me thinking about divorce and its consequences for men, women, and children. Indeed, I have spent almost two decades of my life interviewing families in transition—separating families, divorcing families, and remarried families, all kinds of families with children. It has been a full-time commitment, often running seven days a week.

2   Since 1980, when I founded the Center for the Family in Transition, and in addition to my regular work, I get at least two, sometimes three, telephone calls on an average day from people asking for help in the midst of divorce. Mostly these are strangers who have read my name in a newspaper or heard of my work from a friend. Many of the calls are from parents. Just the other day a man called from Pennsylvania and said, "I'm a teacher. My wife is suing me

for divorce." His voice was strained. "I understand you have written about the importance of fathers, how much their children need to still see them. Can you direct me? Can you send me something to help?"

3   On the same day I got a call from a woman in southern California who told me that the court had ordered her to send her nursing infant to spend every other weekend with the child's father, who lives several hundred miles away. The woman, who must express and freeze extra breast milk to send along with the baby, told me that she was never married to the baby's father, only lived with him briefly, and has no idea what kind of parent he is. She asked, "What should I do?"

4   Shocked by her story—reflecting an intrusion into the most intimate of human relationships, that between a nursing mother and her child—I could say only that there is no psychological research anywhere to support the court's decision but that I knew of no immediate way that I could help. We are staying in touch.

5   Every now and then I get a call from one of the children or parents in our study, usually to announce an important change in his or her life. During this same week, Kedric called to say that he has been accepted into a graduate program in aeronautical engineering—a lifelong dream that he is finally pursuing. And not long ago Denise called from Denmark to say that she is getting married, adding, "You know, I still think about my parents' divorce every day." I made a mental note that she said "every day."

6   The third telephone call on an average day is from a lawyer, usually asking if I will be an expert witness in a custody dispute. Although the practice could be lucrative, I have never accepted any of these invitations because I do not want to compromise my impartiality. My credibility as a researcher might diminish if I became identified with any particular point of view in the courts.

7   My daily correspondence also reflects how deeply I have become involved in the issues surrounding divorce and how widespread the divorce phenomenon has become in our country and throughout the world. Last week, I was invited to speak at the University of Rome for two days, to help shape a study of divorce in Italy. I was also asked to attend a conference on child custody in Wisconsin that will attempt to develop national guidelines on these issues. My primary task for the week was to write the keynote address for a family law conference in Los Angeles involving judges, mediators, and attorneys from all over the United States and Canada.

8   All of these activities—combined with my ongoing long-term research, the work on joint custody, and my close supervision of the various counseling programs at the center—have given me a ringside seat at the drama of changing relationships between the men and women, and the parents and children, in our society. I feel that I have been privileged to observe at first hand, close up, what is undoubtedly one of the most important revolutions of modern times. In looking at divorce, we are looking at the flip side of marriage; and we are gaining new insights into basic family values—what people believe is right

and how people behave toward one another. We are a society in the process of fundamental change in a direction that is entirely new and uncharted.

9   In thinking about these changes, I am reminded of a conversation I had with anthropologist Margaret Mead in 1972. Upset over my early findings at how troubled children are after divorce, I arranged to meet her at the San Francisco airport at midnight. She was on her way to what was to be her last trip to New Guinea, and we had several hours together before she had to leave. She, too, was disturbed by the findings and at one point said, "Judy, there is no society in the world where people have stayed married without enormous community pressure to do so. And I don't think anybody can predict what you will find."

10   Her words continue to impress on me how little we really now about the world we have created in the last twenty years—*a world in which marriage is freely terminable at any time, for the first time in our history*. Perhaps as a clinician and a psychologist I should confess that when we began to look at family changes caused by divorce, we began at ground zero. We lacked, and continue to lack, the psychological theory that we need to understand and to predict the consequences. This is because psychoanalysis, family systems theory, and child development theory have all developed within the context of the two-parent, intact family. Now we are in the awkward position of inventing the theory we need as we discover new facts. So if we've been sashaying back and forth as new findings come to light, it's because that is the state of our knowledge. Only painfully and slowly, essentially since the mid-seventies, have we begun to build a consensus and theory on which we can agree.

11   From the stories of these children and their parents and all the other people I have spoken with over the years, however, several lessons do emerge. They have taught all of us a great deal that we did not know, that we had no way of knowing:

12   ■ Divorce is a wrenching experience for many adults and almost all children. It is almost always more devastating for children than for their parents.

13   ■ Divorce is not an event that stands alone in children's or adults' experience. It is a continuum that begins in the unhappy marriage and extends through the separation, the divorce, and any remarriages and second divorces. Divorce is not the culprit; it may be no more than one of the many experiences that occur in this broad continuum.

14   ■ The effects of divorce are often long-lasting. Children are especially affected because divorce occurs during their formative years. What they see and experience becomes a part of their inner world, their view of themselves, and their view of society. The early experiences in a failing marriage are not erased by divorce. Children who witnessed violence between their parents often found these early images dominating their own relationships ten and fifteen years later. Therefore, while divorce can rescue a parent from an intolerable situation, it can fail to rescue the children.

15 ■ Almost all children of divorce regard their childhood and adolescence as having taken place in the shadow of divorce. Although many agree by adulthood that their parents were wise to part company, they nevertheless feel that they suffered from their parents' mistakes. In many instances, the conditions in the postdivorce family were more stressful and less supportive to the child than the conditions in the failing marriage.

16 ■ Children of divorce come to adulthood eager for enduring love and marriage. They do not take divorce lightly.

17 ■ For the children in our study, the postdivorce years brought the following:

18 —Half saw their mother or father get a second divorce in the ten-year period after the first divorce.

19 —Half grew up in families where parents stayed angry at each other.

20 —One in four experienced a severe and enduring drop in their standard of living and went on to observe a major, lasting discrepancy between economic conditions in their mothers' and fathers' homes. They grew up with their noses pressed against the glass, looking at a way of life that by all rights should have been theirs.

21 —Three in five felt rejected by at least one of the parents, sensing that they were a piece of psychological or economic baggage left over from a regretted journey.

22 —Very few were helped financially with college educations, even though they continued to visit their fathers regularly. But because their fathers were relatively well-off, they were ineligible for scholarships.

23 ■ Many of the children emerged in young adulthood as compassionate, courageous, and competent people. Those who did well were helped along the way by a combination of their own inner resources and supportive relationships with one or both parents, grandparents, stepparents, siblings, or mentors. Some later experienced nurturing love affairs and good marriages of their own making. Some of those who did well were very much helped by the example of parents who had been able to successfully rebuild their lives after divorce. Others did well because they were deliberately able to turn away from the examples set by their parents. A smaller number benefited from the continued relationship with two good parents who—despite their anger and disappointment with each other—were able to cooperate in the tasks of childrearing.

24 ■ In this study, however, almost half of the children entered adulthood as worried, underachieving, self-deprecating, and sometimes angry young men and women. Some felt used in a battle that was never their own. Others felt deprived of the parenting and family protection that they always wanted and never got. Those who were troubled at young adulthood were more depleted by early experiences before and after their parents' divorces, had fewer resources, and often had very little help from their parents or from anybody else. Some children literally brought themselves up, while others were responsible for the welfare of a troubled parent as well.

25   ■ Although boys had a harder time over the years than girls, suffering a wide range of difficulties in school achievements, peer relationships, and the handling of aggression, this disparity in overall adjustment eventually dissipated. As the young women stood at the developmental threshold of young adulthood, when it was time to seek commitment with a young man, many found themselves struggling with anxiety and guilt. This sudden shock, which I describe as a sleeper effect, led to many maladaptive pathways, including multiple relationships and impulsive marriages that ended in early divorce.

26   ■ Adolescence is a period of grave risk for children in divorced families; those who entered adolescence in the immediate wake of their parents' divorces had a particularly hard time. The young people told us time and again how much they needed a family structure, how much they wanted to be protected, and how much they yearned for clear guidelines for moral behavior. They told us they needed more encouragement from parents in the complicated process of growing up and that, failing to get it, they were seduced by the voices of the street. Feeling abandoned at this critical time in their lives, they were haunted by inner doubts and uncertainties about the future. An alarming number of teenagers felt abandoned, physically and emotionally.

27   ■ Finally, and perhaps most important for society, the cumulative effect of the failing marriage and divorce rose to a crescendo as each child entered young adulthood. It was here, as these young men and women faced the developmental task of establishing love and intimacy, that they most felt the lack of a template for a loving, enduring, and moral relationship between a man and a woman. It was here that anxiety carried over from divorced family relationships threatened to bar the young people's ability to create new, enduring families of their own. As these anxieties peak in the children of divorce throughout our society, the full legacy of the past twenty years begins to hit home. The new families that are formed appear vulnerable to the effects of divorce. Although many young people in the study eventually were able to move forward and to establish good relationships and good marriages, this is a critical passage for all.

28   For adults, divorce more often brings an end to an unhappy chapter in their lives. Many of the individuals in our study succeeded in creating a much happier, better way of life for themselves, often but not necessarily within a happy second marriage.

29   More, however, experienced divorce as essentially the beginning of a long-lasting discrepancy between themselves and their former spouses. As the years went by, one person was able to create a better quality of life while the other felt left behind—economically, psychologically, and socially. These are the winners and losers in this book, the ex-husbands and ex-wives who—relative to one another—made better or worse use of their second chances in the decade after divorce.

30   In watching adults take up or fail to take up their second chances, we have learned the following:

31   ■ Many of the second marriages are in fact happier. These adults learn from their earlier experiences and avoid making the same mistakes.

32   ■ Many adults, especially women, show striking growth in competence and self-esteem.

33   ■ Recovery is not a given in adult life. The assumption that all people recover psychologically is not based on evidence. On what basis do we make the assumption that after twenty or twenty-five years of marriage people can inevitably pick themselves back up and start over again?

34   ■ Feelings, especially angry feelings and feelings of hurt and humiliation, can remain in full force for many years after divorce.

35   ■ Some adults are at greater risk than others. Women with young children, especially if they are driven into poverty by divorce, face a Herculean struggle to survive emotionally and physically. The stress of being a single parent with small children, working day shift and nightshift without medical insurance or other backup, is unimaginable to people who have not experienced it. No wonder some women told us that they feel dead inside.

36   ■ Many older men and women coming out of long-term marriages are alone and unhappy, facing older age with rising anxiety. They lean on their children, with mixed feelings, for support and companionship ten and fifteen years after divorce. Opportunities for work, play, sex and marriage decline rapidly with age, especially for women.

37   ■ Younger men are often adrift. Divorce seems to block them from expanding into their adult roles as husbands and fathers.

38   ■ Finally, for adults, the high failure rate of second marriages is serious and, as we discovered, often devastating because it reinforces the first failure many times over.

39   Many of our more baffling findings have to do with changes in parent-child relationships that occur at the time of divorce and in the years that follow. Because children long remain dependent on parents for economic and emotional support, these changes can have serious consequences. Evidently the relationship between parents and children grows best in the rich soil of a happy, intact family. But without this nurturing growth medium, parent-child relationships can become very fragile and are easily broken. What does this mean for families? What have we learned?

40   ■ As in the intact family, the child's continued relationship with good parents who cooperate with each other remains vital to his or her proper development. However, good, cooperative parenting is many times more difficult in the postdivorce family.

41   ▪ When a marriage breaks down, most men and women experience a diminished capacity to parent. They give less time, provide less discipline, and are less sensitive to their children, being caught up themselves in the personal maelstrom of divorce and its aftermath. Many parents are temporarily unable to separate their children's needs from their own. In many families parenting is restored within a year or two after divorce. But in a surprising number of families, the diminished parenting continues, permanently disrupting the child-rearing functions of the family.

42   ▪ Since most children live with their mothers after divorce, the single most important protective factor in a child's psychological development and well-being over the years is the mother's mental health and the quality of her parenting.

43   ▪ We have seen how difficult it is for fathers who have moved out of the house to sustain a close and loving relationship with their children, especially if one or both parents remarry. Yet we have also seen how poignantly the children hold on to an internal image, sometimes a fantasy image, of the absent or even the visiting father and how both fathers and children create phantom relationships with each other.

44   ▪ We have seen that the children's need for their father continues and that it rises with new intensity at adolescence, especially when it is time for the children to leave home. The nature of the father-child relationship, and not the frequency of visiting, is what most influences the child's psychological development.

45   ▪ Many a father seems to have lost the sense that his children are part of his own generational continuity, his defense against mortality. This blunting of the father's relationship to his children is a stunning surprise.

46   ▪ New, unfamiliar parent-child relationships have developed in some families, in which the child is overburdened by responsibility for a parent's psychological welfare or by serving as an instrument of parental rage.

47   ▪ We have learned that good stepparent-child relationships are not assured. They need to be properly nurtured to take root in the minds and hearts of the children. Many children feel excluded from the remarried family.

48   ▪ At the same time, we have seen some mothers and fathers, and even some stepparents, undertake heroic measures of loyalty, selflessness, and devotion to their children.

49   I have asked myself many times if these children and adults who experienced divorce in the early 1970s are different from those who are experiencing divorce today. At the Center for the Family in Transition, we are counseling about thirty new families every month, more than any other agency in the country. Although the divorce rate rose steeply in the 1970s, it reached a plateau in the 1980s, at a level where one in two recent marriages can be expected to end in divorce. Children born in the mid-1980s stand a 38 percent chance of experiencing their parents' divorce before they reach age eighteen.

50   I see surprisingly little change in how adults or children react emotionally to divorce. Parents still have trouble telling the children. Despite the tremendous proliferation of media attention to divorce, nearly 50 percent of the families that we counsel waited until the day of the separation or afterward to tell their children that their familiar world is coming apart.

51   The causes of divorce have not changed, nor have men's and women's feelings changed. The amount of suffering is no less. People like to think that because there are so many divorced families, adults and children will find divorce easier or even easy. But neither parents nor children find comfort in numbers. Divorce is not a more "normal" experience simply because so many people have been touched by it. Our findings reveal that all children suffer from divorce, no matter how many of their friends have gone through it. And although the stigma of divorce has been enormously reduced in recent years, the pain that each child feels is not assuaged. Each and every child cries out, "Why me?"

52   One very worrisome difference between the 1970s and 1980s, based on reports from mental health clinics, is an increase in severe reactions in today's families—more violence, more parental dependence on children, and many more troubled, even suicidal children. I am very worried about the acute depression in many adolescents who functioned well before the divorce. There has been a rise in reports of child abuse and sexual molestation. Although it is sometimes difficult to separate real from fabricated abuse, especially when these are at issue in child custody battles, the problem is alarming. Worse yet, the system set up to deal with the problem is woefully inadequate.

53   We have seen a major shift in the attitudes of fathers, more of whom are trying to maintain an active parenting role in their children's lives. There is also a greater willingness among women to allow this involvement and a wider expectation that it will occur whatever the custody arrangement. On the other hand, we see a small but significant increase in the number of women who are leaving their children, choosing to place them temporarily or entirely in their ex-husbands' care. There are many motives involved in this decision, including the fact that it has become a more acceptable option in our society.

54   Economically, the impact of divorce on women and children continues to be a serious problem. As a result of national legislation passed in 1984, states have more tools to enforce child support payment, but it is too soon to tell how much their efforts are helping children. There continues to be little general support for equalizing the standard of living between the fathers' and mothers' homes in the years after divorce. As a result, children continue to be primarily dependent on their mothers' earning power, which is usually less than their fathers'. Despite the women's movement, few mothers in the 1980s are prepared to enter the marketplace with skills that will maintain them and their children at a comparable or a reasonably good standard of living.

55   One major difference between the 1970s and 1980s has been the rise in joint custody, which can be helpful in families where it has been chosen voluntarily by both parents and is suitable for the child. But there is no evidence to support the notion that "one size fits all" or even most. There is, in fact, a lot of evidence for the idea that different custody models are suitable for different families. The policy job ahead is to find the best match for each family.

56   Sadly, when joint custody is imposed by the court on families fighting over custody of children, the major consequences of the fighting are shifted onto the least able members of the family—the hapless and helpless children. The children can suffer serious psychological injury when this happens. I am in favor of joint custody in many cases, where parents and children can handle it, but it is no panacea. We still have a great deal to learn.

57   Another question I have asked myself: Does the experience in California speak for the rest of the nation? It speaks primarily, in my view, to middle-class America and perhaps to middle-class families in other parts of the postindustrial world. We know much less about the divorce experience of families in other social classes and among other ethnic groups. As for middle-class America, however, my findings have held up well in the light of studies conducted in other parts of the country. When I speak at conferences around the country, in Europe, Latin America, and elsewhere abroad, professionals and parents confirm that the reactions they have observed in children and adults are remarkably in accord with my observations.

58   Although our overall findings are troubling and serious, we should not point the finger of blame at divorce per se. Indeed, divorce is often the only rational solution to a bad marriage. When people ask whether they should stay married for the sake of the children, I have to say, "Of course not." All our evidence shows that children turn out less well adjusted when exposed to open conflict, where parents terrorize or strike one another, than do children from divorced families. And while we lack systematic studies comparing unhappily married families and divorced families, I do know that it is not useful to provide children with a model of adult behavior that avoids problem solving and that stresses martyrdom, violence, or apathy. A divorce undertaken thoughtfully and realistically can teach children how to confront serious life problems with compassion, wisdom, and appropriate action.

59   Our findings do not support those who would turn back the clock. As family issues are flung to the center of our political arena, nostalgic voices from the right argue for a return to a time when divorce was difficult to obtain. But they do not offer solutions to the serious problems that have contributed to the rising divorce rate in the first place. From the left we hear counterarguments that relationships have become more honest and more equal between men and women and that the changes we face simply represent "the new family form." But to say that all family forms are equivalent is to semantically camouflage the truth: All families are *not* alike in the protection they extend to children. Moreover, the voices of our children are not represented in the political arena. Although men and women talk *about* children, it is hard for me to believe that they are necessarily talking *for* children.

60   Like it or not, we are witnessing family changes which are an integral part of the wider changes in our society. We are on a wholly new course, one that gives us unprecedented opportunities for creating better relationships and stronger families—but one that has also brought unprecedented dangers for society, especially for our children.

61   We have reached the brow of the hill at the end of the 1980s. As I survey the landscape, I am encouraged by signs of change for the better:

62   ▪ Society is beginning to pay attention to the economic plight of its women and children, to the so-called feminization of poverty. We are less tolerant of the economic injustice promoted by divorce.

63   ▪ There are strong voices raised in the legislatures and the courts that reflect concern about the unmet needs of all children and families in our society.

64   ▪ There seems to be growing community awareness about the impact of divorce on families and children. Teachers, psychotherapists, clergy, physicians, judges, family lawyers, and parents are more attuned to the special needs of divorcing families.

65   ▪ There has been an increase in divorce services, including mediation in the courts and more psychological counseling services in the community.

66   But these encouraging signs still do not measure up to the magnitude of the problem. Legal, mediation, and mental health services focus almost exclusively on the here and now of the divorce crisis. Child support payment is set in accord with the present and not the changing future needs of the children. Even visiting schedules for the children are established on the basis of current need and age. All of these services assume that if only we can help people settle property, custody, and visitation, all else will follow. This is clearly not the case.

67   If the goal of the legal system is—and I fully believe that it should be—to minimize the impact of divorce on children and to preserve for children as much as possible of the social, economic, and emotional security that existed while their parents' marriage was intact, then we still have very far to go.

68   At a minimum, the variety of supports and services for divorcing families needs to be expanded in scope and over time. These families need education at the time of the divorce about the special problems created by their decision. They need help in making decisions about living arrangements, visiting schedules, and sole or joint custody. And they need help in implementing these decisions over many years—and in modifying them as the children grow and the family changes. Divorcing families need universally available mediation services. They also need specialized counseling over the long haul in those cases where the children are at clear risk, where the parents are still locked in bitter disputes, and where there has been family violence. Divorcing men and women must make realistic provision for the economic support of their children,

backed up by the government when necessary. These provisions should include health care and college education, where it is appropriate.

69   Beyond all this, we need to learn much more about divorce. We need to learn how and why things worked out so badly between divorced men and women who have had children together, most of whom tell us that they married for love. We need to learn how to reduce the unhappiness, anger, and disappointment that is so widespread in the relationships between men and women. And we need to learn more about courtship, marriage, and remarriage and about what makes good marriages work.

70   As a society we have always been quick to respond to individual needs; it was easy and natural for us to rivet our collective attention on the little girl who was recently trapped in an abandoned well. But it is harder for us to face up to the problems affecting our collective selves—and for a very good reason. To echo the immortal words of "Pogo" cartoonist Walt Kelly, "We have met the enemy and he is us." Divorce is not an issue of "we" versus "them." Profound changes have shaken the American family. It is not that we are less virtuous or less concerned for our children and their future, but we have been slow to recognize the magnitude of the needs of children of divorce and their parents. And we have been reluctant to take collective responsibility.

71   A society that allows divorce on demand inevitably takes on certain responsibilities. It is up to us to protect one another, especially our children, to the extent possible against the psychological and economic suffering that divorce can bring. All children in today's world feel less protected. They sense that the institution of the family is weaker than it has ever been before. Children of divorce grow up with the notion that love can be transient and commitment temporary, but all children—even those raised in happy, intact families—worry that their families may come undone as well. Therefore, the task for society in its true and proper perspective is to support and strengthen the family—all families.

72   As I bring this book to a close, a biblical phrase I have not thought of for many years keeps running through my head: "Watchman, what of the night?" We are not, I'm afraid, doing very well on our watch—at least not for our children—and, consequently, not for the future of our society. By avoiding our task, we have unintentionally placed the primary burden of coping with family change onto the children. To state it plainly, we are allowing our children to bear the psychological, economic, and moral brunt of divorce.

73   And from what the children are telling us, they recognize the burdens that have been put on their slender shoulders. When six-year-old John came to our center shortly after his parents' divorce, he would only mumble, "I don't know." He would not answer questions; he played games instead. First John hunted all over the playroom for the baby dolls. When he found a good number of them, he stood the baby dolls firmly on their feet and placed the miniature tables, chairs, beds, and eventually all the playhouse furniture on their heads. John looked at me, satisfied. The babies were supporting a great deal on

their heads. Then, wordlessly, he placed all the mother dolls and father dolls in precarious positions on the steep roof of the dollhouse. As a father doll slid off the roof, John caught him and, looking up at me, said, "He might die." Soon all the mother and father dolls began sliding off the roof. John caught them gently, one by one, saving each from falling to the ground.

74   "Are the babies the strongest?" I asked.

75   "Yes," John shouted excitedly. "The babies are holding up the world."

Understanding Content

1. Why was Wallerstein so affected by Margaret Mead's statement that "'there is no society in the world where people have stayed married without enormous community pressure to do so. And I don't think anybody can predict what you will find'" (Paragraph 9)?
2. Children and adults are affected differently by divorce. Explain how they are affected differently.
3. In paragraph 27, Wallerstein refers to the "cumulative effect of the failing marriage and divorce." What does she mean?
4. How do adolescents react to divorce?
5. Explain how the parent-child relationship is affected by divorce.

Considering Structure and Technique

1. In your own words, write out the thesis of "On the Brow of the Hill." Where in the selection is that thesis best expressed?
2. Several times throughout the selection points are marked with bullets. What purpose do these bullets serve? Do you think they are a good idea? Explain why or why not.
3. What purpose do paragraphs 68 through 71 serve? Do you think the selection would be diminished if those paragraphs were left out? Explain your view.
4. Does the anecdote about John provide an effective conclusion? Explain why or why not.

Exploring Ideas

1. In paragraph 8, Wallerstein says that divorce is "one of the most important revolutions of modern times." Why do you think she believes this? Do you agree? Explain why or why not.
2. In paragraph 59, Wallerstein refers to "the serious problems that have contributed to the rising divorce rate." What do you think some of those problems are?
3. In paragraph 36, Wallerstein notes that opportunities for divorced people "decline rapidly with age, especially for women." Why do you think the decline is greater for divorced women than for divorced men?

4. In paragraphs 61 through 65, Wallerstein displays some optimism. Do you share that optimism? Explain why or why not.

Writing Workshop: Opening with the Author's Credentials

If you have qualifications or credentials that make you particularly well suited to write on a particular subject, you can mention those qualifications or credentials early on. Doing so will impress your audience with your expertise and thus incline your reader to take your points very seriously.

Notice that in the first seven paragraphs of "On the Brow of the Hill," Judith Wallerstein mentions her credentials:

She has spent almost twenty years studying her subject. Paragraph 1

She founded the Center for the Family in Transition. Paragraph 2

She gets many calls from people affected by divorce. Paragraphs 3 through 6

She lectures and attends conferences on her subject. Paragraph 7

To state your credentials in the opening of an essay, you do not have to be a famous researcher like Wallerstein. You probably possess qualifications on a variety of topics. For example, if you played high school basketball for four years, you can cite that credential in an essay about sportsmanship. If you volunteer in a home for the aged, you can cite that credential in a paper about elder care. If you are a single parent, you can cite that credential in a paper calling for day care on campus.

Writing Workshop Activity

List five topics you have credentials to write on. For example, if you are a Little League coach, you have the qualifications to write about the advantages and disadvantages of organized sports for children. Then select one of the topics from your list and write a paragraph that presents your topic and your credentials. For example, if you are a child of divorced parents and have had a happy upbringing, you can cite that qualification in a paragraph that introduces this thesis: Wallerstein presents an unnecessarily pessimistic view of the fate of children of divorce.

Language Notes for Multilingual and Other Writers

Two frequently used idioms derived from references to specific locations appear in "On the Brow of the Hill":

1. *Ringside seat* refers to a place providing a close view. It originally meant the first row of seats on all sides of a boxing or wrestling ring.

   All of these activities . . . have given me a <u>ringside seat</u> at the drama of changing relationships between men and women. . . . Paragraph 8

2. *Ground zero* refers to the beginning of something. It is technically the point at which an atomic or nuclear bomb explodes.

   . . . I should confess that when we began to look at family changes caused by divorce, we began at <u>ground zero</u>. Paragraph 10

From Reading to Writing

In Your Journal: In paragraph 58, Wallerstein says that despite the problems caused by divorce, parents should not remain married for the sake of the children. Do you agree, or do you think it is better for children if their unhappy parents stay together?

With Some Classmates: Write a summary of what Wallerstein says are the effects of divorce on children and parents. (For information on how to write a summary, see p. 14.)

In an Essay

- Interview several people whose parents are divorced (and use your own experience if it is applicable), and then use that information to agree or disagree with one or more of Wallerstein's conclusions.
- If you are from another culture, compare and contrast the views of marriage and divorce in that culture with the views in American culture. If you know someone from another culture, interview that person and then write the comparison and contrast.
- Explain what can be done to help children of divorced parents avoid one of the problems Wallerstein describes. Tell what children can do to help themselves, what parents can do, what teachers can do, and what society and its institutions can do.

Beyond the Writing Class: When you completed the Preview activity for this essay, you learned the current divorce rate. What do you think are the primary causes of that rate? Base your response on your own experience and observation and on information you gather by interviewing sociology and psychology instructors and people you know who have been divorced.

⇥⇥ **CONNECTING THE READINGS**

1. Chapter 3 opens with the statement of Marie von Ebner-Eschenbach, "In youth we learn; in age we understand" (p. 55). Agree or disagree with this statement, drawing on the evidence in the essays in Part 2, along with your own experience and observation.

2. Conflict is a recurring theme in almost all the essays in Part 2. For example, conflict between generations is seen in "The Chase" and "No Turning Back"; conflict between races is seen in "Graduation"; conflict over the transition to different stages of life is seen in "Once More to the Lake" and "Predictable Crises of Adulthood"; cultural conflict is seen in "No Turning Back" and "Hold the Mayonnaise." Discuss the role conflict plays in people's lives. What are the positive and negative aspects of conflict?

3. In "The Chase," "Graduation," "Once More to the Lake," and "The Transmission of Hope," children and adults interact in ways they long remember. Using one or more of those essays and any other information, tell how people are shaped by cross-generational interaction.

4. Several essays in Part 2 lend insight into some of the pressures on the American family. For example, "Hold the Mayonnaise" tells of the challenges faced by stepparents and stepchildren who come from different cultures; "No Turning Back" tells of the pain families experience when children give up the ways of their ancestors for the customs of mainstream society; "On the Brow of the Hill" describes the problems created by divorce; "Stone Soup" tells of some of the perceptions of themselves nontraditional families must face; "Parents Also Have Rights" describes the problems resulting from teenage pregnancy. Drawing on any of these essays and your own experience and observation, discuss one or two of the most serious challenges facing American families. Note the effects of those challenges and go on to suggest ways families can meet them.

5. In "The Predictable Crises of Adulthood," Gail Sheehy describes six stages we go through from age 18 to the forties and fifties. Expand her piece by describing either adolescence or old age. You can draw some of your detail from essays in this section, from interviews, and from your own experience and observation.

6. Both "Graduation" and "The Transmission of Hope" suggest the role ritual may play in our growth. Explain the role ritual plays in life's stages.

PART 3

Society in Transition

© RF/Corbis   © RF/Corbis

CHAPTER 5

THE INDIVIDUAL IN SOCIETY: HOW DO WE FIT IN? HOW DO WE STAND OUT?

"To live is, in itself, a value judgment. To breathe is to judge."

Albert Camus

"Most Americans have never seen the ignorance, degradation, hunger, sickness, and futility in which many other Americans live. . . . They won't become involved in economic or political change until something brings the seriousness of the situation home to them."

Shirley Chisolm

"We are half ruined by conformity, but we should be wholly ruined without it."

Charles Dudley Warner

"We can tell our values by looking at our checkbook stubs."

Gloria Steinem

Screams from Somewhere Else
ROGER ROSENBLATT

Former Harvard professor, columnist for the *Washington Post,* and editor of *U.S. News and World Report,* Roger Rosenblatt is currently an essayist and senior writer for *Time,* as well as a contributing editor and essayist for the *New York Times Magazine, Vanity Fair,* and *The New Republic.* His many awards include an Emmy and a Peabody. "Screams from Somewhere Else" is one of the pieces he wrote for *Time.*

Preview.   In "Screams from Somewhere Else," Rosenblatt notes that the way people react to a scream says a great deal about them and their world. How do we typically react to sounds that should motivate us in some way? Consider fire alarms, car alarms, and, yes, screams. Do we tend to become numb to them and, as a result, to ignore them, or do we spring into action? Explain.

Vocabulary.   If any of the following words from the essay are unfamiliar to you, study their meanings before reading.

indigenous (1) native to or characteristic of a particular place
hysteria (1) an uncontrollable emotional outburst
discerning (2) recognizing
in concert (2) jointly; together
quashed (5) put down or suppressed

The scream is one of the indigenous sounds of city life, like an automobile alarm that whoops and heaves, then stops, leaving the question hanging like a hawk as to whether a car was broken into, or did its owner set off the alarm by accident, and then lay it to rest. With human screams, the question is more complicated, since screams are not mechanical or automatic. Did you hear that, Harry? What could it be? A scream of delight, of fright? Hilarity, Harry? Do you think that someone is laughing too hard? Could it be hysteria, madness? Or is it a scream of blue murder? What should we do, Harry, if it is a scream of murder? And where is it coming from, anyway? Could you tell? I couldn't tell.

2   A Manhattan couple was charged last week with the murder by beating of their six-year-old adopted daughter. Neighbors never had any difficulty telling where the screams were coming from, though sometimes they may have had trouble discerning exactly who was doing the screaming, the six-year-old girl or the woman who lived with the father. The woman is accused of "acting in concert" in the murder, but clearly her own life buckled under regular

punches. She wore dark glasses, and would attribute her recomposed face to a mugging or a fall in the kitchen. Over the years, colleagues and friends chose to believe the mugging and accident stories. Neighbors who heard the screams firsthand placed dozens of telephone calls to the police and to city authorities, who investigated but could prove no harm. The authorities did not hear the screams. After the beatings, the child lay brain dead, and the couple was in custody. Now no one in that building hears the screams.

3   But in other buildings in New York, in other cities, in all the cities, new screams will take up the slack. Sometimes the authorities will respond, sometimes not. The beating of women and children will continue in the hidden boxes of apartments: evil, secret noise. You will hear the scream, and someone else will tell you that it wasn't a scream, it was a kettle whistle; and no one will be sure if there ever was a scream, until a body lies in evidence. How is the citizen-listener to react? Rush wildly through the corridors until the sound is unmistakable? Push open some stranger's door to confront some stranger's scream? Much courage is required for that. Much recklessness as well. The helplessness you feel in such situations is dizzying; and even when you act, someone in power can let you down. You could be wrong. Foolish. You could be sued.

4   Civilization is tested by its screams. One has the choice to hear or not to hear; to detect location or not to detect location; to discover cause; to help or not to help. Along the many lines of choices, excuses and mistakes are possible, even reasonable. One is left with oneself and the screams, like two opponents. The Kitty Genovese case of 1964 keeps coming back, in which a young woman in Queens screamed for help, and everybody heard, and nobody helped. What were we to do? Edvard Munch's famous painting of *The Cry* keeps coming back, equally scary and bewildering. What *are* we to do?

5   You never know how you will react to a scream until you hear one. I can tell you how you will react at first. You will freeze. Your head will snap like an alarmed bird's and your eyes will swell, long before any practical choices begin to form between hiding under the bed and leaping to the rescue. You will freeze because you will recognize the sound. It comes from you; all the panic and the pain; all the screams of one's life, uttered and quashed, there in that dreadful eruption that has scattered the air. All yours.

6   The scream that comes from somewhere else comes from you. You have to go to it. You have to open the door to make it stop.

Understanding Content

1. Why is a scream "complicated"?
2. Throughout the essay, Rosenblatt mentions a number of different responses to a scream. What are they?
3. For what purpose do you think Rosenblatt wrote "Screams from Somewhere Else"? What does he want readers to do? Where is his purpose most clearly stated?

4. Rosenblatt says that "the scream that comes from somewhere else comes from you" (paragraph 6). Obviously, that is not literally true. What point is the author making?

Considering Structure and Technique

1. Paragraph 1 includes a conversation between an unknown person and someone named Harry. What purpose does this conversation serve? What does it contribute to the essay?
2. Why does Rosenblatt tell the story of the 6-year-old girl who was beaten until she was brain-dead?
3. In paragraph 3, Rosenblatt points out all the problems associated with *not* ignoring a scream. Why does he do this?
4. A **simile** is a comparison made using the words *like* or *as*. (See the workshop on p. 121 for an explanation of similes.) For example, in paragraph 1, Rosenblatt uses a simile to compare a particular kind of question to a soaring hawk: "The scream is one of the indigenous sounds of city life, like an automobile alarm that whoops and heaves, then stops, leaving the question hanging like a hawk as to whether a car was broken into. . . . " Identify two other similes in the essay.

Exploring Ideas

1. In paragraph 2, Rosenblatt says that colleagues and friends "chose" to believe the woman's explanations for her injuries. Why does he use the word *chose?*
2. Rosenblatt says that it is both courageous and reckless to "confront some stranger's scream" (paragraph 3). What do you think he means?
3. In paragraph 4, Rosenblatt says, "Civilization is tested by its screams." What do you think he means?
4. When asked why they did not respond to Kitty Genovese's cries for help, people said that they did not want to get involved. Why do you think they felt that way?

Writing Workshop: Describing for Emotional Impact

To have an emotional impact on readers, writers often use description. Consider, for example, the emotions created by the description in paragraph 5 of "Screams from Somewhere Else." Rosenblatt's vivid description of how a person reacts to a scream is powerful because it causes the reader to image the fear and paralysis felt upon hearing the scream. Description has an emotional impact because it is vivid; its power comes from the images it creates in the reader's mind. [See the related workshops on mental images (p. 60) and specific verbs (p. 200).]

Writing Workshop Activity

Rewrite paragraph 5 of "Screams from Somewhere Else" so that it does not include descriptive terms and descriptive language. How do the two versions differ? Do you react differently to each version? Explain.

Language Notes for Multilingual and Other Writers

The following figurative expressions appear in "Screams from Somewhere Else."

1. To *take up the slack* means to act when other people or things have stopped acting. It is a reference to tightening the loose part of a rope.

   But in other buildings in New York, in other cities, in all the cities, new screams <u>will take up the slack</u>. Paragraph 3

2. To *let someone down* means to disappoint that person.

   . . . and even when you act, someone in power can <u>let you down</u>. Paragraph 3

3. To *freeze* means to become unable to move, act, or think.

   You <u>will freeze</u> because you will recognize the sound. Paragraph 5

From Reading to Writing

In Your Journal: If you heard a scream in the night, would you intervene, if doing so would put you at risk? Explain why or why not.

With Some Classmates: In your campus library, locate a photograph of the painting *The Cry*, which is mentioned in paragraph 4. Describe the painting and discuss to what extent it is or is not relevant to modern life. The painting is also frequently reproduced on T-shirts, mugs, and sweatshirts. Explain why you think people like to buy shirts and mugs with this painting on it.

In an Essay

- Write about a time when you or someone you know became involved in a crisis situation. Explain what happened and what can be learned from the situation.
- Explain what kinds of violent and potentially threatening situations exist on college campuses. Then go on to discuss what members of the college community can do to deal with these situations.

- Rosenblatt says, "Civilization is tested by its screams" (paragraph 4). Discuss another thing that tests civilization. Explain what it is, why it is a test, and how civilization passes or fails that test.

Beyond the Writing Class: In the library, find the March 17, 1964, edition of the *New York Times* and read the article by Martin Gansberg called "38 Who Saw Murder Didn't Call Police." This is an account of what happened to Kitty Genovese. Summarize what happened (see p. 14 on summarizing); then go on to explain what can be learned from the incident and what it says about our civilization.

The Teacher Who Changed My Life
NICHOLAS GAGE

When he was nine, Nicholas Gage escaped the civil war in Greece and made it to the United States. His mother, however, did not escape; she was captured and killed by communist guerillas. Gage wrote of his mother in his book *Eleni,* which was made into a critically acclaimed movie of the same name. As its title suggests, the following essay is an account of a teacher who profoundly influenced Gage.

Preview. Individuals *can* make a difference. Consider our teachers, for example, and answer the following questions: How does a teacher affect the lives of students? Have any of your teachers changed your life? In what ways?

Vocabulary.   If any of the following words from this essay are unfamiliar to you, study their meanings before reading.

guerrillas (2) soldiers who are not part of the regular army
• **tenement** (4) apartments in poor condition occupied by poor people
   mentor (5) teacher
• **muse** (5) the inspiration for a writer
• **formidable** (6) overpowering
• **honed** (7) sharpened
   Iron Curtain (9) a barrier to understanding created by hostility between the
      former Soviet Union and countries it was not allied with
• **vocation** (16) job; career

The person who set the course of my life in the new land I entered as a young war refugee—who, in fact, nearly dragged me onto the path that would bring all the blessings I've received in America—was a salty-tongued, no-nonsense schoolteacher named Marjorie Hurd. When I entered her classroom in 1953, I had been to six schools in five years, starting in the Greek village where I was born in 1939.

2   When I stepped off a ship in New York Harbor on a gray March day in 1949, I was an undersized 9-year-old in short pants who had lost his mother and was coming to live with the father he didn't know. My mother, Eleni Gatzoyiannis, had been imprisoned, tortured and shot by Communist guerillas for sending me and three of my four sisters to freedom. She died so that her children could go to their father in the United States.

3   The portly, bald, well-dressed man who met me and my sisters seemed a foreign, authoritarian figure. I secretly resented him for not getting the whole family out of Greece early enough to save my mother. Ultimately, I would grow to love him and appreciate how he dealt with becoming a single parent at the age of 56, but at first our relationship was prickly, full of hostility.

4   As Father drove us to our new home—a tenement in Worcester, Mass.— and pointed out the huge brick building that would be our first school in America, I clutched my Greek notebooks from the refugee camp, hoping that my few years of schooling would impress my teachers in this cold, crowded country. They didn't. When my father led me and my 11-year-old sister to Greendale Elementary School, the grim-faced Yankee principal put the two of us in a class for the mentally retarded. There was no facility in those days for non–English-speaking children.

5   By the time I met Marjorie Hurd four years later, I had learned English, been placed in a normal, graded class and had even been chosen for the college preparatory track in the Worcester public school system. I was 13 years old when our father moved us yet again, and I entered Chandler Junior High shortly after the beginning of the seventh grade. I found myself surrounded by richer, smarter and better-dressed classmates who looked askance at my strange clothes and heavy accent. Shortly after I arrived, we were told to select a hobby to pursue during "club hour" on Fridays. The idea of hobbies and clubs made no sense to my immigrant ears, but I decided to follow the prettiest girl in my class—the blue-eyed daughter of the local Lutheran minister. She led me through the door marked "Newspaper Club" and into the presence of Miss Hurd, the newspaper adviser and English teacher who would become my mentor and my muse.

6   A formidable, solidly built woman with salt-and-pepper hair, a steely eye and a flat Boston accent, Miss Hurd had no patience with layabouts. "What are all you goof-offs doing here?" she bellowed at the would-be journalists. "This is the Newspaper Club! We're going to put out a *newspaper.* So if there's anybody in this room who doesn't like to work, I suggest you go across to the Glee Club now, because you're going to work your tails off here!"

7   I was soon under Miss Hurd's spell. She did indeed teach us to put out a newspaper, skills I honed during my next 25 years as a journalist. Soon I asked the principal to transfer me to her English class as well. There, she drilled us on grammar until I finally began to understand the logic and structure of the English language. She assigned stories for us to read and discuss; not tales of heroes, like the Greek myths I knew, but stories of underdogs—poor people, even immigrants, who seemed ordinary until a crisis drove them to do something extraordinary. She also introduced us to the literary wealth of Greece—giving me a new perspective on my war-ravaged, impoverished homeland. I began to be proud of my origins.

8   One day, after discussing how writers should write about what they know, she assigned us to compose an essay from our own experience. Fixing

me with a stern look, she added, "Nick, I want you to write about what happened to your family in Greece." I had been trying to put those painful memories behind me and left the assignment until the last moment. Then, on a warm spring afternoon, I sat in my room with a yellow pad and pencil and stared out the window at the buds on the trees. I wrote that the coming of spring always reminded me of the last time I said goodbye to my mother on a green and gold day in 1948.

9   I kept writing, one line after another, telling how the Communist guerrillas occupied our village, took our home and food, how my mother started planning our escape when she learned that the children were to be sent to reeducation camps behind the Iron Curtain and how, at the last moment, she couldn't escape with us because the guerrillas sent her with a group of women to thresh wheat in a distant village. She promised she would try to get away on her own, she told me to be brave and hung a silver cross around my neck, and then she kissed me. I watched the line of women being led down into the ravine and up the other side, until they disappeared around the bend—my mother a tiny brown figure at the end who stopped for an instant to raise her hand in one last farewell.

10   I wrote about our nighttime escape down the mountain, across the minefields and into the lines of the Nationalist soldiers, who sent us to a refugee camp. It was there that we learned of our mother's execution. I felt very lucky to have come to America, I concluded, but every year, the coming of spring made me feel sad because it reminded me of the last time I saw my mother.

11   I handed in the essay, hoping never to see it again, but Miss Hurd had it published in the school paper. This mortified me at first, until I saw that my classmates reacted with sympathy and tact to my family's story. Without telling me, Miss Hurd also submitted the essay to a contest sponsored by the Freedoms Foundation at Valley Force, Pa., and it won a medal. The Worcester paper wrote about the award and quoted my essay at length. My father, by then a "five-and-dime-store chef," as the paper described him, was ecstatic with pride, and the Worcester Greek community celebrated the honor to one of its own.

12   For the first time I began to understand the power of the written word. A secret ambition took root in me. One day, I vowed, I would go back to Greece, find out the details of my mother's death and write about her life, so her grandchildren would know of her courage. Perhaps I would even track down the men who killed her and write of their crimes. Fulfilling that ambition would take me 30 years.

13   Meanwhile, I followed the literary path that Miss Hurd had so forcefully set me on. After junior high, I became the editor of my school paper at Classical High School and got a part-time job at the Worcester *Telegram and Gazette*. Although my father could only give me $50 and encouragement toward a college education, I managed to finance four years at Boston University with scholarships and part-time jobs in journalism. During my last year of college, an article I wrote about a friend who had died in the Philippines—the first

person to lose his life working for the Peace Corps—led to my winning the Hearst Award for College Journalism. And the plaque was given to me in the White House by President John F. Kennedy.

14   For a refugee who had never seen a motorized vehicle or indoor plumbing until he was 9, this was an unimaginable honor. When the Worcester paper ran a picture of me standing next to President Kennedy, my father rushed out to buy a new suit in order to be properly dressed to receive the congratulations of the Worcester Greeks. He clipped out the photograph, had it laminated in plastic and carried it in his breast pocket for the rest of his life to show everyone he met. I found the much-worn photo in his pocket on the day he died 20 years later.

15   In our isolated Greek village, my mother had bribed a cousin to teach her to read, for girls were not supposed to attend school beyond a certain age. She had always dreamed of her children receiving an education. She couldn't be there when I graduated from Boston University, but the person who came with my father and shared our joy was my former teacher, Marjorie Hurd. We celebrated not only my bachelor's degree but also the scholarship that paid my way to Columbia's Graduate School of Journalism. There, I met the woman who would eventually become my wife. At our wedding and at the baptisms of our three children, Marjorie Hurd was always there, dancing alongside the Greeks.

16   By then, she was Mrs. Rabidou, for she had married a widower when she was in her early 40s. That didn't distract her from her vocation of introducing young minds to English literature, however. She taught for a total of 41 years and continually would make a "project" of some balky student in whom she spied a spark of potential. Often these were students from the most troubled homes, yet she would alternately bully and charm each one with her own special brand of tough love until the spark caught fire. She retired in 1981 at the age of 62 but still avidly follows the lives and careers of former students while overseeing her adult stepchildren and driving her husband on camping trips to New Hampshire.

17   Miss Hurd was one of the first to call me on Dec. 10, 1987, when President Reagan, in his television address after the summit meeting with Gorbachev, told the nation that Eleni Gatzoyiannis' dying cry, "My children!" had helped inspire him to seek an arms agreement "for all the children of the world."

18   "I can't imagine a better monument for your mother," Miss Hurd said with an uncharacteristic catch in her voice.

19   Although a bad hip makes it impossible for her to join in the Greek dancing, Marjorie Hurd Rabidou is still an honored and enthusiastic guest at all family celebrations, including my 50th birthday picnic last summer, where the shish kebab was cooked on spits, clarinets and *bouzoukis* wailed, and costumed dancers led the guests in a serpentine line around our Colonial farmhouse, only 20 minutes from my first home in Worcester.

20　My sisters and I felt an aching void because my father was not there to lead the line, balancing a glass of wine on his head while he danced, the way he did at every celebration during his 92 years. But Miss Hurd was there, surveying the scene with quiet satisfaction. Although my parents are gone, her presence was a consolation, because I owe her so much.

21　This is truly the land of opportunity, and I would have enjoyed its bounty even if I hadn't walked into Miss Hurd's classroom in 1953. But she was the one who directed my grief and pain into writing, and if it weren't for her I wouldn't have become an investigative reporter and foreign correspondent, recorded the story of my mother's life and death in *Eleni* and now my father's story in *A Place for Us,* which is also a testament to the country that took us in. She was the catalyst that sent me into journalism and indirectly caused all the good things that came after. But Miss Hurd would probably deny this emphatically.

22　A few years ago, I answered the telephone and heard my former teacher's voice telling me, in that won't-take-no-for-an-answer tone of hers, that she had decided I was to write and deliver the eulogy at her funeral. I agreed (she didn't leave me a choice), but that's one assignment I never want to do. I hope, Miss Hurd, that you'll accept this remembrance instead.

Understanding Content

1. When the author first arrived in the United States, how did he feel about his father?
2. How did the author feel about his father later, as an adult? What do you think caused him to change his view?
3. In what ways did Miss Hurd affect Gage's life?
4. Why is spring a difficult time of year for Gage?
5. What is Gage's attitude toward the United States?

Considering Structure and Technique

1. What approach does Gage take to his introduction? Do you like his opening? Explain.
2. Although the essay is about Miss Hurd, Gage provides a great deal of information about the life of his family. Why does he provide this information?
3. In paragraph 5, the author explains how he met Miss Hurd. Is this information important? Why or why not?
4. How does Gage show Miss Hurd's continuing importance in his life as an adult?
5. The essay includes both description and narration. What do each of these contribute?

Exploring Ideas

1. Why do you think Gage responded so positively to Miss Hurd's story assignments, the ones mentioned in paragraph 7?
2. Why was his student essay about Greece so meaningful to Gage? Although it was meaningful, Gage did not want to see the essay again after it was written. Why?
3. How would you describe Miss Hurd's relationship to Gage?
4. Who are the individuals that made a difference in Gage's life? How did they make a difference?

Writing Workshop: Including a Statement of Purpose

Writers write for one or a combination of purposes: to share, to inform, to entertain, to persuade. Most of the time, a writer's purpose is implied, but at times it is specifically stated. This is the case in "The Teacher Who Changed My Life," where Gage's purpose—to write a tribute to his teacher—is stated in the final paragraph: "I hope, Miss Hurd, that you'll accept this remembrance instead."

A word of caution: If you choose to state your purpose, avoid statements like "The purpose of this essay is . . . " or "The following paragraphs will show . . . ." Such expressions are often used in business and technical writing, but they are generally considered weak style in college essays.

Writing Workshop Activity

Read or reread "You're Short, Besides" (p. 356). Which sentence or sentences state the author's purpose?

Language Notes for Multilingual and Other Writers

The word *so* has several uses, three of which are illustrated in "The Teacher Who Changed My Life."

1. To introduce clauses that show purpose (sometimes used with *that*):

   She died <u>so that</u> her children could go to their father in the United States. Paragraph 2

   One day, I vowed, I would go back to Greece, find out the details of my mother's death and write about her life, <u>so</u> her grandchildren would know of her courage. Paragraph 12

2. To introduce clauses and sentences that show result:

"This is the Newspaper Club! We're going to put out a *newspaper*. <u>So</u> if there's anybody in this room who doesn't like to work, I suggest you go across to the Glee Club now. . . . " Paragraph 6

3. To show intensity:

Meanwhile, I followed the literary path that Miss Hurd had <u>so</u> forcefully set me on. Paragraph 13

From Reading to Writing

In Your Journal: Write about an individual who had a significant impact on you, someone who influenced the course your life has taken.

With Some Classmates: Discuss the special circumstances and problems Gage faced as a young student in the United States. Do others today cope with similar circumstances and problems? If so, do you think schools do enough to help these students? Explain.

In an Essay

- As a child, Gage resented his father, but as an adult, he expresses affection and admiration for the man. Compare and contrast how you felt about someone when you were a child and how you feel about that person now.
- Miss Hurd was responsible for Gage's becoming a journalist. Tell about what influenced you to take a particular path in life.
- Gage tells about the first time he met Miss Hurd. Tell about your first encounter with someone who was or is important to you.
- Narrate an account of an ordinary person who is driven by circumstances to "do something extraordinary" (paragraph 7).

Beyond the Writing Class: Write a tribute to a teacher or other person who made a difference in your life. If the person is still alive, mail it to him or her. If the person is a teacher who is deceased, mail it to the school where the person taught. If the person is deceased but was not a teacher, try to locate a relative to mail the tribute to.

So Tsi-fai
SOPHRONIA LIU

An actor, writer, and educator who left Hong Kong for the United States when she was 20, Sophronia Liu earned her master's degree in English from the University of South Dakota. The following selection was first published in *Hurricane Alice,* a feminist journal, in 1986.

Preview.   "So Tsi-fai" is a tragic tale of a peasant's son who did not survive the sixth grade. Was he unlucky, or did social, economic, and educational pressures doom him to failure? Or was he just lazy and uninterested? Before you read to learn the answers, consider the pressures you experience as a student. How much pressure do you feel? What causes the pressure? Do your family and friends help you cope with the pressure? If you do not experience pressure, explain why not.

Vocabulary.   If any of the following words from the selection are unfamiliar to you, study their meanings before reading.

rash (2)   acting quickly, without thinking
defiant (3)   resisting authority and rules
sneer (3)   to smile with hatred or contempt
• **incorrigible** (3)   incapable of being reformed
• **scourge** (4)   a person who bothers others
lenient (4)   easy
grant-in-aid (5)   a form of financial aid used to pay for school
dilated (11)   expanded
ether (12)   a general anesthetic
• **imperceptible** (13)   slight or barely noticeable
• **lusterless** (13)   without shine
green (17)   inexperienced
• **arbitrates** (18)   decides

Voices, images, scenes from the past—twenty-three years ago, when I was in sixth grade:
2   "Let us bow our heads in silent prayer for the soul of So Tsi-fai. Let us pray for God's forgiveness for this boy's rash taking of his own life . . . " Sister Marie (Mung Gu-liang). My sixth-grade English teacher. Missionary nun from Paris. Principal of The Little Flower's School. Disciplinarian, perfectionist, authority figure: awesome and awful in my ten-year-old eyes.

3   "I don't need any supper. I have drunk enough insecticide." So Tsi-fai. My fourteen-year-old classmate. Daredevil; good-for-nothing lazybones (according to Mung Gu-liang). Bright black eyes, disheveled hair, defiant sneer, creased and greasy uniform, dirty hands, careless walk, shuffling feet. Standing in the corner for being late, for forgetting his homework, for talking in class, for using foul language. ("Shame on you! Go wash your mouth with soap!" Mung Gu-liang's sharp command. He did, and came back with a grin.) So Tsi-fai: Sticking his tongue out behind Mung Gu-liang's back, passing secret notes to his friends, kept behind after school, sent to the Principal's office for repeated offense. So Tsi-fai: incorrigible, hopeless, and without hope.

4   It was a Monday, in late November when we heard of his death, returning to school after the weekend with our parents' signatures on our midterm reports. So Tsi-fai also showed his report to his father, we were told later. He flunked three out of fourteen subjects: English Grammar, Arithmetic, and Chinese Dictation. He missed each one by one to three marks. That wasn't so bad. But he was a hopeless case. Overaged, stubborn, and uncooperative; a repeated offender of school rules, scourge of all teachers; who was going to give him a lenient passing grade? Besides, being a few months over the maximum age—fourteen—for sixth graders, he wasn't even allowed to sit for the Secondary School Entrance Exam.

5   All sixth graders in Hong Kong had to pass the SSE before they could obtain a seat in secondary school. In 1964 when I took the exam, there were more than twenty thousand candidates. About seven thousand of us passed: four thousand were sent to government and subsidized schools, the other three thousand to private and grant-in-aid schools. I came in around no. 2000; I was lucky. Without the public exam, there would be no secondary school for So Tsi-fai. His future was sealed.

6   Looking at the report card with three red marks on it, his father was furious. So Tsi-fai was the oldest son. There were three younger children. His father was a vegetable farmer with a few plots of land in Wong Jukhang, by the sea. His mother worked in a local factory. So Tsi-fai helped in the fields, cooked for the family and washed his own clothes. ("Filthy, dirty boy!" gasped Mung Gu-liang. "Grime behind the ears, black rims on the fingernails, dirty collar, crumpled shirt. Why doesn't your mother iron your shirt?") Both his parents were illiterate. So Tsi-fai was their biggest hope: He made it to the sixth grade.

7   Who woke him up for school every morning and had breakfast waiting for him? Nobody. ("Time for school! Get up! Eat your rice!" Ma nagged and screamed. The aroma of steamed rice and Chinese sausages spread all over the house. "Drink your tea! Eat your oranges! Wash your face! And remember to wash behind your ears!") And who helped So Tsi-fai do his homework? Nobody. Did he have older brothers like mine who knew all about the arithmetic of rowing a boat against the currents or with the currents, how to count the feet of chickens and rabbits in the same cage, the present perfect continuous

tense of "to live" and the future perfect tense of "to succeed"? None. Nil. So Tsi-fai was a lost cause.

8   I came first in both terms that year, the star pupil. So Tsi-fai was one of the last in the class: he was lazy; he didn't care. Or did he?

9   When his father scolded him, So Tsi-fai left the house. When he showed up again, late for supper, he announced, "I don't need any supper. I have drunk enough insecticide." Just like another one of his practical jokes. The insecticide was stored in the field for his father's vegetables. He was rushed to the hospital; dead upon arrival.

10   "He gulped for a last breath and was gone," an uncle told us at the \funeral. "But his eyes wouldn't shut. So I said in his ear, 'You go now and rest in peace.' And I smothered my hands over his eyelids. His face was all purple."

11   His face was still purple when we saw him in his coffin. Eyes shut tight, nostrils dilated and white as if fire and anger might shoot out, any minute.

12   In class that Monday, Sister Marie led us in prayer. "Let us pray that God will forgive him for his sins." We said the Lord's Prayer and the Hail Mary. We bowed our heads. I sat in my chair, frozen and dazed, thinking of the deadly chill in the morgue, the smell of disinfectant, ether, and dead flesh.

13   "Bang!" went a gust of wind, forcing open a leaf of the double door leading to the back balcony. "Flap, flap, flap." The door swung in the wind. We could see the treetops by the hillside rustling to and fro against a pale blue sky. An imperceptible presence had drifted in with the wind. The same careless walk and shuffling feet, the same daredevil air—except that the eyes were lusterless, dripping blood; the tongue hanging out, gasping for air. As usual, he was late. But he had come back to claim his place.

14   "I died a tragic death," his voice said. "I have as much right as you to be here. This is my seat." We heard him; we knew he was back.

15   . . . So Tsi-fai: Standing in the corner for being late, for forgetting his homework, for talking in class, for using foul language. So Tsi-fai: palm outstretched, chest sticking out, holding his breath: "Tat. Tat. Tat." Down came the teacher's wooden ruler, twenty times on each hand. Never batting an eyelash: then back to facing the wall in the corner by the door. So Tsi-fai: grimy shirt, disheveled hair, defiant sneer. So Tsi-fai. Incorrigible, hopeless, and without hope.

16   The girls in front gasped and shrank back in their chairs. Mung Gu-liang went to the door, held the doorknob in one hand, poked her head out, and peered into the empty balcony. Then, with a determined jerk, she pulled the door shut. Quickly crossing herself, she returned to the teacher's desk. Her black cross swung upon the front of her gray habit as she hurried across the room. "Don't be silly!" she scolded the frightened girls in the front row.

17   What really happened? After all these years, my mind is still haunted by this scene. What happened to So Tsi-fai? What happened to me? What happened to all of us that year in sixth grade, when we were green and young and

ready to fling our arms out for the world? All of a sudden, death claimed one of us and he was gone.

18   Who arbitrates between life and death? Who decides which life is worth preserving and prospering, and which to nip in its bud? How did it happen that I, at ten, turned out to be the star pupil, the lucky one, while my friend, a peasant's son, was shoveled under the heap and lost forever? How could it happen that this world would close off a young boy's life at fourteen just because he was poor, undisciplined, and lacked training and support to pass his exams? What really happened?

19   Today, twenty-three years later, So Tsi-fai's ghost still haunts me. "I died a tragic death. I have as much right as you to be here. This is my seat." The voice I heard twenty-three years ago in my sixth-grade classroom follows me in my dreams. Is there anything I can do to lay it to rest?

Understanding Content

1. What kinds of pressure was So Tsi-fai experiencing in sixth grade?
2. Using the information in the essay, explain what So Tsi-fai was like.
3. What point do you think Liu is trying to make in "So Tsi-fai"?

Considering Structure and Technique

1. Paragraphs 1, 2, 3, and 15 are made of **sentence fragments** (sentence parts punctuated as if they were sentences). What effect is created with these sentence fragments?
2. In what kinds of order are the details arranged?
3. What contrast is set up in the essay? What purpose does that contrast serve?

Exploring Ideas

1. On the basis of the information in the essay, how would you describe The Little Flower's School that Liu and So Tsi-fai attended?
2. How would you describe So Tsi-fai's relationship with his family?
3. Why do you think So Tsi-fai killed himself?
4. Does the author believe that So Tsi-fai did poorly in school because he was lazy and because he did not care? Explain.
5. Liu and her classmates were haunted by So Tsi-fai after his death, and the last paragraph indicates that Liu continues to be haunted. Why are the author and her classmates unable to shake the memory of So Tsi-fai?

Writing Workshop: Conveying a Dominant Impression

It is impossible to describe every aspect of a subject, so writers make their task manageable by settling on a dominant impression and describing only those features that convey that dominant impression. (The **dominant impression** is the writer's main feeling about what is being described.) Anything unrelated to the dominant impression can be ignored. For example, in paragraph 2, Liu describes only those features of the teacher that show her as stern and frightening to the students. (*Stern* and *frightening* are the dominant impressions.) In paragraph 3, she describes only those features that convey the dominant impression that So Tsi-fai is an outcast who is always in trouble. In paragraphs 7 and 8, she describes only those features that convey the dominant impression that So Tsi-fai is an isolated child struggling through life without support.

Writing Workshop Activity

For each of the following, write a word or phrase that expresses your dominant impression, and then write a sentence that helps convey that impression.

example: a friend

Mario/forgetful: When Mario finally picked his daughter up at school an hour late, he explained that he ran out of gas because he never checked his gas gauge.

a teacher	a boss or coach	a celebrity
a relative	a politician	a friend

Language Notes for Multilingual and Other Writers

In English, many words can function as both nouns and verbs. The part of speech will depend on the way the word is used: as a **noun,** the word will name a person, place, thing or idea; as a **verb,** it will show action. Here are some examples taken from "So Tsi-fai."

chill

noun: I sat in my chair, frozen and dazed, thinking of the deadly <u>chill</u> in the morgue. . . . Paragraph 12

verb: Before serving the dessert, <u>chill</u> it for several hours.

sins

noun: " . . . God will forgive him for his <u>sins.</u>" Paragraph 12

verb: The priest is worried about the child who <u>sins</u> regularly.

walk

noun: The same careless <u>walk</u> and shuffling feet . . . Paragraph 13

verb: Each morning Carlotta and I <u>walk</u> three miles before breakfast.

place

noun: But he had come back to claim his <u>place.</u> Paragraph 13

verb: <u>Place</u> your napkin on your lap before you begin to eat.

hand

noun: Down came the teacher's wooden ruler, twenty times on each <u>hand.</u> Paragraph 15

verb: The waiter asked the diner to <u>hand</u> him the empty water glass.

jerk

noun: Then, with a determined <u>jerk,</u> she pulled the door shut. Paragraph 16

verb: <u>Jerk</u> the cord to open the blinds.

From Reading to Writing

In Your Journal. Why do you think "So Tsi-fai" appears here in the chapter titled "The Individual in Society"?

With Some Classmates: To advance past the sixth grade, students in Hong Kong must pass the Secondary School Entrance Exam. In fact, many countries require students to pass examinations in order to enter high school and/or college. Argue for or against requiring students in the United States to pass certain tests before being allowed to graduate from high school. As an alternative, argue for or against requiring students to pass certain tests before entering college.

In an Essay

- Pick one of your present or former classmates and use description to convey a dominant impression about the kind of student that person was or is. (See paragraph 3 of "So Tsi-fai" for a brief example of using description to convey a dominant impression of a student.) As an alternative, use description to convey a dominant impression of a teacher you have or had in the past. (See paragraph 2 of "So Tsi-fai" for a brief example of using description to convey a dominant impression of a teacher.)
- Compare and contrast So Tsi-fai's life as a student with your own. What pressures do you share, and what circumstances of your academic lives are similar? In what ways is your life as a student different from So Tsi-fai's?
- When you were in elementary and high school, was there someone like So Tsi-fai who was considered to be "hopeless"? That is, was there someone who always seemed to fail and remain on the outside looking in? Describe

that person and narrate a story or two that illustrates what academic life was like for him or her.

- Do you think that students like So Tsi-fai exist in the United States? If so, explain who they are, what their circumstances are, and how their needs should be met. Try to use some description to create a dominant impression.
- In paragraph 18, Liu says that she was the lucky one and So Tsi-fai was the unlucky one. Tell about a circumstance in your life that makes you either lucky or unlucky and explain how you have been affected by this circumstance.

Beyond the Writing Class: Now that you are in college, do you think changes are needed in the school system from which you graduated (or the system your children currently attend)? If so, write a position paper addressed to the local board of education that explains in detail one change that should be made and how that change would improve the schools.

Just Walk On By: A Black Man Ponders His Power to Alter Public Space

BRENT STAPLES

Brent Staples earned his Ph.D. in psychology from the University of Chicago. A member of the *New York Times* editorial board, Staples was also a reporter for the *Chicago Sun-Times.* He has written for the *New York Times Magazine, Harper's,* and *New York Woman.* His memoir *Parallel Time: Growing Up Black and White* was published in 1994. The following selection appeared in *Ms.* magazine in 1986 and in a revised form in *Harper's* in 1987. In it, Staples explains that "being perceived as dangerous is a hazard in itself."

Preview.   People often make assumptions about each other on the basis of appearance. Study yourself in a full-length mirror. On the basis of your physical features (size, skin color, and so forth), the way you dress, and the way you move, what kind of impression do you think a stranger would form of you after seeing you for the first time? How would the stranger judge your age, social class, level of intelligence, economic level, occupation, and such? Why would the stranger draw these conclusions? Respond to these questions in a page or so of your journal.

Vocabulary.   If any of the following words from the selection are unfamiliar to you, study their meanings before reading.

affluent (1)   wealthy
quarry (2)   an animal being hunted
accomplice in tyranny (2)   a person who helps keep others in someone's power
foyer (2)   entrance hall
errant (2)   wrong
SoHo (4)   a section in New York where artists live and show their work
taut (4)   tense
infamous (5)   having a bad reputation
extols (5)   praises highly
warrenlike (6)   crowded (like a warren, where rabbits live)
bandolier (6)   a belt that holds bullets that is worn over the chest and shoulder
retrospect (7)   thinking of the past
bravado (9)   pretended courage

ad hoc (10)   formed for a specific purpose
labyrinthine (10)   like a maze
cursory (11) brief and superficial
constitutionals (14) walks

My first victim was a woman—white, well dressed, probably in her early twenties. I came upon her late one evening on a deserted street in Hyde Park, a relatively affluent neighborhood in an otherwise mean, impoverished section of Chicago. As I swung onto the avenue behind her, there seemed to be a discreet, uninflammatory distance between us. Not so. She cast back a worried glance. To her, the youngish black man—a broad six feet two inches with a beard and billowing hair, both hands shoved into the pockets of a bulky military jacket—seemed menacingly close. After a few more quick glimpses, she picked up her pace and was soon running in earnest. Within seconds she disappeared into a cross street.

2   That was more than a decade ago. I was 22 years old, a graduate student newly arrived at the University of Chicago. It was in the echo of that terrified woman's footfalls that I first began to know the unwieldy inheritance I'd come into—the ability to alter public space in ugly ways. It was clear that she thought herself the quarry of a mugger, a rapist, or worse. Suffering a bout of insomnia, however, I was stalking sleep, not defenseless wayfarers. As a softy who is scarcely able to take a knife to raw chicken—let alone hold it to a person's throat—I was surprised, embarrassed, and dismayed all at once. Her flight made me feel like an accomplice in tyranny. It also made it clear that I was indistinguishable from the muggers who occasionally seeped into the area from the surrounding ghetto. That first encounter, and those that followed, signified that a vast, unnerving gulf lay between nighttime pedestrians—particularly women—and me. And I soon gathered that being perceived as dangerous is a hazard in itself. I only needed to turn a corner into a dicey situation, or crowd some frightened, armed person in a foyer somewhere, or make an errant move after being pulled over by a policeman. Where fear and weapons meet—and they often do in urban America—there is always the possibility of death.

3   In that first year, my first away from my hometown, I was to become thoroughly familiar with the language of fear. At dark, shadowy intersections in Chicago, I could cross in front of a car stopped at a traffic light and elicit the *thunk, thunk, thunk, thunk* of the driver—black, white, male, or female—hammering down on the door locks. On less traveled streets after dark, I grew accustomed to but never comfortable with people who crossed to the other side of the street rather than pass me. Then there were the standard unpleasantries with police, doormen, bouncers, cab drivers, and others whose business it is to screen out troublesome individuals *before* there is any nastiness.

4   I moved to New York nearly two years ago and I have remained an avid night walker. In central Manhattan, the near-constant crowd cover minimizes tense one-on-one street encounters. Elsewhere—visiting friends in SoHo, where sidewalks are narrow and tightly spaced buildings shut out the sky—things can get very taut indeed.

5   Black men have a firm place in New York mugging literature. Norman Podhoretz in his famed (or infamous) 1963 essay, "My Negro Problem—And Ours," recalls growing up in terror of black males; they "were tougher than we were, more ruthless," he writes—and as an adult on the Upper West Side of Manhattan, he continues, he cannot constrain his nervousness when he meets black men on certain streets. Similarly, a decade later, the essayist and novelist Edward Hoagland extols a New York where once "Negro bitterness bore down mainly on other Negroes." Where some see mere panhandlers, Hoagland sees "a mugger who is clearly screwing up his nerve to do more than just *ask* for money." But Hoagland has "the New Yorker's quick-hunch posture for broken-field maneuvering," and the bad guy swerves away.

6   I often witness that "hunch posture," from women after dark on the warrenlike streets of Brooklyn where I live. They seem to set their faces on neutral and, with their purse straps strung across their chests bandolier style, they forge ahead as though bracing themselves against being tackled. I understand, of course, that the danger they perceive is not a hallucination. Women are particularly vulnerable to street violence, and young black males are drastically overrepresented among the perpetrators of that violence. Yet these truths are not solace against the kind of alienation that comes of being ever the suspect, against being set apart, a fearsome entity with whom pedestrians avoid making eye contact.

7   It is not altogether clear to me how I reached the ripe old age of 22 without being conscious of the lethality nighttime pedestrians attributed to me. Perhaps it was because in Chester, Pennsylvania, the small, angry industrial town where I came of age in the 1960s, I was scarcely noticeable against a backdrop of gang warfare, street knifings, and murders. I grew up one of the good boys, had perhaps a half-dozen fist fights. In retrospect, my shyness of combat has clear sources.

8Many things go into the making of a young thug. One of those things is the consummation of the male romance with the power to intimidate. An infant discovers that random flailings send the baby bottle flying out of the crib and crashing to the floor. Delighted, the joyful babe repeats those motions again and again, seeking to duplicate the feat. Just so, I recall the points at which some of my boyhood friends were finally seduced by the perception of themselves as tough guys. When a mark cowered and surrendered his money without resistance, myth and reality merged—and paid off. It is, after all, only manly to embrace the power to frighten and intimidate. We, as men, are not supposed to give an inch of our lane on the highway; we are to seize the fighter's edge in work and in play and even in love; we are to be valiant in the face of hostile forces.

9   Unfortunately, poor and powerless young men seem to take all this nonsense literally. As a boy, I saw countless tough guys locked away; I have since buried several, too. They were babies really—a teenage cousin, a brother of 22, a childhood friend in his mid-twenties—all gone down in episodes of bravado played out in the streets. I came to doubt the virtues of intimidation early on. I chose, perhaps even unconsciously, to remain a shadow—timid, but a survivor.

10   The fearsomeness mistakenly attributed to me in public places often has a perilous flavor. The most frightening of these confusions occurred in the late 1970s and early 1980s when I worked as a journalist in Chicago. One day, rushing into the office of a magazine I was writing for with a deadline story in hand, I was mistaken for a burglar. The office manager called security and, with an ad hoc posse, pursued me through the labyrinthine halls, nearly to my editor's door. I had no way of proving who I was. I could only move briskly toward the company of someone who knew me.

11   Another time I was on assignment for a local paper and killing time before an interview. I entered a jewelry store on the city's affluent Near North Side. The proprietor excused herself and returned with an enormous red Doberman pinscher straining at the end of a leash. She stood, the dog extended toward me, silent to my questions, her eyes bulging nearly out of her head. I took a cursory look around, nodded, and bade her good night. Relatively speaking, however, I never fared as badly as another black male journalist. He went to nearby Waukegan, Illinois, a couple of summers ago to work on a story about a murderer who was born there. Mistaking the reporter for the killer, police hauled him from his car at gunpoint and but for his press credentials would probably have tried to book him. Such episodes are not uncommon. Black men trade tales like this all the time.

12   In "My Negro Problem—And Ours," Podhoretz writes that the hatred he feels for blacks makes itself known to him through a variety of avenues—one being his discomfort with that "special brand of paranoid touchiness" to which he says blacks are prone. No doubt he is speaking here of black men. In time, I learned to smother the rage I felt at so often being taken for a criminal. Not to do so would surely have led to madness—via that special "paranoid touchiness" that so annoyed Podhoretz at the time he wrote the essay.

13   I began to take precautions to make myself less threatening. I move about with care, particularly late in the evening. I give a wide berth to nervous people on subway platforms during the wee hours, particularly when I have exchanged business clothes for jeans. If I happen to be entering a building behind some people who appear skittish, I may walk by, letting them clear the lobby before I return, so as not to seem to be following them. I have been calm and extremely congenial on those rare occasions when I've been pulled over by the police.

14   And on late-evening constitutionals along streets less traveled by, I employ what has proved to be an excellent tension-reducing measure: I whistle melodies from Beethoven and Vivaldi and the more popular classical composers. Even steely New Yorkers hunching toward nighttime destinations seem to relax, and occasionally they even join in the tune. Virtually everybody seems to sense that a mugger wouldn't be warbling bright, sunny selections from Vivaldi's *Four Seasons*. It is my equivalent of the cowbell that hikers wear when they know they are in bear country.

Understanding Content

1. According to Staples, why is it a problem to be perceived as dangerous?
2. How does the perception of him as dangerous pose a threat to Staples? What problems has he encountered as a result?
3. Staples believes that to some extent, the fear of young black males is reasonable. Why?
4. According to Staples, why do some young black males turn to street violence? Why didn't Staples himself fall into a life of violence?
5. What does Staples say causes a young man to become a thug?

Considering Structure and Technique

1. When you read the opening two sentences of the essay, what did you think the essay would be about? Were your expectations fulfilled?
2. In your own words, write out the thesis of "Just Walk On By." Which sentence or sentences in the essay come closest to expressing that thesis?
3. Which paragraphs use brief examples to illustrate a point? (See the workshop on examples on p. 488.) Which paragraphs use narration (a story) to illustrate a point? (See the workshop on narration on p. 79.) What main contrast appears in the essay? (See the workshop on contrast on p. 116.)
4. Why does Staples describe himself in the opening paragraph?

Exploring Ideas

1. What does Staples mean when he refers to his "ability to alter public space in ugly ways" (paragraph 2)?
2. Why do you think Staples refers to Norman Podhoretz's 1963 essay and Edward Hoagland's ideas?
3. Staples says that he "began to take precautions to make [himself] less threatening" (paragraph 13). How successful do you think those precautions are? Explain.
4. How do you suppose Staples has been affected by the fact that he is perceived as a threat?

Writing Workshop: Using Specific Verbs

Verbs often show action, and to make the action vivid (clear and lively), use specific verbs. For example, Staples makes the action vivid by using the following specific verbs (underlined here as a study aid):

As I <u>swung</u> onto the avenue . . . Paragraph 1

. . . I was <u>stalking</u> sleep . . . Paragraph 2

. . . they <u>forge</u> ahead . . . Paragraph 6

Notice how much clearer and livelier these three examples are than the following revisions, written without specific verbs.

As I <u>went</u> onto the avenue . . .

. . . I was <u>looking</u> <u>for</u> sleep . . .

. . . they <u>go</u> ahead . . .

Specific verbs are not always called for, but to make the action clear and lively, specific verbs are a good tool.

Writing Workshop Activity

Look back over "Just Walk On By" and find three examples of specific verbs. Then find at least five examples of specific verbs in other selections in this book. Copy the sentences into your journals and underline the specific verbs.

Language Notes for Multilingual and Other Writers

The **past tense,** which is the verb tense used for actions that began and ended in the past, is often used with time expressions such as *last week, two years ago, yesterday, in January,* and *another day.* Some examples from "Just Walk On By" are given here, with the time expressions and past tense forms underlined as a study aid.

1. <u>In that first year,</u> my first away from my hometown, I <u>was</u> to become thoroughly familiar with the language of fear. Paragraph 3
2. I <u>moved</u> to New York nearly <u>two years ago.</u> . . . Paragraph 4
3. The most frightening of these confusions <u>occurred in the late 1970s.</u> . . . Paragraph 10
4. <u>Another time</u> I <u>was</u> on assignment for a local paper. . . . Paragraph 11
5. He <u>went</u> to nearby Waukegan, Illinois, <u>a couple of summers ago.</u> . . . Paragraph 11

From Reading to Writing

In Your Journal: Do your experience and observation bear out Staples's conclusion that young black males are perceived to be threatening? Try to cite an example or two to support your view.

With Some Classmates: Pick a person from the following list and explain how such a person is perceived by others and how the perception affects that person. If you do not have firsthand knowledge, interview someone for information.

a well-dressed person	a poorly dressed person
a very good-looking person	a very muscular person
a physically disabled person	a very tall person
a very short person	a male with long hair

In an Essay

- In the community where you grew up, could you feel safe walking the streets alone? Explain why or why not.
- In paragraph 8, Staples notes what goes into "the making of a young thug." He explains that it is "only manly to embrace the power to frighten and intimidate." As a result, Staples concludes, "We, as men, are not supposed to give an inch of our lane on the highway; we are to seize the fighter's edge in work and in play and even in love; we are to be valiant in the face of hostile forces." Do you agree that this is how society interprets masculinity? Use examples from your own experience and observation to support your view, and then go on to evaluate the effects of society's concepts of masculinity.
- Tell about a time when you were perceived to he a threat or when you perceived someone else to he a threat. What happened? How did you feel? What if anything, did you learn? As an alternative, tell about a time when you were perceived to be something you are not.

Beyond the Writing Class: In paragraph 6, Staples reports the fact that "young black males are drastically overrepresented among the perpetrators of [street] violence." Interview an instructor in sociology, urban studies, and/or black studies, and then explain why this phenomenon exists. Also, try to offer a solution to the problem.

Growing Up Asian in America
KESAYA E. NODA

Japanese-American Kesaya E. Noda teaches at Lesley College in Massachusetts. After high school she made her first visit to Japan, but since then she has worked and traveled in Japan a number of years. "Growing Up Asian in America" comes from *Making Waves,* which was published in 1989.

Preview. In "Growing Up Asian in America," Kesaya E. Noda describes three aspects of her identity as she attempts to define herself from the inside and from the outside. Try to identify yourself by answering this question in no more than three sentences: Who am I?

Vocabulary. If any of the following words from the selection are unfamiliar to you, study their meanings before reading.

allusions (1)   references to
influx (3)   coming in
Shinto (6)   a Japanese religion
timidity (11)   shyness; a lack of courage
arduously (18)   with difficulty
pluralism (32)   a theory whereby minority groups fully participate in the
    dominant society yet maintain their cultural differences
harangued (32)   scolded or attacked verbally

Sometimes when I was growing up, my identity seemed to hurtle toward me and paste itself right to my face. I felt that way, encountering the stereotypes of my race perpetuated by non-Japanese people (primarily white) who may or may not have had contact with other Japanese in America. "You don't like cheese, do you?" someone would ask. "I know your people don't like cheese." Sometimes questions came making allusions to history. That was another aspect of the identity. Events that had happened quite apart from the me who stood silent in that moment connected my face with an incomprehensible past. "Your parents were in California? Were they in those camps during the war?" And sometimes there were phrases or nicknames: "Lotus Blossom." I was sometimes addressed or referred to as racially Japanese, sometimes as Japanese-American, and sometimes as an Asian woman. Confusions and distortions abounded.

2   How is one to know and define oneself? From the inside—within a context that is self-defined from a grounding in community and a connection with

culture and history that are comfortably accepted? Or from the outside—in terms of messages received from the media and people who are often ignorant? Even as an adult I can still see two sides of my face and past. I can see from the inside out, in freedom. And I can see from the outside in, driven by the old voices of childhood and lost in anger and fear.

3   **I Am Racially Japanese.** A voice from my childhood says: "You are other. You are less than. You are unalterably alien." This voice has its own history. We have indeed been seen as other and alien since the early years of our arrival in the United States. The very first immigrants were welcomed and sought as laborers to replace the dwindling numbers of Chinese, whose influx had been cut off by the Chinese Exclusion Act of 1882. The Japanese fell natural heir to the same anti-Asian prejudice that had arisen against the Chinese. As soon as they began striking for better wages, they were no longer welcomed.

4   I can see myself today as a person historically defined by law and custom as being forever alien. Being neither "free white," nor "African," our people in California were deemed "aliens, ineligible for citizenship," no matter how long they intended to stay here. Aliens ineligible for citizenship were prohibited from owning, buying, or leasing land. They did not and could not belong here. The voice in me remembers that I am always a *Japanese*-American in the eyes of many. A third-generation German-American is an American. A third-generation Japanese-American is a Japanese-American. Being Japanese means being a danger to the country during the war and knowing how to use chopsticks. I wear this history on my face.

5   I move to the other side. I see a different light and claim a different context. My race is a line that stretches across ocean and time to link me to the shrine where my grandmother was raised. Two high, white banners lift in the wind at the top of the stone steps leading to the shrine. It is time for the summer festival. Black characters are written against the sky as boldly as the clouds, as lightly as kites, as sharply as the big black crows I used to see above the fields in New Hampshire. At festival time there is liquor and food, ritual, discipline, and abandonment. There is music and drunkenness and invocation. There is hope. Another season has come. Another season has gone.

6   I am racially Japanese. I have a certain claim to this crazy place where the prayers intoned by a neighboring Shinto priest (standing in for my grandmother's nephew who is sick) are drowned out by the rehearsals for the pop singing contest in which most of the villagers will compete later that night. The village elders, the priest, and I stand respectfully upon the immaculate, shining wooden floor of the outer shrine, bowing our heads before the hidden powers. During the patchy intervals when I can hear him, I notice the priest has a stutter. His voice flutters up to my ears only occasionally because two men and a woman are singing gustily into a microphone in the compound, testing the sound system. A prerecorded tape of guitars, samisens, and drums accompanies them. Rock music and Shinto prayers. That night, to loud applause and

cheers, a young man is given the award for the most *netsuretsu*—passionate, burning—rendition of a song. We roar our approval of the reward. Never mind that his voice had wandered and slid, now slightly above, now slightly below the given line of the melody. Netsurersu. Netsuretsu.

7   In the morning, my grandmother's sister kneels at the foot of the stone stairs to offer her morning prayers. She is too crippled to climb the stairs, so each morning she kneels here upon the path. She shuts her eyes for a few seconds, her motions as matter of fact as when she washes rice. I linger longer than she does, so reluctant to leave, savoring the connection I feel with my grandmother in America, the past, and the power that lives and shines in the morning sun.

8   Our family has served this shrine for generations. The family's need to protect this claim to identity and place outweighs any individual claim to any individual hope. I am Japanese.

9   **I Am a Japanese-American.** "Weak." I hear the voice from my childhood years. "Passive," I hear. Our parents and grandparents were the ones who were put into those camps. They went without resistance; they offered cooperation as proof of loyalty to America. "Victim," I hear. And, "Silent."

10   Our parents are painted as hard workers who were socially uncomfortable and had difficulty expressing even the smallest opinion. Clean, quiet, motivated, and determined to match the American way; that is us, and that is the story of our time here.

11   "Why did you go into those camps?" I raged at my parents, frightened by my own inner silence and timidity. "Why didn't you do anything to resist? Why didn't you name it the injustice it was?" Couldn't our parents even think? Couldn't they? Why were we so passive?

12   I shift my vision and my stance. I am in California. My uncle is in the midst of the sweet potato harvest. He is pressed, trying to get the harvesting crews onto the field as quickly as possible, worried about the flow of equipment and people. His big pickup is pulled off to the side, motor running, door ajar. I see two tractors in the yard in front of an old shed: the flatbed harvesting platform on which the workers will stand has already been brought over from the other field. It's early morning. The workers stand loosely grouped and at ease, but my uncle looks as harried and tense as a police officer trying to unsnarl a New York City traffic jam. Driving toward the shed, I pull my car off the road to make way for an approaching tractor. The front wheels of the car sink luxuriously into the soft, white sand by the roadside and the car slides to a dreamy halt, tail still on the road. I try to move forward. I try to move back. The front bites contentedly into the sand, the back lifts itself at a jaunty angle. My uncle sees me and storms down the road, running. He is shouting before he is even near me.

13   "What's the matter with you?" he screams. "What the hell are you doing?" In his frenzy, he grabs his hat off his head and slashes it through the air

across his knee. He is beside himself. "Don't you know how to drive in sand? What's the matter with you? You've blocked the whole roadway. How am I supposed to get my tractors out of here? Can't you use your head? You've cut off the whole roadway, and we've got to get out of here."

14   I stand on the road before him helplessly thinking, "No, I don't know how to drive in sand. I've never driven in sand."

15   I'm sorry, uncle," I say, burying a smile beneath a look of sincere apology. I notice my deep amusement and my affection for him with great curiosity. I am usually devastated by anger. Not this time.

16   During the several years that follow I learn about the people and the place, and much more about what has happened in this California village where my parents grew up. The issei, our grandparents, made this settlement in the desert. Their first crops were eaten by rabbits and ravaged by insects. The land was so barren that men walking from house to house sometimes got lost. Women came here too. They bore children in 114-degree heat, then carried the babies with them into the fields to nurse when they reached the end of each row of grapes or other truck-farm crops.

17   I had had no idea what it meant to buy this kind of land and make it grow green. Or how, when the war came, there was no space at all for the subtlety of being who we were—Japanese-Americans. Either/or was the way. I hadn't understood that people were literally afraid for their lives then, that their money had been frozen in banks; that there was a five-mile travel limit; that when the early evening curfew came and they were inside their houses, some of them watched helplessly as people they knew went into their barns to steal their belongings. The police were patrolling the road, interested only in violators of curfew. There was no help for them in the face of thievery. I had not been able to imagine before what it must have felt like to be an American— to know absolutely that one is an American—and yet to have almost everyone else deny it. Not only deny it, but challenge that identity with machine guns and troops of white American soldiers. In those circumstances it was difficult to say, "I'm a Japanese-American." "American" had to do.

18   But now I can say that I am a Japanese-American. It means I have a place here in this country, too. I have a place here on the East Coast, where our neighbor is so much a part of our family that my mother never passes her house at night without glancing at the lights to see if she is home and safe; where my parents have hauled hundreds of pounds of rocks from fields and arduously planted Christmas trees and blueberries, lilacs, asparagus, and crab apples, where my father still dreams of angling a stream to a new bed so that he can dig a pond in the field and fill it with water and fish. "The neighbors already came for their Christmas tree?" he asks in December. "Did they like it? Did they like it?"

19   I have a place on the West Coast where my relatives still farm, where I heard the stories of feuds and backbiting, and where I saw that people survived and flourished because fundamentally they trusted and relied upon one an-

other. A death in the family is not just a death in a family; it is a death in the community. I saw people help each other with money, materials, labor, attention, and time. I saw men gather once a year, without fail, to clean the grounds of a ninety-year-old woman who had helped the community before, during, and after the war. I saw her remembering them with birthday cards sent to each of their children.

20   I come from a people with a long memory and a distinctive grace. We live our thanks. And we are Americans. Japanese-Americans.

21   **I Am a Japanese-American Woman.** Woman. The last piece of my identity. It has been easier by far for me to know myself in Japan and to see my place in America than it has been to accept my line of connection with my own mother. She was my dark self, a figure in whom I thought I saw all that I feared most in myself. Growing into womanhood and looking for some model of strength, I turned away from her. Of course, I could not find what I sought. I was looking for a black feminist or a white feminist. My mother is neither white nor black.

22   My mother is a woman who speaks with her life as much as with her tongue. I think of her with her own mother. Grandmother had Parkinson's disease and it had frozen her gait and set her fingers, tongue, and feet jerking and trembling in a terrible dance. My aunts and uncles wanted her to be able to live in her own home. They fed her, bathed her, dressed her, awoke at midnight to take her for one last trip to the bathroom. My aunts (her daughters-in-law) did most of the care, but my mother went from New Hampshire to California each summer to spend a month living with Grandmother because she wanted to and because she wanted to give my aunts at least a small rest. During those hot summer days, mother lay on the couch watching the television or reading, cooking foods that Grandmother liked, and speaking little. Grandmother thrived under her care.

23   The time finally came when it was too dangerous for Grandmother to live alone. My relatives kept finding her on the floor beside her bed when they went to wake her in the mornings. My mother flew to California to help clean the house and make arrangements for Grandmother to enter a local nursing home. On her last day at home, while Grandmother was sitting in her big, overstuffed armchair, hair combed and wearing a green summer dress, my mother went to her and knelt at her feet. "Here, Mamma," she said. "I've polished your shoes." She lifted Grandmother's legs and helped her into the shiny black shoes. My Grandmother looked down and smiled slightly. She left her house walking, supported by her children, carrying her pocket book, and wearing her polished black shoes. "Look, Mamma," my mom had said, kneeling. "I've polished your shoes."

24   Just the other day, my mother came to Boston to visit. She had recently lost a lot of weight and was pleased with her new shape and her feeling of good health. "Look at me, Kes," she exclaimed, turning toward me, front and back,

as naked as the day she was born. I saw her small breasts and the wide, brown scar, belly button to pubic hair, that marked her because my brother and I were both born by Caesarean section. Her hips were small. I was not a large baby, but there was so little room for me in her that when she was carrying me she could not even begin to bend over toward the floor. She hated it, she said.

25   "Don't I look good? Don't you think I look good?"

26   I looked at my mother smiling and as happy as she, thinking of all the times I have seen her naked. I have seen both my parents naked throughout my life, as they have seen me. From childhood through adulthood we've had our naked moments, sharing baths, idle conversations picked up as we moved between showers and closets, hurried moments at the beginning of days, quiet moments at the end of days.

27   I know this to be Japanese, this ease with the physical, and it makes me think of an old Japanese folk song. A young nursemaid, a fifteen-year-old girl, is singing a lullaby to a baby who is strapped to her back. The nursemaid has been sent as a servant to a place far from her own home. "We're the beggars," she says, "and they are the nice people. Nice people wear fine sashes. Nice clothes."

> If I should drop dead,
> bury me by the roadside!
> I'll give a flower
> to everyone who passes.
> What kind of flower?
> The cam-cam-camellia *[tsun-tsun-tsuhaki]*
> watered by Heaven:
> alms water.

28   The nursemaid is the intersection of heaven and earth, the intersection of the human, the natural world, the body, and the soul. In this song, with clear eyes, she looks steadily at life, which is sometimes so very terrible and sad. I think of her while looking at my mother, who is standing on the red and purple carpet before me, laughing, without any clothes.

29   I am my mother's daughter. And I am myself.

30   I am a Japanese-American woman.

31   **Epilogue.** I recently heard a man from West Africa share some memories of his childhood. He was raised Muslim but when he was a young man, he found himself deeply drawn to Christianity. He struggled against his inner impulse for years, trying to avoid the church yet feeling pushed to return to it again and again. "I would have done *anything* to avoid the change," he said. At last, he became Christian. Afterwards he was afraid to go home, fearing that he would not be accepted. The fear was groundless, he discovered, when at last he returned—he had separated himself, but his family and friends (all Muslim) had not separated themselves from him.

32   The man, who is now a professor of religion, said that in the Africa he knew as a child and a young man, pluralism was embraced rather than feared. There was "a kind of tolerance that did not deny your particularity," he said. He alluded to zestful, spontaneous debates that would sometimes loudly erupt between Muslims and Christians in the village's public spaces. His memories of an atheist who harangued the villagers when he came to visit them once a week moved me deeply. Perhaps the man was an agricultural advisor or inspector. He harassed the women. He would say: "Don't go to the fields! Don't even bother to go to the fields. Let God take care of you. He'll send you the food. If you believe in God, why do you need to work? You don't need to work! Let God put the seeds in the ground. Stay home."

33   The professor said, "The women laughed, you know? They just laughed. Their attitude was, 'Here is a child of God. When will he come home?' "

34   The storyteller, the professor of religion, smiled a most fantastic tender smile as he told this story. "In my country, there is a deep affirmation of the oneness of God," he said. "The atheist and the women were having quite different experiences in their encounter, though the atheist did not know this. He saw himself as quite separate from the women. But the women did not see themselves as being separate from him. 'Here is a child of God,' they said. 'When will he come home?' "

Understanding Content

1. According to the author, who is responsible for perpetuating the stereotype of the Japanese?
2. Explain the confusion the author feels about how to identify herself.
3. What are the three components of Noda's identity?
4. What did you learn about the life, history, or culture of Japanese-Americans as a result of reading "Growing Up Asian in America"?

Considering Structure and Technique

1. What is the effect of the single-word sentence fragment that closes paragraph 20? What is the effect of the single-word fragment that opens paragraph 21?
2. What is the function of the narration in paragraphs 21 through 24?
3. What purpose do the ends of paragraphs 8, 20, and 30 serve? What do these paragraphs have in common?
4. An **epilogue** is a concluding statement added on to an essay as an appendix. How does Noda's epilogue relate to the rest of her essay?

Exploring Ideas

1. What do you think Noda means when she says that her "identity seemed to hurtle toward [her] and paste itself right to [her] face" (paragraph 1)?
2. What do paragraphs 3 through 8 suggest about how the Japanese feel about their ancestors?
3. What do you think Noda means when she says that "when the war came there was no space at all for the subtlety of being who we were—Japanese-Americans" (paragraph 17)?
4. Why do you think the author equates her mother with her dark self, "a figure in whom [Noda] thought [she] saw all that [she] feared most in [herself]" (paragraph 21)?

Writing Workshop: Writing Anecdotes

Anecdotes are brief stories that writers use to illustrate their points. For example, in "Growing Up Asian in America," paragraphs 22 and 23 provide an anecdote that illustrates the character of the author's mother and the fact that she "speaks with her life." Paragraphs 24 and 25 contain an anecdote that illustrates Japanese attitudes toward the naked body. In addition to illustrating a point, anecdotes are often lively and interesting, so they help a writer keep the reader's attention. To discover anecdotes to include in your writing, draw on your own experience and those of people you know. Also, draw on your own observations. (For related workshops on narration, see pp. 79 and 87.)

Writing Workshop Activity

Pick a word, phrase, or sentence commonly spoken by you, your family, or your friends. You can select a current slang expression, an ethnic term (such as *chutzpah* or *gringo*), or special term of endearment used in your family. Write an anecdote to illustrate the use of that expression.

Language Notes for Multilingual and Other Writers

Homophones are words that sound alike but that have different meanings, and often different spellings. "Growing Up Asian in America" illustrates the use of three common English homophones: *to, too,* and *two.*

1. *To* can be part of an infinitive or a preposition indicating direction.

> as part of an infinitive: "Why didn't you do anything <u>to resist?</u>" Paragraph 11

> to indicate direction: . . . my identity seemed to hurtle toward me and paste itself right <u>to</u> my face. Paragraph 1

2. *Too* can mean "excessively" or "also."

excessively: She is <u>too</u> crippled to climb the stairs. . . . Paragraph 7

also: It means I have a place here in this country, <u>too.</u> Paragraph 18

3. *Two* is the number.

Even as an adult I can still see <u>two</u> sides of my face and past. Paragraph 2

From Reading to Writing

In Your Journal: In the epilogue, the atheist and the women have two different experiences. What accounts for the difference? Which experience would you have under similar circumstances? What makes you think so?

With Some Classmates: In the library or on the Internet, learn a little about what Japanese-Americans experienced during World War II. Then write a report explaining what happened.

In an Essay

- Who was or is your role model for "growing into womanhood" or manhood (paragraph 21)? Explain why you have that model and specifically how that person has influenced you.
- Noda explains how her identity is defined by her race, gender, and nationality. Pick one of these factors and explain how it has influenced your identity. Use specific examples or anecdotes to illustrate your points.
- In paragraph 3, Noda says that she feels "unalterably alien." That is, she does not feel "American." Explain what you think it means to be "American."

Beyond the Writing Class: Unless you are Native American, your ancestors came to the United States from somewhere else. Speak to one or more of your relatives to learn where your relatives came from and what one or more of them experienced when they came to this country. If you like, you may do some library or Internet reading for information. (If you yourself are not originally from this country, you may write about your own experiences here.)

Beauty: When the Other Dancer Is the Self

ALICE WALKER

Born to Georgia sharecroppers in 1944, Alice Walker is the youngest of eight children. A poet, essayist, and novelist who won a Pulitzer Prize for *The Color Purple* (1982), Walker was active in the civil rights movement and registered voters in Georgia, taught in the Head Start program in Mississippi, and worked in the welfare department in New York City. The autobiographical essay which appears here comes from Walker's *In Search of Our Mothers' Gardens: Womanist Prose* (1983).

Preview.   Walker explains the effects of a disfiguring accident on her self-concept. How do you feel about the way *you* look? Do you like your appearance? How does your view affect the way you interact with others? Does it affect your self-esteem?

Vocabulary.   If any of the following words from the essay are unfamiliar to you, study their meanings before reading.

subversive (1)   tending to go against established beliefs
beribboning (1)   putting ribbons in
faze (2)   disturb
scallop (4)   having rounded edges; shaped like a scallop
crinolines (4)   stiff slips worn to bell out a skirt
Tom Mix, Hopalong Cassidy, Lash LaRue (8)   movie cowboys of the 1930s
damsels (8)   maidens
relegated (8)   placed in an inferior position
throes (14)   violent struggles
boisterous (16)   rough and noisy
reputedly (19)   according to popular belief
abscess (25)   swollen, inflamed tissue with a collection of puss

I t is a bright summer day in 1947. My father, a fat, funny man with beautiful eyes and a subversive wit, is trying to decide which of his eight children he will take with him to the county fair. My mother, of course, will not go. She is knocked out from getting most of us ready. I hold my neck stiff against the pressure of her knuckles as she hastily completes the braiding and beribboning of my hair.

2   My father is the driver for the rich old white lady up the road. Her name is Miss Mey. She owns all the land for miles around, as well as the house in which we live. All I remember about her is that she once offered to pay my mother thirty-five cents for cleaning her house, raking up piles of her magnolia leaves, and washing her family's clothes, and that my mother—she of no money, eight children, and a chronic earache—refused it. But I do not think of this in 1947. I am two and a half years old. I want to go everywhere my daddy goes. I am excited at the prospect of riding in a car. Someone has told me fairs are fun. That there is room in the car for only three of us doesn't faze me at all. Whirling happily in my starchy frock, showing off my biscuit-polished patent-leather shoes and lavender socks, tossing my head in a way that makes my ribbons bounce, I stand hands on hips, before my father. "Take me, Daddy," I say with assurance; "I'm the prettiest!"

3   Later, it does not surprise me to find myself in Miss Mey's shiny black car, sharing the back seat with the other lucky ones. Does not surprise me that I thoroughly enjoy the fair. At home that night I tell the unlucky ones all I can remember about the merry-go-round, the man who eats live chickens, and the teddy bears, until they say: that's enough, baby Alice. Shut up now, and go to sleep.

4   It is Easter Sunday, 1950. I am dressed in a green, flocked, scalloped-hem dress (handmade by my adoring sister Ruth) that has its own smooth satin petticoat and tiny hot-pink roses tucked into each scallop. My shoes, new T-strap patent leather, again highly biscuit-polished. I am six years old and have learned one of the longest Easter speeches to be heard that day, totally unlike the speech I said when I was two: "Easter lilies / pure and white / blossom in / the morning light." When I rise to give my speech I do so on a great wave of love and pride and expectation. People in the church stop rustling their new crinolines. They seem to hold their breath. I can tell they admire my dress, but it is my spirit, bordering on sassiness (womanishness), they secretly applaud.

5   "That girl's a little *mess*," they whisper to each other, pleased.

6   Naturally I say my speech without stammer or pause, unlike those who stutter, stammer, or, worst of all, forget. This is before the word "beautiful" exists in people's vocabulary, but "Oh, isn't she the *cutest* thing!" frequently floats my way. "And got so much sense!" they gratefully add . . . for which thoughtful addition I thank them to this day.

7   *It was great fun being cute. But then, one day, it ended.*

8   I am eight years old and a tomboy. I have a cowboy hat, cowboy boots, checkered shirt and pants, all red. My playmates are my brothers, two and four years older than I. Their colors are black and green, the only difference in the way we are dressed. On Saturday nights we all go the picture show, even my mother; Westerns are her favorite kind of movie. Back home, "on the ranch," we pretend we are Tom Mix, Hopalong Cassidy, Lash LaRue (we've even named one of our dogs Lash LaRue); we chase each other for hours rustling cattle, being outlaws, delivering damsels from distress. Then my parents decide to buy my brothers guns. These are not "real" guns. They shoot "BBs," copper

pellets my brothers say will kill birds. Because I am a girl, I do not get a gun. Instantly I am relegated to the position of Indian. Now there appears a great distance between us. They shoot and shoot at everything with their new guns. I try to keep up with my bow and arrows.

9   One day while I am standing on top of our makeshift "garage"—pieces of tin nailed across some poles—holding my bow and arrow and looking out toward the fields, I feel an incredible blow in my right eye. I look down just in time to see my brother lower his gun.

10   Both brothers rush to my side. My eye stings, and I cover it with my hand. "If you tell," they say, "we will get a whipping. You don't want that to happen, do you?" I do not. "Here is a piece of wire," says the older brother picking it up from the roof; "say you stepped on one end of it and the other flew up and hit you." The pain is beginning to start. "Yes," I say, "Yes, I will say that is what happened." If I do not say this is what happened, I know my brothers will find ways to make me wish I had. But now I will say anything that gets me to my mother.

11   Confronted by our parents we stick to the lie agreed upon. They place me on a bench on the porch and I close my left eye while they examine the right. There is a tree growing from underneath the porch that climbs past the railing to the roof. It is the last thing my right eye sees. I watch as its trunk, its branches, and then its leaves are blotted out by the rising blood.

12   I am in shock. First there is intense fever, which my father tries to break using lily leaves bound around my head. Then there are chills: my mother tries to get me to eat soup. Eventually, I do not now how, my parents learn what has happened. A week after the "accident" they take me to see a doctor. "Why did you wait so long to come?" he asks, looking into my eye and shaking his head. "Eyes are sympathetic," he says. "If one is blind, the other will likely become blind too."

13   This comment of the doctor's terrifies me. But it is really how I look that bothers me most. Where the BB pellet struck there is a glob of whitish scar tissue, a hideous cataract, on my eye. Now when I stare at people—a favorite pastime, up to now—they will stare back. Not at the "cute" little girl, but at her scar. For six years I do not stare at anyone, because I do not raise my head.

14   Years later, in the throes of a mid-life crisis, I ask my mother and sister whether I changed after the "accident." "No," they say, puzzled. "What do you mean?"

15   *What do I mean?*

16   I am eight, and, for the first time, doing poorly in school, where I have been something of a whiz since I was four. We have just moved to the place where the "accident" occurred. We do not know any of the people around us because this is a different county. The only time I see the friends I knew is when we go back to our old church. The new school is the former state penitentiary. It is a large stone building, cold and drafty, crammed to overflowing with boisterous, ill-disciplined children. On the third floor there is a huge circular imprint of some partition that has been torn out.

17   "What used to be here?" I ask a sullen girl next to me on our way past it to lunch.

18   "The electric chair," says she.

19   At night I have nightmares about the electric chair, and about all the people reputedly "fried" in it. I am afraid of the school, where all the students seem to be budding criminals.

20   "What's the matter with your eye?" they ask, critically.

21   When I don't answer (I cannot decide whether it was an "accident" or not), they shove me, insist on a fight.

22   My brother, the one who created the story about the wire, comes to my rescue. But then brags so much about "protecting" me, I become sick.

23   After months of torture at the school, my parents decide to send me back to our old community, to my old school. I live with my grandparents and the teacher they board. But there is no room for Phoebe, my cat. By the time my grandparents decide there *is* room, and I ask for my cat, she cannot be found. Miss Yarborough, the boarding teacher, takes me under her wing, and begins to teach me to play the piano. But soon she marries an African—a "prince," she says—and is whisked away to his continent.

24   At my old school there is at least one teacher who loves me. She is the teacher who "knew me before I was born" and bought my first baby clothes. It is she who makes life bearable. It is her presence that finally helps me turn on the one child at the school who continually calls me "one-eyed bitch." One day I simply grab him by his coat and beat him until I am satisfied. It is my teacher who tells me my mother is ill.

25   My mother is lying in bed in the middle of the day, something I have never seen. She is in too much pain to speak. She has an abscess in her ear. I stand looking down on her, knowing that if she dies, I cannot live. She is being treated with warm oils and hot bricks held against her cheek. Finally a doctor comes. But I must go back to my grandparents' house. The weeks pass but I am hardly aware of it. All I know is that my mother might die, my father is not so jolly, my brothers still have their guns, and I am the one sent away from home.

26   "You did not change," they say.

27   *Did I imagine the anguish of never looking up?*

28   I am twelve. When relatives come to visit I hide in my room. My cousin Brenda, just my age, whose father works in the post office and whose mother is a nurse, comes to find me. "Hello," she says. And then she asks, looking at my recent school picture, which I did not want taken, and on which the "glob," as I think of it, is clearly visible, "You still can't see out of that eye?"

29   "No," I say and flop back on the bed over my book.

30   That night, as I do almost every night, I abuse my eye. I rant and rave at it, in front of the mirror. I plead with it to clear up before morning. I tell it I hate and despise it. I do not pray for sight, I pray for beauty.

31   "You did not change," they say.

32   I am fourteen and baby-sitting for my brother Bill, who lives in Boston. He is my favorite brother and there is a strong bond between us. Understanding my feelings of shame and ugliness he and his wife take me to a local hospital, where the "glob" is removed by a doctor named O. Henry. There is still a small bluish center where the scar tissue was, but the ugly white stuff is gone. Almost immediately I become a different person from the girl who does not raise her head. Or so I think. Now that I've raised my head I win the boyfriend of my dreams. Now that I've raised my head I have plenty of friends. Now that I've raised my head classwork comes from my lips as faultlessly as Easter speeches did, and I leave high school as valedictorian, most popular student, and *queen,* hardly believing my luck. Ironically, the girl who was voted most beautiful in our class (and was) was later shot twice through the chest by a male companion, using a "real" gun, while she was pregnant. But that's another story in itself. Or is it?

33 "You did not change," they say.

34 It is now thirty years since the "accident." A beautiful journalist comes to visit and to interview me. She is going to write a cover story for her magazine that focuses on my latest book. "Decide how you want to look on the cover," she says. "Glamorous, or whatever."

35 Never mind "glamorous," it is the "whatever" that I hear. Suddenly all I can think of is whether I will get enough sleep the night before the photography session: if I don't, my eye will be tired and wander, as blind eyes will.

36 At night in bed with my lover I think up reasons why I should not appear on the cover of a magazine. "My meanest critics will say I've sold out," I say. "My family will now realize I write scandalous books."

37 "But what's the real reason you don't want to do this?" he asks.

38 "Because in all probability," I say in a rush, "my eye won't be straight."

39 "It will be straight enough," he says. Then, "Besides, I thought you'd made your peace with that."

40 And I suddenly remember that I have.

41 *I remember:*

42 I am talking to my brother Jimmy, asking if he remembers anything unusual about the day I was shot. He does not know I consider that day the last time my father, with his sweet home remedy of cool lily leaves, chose me, and that I suffered and raged inside because of this. "Well," he says, "all I remember is standing by the side of the highway with Daddy, trying to flag down a car. A white man stopped, but when Daddy said he needed somebody to take his little girl to the doctor, he drove off."

43 *I remember:*

44 I am in the desert for the first time. I fall totally in love with it. I am so overwhelmed by its beauty, I confront for the first time, consciously, the meaning of the doctor's words years ago: "Eyes are sympathetic. If one is blind, the other will likely become blind too." I realize I have dashed about the world madly, looking at this, looking at that, storing up images against the fading of the light. *But I might have missed seeing the desert!* The shock of that possibility—and gratitude for over twenty-five years of sight—sends me literally to my knees. Poem after poem comes—which is perhaps how poets pray.

45

46

ON SIGHT

I am so thankful I have seen
The Desert
And the creatures in the desert
And the desert Itself.

47

The desert has its own moon
Which I have seen
With my own eye.
There is no flag on it.

48

Trees of the desert have arms
All of which are always up
That is because the moon is up
The sun is up
Also the sky
The stars
Clouds
None with flags.

49

If there *were* flags, I doubt
the trees would point.
Would you?

50   *But mostly, I remember this:*

51   I am twenty-seven, and my baby daughter is almost three. Since her birth I have worried about her discovery that her mother's eyes are different from other people's. Will she be embarrassed? I think. What will she say? Every day she watches a television program called "Big Blue Marble." It begins with a picture of the earth as it appears from the moon. It is bluish, a little battered-looking, but full of light, with whitish clouds swirling around it. Every time I see it I weep with love, as if it is a picture of Grandma's house. One day when I am putting Rebecca down for her nap, she suddenly focuses on my eye. Something inside me cringes, gets ready to try to protect myself. All children are cruel about physical differences. I know from experience, and that they don't always mean to is another matter. I assume Rebecca will be the same.

52   But no-o-o-o. She studies my face intently as we stand, her inside and me outside her crib. She even holds my face maternally between her dimpled little hands. Then, looking every bit as serious and lawyerlike as her father, she says, as if it may just possibly have slipped my attention: "Mommy, there's a *world* in your eye. (As in, "Don't be alarmed, or do anything crazy.") And then, gently, but with great interest: "Mommy, where did you get that world in your eye?"

53   For the most part, the pain left then. (So what, if my brothers grew up to buy even more powerful pellet guns for their sons and to carry real guns themselves. So what, if a young "Morehouse man" once nearly fell off the steps of

Trevor Arnett Library because he thought my eyes were blue.) Crying and laughing I ran to the bathroom, while Rebecca mumbled and sang herself off to sleep. Yes indeed, I realized, looking into the mirror. There *was* a world in my eye. And I saw that it was possible to love it: that in fact, for all it had taught me of shame and anger and inner vision, I did love it. Even to see it drifting out of orbit in boredom, or rolling up out of fatigue, not to mention floating back at attention in excitement (bearing witness, a friend has called it), deeply suitable to my personality, and even characteristic of me.

54   That night I dream I am dancing to Stevie Wonder's song "Always" (the name of the song is really "As," but I hear it as "Always"). As I dance, whirling and joyous, happier than I've ever been in my life, another bright-faced dancer joins me. We dance and kiss each other and hold each other through the night. The other dancer has obviously come through all right, as I have done. She is beautiful, whole and free. And she is also me.

Understanding Content

1. How did Walker see herself before her injury?
2. How is Walker affected by the loss of her eye?
3. How was Walker affected by her daughter's reaction to her eye? Why did the child react the way she did?
4. Why does Walker come to love her eye?
5. What incident of racism is highlighted in the essay?

Considering Structure and Technique

1. Walker opens with two anecdotes (brief stories). What purpose do these anecdotes serve? (For a workshop on anecdotes, see p. 209.)
2. Why do you think Walker includes the poem and her reaction to the desert?
3. Walker repeats the words "You did not change" a number of times. Why does she do this?
4. In what order does Walker arrange the details in "Beauty: When the Other Dancer Is the Self"?

Exploring Ideas

1. Why do you think Walker did poorly in school after the accident, when she had been doing well in school before the accident? Why did she perform well in school again when the scar tissue was removed?
2. How do you explain the meaning of the dream described in the last paragraph?
3. What point about beauty do you think Walker is making in her essay?
4. What do you think the title of the essay means?

Writing Workshop: Using Present Participles as Modifiers

The *-ing* form of a verb (called the **present participle**) can be used as a modifier (descriptive word). This can be seen in the following sentences taken from "Beauty: When the Other Dancer Is the Self." (The *-ing* modifiers are underlined, and an arrow is drawn to the word each describes.)

Whirling happily in my starchy frock, showing off my biscuit-polished patent-leather shoes and lavender socks, tossing my head in a way that makes my ribbons bounce I stand . . . Paragraph 2

Later, It does not surprise me to find myself in Miss Mey's shiny block car, sharing the back seat with the other lucky ones. Paragraph 3

Crying and laughing I ran to the bathroom . . . Paragraph 53

As I dance, whirling and joyous, happier than I've ever been in my life, another bright-faced dancer joins me. Paragraph 54

Notice that in these examples the underlined *-ing* forms are not the main verbs in the sentences but verb forms that act like modifiers describing other words. Including present participles is one way you can vary the structure of your sentences. For more on varying sentence structure, see the workshop on sentence openers on p. 257.

Writing Workshop Activity

Write sentences using the following *-ing* verb forms (present participles). Be sure to include a noun or pronoun that the *-ing* form can describe. (The first two are done as examples.)

1. laughing all the while

   Jill and Kristin worked on their biology project, laughing all the while.

2. speaking quickly

   Speaking quickly, Antoine explained how to get to Route 11.

3. whistling softly
4. finishing before everyone else
5. while listening to the radio
6. feeling drowsy
7. smiling
8. slamming the door with a bang
9. after seeing Dr. Hanks across the room
10. limping slightly

Language Notes for Multilingual and Other Writers

Ordinarily, events that occurred in the past are written about in the **past tense**. However, the **historical present tense** is used for events that occurred in the past when those events are actions in a book, movie, television show, essay, article, or other written material. The historical present tense is used because the action, although written in the past, occurs in the present for the reader.

In *Gone with the Wind*, Scarlett O'Hara <u>vows</u> never to be hungry again.

In her novels, Barbara Kingsolver <u>examines</u> friendship among women.

In "Beauty: When the Other Dancer Is the Self," Alice Walker uses the historical present tense to describe actions that occurred in her past:

It <u>is</u> a bright summer day in 1947. Paragraph 1

I <u>am</u> eight years old and a tomboy. Paragraph 8

At night I <u>have</u> nightmares about the electric chair. . . . Paragraph 19

She <u>studies</u> my face intently as we <u>stand</u>, her inside and me outside and her crib. Paragraph 52

Walker's use of the historical present tense emphasizes that the actions in the essay continue to exist in her present time—they are just that vivid, immediate, and significant to her here and now.

From Reading to Writing

In Your Journal: If Walker could have changed one aspect of her appearance, she would have made her disfigured eye normal again. If you could change one thing about yourself, what would it be? How do you think your interactions with people would change as a result?

With Some Classmates: Use the evidence in the essay to tell what Walker's parents and siblings were like. Also explain how you think her immediate family affected Walker's reaction to her injured eye.

In an Essay

- For Walker, the injury to her eye marked a turning point, a time when everything changed. Write about a turning point in your life or in someone else's. What caused the turning point, and how did things change?

- How does physical appearance influence the way we view ourselves and others? Illustrate your view with examples from your own experience and observation. (Your preview activity may give you some ideas.)
- Some people say that physical beauty can be a curse because it gets in the way of relationships. Other people become jealous, or they do not want to associate with someone who is attractive because they feel inferior. Some also say that very attractive people are not taken seriously; they are thought to be unintelligent and superficial. What do you think? Respond and illustrate your view with examples from your own observation, experience, and television and movie viewing.
- If you had to choose between being very attractive and not very intelligent or being unattractive but very intelligent, which would you choose? Explain why.
- In paragraph 24, Walker mentions the teacher who "ma[de] life bearable" for her. Tell about someone who helped you through a difficult time.

Beyond the Writing Class: Standards of beauty are culturally determined. Thus, different cultures find different physical features "beautiful." Interview someone from another culture and/or do some research. Then compare and contrast the standards for male or female attractiveness in your culture with that of the culture you researched. As an alternative, look at magazines of 30 or more years ago and discuss how standards of beauty have changed over time.

Fighting to Fill the Values Gap
MELISSA HEALY

Melissa Healy, a staff writer for the *Los Angeles Times,* wrote the following selection for that newspaper in 1996. In it, she reports the belief of those who claim the United States is sliding into serious moral decline. Although these people tend to distrust efforts to legislate morality, they do address the problem in their own way.

Preview.   A 1996 Los Angeles Times poll asked Americans if they were satisfied or dissatisfied with current moral values. What percentage of respondents do you think said they were satisfied? What percentage do you think said they were dissatisfied?

Vocabulary.   If any of the following words from the essay are unfamiliar to you, study their meanings before reading.

chastise (2)   scold, discipline
spewing expletives (3)   swearing vigorously
curtail (4)   reduce
bleeding-heart liberal (5)   a negative term for a person on the political left, who is judged to be excessively sympathetic to liberal political beliefs
litany (23)   a long, boring recitation
wrenching (31)   causing mental pain
double-edged sword (32)   an expression that refers to having two ways to think of something
perennial (34)   enduring
demographers (34)   pollsters or statisticians
demographic (34)   relating to population distribution and balance
body politic (34)   group of people under one government
arbiters (37)   judges
flout (41)   scoff at
acrimonious (50)   harsh and biting
exhorts (51)   cautions
bellwethers (61)   leaders or guides

"**V**alues? *Values???*" asks 37-year-old Lila Robinson, her pitch rising as she warms to her subject. "I've been waiting for someone to ask me about this for years! Hold on a sec, let me get my soapbox!"

2   For Robinson, proof of the nation's moral slide is everywhere. She is irked by the kids who tromp down the grass as they cut across the lawn of her

family's new home in Brunswick, Ohio. She gets even more steamed when she dares not chastise the teenage trespassers for fear trouble might ensue.

3   She fumes over a kid punching loaves of bread in the supermarket and over his mother spewing expletives when a stranger suggests he stop. She smolders over a sister's divorce and the fact that the parents play their children off one another.

4   Yet she has little use for politicians and activists who patter on about family values and seek to legislate common virtues, such as civility, compassion, respect and responsibility. She suspects that they would like to curtail some of the freedoms she cherishes.

5   Robinson, a "bleeding-heart liberal who realizes the government can't do it all," prefers to take matters into her own hands. Acknowledging candidly that "some of the things I did when I was single and crazed were wrong," she is determined to teach her children to avoid her mistakes—without denying that she made them.

6   Robinson's worries—as well as her response—put her on the front lines of a social movement that has millions of foot soldiers but few, if any, field marshals. Convinced that the nation is suffering from a values decline of crisis proportions, more and more Americans are fighting back.

7   Some have embraced legislative remedies ranging from tightening up divorce laws to restricting welfare benefits. Others, like Robinson, are wary of government intervention and believe that the answer lies within communities, families and individuals—including themselves.

8   At home, she and others are making more time for their children by returning to family meals or turning off the TV. Others are reaching out to neighbors to organize fathers' groups or plan new school curricula designed to teach good character.

9   While many still tend to blame others for society's ills, a sizable minority says it is willing to change its behavior and accept some limits on civil liberties for the common good. Thus, moved by concern for plunging social standards, they agree to make their kids wear uniforms to public school, or they embrace technologies that would black out unwanted TV programs at home.

10   "There's a growing sense that we stand at a cultural crossroads," said Thomas Lickona, an education professor at the State University of New York, Cortland, and a leader of the character education movement. "Either we reverse the current trends or continue the slide and go down the tubes."

11   For many Americans, particularly baby boomers now entering middle age, the values movement is an attempt to synthesize the best elements of the "do-your-own-thing" philosophy of the 1960s and '70s with the social stability of an earlier era.

12   "We're having a debate now we simply couldn't have 15 years ago," said William Galston, 50, a public administration professor at the University of Maryland and a former domestic policy advisor to President Clinton. "I don't

think we're going to end up back in the 1950s, but I don't think we're going to remain tied to the kind of revolt against the 1950s. We are looking for a new balance."

13   Amitai Etzioni, a George Washington University professor, leads the "communitarian" movement that helped launch the current debate. He asserts that when Americans limit their behavior for the good of the community, they do not feel as if they have made sacrifices or forfeited freedoms. They feel as if their personal choices have helped build a more cohesive, supportive community.

14   "Today, everybody's free to do anything, but it's not what they want," Etzioni said. "It's not liberating; it's not freedom." The debate over values and what to do about them, he adds, "is a clear indication we're groping for new ways to come together and, yes, impose some requirements on ourselves."

15   Mention the V-word across the country and you will hear the hiss and bubble of a thousand stories boiling over the top. Some come from the TV news or the headlines, but most originate in their tellers' backyards, schools and workplaces. Stories of friends on welfare getting pregnant again, of whole college classes conspiring to cheat on a test. Stories of parents worried sick that nice clothes may mark their children for violence.

16   The stories reflect a powerful feeling among Americans that the nation's sense of right and wrong—its moral compass—is dangerously out of kilter. "It just seems like not many people have morals," said Myorka Cummings, a 24-year-old homemaker in Marshalltown, Iowa. "They don't seem to care about their neighbor. They'd just as soon rob him as come over and say hi."

17   Americans, notes pollster Peter Hart, "look at all the basics of our society and see them going in a direction they're uncomfortable with. They look at schools and they see violence. That scares them. They look at the media and they see [TV] programs they find unacceptable and that go beyond bounds of public decency. They look at athletic fields and see behavior they do not consider good sportsmanship. They look at the institution of family and marriage and they see breakups."

18   In a Los Angeles Times Poll conducted nationwide April 13-16, *year?* 78% of respondents said they were dissatisfied with today's moral values. Of that group, 47% identified family issues such as divorce, working parents and undisciplined children as the main causes. Another 34% blamed a breakdown in personal responsibility and community involvement.

19   The anxieties cross lines of race, age, gender, income and region. They spread well beyond the political bounds of religious conservatives, who have dominated debate on family values for much of the past decade.

20   Charles Dewane, a 27-year-old unmarried father in Detroit, says he "is trying to go the right way—the straight and narrow." He is engaged to the mother of his child, he says, and he takes an active role in his care.

21   As he sees it, the trouble with society is "punk parents raising kids, not giving their kids any values or morals." A self-described member of "a lost ed-

FIGURE 1   *Result of the Times Poll on Moral Values*

An overwhelming majority of Americans say they are dissatisfied with the nation's moral values these days. They cite the breakdown of the family unit as one of the top reasons for their discontent. Therefore, it is not surprising that many agree that it is better to raise children in a house where there are two parents and that divorce should be made more difficult to obtain.

Satisfied or dissatisfied?
Would you say you are satisfied or dissatisfied with moral values these days?

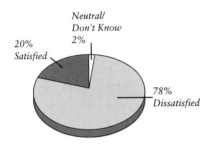

Parents' role
Do you agree or disagree with the following statement: "Parents today are not taking enough responsibility for teaching their kids moral values?"

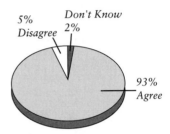

Why they're dissatisfied
Why are you dissatisfied with the nation's moral values? (among respondents who say they are dissatisfied; two answers accepted; net answers shown)

Breakdown in family	47%
Lack of community involvement	34
Crime	12
Too much sex/violence in movies/TV	11
Lack of religion	5
Schools not strict enough/ should teach civics	5

Two-parent families
Do you agree or disagree with the following statement: "It's always best for children to be raised in a home where a married man and woman are living together as father and mother?

Agree	71%
Disagree	28
Don't know	1

Poll also found . . .
   42% believe divorce should be more difficult to obtain (9% say easier).
   83% believe the way TV shows depict sex tends to encourage immorality.
   91% of parents have rules limiting what the children can watch or listen to.*

Source: Los Angeles Times Poll
Note: Numbers may not add up to 100% where more than one response was accepted or not all answer categories are shown.
*Parents with children under 18 responded to this question.

ucation generation," he has decided to do better by 8-month-old Charles Dewane Jr.

22   Although Dewane, who installs heating and cooling systems, has not attended church in years, he plans to send his son to parochial school because "people who send their kids to Catholic schools give a damn."

23   Marsha "Pat" Maliszewski, 49, is a mother of two and until recently a marketing representative for a small computer firm. She quit her job this spring to devote herself full time to organizing a community-wide forum on "character" in Battle Creek, Mich. The wife of a police officer, she hears a daily litany of stories attesting to a moral slide in her city of 35,000.

24   Maybe, she concluded, if she could bring together liberals and conservatives, teachers and church people, artists and bank tellers and corporate leaders from the town's largest employer, Kellogg Co., they could talk about common values. Maybe they could even forge a consensus on how those values could be reinforced in everyday life.

25   As a result, Battle Creek will have its first countywide community meeting on character and ethics June 18-21. The planned sessions, at which almost three dozen community leaders will be trained in ethical decision-making, have drawn an enthusiastic crowd of all stripes. "We're on fire out here," said Maliszewski, who hopes the forum will result in programs in schools, churches, workplaces and athletic fields.

26   The seed was planted when she attended a lecture on teaching children good character. It prompted her to examine the daily compromises and white lies that had chipped away at her own sense of right and wrong. Now, she says, "it is time to walk the walk," and she is determined to take her ethics mission statewide.

27   For the nearly 63 million Americans with children at home, the values debate is both especially urgent and difficult. The bulk of those parents grew up in the 1960s, '70s or '80s, when younger Americans embraced freedom of expression and self-actualization with near-religious fervor.

28   Today, divorce rates have doubled since 1960, crime rates are soaring, educational standards are slipping and civic debate is increasingly uncivil. And these children of a rebellious age are asking themselves if perhaps too many people have chosen to do their own thing. They suspect that their rebellion, while rooting out some of the 1950s' ugliest prejudices and loosening some of its most constricting mores, also might have damaged some of society's basic institutions and erected little to replace them.

29   "Basically I feel I'm very openminded, very liberal," says Emalie Mobarekeh, 45, a mother of two and part-time middle-school teacher in Sarasota, Fla. But groups that she has supported, like the American Civil Liberties Union, "keep wanting to push the norms of society further and further.

30   "I think, how much more are people going to take and say OK to? And I'm not a right-winger! They say you've got to accept this—say, gay girls and

homosexuals adopting kids. All this deviation from the norm? I don't know. It bothers me after a while."

31   Now with children at home, parents like her are painfully aware of their responsibility to impart a sense not only of what is wrong with society but of what is right and wrong for individuals. And for children of the nonjudgmental 1960s and 1970s that often is a wrenching adjustment.

32   "We've engaged in a generation-long experiment, testing the limits of individual freedom and its social consequences," said Galston, the University of Maryland professor. "My sense is that a lot of people about my age are reassessing the balance that our generation struck in its youth and are looking for a new balance. . . . They've discovered that the values and practices and ways of thinking they embraced when young turned out to be a double-edged sword and that raising children calls upon us to reconsider lots of things."

33   As a result, polls today indicate a surprising willingness among Americans to disapprove of other people's personal decisions that they believe have hurt society. Half of Americans, for instance, say they believe that it is always or almost always wrong for a woman to have a child out of wedlock, and 46% say they believe that it is always or almost always wrong to have sex outside of marriage.

34   The conflicting themes of freedom and order are one of democracy's perennial tensions, and demographers argue that surging tides of social conservatism recur at regular intervals in the American body politic. Making the latest outbreak of soul-searching noteworthy are the extreme demographic and societal spikes that have prompted it—a rise in violent crime, a surge in divorce and single-parent families, a stubborn drug problem.

35   Stephen Carter, 41, who teaches law and ethics at Yale University, says there is another factor that makes the current round of moral fretting unique:

36   "This is the first era in our public's history where people feel queasy about discussing publicly notions of right and wrong." In the wake of the 1960s and '70s, he adds, "some people feel incorrectly that public discussion of right and wrong is a threat to individual freedom. It's not. They fear that because they think that if most people are against something, they want to make it illegal. But that's not the point of moral conversation. Only in America do we think that talking about right and wrong means we want to legislate it."

37   While the impulse to legislate morality is a powerful theme in American society, it is counterbalanced by an equally powerful mistrust of the government and of politicians as arbiters of the nation's values. The result, a deep ambivalence about the values debate, helps explain Americans' fitful efforts to effect legislative changes that address the problems they see.

38   The Times Poll dramatically illustrates the conflicts and contradictions that shade Americans' views about public values.

39   A 57% majority, for instance, says that "too many people have lifestyles and beliefs which are harmful to themselves and society" and that those are a greater danger than intolerance for other people's life-styles and beliefs.

40   Cast the question in terms of government intervention, however, and majority support quickly evaporates.

41   The poll asked people to identify which annoyed them more: government intrusion into citizens' private lives or government's protecting activities that flout traditional family values. A slim majority of 52% found government intrusion the greater irritant, while 36% said they are more annoyed by government protection of activities that run counter to "family values."

42   Part of the public's ambivalence about legislative remedies appears to reflect the fact that few Americans blame themselves for having contributed to the social ills they bemoan. As a result, say pollsters, they are reluctant to embrace government interventions that could crimp their own freedoms along with those of the people they blame for the values breakdown.

43   The Times Poll suggested that only 11% of respondents say they believe that their own behavior has contributed to the moral problems the nation faces. Similarly, 96% say they believe that they are doing an excellent or good job teaching their children about morals and values. But those numbers don't square with their perception of how others are behaving: 93% say that parents are not taking enough responsibility for teaching their children moral values.

44   For all of Americans' qualms about government intrusion, an overwhelming majority expect government to do *something* to support families.

45   In a January poll conducted as part of the University of Texas's National Issues Convention, 92% said they would like government to strengthen families and family values with benefits such as child care and preschool. Increasingly, Americans are looking to their public schools to teach and reinforce civic and personal virtues with character education. And large majorities have supported legislation that would give parents the V-chip to limit their children's TV and computer exposure to sex and violence.

46   American parents, says Sen. Joseph I. Lieberman (D-Conn.), "want help" from the government. At a minimum, he adds, "they want to feel that we [politicians] get it, that we understand what they're going through—that there's a values problem in this country and that we're going to do what we can to put ourselves on their side."

47   Americans such as Agnes Shelton, 32, a homemaker from Greeneville, Tenn., echo that sense:

48   "It's hard to say where the government should start at. If they would even honor families being together instead of separate" it would be an improvement.

49   But how much help Americans want, Lieberman adds, "is not yet clear." Inside Congress, he says, "we're hesitant to go too far."

50   Nevertheless, the perceived values crisis has become a potent electoral issue for politicians across the spectrum. Four years ago, Republican Vice President Dan Quayle ignited acrimonious debate when he criticized television's Murphy Brown, an unmarried woman, for having a child.

51   These days, Clinton regularly makes the same point, decrying out-of-wedlock births and popular entertainment that glamorizes sex and single parenthood. He exhorts Americans to teach virtue in public schools, to stay together as families, to be better parents and to "overcome the notion that self-gratification is more important than our obligation to others."

52   And Clinton appears to have met with some success in laying claim to issues that traditionally have belonged to Republicans. The Times Poll found that 39% of respondents say they believe that Democrats have the best ideas for handling family values and morality, while 37% favor Republicans' views.

53   Many Americans appear willing to let politicians take the debate much further than it has gone in decades. They are urging state and national legislators to pass laws addressing what most see as the cause of declining values today—the breakdown of the family:

- In several states, legislatures are debating restrictions on the rights of couples with children to divorce.
- Congress has proposed to cut off welfare payments to women who bear additional children out of wedlock, and many states are proceeding with experimental programs to do so.
- States have adopted aggressive programs to track down divorced spouses who do not pay child support.
- Many politicians say they are determined to get rid of the marriage penalty that is a byproduct of the federal income tax system. Some propose offering stay-at-home spouses tax breaks.

54   On the home front, the debate over the nation's moral standards is less public and less clamorous. But when parents take steps to act on their convictions at home, their actions may well have the greatest impact, for it is here that most Americans agree that children learn their values.

55   While Americans remain reluctant to subject their own behavior to criticism or limitations, many are wrestling with personal decisions that they know have broader social consequences. And many, moved by the conviction that public virtue must begin in private, are making decisions they might not have made in the prevailing climate of a decade ago.

56   Thus when parents stay together for the sake of their children, when they attend school meetings about curriculum changes, when an unmarried woman decides not to have a baby on her own, or a man decides that an office assignment should not take precedence over his daughter's soccer tournament, each—wittingly or not—has taken a stand in a debate over personal and public values.

57   Americans have always made personal choices with powerful public consequences. In the current ferment over values, however, many are explicitly considering broader social concerns as factors in their personal decisions.

58   That is the kind of decision Mike Rademacher, a farmer in Longmont, Colo., and his wife, Vicki, made some years ago. Parents of children who are now 14 and 7, the Rademachers decided that Vicki should quit her job as a secretary, sacrificing an income that in many years outstripped her husband's, so that the children would have a parent available at any time.

59   "Parental involvement is the backbone of our society, and that's been lost" in an economy in which a second income is often necessary to "afford the basics or buy the extras," said Mike Rademacher, one of several Times Poll respondents who discussed his views with a reporter. "It was our decision that raising our family was more important than the monetary value" of Vicki's income.

60   It is a choice, he says, that he would like to see more parents make, although he sees no role for government in prodding such decisions. "It'd be good for everybody," he said, "especially the kids."

61   To many experts, the public policy debates that swirl around the values issues are bellwethers of a larger movement: Americans, they say, appear ready to forfeit some measure of their cherished freedoms in the interest of restoring a lost sense of community.

62   The search for that new balance point may be hinted at in the Times Poll. Asked if they would be willing to abridge civil liberties—such as censoring television—to improve the nation's moral climate, 17% said they would not and more than twice as many—35%—said they would.

63   As Americans experiment with new ways to restore their sense of lost community and family values, some see a corner turned.

64   Brenda Clark, principal of Azalea Elementary School in St. Petersburg, Fla., has struggled to improve the quality of teaching and to restore a sense of accountability among students and teachers. Her latest bid to improve the learning environment involves mandatory uniforms for kids starting in September. She has been heartened by the reaction.

65   "I think people are saying, 'Enough! We've had enough of this! Let's get back to what is right and good,'" she said. "I think we've hit bottom and are heading back."

Understanding Content

1. In your own words, write out the thesis of "Fighting to Fill the Values Gap."
2. What does the essay indicate that the single individual can do to reverse society's moral decline?
3. Although she believes the country is in a moral decline, Lila Robinson opposes legislation that attempts to stop that decline. Why?
4. In paragraph 34, Healy says, "The conflicting themes of freedom and order are one of democracy's perennial tensions." Explain what Healy means and how the statement is relevant to the focus of the essay.

Considering Structure and Technique

1. Healy opens by quoting Lila Robinson and mentioning her belief. Is this an effective opening? Explain.
2. A **metaphor** is a comparison made without using the words *like* or *as*. (For more on metaphors, see p. 121.) What metaphor appears in paragraph 6? In paragraph 15? What purpose do these metaphors serve?
3. In paragraphs 10, 12, 13, 14, 32, and 35, Healy quotes educators. What purpose do these quotations serve? Are they effective? Explain.
4. In addition to quoting authorities, Healy quotes everyday people. Are those quotations effective? Why or why not?
5. Figure 1 on p. 224 provides some information in pie charts and some information in lists. Would any of this information be better presented in one or more paragraphs? Why or why not?

Exploring Ideas

1. What evidence does Lila Robinson offer as proof that "the nation's moral slide is everywhere" (paragraph 2)? Do you think her evidence is convincing? Why or why not?
2. Paragraph 11 refers to the "values movement." Reread that paragraph and explain what you think the values movement is.
3. How would you evaluate the status of values on your campus? Are they in decline or not? Cite examples to support your view.
4. In paragraph 53, Healy notes that many Americans are urging legislation "addressing . . . the breakdown of the family." Do you think our politicians can be trusted to pass laws that will strengthen the family? Explain.

Writing Workshop: Citing Authority and Data

One way to help prove a point is to include the words and ideas of authorities. This technique is persuasive because it provides "expert testimony." For example, in paragraph 10, Healy quotes the *words* of education professor Thomas Lickona, and in paragraph 13 she mentions the *idea* of Professor Amitai Etzioni.

Referring to data is another form of proof that lends a persuasive quality. For example, in paragraph 18, Healy cites statistics from a Los Angeles Times poll, and in paragraph 45, she cites data from the University of Texas's National Issues Convention poll.

You, too, can draw on the words, ideas, and data of others for proof for your points. In fact, you can use many of the essays in this text as a source of support. When you cite an authority or data, be sure to mention the name of the person or source you are citing—as Healy does—and be sure to use quotation marks around a person's exact words. In addition, consult a handbook to learn how to credit the author and source of the borrowing, both in your text and in a list of references. (See p. 19 on paraphrasing and quoting.)

Writing Workshop Activity

List three or four ideas for a paper about divorce in the United States. Using "On the Brow of the Hill" (p. 158), "Fighting to Fill the Values Gap," and material you locate on the Internet or in your library, find some words, some ideas, and some data that could be used to prove one or more of the ideas on your list.

Language Notes for Multilingual and Other Writers

A **compound** is formed when two or more words are put together to form one word, as in these examples from the essay:

paragraph 1: soapbox (soap + box)

paragraph 15: headlines (head + lines)

paragraph 34: outbreak (out + break)

paragraph 59: backbone (back + bone)

When the compound acts as a modifier to describe a noun after it, a hyphen or hyphens often separate the words forming the compound.

paragraph 5: bleeding-heart liberal

paragraph 11: do-your-own-thing philosophy

paragraph 34: single-parent families

paragraph 51: out-of-wedlock births

Check a dictionary when in doubt because there are exceptions, including this one from paragraph 34: outbreak of <u>soul-searching</u>. (For more on this subject, see the writing workshop on hyphens on p. 99).

From Reading to Writing

In Your Journal: Would you be willing to give up some civil liberties to improve the nation's moral climate? For example, would you allow increased censorship of media, laws against profanity, and dress codes? Explain in a page or two.

With Some Classmates: A "random act of kindness" is an unexpected good deed done—often anonymously—and without expectation of reward. It is a deed such as sending an encouraging card to a stranger you read about in the newspaper, picking up litter, leaving a coupon on a grocery shelf for someone to use, leaving flowers on the porch of an elderly stranger. Each of you should perform a random act of kindness and write about how it makes you feel. Then compare your reactions.

In an Essay

- Paragraph 6 states that more and more Americans are "convinced that the nation is suffering from a values decline of crisis proportions." Agree or disagree, citing examples from your experience and observation to support your view.
- In paragraph 14, Healy quotes Amitai Etzioni: "'Today, everybody's free to do anything, but it's not what they want. Its not liberating; it's not freedom.'" Explain the meaning of this statement and use examples to show that it is or is not true. As an alternative, write your own definition of *freedom.*
- Argue for or against the passage of one of the four laws mentioned in the list in paragraph 53.

Beyond the Writing Class: Some people in favor of the values movement advocate school uniforms as a way to combat what they consider moral decline in schools. Research the issue on the Internet or in your school library and write a letter to the editor of your local paper arguing for or against uniforms in public schools.

CHAPTER 6

THE IMPACT OF TECHNOLOGY: WHAT PRICE PROGRESS?

"The new electronic interdependence re-creates the world in the image of a global village."

Marshall McLuhan

"Technology is the science of arranging life so that one need not experience it."

Anonymous

"Any sufficiently advanced technology is indistinguishable from magic."

Arthur C. Clarke

"The computer is only a fast idiot; it has no imagination; it cannot originate action. It is, and will remain, only a tool to man."

American Library Association statement on UNIVAC
computer exhibited at New York World's Fair, 1964

Fear and Longing

MARC ZABLUDOFF

Formerly at *Science Digest* and *Esquire,* Marc Zabludoff is the editor-in-chief of *Discover* magazine. He was the director of that magazine's "Science of Race" issue, which won the 1995 National Magazine award. "Fear and Longing" first appeared in *Discover* in 1998. As you read it, ask yourself how convincing the author's argument is.

Preview.   Cloning used to be the stuff of science fiction. Then, in 1996, a sheep named Dolly was cloned, and, suddenly, cloning became science fact.

Some scientists are even turning their attention to cloning human beings, a prospect that intrigues some people and disturbs others. Is human cloning the same as animal cloning? What is your opinion?

Vocabulary.   If any of the following words from the essay are unfamiliar to you, study their meanings before reading.

mammalian (1)   like a mammal (a warm-blooded animal that produces milk and has a backbone)
conferred (1) given
languorous (1)   slow, lazy
tousled (3)   messy
Salieri (3)   Antonio Salieri, an Italian composer who was Mozart's rival
aria (4)   vocal musical solo
intact (4)   whole, unbroken
garnered (5)   acquired
imperative (5)   requirement
enterprise (5)   undertaking
disquieting (6)   disturbing
genome (6)   the complete set of genetic material

In February [1998], at the annual meeting of the American Association for the Advancement of Science, in Philadelphia, I attended a session entitled "The Rights and Wrongs of Cloning Humans." Among the speakers was Ian Wilmut, of the Roslin Institute in Edinburgh. Now, Ian Wilmut, as the leader of the research team that cloned the famous lamb Dolly, is rightly the "father" of mammalian cloning, if such a title can be conferred. That is to say, Dr. Wilmut is a man who has unblinkingly beheld the concrete future, has seen it take shape under his own guidance. He is a balding, bespectacled, soft-spoken scientist, with Scottish accent characteristically clipped but languorous. For all his world-shattering achievement, he is an undramatic and unemotional speaker. Yet there was no mistaking the passion of his sentiments on this subject. When faced with the prospect of colleagues racing to bring forth a cloned human infant, he was appalled.

2   First of all, he noted, the limits of current technology simply do not allow the attempt: To get one successful birth, many babies would have to die in failed procedures—an absolutely unacceptable price. But even assuming we solve the technical problems, why, he asked, would we *want* to clone ourselves? Even if we truly desire an exact duplicate of someone—ourselves, a lost loved one, a scientific or artistic genius—the plain truth is that we won't get it.

3   We are more than our genes. We are our genes in a particular place and time, whole people interacting with others in an infinitely variable world. Only through that experience do we become who we are. A cloned Einstein reared in twenty-first-century Los Angeles will not become a tousled professor of new physics. A cloned Mozart will not reelevate our souls or drive a cloned Salieri to distraction. A clone of a child tragically and prematurely dead will not replace wholly and without distinction the child who once was. All the clone will be for certain is the bearer of unmet expectation.

4   That cloning won't fully work should be evident to all of us. We are each a half-clone, after all, with respect to either parent. And though we may at some time have heard that we got, say, our singing voice from our mother or our temper from our father, we know it's not strictly true. Talents and temperament aren't really divvied up, trait by trait, and served intact down the genetic line. Not one of us is identical to a parent, not even in the middle of an aria or rage. And we would not be so even if we were the inheritor of all a parent's genes rather than half.

5   To be fair, cloning is not the focus of most biotech research. It has simply garnered the most publicity. But it does most dramatically illustrate what some have called the technological imperative—which means that if we *can* do something, we *will*, whether there is wisdom in the enterprise or not.

6   And cloning is not the only application of biotechnology that even the science-supporting public finds disquieting. Yes, we're eager to have the entire human genome laid out before us. Yes, we're eager to see the day when the genes that cause truly terrible diseases can be repaired. But are we ready for casual tinkering with the genes of plants that feed us? Are we ready for the genetic manipulation of cows and pigs for the sole purpose of human convenience? Are we ready to turn loose all the forces of technology to further—surely unnecessarily—the pace of human reproduction, no matter what the material, societal, and psychological costs?

7   We are preparing for our children a new world, and we don't yet know its borders.

Understanding Content

1. What is the author's view of cloning human beings? How does that view compare to Ian Wilmut's?
2. What reasons does Wilmut have for his view of cloning human beings?
3. In your own words, explain what the "technological imperative" is.
4. How does Zabludoff feel about the focuses of biotechnology, other than cloning of humans?

Considering Structure and Technique

1. Why is Zabludoff so careful in the introduction to establish Wilmut's level of involvement in cloning research?
2. Why does Zabludoff describe Wilmut in paragraph 1?
3. A **rhetorical question** is a question for which no answer is expected because the answer is implied. (See p. 313.) Why does Zabludoff use rhetorical questions in paragraph 6? Do you think they are effective? Explain.
4. Zabludoff opens paragraph 5 by saying, "To be fair. . . . " Do you think he is being fair in the essay? Do you think he is convincing?

Exploring Ideas

1. In what ways are we "more than our genes" (paragraph 3)?
2. Which do you think shapes a person more, an individual's genetic code or the environment the person grows up in? Explain.
3. Reread paragraph 6. What assumption about manipulating genes and influencing human reproduction goes unstated? Is the assumption a fair one? Explain.
4. If you could clone just one person, who would it be? Why?

Writing Workshop: Concluding with a Single Sentence

Rather than conclude with a full paragraph, writers sometimes use just a single sentence to tie off a piece. A single-sentence closing can be particularly appropriate for a short writing, such as a newspaper editorial. The single-sentence conclusion of "Fear and Longing" works well because it is in balance with the rest of the relatively short essay.

Writing Workshop

Select an essay you have already written this term and rewrite the conclusion as a single sentence. Which conclusion do you prefer? Why?

Language Notes for Multilingual and Other Writers

If you are writing a formal piece, your sentences typically should not begin with *and, but,* or *yet.* However, these words can start sentences in semiformal and informal writing, as these sentences from "Fear and Longing" illustrate.

<u>Yet</u> there was no mistaking the passion of his sentiments on this subject. Paragraph 1

<u>And</u> we would not be so even if we were the inheritor of all a parent's genes rather than half. Paragraph 4

<u>But</u> it does most dramatically illustrate what some have called the technological imperative . . . Paragraph 5

From Reading to Writing

In Your Journal: Do you think cloning should be available to couples who are unable to have children? Explain your view.

With Some Classmates: Zabludoff does not discuss any potential benefits to human cloning. Consider what they might be and write a paper that explains the possible benefits.

In an Essay

- Write an essay that argues for or against passing legislation that would ban the cloning of human beings.
- In paragraph 5, Zabludoff notes that the technological imperative states that "if we *can* do something, we *will,* whether there is wisdom in the enterprise or not." Discuss a technological innovation that you think the world would be better off without, something that we were able to do but should not have done.
- In paragraph 3, Zabludoff notes that people become who they are, in part, because of their environment (their experiences, interactions with others, location, and so forth). Explain how you have been shaped by one aspect of your environment. You can discuss order of birth, place of birth, family structure, or any other interaction or experience.

Beyond the Writing Class: If we are more than our genes (paragraph 3), then identical twins raised apart will differ in important ways. Do some research to learn to what extent identical twins raised in different environments are different or the same. Then write up your findings and draw a conclusion.

Stepping through a Computer Screen, Disabled Veterans Savor Freedom

N. R. KLEINFIELD

N. R. Kleinfield is a journalist who wrote this 1995 piece for the *New York Times*. In it, he describes how cutting-edge technology enriches the lives of disabled veterans at the Bronx Veterans Affairs Medical Center. As you read, try to imagine how the veterans feel as they transcend their physical limitations with the aid of virtual reality technology.

Preview.   N. R. Kleinfield describes how virtual reality helps paralyzed veterans have experiences they otherwise could not have. If you know what virtual reality is, write a definition of it. Otherwise, write a definition of what you think it might be.

Vocabulary.   If any of the following words from the essay are unfamiliar to you, study their meanings before reading.

paraplegic (1)   a person paralyzed from the waist down
plush (2)   abundant
quadriplegics (2)   people paralyzed from the neck down
outer envelope (5)   a reference to the limits of something
full-fledged (5)   complete
tantalizing (9)   tempting
troves (13)   hoards
buoyant (16)   cheerful
moored (18)   anchored; secured
prosaic (20)   everyday; ordinary
galvanized (21)   stimulated
novice (24)   an inexperienced person

The other day, Angelo Degree single-handedly lifted a couch and effortlessly hauled it into another room. He moved around a lamp, a crate. He snatched hold of a man and ran outside with him. Ever since he was shot in the head and spine while being robbed in 1981, Mr. Degree has been a paraplegic. His legs are a wheelchair. One day he is hoping to play football. Tackle.

2   The man who plans to suit him up is William Meredith, who is not a doctor with a miracle cure but a recording engineer with a black bag flush with interactive computer technology. His subjects are the paraplegics and quadriplegics in the spinal cord injury ward at the Bronx Veterans Affairs Medical Center.

3   For some 10 years Mr. Meredith has done volunteer work for the Veterans Bedside Network, a 46-year-old organization made up largely of show-business people who try to rally the spirits of sick veterans, engaging them in plays and song-and-dance routines.

4   "But I always felt there was one group who we weren't able to reach that well, and those were the quadriplegics and paraplegics," Mr. Meredith explained. "And so I thought about virtual reality."

5   Virtual reality, for those unfamiliar with the outer envelope of technology, enables people to feel, through interactive computers, as though they are inside a three-dimensional electronic image. In full-fledged systems, they can actually sense that they are moving and feel virtual reality objects. To participate, all that is required is a working mind.

6   The more Mr. Meredith, 52, chewed over the notion, the more provocative it became. "These visions ran through my mind," he said. "These people could fly, which they can't. They could walk, which they can't. They could play sports, which they can't."

7   After winning over officials at the Bronx Veterans Medical Center and getting a $5,000 equipment budget from the Veterans Bedside Network, Mr. Meredith was in business. In mid-October he got his idea off the ground.

8   Every Tuesday and Thursday afternoon, he lugs three laptop computers to the Bronx hospital. He is an Air Force man himself, and teaches virtual reality at various schools as well as uses it in his recording work for films. He usually travels to the hospital with Michael Storch, who recently joined Veterans Bedside Network and is studying to enter the virtual reality field. They report to the first-floor spinal cord injury unit, where there are about 50 patients, and set up their equipment in the physical rehabilitation room.

9   From 2 P.M. to 4:30 P.M., wheelchairs roll up to their corner and patients enter the tantalizing world of virtual reality.

10   The patients use goggles in which they see a three-dimensional image and a glove that is wired to the computer in a way that when they move their hand, they seem to grasp and move things on the computer screen. Mr. Meredith has yet to incorporate equipment that enables patients to feel and smell the virtual world they enter, though he hopes to do so soon.

11   It seemed only a matter of time for this to happen. Virtual reality is being used by therapists to help treat children who have suffered child abuse. It is being used to teach sufferers of muscular dystrophy how to operate a wheelchair. It is being used to help people overcome a fear of heights. They are ushered onto a virtual reality ledge, many stories in the sky. Go on, they are told. Look down.

12   At this early stage in the program, Mr. Meredith is able to offer only limited options to the patients. There are several virtual reality games, including Heretic, which involves wandering through creepy dungeons and staving off demons and menacing creatures. There is a program that allows patients to redecorate a house by moving furniture around through the use of a Power Glove. There is a chess game, which has proved especially popular. And Mr.

Meredith has designed his own virtual reality baseball game, where patients see the field from whichever position they assume.

13   In addition, Mr. Meredith brings along various computer programs that are not virtual reality but enable patients to look up vast troves of information on the computers. One man has been researching the places where he made bomber runs during World War II.

14   The other day, Mr. Degree, 39, finished rearranging the virtual reality house and moved on to Heretic. He was reasonably accomplished. He destroyed quite a few knights and flying beasts before mistakenly grabbing a gas bomb.

15   "You better work on your recognition," Mr. Meredith chided him.

"Next time, I'll give it to them real good," he promised.

16   Mr. Degree was buoyant about the program. "You know why a lot of veterans are in and out of hospitals?" he asked. "Stress. If they want to have any dreams, they have to get them from a bottle. Here, you can have dreams without the bottle. All I can do is look here and see a lot of potential. An angel with a lot of wings."

17   Mike Ableson, the chief of recreation services for the hospital, is equally enthusiastic. "For these guys, it opens up a whole new world," he said. "Physical barriers don't matter. Mobility barriers don't exist."

18   Mr. Meredith has elaborate ambitions. Many veterans relish their trips to the Intrepid Sea-Air-Space Museum aboard the aircraft carrier permanently moored on West 46th Street. Spinal cord patients usually don't go. Mr. Meredith is having a virtual reality tour of the Intrepid designed so patients can experience it from their beds. He hopes it will be ready in July.

19   "Ultimately, I want to have interactive sports," Mr. Meredith said. "I'd like to link up several hospitals and have leagues and everything. They'll play baseball, football, whatever they want. They'll be able to feel every hit."

20   Some patients have employed the computers to assist them in prosaic concerns. "One guy was having problems with the grass on his lawn on Staten Island," Mr. Meredith said, "and so he looked up in one of the data bases in the computer ways of dealing with Bluegrass diseases. I believe he found his answer."

21   Whatever use they make of the technology, the patients find their bedimmed lives galvanized.

22   Wilfred Garcia, 55, was keen to gain knowledge. "I've been looking up where I was stationed in Berlin in 1958," he said. "Brings back the memories. I'm into biography. I looked up Christopher Columbus. I looked up Marco Polo. He was born in the same city as Columbus. I looked up Clark Gable. Man, what an actor."

23   In 1986, Mr. Garcia had an allergic reaction to a tuna sandwich while he was driving on the New York Thruway. He blacked out and his car crashed down an embankment. He was left an "incomplete paraplegic" meaning he can stand up and walk short distances on crutches, but has no balance.

24   Now he is immersed in chess. He was a novice. The computer demolished him. "I might look into boxing on this," he said. "I used to box. At the age of 16, I was going to join the Golden Gloves but my mother wouldn't let me."

25   With limited resources and equipment, Mr. Meredith has been confined to offering his program to those able to come to the rehabilitation room. His goal is to take systems to patient bedsides, which after all, is what Veterans Bedside Network is supposed to be about.

26   There are patients itchy to see that happen. Osvaldo Arias, 35, paralyzed from the neck down since being shot in the back by unseen assailants in the Bronx in 1978, was lying in his room at the Veterans hospital. Recovering from surgery, he could not get to the rehabilitation room.

27   "When you spend a lot of time in bed, you can go crazy," he said. "Right now, I can't get out of bed. I'm bored. You watch TV for a while, then you get tired of it. I try to write letters. An idle mind is the devil's workshop. I want to see that system in here. It's meant for those who can't get out of bed to keep from going stir crazy."

Understanding Content

1. What is the Veterans Bedside Network?
2. According to the essay, what are some of the ways virtual reality has been used?
3. Explain the cause and effect relationship between stress and frequent hospital stays for veterans. How does Meredith's virtual reality program break the stress cycle?
4. What future ambitions does Meredith have for virtual reality technology?

Considering Structure and Technique

1. Is the opening paragraph likely to arouse a reader's interest? Why or why not?
2. Kleinfield includes quotations from the disabled veterans who use the virtual reality technology. What do these quotations contribute to the piece? What, if anything, would be lost if Kleinfield had conveyed the information without using exact words?
3. The selection originally appeared in the *New York Times*. What features make the piece appropriate for the readers of a large metropolitan newspaper?
4. Kleinfield concludes with a statement by a paraplegic who cannot get to the rehabilitation room to use the virtual reality equipment. Is this conclusion effective? Explain.

Exploring Ideas

1. Why were the paraplegics and quadriplegics the one group the Veteran's Bedside Network found it difficult to reach?

2. Why do you think that the virtual reality chess game was so popular among the paraplegics and quadriplegics?
3. What kind of person do you think William Meredith is? List words and phrases that could describe him.
4. What uses for virtual reality, not mentioned in the essay, can you think of?

Writing Workshop: Implying the Thesis

Most writing has a clearly stated **thesis** (statement of the central point; see p. 28). In some cases, though, a writer may *imply* the thesis, rather than write it out. When a thesis is implied successfully, the reader can readily determine what it is from the supporting details. The thesis of "Stepping through a Computer Screen, Disabled Veterans Savor Freedom" is implied rather than stated. It is something like this: Using virtual reality technology, William Meredith has helped paraplegics and quadriplegics experience things they otherwise could not.

If you decide to imply rather than state your thesis, be sure your reader can easily identify your central point—and be sure none of your detail strays from that point.

Writing Workshop Activity

Find one example of a newspaper or magazine article with a stated thesis and one with an implied thesis. Why is the thesis stated in one and implied in the other? Would the piece with the implied thesis be improved or not if the thesis were stated? Explain.

Language Notes for Multilingual and Other Writers

Some of the following expressions from "Stepping through a Computer Screen, Disabled Veterans Savor Freedom" may be unfamiliar to you.
1. *To suit up* means "to outfit or dress."

   The man who plans <u>to suit him up</u> is William Meredith . . . Paragraph 2

2. *To chew over* is an informal way of saying "to think hard about something."

   The more Mr. Meredith, 52, <u>chewed over</u> the notion . . . Paragraph 6.

3. *To win over* is to convince someone to adopt your view. *To be in business* is an informal way of saying "to be able to proceed."

   After <u>winning over</u> officials at the Bronx Veterans Medical Center . . . Mr. Meredith was <u>in business</u>." Paragraph 7

4. *To be itchy* is "to be restless and anxious to do something."

There are patients <u>itchy</u> to see that happen. Paragraph 26

5. *To go stir crazy* is "to become mentally ill as a result of extended confinement."

"It's meant for those who can't get out of bed to keep them from going <u>stir crazy</u>." Paragraph 27

From Reading to Writing

In Your Journal: Tell what you learned about virtual reality and/or quadriplegics and paraplegics as a result of reading the selection.

With Some Classmates: Consider the potential applications of virtual reality on college campuses. Select one or two of those possible applications and explain them and their benefits in a paper.

In an Essay

- In paragraph 11, Kleinfield notes a variety of uses for virtual reality. If you had the opportunity, how would you use virtual reality technology for your own personal benefit? Explain the use and how you would benefit.
- Because William Meredith gives of himself to help others, he enriches the community. To encourage more people to contribute something to their communities, a number of schools require community service as a graduation requirement. What do you think of requiring college students to engage in four hours of community service a month as a requirement for graduation? State and defend your view.
- Argue for or against requiring insurance companies to pay for virtual reality technology in hospitals that treat quadriplegics and paraplegics.

Beyond the Writing Class: Virtual reality can be used to train people to perform a variety of tasks, particularly ones that would otherwise put them at risk. For example, flight simulators use virtual reality technology to train pilots to handle a variety of emergency situations. Research virtual reality applications and write a report on how the technology can be used in the workplace.

Will Tiny Robots Build Diamonds One Atom at a Time?
MICHAEL D. LEMONICK

Michael D. Lemonick is a senior science writer at *Time* magazine. He has also been the executive editor at *Discover* magazine and senior editor at *Science Digest*. Although his first love is astronomy, Lemonick has written on many science subjects, including ocean exploration, Biblical archaeology, brain research, and Egyptology. In the following piece, which first appeared in *Digital Time* in 2000, he looks into the not-so-distant future, where microscopic robots are doing some amazing things.

Preview.　Imagine machines just one billionth of a meter in diameter changing grass clippings into food, fighting disease, and building skyscrapers. Is this science fiction or fact? According to the following essay, these days it is looking more like fact. Knowing that, do you think that the United States government should devote $500 million to further the research? Why or why not?

Vocabulary.　If any of the following words from the essay are unfamiliar to you, study their meaning before reading.

preposterous (1)　absurd
stave off (1)　ward off
proponents (1)　supporters
initiative (2)　undertaking
impeccable (3)　flawless
pedigree (3)　ancestry; background
fabricates (5)　makes
gargantuan (7)　huge
dexterity (9)　manual skill
replicas (11)　duplicates
dystopia (12)　an imaginary place where people are miserable

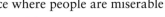

On its face, the notion seems utterly preposterous: a single technology so incredibly versatile that it can fight disease, stave off aging, clean up toxic waste, boost the world's food supply and build roads, automobiles and skyscrapers—and that's only to start with. Yet that's just what the proponents of nanotechnology claim is going to be possible, maybe even before the century is half over.

2　　Crazy though it sounds, the idea of nanotechnology is very much in the scientific mainstream, with research labs all over the world trying to make it work. Last January President Clinton even declared a National Nanotechnology Initiative, promising $500 million for the effort.

3   In fact, nanotechnology has an impeccable and longstanding scientific pedigree. It was back in 1959 that Richard Feynman, arguably the most brilliant theoretical physicist since Einstein, gave a talk titled "There's Plenty of Room at the Bottom," in which he suggested that it would one day be possible to build machines so tiny they would consist of just a few thousand atoms. (The term nanotechnology comes from nanometer, or a billionth of a meter; a typical virus is about 100 nanometers across.)

4   What would such a machine be good for? Construction projects, on the tiniest scale, using molecules and even individual atoms as building blocks. And that in turn means you can make literally anything at all, from scratch— for the altering and rearrangement of molecules is ultimately what chemistry and biology come down to, and manufacturing is simply the process of taking huge collections of molecules and forming them into useful objects.

5   Indeed, every cell is a living example of nanotechnology: not only does it convert fuel into energy, but it also fabricates and pumps out proteins and enzymes according to the software encoded in its DNA. By recombining DNA from different species, genetic engineers have already learned to build new nanodevices—bacterial cells, for example, that pump out medically useful human hormones.

6   But biotechnology is limited by the tasks cells already know how to carry out. Nanotech visionaries have much more ambitious notions. Imagine a nanomachine that could take raw carbon and arrange it, atom by atom, into a perfect diamond. Imagine a machine that dismembers dioxin molecules, one by one, into their component parts. Or a device that cruises the human bloodstream, seeks out cholesterol deposits on vessel walls and disassembles them. Or one that takes grass clippings and remanufactures them into bread. Literally every physical object in the world, from computers to cheese, is made of molecules, and in principle a nanomachine could construct all of them.

7   Going from the principle to the practical will be a tall order, of course, but nanomechanics have already shown that it's possible, using tools like the scanning tunneling electron microscope, to move individual atoms into arrangements they'd never assume in nature: the IBM logo, for example, or a map of the world at one ten-billionth scale, or even a functioning submicroscopic guitar whose strings are a mere 50 nanometers across. They've also designed, though not yet built minuscule gears and motors made of a few score molecules. (These should not be confused with the "tiny" gears and motors, built with millions of molecules, that have already been constructed with conventional chip-etching technique. Those devices are gargantuan compared with what will be built in the future.)

8   Within 25 years, nanotechnologists expect to move beyond these scientific parlor tricks and create real, working nanomachines, complete with tiny "fingers" that can manipulate molecules and with minuscule electronic brains

that tell them how to do it as well as how to search out the necessary raw materials. The fingers may well be made from carbon nanotubes—hairlike carbon molecules, discovered in 1991, that are 100 times as strong as steel and 50,000 times as thin as a human hair.

9   Their electronic brains could themselves he made from nanotubes, which can serve both as transistors and as the wires that connect them. Or they may be made out of DNA, which can be altered to carry instructions that nature never intended. Armed with the proper software and sufficient dexterity, a nanorobot, or nanobot, could construct anything at all.

10   Including copies of itself. To accomplish any sort of useful work, you'd have to unleash huge numbers of nanomachines to do every task—billions in every bloodstream, trillions at every toxic waste site, quadrillions to put a car together. No assembly line could crank out nanobots in such numbers.

11   But nanomachines could do it. Nanotechnologists want to design nanobots that can do two things: carry out their primary tasks, and build perfect replicas of themselves. If the first nanobot makes two copies of itself, and those two make two copies each, you've got a trillion nanobots in no time, each one operating independently to carry out a trillionth of the job.

12   But as any child who's seen Mickey Mouse wrestle with those multiplying broomsticks in *The Sorcerer's Apprentice* can tell you, there's a dystopian shadow that hangs over this rosy picture: What if the nanobots forget to stop replicating? Without some sort of built-in stop signal, the potential for disaster would be incalculable. A first-replicating nanobot circulating inside the human body could spread faster than a cancer, crowding out normal tissues; an out-of-control paper-recycling nanobot could convert the world's libraries to corrugated cardboard; a rogue food-fabricating nanobot could turn the planet's entire biosphere into one huge slab of Gorgonzola cheese.

13   Nanotechnologists don't dismiss the danger, but they believe they can handle it. One idea is to program a nanobot's software to self-destruct after a set number of generations. Another is to design nanobots that can operate only under certain conditions—in the presence of a high concentration of toxic chemicals, for example, or within a very narrow range of temperature and humidity. You might even program nanobots to stop reproducing when too many of their fellows are nearby. It's a strategy nature uses to keep bacteria in check.

14   None of that will help if someone decides to unleash a nanotech weapon of some sort—a prospect that would make computer viruses seem utterly benign by comparison. Indeed, some critics contend that the potential dangers of nanotechnology outweigh any potential benefits. Yet those benefits are so potentially enormous that nanotech, even more than computers or genetic medicine, could be the defining technology of the coming century. It may be that the world will end up needing a nanotech immune system, with police nanobots constantly at microscopic war with destructive bots.

15   One way or another, nanotechnology is coming.

Understanding Content

1. In your own words, define *nanotechnology*. What is nanotechnology good for?
2. Where and with whom did the idea of nanotechnology originate?
3. Why do nanotechnologists want to design nanobots that can reproduce themselves?
4. What danger is associated with self-replication of nanobots? How can the danger be addressed?
5. How far has nanoscience progressed to date?

Considering Structure and Technique

1. Is the thesis of the piece stated or implied? (See the workshop on p. 242 on the implied thesis.) Write out the thesis in your own words.
2. In paragraph 3, Lemonick defines *nanometer* as a billionth of a meter. Why does he go on to illustrate by noting that a virus is 100 nanometers across?
3. A **topic sentence** is a statement that indicates the focus of a body paragraph. (See p. 38 on topic sentences.) The topic sentence of paragraph 4 is a question rather than a statement. Does the question make an effective topic sentence? Explain.
4. Lemonick's essay first appeared in *Time Digital*, a publication meant for the average reader of *Time* magazine. How does Lemonick keep the essay interesting for his particular audience?
5. Ideas coming at the end of an essay are emphasized because they are likely to be remembered—they are the points the reader leaves the essay with. Lemonick places his mention of the dangers of nanotechnology near the end, in paragraph 12. Why do you think he does this?

Exploring Ideas

1. If nanotechnology fulfills its promise, what problems (other than those associated with self-replication) might result?
2. If nanotechnology fulfills its promise, how do you think it will affect the economy?
3. Speculate about the uses of nanotechnology and list three not already mentioned in the essay.
4. Does nanotechnology excite you or worry you? Explain.

Writing Workshop: Opening with a Dramatic or Surprising Statement

To grab a reader's attention as soon as possible and create interest, you can open with a dramatic or surprising statement. Michael Lemonick does this in

"Will Tiny Robots Build Diamonds One Atom at a Time?" by opening with this surprising, attention-grabbing statement:

> On its face, the notion seems utterly preposterous: a single technology so incredibly versatile that it can fight disease, stave off aging, clean up toxic waste, boost the world's food supply and build roads, automobiles and skyscrapers—and that's only to start with.

Writing Workshop Activity

Select a piece you are currently working on or something you have written in the past and draft a dramatic or surprising opening sentence aimed at grabbing your reader's attention. Then ask two classmates to read the sentence and tell you if it makes them want to read on.

Language Notes for Multilingual and Other Writers

A **contraction** is formed by combining two words into one word and omitting one or more letters. An apostrophe (') takes the place of the omitted letter or letters. A number of contractions appear in "Will Tiny Robots Build Diamonds One Atom at a Time?"

1. that's = that is

   Yet <u>that's</u> just what the proponents of nanotechnology claim is going to be possible . . . Paragraph 1

2. there's = there is

   "<u>There's</u> Plenty of Room at the Bottom . . . " Paragraph 3

3. it's = it is

   . . . but nanotechnologists have already shown that <u>it's</u> possible, using tools like the scanning tunneling electron microscope . . . Paragraph 7

4. they'd = they would

   . . . it's possible, using tools like the scanning tunneling electron microscope, to move individual atoms into arrangements <u>they'd</u> never assume in nature . . . Paragraph 7

5. they've = they have

   <u>They've</u> also designed . . . miniscule gears . . . Paragraph 7

6. you'd = you would

   . . . <u>you'd</u> have to unleash huge numbers of nanomachines . . . Paragraph 10

7. you've = you have Paragraph 11

   . . . <u>you've</u> got a trillion nanobots in no time . . . Paragraph 11

8. don't = do not

   Nanotechnologists <u>don't</u> dismiss the danger . . . Paragraph 13

From Reading to Writing

In Your Journal: What do you think of nanotechnology? Does it cause you any concern? Does it excite you? Explain.

With Some Classmates: In paragraph 13 Lemonick says that nanotechnologists believe they can handle the danger of multiplying nanobots. How well have we handled problems associated with some of our other advances? You can consider problems associated with the automobile, computers, mass production, and so forth.

In an Essay

- Many things that were once subjects for science fiction are now fact. For example, before it became a reality, space flight was the subject of Buck Rogers science fiction comic books. Not too many years ago, nanotechnology was the stuff of science fiction, and now it may soon be reality. Write a science fiction story that includes technology not available today that you think might be available in the future.
- In paragraph 7, Lemonick refers to moving atoms into patterns "they'd never assume in nature." In paragraph 9, he refers to altering DNA to "to carry instructions that nature never intended." Do you think nanotechnology should not be pursued because it is unnatural, because it violates the laws of nature? Do other things we already rely on violate laws of nature? Explain your view.
- Paragraph 6 includes some speculation about uses for nanotechnology. Think of a use not mentioned in the selection and write an essay that describes that use as well as its potential benefits and drawbacks.

Beyond the Writing Class: Write a letter to one of your congresspersons urging that person either to give or to withhold support for nanotechnology.

The Future of Computing
MICHAEL L. DERTOUZOS

Professor of Computer Science and Electrical Engineering at Massachusetts Institute of Technology, Michael L. Dertouzos is also the director of the MIT Laboratory for Computer Science, a position he has held for over 25 years. Dertouzos is a pioneering expert in computer science and information technology who is the author of *What Will Be: How the New World of Information Will Change Our Lives* (1997).

Preview. At MIT, Michael Dertouzos and his team are developing the systems for new information technologies of the near future. Their goal is to help people accomplish more with less effort. If you could recommend to Dertouzos and his team two features for the next generation of computers, what would they be? You can consider home, school, and business applications.

Vocabulary. If any of the following words from the selection are unfamiliar to you, study their meanings before reading.

cryptography (2)   secret writing; code
tantamount (8)   equal
altruism (10)   unselfish regard for others
disparities (10)   differences
proffering (10)   offering
kiosk (10)   small, light structure
pervasive (14)   existing everywhere
configurable (15)   capable of being set up or altered
aggregates (18)   groups
protocols (18)   procedures
augments (18)   enlarges, extends
inherent (19)   inborn
hyperlinked (22)   linked electronically to relevant electronic documents
shrink-wrapped (23)   bundled in plastic film that is heated and shrunk to
     provide a tight package
agrarian (27)   related to farming

Last year a few of us from the Laboratory for Computer Science at the Massachusetts Institute of Technology were flying to Taiwan. I had been trying for about three hours to make my new laptop work with one of those cards you plug in to download your calendar. But when the card software was happy, the operating system complained, and vice versa. Frustrated, I turned to Tim Berners-Lee sitting next to me, who graciously offered to assist. After an hour, though, the inventor of the Web admitted that the task was beyond his capabilities.

2   Next I asked Ronald Rivest, the coinventor of RSA public-key cryptography, for his help. Exhibiting his wisdom, he politely declined. At this point, one of our youngest faculty members spoke up: "You guys are too old. Let me do it." But he also gave up after an hour and a half. So I went back to my "expert" approach of typing random entries into the various wizards and lizards that kept popping up on the screen until by sheer accident, I made it work . . . three hours later.

3   Such an ordeal is typical and raises an important issue: for the first 40 years of computer science, we have been preoccupied with catering our technology to what machines want. We design systems and subsystems individually and then throw them at the public, expecting people to make the different components work together. The image this approach evokes for me is that of designing a car in which the driver has to twist dozens of individual knobs to control the fuel mixture, spark advance and valve clearances, among other things—when all he wants to do is go from one place to another.

Doing More by Doing Less

4   We have done enough of this kind of design. It's time we change our machine-oriented mind-set and invent the steering wheel, gas pedal and brakes for people of the Information Age. This idea brings me squarely to the goal of my vision for the near future: people should be able to use the new information technologies to do more by doing less.

5   When I say "doing more by doing less," I mean three things. First, we must bring new technologies into our lives, not vice versa. We will not accomplish more if we leave our current lives, don goggles and bodysuits, and enter some metallic, gigabyte-infested cyberspace. When the industrial revolution came, we didn't go to motorspace. The motors came to us as refrigerators to store our food and cars to transport us. This kind of transition is exactly what I expect will happen with computers and communications: they will come into our lives, and their identities will become synonymous with the useful tasks they perform.

6   Second, new technologies must increase human productivity and ease of use. Imagine if I could pull out a handheld device and say, "Take us to Athens this weekend." My computer would connect to the EasySabre airline reservation system and begin interacting with it, using the same commands that travel agents use. The machine would know that "us" is two people and that we like business class, aisle seats and so forth. It would negotiate with the airline computer for maybe 10 minutes, until it found an acceptable flight and confirmed it. I would have spent three seconds giving my order, whereas my electronic bulldozer—the handheld's software—would have worked for 10 minutes, or 600 seconds. The human productivity improvement in this example is 600 divided by three, which is 200, or, in business terms, 20,000 percent.

7   Such huge gains will not be possible everywhere, of course. But during the 21st century, I expect that we will be able to increase human productivity by 300 percent as we automate routine office activities and offload brain and eyeball work onto our electronic bulldozers. This transformation will happen in the same way that we offloaded muscle work onto bulldozers during the industrial revolution. We have not yet begun to see these gains from the information revolution. Now we click away at our browsers or e-mail screens, squinting our eyeballs and squeezing our brains. In essence, we are still "shoveling," but we don't notice, because we are holding diamond-studded shovels, stamped "high-tech." So our expectations of what computers can do for us must also change if we are to have a true revolution.

8   To date, computer vendors have abused the phrase "ease of use." When they call a system user-friendly, it is tantamount to dressing a chimp in scrubs and earnestly parading it around as a surgeon. When I say "ease of use," I do not mean incorporating more colors and floating animals into our systems. I mean true ease of use, even if the interaction is only via text. It is inconceivable to me that the differences between browsers and operating systems will persist beyond a few more years. Both access information—one at a distance, one locally—and because people need to do the same things with information regardless of where it resides, ease of use demands that we have only one set of commands for both. The current state of affairs is as ridiculous as if your steering wheel turned your car on city streets but applied the brakes out in the country.

9   The final way in which new technologies can enable people to do more by doing less is by including everyone in the word "people." With some 100 million machines interconnected today, we feel pretty smug. Yet that figure represents only 1.6 percent of the world's population. We think the world is communicating widely, but we still cannot hear the voices of billions through anything other than television and government information feeds. Moreover, the information revolution, left to its own devices, will increase the gap between rich and poor, simply because the rich will use their machines to become more productive, hence richer, while the poor stand still.

10   We cannot let this happen—if not for the sake of altruism, then for self-preservation. Such disparities inevitably lead to bloody conflicts. And if we decide to help, the potential is immense: the rich could use the new world of information to buy services and products from the poor, as was done earlier with manufacturing. A Virtual Compassion Corps could for the first time in history match the people proffering human help to those who need it, worldwide. In fact, a small group of undergraduate students at the MIT Laboratory for Computer Science have built a Web site to do precisely that. And help need not always travel from the developed to the developing world. Imagine a doctor in Sri Lanka who makes $20 a day administering health care to homeless people in Boston via a kiosk, equipped with a remote video and medical instrument connection and staffed by a nurse. The service might cost $5 a visit, and although not perfect, it would be superior to no health care at all.

11   This, then, is what I mean when I say that people should be able to do more by doing less: bring the technology into our lives, increase human productivity and ease of use, and offer these gains to all. Given this goal, let's take a look at the computing model over which this vision extends.

The Information Marketplace

12   My model of the information one I've talked about for the past 20 years—the Information Marketplace, the full capability of which is yet to be reached. In the coming decade, half a billion human-operated machines and countless computers—in the form of appliances, sensors, controllers and the like—will be interconnected. And these machines and their users will do three things: buy, sell and freely exchange information and information services. Some $50 billion changes hands over the Internet today. By 2030, I estimate that this flow will amount to 4 trillion of today's dollars, or one-quarter of the world's industrial economy. It will come predominantly from the office sector, which accounts for half of that overall economy. Indeed, a large part of the information services of the future will involve a new type of activity—the purchase and sale of information work. Imagine 1,000 accountants from Beijing doing accounting services for General Motors at $1 per hour.

13   The "free exchange" part of the Information Marketplace will be just as important. It will affect our lives through its family messages; collaborative activities; knowledge-building and accessing capabilities; political, literary and social exchanges; and many new activities.

14   Given the goal of doing more by doing less and the model of the Information Marketplace, how do we get there in practice? To that end, at the Laboratory for Computer Science, we have just launched a major research project. We expect it to result in a radically new hardware and software system called Oxygen, which will be tailored to people and their applications and will become as pervasive—we hope—as the air we breathe. This multimillion-dollar, five-year project involves some 30 faculty members from the Laboratory for Computer Science working in collaboration with the MIT Artificial Intelligence Lab.

Design Oxygen

15   At the heart of the Oxygen system is the Handy 21, which is like a camera, infrared detectors and a computer. The Handy 21 brings the help you need to where you are. Moreover it is all software-configurable in that it can change at the flip of a bit (in any country) from a cell phone to a two-way radio talking to other Handy 21s, to a network node near a high speed wireless office network or to a plain FM radio.

16   The second key technology of Oxygen is the Enviro 21. Unlike the Handy, which follows people, this device stays attached to the environments around people. It is built into the walls of your office and your house and into the trunk of your car. The Enviro 21 bears the same relation to the Handy 21 as does a power socket to a battery. It does everything the Handy 21 does but with greater capacity and speed. Enviro 21s may also be set up to regulate all kinds of devices and appliances, including sensors, controllers, phones, fax machines, and arrays of cameras or microphones.

17   Oxygen interacts with the inanimate physical world in two ways—through these controllable appliances and through the infrared detectors in the Handy 21s. If a door is of interest to your machines, you paste an infrared tag on it. Thereafter, when people point their Handy 21s to that door, the machines read the identity of the door and show what is supposed to be behind it. In other words, the system provides a kind of x-ray vision, helping people relate to the physical objects of interest in their environment.

18   The Handy 21s and Enviro 21s will be linked by way of a novel network, Net 21. Its principal function is to create a secure "collaborative" region among Oxygen users who wish to get together, wherever they may be. The Net 21 must do so on top of the noisy and huge Internet. It must be able to handle constant change as aggregates of participating nodes rise and collapse. It must find you wherever you are. It must connect to numerous appliances. And it must connect to the world's networks. This is no easy task. Oxygen will require a radically new approach to networking protocols that draws on self-organization and adaptation and that augments today's Internet.

19   Oxygen must also involve perceptual resources, especially speech understanding, and address people's inherent need to communicate naturally: we are not born with keyboard and mouse sockets but rather with mouths, ears and eyes. In Oxygen, speech understanding is built-in—and all parts of the system and all the applications will use speech. The systems built by Victor Zue and his group can handle narrow domains of inquiry, such as weather or airlines. We are stitching these narrow domains together—and incorporating vision and graphics where need be—to form a new quilt covering a broader front of human-machine communication.

20   Oxygen's fifth technology deals with people's need to find useful information. We are designing Oxygen so that you can first check your own knowledge stores in ways that are familiar to you. The system will allow you to say simply, "Get me the big red document that came a month ago," forgoing reference numbers and other clues. Oxygen will also check the stores of friends and associates who agree to share their knowledge with you, in the same sense that you might ask a friend or a co-worker a question if you don't know the answer yourself. Finally, Oxygen will search the vast information stores on the Web and "triangulate," relating what it finds there to you and your associates' stored knowledge bases.

21   Oxygen will also let people offload routine and repetitive work onto their electronic bulldozers. It will help users write scripts for automating various jobs, as well as monitor and control the many appliances connected to the Enviro 21s. "Turn up the heat." "Print it there." "Every day at noon, give me the price of my portfolio and the weather in Athens." Oxygen will take care of such instructions using a reason and control loop, which allows a person to guide the machine gently as it carries out automated tasks.

22   The system's collaboration technology will help people keep track of what they do as they move forward. For instance, the system will keep a hyperlinked summary of a meeting, provided by a human secretary, with the help of speech-understanding annotations. When you ask what was decided about, say, a new building's glass roof, it will give you the secretary's three-word summary—"We eliminated it"—but if you desire will also let you probe deeper into the chain of spoken and video input that led up to that conclusion.

23   Last, Oxygen will include customization technology that tailors information to individual needs. There will be no shrink-wrapped software. All software will be downloaded onto the Handy 21s and Enviro 21s from the Net 21 network, triggered by user requests, errors or upgrades. The customization technology will also let people adapt the machines around them to their own needs and habits throughout their use of the other Oxygen technologies.

A Claim and a Wish

24   Oxygen, then, is an integrated collection of eight new technologies: handhelds, wall and trunk computers, a novel net, built-in speech understanding, knowledge access, collaboration automation and customization. The power of Oxygen lies not in any one piece but in the totality of these human-oriented technologies together. They forge a new computing metaphor that we hope will mark an important shift from the desktop and icons of today, as those innovations did from text-only systems.

25   I will now stake a bigger claim: I believe that the five technologies of speech (and other perceptual capabilities), knowledge access, automation, collaboration, and customization are the only new kids on the block. Out of the thousands of things that we can imagine doing in the new world of information, these five are the foundations on which any new activities that help us do more by doing less will be built. For the next few decades at least, they are the steering wheel, the gas pedal and the brakes we seek—as well as the forces leading to a full-fledged Information Marketplace.

26   If this claim is valid, it suggests that people who want to exploit the new world of information should explore the capabilities of the new Oxygen technologies. Every individual and organization will have access to them. The ones who will truly do more by doing less will be the ones who learn how to integrate these technologies and their people into a well-oiled, humming whole. And good Oxygen applications that exploit speech, knowledge access, automation, collaboration, and customization will make it easier for people to reach their full potential. Imagine a health care application built on top of Oxygen: for knowledge access, it might use Medline (a searchable, online database of articles from medical journals, made available by the U.S. National Library of Medicine) and the patient records of hospitals, both available by speech. It could automate routine medical and administrative tasks, help doctors collaborate with one another and much more, taking its application "personality" from the capabilities of the underlying Oxygen system.

27   I hope that this vision, embodied in Oxygen and other systems like it, will help us break away from our 40-year machine preoccupation to a new era of people-oriented computing. And as we focus our technologies increasingly on human needs, perhaps we can make a bigger wish for the future. The first three socioeconomic revolutions were all based on things—the plow for the agrarian revolution, the motor for the industrial revolution, and the computer for the information revolution. Perhaps the time has come for the world to consider a fourth revolution, aimed no longer at objects but at understanding the most precious resource on earth—ourselves.

Understanding Content

1. What approach to computer science has been taken up to now? What is Dertouzos's opinion of that approach?
2. In the near future, Dertouzos believes that information technologies should allow people to do more by doing less. In your own words, explain what he means by "doing more by doing less."
3. What is the Information Marketplace model?
4. What are the chief features of the computer hardware and software system, Oxygen, under development at MIT?
5. What is the author's wish for the future?

Considering Structure and Technique

1. Dertouzos opens with an anecdote (paragraphs 1 and 2). What purpose does that anecdote serve? Do you think it makes an effective opening? Why or why not?
2. A metaphor is a comparison formed without using the words *like* or *as*. (For more on metaphors, see the workshop on p. 121.) For example in paragraph 3, Dertouzos uses a metaphor to compare computer technology to car design. Where else does he use this metaphor? What other metaphors appear in the piece? What do these metaphors contribute?
3. The author is the director of the MIT Laboratory for Computer Science, and he is treating a very technical topic. Yet he writes in a way understandable to a general audience. What techniques does he employ to make his essay readily understandable?
4. How does Dertouzos use examples in the essay?

Exploring Ideas

1. The young faculty member says that the author and his colleagues were unable to solve their technical computer problem because they were too old. Why did he think age was a factor?
2. In paragraphs 9–10, Dertouzos says that we cannot allow computers to widen the gap between the rich and poor because such gaps lead to

"bloody conflicts." Explain how bloody conflicts result from large gaps between the rich and poor.

3. In paragraph 13, Dertouzos tells about the "free-exchange" aspect of the Information Marketplace model he envisions for computer systems of the near future. What aspects of the Information Marketplace already exist? In what form?

4. In paragraph 21, the author says that Oxygen "will help users write scripts for automating various [routine and repetitive] jobs." If you had access to Oxygen, what jobs would you have it take over for you? Why?

Writing Workshop: Varying Sentence Openers

To keep your writing flowing well and to hold your reader's interest, you should vary the way you open sentences. Try opening some sentences with the subject, some with a word before the subject, some with a **phrase** (word group without both a subject and verb) before the subject, and some with a **clause** (word group with a subject and verb) before the subject. These ways to vary sentence openers can be illustrated with sentences from paragraph 1 of "The Future of Computing."

opening with subject:	I had been trying for about three hours to make my new laptop work. . . .
before the subject:	Frustrated, I turned to Tim Berners-Lee sitting next to me. . . .
opening with a phrase before the subject:	Last year a few of us from the Laboratory for Computer Science at the Massachusetts Institute of Technology were flying to Taiwan.
opening with a clause before the subject:	But when the card software was happy, the operating system complained, and vice versa.

Writing Workshop Activity

Form a group with three classmates and take turns reading drafts you are working on or pieces you wrote earlier this term. Does anyone hear any choppiness, any place where the flow would be improved by varying sentence openers? If so, revise to change some of the openings. Now read the passages aloud again. Did varying the openings improve the flow?

Language Notes for Multilingual and Other Writers

When the complete verb of a sentence includes a helping verb, remember that the helping verb (HV) always comes before the action verb (AV) or the linking verb (LV). Here are examples from "The Future of Computing."

Last year a few of us from the Laboratory for Computer Science at the
HV   AV
Massachusetts Institute of Technology were flying to Taiwan. Paragraph 1

HV   AV
. . . computer vendors have abused the phrase "ease of use." Paragraph 8
HV   LV
. . . it would be superior to no health care at all. Paragraph 10

Even when a word that is not a verb separates the helping verb and the ac-
tion or linking verb, the helping verb still comes first:
HV   AV
. . . we have just launched a major research project. Paragraph 14
HV   AV
We have not yet begun to see these gains . . . . Paragraph 7
HV   AV
Oxygen must also involve perceptual resources. . . . Paragraph 19

From Reading to Writing

In Your Journal: List the ways computers affect your life. What would your life be like without computers?

With Some Classmates: If Oxygen is developed in the ways Dertouzos describes and it becomes available to colleges, consider how it will affect the lives of college students. Then write a paper explaining one or more of the effects.

In an Essay

- Dertouzos has a specific hope for the future, one that he expresses in the last paragraph. Tell about your hope for the future and how computers and information technology can help that hope become a reality.
- Some people maintain that as a result of increased computer use, people are becoming more isolated from each other. They believe that the time we spend in front of our computer monitors limits meaningful human interaction. Other people maintain that computers bring people together. E-mail and chat rooms, for example, increase meaningful human interaction. Explain what you think and why.
- Select one computer application (e-mail, distance learning, computer-aided instruction, web surfing, chat rooms, Internet research, and so forth). Explain the role the application plays in your life and how you would like Oxygen to enhance the application and the role it plays.

Beyond the Writing Class: Dertouzos compares the technological revolution with the industrial revolution (paragraph 7), which is a common analogy. Research the industrial revolution in the Internet or in your library and write a paper that compares one or two of its features with features of the technological revolution.

A New Declaration of Independence
CHARLES SIEGEL

"A New Declaration of Independence," adapted from Charles Siegel's *The Preservationist's Manifesto* (1996), was published in the *Utne Reader* in 1996. While many of the other authors in this unit are excited about existing and emerging technology, Siegel is concerned, for he believes we are "calling for more technology to solve the problems caused by technology itself." See if you agree.

Preview. Siegel believes we should scale back our technology and solve a number of social, economic, and political problems as a result. However, such scaling back would not be easy. To do so, for instance, would you be willing to reduce speed limits to 30 miles per hour, limit automobile travel to short local trips, use a train for longer trips, stop shopping at large chain stores, and patronize smaller retail outlets instead?

Vocabulary. If any of the following words from the selection are unfamiliar to you, study their meanings before reading.

progressives (1)   those who favor change
conservatives (1)   those who favor little or no change
entrenched (1)   ingrained and protected
technocratic (2)   controlled by technicians
Mamie Eisenhower (2)   wife of President Eisenhower
autonomy (4)   independence
tack (5)   course
tract housing (6)   similarly designed housing
recede (7)   fall back
pipe dream (9)   fantasy
the left (13)   those who favor changes to help the common person
rhapsodize (14)   speak or write emotionally
indictment (15)   accusation against
paternalistic (17)   the practice of taking care of others
pervasive (17)   existing everywhere

America is at a crucial turning point. We have taken the distinction between progressives and conservatives so much for granted that it is now hard for us to think about politics in any other terms. Yet this way of looking at things was invented 200 years ago, at a time when modernization and progress were sweeping away entrenched privilege and challenging the status quo. It is no longer relevant now that modernization and progress *are* the status quo. . . .

2   Our problem is not modernization itself but technocratic modernism, the blind faith that technology can do everything better. This fascination with technology and growth transformed America during the postwar period when we were the only country with a strong enough economy to move at full speed toward the technological ideal. Mamie Eisenhower would not serve fresh vegetables in the White House because she considered canned and frozen vegetables more modern. Federal, state, and local governments did all they could to promote the construction of freeways, housing subdivisions, and shopping malls rather than neighborhoods where people could walk. Suburban parents sent their children to nursery schools, where they could benefit from special programs designed by experts in educational psychology.

3   Without question, modernization has had great successes—among them, curing disease and reducing poverty—but now we can see that the modernist faith has also failed in many ways. For example, we spend more than twice as much on each child's education than we did in 1960 (after correcting for inflation), but standardized tests show that students learn less than they did then. Or consider this: America's per capita national income is about twice what it was in 1960 (after correcting for inflation), but Americans do not feel that they are twice as well off as they were in 1960. In many ways, we feel worse off.

4   Yet we have not come up with a new political direction that responds to the failures of modernization as it relates to four important aspects of our lives: the physical and social environment of our neighborhoods, our places of business, our families, and our sense of personal autonomy. Instead, we are still calling for more technology to solve the problems caused by technology itself.

5   We should take the opposite tack. Most environmental and social problems we face today exist only because we have had such faith in technology and economic growth in this century that we've rushed headlong to modernize every activity of life, even in many cases when it is obvious that modernization doesn't work. Rather than applying more expertise and spending more money to solve these problems, we should get at their root by limiting technology and growth. We should use modern technology where it works and get the inappropriate technology out of the way.

Revitalizing Our Neighborhoods

6   To build workable neighborhoods, we need to rein in the automobile— and the best way to do this is to reduce the speed limit. How low should we go? Consider the impact of reducing the speed limit to 15 miles per hour for private vehicles within the city limits. It would allow people to use cars for local errands but force them to take higher-speed public transportation for longer trips. As a result, automobiles would no longer dominate the environment, and bicycles and small electric vehicles could easily fit into the flow of traffic. Streets would be friendlier to pedestrians, and safe enough for children to play in them. We would also have to limit the scale of development to make

room for slower forms of transportation. It is hard to get around on a bicycle or in an electric cart, and virtually impossible to walk anywhere, if you inhabit a landscape of tract housing and shopping malls.

7   Another possibility would be to cut the speed limit to 30 miles per hour. That would shift long-distance commuting from the freeways to high-speed rail systems. Commercial development would cluster around the rail stations to take advantage of the new customer base; freeway-oriented shopping malls would make way for mixed-use shopping and office complexes (with plenty of parking) at rail stations. Some of the suburban sprawl at the edges of metropolitan areas would also recede because it is totally dependent on high-speed freeway access.

8   Yet, if the city bad a high-speed rail system, this change would still allow everyone to live in a suburban neighborhood. The big differences from today's suburbs would be that people would shop and work in mixed-use complexes, which are far more interesting than shopping malls and office parks, and most commutes would be less grueling. This change would also cut automobile use roughly in half, dramatically reducing the city's environmental problems.

9   Are these ideas a mere pipe dream? Not necessarily. Cities all over the world are "calming" traffic on residential streets. In the 1980s, Germany began an ambitious experiment that went further, slowing traffic on both residential and arterial streets in areas ranging from a neighborhood in Berlin with 30,000 residents to a small town of 2,300 residents. The government cut the speed limit in half but discovered that the time for the average trip increased by just a bit over 10 percent. Obviously, one result of traffic calming was to shorten the length of the average trip. In addition, noise levels and injuries from automobile accidents dropped dramatically. The German automobile association, which was skeptical about the government's data, conducted its own interviews and found that, after speeds were lowered, 67 percent of motorists and even higher proportions of residents approved of the change. The experiment was so successful, in fact, that it has since been imitated in cities in Denmark, Sweden, the Netherlands, Italy, Switzerland, Austria, and Japan.

Protecting Our Small Businesses

10   To promote civic life, it would also be useful to phase out chain stores and reduce the overall scale of retail outlets, so that national megastores could not displace locally owned businesses. Some cities already have zoning laws that restrict chains, but it would be more effective to have a national law limiting the number of stores that one company could own—to break up existing chains and reduce the mind-numbing sameness that now blankets most of the United States.

11   Eliminating chains would increase some costs. Obviously, chains and superstores are more efficient than most independently owned stores because of their vast economies of scale. In some cases—supermarkets, for example—the economic benefits of chains might outweigh their social costs. But in others—

most notably book-selling—quality, diversity, and the free flow of ideas are so important that it is urgent to get rid of the chains, even if the costs increase.

12   Replacing chains with small businesses would lower overall productivity, but retailing is one of the few industries that can stay small without hurting a country's economic position internationally. Virtually all of Japan's retailing is done by mom-and-pop businesses, but it hasn't prevented Japan from becoming one of the most prosperous countries in the world.

Making Our Families Work

13   Moving from the storefront to the home front, it is clear that some of our most deep-seated social problems result from the modernization of the family. Few would dispute that there is a "parenting deficit" in America today. Children are suffering not only because families are breaking up but also because, even in intact families, both parents must work full time to keep up financially. The left generally ignores this new problem and continues to push for family policies from early in the century: more money for day care, Head Start, and schooling. These ideas made sense in the 1950s, when stable families were the norm and most people believed in progressive methods of raising children. But today even the left is disillusioned with them. They support these programs to help cope with family breakdown, but they have no vision of a better future.

14   By default, this territory now belongs to the conservatives who rhapsodize about "the traditional family" (by which they really mean the early modern family, with a husband who goes to work in a factory or office and a wife who stays home). The conservatives strike a chord with many voters because they don't deny the damage done by the decline of the family during the past few decades, but they can't go any farther than that because they are also champions of economic growth.

15   The fact that parents no longer have time for their children is the worst possible indictment of the modern economy. Rather than demanding more day care and schooling to help families conform to the economy, the left should be demanding radical changes in the growth economy to make it work for families. One practical approach would be to change the current tax laws—and corporate subsidy programs—which discriminate against parents who take care of their own children. Many parents already get tax credits and subsidies to help pay for day care. Why not give parents who forgo day care equivalent benefits? In many cases, equal benefits would make it possible for parents to cut back their work hours and raise their children on their own.

16   But larger economic changes are also needed. In 1950, one parent working 40 hours a week was enough to support a typical family. If we had been more sensible, we could have used the phenomenal rise of women in the workforce from the 1960s onward to create families supported by two parents, each working 20 hours a week. The original promise of modernization was that higher productivity would give people more leisure, but the economy has not kept this promise.

Restoring Our Personal Autonomy

17 Technocratic modernism undermines autonomy in the same way that it undermines the neighborhood and the family. Economic planners, urban planners, and social planners take over individuals' personal decisions by redefining them as technical problems that only "the experts" can deal with. The tone is usually paternalistic. The experts themselves believe they are using modern methods to "help" people, but, in reality, they are controlling people and increasing the feelings of powerlessness and dependence that are pervasive in modern society.

18 The most astounding example of the way that we allow bureaucracies to control our live is our commitment to the idea that the economic system must "help" people by "providing jobs." This idea made sense in the early part of the century when most people needed more income to buy necessities. But now that we no longer have that problem, we need to give people the ability to choose their own standard of living. In a surplus economy, the idea that we must provide jobs for people forces us to promote economic growth, even if most of the products we produce are useless.

19 Not surprisingly, we think about work like consumers. We think in terms of *having* jobs, not in terms of *doing* jobs because they are useful. We demand more jobs just as we demand more transportation, education, health care, child care, and more of any "service" that we expect the system to provide. And, in the process, we lose sight of the fact that we are actually demanding to do unnecessary work.

20 It is reasonable to work until you produce what you want, then stop. But, as a culture, we believe in creating demand for products that people don't really want purely to create extra work for ourselves. To put the economy back on a rational basis, to produce the goods and services that people actually want, we need to offer job seekers more flexible work hours. One way would be to give employers tax incentives to create more part-time jobs and accommodate different work schedules without penalizing part-time workers with lower hourly pay, restricted benefits, or fewer promotion opportunities. Federal, state, and local governments should act as a model by offering their own employees work hours that are as flexible as possible.

21 We can't expect employers to take advantage of flexible work hours, though, unless we limit the demands that the consumer economy makes on them. In part, this would involve changing personal behavior—getting people to go beyond the "shop till you drop" mindset that makes Americans spend three to four times as many hours shopping as Europeans do. But it also would require larger political changes, such as rebuilding American cities, where it now is absolutely essential for most families to own two cars.

Humanizing the Economy

22 We can use the law to control growth if we learn to think about technology in human terms, rather than focusing on the abstractions that only "the

experts" can work with. As long as we think of transportation, land use, and pollution control as "urban problems," we will surrender to the city planners and let them decide what kinds of neighborhoods we live in. But if we can focus on the human purpose of our cities—they are the places where we live—it will become obvious that the people themselves should make the political and personal decisions that will shape the city's design.

23   Similarly, as long as we think of unemployment and inflation as "economic problems," we will allow economists to decide what our standard of living should be. But when we think about the human purpose of the economy—to produce things that we actually want —it becomes obvious that workers should chose their own work schedules and standard of living. Planning is useful to control the business cycles and fine tune the economy, but this planning should be subordinate to the human question of what we want to consume, which individuals should decide for themselves.

24   The bias of the consumer economy has crippled our politics. Real change will be possible when people act as citizens who use the law to govern themselves—not as clients demanding more services from the system and voting for the politicians they think will do the best job of providing them with more education, more health care, more transportation, and, most important, more jobs. The moral advantage of limiting technology is that it increases individual freedom and responsibility, which have been eroded by modernization. Someone always objects that limiting technology is unrealistic—for example, that Americans will never vote to lower the speed limit. That may be true today, but only because people believe that building livable cities is a technical problem that the planners must solve for them, and that their role is just to demand services from the planners. People will act differently if they see that, in order to have decent cities to live in, well-educated children, and an economy that produces things they want, they must consume less and do more for themselves.

Understanding Content

1. First Lady Mamie Eisenhower served canned and frozen vegetables, rather than fresh, in the White House. Why? What does her preference suggest about our view of technology?
2. What does Siegel think has caused our environmental and social problems?
3. According to Siegel, how will reducing the speed limit improve our neighborhoods?
4. What does the author see wrong with the way we think about work?
5. Siegel says that we should think about technology in human terms. What does he mean?

Considering Structure and Technique

1. Which sentence in the essay best expresses the thesis of the "The New Declaration of Independence?
2. A number of paragraphs come before the thesis. What purpose do they serve?
3. In **problem-solution order,** a writer states a problem early on and devotes one or more body paragraphs to explaining one or more solutions to the problem. How does Siegel use problem-solution order?
4. In paragraphs 9 and 12, Siegel cites the experiences of other countries as examples. Do these examples provide effective support? Why or why not?
5. As part of a **persuasive strategy,** writers can mention the views of people who disagree with them and then go on to counter the objections in some way. What objection does Siegel acknowledge in paragraph 24? How does he deal with that objection?

Exploring Ideas

1. Do you agree with Siegel that our neighborhoods are not workable? Explain why or why not.
2. Siegel advocates federal legislation to eliminate chain stores. What do you think of this idea? Is such legislation possible?
3. In paragraph 15, Siegel says, "The fact that parents no longer have time for their children is the worst possible indictment of the modern economy." Do you believe it is a fact that parents have no time for their children? Explain.
4. In paragraph 24, Siegel says that Americans will agree to limit technology when they are shown the benefits of doing so. Do you agree? Explain your view.
5. Did Siegel convince you that we should scale back technology? Why or why not?

Writing Workshop: Concluding with a New, Related Idea

You can sometimes write an effective conclusion by introducing a new idea that is closely related to the ideas already discussed. For example, in "The New Declaration of Independence," Siegel concludes by restating a number of previously mentioned points, but he also states an idea not previously discussed: that people will limit technology when they realize what the benefits of doing so are.

Writing Workshop Activity

With some classmates, rewrite the conclusion of "The New Declaration of Independence" so that it expresses a new, related idea—but not the same one currently expressed. Be sure the idea is closely related to the rest of the essay.

Language Notes for Multilingual and Other Writers

In some languages, a pronoun before the verb restates the subject. In English, however, the subject is stated once in each clause—no pronoun restatement is used.

yes: America is at a crucial turning point.

 no: America <u>it</u> is at a crucial turning point.

yes: This fascination with technology and growth transformed America.

 no: This fascination with technology and growth <u>it</u> transformed America.

From Reading to Writing

In Your Journal: Discuss one or two ways that technology has improved your life and one or two ways it has detracted from your quality of life.

With Some Classmates: Imagine a 10-minute discussion about technology between Charles Siegel and Bill Gates. Write a transcript of that discussion.

In an Essay

- Summarize "The New Declaration of Independence" and then evaluate the strength or weakness of one of Siegel's ideas.
- In paragraph 16, Siegel advocates the idea of "families supported by two parents, each working 20 hours a week." What do you think of this idea?
- Using a problem-solution organization (see above, "Considering Structure and Technique," question 3), state and suggest a solution to a technology-related problem not mentioned in "The New Declaration of Independence."
- Siegel takes exception to our "blind faith that technology can do everything better." Discuss one or more things that technology does not do better, focusing on specifics not mentioned in "The New Declaration of Independence."

Beyond the Writing Class: Evaluate one or more uses of technology on your campus, and write a letter to the editor of your campus newspaper praising or criticizing the use(s). Be sure to give reasons for your view.

Virtual Love
MEGHAN DAUM

A contributing editor at *Harper's Bazaar,* Megan Daum has written for the *New York Times Book Review, GQ, Vogue,* and other publications. She also has written a collection of essays called *Let the Trinkets Do the Talking.* "Virtual Love," a narrative account of her e-mail romance, first appeared in *The New Yorker* in 1997.

Preview.   Meghan Daum was not "a computer person," but she found herself involved in a cyber-romance. Then she met the object of her affection face-to-face. How do you think the meeting affected their relationship? Why do you think this?

Vocabulary.   If any of the following words from the selection are unfamiliar to you, study their meanings before reading.

construed (1)   interpreted
icon (2)   symbol
palpable (5)   unmistakable
volatile (5)   short-lived
innocuous (6)   harmless, inoffensive
conceit (6)   fanciful idea
Howard Stern (11)   a controversial radio personality
oxymoron (12)   a contradiction
periphery (12)   edge; border
requisite (14)   required
inertia (14)   lack of motion; passiveness
systemic (16)   affecting the whole body
narcissism (18)   self-admiration
epistolary (18)   relating to letters, especially ones that became part of the
   New Testament
tarmac (25)   a runway
epistle (31)   a letter, especially one that became part of the New Testament

It was last November; fall was drifting away into an intolerable chill. I was at the end of my twenty-sixth year, and was living in New York City, trying to support myself as a writer, and taking part in the kind of urban life that might be construed as glamorous were it to appear in a memoir in the distant future. At the time, however, my days felt more like a grind than like an adventure: hours of work strung between the motions of waking up, getting the mail, watching TV with my roommates, and going to bed. One morning, I logged on to my America Online account to find a message under the heading "is this the real meghan daum?" It came from someone with the screen name PFSlider. The body of the message consisted of five sentences, written entirely in lower-case letters, of perfectly turned flattery: something about PFSlider's admiration of some newspaper and magazine articles I had published over the last year and a half, something about his resulting infatuation with me, and something about his being a sportswriter in California.

2   I was engaged for the thirty seconds that it took me to read the message and fashion a reply. Though it felt strange to be in the position of confirming that I was indeed "the real meghan daum," I managed to say, "Yes, it's me. Thank you for writing." I clicked the "Send Now" icon, shot my words into the void, and forgot about PFSlider until the next day, when I received another message, this one headed "eureka."

3   "wow, it is you," he wrote, still in lower case. He chronicled the various conditions under which he'd read my few-and-far-between articles—a board-walk in Laguna Beach, the spring-training pressroom for a baseball team that he covered for a Los Angeles newspaper. He confessed to having a crush on me. He referred to me as "princess daum." He said he wanted to have lunch with me during one of his two annual trips to New York.

4   The letter was outrageous and endearingly pathetic, possibly the practical joke of a friend trying to rouse me out of a temporary writer's block. But the kindness pouring forth from my computer screen was bizarrely exciting, and I logged off and thought about it for a few hours before writing back to express how flattered and "touched"—this was probably the first time I had ever used that word in earnest—I was by his message.

5   I am not what most people would call a computer person. I have no interest in chat rooms, newsgroups, or most Web sites. I derive a palpable thrill from sticking a letter in the United Starts mail. But I have a constant low-grade fear of the telephone, and I often call people with the intention of getting their answering machines. There is something about the live voice that I have come to find unnervingly organic, as volatile as live television. E-mail provides a useful antidote for my particular communication anxieties. Though I generally send and receive only a few messages a week, I take comfort in their silence and their boundaries.

6   PFSlider and I tossed a few innocuous, smart-assed notes back and forth over the week following his first message. Let's say his name was Pete. He was twenty-nine, and single. I revealed very little about myself, relying instead on the ironic commentary and forced witticisms that are the conceit of so many E-mail messages. But I quickly developed an oblique affection for PFSlider. I was excited when there was a message from him, mildly depressed when there wasn't. After a few weeks, he gave me his phone number. I did not give him mine, but he looked it up and called me one Friday night. I was home. I picked up the phone. His voice was jarring, yet not unpleasant. He held up more than

his end of the conversation for an hour, and when he asked permission to call me again I granted it, as though we were of an earlier era.

7   Pete—I could never wrap my mind around his name, privately thinking of him as PFSlider, "E-mail guy"," or even "baseball boy"—began phoning me two or three times a week. He asked if he could meet me, and I said that that would be O.K. Christmas was a week away, and he told me that he would be coming back East to see his family. From there, he would take a short flight to New York and have lunch with me.

8   "It is my off-season mission to meet you," he said.

9   "There will probably be a snowstorm," I said.

10   "I'll take a team of sled dogs," he answered.

11   We talked about our work and our families, about baseball and Howard Stern and sex, about his hatred for Los Angeles and how much he wanted a new job. Sometimes we'd find each other logged on simultaneously and type back and forth for hours.

12   I had previously considered cyber-communication an oxymoron, a fast road to the breakdown of humanity. But, curiously, the Internet—at least in the limited form in which I was using it—felt anything but dehumanizing. My interaction with PFSlider seemed more authentic than much of what I experienced in the daylight realm of living beings. I was certainly putting more energy into the relationship than I had put into many others. I also was giving Pete attention that was by definition undivided, and relishing the safety of the distance between us by opting to be truthful instead of doling out the white lies that have become the staple of real life. The outside world— the place where I walked around avoiding people I didn't want to deal with, peppering my casual conversations with half-truths, and applying my motto "Let the machine take it" to almost any scenario—was sliding into the periphery of my mind.

13   For me, the time online with Pete was far superior to the phone. There were no background noises, no interruptions from "call waiting," no long distance charges. Through typos and misspellings, he flirted maniacally." I have an absurd crush on you," he said. "If I like you in person, you must promise to marry me." I was coy and conceited, telling him to get a life, baiting him into complimenting me further, teasing him in a way I would never have dared to do in person, or even on the phone. I would stay up until 3 A.M. typing with him, smiling at the screen, getting so giddy that when I quit I couldn't fall asleep. I was having difficulty recalling what I used to do at night. It was as if he and I lived together in our own quiet space—a space made all the more intimate because of our conscious decision to block everyone else out. My phone was tied up for hours at a time. No one in the real world could reach me, and I didn't really care.

14   Since my last serious relationship, I'd had the requisite number of false starts and five-night stands, dates that I wasn't sure were dates, and emphatically casual affairs that buckled under their own inertia. With PFSlider, on the other hand, I may not have known my suitor, but, for the first time in my life,

I knew the deal: I was a desired person, the object of a blind man's gaze. He called not only when he said he would call but unexpectedly, just to say hello. He was protected by the shield of the Internet; his guard was not merely down but nonexistent. He let his phone bill grow to towering proportions. He told me that he thought about me all the time, though we both knew that the "me" in his mind consisted largely of himself. He talked about me to his friends, and admitted it. He arranged his holiday schedule around our impending date. He managed to charm me with sports analogies. He didn't hesitate. He was unblinking and unapologetic.

15   And so PFSlider became my everyday life. All the tangible stuff fell away. My body did not exist. I had no skin, no hair, no bones. All desire had converted itself into a cerebral current that reached nothing but my frontal lobe. There was no outdoors, no social life, no weather. There was only the computer screen and the phone, my chair, and maybe a glass of water. Most mornings, I would wake up to find a message from PFSlider, composed in Pacific time while I slept in the wee hours. "I had a date last night," he wrote. "And I am not ashamed to say it was doomed from the start because I couldn't stop thinking about you."

16   I fired back a message slapping his hand. "We must be careful where we tread," I said. This was true but not sincere. I wanted it, all of it. I wanted unfettered affection, soul-mating, true romance. In the weeks that had elapsed since I picked up "is this the real meghan daum?" the real me had undergone some kind of meltdown—a systemic rejection of all the savvy and independence I had worn for years, like a grownup Girl Scout badge.

17   Pete knew nothing of my scattered, juvenile self, and I did my best to keep it that way. Even though I was heading into my late twenties, I was still a child, ignorant of dance steps and health insurance, a prisoner of credit-card debt and student loans and the nagging feeling that I didn't want anyone to find me until I had pulled myself into some semblance of an adult. The act that Pete had literally seemed to discover me, as if by turning over a rock, lent us an aura of fate which I actually took half-seriously. Though skepticism seemed like the obvious choice in this strange situation, I discarded it precisely because it was the obvious choice, because I wanted a more interesting narrative than cynicism would ever allow. I was a true believer in the urban dream: the dream of years of struggle, of getting a break, or making it. Like most of my friends, I wanted someone to love me, but I wasn't supposed to need it. To admit to loneliness was to smack the face of progress, to betray the times in which we lived. But PFSlider derailed me. He gave me all of what I'd never even realized I wanted.

18   My addiction to PFSlider's messages indicated a monstrous narcissism, but it also revealed a subtler desire, which I didn't fully understand at the time. My need to experience an old-fashioned kind of courtship was stronger than I had ever imagined. And the fact that technology was providing an avenue for such archaic discourse was a paradox that both fascinated and repelled me. Our relationship had an epistolary quality that put our communication closer to the eighteenth century than to the impending millennium. Thanks to the

computer, I was involved in a well-defined courtship, a neat little space in which he and I were both safe to express the panic and the fascination of our mutual affection. Our interaction was refreshingly orderly, noble in its vigor, dignified despite its shamelessness. It was far removed from the randomness of real-life relationships. We had an intimacy that seemed custom-made for our strange, lonely times. It seemed custom-made for me.

19   The day of our date, a week before Christmas, was frigid and sunny. Pete was sitting at the bar of the restaurant when I arrived. We shook hands. For a split second, he leaned toward me with his chin, as if to kiss me. He was shorter than I had pictured, though he was not short. He struck me as clean-cut. He had very nice hands. He wore a very nice shirt. We were seated at a very nice table. I scanned the restaurant for people I knew, saw none, and couldn't decide how I felt about that.

20   He talked, and I heard nothing he said. I stared at his profile and tried to figure out whether I liked him. He seemed to be saying nothing in particular, but he went on forever. Later, we went to the Museum of Natural History and watched a science film about storm chasers. We walked around looking for the dinosaurs, and he talked so much that I wanted to cry. Outside, walking along Central Park West at dusk, through the leaves, past the yellow cabs and the splendid lights of Manhattan at Christmas, he grabbed my hand to kiss me and I didn't let him. I felt as if my brain had been stuffed with cotton. Then, for some reason, I invited him back to my apartment. I gave him a few beers and finally let him kiss me on the lumpy futon in my bedroom. The radiator clanked. The phone rang and the machine picked up. A car alarm blared outside. A key turned in the door as one of my roommates came home. I had no sensation at all—only a clear conviction that I wanted Pete out of my apartment. I wanted to hand him his coat, close the door behind him, and fight the ensuing emptiness by turning on the computer and taking comfort in PFSlider.

21   When Pete finally did leave, I berated myself from every angle: for not kissing him on Central Park West, for not letting him kiss me at all, for not liking him, for wanting to like him more than I had wanted anything in such a long time. I was horrified by the realization that I had invested so heavily in a made-up character—a character in whose creation I'd had a greater hand than even Pete himself. How could I, a person so self-congratulatingly reasonable, have been sucked into a scenario that was more akin to a television talk show than to the relatively full and sophisticated life I was so convinced I led? How could I have received a fan letter and allowed it to go this far?

22   The next day, a huge bouquet of FTD flowers arrived from him. No one had ever sent me flowers before. I forgave him. As human beings with actual flesh and hand gestures and Gap clothing, Pete and I were utterly incompatible, but I decided to pretend otherwise. He returned home and we fell back into the computer and the phone, and I continued to keep the real world safely away from the desk that held them. Instead of blaming him for my disap-

pointment, I blamed the earth itself, the invasion of roommates and ringing phones into the immaculate communication that PFSlider and I had created.

23   When I pictured him in the weeks that followed, I saw the image of a plane lifting off over an overcast city. PFSlider was otherworldly, more a concept than a person. His romance lay in the notion of flight, the physics of gravity defiance. So when he offered to send me a plane ticket to spend the weekend with him in Los Angeles I took it as an extension of our blissful remoteness, a dimensional E-mail message lasting an entire weekend.

24   The temperature on the runway at J.F.K. was seven degrees Fahrenheit. Our DC-10 sat for three hours waiting for deicing. Finally, it took off over the frozen city, and the ground below shrank into a drawing of itself. Phone calls were made, laptop computers were plopped onto tray tables. The recirculating air dried out my contact lenses. I watched movies without the sound and told myself that they were probably better that way. Something about the plastic interior of the fuselage and the plastic forks and the din of the air and the engines was soothing and strangely sexy.

25   Then we descended into LAX. We hit the tarmac, and the seatbelt signs blinked off. I hadn't moved my body in eight hours, and now I was walking through the tunnel to the gate, my clothes wrinkled, my hair matted, my hands shaking. When I saw Pete in the terminal, his face seemed to me just as blank and easy to miss as it had the first time I'd met him. He kissed me chastely. On the way out to the parking lot, he told me that he was being seriously considered for a job in New York. He was flying back there next week. If he got the job, he'd be moving within the month. I looked at him in astonishment. Something silent and invisible seemed to fall on us. Outside, the wind was warm, and the Avis arid Hertz buses ambled alongside the curb of Terminal 5. The palm trees shook, and the air seemed heavy and palpable as Pete's hand, which held mine for a few seconds before dropping it to get his car keys out of his pocket. He stood before me, all flesh and preoccupation, and for this I could not forgive him.

26   Gone were the computer, the erotic darkness of the telephone, the clean, single dimension of Pete's voice at 1 A.M. It was nighttime, yet the combination or sight and sound was blinding. It scared me. It turned me off. We went to a restaurant and ate outside on the sidewalk. We strained for conversation, and I tried not to care that we had to. We drove to his apartment and stood under the ceiling light not really looking at each other. Something was happening that we needed to snap out of. Any moment now, I thought. Any moment and we'll be all right. These moments were crowded with elements, with carpet fibres and automobiles and the smells of everything that had a smell. It was all wrong. The physical world had invaded our space.

27   For three days, we crawled along the ground and tried to pull ourselves up. We talked about things that I can no longer remember. We read the Los Angeles *Times* over breakfast. We drove north past Santa Barbara to tour the wine country. I felt like an object that could not be lifted, something that

secretly weighed more than the world itself. Everything and everyone around us seemed imbued with a California lightness. I stomped around the countryside, an idiot New Yorker in my chunky shoes and black leather jacket. Not until I studied myself in the bathroom mirror of a highway rest stop did I fully realize the preposterousness of my uniform. I was dressed for war. I was dressed for my regular life.

28   That night, in a tiny town called Solvang, we ate an expensive dinner. We checked into a Marriott and watched television. Pete talked at me and through me and past me. I tried to listen. I tried to talk. But I bored myself and irritated him. Our conversation was a needle that could not be threaded. Still, we played nice. We tried to care, and pretended to keep trying long after we had given up. In the car on the way home, he told me that I was cynical, and I didn't have the presence of mind to ask him just how many cynics he had met who would travel three thousand miles to see someone they barely knew.

29   Pete drove me to the airport at 7 A.M. so I could make my eight-o'clock flight home. He kissed me goodbye—another chaste peck that I recognized from countless dinner parties and dud dates. He said that he'd call me in a few days when he got to New York for his job interview, which we had discussed only in passing and with no reference to the fact that New York was where I happened to live. I returned home to frozen January. A few days later, he came to New York, and we didn't see each other. He called me from the plane taking him back to Los Angeles to tell me, through the static, that he had got the job. He was moving to my city.

30   PFSlider was dead. There would be no meeting him in distant hotel lobbies during the baseball season. There would be no more phone calls or E-mail messages. In a single moment, Pete had completed his journey out of our mating dance and officially stepped into the regular world—the world that gnawed at me daily, the world that fostered those five-night stands, the world where romance could not be sustained, because so many of us simply did not know how to do it. Instead, we were all chitchat and leather jackets, bold proclaimers of all that we did not need. But what struck me most about this affair was the unpredictable nature of our demise. Unlike most cyber-romances, which seem to come fully equipped with the inevitable set of misrepresentations and false expectations, PFSlider and I had played it fairly straight. Neither of us had lied. We'd done the best we could. Our affair had died from natural causes rather than virtual ones.

31   Within a two-week period after I returned from Los Angeles, at least seven people confessed to me the vagaries of their own E-mail affairs. This topic arose, unprompted, in the course of normal conversation. I heard most of these stories in the close confines of smoky bars and crowded restaurants, and we all shook our heads in bewilderment as we told our tales, our eyes focussed on some point in the distance. Four of these people had met their correspondents, by travelling from New Haven to Baltimore, from New York to Montana, from Texas to Virginia, and from New York to Johannesburg. These were normal people, writers and lawyers and scientists. They were all smart,

attractive, and more than a little sheepish about admitting just how deeply they had been sucked in. Mostly, it was the courtship ritual that had seduced us. E-mail had become an electronic epistle, a yearned-for rule book. It allowed us to do what was necessary to experience love. The Internet was not responsible for our remote, fragmented lives. The problem was life itself.

32   The story of PFSlider still makes me sad, not so much because we no longer have anything to do with each other but because it forces me to see the limits and the perils of daily life with more clarity than I used to. After I realized that our relationship would never transcend the screen and the phone—that, in fact, our face-to-face knowledge of each other had permanently contaminated the screen and the phone—I hit the pavement again, went through the motions of everyday life, said hello and goodbye to people in the regular way. If Pete and I had met at a party, we probably wouldn't have spoken to each other for more than ten minutes, and that would have made life easier but also less interesting. At the same time, it terrifies me to admit to a firsthand understanding of the way the heart and the ego are snarled and entwined like diseased trees that have folded in on each other. Our need to worship somehow fuses with our need to be worshipped. It upsets me still further to see how inaccessibility can make this entanglement so much more intoxicating. But I'm also thankful that I was forced to unpack the raw truth of my need and stare at it for a while. It was a dare I wouldn't have taken in three dimensions.

33   The last time I saw Pete, he was in New York, three thousand miles away from what had been his home, and a million miles away from PFSlider. In a final gesture of decency, in what I later realized was the most ordinary kind of closure, he took me out to dinner. As the few remaining traces of affection turned into embarrassed regret, we talked about nothing. He paid the bill. He drove me home in a rental car that felt as arbitrary and impersonal as what we now were to each other.

34   Pete had known how to get me where I lived until he came to where I lived: then he became as unmysterious as anyone next door. The world had proved to be too cluttered and too fast for us, too polluted to allow the thing we'd attempted through technology ever to grow in the earth. PFSlider and I had joined the angry and exhausted living. Even if we met on the street, we wouldn't recognize each other, our particular version of intimacy now obscured by the branches and bodies and falling debris that make up the physical world.

Understanding Content

1. How did Daum react to PFSlider's first two e-mails?
2. How did Daum's initial view of her e-mail correspondence with PFSlider change? Trace the course of her view of the correspondence.
3. How did Daum feel about PFSlider on their first date?
4. How did she react to the news that he might move to New York? Why did she react that way?
5. What did the author learn from her cyber-romance?

Considering Structure and Technique

1. Explain the meaning of the title. Do you think the title is effective? Why or why not?
2. Because "Virtual Love" tells a story, it is a **narration.** Narration is often enhanced by description that helps the reader form a mental image of people and places important to the story. For example, in paragraph 1 the scene is set with this description: "It was November; fall was drifting away into an intolerable chill." Cite three other examples of description that you find particularly effective.
3. **Transitions** are words and phrases that signal how ideas relate to each other. (For more on transitions, see p. 35.) Because Daum's narrative details are arranged in **chronological** (time) order, a number of paragraphs open with transitions that signal that chronological order. Identify the paragraphs that open with transitions to signal chronological order and identify the transitions.
4. Daum uses repetition for particular effects. For example, in paragraph 14, the third and subsequent sentences begin with "He." Read those sentences aloud. What effect does the repetition create? What is the effect of the repetition of "very nice" in paragraph 19?

Exploring Ideas

1. PFSlider wrote all in lower-case letters, a practice becoming increasingly common in casual e-mail correspondence. Why do you think that practice is becoming common?
2. In paragraph 6, Daum says that in her first messages to PFSlider, she "revealed very little about [her]self, relying instead on the ironic commentary and forced witticisms that are the conceit of so many E-mail messages." Explain what Daum means.
3. Why did Daum become so involved in the e-mail correspondence with PFSlider?
4. How does the essay point out that "virtual love" can be both safe and dangerous?

Writing Workshop: Concluding by Explaining Why Events Happened

One way to conclude a narration is to explain why the events happened as they did. Meghan Daum does this in the final paragraph of "Virtual Love." First she explains why she began the correspondence: "Pete had known how to get me where I lived." Then she explains why the relationship failed: " . . . he became as unmysterious as anyone next door. The world had proved to be too cluttered and too fast for us." Finally, she explains why she and Pete would no longer recognize each other: " . . . our particular version of intimacy was now obscured by the . . . physical world."

Writing Activity Workshop

Read or reread "No Turning Back" on p. 133. Add a paragraph at the end that explains why one or more of the events happened. What do you think of this new conclusion?

Language Notes for Multilingual and Other Writers

A number of expressions in "Virtual Love" relate to the way people think or feel.

1. *To wrap your mind around* means "to comprehend."

   I could never <u>wrap my mind around</u> his name, privately thinking of him as PFSlider . . . Paragraph 7

2. *To be turned off* means "to lose interest or to be bothered by something."

   It scared me. It <u>turned me off</u>. Paragraph 26

3. *To snap out of* means "to regain one's composure."

   Something was happening that we needed <u>to snap out of</u>. Paragraph 26

4. *To get you where you live* means "to affect your emotions deeply."

   Pete had known how <u>to get me where I lived</u> until he came to where I lived . . . " Paragraph 34

From Reading to Writing

In Your Journal: Describe your own e-mail, chat room, listserv, or message-board relationships with others, if you involve yourself in any of these activities. If not, explain why you think so many people experience "virtual relationships."

With Some Classmates: Daum says, "We had an intimacy that seemed custom-made for our strange, lonely times." Do you think our times are "strange and lonely"? Explain why or why not.

In an Essay

- In paragraph 5, Daum says she is not "what most people would call a computer person." Write an essay that defines a computer person. Present and illustrate the characteristics of a such a person. If you like, you can make this humorous.
- In paragraph 12, Daum states that her "interaction with PFSlider seemed more authentic than much of what [she] experienced in the daylight realm of living beings." Evaluate the authenticity of Internet communication (e-mail, chatrooms, message boards, and listservs).
- In paragraph 31, Daum blames "life itself" for her situation. Do you agree? Why or why not?

Beyond the Writing Class: Research the danger to young people who engage in e-mail correspondences and chat room communications with a stranger and then meet the person. Write a paper for young people explaining the dangers and providing safety guidelines for Internet use.

⇒ CONNECTING THE READINGS

1. In "Fighting to Fill the Values Gap (p. 221)," Melissa Healy writes of the values movement. Discuss how proponents of the values movement would view the family structures described in "Hold the Mayonnaise" (p. 118) and "Stone Soup" (p. 148).

2. In "Just Walk on By" (p. 195), Brent Staples discusses the way our physical appearance affects how others perceive and treat us. In "Beauty: When the Other Dancer Is the Self" (p. 211), Alice Walker discusses the way our physical appearance affects our view of ourselves. How conditioned are we to "judge a book by its cover"? What can we do to counter the forces that incline us to make judgments based on appearance? Respond in an essay.

3. Nicholas Gage thrived as a result of his school experience ("The Teacher Who Changed My Life," p. 181); So Tsi-fai ("So Tsi-fai," p. 188) did not. Account for the difference in their experiences, and explain what the difference points out about formal education.

4. According to Lila Robinson ("Fighting to Fill the Values Gap," p. 221), the United States is experiencing a moral decline. Using the ideas in this essay and those in any of the essays in Chapter 6, discuss how you think Robinson would evaluate the effect of technology on our values.

5. Chapter 6 opens with this quote from Marshall McLuhan: "The new electronic interdependence recreates the world in the image of a global village." Discuss one important way "electronic interdependence" and the "global village" affect the individual in society. Draw on your own experience and observation and the readings in Chapters 5 and 6.

PART 4

Culture in Transition

Chapter 7
Gender Issues: What Does It Mean to Be Male or Female?

Chapter 8
Diversity: How Do We Respond to Difference?

The Library of Congress/Photo Researchers

© RF/Corbis

GENDER ISSUES: WHAT DOES IT MEAN TO BE MALE OR FEMALE?

"The great question . . . which I have not been able to answer, despite my thirty years of research into the feminine soul, is 'What does a woman want?'"

Sigmund Freud

"We are living at an important and fruitful moment now, for it is clear to men that the images of adult manhood given by the popular culture are worn out; a man can no longer depend on them. By the time a man is thirty-five he knows that the images of the right man, the tough man, the true man which he received in high school do not work in life."

Robert Bly

"The finest people marry the two sexes in their own person."

Ralph Waldo Emerson

"Men and women, women and men. It will never work."

Erica Jong

Anti-Male Bias Increasingly Pervades Our Culture
JOHN LEO

A contributing editor for *U.S. News and World Report,* John Leo has also been a reporter for the *New York Times* and an associate editor and senior writer at *Time* magazine. Before that, he held positions at the *Village Voice* and *Commonweal.* The following piece first appeared in *Jewish World Review* in July 2000. In it, Leo claims that popular culture encourages a bias not often spoken of: a bias against males.

Preview.   Some greeting card companies have successful lines of cards that ridicule men. These cards are purchased by women. Think about that and answer the following questions: Is it okay for greeting cards to make fun of men? Could the same companies also sell cards that ridicule women? Why do you think the male-bashing cards sell so well?

Vocabulary.   If any of the following words from the selection are unfamiliar to you, study their meanings before reading.

Thelma and Louise (3)   characters in the 1991 movie of the same name; they
    shoot a rapist and take off in a Thunderbird
double-standard (5)   a set of principles applied to one group but not another
aggrieved (7)   having a grievance
jilted (7)   rejected
castration (7)   removal of the testes
graphic (9)   vivid, detailed
JWR (10)   *Jewish World Review,* the publication this article originally
    appeared in
pervading (10)   filling
antagonism (11)   conflict
fervently (11)   intensely

A famous television newswoman told this joke last month at a fund-raising dinner for a women's college: A woman needed a brain transplant. Her doctor said two brains were available, a woman's brain for $500 and a man's brain for $5,000. Why the big price difference? Answer: The woman's brain has been used.

2   Most in the audience laughed, but one man stood up and booed. What's wrong? asked a woman at his table. The man said, "Just substitute woman, black or Jew for 'man' in that joke, and tell me how it sounds."

3   At about the same time, American Greeting Cards launched an ad campaign in *Newsweek, Life* and other magazines. One ad featured a "Thelma and Louise" greeting card, pasted into the magazines, that said on the front: "Men are always whining about how we are suffocating them." The punch line inside the card was this: "Personally, I think if you can hear them whining, you're not pressing hard enough on the pillow."

4   The newswoman, who is a friend, seemed shocked when I phoned and raised questions about her joke. "The poor, sensitive white male," she said. A spokesman for the greeting card company saw nothing wrong with a humorous card about a woman killing a man. He faxed a statement saying the card had been pretested successfully, and besides, "We've heard no protests from consumers who are buying and using this card." But would American Greetings print a card with the sexes reversed, so the humor came from men joking about suffocating a woman? No, said the spokesman, because 85 percent to 90 percent of cards are bought by women. There is no market for a reverse card.

5   In truth, no man could get up at a fancy banquet and tell a joke about how stupid women are. And a greeting card joking about a woman's murder would be very unlikely, even if surveys showed that millions of males were eager to exchange lighthearted gender-killing greetings. The obvious is true: A sturdy double standard has emerged in the gender wars.

6   "There used to be a certain level of good-natured teasing between the sexes," says Christina Sommers, author of *Who Stole Feminism?* "Now even the most innocent remark about women will get you in trouble, but there's no limit at all to what you can say about men."

7   Men's rights groups phone me a lot, and I tell them my general position on these matters: The last thing we need in America is yet another victim group, this one made up of seriously aggrieved males. But these groups do have an unmissable point about double standards. On the "Today" show last November, Katie Couric suddenly deviated from perkiness and asked a jilted bride, "Have you considered castration as an option?" Nobody seemed to object. Fred Hayward, a men's rights organizer, says: "Imagine the reaction if Matt Lauer had asked a jilted groom, 'Wouldn't you just like to rip her uterus out?'"

8   The double standard is rooted in identity politics and fashionable theories about victimization: Men as a group are oppressors; jokes that oppressors use to degrade the oppressed must be taken seriously and suppressed. Jokes by the oppressed against oppressors, however, are liberating and progressive. So while sexual harassment doctrine cracks down on the most harmless jokes about women, very hostile humor about men keeps expanding with almost no objections.

9   Until recently, for example, the 3M company put out post-it notes with the printed message: "Men have only two faults: everything they say and everything they do." Anti-male greeting cards are increasingly graphic, with some of the most hostile coming from Hallmark Cards' Shoebox Division.

10   (Sample: "Men are scum . . . Excuse me. For a second there I was feeling generous.") JWR columnist Cathy Young sees a rising tide of male-bashing, in-

cluding "All Men Are Bastards" and "Men We Love to Hate" calendars, and a resentful "It's-always-his-fault" attitude pervading women's magazines.

11   Commercial attempts to increase the amount of sexual antagonism in America are never a good idea. And if you keep attacking men as a group, they will eventually start acting as a group, something we should fervently avoid. But the worst impact of all the male-bashing is on the young.

12   Barbara Wilder-Smith, a teacher and researcher in the Boston area, was recently quoted in several newspapers on how deeply anti-male attitudes have affected the schools. When she made "Boys Are Good" T-shirts for boys in her class, all 10 of the female student teachers under her supervision objected to the message. (One, she said, was wearing a button saying "So many men, so little intelligence.")

13   "My son can't even wear the shirt out in his back yard," she said. "People see it and object strongly and shout things." On the other hand, she says, nobody objects when the girls wear shirts that say "Girls Rule" or when they taunt boys with a chant that goes, "Boys go to Jupiter to get more stupider; girls go to college to get more knowledge." Worse, she says, many adolescent boys object to the "Boys Are Good" shirts too, because they have come to accept the cultural message that something is seriously wrong with being a male.

14   "The time is ripe for people to think about the unspoken anti-male 'ism' in our colleges and schools," she says. And in the rest of the popular culture as well.

Understanding Content

1. What is the double standard that Leo says exists in the gender wars?
2. What reason does Leo give for the double standard?
3. What does Leo consider to be the most serious effect of anti-male bias?

Considering Structure and Technique

1. Which sentence is the thesis of the essay?
2. Because the essay is written in the journalistic style often used in newspapers, the paragraphs are short. Why does journalistic style typically call for short paragraphs? If you were to reformat the piece into a more traditional essay style with longer paragraphs, which paragraphs would you combine?
3. Which paragraphs include examples? What do the examples contribute to the piece?

Exploring Ideas

1. A spokesperson for American Greeting Cards defends the company's card about a woman killing a man by stating that buyers of the card do not object to it. What do you think of this defense?
2. What are the gender wars that Leo refers to in paragraph 5?

3. In paragraph 7, Leo asks the reader to imagine the reaction if Matt Lauer asked a man a question like the one Katie Couric asked a woman. What do you think the reaction would be?
4. Do you think male-bashing is a problem in our society? Explain.

Writing Workshop: Using Induction and Deduction

Induction moves from specific evidence to a general conclusion. For example, in paragraphs 1-5, Leo uses induction by citing specific examples of the double standard and then drawing this conclusion: "A sturdy double standard has emerged in the gender wars." **Deduction** moves from a general statement to specific evidence. Leo uses deduction in paragraph 12. First, he opens the paragraph with a general statement indicating that "anti-male attitudes have affected the schools." Then he cites a specific example as proof: female student teachers objected to boys wearing "Boys Are Good" T-shirts.

Writing Workshop Activity

Examine this book, newsmagazines, or a local newspaper. Find a passage of one or more paragraphs illustrating *induction* and a passage of one or more paragraphs illustrating *deduction*.

Language Notes for Multilingual and Other Writers

Many rules govern the use of *a*, *an*, and *the*. Here are four of them.

1. Use *a* and *an* with singular **count nouns** (nouns such as *dog* and *hat* that can be made plural) when the identity of the noun is unknown to the reader.

   Her doctor said two brains were available, a woman's brain for $500 and a man's brain for $5,000. Paragraph 1

2. Use *the* with specific singular and plural count nouns.

   A spokesman for the greeting card company saw nothing wrong with a humorous card about a woman killing a man. Paragraph 4

   But would American Greetings print a card with the sexes reversed . . . ? Paragraph 4

3. Use *the* with a singular count noun whose identity is known.

   The newswoman, who is a friend, seemed shocked . . . Paragraph 4

4. Do not use *a* or *an* with plural nouns.

    yes: A sturdy double standard has emerged in <u>the</u> gender wars.
    Paragraph 5

    no: A sturdy double standard has emerged in <u>a</u> gender wars.

5. Do not use any article with nouns used to name people, places, things, or ideas *in general.*

So while sexual harassment doctrine cracks down on the most harmless jokes about <u>women</u>, very hostile humor about <u>men</u> keeps expanding with almost no objections. Paragraph 8

From Reading to Writing

In Your Journal: Think about the last time you heard an anti-male or "dumb blonde" joke. What was your reaction? Why did you react that way?

With Some Classmates: In paragraph 11, Leo says that if men continue to be attacked as a group, "they will eventually start acting as a group." Explain how they might start acting.

In an Essay

- Do you agree with Leo that a "double standard has emerged in the gender wars" (paragraph 5)? Cite examples to support your view.
- Define and illustrate *male-bashing.* As an alternative, define and illustrate *sexual harassment.*
- Paragraph 10 refers to "a resentful 'It's-always-his-fault' attitude pervading women's magazines." Review four or more women's magazines on the Internet or in your library and report on the nature and amount of anti-male sentiment in the advertising and articles.

Beyond the Writing Class: Develop a set of specific guidelines for the behavior of teachers and students, guidelines meant to help prevent sexual harassment and male-bashing and to promote gender equality. Do you think these guidelines should be adopted by your school? Explain.

Only daughter
SANDRA CISNEROS

Novelist, short-story writer, and poet, Sandra Cisneros is one of the first Hispanic-American writers to achieve commercial success as well as critical acclaim. She is the only daughter in a family of seven children born to a Mexican father and a Mexican-American mother. As the selection (which first appeared in *Glamour* in 1990) reveals, being the only female child has had a profound impact on her. As you read, ask yourself to what extent that impact has been positive and to what extent it has been negative.

Preview. Assume that one of your writings has been selected to appear in a campus publication of student writings and that you have been asked to compose a few sentences about yourself for a headnote before the selection. Write the headnote.

Vocabulary. If any of the following words from the essay are unfamiliar to you, study their meanings before reading.

philandering (7) cheating by committing adultery
woo (8) to attempt to win the favor or affection of someone
nostalgia (9) a sentimental longing for the past
flat (9) an apartment
[Federico] Fellini (16) an Italian filmmaker
vials (18) glass containers

Once, several years ago, when I was just starting out my writing career, I was asked to write my own contributor's note for an anthology. I wrote: "I am the only daughter in a family of six sons. *That* explains everything."

2   Well, I've thought that ever since, and yes, it explains a lot to me, but for the reader's sake I should have written: "I am the only daughter in a *Mexican* family of six sons." Or even: "I am the only daughter of a Mexican father and a Mexican-American mother." Or: "I am the only daughter of a working-class family of nine." All of these had everything to do with who I am today.

3   I was/am the only daughter and *only* a daughter. Being an only daughter in a family of six sons forced me by circumstance to spend a lot of time by myself because my brothers felt it beneath them to play with a *girl* in public. But that aloneness, that loneliness, was good for a would-be writer—it allowed me time to think and think, to imagine, to read and prepare myself.

4   Being only a daughter for my father meant my destiny would lead me to become someone's wife. That's what he believed. But when I was in the fifth

grade and shared my plans for college with him, I was sure he understood. I remember my father saying, *"Que bueno, mi'ja,* that's good." That meant a lot to me, especially since my brothers thought the idea hilarious. What I didn't realize was that my father thought college was good for girls—good for finding a husband. After four years in college and two more in graduate school, and still no husband, my father shakes his head even now and says I wasted all that education.

5   In retrospect, I'm lucky my father believed daughters were meant for husbands. It meant it didn't matter if I majored in something silly like English. After all, I'd find a nice professional eventually, right? This allowed me the liberty to putter about embroidering my little poems and stories without my father interrupting with so much as a "What's that you're writing?"

6   But the truth is, I wanted him to interrupt. I wanted my father to understand what it was I was scribbling, to introduce me as "My only daughter, the writer." Not as "This is my only daughter. She teaches." *Es maestra*—teacher. Not even *profesora.*

7   In a sense, everything I have ever written has been for him, to win his approval even though I know my father can't read English words, even though my father's only reading includes the brown-ink *Esto* sports magazines from Mexico City and the bloody *¡Alarma!* magazines that feature yet another sighting of *La Virgen de Guadalupe* on a tortilla or a wife's revenge on her philandering husband by bashing his skull in with a *molcajete* (a kitchen mortar made of volcanic rock). Or the *fotonovelas,* the little picture paperbacks with tragedy and trauma erupting from the characters' mouths in bubbles.

8   A father represents, then, the public majority. A public who is disinterested in reading, and yet one whom I am writing about and for, and privately trying to woo.

9   When we were growing up in Chicago, we moved a lot because of my father. He suffered bouts of nostalgia. Then we'd have to let go of our flat, store the furniture with mother's relatives, load the station wagon with baggage and bologna sandwiches and head south. To Mexico City.

10   We came back, of course. To yet another Chicago flat, another Chicago neighborhood, another Catholic school. Each time, my father would seek out the parish priest in order to get a tuition break, and complain or boast: "I have seven sons."

11   He meant *siete hijos,* seven children, but he translated it as "sons." "I have seven sons." To anyone who would listen. The Sears Roebuck employee who sold us the washing machine. The short-order cook where my father ate his ham-and-eggs breakfasts. "I have seven sons." As if he deserved a medal from the state.

12   My papa. He didn't mean anything by that mistranslation, I'm sure. But somehow I could feel myself being erased. I'd tug my father's sleeve and whisper: "Not seven sons. Six! and *one daughter.*"

13   When my oldest brother graduated from medical school, he fulfilled my father's dream that we study hard and use this—our heads, instead of this—

our hands. Even now my father's hands are thick and yellow, stubbed by a history of hammer and nails and twine and coils and springs. "Use this," my father said, tapping his head, "and not this," showing us those hands. He always looked tired when he said it.

14   Wasn't college an investment? And hadn't I spent all those years in college? And if I didn't marry, what was it all for? Why would anyone go to college and then choose to be poor? Especially someone who had always been poor.

15   Last year, after ten years of writing professionally, the financial rewards started to trickle in. My second National Endowment for the Arts Fellowship. A guest professorship at the University of California, Berkeley. My book, which sold to a major New York publishing house.

16   At Christmas, I flew home to Chicago. The house was throbbing, same as always; hot *tamales* and sweet *tamales* hissing in my mother's pressure cooker, and everybody—my mother, six brothers, wives, babies, aunts, cousins—talking too loud and at the same time, like in a Fellini film, because that's just how we are.

17   I went upstairs to my father's room. One of my stories had just been translated into Spanish and published in an anthology of Chicano writing, and I wanted to show it to him. Ever since he recovered from a stroke two years ago, my father likes to spend his leisure hours horizontally. And that's how I found him, watching a Pedro Infante movie on Galavision and eating rice pudding.

18   There was a glass filmed with milk on the bedside table. There were several vials of pills and balled Kleenex. And on the floor, one black sock and a plastic urinal that I didn't want to look at but looked at anyway. Pedro Infante was about to burst into song, and my father was laughing.

19   I'm not sure if it was because my story was translated into Spanish, or because it was published in Mexico, or perhaps because the story dealt with Tepeyac, the *colonia* my father was raised in and the house he grew up in, but at any rate, my father punched the mute button on his remote control and read my story.

20   I sat on the bed next to my father and waited. He read it very slowly. As if he were reading each line over and over. He laughed at all the right places and read lines he liked out loud. He pointed and asked questions: "Is this So-and-so?" "Yes," I said. He kept reading.

21   When he was finally finished, after what seemed like hours, my father looked up and asked: "Where can we get more copies of this for the relatives?"

22   Of all the wonderful things that happened to me last year, that was the most wonderful.

Understanding Content

1. How was the author affected by being the only daughter in her family?
2. Why does Cisneros write for her father, even though he cannot read what she writes because it is in English?

3. Why did the author's father want his children to go to college?
4. What differences are there in the way Cisneros's father views his sons and his daughter?

Considering Structure and Technique

1. In the title of the essay, Cisneros chose not to capitalize the *d* in *daughter.* What is the significance of that lowercase letter?
2. "Only daughter" originally appeared in *Glamour* magazine. Is the essay well suited to its original audience? Explain.
3. For what purpose do you think Cisneros wrote "Only daughter"?
4. Why do you think the author italicizes "that" in paragraph 1, "only" and "girl" in paragraph 3, and "one daughter" in paragraph 12?
5. Rhetorical questions appear in paragraphs 5 and 14. (**Rhetorical questions** are questions for which the author expects no answer; see the workshop on p. 313.) What purpose do these questions serve?

Exploring Ideas

1. In the opening paragraph, Cisneros says the fact that she is the only daughter in a family with six sons explains everything. What specifically does it explain?
2. What attitude does Cisneros convey about her profession when she describes writing as "embroidering my little poems and stories" in paragraph 5? Why do you think she uses this phrase?
3. Cisneros mentions that she moved around quite a bit as a child. The effects of this move on her are not discussed much. Do you think she was influenced much by the moves? Explain.

Writing Workshop: Becoming Increasingly Specific

To back up your points, you know that you must offer specific evidence (see p. 30). Sometimes you can do this by becoming increasingly specific, a strategy apparent in "Only daughter." The essay opens with this general statement:

I am the only daughter in a family of six sons. *That* explains everything.

To prove that her female status in her family explains her behavior and that of others, the author follows that general statement with one at the beginning of paragraph 4 that notes one specific influence:

Being only a daughter for my father meant my destiny would lead me to become someone's wife.

Later in paragraph 4 and also in paragraph 5, the author gets even more specific by focusing the essay on a single, specific way she was affected by the view that she would be someone's wife.

But when I was in the fifth grade and shared my plans for college . . . I remember my father saying . . . "that's good." . . . What I didn't realize was that my father thought college was good for girls—good for finding a husband.

In retrospect, I'm lucky my father believed daughters were meant for husbands. It meant it didn't matter if I majored in something silly like English.

A diagram of this general-to-specific pattern looks like this:

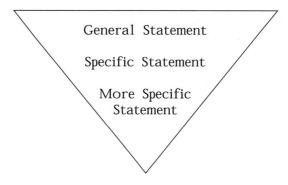

General Statement

Specific Statement

More Specific
Statement

Writing Workshop Activity

Fill in the blanks in the following paragraph according to the directions given in brackets. When you are through, you will have a paragraph that becomes increasingly specific.

Everyone has embarrassing moments. For example, _____

_____

_____

[Fill in the blanks with examples of embarrassing situations many people have encountered, situations like forgetting someone's name or wearing socks that don't match.]

My most embarrassing moment occurred when _____

_____

_____

[Fill in the blanks with a specific instance of a time when you were embarrassed.]

Language Notes for Multilingual and Other Writers

Some languages require nouns and adjectives to agree in number. In English, however, adjectives have only a singular, or nonnumbered, form, as the following examples from "Only daughter" illustrate.

1. This allowed me the liberty to putter about embroidering my <u>little poems and stories</u> [not *littles poems and stories*]. . . . Paragraph 5
2. Then we'd have to let go of our flat, . . . load the station wagon with baggage and <u>bologna sandwiches</u> [not *bolognas sandwiches*] and head south. Paragraph 9
3. Last year, after <u>ten years</u> [not *tens years*] of writing professionally, the <u>financial rewards</u> [not *financials rewards*] started to trickle in. Paragraph 15

From Reading to Writing

In Your Journal: Based on what you know about Cisneros from "Only daughter," would you like to have her for a friend? Explain why or why not in about a page.

With Some Classmates: Discuss whether or not there are different expectations for males and females in the United States. Then state your conclusion in an essay and illustrate it with specific examples.

In an Essay

- As you were growing up, did you feel valued in your family? Like Cisneros, explain how you felt, why you felt that way, and how you have been affected as a result.
- In paragraph 2, Cisneros mentions the factors that "had everything to do with who [she is] today." Explain the factors and influences that have everything to do with who you are today.
- In paragraph 12, Cisneros says she felt "erased." Tell about a time you felt erased. Be sure to provide specific detail so your reader understands exactly why you felt the way you did.
- Are boys treated differently from girls in your family? Cite specific examples to illustrate that they are or are not treated differently.

Beyond the Writing Class: Cisneros explains how she was affected by her family's view of her gender. However, gender views are just one of many factors that influence us. Research how we are affected by birth order and write a paper suitable for either a child psychology class or an education class that notes one or more of the significant ways personality is shaped by birth order. Then go on to explain what you think the implications of birth order are for educators.

One Man's Kids

DANIEL MEIER

Daniel Meier, who has a master's degree from Harvard's Graduate School of Education, wrote "One Man's Kids" for the *New York Times Magazine*. In it, he describes the awkward situation he finds himself in because the work he loves to do is considered a "woman's job." As you read, ask yourself why we associate certain jobs with certain genders.

Preview. Did you have any male teachers when you were in elementary school? If so, did you like having a male teacher? If not, do you think you would have liked having a male teacher? Can you think of any careers that are dominated by one gender? Answer these questions in your journal.

Vocabulary. If any of the following words from the selection are unfamiliar to you, study their meanings before reading.

singular (5)   traveling one path; one-track or one-sided
pursuit (5)   occupation
expertise (5)   expert skill or knowledge
consoling (6)   soothing; lessening sorrow
exult (6)   to show or feel joy

I teach first graders. I live in a world of skinned knees, double-knotted shoelaces, riddles that I've heard a dozen times, stale birthday cakes, hurt feelings, wandering stories, and one lost shoe ("and if you don't find it my mother'll kill me"). My work is dominated by 6-year-olds.

2   It's 10:45, the middle of snack, and I'm helping Emily open her milk carton. She has already tried the other end without success, and now there's so much paint and ink on the carton from her fingers that I'm not sure she should drink it at all. But I open it. Then I turn to help Scott clean up some milk he has just spilled onto Rebecca's whale crossword puzzle.

3   While I wipe my milk- and paint-covered hands, Jenny wants to know if I've seen that funny book about penguins that I read in class. As I hunt for it in a messy pile of books, Jason wants to know if there is a new seating arrangement for lunch tables. I find the book, turn to answer Jason, then face Maya, who is fast approaching with a new knock-knock joke. After what seems like the 10th "Who's there?" I laugh and Maya is pleased.

4   Then Andrew wants to know how to spell "flukes" for his crossword. As I get to "u," I give a hand signal for Sarah to take away the snack. But just as Sarah is almost out the door, two children complain that "we haven't even had ours yet." I stop the snack mid-flight, complying with their request for graham

crackers. I then return to Andrew, noticing that he has put "flu" for 9 Down, rather than 9 Across. It's now 10:50.

5   My work is not traditional male work. It's not a singular pursuit. There is not a large pile of paper to get through or one deal to transact. I don't have one area of expertise or knowledge. I don't have the singular power over language of a lawyer, the physical force of a construction worker, the command over fellow workers of a surgeon, the wheeling and dealing transactions of a businessman. My energy is not spent in pursuing, climbing, achieving, conquering, or cornering some goal or object.

6   My energy is spent in encouraging, supporting, consoling, and praising my children. In teaching, the inner rewards come from without. On any given day, quite apart from teaching reading and spelling, I bandage a cut, dry a tear, erase a frown, tape a torn doll, and locate a long-lost boot. The day is really won through matters of the heart. As my students groan, laugh, shudder, cry, exult, and wonder, I do too. I have to be soft around the edges.

7   A few years ago, when I was interviewing for an elementary-school teaching position, every principal told me with confidence that, as a male, I had an advantage over female applicants because of the lack of male teachers. But in the next breath, they asked with a hint of suspicion why I chose to work with young children. I told them that I wanted to observe and contribute to the intellectual growth of a maturing mind. What I really felt like saying, but didn't, was that I loved helping a child learn to write his name for the first time, finding someone a new friend, or sharing in the hilarity of reading about Winnie the Pooh getting so stuck in a hole that only his head and rear show.

8   I gave that answer to those principals, who were mostly male, because I thought they wanted a "male" response. This meant talking about intellectual matters. If I had taken a different course and talked about my interest in helping children in their emotional development, it would have been seen as closer to a "female" answer. I even altered my language, not once mentioning the word "love" to describe what I do indeed love about teaching. My answer worked; every principal nodded approvingly.

9   Some of the principals also asked what I saw myself doing later in my career. They wanted to know if I eventually wanted to go into educational administration. Becoming a dean of students or a principal has never been one of my goals, but they seemed to expect me, as a male, to want to climb higher on the career stepladder. So I mentioned that, at some point, I would be interested in working with teachers as a curriculum coordinator. Again, they nodded approvingly.

10   If those principals had been female instead of male, I wonder whether their questions, and my answers, would have been different. My guess is that they would have been.

11   At other times, when I'm at a party or a dinner and tell someone that I teach young children, I've found that men and women respond differently. Most men ask about the subjects I teach and the courses I took in my training. Then, unless they bring up an issue such as merit pay, the conversation stops.

Most women, on the other hand, begin the conversation on a more immediate and personal level. They say things like "those kids must love having a male teacher" or "that age is just wonderful, you must love it." Then, more often than not, they'll talk about their own kids or ask me specific questions about what I do. We're then off and talking shop.

12   Possibly, men would have more to say to me, and I to them, if my job had more of the trappings and benefits of more traditional male jobs. But my job has no bonuses or promotions. No complimentary box seats at the ball park. No cab fare home. No drinking buddies after work. No briefcase. No suit. (Ties get stuck in paint jars.) No power lunches. (I eat peanut butter and jelly, chips, milk, and cookies with the kids.) No taking clients out for cocktails. The only place I take my kids is to the playground.

13   Although I could have pursued a career in law or business as several of my friends did, I chose teaching instead. My job has benefits all its own. I'm able to bake cookies without getting them stuck together as they cool, buy cheap sewing materials, take out splinters, and search just the right trash cans for useful odds and ends. I'm sometimes called "Daddy" and even "Mommy" by my students, and if there's ever a lull in the conversation at a dinner party, I can always ask those assembled if they've heard the latest riddle about why the turkey crossed the road. (He thought he was a chicken.)

Understanding Content

1. What does Meier explain to be the differences between his job as a first grade teacher and a traditional male job?
2. During the interview for his teaching job, why did Meier mention that he would be interested in becoming a curriculum coordinator?
3. In what ways do men and women respond differently when they learn that the author teaches young children?
4. Is the author angry or bitter about the fact that his job is perceived to be a "female job"? Explain.

Considering Structure and Technique

1. Paragraphs 1 through 4 describe a few minutes in the author's day. Why does Meier provide this description?
2. In paragraphs 1, 6, and 12, Meier lists some of the characteristics of his job. What is the effect of these lists?
3. What is the thesis of "One Man's Kids"? Is that thesis stated or implied?
4. Paragraphs 2 through 4 are written in the present tense, even though the events described do not occur in the present. Why is the present tense used?

Exploring Ideas

1. In paragraph 7, the author notes that during job interviews he was viewed with a hint of suspicion. Why do you think he was viewed this way?

2. Why do you think that teaching in elementary school is *not* a "male job," but teaching in high school and college *are* "male jobs"?
3. For what purpose do you think Meier wrote "One Man's Kids"? Do you think the essay fulfills that purpose? Explain.
4. In paragraph 6, Meier says, "The day is really won through matters of the heart." Explain what you think he means.

Writing Workshop: Using Short Sentences for Impact or Emphasis

An essay filled with short sentences will appear to have an immature style. However, a judiciously placed short sentence can emphasize a point or lend impact, especially when that short sentence comes before or after a longer one. Here are some examples from "One Man's Kids." (The short sentences are underlined as a study aid.)

I teach first graders. I live in a world of skinned knees, double-knotted shoelaces, riddles that I've heard a dozen times, stale birthday cakes, hurt feelings, wandering stories, and one lost shoe ("and if you don't find it, my mother'll kill me"). Paragraph 1

So I mentioned that, at some point, I would be interested in working with teachers as a curriculum coordinator. Again, they nodded approvingly. Paragraph 9

If those principals had been female instead of male, I wonder whether their questions, and my answers, would have been different. My guess is that they would have been. Paragraph 10

Then, more often than not, they'll talk about their own kids or ask me specific questions about what I do. We're then off and talking shop. Paragraph 11

Writing Workshop Activity

Using the readings in this text, local and campus newspapers, or magazines, find three examples of using short sentences for emphasis or impact. Share your sentences with the rest of your class.

Language Notes for Multilingual and Other Writers

"One Man's Kids" includes two references to jokes and riddles that you may be unfamiliar with if English is your second language.

1. Paragraph 3 refers to a *knock-knock joke,* which is a common children's joke format involving word play. Here is one example:

    JOKE TELLER: Knock, knock.

    RESPONDENT: Who's there?

    JOKE TELLER: Boo.

    RESPONDENT: Boo Who?

    JOKE TELLER: Please don't cry.

2. Paragraph 13 closes with a riddle that is a reference to this common children's riddle:

    RIDDLE: "Why did the chicken cross the road?"

    ANSWER: "To get to the other side."

From Reading to Writing

In Your Journal: How do you think you would feel if you held a job dominated by members of the opposite sex? For example, consider how you would feel on a construction crew if you are female or as a flight attendant if you are male.

With Some Classmates: Write out a transcript of the questions and answers that might have occurred in one of the author's teaching interviews with a male principal. Then write out a transcript of the questions and answers that might occur between the same principal and a female applicant.

In an Essay

- Do you think Meier is successful? Write a definition of success, and illustrate your definition with examples of successful people you know, being sure to explain what makes them successful. Then explain whether or not Meier is successful according to your definition.
- If you are from another culture, explain the traditional male and female occupations or roles in your culture. If you are not from another culture, interview someone who is and then write the essay.
- Have you ever participated in an activity or held a job that was dominated by members of the opposite sex? If so, explain how you and those around you felt and behaved.
- Meier describes an instance of gender stereotyping when he notes that teaching young children is a female job. Discuss one or more other examples of gender stereotyping in the workplace. Does such stereotyping create problems? Explain.

Beyond the Writing Class: As part of your career search, select a job that interests you for any reason and research the qualities needed for success in that job (qualities such as patience, critical thinking ability, creativity, high frustration tolerance, and so forth). You can do your research by talking to people in your career services department, by interviewing people who hold the job that interests you, and by looking in the library or on the Internet. After your research, decide whether the job is traditionally "male," "female," or "gender-neutral," and write a report explaining why.

Nora Quealey
JEAN REITH SCHROEDEL

Jean Reith Schroedel is an associate professor in the Center for Politics and Economics of the Claremont Graduate School. The following selection came from *Alone in a Crowd* (1985), a collection of interviews with blue-collar working women. As you read, notice that more than one kind of discrimination is described.

Preview.   In your journal, react to this quotation: "You can still be treated like a lady and act like a lady and work like a man." What do you think this statement means? Do you agree with it? What does it say about women in the workplace?

Vocabulary.   If any of the following words from the selection are unfamiliar to you, study their meanings before reading.

Boeing (3)   a manufacturer of airplanes
G.E.D. (3)   general equivalency diploma: a high school equivalency
   certificate given to those who have not graduated from high school but
   who have passed the appropriate test
Bangor (4)   site of a nuclear submarine base in Washington State
reamers (6)   tools for enlarging holes in metal
freon (7)   the chemical coolant in air conditioners
dolly (7)   a two-wheeled cart for moving heavy things
journeyman (10)   a person who has had enough training to work in a trade
shop steward (11)   a union member who represents the department (shop)
   with the employer
spasms (12)   muscle contractions

I was a housewife until five years ago. The best part was being home when my three kids came in from school. Their papers and their junk that they made from kindergarten on up—they were my total, whole life. And then one day I realized when they were grown up and gone, graduated and married, I was going to be left with nothing. I think there's a lot of women that way, housewives, that never knew there were other things and people outside of the neighborhood. I mean the block got together once a week for coffee and maybe went bowling, but that was it. My whole life was being there when the kids came home from school.

2   I never disliked anything. It was just like everything else in a marriage, there never was enough money to do things that you wanted—never to take a week's vacation away from the kids. If we did anything, it was just to take the car on Saturday or Sunday for a little, short drive. But there was never enough money. The extra money was the reason I decided to go out and get a job. The kids were getting older, needed more, wanted more, and there was just not enough.

3   See, I don't have a high school diploma, so when I went to Boeing and put an application in, they told me not to come back until I had a diploma or a G.E.D. On the truck line they didn't mind that I hadn't finished school. I put an application in and got hired on the spot.

4   My dad works over at Bangor in the ammunition depot, so I asked him what it would be like working with all men. The only thing he told me was if I was gonna work with a lot of men, then I would have to *listen* to swear words and some of the obscene things, but still *act* like a lady, or I'd never fit in. You can still be treated like a lady and act like a lady and work like a man. So I just tried to fit in. It's worked too. The guys come up and they'll tell me jokes and tease me and a lot of them told me that I'm just like one of the guys. Yet they like to have me around because I wear make-up and I do curl my hair, and I try to wear not really frilly blouses, see-through stuff, but nice blouses.

5   We had one episode where a gal wore a tank top and when she bent over the guys could see her boobs or whatever you call it, all the way down. Myself and a couple other women went and tried to complain about it. We wanted personnel to ask her to please wear a bra, or at least no tank tops. We were getting a lot of comebacks from the guys like, "When are *you* gonna dress like so-and-so," or "When are *you* gonna go without a bra," and "We wanna see what *you've* got." And I don't feel any need to show off; you know, I know what I've got. There were only a few women there, so that one gal made a very bad impression. But personnel said there was nothing they could do about it.

6   But in general the guys were really good. I started out in cab building hanging radio brackets and putting heaters in. It was all hand work, and at first I really struggled with the power screwdrivers and big reamers, but the guy training me was super neato. I would think, "Oh, dear, can I ever do this, can I really prove myself or come up to their expectations?" But the guys never gave me the feeling that I was taking the job from a man or food from his family's mouth. If I needed help, I didn't even have to ask, if they saw me struggling, they'd come right over to help.

7   I've worked in a lot of different places since I went to work there, I was in cab build for I don't know how long, maybe six months, eight months. Then they took me over to sleeper boxes, where I stayed for about two-and-one-half years. I put in upholstery, lined the head liners and the floor mats. After that I went on the line and did air conditioning. When the truck came to me, it had hoses already on it, and I'd have to hook up a little air-condition-pump-type thing and a suction that draws all the dust and dirt from the lines. Then you close that off, put freon in, and tie down the line.

Then I'd tie together a bunch of color-coded electrical wires with tie straps and electrical tape to hook the firewall to the engine. Sometimes I also worked on the sleeper boxes by crawling underneath and tightening down big bolts and washers. Next they sent me over to the radiator shop. I was the first woman ever to do radiators. That I liked. A driver would bring in the radiators and you'd put it on a hoist, pick it up and put it on a sling, and work on one side putting your fittings on and wiring and putting in plugs. Then they bounced me back to sleeper boxes for a while and finally ended up putting me in the motor department, where I am now. The motors are brought in on a dolly. The guy behind me hangs the transmission and I hang the pipe with the shift levers and a few other little things and that's about it. Except that we have to work terribly fast.

8   I was moved into the motor department after the big layoff. At that time we were doing ten motors a day. Now we're up to fourteen without any additional help. When we were down, the supervisor came to me and said we had to help fill in and give extra help to the other guys, which is fine. But the minute production went up, I still had to do my own job plus putting on parts for three different guys. These last two weeks have been really tough. I've been way behind. They've got two guys that are supposed to fill in when you get behind, but I'm stubborn enough that I won't go over and ask for help. The supervisor should be able to see that I'm working super-duper hard while some other guys are taking forty-five minutes in the can and have a sandwich and two cups of coffee. Sometimes I push myself so hard that I'm actually in a trance. And I have to stop every once in a while and ask, "What did I do?" I don't even remember putting parts on, I just go from one to the other, just block everything out—just go, go, go, go. And that is bad, for myself, my own sanity, my own health. I don't take breaks. I don't go to the bathroom. There's so much pressure on me, physical and mental stress. It's hard to handle because then I go home and do a lot of crying and that's bad for my kids because I do a lot of snapping and growling at them. When I'm down, depressed, aching, and sore, to come home and do that to the kids is not fair at all. The last couple of days the attitude I've had is, I don't care whether I get the job done or not. If they can't see I'm going under, then I don't care. And I'll take five or ten minutes to just go to the bathroom, sit on the floor, and take a couple of deep breaths, just anything to get away.

9   The company doesn't care about us at all. Let me give you an example. When we were having all this hot weather, I asked them please if we couldn't get some fans in here. Extension cords even, because some guys had their own fans. I wasn't just asking for myself, but those guys over working by the oven. They've got a thermometer there and it gets to a hundred and fifteen degrees by that oven! They've got their mouths open, can hardly breathe, and they're barely moving. So I said to the supervisor, "Why can't we have a fan to at least circulate the air?" "Oh, yeah, we'll look at it," was as far as it went. We're human. We have no right to be treated like animals. I mean you go out to a dairy farm and you've got air conditioning and music for those cows. I'm a person,

and I don't like feeling weak and sick to my stomach and not feel like eating. Then to have the supervisor expect me to put out production as if I was mechanical—a thing, just a robot. I'm human.

10   You know, I don't even know what my job title is. I'm not sure if it's trainee or not. But I do know I'll never make journeyman. I'll never make anything. I tried for inspection—took all the classes they offered at the plant, went to South Seattle Community College on my own time, studied blueprinting, and worked in all the different areas like they said I had to. I broke ground for the other girls, but they won't let me move up. And it all comes down to one thing, because I associated with a black man. I've had people in personnel tell me to stop riding to work with the man, even if it meant taking the bus to and from work. I said no one will make my decisions as to who I ride with and who my friends are. Because you walk into a building with a person, have lunch with him, let him buy you a cup of coffee, people condemn you. They're crazy, because when I have a friend, I don't turn my back on them just because of what people think. What I do outside the plant after quitting time is my own business. If they don't like it, that's their problem. But in that plant I've conducted myself as a lady and have nothing to be ashamed of. I plant my feet firmly and I stand by it.

11   Early on, I hurt my neck, back, and shoulder while working on sleeper boxes. When I went into the motor department I damaged them more by working with power tools above my head and reaching all day long. I was out for two weeks and then had a ten-week restriction. Personnel said I had to go back to my old job, and if I couldn't handle it I would have to go home. They wouldn't put me anywhere else, which is ridiculous with all the small parts areas that people can sit down and work in while they are restricted. My doctor said if I went back to doing what I was doing when I got hurt, I had a fifty-fifty chance of completely paralyzing myself from the waist down. But like a fool I went back. Some of the guys helped me with the bending and stooping over. Then the supervisor borrowed a ladder with three steps and on rollers from the paint department. He wanted me to stand on the top step while working on motors which are on dollies on a moving chain. I'd be using two press-wrenches to tighten fittings down while my right knee was on the transmission and the left leg standing up straight. All this from the top step of a ladder on rollers. One slip and it would be all over. I backed off and said it wouldn't work. By this time I'd gotten the shop steward there, but he didn't do anything. In fact, the next day he left on three weeks' vacation without doing anything to help me. I called the union hall and was told they'd send a business rep down the next day. I never saw or heard from the man.

12   Anyhow, I'm still doing the same job as when I got hurt. I can feel the tension in my back and shoulder coming up. I can feel the spasms start and muscles tightening up. Things just keep gettin' worse and they don't care. People could be rotated and moved rather than being cramped in the same position, like in the sleeper boxes, where you never stand up straight and stretch your

neck out. It's eight, ten, twelve hours a day all hunched over. In the next two years I've got to quit. I don't know what I'll do. If I end up paralyzed from the neck down, the company doesn't give a damn, the union doesn't give a damn, who's gonna take care of me? Who's gonna take care of my girls? I'm gonna be put in some moldy, old, stinkin' nursing home. I'm thirty-seven years old. I could live another thirty, forty years. And who's gonna really care about me?

13   I mean my husband left me. He was very jealous of my working with a lot of men and used to follow me to work. When I joined the bowling team, I tried to get him to come and meet the guys I work with. He came but felt left out because there was always an inside joke or something that he couldn't understand. He resented that and the fact that I made more money than he did. And my not being home bothered him. But he never said, "I want you to quit," or "We'll make it on what I get." If he had said that I probably would have quit. Instead we just muddled on. With me working, the whole family had to pitch in and help. When I come home at night my daughter has dinner waiting, and I do a couple loads of wash and everybody folds their own clothes. My husband pitched in for a while. Then he just stopped coming home. He found another lady that didn't work, had four kids, and was on welfare.

14   It really hurt and I get very confused still. I don't have the confidence and self-assurance I used to have. I think, "Why did I do that," or "Maybe I shouldn't have done it," and I have to force myself to say, "Hey, I felt and said what I wanted to and there's no turning back." It came out of me and I can't be apologizing for everything that I do. And, oh, I don't know, I guess I'm in a spell right now where I'm tired of being dirty. I want my fingernails long and clean. I want to not go up to the bathroom and find a big smudge of grease across my forehead. I want to sit down and be pampered and pretty all day. Maybe that wouldn't satisfy me, but I just can't imagine myself at fifty or sixty or seventy years old trying to climb on these trucks. I've been there for five years. I'm thirty-seven and I want to be out of there before I'm forty. And maybe I will. I've met this nice guy and he's talking of getting married. At the most, I would have to work for one more year and then I could stay at home, go back to being a housewife.

Understanding Content

1. How did Nora Quealey feel about being a housewife?
2. What prompted Nora Quealey to go to work outside her home? Do you think her reason was a good one?
3. What did Quealey do in order to cope with working in a predominately male environment?
4. In general, what is the company's attitude toward its employees? Which paragraphs do you think make this attitude clear?
5. How many different kinds of discrimination are revealed in "Nora Quealey"? What are they?

Considering Structure and Technique

1. Does "Nora Quealey" hold your interest? Why or why not?
2. Paragraph 5 tells about a woman who did not dress appropriately for work. What does this paragraph contribute? Would anything be lost if this paragraph were omitted? Explain.
3. "Nora Quealey" is taken from an interview. Cite three examples of conversational phrasings that seem more characteristic of speech than writing.
4. How are the introduction and conclusion connected?

Exploring Ideas

1. What do you think of Quealey's method of "fitting in" and dealing with men in the workplace?
2. Do you think that Quealey is a good employee? Explain why or why not.
3. Why are the circumstances of Nora Quealey's life so difficult? That is, what social forces and personal conditions have affected her?
4. To what extent do you think that Quealey's lack of money affects how much discrimination she must put up with?
5. Do you think that Nora Quealey is an everyday hero and a role model? Explain why or why not.

Writing Workshop: Speaking and Writing

Speaking and writing can be very different from each other. When you speak, your tone of voice and gestures help you convey meaning, and your listener can interrupt to ask a question if something is unclear. When you write, you do not have the benefit of tone of voice, gestures, and a listener who can question, so you must be very attentive to word choice and detail. Also, while speakers need not worry about capitalization, punctuation, and spelling, writers must attend to these. As a result, writers go back over what they have said and rewrite carefully to cut unnecessary material, add transitions, correct mistakes, clarify points, and improve their writing any other way they can. After all, they have no tone of voice, gestures, or listener questions to help them. Because "Nora Quealey" is the reproduction of an interview, you may have noticed that some of it is more suited to speech than writing.

Writing Workshop Activity

1. If you were to revise and edit "Nora Quealey" to make it more like a written essay, what changes would you make?
2. Would your changes make the piece more or less powerful? Explain.

Language Notes for Multilingual and Other Writers

If you speak English as a second language, a number of expressions in "Nora Quealey" may be unfamiliar to you.

1. *On the spot* means "immediately."

   I put an application in and got hired <u>on the spot.</u> Paragraph 3

2. To *fit in* means "to belong."

   . . . I would have to *listen* to swear words and some of the obscene things, but still *act* like a lady, or I'd never <u>fit in.</u> Paragraph 4

3. To *turn one's back* means "to abandon, ignore, or reject."

   . . . when I have a friend, I don't <u>turn my back</u> on them. . . . Paragraph 10

4. To *pitch in* means "to help."

   My husband <u>pitched in</u> for awhile. Paragraph 13

From Reading to Writing

In Your Journal: Do you think that Nora Quealey is someone to respect and admire? Why or why not?

With Some Classmates: If Nora Quealey asked you for help, what would you tell her? Compose at least two pages of advice.

In an Essay

- What can be learned from reading "Nora Quealey" about the relationship between men and women in the workplace? Consider the effects of the woman wearing a tank top without a bra, instances of sexual harassment, Quealey's remark that she had to work like a man but act like a lady, and anything else in the selection that you think is significant.
- Using the clues in the selection, describe the kind of person Nora Quealey is. Back up your conclusions with evidence from the interview. Do you think she should be considered a role model? Why or why not?
- Have you ever been the victim of sexual harassment in the workplace, or have you ever witnessed sexual harassment in the workplace? If so, tell what happened and explain the effects it had on the victim and other employees.

- Tell about an unpleasant work experience that you have had. Explain what the problem was, how you reacted to the problem, and how you were affected by the situation. Also, if there is anything to be learned from your experience, mention what that is.

Beyond the Writing Class: Ask your classmates and other people you know whether they have been the victims of sexual harassment in the workplace or whether they have ever witnessed it. Find two people who answer yes and interview them for responses to these and any other follow-up questions you care to ask:

What happened? Describe the incident of harassment.

Why do you think the harassment occurred?

How did the harassment make you feel?

Why do you think you felt the way you did?

What effect did the harassment have on you or (if you were not the victim) the victim?

What effect did the harassment have on others in the workplace? Tape-record your interviews or write out the answers carefully. Then reproduce the interviews in an essay about sexual harassment and try to draw a conclusion from them about the causes and effects of sexual harassment.

As an alternative, discover your college's specific written policies on harassment. Are they adequate, in your opinion? Explain.

India: A Widow's Devastating Choice
JUTHICA STANGL

In this 1984 *Ms.* essay, Juthica Stangl writes of *suttee* (also called *sati*), a practice whereby widows in India kill themselves in order to follow their husbands into death. As the piece points out, suttee is not just an ancient tradition; it is an ongoing issue.

Preview. In your journal, write an ending to this story: A man dies and leaves his young wife and 14-year-old son penniless. The woman is unable to find a job, and because of long-standing bad feelings, both her family and her in-laws refuse to give any help. Without money, the woman and her son face the worst kind of poverty, including homelessness and hunger. What happens?

Vocabulary. If any of the following words from the selection are unfamiliar to you, study their meanings before reading.

Delhi (1)   a city in India
meticulous (4)   with attention to detail
sari (6)   the outer garment worn by Hindu women; a long piece of cotton or silk worn around the body with one end draped over the shoulder
garb (6)   clothes
Bengali (11)   a language spoken in India
Hindu (13)   pertaining to the religion of Hinduism, practiced in India
Brahmin (13)   the highest social caste (group) in India
caste (13)   one of four social groups into which Hindu society is rigidly divided
boisterous (14)   rough and noisy
dowry (20)   the money or goods paid by the bride's family to the groom's family
destitute (33)   penniless
funeral pyre (37)   a pile of wood used for cremations (burning dead bodies)
superfluous (38)   extra; unnecessary
atone (38)   to make up for

On October 26, 1981, while Delhi prepared for Deevali, the festival of lights, Anjali Banerji* and her 14-year-old son Ashok each swallowed a lethal handful of sleeping pills. They had already fed a dose to the family dog, Tepi.

*The names have been fictionalized.

2   Anjali Banerji died four days later; Ashok and Tepi survived, thanks to police officers who pumped their stomachs after the attempt.

3   A November issue of *India Today* magazine reported the suicide. Anjali Banerji's husband, Rajib, a doctor at the Hindu Rao Hospital, had been hit by a car and, after a lengthy hospitalization, had died the previous January. In time, the widow began searching for work. She had a degree in social work and 14 years experience in West Bengal, but no job came her way. She received little sympathy from her family and from friends—only the advice to move in with relatives. After 10 frustrating months, she decided to follow her husband in death, and to take the rest of the family with her.

4   The reporter noted her meticulous preparations—notes written to the police and her brother, the refrigerator emptied and defrosted, kitchen stocked with food for relatives or whoever came to take care of the possessions left behind.

5   Two weeks after her death, friends sent the clipping to me in California.

6   Anjali had been very special to me. We were both about 16 when we met outside a classroom on the first day of college at the University of Calcutta. I still remember it clearly. I was standing alone in an archway, watching a crow feed her little ones. Suddenly I heard footsteps and there was a tall, slender girl with two short braids, wearing a well-starched white sari. Like me, she wore no jewelry, not even the customary thin gold bracelets every middle-class girl wore like a uniform. I had not met anyone before who also rebelled against the prescribed dress code. What we were wearing would be considered a widow's garb. I felt close to her instantly.

7   I smiled and asked if she was also waiting for room three. She nodded with a smile and said, "Yes, and am I glad to find someone to talk to. None of my friends got into this college. I was so nervous when my father dropped me off at the gate that I didn't sleep all night."

8   "I can understand that, since I have no old friends here either. My name is Juthica, but everyone calls me Julie."

9   She stared at me for a few seconds, then told me her name and that she had attended a large school. She hadn't really expected to get into such a good college. She also asked where I had gone to high school. I was sure she had never heard of my school, so I told her it was a small, British missionary boarding school. My graduating class had only 13 students.

10   "You must be Christian with a name like Julie," she said.

11   I found myself apologizing: "It is only my nickname. I do have a real, honest-to-goodness Bengali name, too."

12   She laughed and said, "Oh, it doesn't bother me a bit that you are Christian. As a matter of fact, many people think I'm one too, because of the way I dress."

13   I tried to explain that I wasn't wearing white because of my religion, but simply because I liked it. I realized we both had many misconceptions about each other's communities. She came from a Hindu Brahmin family, the highest

caste, I from a Christian middle-class one. We spoke the same language, but our cultures were very different.

14 From then on, for four years, we were inseparable. We took the same classes, joined the National Cadet Corps, helped each other learn to ride bikes, and visited each other after school. I always invited her home for Christmas dinner, and spent Hindu feasts at hers. We covered for each other, telling little white lies when doing something or going somewhere our families wouldn't approve. We comforted each other through difficult times, and teased and poked fun at each other. She was quiet and sensible, with an irresistible sense of humor. I was wild, impulsive, and boisterous—we complemented each other well.

15 Now she is dead.

16 All those times when I felt that the world had come to an end, that my great love was over, or that I would surely flunk the final, she would patiently listen to my stories, then put her arm around me and reassure me. Even now, 30 years later, the memory of her strength pulls me through difficult times. What could have happened to her strength, her confidence, her optimism?

17 As I read through the clipping, I found I couldn't help blaming myself that I wasn't there when she really needed someone. I began to feel angry at her family.

18 Traditionally, the extended Indian family comes to the rescue in times of trouble. What had happened to them? Her father was a scholarly gentleman who taught high school. She had two older brothers, one an army doctor, the other an engineer, and an older sister, who was already married and out of the house by the time I met her. Anytime I was visiting I was always struck by how quiet and peaceful the household was. They all spoke in gentle voices. It seemed unnatural to me, being used to seven children playing, laughing, fighting, and loving in my family. When I commented once on this, she said it was true, nothing much was ever going on. Her father spent most of the time in his study, her mother kept the house. I had an image of trees in the forest, growing near, but never touching, except in a big storm, when the contact results in a broken limb.

19 Anjali did produce a storm when she married Rajib. She went against her family's expectations by finding her own future husband, rather than waiting for her match to be arranged. What's more, he was from a lower caste.

20 Rajib's family was even more resentful. Even though Anjali was higher caste, which on one level meant social achievement, the family missed out on a potentially major dowry. Had Rajib married within his own caste, the family would have been offered clothes, jewelry, and money, and considering that he was a doctor, perhaps even a car or house. His family counted on this; it would have helped with providing Rajib's sisters' dowries. The loss was significant.

21 In the wake of the storm, both Anjali and Rajib ended up as limbs broken off family trees. They established themselves on their own. Except for a few sticks of furniture they had nothing, but seemed very happy. By then I was living in California; I visited her each time I was in India, sometimes really

going out of my way to do so to catch up with their frequent moves. Each time I saw them I was impressed with the intimacy of their relationship. They were two people who genuinely enjoyed and respected each other, who truly shared their life in the best sense of the word. I kept up with her every way I could.

22   She was overjoyed when her son was born. Her family, at last, showed some interest in the new grandson. However, Rajib's family did not respond even then. She was determined, with or without the families' support, to continue providing a happy home. From everything I saw, she succeeded. But underneath it, I could tell that she was hurt by her isolation from her family; a feeling of sadness remained for not being accepted by her in-laws.

23   The last time I saw her was in a hotel room in Delhi. Rajib, Anjali, and Ashok lived outside of town at that point; they took a long bus drive to come to see me and my family. She brought some fried fish, my favorite kind, which she remembered from our college days. Her son by this time was about 12, very bright and friendly. I fantasized about our children developing the kind of friendship Anjali and I had, knowing full well that with the distance between us that would not be possible. The relationship I had been impressed with over the years between Anjali and Rajib obviously was still there, and now included their son. I was particularly happy to see that our children and Ashok got along well.

24   We parted with the promise of writing more often. We even talked about her sending Ashok to the United States for a year, when he would stay with us.

25   Is it possible that the article in my hand was about the same Anjali? Suddenly I was furious with her. How could this wonderful woman, this pillar of strength, this model friend and mother, simply do away with herself? What about the promises? How could she just abandon everything, including me?

26   When I was still in India with my family, I got a letter from her about her husband's car accident. I left India knowing only that he was seriously injured and in the hospital. For months I had had no news, despite my many letters to Anjali. I would have called, but they could never afford a telephone. I felt helpless, but not knowing anyone in the area where they were living at the time, there was nothing I could do.

27   The next news came in the form of an invitation to a memorial service for Rajib. It was signed by Ashok, as is the custom. The eldest son takes matters into his hands on the father's death. At this time he was barely 14. I could not imagine my own son, three years younger—having to—or being able to do this. But knowing Anjali I knew that if Ashok was anything like his mother, he would perform his duty admirably.

28   All I could do was to write, offering my help and whatever support I could, long distance. I felt I had failed her completely; I was never there when I might have been able to help.

29   I never heard from her again. I wrote to all our common acquaintances trying to get news. No one seemed to be in touch with her.

30   But the *India Today* reporter described the last nine months of her life in great detail. The family had had a comfortable existence, but their modest sav-

ings were used up quickly during Rajib's hospitalization after the hit-and-run accident.

31   In India, of course, accident insurance is uncommon. The application for his life insurance benefit was lost by the company. After months, the company had not responded to the duplicate application. The promised assistance from her husband's employer had not come through despite her repeated appeals. Within weeks she was totally without funds.

32   Given India's unemployment problem, there were few jobs available even to experienced and highly educated men. It is not surprising then that a woman, out of the job market as long as Anjali had been, was not seriously considered by most employers. Further, she did not have the necessary personal connections, or the know-how to pay bribes to secure a job.

33   The prospect of being destitute, with no source of support for herself, her son, or even the dog, must have been devastating to her. India is, of course, best known for its poverty. But perhaps just because of this, extreme poverty is even more unthinkable for someone like Anjali who had never before had to worry about it.

34   The article told of her difficulties with the bureaucratic maze and her resulting depression and loneliness. Her family, whom, according to the article, she had abandoned to marry the man she chose, did not come to her. Her parents had died by now, only her brothers and sisters remained. It is less surprising that her in-laws did not respond either. They considered their son dead once he had married against their wishes.

35   A reporter interviewed Anjali's brother after the tragedy, and he claimed the family never knew what kind of difficulty she was in. Perhaps her pride kept her from turning to them. Rejected once, she did not want to risk it again.

36   Anjali's whole life had revolved around her husband and son. She simply couldn't imagine leaving Ashok to other people's mercy. Once she decided to end her life she saw no other way but to take her son with her.

37   I suddenly realized that, as I was reading on, the image the article conjured up was not of Anjali, but of a women's demonstration I had seen in Delhi during my last trip to India. Hundreds of angry women, mostly villagers, marched with banners, demanding the reinstatement of suttee, the ancient custom in which a widow is to throw herself onto her husband's funeral pyre. The British had outlawed suttee in 1829.

38   The custom is a testimony to the fact that the life of a widow is superfluous. Once the man is dead, there is no further purpose for the woman. Her role is to bear children; with her husband's death that job is done. Religious tradition holds that her sacrifice helps her husband atone for his sins and for this she becomes a saint.

39   Despite the established tradition, not all widows had always willingly killed themselves in this way. Village elders and family members often had to force a young wife to follow her husband into death. They would do so not just for religious or traditional reasons, but because the burden of supporting the surviving wife was usually too much for the family.

40 When I saw that demonstration, I could hardly believe my eyes. How could women, in this day and age, especially in a country where the prime minister is a woman, actually campaign for the right to commit suicide just because their husbands had died?

41 The demonstration dramatized the fact that the ancient custom still has social and economic relevance today. The marching women realized that by outlawing the custom, the British had succeeded only in making it illegal, not in removing its significance. Even today, India's society has no mechanism to help a woman in a traditional role develop her own identity and avoid becoming a burden. The women were making a statement that suicide is the easier alternative to a life of dependency on unwilling families.

42 Anjali was an educated and sophisticated woman, with a background and social circle totally different from that of the demonstrators. For her, living in 20th-century Delhi, suttee, in its traditional form, was unthinkable. But, in the end, didn't she find herself forced onto her husband's funeral pyre anyway?

Understanding Content

1. Why were Anjali's parents upset about her marriage? Why were Rajib's parents upset?
2. As schoolgirls, what did the author and Anjali have in common?
3. As schoolgirls, how were the author and Anjali different?
4. Why did the author blame herself for Anjali's suicide? Why did she blame Anjali's family?

Considering Structure and Technique

1. Does the opening paragraph arouse your interest and make you want to read further? Explain why or why not.
2. Paragraphs 5 and 15 are each composed of just one sentence. What is the effect of each single-sentence paragraph?
3. Stangl's essay includes some conversation but not a great deal, considering the length of the narration. Why do you think the author uses so little conversation? Would the essay have benefited from more conversation? Explain.
4. Why does Stangl tell about the women's demonstration to reinstate suttee? How do you think that demonstration relates to the rest of the essay?

Exploring Ideas

1. Why did Anjali kill herself? Do you think she had any alternatives to suicide? Explain.
2. Using the evidence in the essay as clues, explain how you think that Anjali's Hindu view of suicide is the same as or different from the author's Judeo-Christian view of suicide?

3. What is your opinion of Anjali's attempting to take her son with her in suicide? What were her considerations when she did this? Is it possible to defend her action? Explain.
4. Who or what do you feel is responsible for Anjali's suicide? How do you answer the question at the end of the essay?

Writing Workshop: Asking Rhetorical Questions

A **rhetorical question** is a question for which no answer is expected. A writer asks a rhetorical question to emphasize a point, to arouse the reader's interest, or to get the reader to think about something. For example, the rhetorical question in paragraph 16 of "India: A Widow's Devastating Choice" ("What could have happened to her strength, her confidence, her optimism?") gets the reader to think about why Anjali killed herself. Rhetorical questions also appear in paragraphs 18, 25, 40, and 42 of the essay.

Writing Workshop Activity

Take a look at the rhetorical questions in paragraphs 25, 40, and 42. Then decide which of these purposes each question serves: to emphasize a point, to arouse the reader's interest, or to get the reader to think about something. (A rhetorical question may serve more than one purpose.)

Language Notes for Multilingual and Other Writers

The **past tense** is used for actions that began and ended in the past. As the following examples from the essay reveal, the past tense often appears with time expressions that point to the past. (The time expressions and past tense verbs are underlined as a study aid.)

1. <u>On October 26, 1981</u>, while Delhi <u>prepared</u> for Deevali, . . . Anjali Banerji . . . <u>swallowed</u> a lethal handful of sleeping pills. Paragraph 1
2. Anjali Banerji <u>died four days later</u> . . . . Paragraph 2
3. <u>After 10 frustrating months,</u> she <u>decided</u> to follow her husband in death. . . . Paragraph 3

The time expressions accompanying the past tense are often sequence expressions.

1. <u>From then on,</u> for four years, we <u>were</u> inseparable. Paragraph 14
2. Her family, <u>at last, showed</u> some interest in the new grandson. Paragraph 22
3. <u>The last time</u> I <u>saw</u> her <u>was</u> in a hotel room in Delhi. Paragraph 23
4. The <u>next</u> news <u>came</u> in the form of an invitation to a memorial service. . . . Paragraph 27

From Reading to Writing

In Your Journal: In paragraph 18, Stangl says she had an image of trees in a forest. Explain that image and its significance.

With Some Classmates: Using the information in the essay, write a character sketch of Anjali. (A **character sketch** tells what someone is like.) Give her personality traits and explain what motivated her. Then go on to compare your sketch to the perception the following people had of Anjali: Stangl, Anjali's family and in-laws, and Indian society.

In an Essay

- Compare and contrast the way Anjali was treated by her family with the way Polingaysi was treated by her family (see "No Turning Back" on p. 133).
- In paragraph 13, Stangl says that at first she and Anjali had misconceptions about each other's communities. Select two groups from this country (whites and blacks, men and women, southerners and northerners, urban and rural dwellers, and so forth) and tell about some of the misconceptions these groups have about each other. As an alternative, tell about one or more misconceptions you had about another person.
- In paragraph 16, Stangl says that "the memory of [Anjali's] strength pulls [her] through difficult times." Is there someone who gets you through difficult times? If so, tell about that person and how he or she helps you.
- In paragraph 13, Stangl refers to the different castes (classes) in Indian society. Describe the social classes in the United States and discuss to what extent it is or is not possible to move between the classes. Also explain the effects the classes have on individuals.
- In the library or on the Internet, learn about the caste system in India, including its history and present status. Then write up your findings in a paper suitable for a cultural anthropology course with a focus on describing the social organizations of different cultures.

High School Controversial
MARC PEYSER AND DONATELLA LORCH

"High School Controversial" is part of a March 2000 *Newsweek* special report called "Shades of Gay." The report looks at levels of acceptance of homosexuals in schools, churches, offices, and families. Overall, the report concludes that the news is mixed: In some areas, gays have gained acceptance, but in others they still meet with resistance.

Preview. "High School Controversial" tells of the struggle of two Louisiana students who fought to bring a Gay-Straight Alliance to their school. In the process, they learned something about activism and tolerance. Take a moment and think about your own views by answering the following: (1) Is homosexuality a sin? (2) Should the government sanction same-sex marriages? (3) Should homosexuals be permitted to serve in the military? (4) Should homosexual couples be able to adopt children?

Vocabulary.   If any of the following words from the selection are unfamiliar to you, study their meanings before reading.

melee (1)   fight
• **bulwark** (2)   barrier
homophobia (2)   fear of homosexuals or homosexuality
• **Matthew Shepard** (2)   a gay college student who was beaten and left to die in Wyoming
dichotomy (2)   division into two
contentious (3)   hostile, antagonistic
detox (4)   short for "detoxification," to eliminate drug or alcohol from an addict's system
abomination (4)   a wickedness or hatred
contingent (5)   group
brazen (6)   overly bold
raucous (6)   loud and rowdy

It was only first period at McKinley High School in Baton Rouge when 17-year-old Leslie-Claire Spillman sensed that something was wrong. The door to her classroom burst open, a girl jumped in and yelled, "It's time!" Spillman soon heard students murmuring and slamming lockers in the halls. As she edged her way outside, she realized that all the commotion was about—her. "No Gay Clubs!" the kids were chanting as the crowds began to grow thicker and meaner in the halls. Spillman is the openly bisexual cochairman of the

Gay-Straight Alliance, a group she and her friend Martin Pfeiffer, also 17, had fought for six months to form. They had started with the school's principal and battled all the way to Louisiana's East Baton Rouge Parish School Board. But the morning's mini-melee was tougher than any of those fights. A girl walked up to Spillman and said, "Watch your back. I'm going to f---ing beat your a--" One of Pfeiffer's teachers barricaded him in a classroom. When it was all over, the school suspended 36 anti-gay protesters. Yet that didn't make it any easier for Spillman and Pfeiffer. "The kid lives in a pressure cooker," says Pfeiffer's mom, Molly. "I don't know how he gets up every morning."

2   It's not always this dangerous to be openly gay in high school. In fact, it may never have been easier. Gay-Straight Alliances have been a major factor in helping teenagers create openly gay lives. First established in 1988, GSAs were designed as both support groups for gay students and—with the help of the sympathetic straight students—a bulwark against homophobia. The Gay, Lesbian, Straight Teacher Network estimates there are about 700 GSAs nationwide, most of which were formed—peacefully—in the wake of the 1998 murder of Matthew Shepard. But the move out of the classroom closet isn't always smooth—or predictable. In Orange County, Calif., pro- and anti-gay forces have been fighting for months over El Modena High School's GSA, even though a federal judge ruled last fall that the group must be allowed to meet on campus. On the other hand, Decatur High—smack in the middle of the Georgia Bible belt—has had a GSA for two years with practically no dissent. "Kids who are out are the class president, the star athlete. Same-sex couples at proms aren't even a weirdo thing anymore," says Ritch Savin-Williams, a Cornell psychology professor. "There's an interesting dichotomy today. It's really bad for some, but many gay kids are doing well."

3   For Pfeiffer and Spillman, the road has been rocky. It was Pfeiffer's idea to start the GSA. He'd been taunted by kids since middle school—long before, at 15, he came out to his mom at Wal-Mart—and decided a support group would help gay students and foster tolerance. When Pfeiffer went to the McKinley principal last October to talk about starting a GSA, she said no. Next Pfeiffer went to the school superintendent. After placing 25 unreturned phone calls over a month, he finally got a response: "inappropriate." So he went to the school board, which held a series of continuous meetings.

4   Pfeiffer—with his bleached-blond hair, pierced ears and a choker necklace adorned with his boyfriend's school ring—spoke about how the years of harassment had once made him suicidal. Spillman says she actually dropped out of school, became a heroin addict and spent five weeks in detox after the gay taunts became so unrelenting. Perhaps it's not surprising that, while it's easier for many kids to be open about their sexuality today, the suicide rate of gay teens is alarmingly high. A 1997 study of Massachusetts high-school students found that 46 percent of the gay, lesbian and bisexual kids surveyed had attempted suicide in the last year. "If you're in a society that tells you you are an abomination, right or wrong it's what you believe," Pfeiffer says.

5   The anti-GSA contingent used that fear factor, too. They brought in an "ex" lesbian and gay man to the decisive board meeting to talk about how miserable they were before they adjusted their sexual orientation. "Dresses! Some of them [the boys] wear dresses. What are you going to do?" the ex-lesbian warned. At one point, Spillman started to cry. After five hours of debate, the 12-member board came up only one vote short of the seven needed to pass the policy allowing the GSA on campus. But the school superintendent—perhaps mindful of the 1984 Equal Access Law that prohibits schools from selectively prohibiting extracurricular groups from meeting on campus—decided not to stand in the way of Pfeiffer and Spillman's group after all. (The principal did not return calls requesting an interview.)

6   And that was the easy part. Once Pfeiffer and Spillman got the go-ahead from their principal, the anti-gay pressure at school intensified. Pfeiffer says one boy was brazen enough to taunt him—"Hey, gay boy!"—right in front of the main office. "People like you are the reason I am starting this club," replied Pfeiffer. For all his brashness, he started having friends escort him to classes. On the raucous day last February, Spillman and Pfeiffer saw the student protestors on the front lawn carrying signs with that old line, GOD MADE ADAM AND EVE, NOT ADAM AND STEVE. But they had no idea that students planned to demonstrate inside as well. It got very noisy very quickly. Pfeiffer's English teacher immediately locked the door and told him to keep his easy-to-spot blond head away from the window. "We have the right to speak freely," says Chiquita Harris, one of the students who was suspended for three days because of the incident. "School is not a place for a gay club." It will be soon. McKinley's 20-member GSA is scheduled to have its first on-campus meeting on March 22. What will happen then is anyone's guess. Ironically, while Spillman and Pfeiffer were fighting the good fight, another high school in the parish, Scotlandville, already had its first SGA meeting, uneventfully. "I think 20 years from now, the environment will be so much different in Baton Rouge because of these clubs," Pfeiffer says.

7   It has already changed the two gay teens who fought to make it happen. Despite the battle scars, Spillman and Pfeiffer say their crusade to bring a gay-support group to their school has made them better, stronger people. "I feel this activated feeling," says Spillman, who, despite the year she lost when she dropped out, is expected to graduate this spring. "I used to count the days to escape Baton Rouge—that's where the work needs to be done. I have a voice I can use." Pfeiffer, a straight-A student who is already taking courses at nearby Louisiana State University, also plans to continue to work as an activist. "People can't break me anymore. I've got something in me that no one can take away, no matter how violent and vicious they are," says Pfeiffer, who has applied to Harvard and Boston University. "I don't want to leave this high school without leaving something behind." He already has.

Understanding Content

1. What purpose do high school Gay-Straight Alliances serve?
2. Pfeiffer and Spillman endured considerable harassment because of their sexual orientations. How were they affected by that harassment?
3. Why is the suicide rate so high for gay teenagers?
4. Why did the superintendent of McKinley High School finally allow the formation of the Gay-Straight Alliance?

Considering Structure and Technique

1. What approach do the authors take to their opening? Does that opening engage your interest? Why or why not?
2. Why do the authors mention Spillman's drug addiction and dropping out of school and Pfeiffer's suicidal feelings?
3. Is the essay unbiased, or do the authors reveal their points of view? Cite evidence to support your evaluation.
4. Paragraph 6 opens with a short sentence: "And that was the easy part." Later in the paragraph, there is another short sentence: "It will be soon." Finally, the essay ends with a short sentence: "He already has." What effect do these short sentences have on the reader?

Exploring Ideas

1. Martin Pfeiffer's mother says that her son "'lives in a pressure cooker'" (paragraph 1). What are the sources of his pressure? What do you think the long-term effects of the pressure will be?
2. Pfeiffer told his mother in Wal-Mart that he is gay. Speculate about what could have prompted him to make such an important statement in that location.
3. Why do you think the McKinley High School principal and the school board said no to Pfeiffer's initial request to form the GSA?
4. In addition to "homosexual" and related words, what words and phrases describe Pfeiffer and Spillman?

Writing Workshop: Opening with a Story

A story makes a good opening when it is likely to stimulate a reader's interest and in some way illustrate a point made in the essay or provide helpful background information. In "High School Controversial," for example, the opening story engages interest because it is suspenseful. It also provides important background information about and an illustration of the harassment gay students have experienced in McKinley High School.

Writing Workshop Activity

Assume you are writing an essay with this thesis: "High school is a time of _____ for many teenagers" [You fill in the blank.] Draft an opening for the essay that tells a story.

Language Notes for Multilingual and Other Writers

Four common expressions appear in "High School Controversial."

1. A *pressure cooker* is a device that cooks food quickly using superheated steam under pressure. *To be in a pressure cooker* is "to be in a situation that causes considerable social or emotional stress."

    The kid lives in <u>a pressure cooker</u>. Paragraph 1

2. *To come out of the closet* or *to come out* means "to live publicly as a homosexual." *To be in the closet* means "to keep one's homosexuality a secret."

    But the move <u>out of the classroom closet</u> isn't always smooth—or predictable. Paragraph 2

    . . . he <u>came out</u> to his mom at Wal-Mart . . . Paragraph 3

3. The *Bible belt* is a name given to an area chiefly in the southern United States where many people are said to accept a literal interpretation of the Bible.

    On the other hand, Decatur High—smack in the middle of the Georgia <u>Bible belt</u>—has had a GSA for two years with practically no dissent. Paragraph 2

From Reading to Writing

In Your Journal: If you had been the principal of McKinley High School, how would you have responded to the initial request for a Gay-Straight Alliance? Why?

With Some Classmates: Paragraph 5 refers to a "fear factor." Explain the role fear plays in the relations between gays and straights.

In an Essay

- In paragraph 6, Martin Pfeiffer, is quoted as saying, "'I think 20 years from now, the environment will be so much different in Baton Rouge because of these clubs.'" Do you agree? If so, look 20 years into the future and tell what changes are likely to have occurred and why the changes came about. If you do not agree, explain why not.
- What would the reaction have been at your high school if students tried to form a Gay-Straight Alliance? Why? If such a group did exist at your school, tell how it was received by nonmembers.
- Leslie-Claire Spillman and Martin Pfeiffer say they are "better, stronger people" as a result of their struggle to form the GSA. Drawing on your own experience and observation, discuss the fact that adversity can strengthen people.

Beyond the Writing Class: Read newspaper reports on the killing of Matthew Shepard and what happened afterward. Then, in your own words, write an account of what happened and the aftermath. Draw one or more conclusions from the events.

CHAPTER 8

DIVERSITY: HOW DO WE RESPOND TO DIFFERENCE?

"Differences challenge assumptions."

Anne Wilson Schaef

"The real death of America will come when everyone is alike."

James T. Ellison

"Give me your tired, your poor,/Your huddled masses yearning to breathe free,/The wretched refuse of your teeming shore./Send these, the homeless, tempest-tost to me,/I lift my lamp beside the golden door!"

from "The New Colossus," a poem by Emma Lazarus;
inscribed on the base of The Statue of Liberty

"Why do you have to be a nonconformist like everybody else?"

James Thurber

Black *and* Latino

ROBERTO SANTIAGO

Award-winning writer and journalist Roberto Santiago is currently a contributing editor for *Time Out* magazine. He also conducts workshops on the roots of racial stereotypes and how they prevent growth. In 1991, he interviewed Fidel Castro for a piece that earned him the Inter-American Press Association Award. "Black *and* Latino," which originally appeared in *Essence,* explores what can happen when two aspects of a person's identity conflict with each other.

Preview.   Like Santiago, consider a time when you felt caught between two worlds, as though you belonged to both but were not fully accepted or comfortable in either. Perhaps you have been caught between the culture you live in and the one your parents were raised in, between the worlds of divorced parents or two religious traditions. Or consider roles that sometimes conflict: student and athlete or that of mother and student, for example.

Vocabulary.   If any of the following words from the essay are unfamiliar to you, study their meanings before reading.

parody (4) a ridiculous imitation
eons (6)   periods of geologic time, commonly used to mean long periods of time
categorically (6)   related to a category or division
predominant (6)   main
determinant (6)   deciding
searing (6)   burning and painful
bridle path (7)   a wide path for riding horses
slur (8)   insult
solace (9)   comfort
hang-up (9)   a personal or emotional problem
iconoclast (11)   a person who attacks or disregards cherished beliefs

❝There is no way that you can be black and Puerto Rican at the same time." What? Despite the many times I've heard this over the years, that statement still perplexes me. I *am* both and always have been. My color is a blend of my mother's rich, dark skin tone and my father's white complexion. As they were both Puerto Rican, I spoke Spanish before English, but I am totally bilingual. My life has been shaped by my black and Latino heritages, and despite other people's confusion, I don't feel I have to choose one or the other. To do so would be to deny a part of myself.

2   There has not been a moment in my life when I did not know that I looked black—and I never thought that others did not see it, too. But growing up in East Harlem, I was also aware that I did not "act black," according to the African-American boys on the block.

3   My lighter-skinned Puerto Rican friends were less of a help in this department. "You're not black," they would whine, shaking their heads. "You're a *boriqua* [slang for Puerto Rican], you ain't no *moreno* [black]." If that was true, why did my mirror defy the rules of logic? And most of all, why did I feel that there was some serious unknown force trying to make me choose sides?

4   *Acting black. Looking black. Being a real black.* This debate among us is almost a parody. The fact is that I am black, so why do I need to prove it?

5   The island of Puerto Rico is only a stone's throw away from Haiti, and, no fooling, if you climb a palm tree, you can see Jamaica bobbing on the Atlantic. The slave trade ran through the Caribbean basin, and virtually all Puerto Rican citizens have some African blood in their veins. My grandparents on my mother's side were the classic *negro como carbon* (black as carbon) people, but despite the fact that they were as dark as can be, they are officially not considered black.

6   There is an explanation for this, but not one that makes much sense, or difference, to a working-class kid from Harlem. Puerto Ricans identify themselves as Hispanics—part of a worldwide race that originated from eons of white Spanish conquests—a mixture of white, African, and *Indio* blood, which, categorically, is apart from black. In other words, the culture is the predominant and determinant factor. But there are frustrations in being caught in a duo-culture, where your skin color does not necessarily dictate what you are. When I read Piri Thomas's searing autobiography, *Down These Mean Streets,* in my early teens, I saw that he couldn't figure out other people's attitudes toward his blackness, either.

7   My first encounter with this attitude about the race thing rode on horseback. I had just turned six years old and ran toward the bridle path in Central Park as I saw two horses about to trot past. "Yea! Horsie! Yea!" I yelled. Then I noticed one figure on horseback. She was white, and she shouted, "Shut up, you f-----g nigger! Shut up!" She pulled back on the reins and twisted the horse in my direction. I can still feel the spray of gravel that the horse kicked at my chest. And suddenly she was gone. I looked back and, in the distance, saw my parents playing Whiffle Ball with my sister. They seemed miles away.

8   They still don't know about this incident. But I told my Aunt Aurelia almost immediately. She explained what the words meant and why they were said. Ever since then I have been able to express my anger appropriately through words or action in similar situations. Self-preservation, ego, and pride forbid men from ever ignoring, much less forgetting, a slur.

9   Aunt Aurelia became, unintentionally, my source for answers I needed about color and race. I never sought her out. She just seemed to appear at my home during the points in my childhood when I most needed her for solace. "Puerto Ricans are different from American blacks," she told me once. "There

is no racism between what you call white and black. Nobody even considers the marriages interracial." She then pointed out the difference in color between my father and mother. "You never noticed that," she said, "because you were not raised with that hang-up."

10   Aunt Aurelia passed away before I could follow up on her observation. But she had made an important point. It's why I never liked the attitude that says I should be exclusive to one race.

11   My behavior toward this race thing pegged me as an iconoclast of sorts. Children from mixed marriages, from my experience, also share this attitude. If I have to bear the label of iconoclast because the world wants people to be in set categories and I don't want to, then I will.

12   A month before Aunt Aurelia died, she saw I was a little down about the whole race thing, and she said, "Roberto, don't worry. Even if—no matter what you do—black people in this country don't, you can always depend on white people to treat you like a black."

Understanding Content

1. What is the basic conflict that Santiago faces? How does he resolve that conflict?
2. Santiago's aunt says there is no racism between whites and blacks in Puerto Rico. Why does Santiago say that this racism exists in the United States but not in Puerto Rico?
3. In what way or ways is Santiago a victim of bias and discrimination?

Considering Structure and Technique

1. Paragraph 1 is the introduction of "Black *and* Latino." In that introduction, Santiago provides background information, a technique that is discussed in the workshop in this chapter. However, he also uses another approach to stimulate interest in his essay. What is that approach?
2. Which sentence or sentences do you think best express Santiago's thesis?
3. Which paragraph makes use of an anecdote (brief story). What purpose does the anecdote serve?

Exploring Ideas

1. In paragraph 1, Santiago says his identity confuses people. Why do you think people are confused?
2. Why do you think the author did not tell his parents about the racist incident in Central Park when it happened? Why do you think he has not told them to this day?
3. Why does the author resist the pressure to choose one of his identities over the other?
4. Explain the meaning of the aunt's words in paragraph 12.

Writing Workshop: Providing Background Information in the Introduction

If the reader needs certain information in order to appreciate or understand ideas in your essay, you can put that information in the introduction. In his introduction, Santiago provides the following background information: he is black and Puerto Rican; he is bilingual; he has been shaped by both of his cultural heritages. To be successful, an introduction that provides background information should do two things: create interest in the essay and give helpful information.

Writing Workshop Activity

Look through this book, magazines, newspaper editorial pages, and books of essays to find an essay with background information in the introduction. Decide why the author thought it was necessary to provide the reader with this background.

Language Notes for Multilingual and Other Writers

Two interesting expressions appear in "Black *and* Latino."

1. *Stone's throw* refers to something nearby, that is, to something so close that you can hit it if you throw a stone in its direction.

   The island of Puerto Rico is only <u>a stone's throw away</u> from Haiti. . . . Paragraph 5

2. *Pegged* is an informal usage meaning to identify.

   My behavior toward this race thing <u>pegged</u> me as an iconoclast of sorts. Paragraph 11

From Reading to Writing

In Your Journal: In paragraph 9, Santiago's aunt points out that Santiago did not notice the difference in his parents' skin color because he was not raised to notice racial distinctions. In a page or two, explain how your upbringing influenced your attitude about race.

With Some Classmates: Some people argue that black children should not be adopted by white parents because the children will not learn enough about their black heritage and because they will be caught between worlds, never feeling like they fully belong in either. Using the information in "Black *and* Latino" and your own thinking on the subject, explain either why it is not a good idea for white parents to adopt black children, or why such adoptions should not be discouraged.

In an Essay

- In paragraph 7, Santiago tells a brief story (an anecdote) that illustrates his "first encounter with [some people's] attitude about the race thing." Tell an anecdote of your own that illustrates an attitude about race. Your story can be about something you experienced or observed or about something experienced or observed by someone you know.
- Write an essay with the title ＿＿＿＿＿＿＿＿ and ＿＿＿＿＿＿＿＿, filling in the blanks with two conflicting aspects of your identity. For example, one of the following might apply:

Wife *and* Student	City Dweller *and* Country Boy
Catholic *and* Jewish	Student *and* Athlete
Father *and* Son	Student *and* Full-time Employee

Like Santiago, explain the nature of the conflict you experience, any pressures people bring to bear, and how you resolve the conflict. If possible, tell a brief story (an anecdote) that serves as an example, the way Santiago does in paragraph 7.

- Assume you have a child who is planning to marry a person of a different race. Is this interracial marriage a positive, negative, or neutral thing? Explain your answer in an essay.
- In paragraph 1, Santiago says, "My life has been shaped by my black and Latino heritages." Tell what aspects of your heritage have shaped your life, and explain in what ways you have been shaped.
- If you are from another culture, tell how American culture has shaped you. Like Santiago, do you sometimes experience a conflict?

Beyond the Writing Class: Research the slave trade in Puerto Rico and write a summary of the trade's history and an explanation for why most Puerto Ricans have some African ancestry.

It Is Time to Stop Playing Indians
ARLENE HIRSCHFELDER

Author and historian Arlene Hirschfelder is a scholar of Native American studies who has also written extensively on smoking and tobacco. She has combined these areas of interest into her study of Native American ceremonial tobacco use and abuse. In the following piece, which first appeared in the *Los Angeles Times,* Hirschfelder says we should rethink the symbols of our sports teams, as well as our symbols of Thanksgiving and Halloween celebrations.

Preview.   Using a general knowledge encyclopedia from your campus library or the Internet, look up the role Native Americans played in the survival of the Pilgrims at Plymouth in 1620 and 1621. (The first Thanksgiving is relevant here.) How did we thank the Native Americans over the years for their role in our survival? A good starting point is to check these headings: "Plymouth Colony," "Thanksgiving," "Squanto," "Pilgrims."

Vocabulary.   If any of the following words from the selection are unfamiliar to you, study their meanings before reading.

pseudo (1)   false or pretended
innocuous (3)   harmless
trappings (3)   ornaments of dress
per capita (4)   per person
ersatz (4)   artificial
mayhem (6)   causing injury
impede (7)   to slow progress
inadvertently (7)   unintentionally; without meaning to
denigrate (7)   to speak damagingly

It is predictable. At Halloween, thousands of children trick-or-treat in Indian costumes. At Thanksgiving, thousands of children parade in school pageants wearing plastic headdresses and pseudo-buckskin clothing. Thousands of card shops stock Thanksgiving greeting cards with images of cartoon animals wearing feathered headbands. Thousands of teachers and librarians trim bulletin boards with Anglo-featured, feathered Indian boys and girls. Thousands of gift shops load their shelves with Indian figurines and jewelry.

2   Fall and winter are also the seasons when hundreds of thousands of sports fans root for professional, college and public school teams with names that summon up Indians—"Braves," "Redskins," "Chiefs." (In New York State, one out of eight junior and senior high school teams call themselves "Indians,"

"Tomahawks" and the like.) War-whooping team mascots are imprinted on school uniforms, postcards, notebooks, tote bags and car floor mats.

3   All of this seems innocuous; why make a fuss about it? Because these trappings and holiday symbols offend tens of thousands of other Americans— the Native American people. Because these invented images prevent millions of us from understanding the authentic Indian America, both long ago and today. Because this image-making prevents Indians from being a relevant part of the nation's social fabric.

4   Halloween costumes mask the reality of high mortality rates, high diabetes rates, high unemployment rates. They hide low average life spans, low per capita incomes and low educational levels. Plastic war bonnets and ersatz buckskin deprive people from knowing the complexity of Native American heritage—that Indians belong to hundreds of nations that have intricate social organizations, governments, languages, religions, and sacred rituals, ancient stories, unique arts and music forms.

5   Thanksgiving school units and plays mask history. They do not tell how Europeans mistreated Wampanoags and other East Coast Indian peoples during the 17th century. Social studies units don't mention that, to many Indians, Thanksgiving is a day of mourning, the beginning of broken promises, land theft, near extinction of their religions and languages at the hands of invading Europeans.

6   Athletic team nicknames and mascots disguise real people. Warpainted, buckskin-clad, feathered characters keep the fictitious Indian circulating on decals, pennants and team clothing. Toy companies mask Indian identity and trivialize sacred beliefs by manufacturing Indian costumes and headdresses, peacepipes and trick-arrow-through-the-head gags that equate Indianness with playtime. Indian figures equipped with arrows, guns and tomahawks give youngsters the harmful message that Indians favor mayhem. Many Indian people can tell about children screaming in fear after being introduced to them.

7   It is time to consider how these images impede the efforts of Indian parents and communities to raise their children with positive information about their heritage. It is time to get rid of stereotypes that, whether deliberately or inadvertently, denigrate Indian cultures and people.

8   It is time to bury the Halloween costumes, trick arrows, bulletin-board pin-ups, headdresses and mascots. It has been done before. In the 1970s, after student protests, Marquette University dropped its "Willie Wampum," Stanford University retired its mascot, "Prince Lightfoot," and Eastern Michigan University and Florida State modified their savage-looking mascots to reduce criticism.

9   It is time to stop playing Indians. It is time to abolish Indian images that sell merchandise. It is time to stop offending Indian people whose lives are all too often filled with economic deprivation, powerlessness, discrimination and gross injustice. This time next year, let's find more appropriate symbols for the holiday and sports seasons.

Understanding Content

1. According to the essay, what are the effects of the fact that we continue to "play Indians"?
2. How do toy companies "mask Indian identity and trivialize sacred beliefs"?
3. How do schools contribute to the problem Hirschfelder describes in the essay?

Considering Structure and Technique

1. How do you react to the opening sentence of "It Is Time to Stop Playing Indians"? Do you think that opening is a good way to begin? Why or why not?
2. Which paragraph do you think best expresses Hirschfelder's thesis?
3. In which paragraph does Hirschfelder use examples to back up her points?

Exploring Ideas

1. What do you think Hirschfelder means in paragraph 5 when she says, "Thanksgiving school units and plays mask history"? What is interesting about her use of the word *mask?*
2. In paragraph 7, Hirschfelder says the images of Indians in our culture "impede the efforts of Indian parents and communities to raise their children with positive information about their heritage." Why do you think Hirschfelder thinks this is the case?
3. Explain the significance of the phrase "Playing Indians" in the essay's title.

Writing Workshop: Listing Examples

Sometimes writers provide an example and then go on to explain that example. In her essay, however, Hirschfelder does something different: She piles one example on top of another with no explanation of any single one. What she is really doing is listing examples. For instance, paragraph 1 is a list of examples of injustices against Indians at Halloween; paragraph 4 is a list of realities hidden by Halloween masks. More lists appear in paragraphs 5, 6, and 8. Read these paragraphs and you will notice that the lists have a particular effect—they provide the support that comes from the sheer force of numbers. A word of caution is in order here: If you have only a few examples, then you must provide explanation of them so your detail is specific. Only when you are listing many examples can you rely on the weight of numbers—rather than the weight of explanatory detail—to make your point.

Writing Workshop Activity

With two or three classmates, write a sentence that expresses something that is wrong with the way we celebrate a particular holiday. Here are two examples. You may use one of these or one that you compose.

Each year, Christmas spirit gives way to materialism.

On Memorial Day, we do everything but what we *should* do: remember those who died in wars to protect our country.

After deciding on a sentence, make a list of as many examples as you can think of to illustrate how we celebrate inappropriately.

Language Notes for Multilingual and Other Writers

"It Is Time to Stop Playing Indians" includes some references to American holidays you may not be familiar with if English is your second language.

1. *Halloween* falls on the evening of October 31. Strictly speaking, it once had a religious significance as the eve of All Saints Day, but in actual practice Halloween is a children's holiday with no overt religious observance. On Halloween, children dress up in scary costumes and go from house to house asking for candy and other treats. They shout, "Trick or treat," meaning if they do not get a treat they may play some kind of a trick on the person who failed to give them candy or other sweets.
2. *Thanksgiving* is a national holiday of feasting and giving thanks, celebrated on the fourth Thursday in November. The first Thanksgiving was celebrated after the Plymouth colonists' first difficult winter in Massachusetts. Nearly half the colonists died, but a bountiful corn harvest brought rejoicing, so a three-day feast was held.

From Reading to Writing

In Your Journal: Think back to the American history classes you have taken. Did your texts and teachers tell you much about the Native American experience and culture? Do you think history texts and classes should be revised to emphasize Native American suffering at the hands of white settlers? Why or why not?

With Some Classmates: In her conclusion, Hirschfelder says, "This time next year, let's find more appropriate symbols for the holiday and sports seasons."

Mention one or more holiday and/or sports symbols that you find inappropriate. Explain why you find the symbol(s) inappropriate and go on to suggest suitable replacements.

In an Essay

- Describe the image of the Native Americans as depicted in the media, stories, and textbooks. What effect does this image have on our perception of Native Americans and their role in history?
- Do you think athletic teams like the Cleveland Indians, the Washington Redskins, and the Florida State Seminoles should be forced to change their nicknames and mascots? State and defend your opinion, drawing on your own ideas and those in the essay. Try to consider a number of factors, such as justice, fan reaction, financial effects, team recognition, and merchandising.
- Describe your family's celebration of Halloween or Thanksgiving, and tell to what extent it perpetuates the stereotype of Native Americans.
- Pick a holiday that you think we celebrate inappropriately, and, like Hirschfelder, use lists of examples to illustrate what is wrong with the way we celebrate.

Beyond the Writing Class: Write a set of guidelines explaining appropriate and inappropriate celebrations and classroom lessons for Thanksgiving and Halloween. Send the guidelines to your local school board.

Honor Bound

JOSEPH STEFFAN

Now an attorney, in 1987 Joseph Steffan was a senior when he was expelled from the United States Naval Academy for being a homosexual. Choosing to fight his expulsion, he filed a lawsuit and was thereafter in the foreground of the battle against banning homosexuals from serving in the military. He recounts his experiences at the academy in *Honor Bound* (1992), from which this excerpt is taken.

Preview.   Perhaps the most difficult moments in life are when we face moral dilemmas, painful choices we must make between right and wrong when the choices are not easy or clear-cut. Consider this moral dilemma: If you knew that telling the truth about yourself would end your career goals, would you lie, knowing that no one would get hurt as a result of your lie?

Vocabulary.   If any of the following words from the selection are unfamiliar to you, study their meanings before reading.

permeate (1)   penetrate
brigade (1)   a military unit
opulent (3)   rich, showing wealth
stickler (6)   a person who insists on something rigidly
inherent (7)   built-in
midshipmen (7)   students at the Naval Academy
moment of truth (11)   a critical time
coming out (15)   announcing one's homosexuality
persevere (15)   to continue in spite of difficulties
tenet (16)   belief
Annapolis (16)   The U.S. Naval Academy
tangible (18)   touchable
imminent (20)   close at hand
in retrospect (21)   looking back
inducted (22)   admitted

I walked into the commandant's outer office and reported to his executive assistant, a junior officer assigned to serve as his aide. He said the commandant would be right with me, and asked me to take a seat. The strange quietness of the hallway seemed to permeate everything, and although the EA's greeting had been cordial, there was an obvious tension in the air. He undoubtedly knew the purpose of this meeting as well, and I began to wonder how long it would take before it leaked to the rest of the brigade.

2   I tried to keep calm, but it was difficult to ignore the obvious importance of this meeting. What would happen in the next few moments would likely determine, to a very large extent, the rest of my life. My feelings were a strange mixture of fear, anger, and pride, and I was determined that, no matter what, I was going to maintain my sense of dignity.

3   Finally, the EA signaled that the commandant was ready and led me into his office. The commandant of midshipmen, Captain Howard Habermeyer, was waiting just inside the door as we entered. He greeted me, shaking my hand, and motioned for me to sit as he returned to his desk. The office was relatively opulent by military standards, with dark wood paneling and blue carpeting. Behind the commandant's large wooden desk stood the United States flag and the blue-and-gold flag of the Brigade of Midshipmen. The walls were covered with pictures and plaques, memorabilia from his service as an officer in the submarine service.

4   Captain Habermeyer was tall, bespectacled, and quite thin, almost to the point of frailty. He and the superintendent had taken over during the previous summer, replacing Captain Chadwick and Admiral Larson, both of whom I had come to know quite well during my previous years. I regretted that they were not here now, and that my fate rested in the hands of two officers who barely knew me. I sometimes wonder if they had been there instead whether it would have changed the outcome at all. Perhaps it would at least have been more difficult for them.

5   I had first met Captain Habermeyer at a small leadership retreat held for the top incoming stripers of my class. The retreat was relatively informal and was held at an Annapolis hotel. At the time, he impressed me as an intelligent and articulate officer, and we had shared a conversation about his admiration of Japanese culture. It was an interest that had grown through several tours of duty he had in Japan.

6   I had heard since then that Captain Habermeyer was a stickler for regulations. He played everything exactly by the book. My suspicion was confirmed when the EA remained standing in the doorway as the commandant began to question me about my request. He had apparently been ordered to remain as witness to the conversation. Despite an outward sense of cordiality, I was beginning to feel like a criminal under interrogation.

7   As with the previous officers, I refused to discuss the purpose of my request with the commandant, but he continued to question me. He finally stated that no one in the military has an inherent right to meet with anyone above his own commanding officer, which for midshipmen is technically the commandant. If I refused to disclose the purpose of the meeting, he would deny my request. When he again questioned me, I finally answered, "The meeting concerns a situation of which you are already aware."

8   "You're referring to the NIS investigation presently under way?" he asked.

9   "Yes, sir."

10   He responded, "Are you willing to state at this time that you are a homosexual?"

11   The moment of truth had arrived. In a way, I was surprised that he was even asking the question. Captain Holderby had already basically told him the answer. Was he offering me an out, a chance to deny it, to say that it was all a big misunderstanding? Was he offering me a chance to lie?

12   I looked him straight in the eye and answered, "Yes sir, I am."

13   It was a moment I will never forget, one of agony and intense pride. In that one statement, I had given up my dreams, the goals I had spent the last four years of my life laboring to attain. But in exchange, I retained something more valuable—my honor and my self-esteem.

14   In many ways, the commandant's words were more than a simple question—they were a challenge to everything I believed in, and to the identity I had struggled to accept. In giving me the opportunity to deny my sexuality, the commandant was challenging that identity. He could just as well have asked, "Are you ashamed enough to deny your true identity in order to graduate?" More than anything I have ever wanted in my entire life, I wanted to be an outstanding midshipman and to graduate from the Naval Academy. And I firmly believe that if I had been willing to lie about my sexuality, to deny my true identity, I would have been allowed to graduate.

15   I had come to the academy to achieve my potential as an individual. These four years had been filled with trials and lessons from which I learned a great deal about life and about myself. But none of these lessons was more difficult, important, or meaningful than coming to understand and accept my sexuality—in essence, to accept my true identity. By coming out to myself, I gained the strength that can come only from self-acceptance, and it was with that added strength that I had been able to persevere through the many trials and difficulties of life at Annapolis.

16   The commandant's question was also a challenge to my honor as a midshipman. The Honor Concept at Annapolis is based on the tenet that personal honor is an absolute—you either have honor or you do not. No one can take it from you; it can only be surrendered willingly. And once it is surrendered, once it is compromised, it can never again be fully regained.

17   I knew that my graduation would mean absolutely nothing if I had to lie to achieve it, especially if that lie was designed to hide the very fact of my own identity. I would have given up my honor, destroying everything it means to be a midshipman. And I would have given up my identity and pride—everything it means to be a person.

18   The only way to retain my honor and identity, both as a midshipman and a person, was to tell the truth. I was honor bound not simply by the Honor Concept, but by its foundation: the respect for fundamental human dignity. The academy had the power to take away everything tangible that I had attained, but only I had the power to destroy my honor. Even if the academy discharged me for being gay, I could live with the knowledge that I had passed the

ultimate test. I was willing to give up everything tangible to retain something intangible but far more meaningful: my honor and my identity. Even the military could not take them away from me now.

19   Captain Habermeyer said that he could not grant my request to speak with the superintendent because he would eventually sit in judgment over me. A performance board would be scheduled the next day, the first step toward discharge from Annapolis. Although I explained that I still desired to graduate, the commandant assured me that he did not believe the superintendent would allow it.

20   Before leaving, I looked at the commandant and said, "I'm sorry it had to end this way." He answered, "So am I." Truly I believed him, which didn't make the imminent destruction of my life much easier to deal with. It would have been so much easier to have someone to hate, a person to blame for everything that was happening. But there was not one to blame. I couldn't blame myself because I had done what I believed right. There was only a military policy, a rule like countless others that define life in the military, rules that we learn to instinctively enforce and obey.

21   My perception of what was happening seemed almost detached at times, and I wondered how long it would be before I woke up to realize this was all a horrible dream. In retrospect, I don't doubt that I was suffering from shock, so completely overcome by emotion that I couldn't feel anything at all. I wanted to scream or cry or something, but there was too much to deal with, and I wondered if I would be able to stop once I started.

22   Not only was the nature of my life changing rapidly, but I was also anticipating how each of my relationships with other people would change. Would my parents and friends reject me as I had feared for so long, or was I not giving them enough credit? In any case, I knew it would be only a short time until the news of my disclosure would leak to the brigade, and I had to be prepared before then. I had heard a story about two male mids who were caught in bed together a year or two before I was inducted. That evening, they were both dragged from their rooms, wrapped in blankets and beaten by other mids in what was called a "blanket party." In a way, I doubted whether anyone would dare do that to me, but I wasn't too excited about the possibility.

23   There was no doubt in my mind that the story would leak, probably within twenty-four hours. After that, it would spread like wildfire. Annapolis is such a rumor mill that I could expect to hear about five hundred colorful variations of the story within a few hours. I decided that the best way to combat this inevitability was through a controlled release of information, and that release had to start with my closest friends at the academy.

24   I spent the rest of the afternoon telling six of my friends what was going on. Each of them was shocked and surprised, but they were universally supportive, even more so than I had hoped. I told them I wanted them to hear it from me first, but that they should keep it under wraps for now. I also took the time to go to each of the teachers I had in classes that semester to inform them

personally. I felt a need to do this first out of respect for them, and second, to make sure that they knew I was not ashamed to face them. If I was going to leave the academy, I wanted it to be with the same level of pride I felt as a battalion commander. I didn't want anyone to think I was running away, departing under a cloak of deserved shame. I wanted to show them I was the same person as before—exactly the same.

Understanding Content

1. In response to Captain Habermeyer's question, the author admitted to being a homosexual. The answer was a moment "of agony and intense pride." Explain the nature of the author's conflict.
2. Steffan believes that Captain Habermeyer's question had a hidden significance. What was it?
3. Explain the Honor Concept at Annapolis. How did the Honor Concept influence Steffan's decision not to lie about his sexuality?
4. Why did Steffan tell his friends and classmates about his meeting in Captain Habermeyer's office?

Considering Structure and Technique

1. The first nine paragraphs create an air of suspense. How do they do that?
2. When narrating a story writers can use **transitions** (connecting words and phrases) to signal the chronology (time order) and keep the reader oriented in time. (For more on transitions, see p. 35.) What transitions in paragraph 3 signal the chronology? In paragraph 5? In paragraph 20? In paragraph 25?
3. What purpose does the description in paragraph 3 serve?
4. Rather than narrate actual events, much of the piece gives the author's comments on events and his reaction to them. Why is this the case?

Exploring Ideas

1. Do you think Steffan should have lied about his sexuality so he could have stayed at Annapolis and in the military and, perhaps, gone on to work to change policy about homosexuals? Explain your view.
2. Steffan notes that Captain Habermeyer was "a stickler for regulations" who "played everything exactly by the book" (paragraph 6). Why are these aspects of Habermeyer's style of command significant?
3. Currently, the military policy is "Don't ask; don't tell," which means that people cannot be asked about their sexuality, nor volunteer information because it can be grounds for discharge. Does this policy violate a homosexual's honor, as honor is understood by Steffan? Explain.

4. Since the military did not permit homosexuality at the time Steffan came out, was Captain Habermeyer honor bound to help Steffan or to enforce the rules? Explain.

Writing Workshop: Using Commas with Appositives

An **appositive** is a word or word group that renames something that comes before it. Appositives are typically set off with commas. To help you see what appositives are and how commas are used with them, study the following examples taken from "Honor Bound." As a study aid, the appositives are underlined and an arrow is drawn to the word renamed.

I walked into the commandant's outer office and reported to his executive assistant, <u>a junior officer assigned to serve as his aide</u>. Paragraph 1

The commandant of midshipmen, <u>Captain Howard Habermeyer</u>, was waiting just inside the door as we entered. Paragraph 3

In that one statement, I had given up my dreams, <u>the goals I had spent the last four years of my life laboring to attain.</u> Paragraph 13

Writing Workshop Activity

Use each of the following words and accompanying appositives in a sentence, being careful to use commas as needed.

Example:

my third grade teacher/Ms. Rodriguez

My third grade teacher, Ms. Rodriguez, is being honored as teacher of the year.

1. Tony Montgomery/the second-string quarterback for the team

2. an ancient superstition/throwing salt over the shoulder

3. my latest roommate/a 100-pound German shepherd

4. the chief of police/Chris Novotny

5. Louisa Seinfeld/my oldest friend

Language Notes for Multilingual and Other Writers

Do not use a pronoun to refer to a word already referred to by *who, whom, which,* or *that.*

yes: . . . my fate rested in the hands of two officers who barely knew me. Paragraph 4

no: . . . my fate rested in the hands of two officers who they barely knew me.

yes: He . . . had taken over . . . , replacing Captain Chadwick and Admiral Larson, both of whom I had come to know quite well . . . . Paragraph 4

no: He . . . had taken over . . . , replacing Captain Chadwick and Admiral Larson, both of whom I had come to know them quite well. . . .

yes: Truly I believed him, which didn't make the imminent destruction of my life much easier to deal with. Paragraph 20

no: Truly I believed him, which it didn't make the imminent destruction of my life much easier to deal with.

yes: It would have been so much easier to have someone to hate, a person to blame for everything that was happening. Paragraph 20

no: It would have been so much easier to have someone to hate, a person to blame for everything that it was happening.

From Reading to Writing

In Your Journal: Did Annapolis's honor code do Steffan more harm than good? Explain your view.

With Some Classmates: There has been controversy over whether homosexuals should be permitted to be boy scouts or scout leaders. What do you think? Why?

In an Essay

- Paragraph 11 notes that Steffan experienced a "moment of truth" when asked if he were willing to state he was a homosexual. Tell about a time you or someone close to you faced a moment of truth.
- Write your own definition of *honor,* one that explores many of its aspects. Use examples to illustrate those aspects.
- Steffan says that there are rules that "we learn to instinctively enforce and obey" (paragraph 20). However, if a person believes a particular rule or law is harmful or immoral, should that person violate it? Support your view with examples.

Beyond the Writing Class: The current policy governing gays in the military is "Don't ask; don't tell." The effectiveness of this policy is a matter of debate. Look up the policy, read about some of its strengths and weaknesses, and then argue for or against it.

Race in America
GEORGE HENDERSON

George Henderson, Dean of the College of Liberal Arts at the University of Oklahoma, is a professor of human relations, education, and sociology. A race-relations consultant, Henderson is also widely published. His most recent work is *Our Souls to Keep: Black/White Relations in America* (1999). The following essay first appeared in the spring 2000 issue of *National Forum: Phi Kappa Phi Journal.*

Preview.   In "Race in America," George Henderson says that "at different times, all ethnic groups have been both the oppressed and the oppressors." What do you think is the cause of the oppression and discrimination that ethnic groups have experienced in the United States?

Vocabulary.   If any of the following words from the essay are unfamiliar to you, study their meanings before reading.

lineage (2)   ancestry
nondescript (2)   common, undistinguished
pervasive (2)   existing everywhere
disparate (2)   different
schisms (3)   splits
dictum (4)   pronouncement
genocide (5)   the killing of a people
assimilation (5)   changing to fit in to the dominant culture
homogeneous (6)   being alike
Eurocentric (6)   the belief in the superiority of all things European
enclaves (7)   territories surrounded by other territories
nativist (7)   the policy of protecting existing interests from immigrants
miscegenation (9)   marriage or cohabitation between men and women of
    different races
amalgamated (9)   blended
ethnocentrism (9)   the belief that one's own group is superior
indigenous (9)   native
pariahs (13)   social outcasts
demographic (14)   related to population statistics
pernicious (17)   harmful
culpability (18)   blame
purveyors (19)   providers

From the outset of colonialization, America has been a haven for the persecuted, the ambitious, and the homeless peoples of the world. "The New Colossus," a poem by Emma Lazarus inscribed on a tablet in the pedestal of the Statue of Liberty, captures the essence of the United States of America. It promises freedom and justice for all. As the tired, poor, and huddled masses have come to this country and contributed to its development, it is clear to most observers that we are a nation of migrants, immigrants and [former] slaves.

2   Because of intermarriage, most Americans have multiple ethnic and racial identities. Some persons of mixed lineage prefer to assume culturally nondescript identities. For example, they have become "white people," "black people," "Indians," "Latinos," "Asians," or just plain "Americans" in order to somehow deflect from themselves any connection with their ancestors. The task of tracing their families has become too taxing or too insignificant. Even so, the effects of ethnicity and race are pervasive: disparate patterns of community relationships and economic opportunities haunt us. At some time in their history, all ethnic groups in the United States have been the underclass. Also, at different times, all ethnic groups have been both the oppressed and the oppressors.

3   Ethnicity is the most distinguishing characteristic of Americans, where we are sorted primarily on the basis of our cultural identities or nationalities. An ethnic group is a culturally distinct population whose members share a collective identity and a common heritage. Historically, the overwhelming majority of ethnic groups emerged in the United States as a result of one of several responses to the following processes: (1) migration, (2) consolidation of group forces in the face of an impending threat from an aggressor, (3) annexation or changes in political boundary lines, or (4) schisms within a church. Hence, "ethnic minority" presupposes people different from the mainstream or dominant cultured persons.

4   But it is the erroneous belief that people who come to America can be placed in categories based on their unique gene pools that has resulted in the most blatant instances of discrimination. Races, however defined, do not correspond to genetic reality because inbreeding world populations share a common gene pool. A much more practical dictum, and one that has often been ignored throughout American history, is that all people belong to the same species. Unfortunately, too few individuals believe that the only race of any significance is the human race.

A Brief History

5   At the time of the American Revolution, the American population was largely composed of English Protestants who had absorbed a substantial number of German and Scotch-Irish settlers and a smaller number of French, Dutch, Swedes, Poles, Swiss, Irish, and other immigrants. The colonies had a modest number of Catholics, and a smaller number of Jews. Excluding Quakers and Swedes, the colonists treated Native Americans with contempt and hostility, and engaged in wars against them that bordered on genocide. They

drove natives from the coastal plains in order to make way for a massive white movement to the West. Although Africans, most of whom were slaves, comprised one-fifth of the American population during the Revolution, they, similar to Indians, were not perceived by most white colonists as being worthy of assimilation.

6   The white peoples of the new nation had long since crossed Caucasian lines to create a conglomerate but culturally homogeneous society. People of different ethnic groups—English, Irish, German, Huguenot, Dutch, Swedish—mingled and intermarried. English settlers and peoples from western and northern Europe had begun a process of ethnic assimilation that caused some writers to incorrectly describe the nation as melted into one ethnic group: American. In reality, non-Caucasian Americans were not included in the Eurocentric cultural pot.

7   During the 150 years immediately following the Revolution, large numbers of immigrants came to the United States from eastern European countries. They were the so-called "new immigrants." During the latter part of that period, slaves were emancipated, numerous Indian tribes were conquered and forced to relocate to reservations, portions of Mexico's land were taken, and Asians began emigrating to the United States. The English language and English-oriented cultural patterns grew even more dominant. Despite a proliferation of cultural diversity within the growing ethnic enclaves, Anglo-conformity ideology spawned racist notions about Nordic and Aryan racial superiority. This ideology gave rise to nativist political agendas and exclusionist immigration policies favoring western and northern European immigrants.

8   Non–English-speaking western Europeans and northern Europeans were also discriminated against. The slowness of some of those immigrants, particularly Germans, to learn English, their tendency to live in enclaves, and their establishment of ethnic-language newspapers were friction points. Such ethnic-oriented lifestyles prompted many Americanized people to chide: "If they don't like it here, they can go back to where they came from." But that solution was too simplistic. Immigrants from all countries and cultures, even those who were deemed socially and religiously undesirable, were needed to help build a nation—to work the farms, dig the ore, build the railroads and canals, settle the prairies, and otherwise provide human resources.

9   Beginning in the 1890s, immigrants from eastern and southern Europe were numerically dominant. That set the stage for racist statements about inferior, darker people threatening the purity of blond, blue-eyed Nordics or Aryans through miscegenation. Intermixture was perceived as a deadly plague. Although the immigrants from eastern and southern Europe were not suitable marriage partners, their critics stated, they could be properly assimilated and amalgamated. This kind of ethnocentrism prevented large numbers of other immigrants and indigenous peoples of color from becoming fully functioning citizens. And the legacy for the children of people denied equal opportunities was second-class citizenship. We can easily document the negative effects of

second-class citizenship: abhorrent inequalities, unwarranted exclusions, and atmospheres of rejection.

10   Immigrants who lived in remote, isolated areas were able to maintain some semblance of being ethnic nations within America. But the growth of cities brought about the decline of farming populations and ethnic colonies. A short time was required for the white immigrants who settled in cities to discard their native languages and cultures. But it is erroneous to think of any ethnic group as melting away without leaving a trace of its cultural heritage. All ethnic groups have infused portions of their cultures into the tapestry of American history.

11   Early twentieth-century eastern European immigrants were a very disparate mixture of peoples. They came from nations that were trying to become states—Poland, Czechoslovakia, Lithuania, and Yugoslavia; from states trying to become nations—Italy, Turkey, and Greece; and from areas outside the Western concept of either state or nation. All of them included people such as Jews who did not easily fit into any of those categories. Through social and educational movements, laws, and superordinate goals such as winning wars and establishing economic world superiority, eastern Europeans and other white ethnic groups were able to enter mainstream America.

12   The cultures and colors of Third World ethnic groups were in stark contrast to European immigrants. Those differences became obstacles to assimilation and, more importantly, to people of color achieving equal opportunities. Nonwhite groups in the United States occupied specific low-status niches in the workplace, which in turn resulted in similarities among their members in such things as occupations, standard of living, level of education, place of residence, access to political power, and quality of health care. Likenesses within those groups facilitated the formation of stereotypes and prejudices that inhibited the full citizenship of non-white minorities.

13   Immigrants who held highly esteemed occupations—lawyers, artists, engineers, scientists, and physicians—became Americanized much faster than those who held less esteemed positions—unskilled laborers, farm workers, coal miners, and stock clerks. But even in those instances there were pro-European biases and stereotypes. For example, French chefs, Italian opera singers, Polish teachers, German conductors, and Russian scientists were more highly recruited than Africans, Hispanics, and Asians who had the same skills. Racial and quasi-racial groups—including American Indians, Mexican Americans, Asian Americans, African Americans, and Puerto Ricans—were not nearly so readily absorbed as various Caucasian ethnic groups. And that is generally the situation today. Despite numerous and impressive gains during the past century, a disproportionate number of peoples of color are still treated like pariahs.

What Does the Future Hold?

14   If U.S. Census Bureau population projections are correct, our nation is undergoing mind-boggling demographic changes: Hispanics will triple in num-

bers, from 31.4 million in 1999 to 98.2 million in 2050; blacks will increase 70 percent, from 34.9 million to 59.2 million; Asians and Pacific Islanders will triple, from 10.9 million to 37.6 million; Native Americans and Alaska Natives will increase from approximately 2.2 million to 2.6 million. During the same period, the non-Hispanic white population will increase from 196.1 million to 213 million. Also, the foreign-born population, most of them coming from Asia and Latin America, will increase from 26 million to 53.8 million. The non-Hispanic white population will decrease from 72 percent of the total population in 1999 to 52 percent in 2050, and the nation's workforce will be composed of over 50 percent racial and ethnic minorities and immigrants. Who then will be the pariahs?

15   Without equal opportunities, the melting pot will continue to be an unreachable mirage, a dream of equality deferred, for too many people of color. This does not in any way detract from the significance of the things minorities have achieved. Ethnic-group histories and lists of cultural contributions support the contention that each group is an integral part of a whole nation. Although all American ethnic minority groups have experienced continuous socioeconomic gains, the so-called "playing field" that includes white participants is not yet level. Simply stated, the rising tide of economic prosperity has not yet lifted the masses of people of color. Whatever our life circumstances, the citizens of the United States are bound together not as separate ethnic groups but as members of different ethnic groups united in spirit and behavior and locked into a common destiny.

16   There is little doubt that our nation is at a crossroads in its race relations. Where we go from here is up to all of us. We can try segregation again, continuance of the status quo, silence in the face of prejudice and discriminatory practices, or activism. The choice is ours.

17   Segregation of ethnic minorities is not a redeeming choice for the United States. It did not work during earlier times, and it will not work now. There have never been separate but equal majority-group and minority-group communities in the United States And the pretense of such a condition would once again be a particularly pernicious injustice to all citizens. Racial segregation diminishes both the perpetrators and their victims. Preserving the status quo in education, employment, health care, and housing, which so often is little more than codified racial discrimination, is not justice for minorities either.

18   Inaction by people who witness oppressive acts is equally unacceptable. Even though they may be shocked and frustrated by the problems, standing in wide-eyed horror is not an adequate posture to assume. While they may be legally absolved of any wrongdoing, these silent people must come to terms with what others believe to be their moral culpability. Of course, silence may be prudent. Usually, there is a high price to be paid by those who would challenge racism in community institutions. Friends, jobs, promotions, and prestige may be lost. Furthermore, few victories come easily, and most of the victors are unsung heroes.

19   Individuals who choose to challenge purveyors of bigotry and unequal opportunities must also take care that in their actions to redress racial injustices, they do not emulate the oppressors whom they deplore. That might makes right, that blood washes out injustices—these too are false strategies for achieving justice. "It does not matter much to a slave what the color of his master is," a wise black janitor once said. We, the descendants of migrants, immigrants, and slaves, can build a better nation—a place where all people have safe housing, get a top-quality education, do meaningful work for adequate wages, are treated fairly in criminal-justice systems, have their medical needs met, and in the end die a timely death unhurried by bigots. This is the kind of history that should be made.

Understanding Content

1. How does Henderson define *ethnic group?*
2. What does Henderson say causes discrimination in the United States?
3. At the time of the Revolution, was the United States a nation of people melted into the single ethnic group, called American? Explain. Is it accurate to consider the United States a melting pot today? Why or why not?
4. Henderson says we are at a crossroads and have four courses of action. Why are we at a crossroads, and what are the possible courses of action?

Considering Structure and Technique

1. What are the three main parts of "Race in America"? That is, what three main areas does Henderson discuss?
2. For what purpose do you think Henderson wrote "Race in America"?
3. Paragraphs 5–14 are a history of United States immigration and the accompanying pattern of discrimination. Why does Henderson devote so much of his essay to presenting this information?
4. A **metaphor** is a comparison formed without using the words *like* or *as.* (See p. 121.) What four metaphors appear in paragraph 15?

Exploring Ideas

1. In paragraph 10, Henderson refers to "the tapestry of American history." Why does he use the image of a tapestry to describe American history?
2. Some people refer to the United States as a melting pot, and others think of it more as a cultural stew. Which image do you think is more appropriate? Why?
3. After reading paragraphs 5–14, what can you conclude about the way Americans respond to immigrants?
4. Henderson notes a pattern of discrimination and prejudice in the United States, one that reemerges with each wave of immigration. Why do you think the discrimination occurs?

Writing Workshop: Guiding the Reader with Transitional Paragraphs

A **transition** is a connecting device that shows how ideas relate to each other. Most often, transitions are words or phrases (see p. 35). However, when an essay is long, has distinct parts, or complex ideas, a **transitional paragraph** can help the reader keep things straight. It does so by restating some of what has already been said and then pointing to what is to come. Paragraph 16 of "Race in America" is an example.

[There is little doubt that our nation is at a crossroads in its race relations.] [Where we go from here is up to all of us. We can try segregation again, continuance of the status quo, silence in the face of prejudice and discriminatory practices, or activism. The choice is ours.]

Reference to points made in paragraphs 14 and 15.

Reference to what is discussed in paragraphs 17, 18, and 19.

Writing Workshop Activity

Find an example of a transitional paragraph in this book or any other published work, or in your own writing. Label the part that mentions what came before and the part that mentions what is about to come.

Language Notes for Multilingual and Other Writers

When you are writing about events that occur in a particular time order, you can often use time expressions (known as **transitions**—see p. 35) to open paragraphs. Doing so helps your reader follow the time sequence and at the same time allows you to move smoothly from one paragraph to the next.

The following sentences, which open paragraphs in "Race in America," illustrate the use of time transitions (underlined as a study aid).

At the time of the American Revolution, the American population was largely composed of English Protestants who had absorbed a substantial number of German and Scotch-Irish settlers and a smaller number of French, Dutch, Swedes, Poles, Swiss, Irish, and other immigrants. Paragraph 5

The white peoples of the new nation had long since crossed Caucasian lines to create a conglomerate but culturally homogeneous society. Paragraph 6

During the 150 years immediately following the Revolution, large numbers of immigrants came to the United States from eastern European countries. Paragraph 7

Beginning in the 1980s, immigrants from eastern and southern Europe were numerically dominant. Paragraph 9

From Reading to Writing

In Your Journal: What did you learn as a result of reading "Race in America"? Did this new information surprise you? Why or why not?

With Some Classmates: Is the United States, as Henderson says in paragraph 1, "a haven for the persecuted, the ambitious, and the homeless peoples of the world"? Use the information in the essay, along with your own knowledge, experience, and observation, to support your view.

In an Essay

- Paragraph 1 presents one view of "the essence of the United States of America." Explain and illustrate your view of the essence of the United States.
- Explain how your particular racial and ethnic identity has affected your place in the world and your interactions with people.
- Paragraph 19 notes that an individual can pay a high price for activism. Tell about a time you or someone you know paid a price for taking action and whether you or that person would do the same thing again.

Beyond the Writing Class: In an effort to address discrimination, a number of laws have been passed, including the 1964 Civil Rights Act, the 1965 Voting Rights Act, and the 1968 Fair Housing Act. Pick one of these, look it up, and tell what it has accomplished.

Don't Just Stand There
DIANE COLE

When someone tells an ethnic joke, do you stand frozen, uncomfortable, and unsure how to react? Or have you ever responded angrily to a racial insult and later felt that you could have handled the situation better? If you answer yes to either of these questions, "Don't Just Stand There" is for you. In this piece, which was originally part of a special supplement to the *New York Times*, Diane Cole explains how to respond to racist, ethnic, religious, and sexist remarks.

Preview.   In your journal, write about the last time you heard someone tell a joke that insulted a particular group of people (African-Americans, Polish people, Jews, blondes, and so forth). Or tell about a time someone made an insulting remark about a person's race, sex, religion, or ethnic background. Explain how you felt when the joke was told or when the remark was made. Did you respond? If so, how? Were you satisfied with your response? Why or why not? If you did not respond, explain why.

Vocabulary.   If any of the following words from the essay are unfamiliar to you, study their meanings before reading.

- **ebullience** (1)   enthusiasm
  tinged with (1)   colored with
  anti-Semitic (1)   hostile to Jews
  slurs (4)   insults
  analogy (5)   comparison
  vulnerable (8, 31)   capable of being wounded or hurt
- **ante** (9)   to pay (a poker term for the amount each player puts in the pot)
  rift (17)   a break in friendly relations
  discreetly (28)   being careful about delicate matters
  volatile (33)   capable of breaking out in violence

It was my office farewell party, and colleagues at the job I was about to leave were wishing me well. My mood was one of ebullience tinged with regret, and it was in this spirit that I spoke to the office neighbor to whom I had waved hello every morning for the past two years. He smiled broadly as he launched into a long, rambling story, pausing only after he delivered the punch line. It was a very long pause because, although he laughed, I did not: This joke was unmistakably anti-Semitic.

2   I froze. Everyone in the office knew I was Jewish; what could he have possibly meant? Shaken and hurt, not knowing what else to do, I turned in stunned silence to the next well-wisher. Later, still angry, I wondered, what else should I—could I—have done?

3   Prejudice can make its presence felt in any setting, but hearing its nasty voice in this way can be particularly unnerving. We do not know what to do and often we feel another form of paralysis as well: We think, "Nothing I say or do will change this person's attitude, so why bother?"

4   But left unchecked, racial slurs and offensive ethnic jokes "can poison the atmosphere," says Michael McQuillan, adviser for racial/ethnic affairs for the Brooklyn borough president's office. "Hearing these remarks conditions us to accept them; and if we accept these, we can become accepting of other acts."

5   Speaking up may not magically change a biased attitude, but it can change a person's behavior by putting a strong message across. And the more messages there are, the more likely a person is to change that behavior, says Arnold Kahn, professor of psychology at James Madison University, Harrisonburg, Va., who makes this analogy: "You can't keep people from smoking in *their* house, but you can ask them not to smoke in *your* house."

6   At the same time, "Even if the other party ignores or discounts what you say, people always reflect on how others perceive them. Speaking up always counts," says LeNorman Strong, director of campus life at George Washington University, Washington, D.C.

7   Finally, learning to respond effectively also helps people feel better about themselves, asserts Cherie Brown, executive director of the National Coalition Building Institute, a Boston-based training organization. "We've found that, when people felt they could at least in this small way make a difference, that made them more eager to take on other activities on a larger scale," she says. Although there is no "cookbook approach" to confronting such remarks— every situation is different, experts stress—[the following] are some effective strategies.

8   When the "joke" turns on who you are—as a member of an ethnic or religious group, a person of color, a woman, a gay or lesbian, an elderly person, or someone with a physical handicap—shocked paralysis is often the first response. Then, wounded and vulnerable, on some level you want to strike back.

9   Lashing out or responding in kind is seldom the most effective response, however. "That can give you momentary satisfaction, but you also feel as if you've lowered yourself to that other person's level," Mr. McQuillan explains. Such a response may further label you in the speaker's mind as thin-skinned, someone not to be taken seriously. Or it may up the ante, making the speaker, and then you, reach for new insults—or physical blows.

10   "If you don't laugh at the joke, or fight, or respond in kind to the slur," says Mr. McQuillan, "that will take the person by surprise, and that can give you more control over the situation." Therefore, in situations like the one in

which I found myself—a private conversation in which I knew the person making the remark—he suggests voicing your anger calmly but pointedly: "I don't know if you realize what that sounded like to me. If that's what you meant, it really hurt me."

11   State how *you* feel, rather than making an abstract statement like, "Not everyone who hears that joke might find it funny." Counsels Mr. Strong: "Personalize the sense of 'this is how I feel when you say this.' That makes it very concrete"—and harder to dismiss.

12   Make sure you heard the words and their intent correctly by repeating or rephrasing the statement: "This is what I heard you say. Is that what you meant?" It's important to give the other person the benefit of the doubt because, in fact, he may *not* have realized that the comment was offensive and, if you had not spoken up, would have had no idea of its impact on you.

13   For instance, Professor Kahn relates that he used to include in his exams multiple-choice questions that occasionally contained "incorrect funny answers." After one exam, a student came up to him in private and said, "I don't think you intended this, but I found a number of those jokes offensive to me as a woman." She explained why. "What she said made immediate sense to me," he says. "I apologized at the next class, and I never did it again."

14   But what if the speaker dismisses your objection, saying, "Oh, you're just being sensitive. Can't you take a joke?" In that case, you might say, "I'm not so sure about that, let's talk about that a little more." The key, Mr. Strong says, is to continue the dialogue, hear the other person's concerns, and point out your own. "There are times when you're just going to have to admit defeat and end it," he adds, "but I have to feel that I did the best I could."

15   When the offending remark is made in the presence of others—at a staff meeting, for example—it can be even more distressing than an insult made privately.

16   "You have two options," says William Newlin, director of field services for the Community Relations division of the New York City Commission on Human Rights. "You can respond immediately at the meeting, or you can delay your response until afterward in private. But a response has to come."

17   Some remarks or actions may be so outrageous that they cannot go unnoted at the moment, regardless of the speaker or the setting. But in general, psychologists say, shaming a person in public may have the opposite effect of the one you want: The speaker will deny his offense all the more strongly in order to save face. Further, few people enjoy being put on the spot, and if the remark really was not intended to be offensive, publicly embarrassing the person who made it may cause an unnecessary rift or further misunderstanding. Finally, most people just don't react as well or thoughtfully under a public spotlight as they would in private.

18   Keeping that in mind, an excellent alternative is to take the offender aside afterward: "Could we talk for a minute in private?" Then use the strategies suggested above for calmly stating how you feel, giving the speaker the benefit of the doubt, and proceeding from there.

19   At a large meeting or public talk, you might consider passing the speaker a note, says David Wertheimer, executive director of the New York City Gay and Lesbian Anti-Violence Project: You could write, "You may not realize it, but your remarks were offensive because. . . ."

20   "Think of your role as that of an educator," suggests James M. Jones, Ph.D., executive director for public interest at the American Psychological Association. "You have to be controlled."

21   Regardless of the setting or situation, speaking up always raises the risk of rocking the boat. If the person who made the offending remark is your boss, there may be an even bigger risk to consider: How will this affect my job? Several things can help minimize the risk, however. First, know what other resources you may have at work, suggests Caryl Stern, director of the A World of Difference-New York City campaign: Does your personnel office handle discrimination complaints? Are other grievance procedures in place?

22   You won't necessarily need to use any of these procedures, Ms. Stern stresses. In fact, she advises, "It's usually better to try a one-on-one approach first." But simply knowing a formal system exists can make you feel secure enough to set up that meeting.

23   You can also raise the issue with other colleagues who heard the remark: Did they feel the same way you did? The more support you have, the less alone you will feel. Your point will also carry more validity and be more difficult to shrug off. Finally, give your boss credit—and the benefit of the doubt: "I know you've worked hard for the company's affirmative action programs, so I'm sure you didn't realize what those remarks sounded like to me as well as the others at the meeting last week. . . ."

24   If, even after this discussion, the problem persists, go back for another meeting, Ms. Stern advises. And if that, too, fails, you'll know what other options are available to you.

25   It's a spirited dinner party, and everyone's having a good time, until one guest starts reciting a racist joke. Everyone at the table is white, including you. The others are still laughing, as you wonder what to say or do.

26   No one likes being seen as the party-pooper, but before deciding that you'd prefer not to take on this role, you might remember that the person who told the offensive joke has already ruined your good time.

27   If it's a group that you feel comfortable in—a family gathering for instance—you will feel freer to speak up. Still, shaming the person by shouting "You're wrong!" or "That's not funny!" probably won't get your point across as effectively as other strategies. "If you interrupt people to condemn them, it just makes it harder," says Cherie Brown. She suggests trying to get at the resentments that lie beneath the joke by asking open-ended questions: "Grandpa, I know you always treat everyone with such respect. Why do people in our family talk that way about black people?" The key, Ms. Brown says, "is to listen to them first, so they will be more likely to listen to you."

28   If you don't know your fellow guests well, before speaking up you could turn discreetly to your neighbors (or excuse yourself to help the host or hostess in the kitchen) to get a reading on how they felt, and whether or not you'll find support for speaking up. The less alone you feel, the more comfortable you'll be speaking up: "I know you probably didn't mean anything by that joke, Jim, but it really offended me. . . . " It's important to say that *you* were offended—not state how the group that is the butt of the joke would feel. "Otherwise," LeNorman Strong says, "you risk coming off as a goody two-shoes."

29   If you yourself are the host, you can exercise more control; you are, after all, the one who sets the rules and the tone of behavior in your home. Once, when Professor Kahn's party guests began singing offensive, racist songs, for instance, he kicked them all out, saying, "You don't sing songs like that in my house!" And, he adds, "they never did again."

30   At school one day, a friend comes over and says, "Who do you think you are, hanging out with Joe? If you can be friends with those people, I'm through with you!"

31   Peer pressure can weigh heavily on kids. They feel vulnerable and, because they are kids, they aren't as able to control the urge to fight. "But if you learn to handle these situations as kids, you'll be better able to handle them as an adult," William Newlin points out.

32   Begin by redefining to yourself what a friend is and examining what friendship means, advises Amy Lee, a human relations specialist at Panel of Americans, an intergroup-relations training and educational organization. If that person from a different group fits your requirement for a friend, ask, "Why shouldn't I be friends with Joe? We have a lot in common." Try to get more information about whatever stereotypes or resentments lie beneath your friend's statement. Ms. Lee suggests: "What makes you think they're so different from us? Where did you get that information?" She explains: "People are learning these stereotypes from somewhere, and they cannot be blamed for that. So examine where these ideas came from." Then talk about how your own experience rebuts them.

33   Kids, like adults, should also be aware of other resources to back them up: Does the school offer special programs for fighting prejudice? How supportive will the principal, the teachers, or other students be? If the school atmosphere is volatile, experts warn, make sure that taking a stand at that moment won't put you in physical danger. If that is the case, it's better to look for other alternatives.

34   These can include programs or organizations that bring kids from different backgrounds together. "When kids work together across race lines, that is how you break down the barriers and see that the stereotypes are not true," says Laurie Meadoff, president of CityKids Foundation, a nonprofit group whose programs attempt to do just that. Such programs can also provide what

Cherie Brown calls a "safe place" to express the anger and pain that slurs and other offenses cause, whether the bigotry is directed against you or others.

35 In learning to speak up, everyone will develop a different style and slightly different message to get across, experts agree. But it would be hard to do better than these two messages suggested by teenagers at CityKids: "Everyone on the face of the earth has the same intestines," said one. Another added, "Cross over the bridge. There's a lot of love on the streets."

Understanding Content

1. According to the essay, why is it important for us to respond appropriately to ethnic jokes and racial slurs? Do you agree? Explain.
2. Why shouldn't you let your anger show when you hear a joke that insults your own race, sex, religion, or background? What is the best way to handle the situation? Do you agree with the approach described in the essay? Explain.
3. How is a person who makes an offensive remark likely to react if confronted and shamed in public?
4. When an offensive joke is told in public, what risk do you run if you publicly shame the person?

Considering Structure and Technique

1. In your own words, write out the thesis of "Don't Just Stand There." How does the title relate to that thesis?
2. The opening two paragraphs as well as paragraphs 13, 18, 19, and 29 include examples. What do these examples contribute?
3. At times, Cole explains what a person should *not* do. For example, in paragraph 27, she says not to interrupt or shame the offending speaker. Cite another example of explaining what *not* to do. What purpose is served by explaining what *not* to do?
4. Cole cites a number of authorities in her essay, frequently quoting their words. What does citing authorities add to the essay?
5. Why do you think Cole devotes five paragraphs at the end of the essay to how children can deal with ethnic insults?

Exploring Ideas

1. Why do you think racial, ethnic, and sexist jokes remain popular?
2. Why do you think more people who take offense at racial, ethnic, and sexist jokes do not speak up?
3. How realistic do you find Cole's advice? Are some pieces of her advice more realistic than others? Explain.
4. What do you think Cole would say to a person who routinely did nothing when he or she heard racial or ethnic jokes?

Writing Workshop: Using Process Analysis

Process analysis explains how to do something. For example, an article in your campus newspaper that explains how to prepare for final examinations is a process analysis. You can rely on process analysis when you want to go beyond *telling* your reader to do something to *showing* your reader how to do it. In "Don't Just Stand There," Diane Cole uses process analysis to show the reader how to respond to insults. For example, in paragraphs 10 through 12, she tells how to respond to an insulting joke; in paragraphs 18 through 20, she explains the process for talking to the offender in private; in paragraphs 21 through 24, she tells how to handle an insult made by a boss; and in paragraphs 32 through 34, she explains how to help children deal with insulting remarks.

Writing Workshop Activity

If you disagree with one or more of Cole's suggestions, list the steps in a process *you* recommend for dealing with insulting remarks or jokes. As an alternative, list the steps in a process to solve one of these problems:

ageism	discrimination against	sexism
homophobia	the disabled	sexual harassment

Language Notes for Multilingual and Other Writers

A number of figurative expressions appear in "Don't Just Stand There."

1. *Lashing out* means scolding or showing anger.

   <u>Lashing out</u> or responding in kind is seldom the most effective response, however. Paragraph 9

2. *Thin-skinned* means easily offended.

   Such a response may further label you in the speaker's mind as <u>thin-skinned</u>, someone not to be taken seriously. Paragraph 9

3. *Shrug off* means disregard or minimize.

   Your point will also carry more validity and be more difficult to <u>shrug off.</u> Paragraph 23

4. *Party-pooper* means a person who spoils the enjoyment of others.

   No one likes being seen as the <u>party-pooper.</u> . . . Paragraph 26

From Reading to Writing

In Your Journal: Cole suggests that we have a private conversation with a person who makes an insulting remark in order to explain how the remark makes us feel. What do you think of this advice? Would you be able to follow it? Explain in one or two pages.

With Some Classmates: Consider to what extent the media encourage or discourage the tendency to tell insulting jokes. You can consider one or more of the following: television programs, movies, radio shows, newspaper articles, and magazine articles.

In an Essay

- Why do people tell ethnic, racial, and sexist jokes? Explain what you think the motivation is, including why you think Cole's colleague told an anti-Semitic joke when he knew she was Jewish.
- If you disagree with some aspect of Cole's advice, explain why you disagree. Then go on to give what you think is better advice. If possible, use process analysis to describe the better process.
- Tell about a time you made an insulting remark or about a time you witnessed someone else doing so. Narrate what happened and the effect it had on people. Explain how you reacted and whether you would react differently now as a result of reading "Don't Just Stand There."
- Like Cole, write an essay with the title "Don't Just Stand There." However, instead of describing a process for dealing with insulting remarks, describe a process for dealing with another problem: sexual harassment, sexism, homophobia, avoidance of the disabled, ageism, and so forth. Also, like Cole, use examples to clarify your points.

Beyond the Writing Class: Write a policy on the use of ethnic humor on your campus. Include an explanation of what is and is not acceptable along with an explanation of what should be done about violations of the policy. Consider submitting the policy to the appropriate campus administrators.

You're Short, Besides
SUCHENG CHAN

Scholar, award-winning author, and award-winning professor of Asian–American Studies at the University of California, Sucheng Chan is the victim of childhood polio and physically disabled. Although remarkably talented, she wonders whether people can look past her disability to see her ability.

Preview. If you were or are physically disabled and had to choose between living an active life that would cause you to be in a wheelchair in 10 years, or living a quiet life that would not lead to a wheelchair, which would you choose? Explain why.

Vocabulary.   If any of the following words from the selection are unfamiliar to you, study their meanings before reading.

salient (1)   obvious
presumptuous (2)   too bold
chaste (2)   decent and pure
atrophied (2)   wasted away
rambunctious (2)   disorderly and unruly
precocious (2)   matured earlier than usual
retribution (4)   punishment
assuage (4)   soothe or relieve
chagrin (5)   embarrassment due to failure or disappointment
Seventh-Day Adventists (6)   a Protestant religious group
eschew (11)   avoid
agnostic (19)   a person who believes it is impossible to know whether God
    exists
acculturation (23)   adapting to a particular culture
incorrigible (25)   incapable of being reformed
sardonically (30)   sarcastically

When asked to write about being a physically handicapped Asian American woman, I considered it an insult. After all, my accomplishments are many, yet I was not asked to write about any of them. Is being handicapped the most salient feature about me? The fact that it might be in the eyes of others made me decide to write the essay as requested. I realized that the way I think about myself may differ considerably from the way others perceive me. And maybe that's what being physically handicapped is all about.

2   I was stricken simultaneously with pneumonia and polio at the age of four. Uncertain whether I had polio of the lungs, seven of the eight doctors

who attended me—all practitioners of Western medicine—told my parents they should not feel optimistic about my survival. A Chinese fortune teller my mother consulted also gave a grim prognosis, but for an entirely different reason: I had been stricken because my name was offensive to the gods. My grandmother had named me "grandchild of wisdom," a name that the fortune teller said was too presumptuous for a girl. So he advised my parents to change my name to "chaste virgin." All these pessimistic predictions notwithstanding, I hung onto life, if only by a thread. For three years, my body was periodically pierced with electric shocks as the muscles of my legs atrophied. Before my illness, I had been an active, rambunctious, precocious, and very curious child. Being confined to bed was thus a mental agony as great as my physical pain. Living in war-torn China, I received little medical attention; physical therapy was unheard of. But I was determined to walk. So one day, when I was six or seven, I instructed my mother to set up two rows of chairs to face each other so that I could use them as I would parallel bars. I attempted to walk by holding my body up and moving it forward with my arms while dragging my legs along behind. Each time I fell, my mother gasped, but I badgered her until she let me try again. After four nonambulatory years, I finally walked once more by pressing my hands against my thighs, so my knees wouldn't buckle.

3   My father had been away from home during most of those years because of the war. When he returned, I had to confront the guilt he felt about my condition. In many East Asian cultures, there is a strong folk belief that a person's physical state in this life is a reflection of how morally or sinfully he or she lived in previous lives. Furthermore, because of the tendency to view the family as a single unit, it is believed that the fate of one member can be caused by the behavior of another. Some of my father's relatives told him that my illness had doubtless been caused by the wild carousing he did in his youth. A well-meaning but somewhat simple man, my father believed them.

4   Throughout my childhood, he sometimes apologized to me for having to suffer retribution for his former bad behavior. This upset me; it was bad enough that I had to deal with the anguish of not being able to walk, but to have to assuage his guilt as well was a real burden! In other ways, my father was very good to me. He took me out often, carrying me on his shoulders or back, to give me fresh air and sunshine. He did this until I was too large and heavy for him to carry. And ever since I can remember, he has told me that I am pretty.

5   After getting over her anxieties about my constant falls, my mother decided to send me to school. I had already learned to read some words of Chinese at the age of three by asking my parents to teach me the sounds and meaning of various characters in the daily newspaper. But between the ages of four and eight, I received no education since just staying alive was a full-time job. Much to her chagrin, my mother found no school in Shanghai, where we lived at the time, which would accept me as a student. Finally, as a last resort, she approached the American School which agreed to enroll me only if my family kept an *amah* (a servant who takes care of children) by my side at all

times. The tuition at the school was twenty U.S. dollars per month—a huge sum of money during those years of runaway inflation in China—and payable only in U.S. dollars. My family afforded the high cost of tuition and the expense of employing a full-time *amah* for less than a year.

6   We left China as the Communist forces swept across the country in victory. We found an apartment in Hong Kong across the street from a school run by Seventh-Day Adventists. By that time I could walk a little, so the principal was persuaded to accept me. An *amah* now had to take care of me only during recess when my classmates might easily knock me over as they ran about the playground.

7   After a year and a half in Hong Kong, we moved to Malaysia, where my father's family had lived for four generations. There I learned to swim in the lovely warm waters of the tropics and fell in love with the sea. On land I was a cripple; in the ocean I could move with the grace of a fish. I liked the freedom of being in the water so much that many years later, when I was a graduate student in Hawaii, I became greatly enamored with a man just because he called me a "Polynesian water nymph."

8   As my overall health improved, my mother became less anxious about all aspects of my life. She did everything possible to enable me to lead as normal a life as possible. I remember how once some of her colleagues in the high school where she taught criticized her for letting me wear short skirts. They felt my legs should not be exposed to public view. My mother's response was, "All girls her age wear short skirts, so why shouldn't she?"

9   The years in Malaysia were the happiest of my childhood, even though I was constantly fending off children who ran after me calling, *"Baikah! Baikah!"* ("Cripple! Cripple!" in the Hokkien dialect commonly spoken in Malaysia). The taunts of children mattered little because I was a star pupil. I won one award after another for general scholarship as well as for art and public speaking. Whenever the school had important visitors my teacher always called on me to recite in front of the class.

10   A significant event that marked me indelibly occurred when I was twelve. That year my school held a music recital and I was one of the students chosen to play the piano. I managed to get up the steps to the stage without any problem, but as I walked across the stage, I fell. Out of the audience, a voice said loudly and clearly, "Ayah! A *baikah* shouldn't be allowed to perform in public." I got up before anyone could get on stage to help me and, with tears streaming uncontrollably down my face, I rushed to the piano and began to play. Beethoven's "Für Elise" had never been played so fiendishly fast before or since, but I managed to finish the whole piece. That I managed to do so made me feel really strong. I never again feared ridicule.

11   In later years I was reminded of this experience from time to time. During my fourth year as an assistant professor at the University of California at Berkeley, I won a distinguished teaching award. Some weeks later I ran into a former professor who congratulated me enthusiastically. But I said to him,

"You know what? I became a distinguished teacher by *limping* across the stage of Dwinelle 155!" (Dwinelle 155 is a large, cold, classroom that most colleagues of mine hate to teach in.) I was rude not because I lacked graciousness but because this man, who had told me that my dissertation was the finest piece of work he had read in fifteen years, had nevertheless advised me to eschew a teaching career.

12   "Why?" I asked.

13   "Your leg . . ." he responded.

14   "What about my leg?" I said, puzzled.

15   "Well, how would you feel standing in front of a large lecture class?"

16   "If it makes any difference, I want you to know I've won a number of speech contests in my life, and I am not the least bit self-conscious about speaking in front of large audiences. . . . Look, why don't you write me a letter of recommendation to tell people how brilliant I am, and let *me* worry about my leg!"

17   This incident is worth recounting only because it illustrates a dilemma that handicapped persons face frequently: those who care about us sometimes get so protective that they unwittingly limit our growth. This former professor of mine had been one of my greatest supporters for two decades. Time after time, he had written glowing letters of recommendation on my behalf. He had spoken as he did because he thought he had my best interests at heart; he thought that if I got a desk job rather than one that required me to be a visible, public person, I would be spared the misery of being stared at.

18   Americans, for the most part, do not believe as Asians do that physically handicapped persons are morally flawed. But they are equally inept at interacting with those of us who are not able-bodied. Cultural differences in the perception and treatment of handicapped people are most clearly expressed by adults. Children, regardless of where they are, tend to be openly curious about people who do not look "normal." Adults in Asia have no hesitation in asking visibly handicapped people what is wrong with them, often expressing their sympathy with looks of pity, whereas adults in the United States try desperately to be polite by pretending not to notice.

19   One interesting response I often elicited from people in Asia but have never encountered in America is the attempt to link my physical condition to the state of my soul. Many a time while living and traveling in Asia people would ask me what religion I belonged to. I would tell them that my mother is a devout Buddhist, that my father was baptized a Catholic but has never practiced Catholicism, and that I am an agnostic. Upon hearing this, people would try strenuously to convert me to their religion so that whichever God they believed in could bless me. If I would only attend this church or that temple regularly, they urged, I would surely get cured. Catholics and Buddhists alike have pressed religious medallions into my palm, telling me if I would wear these, the relevant deity or saint would make me well. Once while visiting the tomb of Muhammad Ali Jinnah in Karachi, Pakistan, an old Muslim, after finishing his

evening prayers, spotted me, gestured toward my legs, raised his arms heaven-ward, and began a new round of prayers, apparently on my behalf.

20   In the United States adults who try to act "civilized" towards handi-capped people by pretending they don't notice anything unusual sometimes end up ignoring handicapped people completely. In the first few months I lived in this country, I was struck by the fact that whenever children asked me what was the matter with my leg, their adult companions would hurriedly shush them up, furtively look at me, mumble apologies, and rush their children away. After a few months of such encounters, I decided it was my responsibility to educate these people. So I would say to the flustered adults, "It's okay, let the kid ask." Turning to the child, I would say, "When I was a little girl, no bigger than you are, I became sick with something called polio. The muscles of my leg shrank up and I couldn't walk very well. You're much luckier than I am be-cause now you can get a vaccine to make sure you never get my disease. So don't cry when your mommy takes you to get a polio vaccine, okay?" Some adults and their little companions I talked to this way were glad to be rescued from embarrassment; others thought I was strange.

21   Americans have another way of covering up their uneasiness: they become jovially patronizing. Sometimes when people spot my crutch, they ask if I've had a skiing accident. When I answer that unfortunately it is something less glamorous than that, they say, "I bet you *could* ski if you put your mind to it!" Alternately, at parties where people dance, men who ask me to dance with them get almost belligerent when I decline their invitation. They say, "Of course you can dance if you *want* to!" Some have given me pep talks about how if I would only develop the right mental attitude, I would have more fun in life.

22   Different cultural attitudes toward handicapped persons came out clearly during my wedding. My father-in-law, as solid a representative of middle America as could be found, had no qualms about objecting to the marriage on racial grounds, but he could bring himself to comment on my handicap only indirectly. He wondered why his son, who had dated numerous high school and college beauty queens, couldn't marry one of them instead of me. My mother-in-law, a devout Christian, did not share her husband's prejudices but she worried aloud about whether I could have children. Some Chinese friends of my parents, on the other hand, said that I was lucky to have found such a noble man, one who would marry me despite my handicap. I, for my part, ap-peared in church in a white lace wedding dress I had designed and made my-self—a miniskirt!

23   How Asian Americans treat me with respect to my handicap tells me a great deal about their degree of acculturation. Recent immigrants behave just like Asians in Asia; those who have been here longer or who grew up in the United States behave more like their white counterparts. I have not encoun-tered any distinctly Asian American pattern of response. What makes the experience of Asian American handicapped people unique is the duality of responses we elicit.

24   Regardless of racial or cultural background, most handicapped people have to learn to find a balance between the desire to attain physical independence and the need to take care of ourselves by not overtaxing our bodies. In my case, I've had to learn to accept the fact that leading an active life has its price. Between the ages of eight and eighteen, I walked without using crutches or braces but the effort caused my right leg to become badly misaligned. Soon after I came to the United States, I had a series of operations to straighten out the bones of my right leg; afterwards though my leg looked straighter and presumably better, I could no longer walk on my own. Initially my doctors fitted me with a brace, but I found wearing one cumbersome and soon gave it up. I could move around much more easily—and more important, faster—by using one crutch. One orthopedist after another warned me that using a single crutch was a bad practice. They were right. Over the years my spine developed a double-S curve and for the last twenty years I have suffered from severe, chronic back pains, which neither conventional physical therapy nor a lighter work load can eliminate.

25   The only thing that helps my backaches is a good massage, but the soothing effect lasts no more than a day or two. Massages are expensive, especially when one needs them three times a week. So I found a job that pays better, but at which I have to work longer hours, consequently increasing the physical strain on my body—a sort of vicious circle. When I was in my thirties, my doctors told me that if I kept leading the strenuous life I did, I would be in a wheelchair by the time I was forty. They were right on target: I bought myself a wheelchair when I was forty-one. But being the incorrigible character that I am, I use it only when I am *not* in a hurry!

26   It is a good thing, however, that I am too busy to think much about my handicap or my backaches because pain can physically debilitate as well as cause depression. And there are days when my spirits get rather low. What has helped me is realizing that being handicapped is akin to growing old at an accelerated rate. The contradiction I experience is that often my mind races along as though I'm only twenty while my body feels about sixty. But fifteen or twenty years hence, unlike my peers who will have to cope with aging for the first time, I shall be full of cheer because I will have already fought, and I hope won, that battle long ago.

27   Beyond learning how to be physically independent and, for some of us, living with chronic pain or other kinds of discomfort, the most difficult thing a handicapped person has to deal with, especially during puberty and early adulthood, is relating to potential sexual partners. Because American culture places so much emphasis on physical attractiveness, a person with a shriveled limb, or a tilt to the head, or the inability to speak clearly, experiences great uncertainty—indeed trauma—when interacting with someone to whom he or she is attracted. My problem was that I was not only physically handicapped, small, and short, but worse, I also wore glasses and was smarter than all the boys I knew! Alas, an insurmountable combination. Yet somehow I have

managed to have intimate relationships, all of them with extraordinary men. Not surprisingly, there have also been countless men who broke my heart—men who enjoyed my company "as a friend," but who never found the courage to date or make love with me, although I am sure my experience in this regard is no different from that of many able-bodied persons.

28   The day came when my backaches got in the way of having an active sex life. Surprisingly that development was liberating because I stopped worrying about being attractive to men. No matter how headstrong I had been, I, like most women of my generation, had had the desire to be alluring to men ingrained into me. And that longing had always worked like a brake on my behavior. When what men think of me ceased to be compelling, I gained greater freedom to be myself.

29   I've often wondered if I would have been a different person had I not been physically handicapped. I really don't know, though there is no question that being handicapped has marked me. But at the same time I usually do not *feel* handicapped—and consequently, I do not *act* handicapped. People are therefore less likely to treat me as a handicapped person. There is no doubt, however, that the lives of my parents, sister, husband, other family members, and some close friends have been affected by my physical condition. They have had to learn not to hide me away at home, not to feel embarrassed by how I look or react to people who say silly things to me, and not to resent me for the extra demands my condition makes on them. Perhaps the hardest thing for those who live with handicapped people is to know when and how to offer help. There are no guidelines applicable to all situations. My advice is, when in doubt, ask, but ask in a way that does not smack of pity or embarrassment. Most important, please don't talk to us as though we are children.

30   So, has being physically handicapped been a handicap? It all depends on one's attitude. Some years ago, I told a friend that I had once said to an affirmative action compliance officer (somewhat sardonically since I do not believe in the head count approach to affirmative action) that the institution which employs me is triply lucky because it can count me as nonwhite, female, and handicapped. He responded, "Why don't you tell them to count you four times? . . . Remember, you're short, besides!"

Understanding Content

1. According to Western medicine, what caused the author's disability? How did the Chinese fortune-teller explain the author's illness?
2. Why did Chan's father feel guilty about her illness and disability? How did Chan react to her father's guilt? Why?
3. Why was the school music recital an event that "marked [Chan] indelibly" (paragraph 10)?
4. Why did Chan's professor try to discourage her from being a teacher? What does his attempt illustrate?

5. What differences exist between the Asian and American views of handicapped people?

Considering Structure and Technique

1. What approach does Chan take to her introduction? Does that introduction engage your interest? Why or why not?
2. Which sentences best express the thesis of "You're Short, Besides"?
3. Chan uses conversation in the essay. What does this conversation contribute?
4. What element of contrast appears in the essay?
5. How do you react to the humor at the end of the essay? Does it bring the writing to a satisfying finish, or does it seem inappropriate because of the serious subject matter?

Exploring Ideas

1. In paragraph 1, Chan asks if being handicapped is the most noticeable thing about her. Do you think that people notice the handicaps of others and overlook their abilities? Explain.
2. Do you think Chan should have worn short skirts in school and a miniskirt for her wedding? Explain your view.
3. In paragraphs 20 and 21, Chan says that adults in the United States often ignore the physically disabled or "become jovially patronizing." Why do you think Americans act as they do?
4. Do you think that Sucheng Chan is a hero? Explain your view.

Writing Workshop: Using Semicolons to Separate Main Clauses

The semicolon (;) can separate word groups capable of standing alone as sentences. (Such word groups are called **main clauses.**) Here is an example from "You're Short, Besides":

Living in war-torn China, I received little medical attention; physical therapy was unheard of. Paragraph 2

In this example, each of the main clauses separated by the semicolon could stand as a sentence:

Living in war-torn China, I received little medical attention. Physical therapy was unheard of.

Here is another example. Notice that the word groups on each side of the semicolon (the main clauses) could stand alone as sentences.

Some adults and their little companions I talked to this way were glad to be rescued from embarrassment; others thought I was strange. Paragraph 20

If you do not properly separate main clauses, you will have a problem called a **run-on sentence**. Here is an example:

> *run-on:* The distance runner was careful to eat carbohydrates two days before the race she also avoided chocolate and sugar.
> *correction:* The distance runner was careful to eat carbohydrates two days before the race; she also avoided chocolate and sugar.

Main clauses can also be separated by one of these words: *and, but, or, nor, for, so, yet,* and *because*. But they cannot be separated by a comma alone.

> *incorrect:* The distance runner was careful to eat carbohydrates two days before the race, she also avoided chocolate and sugar.
> *correction:* The distance runner was careful to eat carbohydrates two days before the race, and she also avoided chocolate and sugar.

Writing Workshop Activity

Write five sentences using a semicolon to separate main clauses.

Language Notes for Multilingual and Other Writers

When you want to show that two ideas contrast with each other, you have a number of options. Four of them are illustrated in "You're Short, Besides."

1. Use *but*.

   I bought myself a wheelchair when I was forty-one. <u>But</u> being the incorrigible character that I am, I use it only when I am *not* in a hurry! Paragraph 25

2. Use *however*.

   . . . I usually do not *feel* handicapped—and consequently, I do not *act* handicapped. People are therefore less likely to treat me as a handicapped person. There is no doubt, <u>however,</u> that the lives of my parents, sister, husband, other family members, and some close friends have been affected by my physical condition. Paragraph 29

3. Use *unlike*.

   But fifteen or twenty years hence, <u>unlike</u> my peers who have to cope with aging for the first time, I shall be full of cheer because I will have already fought, and I hope won, that battle long ago. Paragraph 26

4. Use *yet*.

   My problem was that I was not only physically handicapped, small, and short, but worse, I also wore glasses and was smarter than all the boys I knew! Alas, an insurmountable combination. <u>Yet,</u> somehow I have managed to have intimate relationships. . . . Paragraph 27

From Reading to Writing

In Your Journal: In paragraph 20, Chan says that American adults pretend they do not notice physical disability, and thus they end up ignoring disabled people. Tell about your own behavior toward disabled people.

With Some Classmates: Using the information in "You're Short, Besides", along with your own thinking, explain how people respond to the physically disabled. Why do we respond that way? What can be done to improve the way we respond?

In an Essay:

- In paragraph 10, Chan tells of a "significant event that marked [her] indelibly." If there has been such an event in your life, tell what it was, how it affected you, and why it affected you the way it did.
- If Chan's essay has changed your thinking about disabled people, compare and contrast your attitudes before and after reading her essay.
- Much of Chan's essay explains how she copes with her disability. If there is something in your life that you must cope with (an illness, a learning disability, money problems, stress, being very tall, etc.), tell how you are affected and how you cope.
- If a member of your family has a disability, a health problem, or some other problem, tell how the difficulty affects the rest of the family.

Beyond the Writing Class: In paragraph 5, Chan tells of the difficulty involved with enrolling in school. Currently, schools in the United States practice "inclusion," which means the physically and mentally disabled are included in classrooms with students who are not disabled. Research inclusion and write a paper that explains some of its chief advantages and/or disadvantages.

Growing Up, Growing Apart
TAMAR LEWIN

New York Times national correspondent Tamar Lewin wrote "Growing Up, Growing Apart" (June 2000) as part of the newspaper's lengthy series "How Race Is Lived in America." In the piece, she examines what brings young people of different races together—and what drives them apart. As you read, consider your own school experiences with classmates of different races and backgrounds.

Preview.   Friendships can have a natural ebb and flow, causing people to come together and separate for a variety of understandable reasons. Think back to your earlier school years. Were you close to any classmates in elementary or middle school that you did not stay close to in high school? If so, explain what led to the split. If not, what kept you together?

Vocabulary.   If any of the following words from the essay are unfamiliar to you, study their meanings before reading.

ebb (9)   decline
diverging (11)   separating
fault line (11)   a weakness [in the earth's crust]
Greek chorus (12)   in ancient Greek drama, the players who commented on the action
imam (23)   a Muslim religious leader
axis (38)   a central line
bat mitzvah (46)   a Jewish religious ceremony that marks a girl's passage into religious adulthood
consensus (52)   agreement
oblivious (56)   being unaware
breach (57)   break
profound (65)   extreme
commerce (68)   dealings
affluent (93)   wealthy
corrosive (104)   destructive
emulate (104)   imitate
skew (114)   distortion
adamant (115)   firm
dextrous (121)   skillful
Oreo (132)   like the cookie of the same name: black on the outside and white on the inside

- **Ramadan** (140)   in Islam, the daily fast that takes place during the month of the same name

  logistics (144)   a military term referring to the movement of troops, equipment, and supplies
- **gibes** (147)   ridicule

Back in eighth grade, Kelly Regan, Aqeelah Mateen and Johanna Perez-Fox spent New Year's Eve at Johanna's house, swing-dancing until they fell down laughing, banging pots and pans, watching the midnight fireworks beyond the trees in the park at the center of town.

2   They had been a tight threesome all through Maplewood Middle School—Kelly, a tall, coltish Irish-Catholic girl; Aqeelah, a small, earnest African-American Muslim girl, and Johanna, a light-coffee-colored girl who is half Jewish and half Puerto Rican and famous for knowing just about everyone.

3   It had been a great night, they agreed, a whole lot simpler than Johanna's birthday party three nights before. Johanna had invited all their friends, white and black. But the mixing did not go as she had wished.

4   "The black kids stayed down in the basement and danced, and the white kids went outside on the stoop and talked," Johanna said. "I went out and said, Why don't you guys come downstairs? and they said they didn't want to, that they just wanted to talk out there. It was just split up, like two parties."

5   The same thing happened at Kelly's back-to-school party a few months earlier.

6   "It was so stressful," Kelly said. "There I was, the hostess, and I couldn't get everybody together."

7   "Oh, man, I was, like, trying to help her," Aqeelah said. "I went up and down and up and down. But it was boring outside, so finally I just gave up and went down and danced."

8   This year the girls started high school, and what with the difficulty of mixing their black and white friends, none took on the challenge of a birthday party.

9   It happens everywhere, in the confusions of adolescence and the yearning for identity, when the most important thing in life is choosing a group and fitting in: Black children and white children come apart. They move into separate worlds. Friendships ebb and end.

10   It happens everywhere, but what is striking is that it happens even here. In a nation of increasingly segregated schools, the South Orange-Maplewood district is extraordinarily mixed. Not only is the student body about half black and half white, but in the last census, blacks had an economic edge. This is the kind of place where people—black and white—talk a lot about the virtues of

diversity and worry about white flight, where hundreds will turn out to discuss the book "Why Are All the Black Kids Sitting Together in the Cafeteria?" People here care about race.

11   But even here, as if pulled by internal magnets, black and white children begin to separate at sixth grade. These are children who walked to school together, learned to read together, slept over at each other's houses. But despite all the personal history, all the community good will, race divides them as they grow up. As racial consciousness develops—and the practice of grouping students by perceived ability sends them on diverging academic paths—race becomes as much a fault line in their world as in the one their parents hoped to move beyond.

12   As they began high school, Kelly, Johanna and Aqeelah had so far managed to be exceptions. While the world around them had increasingly divided along racial lines, they had stuck together. But where their friendship would go was hard to say. And like a Greek chorus, the voices of other young people warned of tricky currents ahead.

Different but Inseparable

13   On her first day at Columbia High School, Kelly Regan took a seat in homeroom and introduced herself to the black boy at the next desk.

14   "I was trying to be friendly," she explained. "But he answered in like one word, and looked away. I think he just thought I was a normal white person, and that's all he saw."

15   She certainly looks like a normal white person, with her pale skin and straight brown hair. But in middle school, she trooped with Aqeelah and Johanna to Martin Luther King Association meetings; there were only a handful of white girls, but Kelly says she never felt out of place. "Some people say I'm ghetto," she said shrugging. "I don't care."

16   She had always had a mixed group of friends, and since the middle of the eighth grade had been dating a mixed-race classmate, Jared Watts. Even so, she expected that it would be harder to make black friends in the ninth grade. "It's not because of the person I am," she said, "it's just how it is."

17   Kelly's mother, Kathy, is fascinated by her daughter's multiracial world.

18   "It's so different from how I grew up," said Ms. Regan, a nurse who met Kelly's father, from whom she is divorced, at a virtually all-white Catholic school. "Sometimes, in front of the high school, I feel a little intimidated when I see all the black kids. But then so many of them know me, from my oldest daughter or now from Kelly, and they say such a nice, 'Hi, Mrs. Regan,' that the feeling goes away."

19   Johanna Perez-Fox is intensely sociable; her mane of long black curls can often be sighted at the center of a rushed gossip session in the last seconds before class. As she sees it, her mixed background gives her a choice of racial identity and access to everybody. "I like that I can go both ways," said Johanna, whose mother is a special-education teacher and whose father owns a car service.

20   Johanna has a certain otherness among her black friends. "If they say something about white people, they'll always say, 'Oh, sorry, Johanna,'" she said. "I think it's good. It makes them more aware of their stereotypes."

21   Still, she was put off when a new black friend asked what race she was.

22   "People are always asking, 'What are you?' and I don't really like it," she said. "I told him I'm half white and half Puerto Rican, and he said, 'But you act black.' I told him you can't act like a race. I hate that idea. He defended it, though. He said I would have a point if he'd said African-American, because that's a race, but black is a way of acting. I've thought about it, and I think he's right."

23   Aqeelah Mateen's parents are divorced, and she lives in a mostly black section of Maplewood with her mother, who works for AT&T. She also sees a lot of her father, a skycap at Newark Airport, and often goes with him to the Newark mosque where he is an imam.

24   Aqeelah is a girl of multiple enthusiasms, and in middle school, her gutsy good cheer kept her close to black and white friends alike. But in high school, the issue of "acting black" was starting to become a persistent irritant.

25   After school one day, Aqeelah and two other black girls were running down the hall when one of them accidentally knocked a corkboard off the wall. Aqeelah told her to pick it up, but the girl kept going.

26   "What's the matter with you?" Aqeelah asked. "You knocked it over, you pick it up."

27   Why do you have to be like a white person? her friend retorted. Just leave it there.

28   But Aqeelah picked it up.

29   "There's stuff like that all the time, and it gets on my nerves," she said later. "Like at track, in the locker room, there's people telling a Caucasian girl she has a big butt for a white person, and I'm like, 'Who cares, shut up.'"

On an Even Playground

30   Johanna and Aqeelah met in kindergarten and have been friends from Day 1; Kelly joined the group in fifth grade.

31   "Nobody cared about race when we were little," Johanna said. "No one thought about it."

32   On a winter afternoon at South Mountain Elementary School, that still seemed to be the case. There were white and black pockets, but mostly the playground was a picture postcard of racial harmony, white girls and black girls playing clapping games, black boys and white boys shooting space aliens. And when they were asked about race and friendships, there was no self-consciousness. They just said what they had to say.

33   "Making friends, it just depends on what you like to do, and who likes to do those things," said Carolyn Goldstein, a white third grader.

34   "I've known Carolyn G. since kindergarten," said a black girl named Carolyn Morton. "She lives on my block. She's in my class. We even have the same name. We have so many things the same!"

35   As for how they might be different, Carolyn Goldstein groped for an answer: "Well, she has a mom at home and my mom works, and she has a sister, and I don't."

36   They know race matters in the world, they said, but not here.

37   "Some people in some places still feel prejudiced, so I guess it's still a kind of an issue, because Martin Luther King was trying to save the world from slaves and bad people and there still are bad people in jail," Carolyn Morton said, finishing up grandly. "I hope by the year 3000, the world will have peace, and the guys who watch the prisoners can finally go home and spend some time with their families."

A Shifting Sandbox

38   All through middle school, Johanna, Kelly and Aqeelah ate lunch together in a corner of the cafeteria where they could see everyone. The main axis of their friendship was changeable: In seventh grade, Johanna and Kelly were the closest. In eighth grade, as Kelly spent more time with Jared, Johanna and Aqeelah were the tightest.

39   But at the end of middle school, the three were nominated as class "best friends." And while they saw their classmates dividing along racial lines, they tried to ignore it. "In middle school, I didn't want to be aware of the separation," Kelly said. "I didn't see why it had to happen."

40   Most young people here seem to accept the racial split as inevitable. It's just how it is, they say. Or, it just happens. Or, it's just easier to be with your own kind.

41   When Sierre Monk, who is black, graduated from South Mountain, she had friends of all races. But since then, she has moved away from the whites and closer to the blacks. Now, in eighth grade, she referred to the shift, sometimes, as "my drift," as in, "After my drift, I began to notice more how the black kids talk differently from the white kids."

42   Sierre said her drift began after a sixth-grade argument.

43   "They said, 'You don't even act like you're black,'" she remembered. "I hadn't thought much about it until then, because I was too young. And I guess it was mean what they said, but it helped me. I found I wanted to behave differently after that."

44   Sierre (pronounced see-AIR-ah) had come from a mostly white private school in Brooklyn. She is the granddaughter of Thelonius Monk, the great jazz pianist, and more than most families, her parents—Thelonius, a drummer, and Gale, who manages her husband's career and father-in-law's estate—have an integrated social life.

45   For Gale Monk, it has come as something of a surprise to hear Sierre talk about her new distance from her white friends.

46   What about the bat mitzvah this weekend? Ms. Monk asked.

47   Well, that's just because we used to be friends, Sierre said.

48   "What do you mean? She's in and out of this house all the time. I can't remember how many times she's slept over or been in my kitchen."

49   "That was last year, Mom. This year's different. Things have changed."

50   And Sierre's mother allows that some separation may be healthy.

51   "I don't have any problem with the black kids hanging together," she said. "I think you need to know your own group to feel proud of yourself."

52   There is a consensus that the split is mostly, though hardly exclusively, a matter of blacks' pulling away.

53   Marian Flaxman, a white girl in Sierre's homeroom, puts it this way: "You know, you come to a new school and you're all little and scared, and everybody's looking for a way to fit in, for people to like them. At that point, I think we were just white kids, blah, and they were just black kids, blah, and we were all just kids. And then a few black kids began thinking, 'Hey, we're *black* kids.' I think the black kids feel like they're black and the white kids feel like they're white kids because the black kids feel like they're black."

54   And Sierre does not really disagree: "Everybody gets along, but I think the white kids are more friendly toward black or interracial kids, and the black kids aren't as interested back, just because of stupid stereotypical stuff like music and style."

55   What they cannot quite articulate, though, is how much the divide owes to their growing awareness of the larger society, to negative messages about race and about things like violence and academic success. They may not connect the dots, but that sensitivity makes them intensely alert to slights from friends of another race, likely to pull away at even a hint of rejection.

56   Sometimes it is simply a misread cue, as when a black girl, sitting with other black girls, holds up a hand to greet a white friend, and the white girl thinks her greeting means, "I see you, but don't join us." Sometimes it is an obvious, if oblivious, offense: A black boy drops a white friend after discovering that the friend has told another white boy that the black family's food is weird.

57   And occasionally, the breach is startlingly painful: A white seventh grader considers changing schools after her best friend tells her she can no longer afford white friends. Months later, the white girl talked uncomfortably about how unreachable her former friend seemed.

58   "I'm not going to go sit with her at the 'homey' table," she said, then flushed in intense embarrassment: "I'm not sure I'm supposed to say 'homey.' I'm not sure that's what they call themselves; maybe it sounds racist."

59   And indeed, the black girl believed that some of the things her former friend had said did fall between insensitive and racist.

60   For their part, both mothers, in identical tones, expressed anger and hurt about how badly their daughters had been treated. Each, again in identical tones, said her daughter had been blameless. But the mothers had never been friends, and like their daughters, never talked about what happened, never heard the other side.

61   Marian Flaxman went to a mostly black preschool, and several black friends from those days remain classmates. But, she said, it has been years since she visited a black friend's home.

62   "Sometimes I feel like I'm the only one who remembers that we used to be friends," she said. "Now we don't say hello in the halls, and the most we'd say in class is something like, 'Can I borrow your eraser?'"

63   Asked if she knew of any close and lasting cross-race friendships, she was stumped, paging through her yearbook and offering up a few tight friendships between white and mixed-race classmates.

64   Diane Hughes, a New York University psychology professor who lives in South Orange, has studied the changing friendships of children here. In the first year of middle school, she found, black children were only half as likely as they had been two years before to name a white child as a best friend. Whites had fewer black friends to start with, but their friendships changed less. But blacks and whites, on reaching middle school, were only half as likely as third graders to say they had invited a friend of a different race home recently.

65   By the end of middle school, the separation is profound.

66   At 10 P.M. on a Friday in October, 153 revved-up 13-year-olds squealed and hugged their way into the South Orange Middle School cafeteria for the Eighth Grade Sleepover. At 11 they were grouped by birthday month, each group to write what they loved about school.

67   They loved Skittles at lunch . . . the Eighth Grade Sleepover . . . Ms. Wright, the health teacher/basketball coach/Martin Luther King Club adviser. And at the March table, a white boy wrote "interracial friendships."

68   But the moment the organized activities ended, the black and white eighth graders separated. And at 2 A.M., when the girls' sleeping bags covered the library floor and the boys' the gym, they formed a map of racial boundaries. The borders were peaceful, but there was little commerce across territorial lines. After lights out, some black girls stood and started a clapping chant.

69   "I can't," one girl called.

70   "Why not?" the group called back.

71   "I can't"

72   "Why not?"

73   "My back's hurting and my bra's too tight."

74   It grew louder as other black girls threaded their way through the darkness to join in.

75   "I can't"

76   "Why not?"

77   "I shake my booty from left to right."

78   Marian, in her green parrot slippers, was in a group of white girls up front, enjoying, listening, but quiet.

79   "It's cool, when they start stuff like that, or in the lunchroom when they start rumbling on the table and we all pick it up," she said. "It's just louder. One time in class this year, someone was acting up, and when the teacher said sit down, the boy said, 'It's because I'm black, isn't it?' I thought no, it's not be-

cause you're black; that's stupid. It's because you're being really noisy and obnoxious. And it made me feel really white. And then I began thinking, well, maybe it is because he's black, because being noisy may be part of that culture, and then I didn't know what to think.'"

Jostling for Position

80   Aqeelah, Kelly and Johanna refuse to characterize behavior as black or white; they just hate it, they insist, when anyone categorizes them in racial terms.

81   "I think what makes Kelly and Johanna and me different is that we're what people don't expect," Aqeelah said. "I'm the only Muslim most people know, and one of two African-Americans on my softball team. There's Kelly, a white girl playing basketball, and Johanna, when people ask if she's white or Puerto-Rican, saying, 'Both.'"

82   Most students are acutely aware of the signposts of Columbia High's coexisting cultures. The popular wisdom has it that the black kids dominate football and basketball, the white kids soccer, softball and lacrosse. Black kids throw big dancing parties in rented spaces; white parties are more often in people's homes, with a lot of drinking. Everyone wears jeans, but the white kids are more preppy, the black kids more hip-hop. Black kids listen to Hot 97, a hip-hop station, or WBLS, which plays rhythm and blues; white kids favor rock stations like Z100 or K-Rock.

83   "I know a lot of Caucasians listen to Hot 97, too," Aqeelah said, "but even if I had a list of 200 Caucasians who listen to it, everyone still thinks it's an African-American thing."

84   Even though the two cultures are in constant, casual contact—and a few students cross back and forth easily—in the end, they are quite separate.

85   Jason Coleman, a black graduate who just finished his freshman year at Howard University, remembers how the cultures diverged, separating him from the white boy with whom he once walked to school.

86   "The summer before high school, we just went different ways," he said. "We listened to different music, we played different sports, we got interested in different girls. And we didn't have much to say to each other anymore. That's the time you begin to develop your own style, and mine was a different style than his."

87   Jason's style included heavy gold chains, a diamond ear stud, baggy pants and hair in short twists. Asked to define that style, he hesitated, then said, "I guess what bothers me least is if you say that I follow hip-hop fashion."

88   At the start of high school, much of Jason's energy went toward straddling the divide between hip-hop kid and honors student. He was in frequent physical fights, though never with white students; that doesn't seem to happen. Although blacks are now a slight majority at the school, he, like many of the black students, felt an underlying jostling about who really owns the school. And he felt dismissed, intellectually and socially, by some teachers and classmates.

89   "African-Americans may be the majority, but I don't think they feel like the majority because they don't feel they get treated fairly," he said. "You see who gets suspended, and it's the African-American kids. I had one friend suspended for eating a bagel in homeroom because his teacher said he had an attitude. That just wouldn't happen to a Caucasian boy. It doesn't have to be a big thing to make you feel like it's not really your school. We can all hold hands and talk about how united we are, but if the next day you run into a girl from your classes at the mall with her mother and she doesn't say hello, what's that?"

90   To avoid these issues, Jason chose a predominantly black college, Howard, and he seemed relaxed there this year. The gold chains and diamond were gone, and he was studying hard to go to medical school, as his father and brother had.

91   White students at Columbia High have their own issues. Many feel intimidated by the awareness that they are becoming a minority at the school, that they tend not to share academic classes, or culturally much else, with a lot of the black students. It is striking that while there are usually a few black or multiracial children in the school's white groups, whites rarely enter the black groups. Many white students are reluctant to be quoted about the racial climate, lest they seem racist. But some recent graduates are more forthcoming.

92   "A lot of the black kids, it was like they had a really big chip on their shoulder, and they were mad at the world and mad at whites for running the world," said Jean Caviness, a white graduate who attends Columbia University. "One time, in 10th grade, in the hall, this black kid shoved me and said, 'Get out of the way, white crack bitch.' I moved because he was big, but I was thinking how if I said something racial back, I would have been attacked. It was very polarized sometimes."

93   She and others, however, say the cultural jockeying has an upside—a freedom from the rigid social hierarchy that plagues many affluent suburban high schools.

94   "If you're different here, it doesn't matter because there's so many kinds of differences already," Johanna explained when asked to identify the cool kids, the in crowd. "There's no one best way to be."

95   In Johanna's commercial art class one day, there was a table of black boys, a table of white girls and a mixed table, where two black girls were humming as they worked. A white girl asked what the song was.

96   They told her, and she said, "It's really wack."

97   Yeah, one answered, "You don't know music like we know music."

98   "Yeah, and you don't know music like I know music."

99   "I know," the black girl said, smiling. "It's like two completely different tastes."

Acting Black, Acting White

100   Aqeelah, Kelly and Johanna did not have many classes together this year, but they had grown up in a shared academic world. While they are not superstars, they do their work and are mostly in honors classes. But if that common ground has so far helped keep them together, the system of academic tracking more often helps pull black and white children apart.

101   Whenever people talk about race and school, the elephant in the room—rarely mentioned, impossible to ignore—is the racial imbalance that appears when so-called ability grouping begins. Almost all American school districts begin tracking sometime before high school. And when they do, white students are far more likely than blacks to be placed in higher-level classes, based on test scores and teacher recommendations.

102   Nationwide, by any measure of academic performance, be it grades, tests or graduation rates, whites on average do better than blacks. To some extent, it is a matter of differences in parents' income and education. But the gap remains even when such things are factored out, even in places like this. Experts have no simple explanation, citing a tangle of parents' attitudes, low expectations of mostly white teaching staffs and some white classmates, and negative pressure from black students who believe that doing well isn't cool, that smart is white and street is black.

103   It can be a vicious circle—and a powerful influence on friendships.

104   Inevitably, as students notice that honors classes are mostly white and lower-level ones mostly black, they develop a corrosive sense that behaving like honors students is "acting white," while "acting black" demands they emulate lower-level students. Little wonder that sixth grade, when ability grouping starts here, is also when many interracial friendships begin to come apart.

105   "It sometimes bothers me to see how many of my African-American friends aren't in the higher-level classes, and how they try to be cool around their friends by acting up and trying to be silly and getting in fights," said Sierre, who this year moved up to honors in everything but math. "A lot of them just aren't trying. They're my friends, but I look at them and think, 'Why can't you just be cool and do your work?'"

106   The district does not release racial breakdowns of its classes. But at Columbia High, which is 45 percent white, ninth-grade honors classes usually seem to be about two-thirds white, middle-level classes more than two-thirds black, and the lowest level—"basic skills"—almost entirely black. The imbalance is at least as great at Marian and Sierre's middle school.

107   Honors is where students mix most.

108   "You really see the difference when you're not in honors," said Kelly, who was in middle-level English this year. "In middle level, there aren't so many white kids, and whenever you break into groups, people stick with their own race."

109   The contrasts are stark. In Aqeelah's mostly white honors history class, the students argued passionately about the nature of man as they compared Hobbes, Locke, Voltaire and Rousseau. But the next period, when the all-black basic-skills class arrived, the students headed up to the library to learn how to look up facts for a report on a foreign country.

110   "I'm still taken aback, shocked, each time I walk into a class and see the complexion," said LuElla Peniston, a black guidance counselor at the school. "It should be more balanced."

111   The issue has become especially delicate as the district has become progressively blacker, as more students have moved in from poorer neighboring towns with troubled schools, and as the ranking on state tests has slipped. Five years ago, a quarter of the district's children were black; now, with blacks a slight majority, many people worry that the district could tip too far. (Of course, black and white parents tend to have different ideas about how far is too far.)

112   The schools are still impressive. Columbia High always sends dozens of graduates, black and white, to top colleges. It produced Carla Peterman, a black Rhodes scholar, and Lauryn Hill, the hip-hop star, who still lives in town. This year Columbia had more National Achievement Scholarship semifinalists—an honor for top-scoring black seniors in the National Merit Scholarship Program—than any school in the state. And last year it had an 88 percent passing rate on the state high school proficiency test, three points above average.

113   Still, in a society that often associates racial minorities with stereotypes of poverty, the district has an image problem. Many parents—whites, but also some blacks—talk nervously about "those kids with the boomboxes out in front of school," and wonder if they should start checking out private schools or another district.

114   The district's administrators have been grappling with questions of racial balance and ability grouping for years. In middle school, for example, students can temporarily move up a level, to try more challenging work. But the program is used mostly by white families—to push their child or remove him or her from a mostly black classroom—so it has only increased the skew.

115   Many white parents, Ms. Peniston says, are adamant about not letting their children be anywhere below honors. "They either push very hard to get their children into the level where they want them, or they leave," she said.

116   It is not an issue only for whites. Many black parents worry that the schools somehow associate darker-skinned children with lower-level classes.

117   When Kelly's boyfriend, Jared Watts, transferred from South Orange Middle School to Maplewood Middle, he was placed in lower-level classes, something his parents discovered only on parents' night.

118   "There were all these African-American families, asking all these basic questions," said Jared's mother, Debby Watts. "I looked around and realized they'd put him in the wrong group. I was so upset I made my husband do the calling the next day. They moved him up right away. But you can't help but wonder if it would have happened if he'd been white."

119   Sierre Monk's parents are watching her grades, and thinking that unless she is put in honors classes in high school next year, they will move her to private school.

120   Sierre says she is comfortable with her white honors classmates, even if her best friends are now black.

121 "I feel friendly to a lot of the white kids, and still e-mail some of them," she said. As she sees it, she can be a good student without compromising her African-American credentials. Not everyone, she observes, has been so culturally dextrous.

122 "A lot of people think of the black kids in the top classes, the ones who don't hang out with a lot of African-Americans, as the 'white' black kids," she said. "I'd never say it to them, but in my head I call them the white black kids, too."

123 Still, she said, she was happiest in her middle-level math class, where every student but one was black.

124 "It's my favorite, because I can do well there without struggling," she said. "And I feel closest to that class, because I have so many friends there. Once I was waiting outside, alone, when I heard a group of white kids talking about, 'Oh, those kids in Level 3, they must be stupid.' I don't want to associate with people who think like that."

Fissures, Chasms, Islands

125 It was hard for Aqeelah, Kelly and Johanna to get together this year. They had different lunch periods, different study halls. Only Johanna and Kelly had any classes together. Johanna was on the varsity swim team, Kelly was on the ninth-grade basketball team and Aqeelah ran indoor track. The three could go weeks without getting together.

126 But they were still close. In the fall, when Johanna had big news to share about a boy she liked, she was on two phone lines simultaneously, telling Kelly and Aqeelah the latest.

127 When they finally met for dinner at Arturo's Pizza in November, their pleasure in being together was visible.

128 Aqeelah was a little late, so Kelly chose an orange soda for her. When she arrived, they were their usual frisky selves, waving to everyone who walked by and talking about the old friends they didn't see anymore and the new people they felt friendly with but would not yet ask to the movies.

129 They were still in giggle mode when Aqeelah said, "I get made fun of by everybody," and Johanna broke in, "Why, because you're short?" and they collapsed into laughter.

130 But a second later, Aqeelah was not laughing. She had her head down and her eyes covered, and when she looked up, a tear was leaking down her cheek.

131 "No it's really confusing this year," she said. "I'm too white to be black, and I'm too black to be white. If I'm talking to a white boy, a black kid walks by and says, 'Oh, there's Aqeelah, she likes white boys.' And in class, these Caucasian boys I've been friends with for years say hi, and then the next thing they say is, 'Yo, Aqeelah, what up?' as if I won't understand them unless they use that kind of slang. Or they'll tell me they really like 'Back That Thing Up'

by Juvenile. I don't care if they like a rapper, but it seems like they think that's the only connection they have with me.

132   "Last year this stuff didn't bother me, but now it does bother me, because some of the African-American kids, joking around, say I'm an Oreo."

133   Johanna and Kelly were surprised by her pain; they had not heard this before. But they did sense her increasing distance from them.

134   "It's like she got lost or something," Kelly said. "I never see her."

135   Aqeelah had always been the strongest student of the three, the only one in a special math class, one rung above honors. But by winter, she was getting disappointing grades, especially in history, and beginning to worry about being moved down a level. Math was not going so well either, and so she dropped track to focus on homework. She was hoping to make the softball team, and disappointed that neither of her friends was trying out. "I'll never see you," she complained.

136   All three, of course, have always had other friends, and they still did.

137   Much of Kelly's social life was with her racially mixed lunch group. She felt herself moving further from some of her white friends, the ones who hang out only with whites. "It seems like they have their whole clique," she said, and she was not terribly interested in them. Against the grain, she was still working to make friends with blacks, particularly with a basketball teammate.

138   Johanna found herself hanging out more with blacks, much as her older sister had—though not her brother, a college freshman whose high school friends were mostly white.

139   "In middle school, there were black and white tables in the cafeteria and everything, but people talked together in the hallways," Johanna said. "Now there's so many people, you don't even say hi to everybody, and sometimes it seems like the black and white people live in such different worlds that they wouldn't know how to have fun together anymore."

140   The three girls celebrated separately this New Year's Eve—Kelly with Jared, Johanna at a party with her family, Aqeelah at her father's mosque for Ramadan.

141   Kelly still tried to bring them together. One Friday night, she called Johanna and Aqeelah on the spur of the moment, and they came over in their pajamas. And at Kelly's last basketball game, in late February, Johanna and Aqeelah sat and joked with Jared, Kelly's mother, her grandmother and little brother.

142   The next day Kelly and Jared broke up. Kelly said she was sad and working hard to keep up her friendship with Jared, but that's about all she was saying.

143   And as spring arrived, Kelly, Johanna and Aqeelah acknowledged that, at least for now, their threesome had pretty much become a twosome.

144   Johanna and Kelly were still very tight, and did something together almost every weekend. But these days Aqeelah talked most to a black girl, a

longtime family friend. It was partly logistics: Aqeelah would run into her daily at sixth period and after school, at her locker.

145   "I don't know why I don't call Johanna or Kelly," she said. "They'll always have the place in my heart, but not so much physically in my life these days. It seems like I have no real friends this year. You know how you can have a lot of friends, but you have no one? Everyone seems to be settled in their cliques and I'm just searching. And the more I get to know some people, the more I want to withdraw. I'm spending a lot more time with my family this year."

146   It's not that Aqeelah was falling apart. She was still her solid self, with all her enthusiasms—for "Dawson's Creek," movies, and the Friday noon service at the mosque. But increasingly, the gibes about being too white were getting to her. One day, walking to class with a black boy who was an old friend, she blew up when he told her she had "white people's hair."

147   "I just began screaming, 'What's wrong with these people in this school?' and everyone stared at me like I was crazy," she said. "Everyone, every single person, gets on my nerves."

Lessons and Legacies

148   The story of Aqeelah, Kelly and Johanna is still unfolding. But those who have gone before know something about where they may be headed.

149   Aqeelah's struggle is deeply familiar to Malika Oglesby, who arrived from a mostly white school in Virginia in fifth grade and quickly found white friends. Several black boys began to follow her around, taunting her. Lowering her eyes, she recited the chant that plagued her middle-school years: "Cotton candy, sweet as gold, Malika is an Oreo."

150   "I don't think I knew what it meant the first time, but I figured it out pretty fast," she said.

151   Jenn Caviness, one of her white friends from that time, clearly remembers Malika's pain.

152   "Malika was in tears every other day, they just tormented her," she said. "We all felt very protective, but we didn't know how to stop it."

153   Malika felt powerless, too.

154   "I didn't tell my parents about it, I didn't tell my sister, but it was a hard time," she said. "If you'd asked me about it at the time, I would have said that there was absolutely no issue at all about my having chosen all those white friends. But that's not true. By the end of seventh grade, I was starting to be uncomfortable. Everybody was having little crushes on everybody among my friends, but of course nobody was having a crush on me. I began to feel like I was falling behind, I was just the standby."

155   The summer before high school, she eased into a black social group.

156   "I found a black boyfriend, and I kind of lost contact with everyone else," said Malika, who now attends Howard.

157　And yet, when Malika finished talking about her Oreo problem, when Jason recalled his fighting days, when others finished describing difficult racial experiences, a strange thing happened. They looked up, unprompted, and said how much they loved the racial mix here and the window it opened onto a different culture.

158　"Columbia High School was so important and useful to me," said Jenn, immediately after recounting how she had been pushed in the hall by a black boy. "It shaped a lot of parts of my personality."

159　She and others remembered a newfound ease as high school was ending, when the racial divide began to fade.

160　"Senior year was wonderful, when the black kids and the white kids got to be friends again, and the graduation parties where everyone mixed," said Malika. "It was so much better."

161　Many parents say that is a common pattern.

162　"It is an ebb and flow," said Carol Barry-Austin, the biracial mother of three African-American children. "Middle school kids need time to separate and feel comfortable in their racial identity, and then they can come back together. I remember when I wanted to give my oldest daughter a sweet-16 party, she said no, because she couldn't mix her black and white friends. But by the time she got to a graduation party, she could."

163　This year, among the seniors, there was a striking friendship between Jordan BarAm, the white student council president, and Ari Onugha, the black homecoming king.

164　They met in ninth grade when Jordan was running for class president and knew he needed the black vote. Ari, he had heard, was the coolest kid in school, and he went to him in such a low-key and humorous way that Ari was happy to help out. From that unlikely start, a genuine friendship began when both were in Advanced Placement physics the next year.

165　This year they had several Advanced Placement classes together, and they talked on the phone most nights, Jordan said, "about everything"—homework, girls, college. Ari was admitted to the University of Pennsylvania's Wharton School and Jordan to Harvard.

166　"No one looking at me would ever think I'm in Advanced Placement," said Ari, who wears baggy Gibaud pants, a pyramid ring and a big metal watch. "Most of the black kids in the honors classes identify with white culture. I'm more comfortable in black culture, with kids who dress like me and talk like me and listen to the same music I do."

167　Ari and Jordan have a real friendship, but one with limits. On weekends, Ari mostly hangs out with black friends from lower-level classes, Jordan with a mostly white group of top students. When Ari and his friends performed a wildly successful hip-hop dance routine at the Martin Luther King Association fashion show, Jordan, like most white students, did not go. And when Jordan and his friends put together a fund-raising dance for a classmate with multiple sclerosis, Ari did not show up.

168 "We've tried to get him to white parties, everyone wants him there, but he either doesn't come or doesn't stay long," Jordan said.

169 Jordan thinks a lot about race and has been active in school groups to promote better racial understanding—something he has tried unsuccessfully to draw Ari into.

170 And while Ari often visits Jordan's home, Jordan has only rarely, and briefly, been to Ari's

171 Ari laughed. "Hey, dude, you could come."

Understanding Content

1. What common phenomenon was reflected in the fact that white and black students would not mix at Johanna's birthday party?
2. Why was the occurrence of this phenomenon surprising for this particular group of students?
3. How do the students themselves explain the separation that occurs between whites and blacks after years of friendship?
4. What is ability grouping? What effect does it have on whites and blacks in Columbia High School?
5. How is Columbia High School changing? How is the friendship of Johanna, Aqeelah, and Kelly changing?

Considering Structure and Technique

1. What contrast does Lewin set up in the first seven paragraphs? What purpose does this contrast serve?
2. Lewin often reports the students' views on race with their own words. What do you think of this technique? Why?
3. Examples can provide excellent support for a topic sentence. What is the topic sentence of paragraph 112? What examples support that topic sentence? Do the examples provide adequate support? Explain.
4. What do you think of the way Lewin's article ends? Why?

Exploring Ideas

1. In paragraph 14, Kelly Regan defends her black classmate's one-word response by explaining that he may have viewed her as "a normal white person." What does Kelly mean?
2. Reread paragraph 18. What does it suggest about the way some whites react to blacks?
3. List the examples of stereotypical thinking apparent in the essay.
4. Do you think the white girl's remarks in paragraph 58 are racist? Explain.
5. Why do you think Jordan has seldom visited Ari's home?

Writing Workshop: Using Single Quotation Marks

You already know to use quotation marks around a person's exact words. But do you know what to do when a person's exact words include a quotation of their own? The answer is to use single quotation marks to indicate the quote within a quote. Here are two examples from the essay. The double quotation marks indicate that Lewin is quoting, and the single quotation marks indicate that the person Lewin is quoting is quoting a third party.

1. "People are always asking, 'What are you?' and I don't really like it," she said. Paragraph 22

2. "They said, 'You don't even act like you're black,'" she remembered. Paragraph 43

Writing Workshop Activity

Explain the use of double and single quotation marks in paragraph 53.

Language Notes for Multilingual and Other Writers

The rules for capitalization often vary from language to language. A number of the English rules are illustrated in "Growing Up, Growing Apart."

1. Capitalize the names of people: *Kelly Regan, Aqeelah Mateen, Johanna's* (paragraph 1).
2. Capitalize months, days of the week, and holidays: *Friday in October* (paragraph 66), *New Year's Eve* (paragraph 1), *Ramadan* (paragraph 140).
3. Capitalize the names of schools and companies: *Maplewood Middle School* (paragraph 2), *New York University* (paragraph 64), *AT&T* (paragraph 23).
4. Capitalize nationalities, races, and religions: *Puerto Rican, Irish-Catholic, Jewish* (paragraph 2), *African-American, Caucasian* (paragraph 89), *Greek chorus* (paragraph 12).
5. Capitalize cities: *South Orange* (paragraph 64)
6. Capitalize brand names of products: *Oreo* (paragraph 149).

From Reading to Writing

In Your Journal: After reading "Growing Up, Growing Apart," are you interested in reading the rest of the *New York Times* series, "How Race Is Lived in America"? Explain why or why not.

With Some Classmates: The United States is often referred to as a "melting pot." Explain what that means and go on to tell whether or not you think the description is currently accurate.

In an Essay

- Gale Monk believes that people need to know their own group to feel a sense of pride (paragraph 51). How well do you know your own racial, ethnic, or religious group? How are you affected by your knowledge or lack of knowledge?
- How much racial diversity was there at your high school? Explain the effects of that diversity (or lack of it).
- What does Lewin's article tell us about the state of race relations, years after the end of legal discrimination? What do you think can be done to take us to the next level of improvement?
- In paragraph 22, Johanna says it is possible for a person to act black. Is this point of view racist? Explain why or why not.

Beyond the Writing Class: Research the advantages and disadvantages of ability grouping and then argue for or against using it in high schools.

⇛ CONNECTING THE READINGS

1. Using the information in "High School Controversial" (p. 315) and "Honor Bound" (p. 332), along with your own experience and observation, describe one or more of the attitudes of Americans toward homosexuals. Explain what you think causes the attitude(s) as well as the effect of the attitude(s) on society.
2. Using the readings in Part 4, along with your own experience and observation, describe the stereotypes of men and women in a paper that would be suitable for a social psychology class. Go on to explain the effects of the stereotypes on people and society.
3. Explain and illustrate one or more of the issues that often divide the genders (equal employment opportunities, day care, child custody laws, divorce laws, and so forth). Go on to suggest what can be done to bridge the gender divide. The readings in Chapter 7 may help you, along with "Beauty: When the Other Dancer Is the Self" (p. 211) and "Virtual Love" (p. 267).
4. "Honor Bound," "Don't Just Stand There," "It Is Time to Stop Playing Indian" and "Racism in America" tell about individuals working to combat discrimination or advocating that we all take up the effort:. Using the ideas in these readings and your own thoughts, write a letter to your campus newspaper encouraging students to fight discrimination on an individual basis and explaining how they can do that.
5. Design a course called "Issues in Diversity" to be taught at your school. Explain specifically what the course will cover and why it will cover that particular material. Lay out the goals for the course, whether the course is a requirement or an elective and why, and in what year students should take the course.
6. Explain how people react to those who are physically or cosmetically impaired in some way and why we react as we do. "Beauty: When the Other Dancer Is the Self" (p. 211) and "You're Short, Besides" (p. 356) may give you some ideas.

Learning and Language in Transition

F. S. Lincoln/FPG

©RF/Corbis

CHAPTER 9

ISSUES IN EDUCATION: HOW DO WE LEARN? WHAT DO WE LEARN?

"An education is like a crumbling building that needs constant upkeep with repairs and additions."

Edith Wharton

"Education is what survives when what has been learned has been forgotten."

B. F. Skinner

"This is the great vice of academicism, that it is concerned with ideas rather than with thinking."

Lionel Trilling

"A professor is one who talks in someone else's sleep."

W. H. Auden

Learning to Write
RUSSELL BAKER

Russell Baker was a reporter for the *Baltimore Sun* before joining the *New York Times* to write his popular "The Observer" column. In 1979, he won a Pulitzer Prize for journalism. "Learning to Write" is part of his two-volume autobiography, *Growing Up* (1982), for which he won another Pulitzer.

Preview.   Baker expected "another grim year in the dreariest of subjects," but eleventh grade English proved to be a turning point. What kinds of experiences (positive and negative) did you have in high school English classes? How did those experiences affect your attitude toward English studies? Answer these questions in a page or so of your journal. (If you are from a non-English speaking country answer these questions about classes in your native language.)

Vocabulary.   If any of the following words from the selection are unfamiliar to you, study their meanings before reading.

notorious (1) widely known, with a bad reputation
prim (1) stiff and formal
listless (2) showing no interest in anything
unfruitful (2) unproductive
ferocity (2) fierceness
irrepressible (2) uncontrollable
essence (3) the basic nature of something
antecedent (4) the noun a pronoun replaces
exotic (6) unusual
reminiscence (8) an account of a memorable experience
repress (10) hold back

When our class was assigned to Mr. Fleagle for third-year English I anticipated another grim year in that dreariest of subjects. Mr. Fleagle was notorious among City students for dullness and inability to inspire. He was said to be stuffy, dull, and hopelessly out of date. To me he looked to be sixty or seventy and prim to a fault. He wore primly severe glasses, his wavy hair was primly cut and primly combed. He wore prim vested suits with neckties blocked primly against the collar buttons of his primly starched white shirts. He had a primly pointed jaw, a primly straight nose, and a prim manner of speaking that was so correct, so gentlemanly, that he seemed a comic antique.

2   I anticipated a listless, unfruitful year with Mr. Fleagle and for a long time was not disappointed. We read *Macbeth*. Mr. Fleagle loved *Macbeth* and

wanted us to love it too, but he lacked the gift of infecting others with his own passion. He tried to convey the murderous ferocity of Lady Macbeth one day by reading aloud the passage that concludes

> . . . I have given suck, and know
> How tender 'tis to love the babe that milks me.
> I would, while it was smiling in my face,
> Have plucked my nipple from his boneless gums . . .

The idea of prim Mr. Fleagle plucking his nipple from boneless gums was too much for the class. We burst into gasps of irrepressible snickering. Mr. Fleagle stopped.

3   "There is nothing funny, boys, about giving suck to a babe. It is the—the very essence of motherhood, don't you see."

4   He constantly sprinkled his sentences with "don't you see." It wasn't a question but an exclamation of mild surprise at our ignorance. "Your pronoun needs an antecedent, don't you see," he would say, very primly. "The purpose of the Porter's scene, boys, is to provide comic relief from the horror, don't you see."

5   Late in the year we tackled the informal essay. "The essay, don't you see, is the . . . " My mind went numb. Of all forms of writing, none seemed so boring as the essay. Naturally we would have to write informal essays. Mr. Fleagle distributed a homework sheet offering us a choice of topics. None was quite so simpleminded as "What I Did on My Summer Vacation," but most seemed to be almost as dull. I took the list home and dawdled until the night before the essay was due. Sprawled on the sofa, I finally faced up to the grim task, took the list out of my notebook, and scanned it. The topic on which my eye stopped was "The Art of Eating Spaghetti."

6   This title produced an extraordinary sequence of mental images. Surging up out of the depths of memory came a vivid recollection of a night in Belleville when all of us were seated around the supper table—Uncle Allen, my mother, Uncle Charlie, Doris, Uncle Hal—and Aunt Pat served spaghetti for supper. Spaghetti was an exotic treat in those days. Neither Doris nor I had ever eaten spaghetti, and none of the adults had enough experience to be good at it. All the good humor of Uncle Allen's house reawoke in my mind as I recalled the laughing arguments we had that night about the socially respectable method for moving spaghetti from plate to mouth.

7   Suddenly I wanted to write about that, about the warmth and good feeling of it, but I wanted to put it down simply for my own joy, not for Mr. Fleagle. It was a moment I wanted to recapture and hold for myself. I wanted to relive the pleasure of an evening at New Street. To write it as I wanted, however, would violate all the rules of formal composition I'd learned in school, and Mr. Fleagle would surely give it a failing grade. Never mind. I would write something else for Mr. Fleagle after I had written this thing for myself.

8   When I finished it the night was half gone and there was no time left to compose a proper, respectable essay for Mr. Fleagle. There was no choice next

morning but to turn in my private reminiscence of Belleville. Two days passed before Mr. Fleagle returned the graded papers, and he returned everyone's but mine. I was bracing myself for a command to report to Mr. Fleagle immediately after school for discipline when I saw him lift my paper from his desk and rap for the class's attention.

9   "Now, boys," he said, "I want to read you an essay. This is titled 'The Art of Eating Spaghetti.'"

10   And he started to read. My words! He was reading *my words* out loud to the entire class. What's more, the entire class was listening. Listening attentively. Then somebody laughed, then the entire class was laughing, and not in contempt and ridicule, but with openhearted enjoyment. Even Mr. Fleagle stopped two or three times to repress a small prim smile.

11   I did my best to avoid showing pleasure, but what I was feeling was pure ecstasy at this startling demonstration that my words had the power to make people laugh. In the eleventh grade, at the eleventh hour as it were, I had discovered a calling. It was the happiest moment of my entire school career. When Mr. Fleagle finished he put the final seal on my happiness by saying, "Now that, boys, is an essay, don't you see. It's—don't you see—it's of the very essence of the essay, don't you see. Congratulations, Mr. Baker."

Understanding Content

1. How did Russell Baker feel about writing before he was inspired to write "The Art of Eating Spaghetti"?
2. At first Baker was not interested in writing his school essay, but later he became excited about it. What caused him to feel differently?
3. For whom did Baker write his school essay, "The Art of Eating Spaghetti"? That is, who was his primary audience? Why did he write the essay? That is, what was his primary purpose?
4. How did Baker feel about writing after he wrote "The Art of Eating Spaghetti"?

Considering Structure and Technique

1. Baker uses a great deal of specific descriptive language in "Learning to Write." For example, in paragraph 1 he refers to a "grim" year and the "dreariest" of subjects. Cite three other examples of specific descriptive language. What does the description contribute to the essay?
2. In paragraph 1, Baker frequently repeats the words *prim* and *primly.* Why does he do so?
3. What kind of order are Baker's details arranged in: chronological (time) order, spatial (space) order, or progressive (order of importance) order? Why is this order suitable?
4. For what purpose do you think Baker wrote "Learning to Write"?

Exploring Ideas

1. Baker says that Mr. Fleagle "lacked the gift of infecting others with his own passion" (paragraph 2). Do you think the "gift of infecting others" with passion is important to a teacher? Explain.
2. Would you consider Mr. Fleagle a good teacher? Why or why not?
3. What advice for English teachers is implied in "Learning to Write"?
4. What did Baker learn about writing as a result of writing "The Art of Eating Spaghetti"?

Writing Workshop: Using Sentence Fragments for Effect

A **sentence fragment** begins with a capital letter and ends with a period, but it is not really a sentence. Instead, it is a piece (a fragment) of a sentence. Ordinarily, sentence fragments are errors, and they should be avoided. However, on rare occasions, fragments can be written intentionally for emphasis or dramatic effect. In paragraph 10, Baker uses these fragments for emphasis:

My words!

Listening attentively.

In your writing, you should edit carefully to eliminate sentence fragments. However, if you want to use one on purpose to create a special effect, consult with your instructor to be sure you are creating the effect you are after.

Writing Workshop Activity

Form a group with two or three classmates. Each of you should find three examples of sentence fragments in his or her own drafts and/or in published writing. ("Complexion" on p. 63 is a good starting point.) Then, as a group, evaluate each fragment in its context and decide whether each should be edited out or remain to create a desirable effect.

Language Notes for Multilingual and Other Writers

The workshop in this chapter discusses using sentence fragments to achieve a particular effect. However, fragments should be used sparingly and very carefully. Ordinarily you should write complete sentences by keeping the following points in mind.

1. In some languages, sentences do not have subjects. In English, however, a sentence must have a subject; otherwise, the word group is a fragment.
2. In some languages, sentences do not have verbs. In English, however, a sentence without a verb is a fragment.

3. Sometimes a main verb requires a helping verb. If the helping verb is omitted, the result is a fragment.

fragment: The tree near the street <u>hit</u> by a car.

sentence: The tree near the street <u>was hit</u> by a car.

From Reading to Writing

In Your Journal: Assume you are the principal of the high school where Mr. Fleagle teaches. On the basis of the information in Baker's essay, write an evaluation of Mr. Fleagle for his personnel file.

With Some Classmates: Using the information in the essay, your preview journal entries and any other ideas you wish, write an essay with the title "Advice for English Teachers." Your goal is to offer helpful suggestions for teachers from a student's perspective, in order to help teachers do a better job.

In an Essay

- Paragraph 1 of "Learning to Write" is an unflattering description of Mr. Fleagle. Pick one of your former teachers and write either a flattering or unflattering description. The workshop on mental images (p. 60) may help you.
- Baker expected eleventh grade English to be grim, but it proved exciting. In fact, it produced the happiest moment in his school career. Think of a time in your own life when things did not go as you expected them to, and contrast what you expected to happen with what really did happen.
- Tell a story about a happy moment in your school career or about an unhappy moment in your school career.
- In eleventh grade English, Baker had a moment of discovery—he realized he wanted to be a writer. Tell about a moment of discovery, a time when you saw something clearly.
- Explain how you feel about writing and why. If, like Baker, you changed your view about writing, also tell about that change.

Beyond the Writing Class: Russell Baker says that he "discovered" a calling in eleventh grade when Mr. Fleagle read his essay to the class (paragraph 11). Baker went on to become a professional writer. Interview six professional people about how they "discovered a calling" (that is, about how they chose their careers). Be sure to ask these people what role school played in their selection. Then write an essay to present your interview results and draw conclusions about how school can and does influence career choice.

In Praise of the F Word

MARY SHERRY

Mary Sherry teaches literacy skills to high school graduates who did not learn what they should have learned in high school. After years of doing so, Sherry has decided that there is an alternative to granting diplomas to undereducated students. See if you agree with her plan, which is explained in this *Newsweek* essay.

Preview. With two or three classmates, visit your college's registrar or other appropriate official to learn what percentage of your school's freshmen must take remedial reading, writing, or mathematics courses. Consider the statistic and draw a conclusion or two about its significance.

Vocabulary. If any of the following words from the essay are unfamiliar to you, study their meanings before reading.

validity (1) soundness
semiliterate (1) only partly able to read and write
adult-literacy (2) pertaining to the ability of adults to read and write
trump card (4) a card-playing term that refers to a card that gives a player an advantage
composure (6) self-control
radical (6) extreme
illiteracy (11) the inability to read and write
conspiracy (11) plot

Tens of thousands of eighteen-year-olds will graduate this year and be handed meaningless diplomas. These diplomas won't look any different from those awarded their luckier classmates. Their validity will be questioned only when their employers discover that these graduates are semiliterate.

2   Eventually a fortunate few will find their way into educational-repair shops—adult-literacy programs, such as the one where I teach basic grammar and writing. There, high-school graduates and high-school dropouts pursuing graduate-equivalency certificates will learn the skills they should have learned in school. They will also discover they have been cheated by our educational system.

3   As I teach, I learn a lot about our schools. Early in each session I ask my students to write about an unpleasant experience they had in school. No writers' block here! "I wish someone would have had made me stop doing drugs and made me study." "I liked to party and no one seemed to care." "I was a good kid and didn't cause any trouble, so they just passed me along even though I didn't read well and couldn't write." And so on.

4   I am your basic do-gooder, and prior to teaching this class I blamed the poor academic skills our kids have today on drugs, divorce and other impediments to concentration necessary for doing well in school. But, as I rediscover each time I walk into the classroom, before a teacher can expect students to concentrate, he has to get their attention, no matter what distractions may be at hand. There are many ways to do this, and they have much to do with teaching style. However, if style alone won't do it, there is another way to show who holds the winning hand in the classroom. That is to reveal the trump card of failure.

5   I will never forget a teacher who played that card to get the attention of one of my children. Our youngest, a world-class charmer, did little to develop his intellectual talents but always got by. Until Mrs. Stifter.

6   Our son was a high-school senior when he had her for English. "He sits in the back of the room talking to his friends," she told me. "Why don't you move him to the front row?" I urged, believing the embarrassment would get him to settle down. Mrs. Stifter looked at me steely-eyed over her glasses. "I don't move seniors," she said. "I flunk them." I was flustered. Our son's academic life flashed before my eyes. No teacher had ever threatened him with that before. I regained my composure and managed to say that I thought she was right. By the time I got home I was feeling pretty good about this. It was a radical approach for these times, but, well, why not? "She's going to flunk you," I told my son. I did not discuss it any further. Suddenly English became a priority in his life. He finished out the semester with an A.

7   I know one example doesn't make a case, but at night I see a parade of students who are angry and resentful for having been passed along until they could no longer even pretend to keep up. Of average intelligence or better, they eventually quit school, concluding they were too dumb to finish. "I should have been held back," is a comment I hear frequently. Even sadder are those students who are high-school graduates who say to me after a few weeks of class, "I don't know how I ever got a high-school diploma."

8   Passing students who have not mastered the work cheats them and the employers who expect graduates to have basic skills. We excuse this dishonest behavior by saying kids can't learn if they come from terrible environments. No one seems to stop to think that—no matter what environments they come from—most kids don't put school first on their list unless they perceive something is at stake. They'd rather be sailing.

9   Many students I see at night could give expert testimony on unemployment, chemical dependency, abusive relationships. In spite of these difficulties, they have decided to make education a priority. They are motivated by the desire for a better job or the need to hang on to the one they've got. They have a healthy fear of failure.

10   People of all ages can rise above their problems, but they need to have a reason to do so. Young people generally don't have the maturity to value education in the same way my adult students value it. But fear of failure, whether economic or academic, can motivate both.

11   Flunking as a regular policy has just as much merit today as it did two generations ago. We must review the threat of flunking and see it as it really is—a positive teaching tool. It is an expression of confidence by both teachers and parents that the students have the ability to learn the material presented to them. However, making it work again would take a dedicated, caring conspiracy between teachers and parents. It would mean facing the tough reality that passing kids who haven't learned the material—while it might save them grief for the short term—dooms them to long-term illiteracy. It would mean that teachers would have to follow through on their threats, and parents would have to stand behind them, knowing their children's best interests are indeed at stake. This means no more doing Scott's assignments for him because he might fail. No more passing Jodi because she's such a nice kid.

12   This is a policy that worked in the past and can work today. A wise teacher . . . gave our son the opportunity to succeed—or fail. It's time we return this choice to all students.

Understanding Content

1. Why does Mary Sherry think that today's high school diplomas are "meaningless" (paragraph 1)?
2. According to Mary Sherry, what excuse has been used to justify passing students who have not learned what they should?
3. What does Sherry think motivates students to succeed in school?
4. If flunking students is to be a positive educational tool, what conditions does the author think must exist?

Considering Structure and Technique

1. What approach does Sherry take to her introduction? Does that introduction engage your interest? Why or why not?
2. Where is the thesis of "In Praise of the F Word" stated?
3. For what purpose does Sherry tell the anecdote (brief story) about her son?
4. What do you think of the title of the essay? What effect is it likely to have on the reader?
5. Sherry states what qualifies her to write on her subject. What are her credentials? What purpose does it serve to state them?

Exploring Ideas

1. In paragraph 2, Sherry says that high school graduates often "have been cheated by our educational system." What do you think she means? Do you agree with her? Explain.
2. In paragraph 10, Sherry says adults value education more than children do. Do you agree that this is the case? Why?

3. When asked to write about their negative school experiences, the author's students did not experience writer's block. Why do you think that was the case?
4. Would you like to have Mary Sherry as a teacher? Explain why or why not.

Writing Workshop: Using the Dash

The dash (—), which signals a long pause, is used for emphasis or dramatic effect. (To make a dash on a computer keyboard, strike the hyphen key twice.) Use one dash to set off something at the end of a sentence and a pair of dashes to set off something in the middle of a sentence. In "In Praise of the F Word," the dash is used a number of times.

1. Eventually a fortunate few will find their way into educational-repair shops—adult-literacy programs, such as the one where I teach basic grammar and writing. Paragraph 2

2. No one seems to stop to think that—no matter what environments they come from—most kids don't put school first on their list unless they perceive something is at stake. Paragraph 8

3. We must review the threat of flunking and see it as it really is—a positive teaching tool. Paragraph 11

4. It would mean facing the tough reality that passing kids who haven't learned the material—while it might save them grief for the short term—dooms them to long-term illiteracy. Paragraph 11

5. A wise teacher . . . gave our son the opportunity to succeed—or fail. Paragraph 12

Use the dash sparingly. Overuse weakens its impact.

Writing Workshop Activity

Find two example of dashes used elsewhere in this text and explain how they provide emphasis or dramatic impact.

Language Notes for Multilingual and Other Writers

Expletives include these constructions:

it is (it's)	there is (there's)	there was	here is (here's)
it was	there are	there were	here are

Here is an example (By the way, "Here is an example" itself includes an expletive):

There is a credit card on the kitchen table.

Speakers of some romance languages may be tempted to leave off *it, there,* or *here* before the verb. Be careful not to do that. Here are some examples from "In Praise of the F Word":

yes: There are many ways to do this. . . . Paragraph 4

  no: Are many ways to do this . . .

yes: However, if style alone won't do it, there is another way to show who holds the winning hand. Paragraph 4

  no: However, if style alone won't do it, is another way to show who holds the winning hand.

yes: It is an expression of confidence by both teachers and parents. . . . Paragraph 11

  no: Is an expression of confidence by both teachers and parents . . .

yes: It's time we return this choice to all students. Paragraph 12

  no: Is time we return this choice to all students.

From Reading to Writing

In Your Journal: Do you think your high school diploma is "meaningless"? In a page or two of your journal explain why or why not.

With Some Classmates: Mary Sherry claims that teachers often pass students who do not deserve to pass, and they do so for a variety of reasons. Interview one high school teacher and one college teacher. Ask each if teachers ever pass undeserving students. If so, find out why that happens. If not, find out how it is prevented. Then write up your findings, along with recommendations and conclusions.

In an Essay

- Summarize why Mary Sherry believes that flunking is a positive educational experience, and then agree or disagree with her. You may draw on your own experience and observation for some of your details.

- Sherry believes that reinstating the threat of flunking will help students learn. What else do you think can improve the performance of students in school? Mention one strategy and explain how it would help.
- Sherry criticizes one aspect of our educational system. Point out something else that you think is a problem in education (student athletics, teacher training, curriculum, textbooks, length of the school year, and so forth). Describe the nature and extent of the problem and then offer a suggestion for improvement.
- Have you ever been "cheated by our educational system" (paragraph 2)? If so, explain how you have been cheated and the effect on you. Be sure to note how serious the impact is. If you wish, discuss why you think you were cheated and what you can do to lessen the impact on you.

Beyond the Writing Class: Write an evaluation of your high school education to be sent to the board of education in order to provide the members with important feedback. Indicate whether or not you think you were adequately prepared for college. State specifically what aspects of your high school education *did* prepare you and what aspects *did not.* Also, offer suggestions for changes that can remedy any problems you mention.

Life Is Not Measured by Grade-Point Averages

H. BRUCE MILLER

In this article, which originally appeared in the San Jose, California, *Mercury News*, H. Bruce Miller criticizes a common idea of what a college education is all about. Then he goes on to offer advice directly to you, the student. As you read, consider whether you can (and should) follow his advice.

Preview. In your journal, consider the role grades play in your life: how important they are to you, how much you worry about them, how they affect the quality of your life, how often you think about them, and how much pressure you feel to get certain grades.

Vocabulary. If any of the following words from the essay are unfamiliar to you, study their meanings before reading.

littoral (1) a region along the shore
alma mater (1) the college or school that a person attended
litigation (3) lawsuits
hitherto (3) until this time
sacrosanct (3) sacred
precincts (3) regions
Ivy League (3) a group of long-established Eastern U.S. colleges with a
    reputation for high academic achievement
entree (4) the right to enter
finishing-school-cum-country-club (5) a place for the rich that is partly a
    school, partly a playground
upward mobility (5) movement up the social and economic ladder
socioeconomic (5) related to social and economic class

The New Jersey dateline on last Tuesday's story caught my eye; it's not too often that news from my old home state makes its way to this sun-washed littoral. I read a bit further and discovered that the story was about my alma mater, Princeton University. The story reported that a Princeton senior, Gabrielle Napolitano, is embroiled in a lawsuit against the university. Napolitano wrote a paper in a Spanish literature course in which she quoted extensively from a certain scholarly work. It seems that in some places Napolitano accompanied the quotations with quotation marks and footnotes and in many other places she didn't. A faculty-student committee ruled that Napolitano had committed plagiarism and that her diploma should be withheld for a year.

2   Napolitano, whose grade-point average is an impressive 3.7 out of a possible 4.0 and who is awaiting admission to law school, wasn't about to take that without a fight. She hired a lawyer and went to court, claiming that, in the first place, she had committed only a "technical error" rather than deliberate plagiarism and, in the second place, the punishment was out of proportion to the alleged offense. At last report a county judge had ordered the university committee to reconsider the Napolitano case, and the committee had reconsidered and reaffirmed it original decision. Whether Napolitano will appeal to the courts again is not known.

3   I can't attempt, on the basis of very limited knowledge of the circumstances and no knowledge at all of Napolitano, to judge the right and wrong of this case. The significant—and depressing—thing about it to me is what it seems to be saying about the place of education in modern America. Napolitano's lawsuit is just another variation on what's getting to be a common theme. Students get a lower grade in a course than they think they deserve; they sue. Students graduate and fail to get a job, or as good a job as they expected; they sue. The junior colleges and state universities have been getting hit by such litigation for years; now it looks like the plague has invaded the hitherto sacrosanct precincts of the Ivy League.

4   When you think about it, it's obvious that such lawsuits are a natural result of the way modern Americans look at education. We assume that the purpose of school is to provide job training, and the purpose of universities and graduate and professional schools is to provide advanced, specialized job training. The student (or the student's parents) invests a lot of money, time and work in the process; in return the educational institution is expected to deliver the goods—i.e., a degree that will provide entree to a high-paying, prestigious career. When it fails to deliver, what's more logical than to sue?

5   It was not always thus. Well into this century, the American university was basically either a glorified finishing-school-cum-country-club for the sons of the wealthy or a place to prepare for a career in the pulpit or the classroom, neither of which promised much in the way of what we nowadays call upward mobility. Ironically enough, Napolitano's university and mine was founded in the 1740s for the purpose of training Presbyterian clergyman. Only in the last 50 or 60 years has the American university assumed the role of springboard for socioeconomic climbers. The notion that the principal, or only, purpose of going to college is to win a ticket of admission to the great upper middle class is a fairly recent growth.

6   With that notion has come the frantic competitiveness, the obsession with getting into the best graduate and professional schools, the grade-grubbing—and, inevitably, the ethical corner-cutting. What seems to have all but vanished is the love of learning for its own sake, the idea that to increase one's knowledge and understanding is a worthwhile pursuit in itself.

7   I'd be the last one to lobby for a return to the country-club university, but it seems to me that today's college students might be happier and healthier for

a little dose of some of its values. There's something terribly depressing about the thought of all those bright young people in the nation's greatest universities drudging their student years away, never lifting their eyes from the grade-point average long enough to glimpse the wonder and excitement of the intellectual world around them.

8   Since this is the season when the middle-aged give advice to young men and women who are leaving high school or college and are about to enter college or graduate school, here's my two cents' worth for Gabrielle Napolitano and the rest of her generation: Don't worry so much about your grades. Your life will not be permanently blighted if you get a B-plus instead of an A in Organic Chemistry 101. I can personally assure you that 15 years from now you're not going to remember the names of most of the courses you took, much less what grades you got. And don't worry so much about making money, either. You are an intelligent and capable person; you will not starve. You will not be a failure if you're not making $35,000 a year by the time you're 24. Money is overrated anyway. As William James observed, it's not lack of money but the fear of the lack of money that enslaves us.

9   Don't be in such a hurry to step onto the career treadmill. Don't take only the courses that you need to get into business school or that will impress the corporate recruiters. Take a few courses just because they interest you, or because they look like fun. Don't always ask, "What can I do with this?" Try asking, "What can I learn from this?" It's a beautiful and fascinating world. Enjoy it, learn about it, learn about yourself. Perhaps never again in your crowded lifetime will you have such a chance.

Understanding Content

1. In your own words, write a sentence or two that expresses the thesis of "Life Is Not Measured by Grade-Point Averages."
2. Miller cites a contrast between the way universities are now and the way they used to be. What is that contrast?
3. What does Miller find so depressing about the Napolitano case?
4. What is Miller's view of money?

Considering Structure and Technique

1. Why do you think Miller opens his essay with the story about Gabrielle Napolitano?
2. Which sentence marks Miller's movement into a contrast?
3. Which paragraphs have the quality of a speech, where the speaker-writer directly addresses the listener-reader? What gives the paragraphs their speechlike quality?
4. What do you think of the way Miller ends "Life Is Not Measured by Grade-Point Averages"?

Exploring Ideas

1. Miller wrote "Life Is Not Measured by Grade-Point Averages" for the San Jose, California, *Mercury News*. Which group of newspaper readers was he trying to reach? Do you think these readers were receptive to his message? Why or why not?
2. Miller describes universities now and in the past. Which way do you think is better—the way universities are today or the way they used to be? Exaplain your view.
3. Do you agree or disagree with Miller's attitude toward money? Explain your view.
4. Do you think that the primary role of college should be to provide job training, or to provide intellectual stimulation and development? Explain.

Writing Workshop: Opening with an Illustration

Writers often state their thesis and then go on to illustrate the truth of that thesis with some well-chosen examples. In "Life Is Not Measured by Grade-Point Averages," Miller does the opposite: he opens with an illustration that bears out the truth of his thesis, but the thesis is not apparent until later. Opening with an illustration can be a dramatic way to lead up to the thesis and at the same time help demonstrate its truth.

Writing Workshop Activity

The following essays open with an illustration of the thesis: "Beauty: When the Other Dancer Is the Self" (p. 211) and "Just Walk On By: A Black Man Ponders His Power to Alter Public Space" (p. 195). Read one of these essays, identify the thesis, and explain how the opening example illustrates that thesis.

Language Notes for Multilingual and Other Writers

Several figurative expressions appear in "Life Is Not Measured by Grade-Point Averages":

1. *To catch someone's eye* means to get someone's attention.

    The New Jersey dateline on last Tuesday's story <u>caught my eye</u>. . . . Paragraph 1

2. *To take something without a fight* means to give in without any resistance.

    Napolitano . . . wasn't about <u>to take that without a fight.</u> Paragraph 2

3. *To be hit by something* means to be affected in a negative way.

The junior colleges and state universities <u>have been getting hit</u> by such litigation for years. . . . Paragraph 3

4. A person's *two cents' worth* is that person's opinion.

. . . here's my <u>two cents' worth</u> for Gabrielle Napolitano and the rest of her generation: Don't worry so much about your grades. Paragraph 8

From Reading to Writing

In Your Journal: Why are you in college? Explain your education goals and what college is responsible for providing you. Also explain what you are responsible for bringing to your college education.

With Some Classmates: In paragraph 4, Miller gives his views of how modern Americans define education. Discuss what you think the goals of education are and what they should be. Then write your own definition of education by focusing either on what education is or what it should be.

In an Essay

- Assume that you were a member of the faculty-student committee that ruled on the Napolitano case. What was your decision? Explain why.
- In paragraph 8, Miller offers college students some advice: "Don't worry so much about your grades." How realistic is this advice? Consider to what extent grades rule your life and how possible it is to free yourself from the pressure for grades. Also, what would happen if you did take Miller's advice? Your Preview journal entry may help you with this essay.
- Argue for or against abolishing grading after considering what college would be like without grades and how well grades measure student achievement. Also consider whether there are satisfactory alternatives to grading.
- In paragraph 6, Miller refers to the "frantic competitiveness" of college. Describe the nature of this competitiveness and the effect it has on students and/or the institution. Use examples to illustrate your points.
- Have you ever challenged a grade or evaluation given by a teacher? If so, tell what happened and what the outcome was.
- If you are from a different country, compare and contrast the role of grades in the educational system in your country with the role of grades in American education. Is one system better than the other? Explain. As an alternative, interview someone from another country and then write the essay.

Beyond the Writing Class: Check your student handbook and find out how your school defines plagiarism and how it penalizes it. Then write an essay that argues for keeping the policy as it is or altering it in some way.

Reading for Success
RICHARD RODRIGUEZ

Winner of television's George Foster Peabody Award for his *NewsHour* essays on American Life, Richard Rodriguez is an editor at Pacific News Service and a contributing editor to various publications, including *Harper's, U.S. News and World Report,* and the "Opinion" section of the *Los Angeles Times.* He has also written for the *New York Times, The Wall Street Journal, Mother Jones,* and *The New Republic.* Raised in Mexican-American household, Rodriguez spoke only Spanish until he was 6-years old. In "Reading for Success," from his 1981 autobiography *The Hunger of Memory,* he describes both his attraction to reading books in English and the isolation this activity caused him.

Preview.   To determine the role reading plays in your life, answer these questions.

1. In a typical week, approximately how many hours do you spend reading school-related material?
2. Do you read for pleasure? If so, approximately how many hours a week? What do you like to read?
3. What is the title of the last book you read? What did you think of it? Why did you read it?
4. If you got a $100 gift certificate to a bookstore, what would you buy?
5. Do you read fast enough to cope with reading tasks required of you?
6. Do you understand what you read well enough?
7. Is there a reading lab or other place on your campus that helps students improve their reading skills? If so, find out if the lab offers any services you could benefit from.

Vocabulary.   If any of the following words from the selection are unfamiliar to you, study their meanings before reading.

remedial (3) meant to improve a person's skill
National Geographic (4) a magazine featuring articles and photographs on subjects from around the world
literacy (5) being able to read and write
grandiose (6) grand in an impressive way
basked (6) exposed oneself to a pleasant atmosphere
initially (6) at first
appraisals (8) evaluations
constituted (8) formed; made up
breadth (10) width or size in general
epigrams (11) brief witty or meaningful statements
irony (11) a meaning opposite of what is expressed

⇒⟩⟩

From an early age I knew that my mother and father could read and write both Spanish and English. I had observed my father making his way through what, I now suppose, must have been income tax forms. On other occasions I waited apprehensively while my mother read onion-paper letters airmailed from Mexico with news of a relative's illness or death. For both my parents, however, reading was something done out of necessity and as quickly as possible. Never did I see either of them read an entire book. Nor did I see them read for pleasure. Their reading consisted of work manuals, prayer books, newspapers, recipes. . . .

2   In our house each school year would begin with my mother's careful instruction: "Don't write in your books so we can sell them at the end of the year." The remark was echoed in public by my teachers, but only in part: "Boys and girls, don't write in your books. You must learn to treat them with great care and respect."

3   OPEN THE DOORS OF YOUR MIND WITH BOOKS, read the red and white poster over the nun's desk in early September. It soon was apparent to me that reading was the classroom's central activity. Each course had its own book. And the information gathered from a book was unquestioned. READ TO LEARN, the sign on the wall advised in December. I privately wondered: What was the connection between reading and learning? Did one learn something only by reading it? Was an idea only an idea if it could be written down? In June, CONSIDER BOOKS YOUR BEST FRIENDS. Friends? Reading was, at best, only a chore. I needed to look up whole paragraphs of words in a dictionary. Lines of type were dizzying, the eye having to move slowly across the page, then down, and across. . . . The sentences of the first books I read were coolly impersonal. Toned hard. What most bothered me, however, was the isolation reading required. To console myself for the loneliness I'd feel when I read, I tried reading in a very soft voice. Until: "Who is doing all the talking to his neighbor?" Shortly after, remedial reading classes were arranged for me with a very old nun.

4   At the end of each school day, for nearly six months, I would meet with her in the tiny room that served as the school's library but was actually only a storeroom for used textbooks and a vast collection of *National Geographics*. Everything about our sessions pleased me: the smallness of the room; the noise of the janitor's broom hitting the edge of the long hallway outside the door; the green of the sun, lighting the wall; and the old woman's face blurred white with a beard. Most of the time we took turns. I began with my elementary text. Sentences of astonishing simplicity seemed to me lifeless and drab. "The boys ran from the rain. . . . She wanted to sing. . . . The kite rose in the blue." Then the old nun would read from her favorite books, usually biographies of early American presidents. Playfully she ran through complex sentences, calling the words alive with her voice, making it seem that the author somehow was speaking directly to me. I smiled just to listen to her. I sat there and sensed for

the very first time some possibility of fellowship between a reader and a writer, a communication, never *intimate* like that I heard spoken words at home convey, but one nonetheless *personal*.

5   One day the nun concluded a session by asking me why I was so reluctant to read by myself. I tried to explain: said something about the way written words made me feel all alone—almost, I wanted to add but didn't, as when I spoke to myself in a room just emptied of furniture. She studied my face as I spoke; she seemed to be watching more than listening. In an uneventful voice she replied that I had nothing to fear. Didn't I realize that reading would open up whole new worlds? A book could open doors for me. It could introduce me to people and show me places I never imagined existed. She gestured toward the bookshelves. (Bare-breasted African women danced, and the shiny hubcaps of automobiles on the back covers of the *Geographic* gleamed in my mind.) I listened with respect. But her words were not very influential. I was thinking then of another consequence of literacy, one I was too shy to admit but nonetheless trusted. Books were going to make me "educated." *That* confidence enabled me, several months later, to overcome my fear of the silence.

6   In fourth grade I embarked upon a grandiose reading program. "Give me the names of important books," I would say to startled teachers. They soon found out that I had in mind "adult books." I ignored their suggestion of anything I suspected was written for children. (Not until I was in college, as a result, did I read *Huckleberry Finn* or *Alice's Adventures in Wonderland.*) Instead, I read *The Scarlet Letter,* and Franklin's *Autobiography.* And whatever I read I read for extra credit. Each time I finished a book, I reported the achievement to a teacher and basked in the praise my effort earned. Despite my best efforts, however, there seemed to be more and more books I needed to read. At the library I would literally tremble as I came upon whole shelves of books I hadn't read. So I read and I read and I read: *Great Expectations;* all the short stories of Kipling; *The Babe Ruth Story;* the entire first volume of the *Encyclopedia Britannica* (A-ANSTEY); the *Iliad; Moby Dick; Gone with the Wind; The Good Earth; Ramona; Forever Amber; The Lives of the Saints; Crime and Punishment; The Pearl.* . . . Librarians who initially frowned when I checked out the maximum ten books at a time started saving books they thought I might like. Teachers would say to the rest of the class, "I only wish the rest of you took reading as seriously as Richard obviously does."

7   But at home I would hear my mother wondering, "What do you see in your books?" (Was reading a hobby like her knitting? Was so much reading even healthy for a boy? Was it the sign of "brains"? Or was it just a convenient excuse for not helping around the house on Saturday mornings?) Always, "What do you see . . . ?"

8   What *did* I see in my books? I had the idea that they were crucial for my academic success, though I couldn't have said exactly how or why. In the sixth grade I simply concluded that what gave a book its value was some major idea or theme it contained. If that core essence could be mined and memorized, I

would become learned like my teachers. I decided to record in a notebook the themes of the books that I read. After reading *Robinson Crusoe,* I wrote that its theme was "the value of learning to live by oneself." When I completed *Wuthering Heights,* I noted the danger of "letting emotions get out of control." Rereading these brief moralistic appraisals usually left me disheartened. I couldn't believe that they were really the source of reading's value. But for many years, they constituted the only means I had of describing to myself the educational value of books.

9   In spite of my earnestness, I found reading a pleasurable activity. I came to enjoy the lonely good company of books. Early on weekday mornings, I'd read in my bed. I'd feel a mysterious comfort then, reading in the dawn quiet— the blue-gray silence interrupted by the occasional churning of the refrigerator motor a few rooms away or the more distant sounds of a city bus beginning its run. On weekends I'd go to the public library to read, surrounded by old men and women. Or, if the weather was fine, I would take my books to the park and read in the shade of a tree. Neighbors would leave for vacation and I would water their lawns. I would sit through the twilight on the front porches or in backyards, reading to the cool, whirling sounds of the sprinklers.

10   I also had favorite writers. But often those writers I enjoyed most I was least able to value. When I read William Saroyan's *The Human Comedy,* I was immediately pleased by the narrator's warmth and the charm of his story. But as quickly I became suspicious. A book so enjoyable to read couldn't be very "important." Another summer I determined to read all the novels of Dickens. Reading his fat novels, I loved the feeling I got—after the first hundred pages— of being at home in a fictional world where I knew the names of the characters and cared about what was going to happen to them. And it bothered me that I was forced away at the conclusion, when the fiction closed tight, like a fortune-teller's fist—the futures of all the major characters neatly resolved. I never knew how to take such feelings seriously, however. Nor did I suspect that these experiences could be part of a novel's meaning. Still, there were pleasures to sustain me after I'd finish my books. Carrying a volume back to library, I would be pleased by its weight. I'd run my fingers along the edge of the pages and marvel at the breadth of my achievement. Around my room, growing stacks of paperback books reinforced my assurance.

11   I entered high school having read hundreds of books. My habit of reading made me a confident speaker and writer of English. Reading also enabled me to sense something of the shape, the major concerns, of Western thought. (I was able to say something about Dante and Descartes and Engels and James Baldwin in my high school term papers.) In these various ways, books brought me academic success as I hoped that they would. But I was not a good reader. Merely bookish, I lacked a point of view when I read. Rather, I read in order to acquire a point of view. I vacuumed books for epigrams, scraps of information, ideas, themes—anything to fill the hollow within me and make me feel educated. When one of my teachers suggested to his drowsy tenth-grade Eng-

lish class that a person could not have a "complicated idea" until he had read at least two thousand books, I heard the remark without detecting either its irony or its very complicated truth. I merely determined to compile a list of all the books I had ever read. Harsh with myself, I included only once a title I might have read several times. (How, after all, could one read a book more than once?) And I included only those books over a hundred pages in length. (Could anything shorter be a book?)

12   There was yet another high school list I compiled. One day I came across a newspaper article about the retirement of an English professor at a nearby state college. The article was accompanied by a list of the "hundred most important books of Western Civilization." "More than anything else in my life," the professor told the reporter with finality, "these books have made me all that I am." That was the kind of remark I couldn't ignore. I clipped out the list and kept it for the several months it took me to read all of the titles. Most books, of course, I barely understood. While reading Plato's *Republic* for instance, I needed to keep looking at the book jacket comments to remind myself what the text was about. Nevertheless, with the special patience and superstition of a scholarship boy, I looked at every word of the text. And by the time I reached the last word, relieved, I convinced myself that I had read *The Republic*. In a ceremony of great pride, I solemnly crossed Plato off my list.

Understanding Content

1. What were Rodriguez's early feelings about reading? Why do you think he felt like this?
2. Why did Rodriguez become a passionate reader despite the fact that he did not enjoy reading at first?
3. What effects did reading have on Rodriguez?
4. Despite the great amount of reading that Rodriguez did, he says in paragraph 11 that he "was not a good reader." Why does he think he was not a good reader?

Considering Structure and Technique

1. Rodriguez uses a considerable amount of descriptive language in "Reading for Success." For example, in paragraph 3, he says, "Lines of type were dizzying." Cite two other examples of description. What does this description contribute?
2. In what order does Rodriguez arrange details? Why is this a suitable order?
3. What element of cause-and-effect analysis appears in the selection?

Exploring Ideas

1. In paragraph 8, Rodriguez says that as a child he thought that books had ideas that "could be mined and memorized." As a result, he would record

in a notebook the themes of the books he had read. Read "Facts about Reading that May Surprise You" (p. 2). How does Rodriguez's early point of view contrast with the view in that section of this book?

2. In paragraph 10, Rodriguez says that he believed an *enjoyable* book could not be an *important* book. Why do you think he believed that? Do you agree or disagree with his view? Explain.

3. Do you agree or disagree with Rodriguez's assessment in paragraph 11 that he was not a good reader? Explain.

4. Explain the significance of the fact that Rodriguez crossed a book off his list after he read it.

Writing Workshop: Using the Colon

"Reading for Success" illustrates three common uses of the colon:

1. A colon can follow an introduction to a quotation when the introduction is an independent clause.

   In our house each school year would begin with my mother's careful instruction: "Don't write in your books so we can sell them at the end of the year." The remark was echoed in public by my teachers, but only in part: "Boys and girls, don't write in your books. You must learn to treat them with great care and respect." Paragraph 2

2. A colon can indicate that what comes after it summarizes, explains, or illustrates what comes before it.

   I tried to explain: said something about the way written words made me feel all alone—almost, I wanted to add but didn't, as when I spoke to myself in a room just emptied of furniture. Paragraph 5

3. A colon can follow an independent clause that introduces a list.

   So I read and I read and I read: *Great Expectations*; all the short stories of Kipling; *The Babe Ruth Story*; the entire first volume of the *Encyclopedia Britannica* (A-ANSTEY); the *Iliad*; *Moby Dick*; *Gone with the Wind*; *The Good Earth*; *Ramona*; *Forever Amber*; *The Lives of the Saints*; *Crime and Punishment*; *The Pearl*. . . . Paragraph 6

Writing Workshop Activity

Write sentences illustrating each of the above three uses of the colon.

Language Notes for Multilingual and Other Writers

Verb tenses and pronouns are affected by whether a sentence is an indirect quotation or a direct quotation, as these examples from "Reading for Success" show.

indirect quotation: One day the nun concluded a session by asking <u>me</u> why I <u>was</u> so reluctant to read by <u>myself.</u> Paragraph 5

direct quotation: The nun asked, "Why <u>are you</u> so reluctant to read by <u>yourself?</u>"

indirect quotation: In an uneventful voice she replied that <u>I had</u> nothing to fear. Paragraph 5

direct quotation: In an uneventful voice she replied, "<u>You have</u> nothing to fear."

From Reading to Writing

In Your Journal: In paragraph 3, Rodriguez tells about his early experiences with reading and his feelings about reading. Tell about your early experiences with and feelings about reading.

With Some Classmates: Compare and contrast the directions Rodriguez's mother gave him (paragraph 2) and the ideas in the school's signs (paragraph 3) with the suggestions for active reading given on pages 6 through 9.

In an Essay

- Rodriguez tells about the nature and extent of the reading done by his parents. Tell how much reading was done in your house when you were growing up and what kind of reading that was. How were you influenced as a result of that reading? If little or no reading occurred, explain why and tell how you were affected by the lack of reading.
- A turning point in Rodriguez's education occurred when the nun read aloud and he "sensed for the very first time some possibility of fellowship between a reader and a writer" (paragraph 4), After that, Rodriguez realized that reading could help him become educated. Tell about some turning point in your education, a time when you realized something you did not know before. Explain what caused the turning point and what your life was like before and after it.
- What view of education does "Reading for Success" present? That is, what does it say about the role of teachers, students, and books? Do you think this is an accurate view? Is it a desirable view? Explain why or why not.
- Like Rodriguez, tell how you have felt (positively and/or negatively) about reading over the years. If appropriate, tell how your feelings have changed

and why they have changed. Also tell what effect reading has had on you. (As an alternative, discuss some other subject—math, history, physical education, and so forth.)

- In paragraph 7, Rodriguez explains that his mother did not understand why he liked to read. If you have been involved in a school-related activity and someone else did not understand why you were interested, explain how your interest affected your relationship with that person.

- If you speak English as a second language, tell how you felt and what you did when you first found yourself in an English-speaking classroom.

Beyond the Writing Class: Assume you are a student member of your school's curriculum committee and that the committee has been asked to develop a list of 50 things all students should read before graduation. The list can include material from any field: literature, history, philosophy, science, politics, psychology, and so forth. Decide on one or two selections that you believe should be on the list and propose them to the rest of the committee along with your written rationale for their inclusion.

Is That Your Final Answer?
JODIE MORSE

Jodie Morse frequently writes on education topics for *Time* magazine. In "Is That Your Final Answer?" which originally appeared in *Time* in June 2000, Morse reports on student, teacher, and parental resistance to standardized tests given to high school students just prior to graduation.

Preview. "Is That Your Final Answer?" presents a number of objections to "high-stakes" standardized tests. What do you think those objections are?

Vocabulary. If any of the following words from the essay are unfamiliar to you, study their meanings before reading.

Freedom Trail (1) the walking path in Boston that passes such historic sites as The Old North Church, Bunker Hill Monument, and the First Public School site

bubble tests (2) multiple choice tests that require students to mark correct answers by darkening a circle (bubble) that corresponds to the correct answer

allegations (3) assertions

roiled (3) bothered

en masse (4) as a whole

picayune (4) trivial, insignificant

factoids (4) unimportant fact

curtail (4) reduce, decrease

mandated (7) ordered

emeritus (7) a person retired from professional life but allowed to keep his or her title

kitty (8) a sum of money kept in a pool

moratorium (11) a break

touting (12) talking up, praising

The 25 Boston teenagers marched last Monday down the city's famed Freedom Trail, past Paul Revere's home, to the office of Massachusetts Governor Paul Cellucci. They were armed with 800 letters of protest and a simple demand: that the Governor sit for the standardized test that will soon decide which students graduate from the state's public high schools. When an aide told them there was no time in his schedule—the test takes more than 18 hours—the students handed over a poster-size report card on the Governor's program to raise academic performance. His marks: an incomplete, a D-minus and two F's.

2   As shots go, theirs wasn't heard round the world. But the students are foot soldiers in a growing revolt being waged in classrooms, car-pool lines and state-houses across the U.S. The enemy? The standardized exams being taken by so many kids in the final days of the school year. Unlike the fill-in-the-bubble tests of yesteryear, which often did little more than single out kids for accelerated classes, this exhaustive new breed of tests is increasingly used to determine not only whether students get diplomas but also whether the school gets funding and teachers get raises—not to mention whether students will spend their upcoming vacation sunning on the beach or sweating out summer school.

3   As the stakes have risen, so has the pressure to perform—and the frustration among parents, students and educators. In the past year, protest-the-test groups have sprouted in at least 36 states. In Colorado, more than a thousand parents, teachers and students surrounded the state capitol in March and demanded that Governor Bill Owens take the test. (He too declined.) Parents in Louisiana, Indiana, and California have gone a step further, filing lawsuits alleging that the tests violate their children's civil rights. In Illinois, 200 students claimed they flunked the test on purpose. Teachers are taking to the streets, with some walking out of exams or quitting the profession entirely. Even worse, some are trying to beat the tests by any means available. In the past few months alone, allegations of teacher-assisted cheating have roiled schools in California, Florida, Maryland, New York and Ohio. A common line of defense among these teachers: they cracked under the pressure.

4   While few dispute the need to gauge student achievement, many are beginning to challenge the calculators. In practice, the tests have spawned an epidemic of distressing headlines: students failing—and being held back—en masse; frenzied parents enrolling first-graders in professional test-prep courses; property values being influenced by test scores in local schools. Even those schools that have posted gains say the success has come at a hefty price. Educators say they have had to dumb down their lessons to teach the often picayune factoids covered by the exams. A study released last month by the University of Virginia found that while some schools had boosted their performance on Virginia's exam, teachers had to curtail field trips, elective courses and even student visits to the bathroom—all in an effort to cram more test prep into the school day. Says the study's author, education professor Daniel Duke: "These schools have become battlefield units."

5   And it is parents who are heeding the call to arms. They charge that too much is riding on a single testing session where questions often resemble those in Trivial Pursuit. "In many ways, it's not an academically rigorous test," says Rob Riordan, a former teacher and father of a Boston 10th-grader. "It's full of trivialities. It's a crapshoot." A sample question from the Massachusetts exam for 10th grade: The Song dynasty in China was brought to an end in the 13th century by: a) an extended civil war, b) the Mongol invasion, c) economic collapse or d) a military revolt. No wonder Governor Cellucci was so busy the other day. (The correct answer is b.)

6   Another criticism is that because many testing companies find it economical to recycle test questions, the firms seldom allow schools to return copies of their graded exams to students so they, and their teachers, might learn from their mistakes.

7   While high scores translate into bonuses and raises for teachers, a low performance can put their jobs—and their pride—on the line. Last month the Massachusetts board of education mandated that math teachers in any school in which more than 30% of students fail the state math test must prove they can pass a competency exam. As a result, an excellent math teacher in a low-scoring inner-city school must prove her knowledge, while an incompetent teacher at a suburban school with higher-scoring students will be spared that indignity. Thus recruiting and retention of good teachers for inner-city schools will be made that much harder. Colorado has already seen a flurry of resignations and transfer requests by teachers in its poorer pockets. Laments James Popham, professor emeritus at UCLA's Graduate School of Education: "Standardized tests are putting educators under pressure in a game they can't win."

8   Unless, of course, they play by their own rules. That's apparently what happened at Maryland's Potomac Elementary School, where students donned "We're No. 1" buttons—and the school won a slice of a $2.75 million state kitty—after ranking the best in their county on last year's exam. The school's principal Karen Karch resigned last month amid allegations that she coached students on examinations and gave them extra time. The matter is currently the subject of a state investigation. "People don't cheat when there's a level playing field," says Lynn Winters, a researcher for the Long Beach, Calif., school district. "But when teachers feel backed into a corner, who knows what's going to happen?"

9   Many teachers maintain it can be difficult to draw the line between helping students do their best and outright cheating. A report in May by New York City's school investigator Edward Stancik offers a case in point. It cited a fourth-grade teacher whose "use of voice inflection" in asking questions—and emphasizing certain key words—gave the class an unfair advantage on the city's English exam.

10   Advocates of greater accountability in the schools contend that teachers—not the tests—are to blame for the cheating. But even some backers of tough standards are taking a second look at the tests. "Research shows that using test scores in combination with grades results in a more valid decision," says Walt Haney, a senior research associate at Boston College's Center for the Study of Testing. "The clear solution is to reduce the stakes." Such wisdom is swaying some politicians. Conceding that some tests have begun "to crowd out all other [classroom] endeavors," President Clinton this spring said testing is due for a "mid-course review." And on Capitol Hill, Minnesota Senator Paul Wellstone proposed legislation that would penalize states financially for using exams as the sole measure of a student.

11   The bill is unlikely to pass in the Republican-controlled Congress. But several states are pursuing similar reforms. Ohio legislators introduced a bill this spring calling for a moratorium on the state's testing. After parent protests, Wisconsin shelved its all-or-nothing graduation test; the state now judges students on a portfolio of their work, including test scores, grades and letters of recommendation. Legislators in Massachusetts are considering a similar proposal. Florida has forsaken rote multiple-choice exams in favor of tests with longer essay questions and math problems requiring students to show their work.

12   The debate is unlikely to subside, especially in an election year. Both Al Gore and George W. Bush are touting proposals that tie federal money to test scores. On the other side, California's largest teachers' union is considering a statewide boycott of next year's exam. "When parents start to realize their [child's] going to take a test and may not get a high school diploma, more and more people will start raising their voices," predicts Jim Bougas, a middle school history teacher from Cape Cod, Mass., who was suspended twice for boycotting the state exam. Back in Boston, the protesting students are amplifying their rebel yell. Their summer plans include gathering signatures on petitions, lobbying state politicians and taking a few more treks up the Freedom Trail. Maybe by that time, Cellucci will have loosened up his schedule—and brushed up on his 13th century Chinese history.

Understanding Content

1. In your own words, write out the thesis of "Is That Your Final Answer?"
2. Many of the standardized tests given at the end of the school year are "high-stakes" tests because much of importance rests on their outcome. What is at stake?
3. In some cases, standardized tests have negative effects. What are they?
4. How are math teachers in Massachusetts affected by students' performance on the state math test? How are teachers responding as a result?

Considering Structure and Technique

1. When writers use **figurative language**, they refer to one thing in terms of another. In "Is That Your Final Answer?" Morse often uses figurative language by using the language of war to refer to opposition to standardized tests. For example, in paragraph 2, she calls student protestors "foot soldiers." Cite other examples in the essay of the figurative language of war.
2. Is the language of war appropriate in this essay? Why or why not?
3. In paragraphs 4, 5, 8, 10, 11, and 12, Morse includes quotations. Are these quotations effective supporting details? Explain.
4. Does Morse give a balanced presentation of the testing issue? That is, are both sides presented adequately? Explain.

Exploring Ideas

1. Do you think Governor Cellucci should have agreed to take the Massachusetts standardized test? Why or why not?

2. Do you agree that "it can be difficult to draw the line between helping students do their best and outright cheating" (paragraph 9)? Explain.

3. If teachers really *are* cheating to help their students perform better, where does the blame rest: with the teachers or with the tests? Explain.

4. What do you think is motivating the push to test students in the fashion described in "Is That Your Final Answer?"

Writing Workshop Activity: Concluding by Looking Ahead

One way to end an essay is to look forward to a time beyond the period dealt with in the essay. For example, Morse concludes by looking to the future and how she expects things to turn out. She says, "The debate is unlikely to subside," and she quotes a teacher who predicts that more people will join the protest in the future. Also, she looks ahead to the summer and a time of more student activism.

Writing Workshop Activity

Read or reread "Stepping through a Computer Screen, Disabled Veterans Savor Freedom" on p. 238. Then add a paragraph at the end that looks ahead. Which ending do you prefer, the original or yours? Why?

Language Notes for Multilingual and Other Writers

Three references to games and sport you may not be familiar with appear in "Is That Your Final Answer?"

1. *Trivial Pursuit* is a board game. Players advance around the board by correctly answering trivia questions on a variety of topics.

> They charge that too much is riding on a single testing session where questions often resemble those in <u>Trivial Pursuit</u>. Paragraph 5

2. A *crapshoot* is a risky venture. The term is from a game of chance, called "craps," played with dice.

> "It's full of trivialities. It's a <u>crapshoot</u>." Paragraph 5

3. A *playing field* is an area where sports or games are played. A *level playing field* means that opponents have equal playing conditions and, therefore, an equal chance to win.

> "People don't cheat when there's <u>a level playing field</u>." Paragraph 8

From Reading to Writing

In Your Journal: In a page or so, record your feelings about tests. Do they make you anxious? Do they allow you to show what you know?

With Some Classmates: Devise a plan that is an alternative to testing for determining one or more of the following: who graduates, which teachers get raises, and how schools get funded.

In an Essay

- Tell something about your experience with tests. What does that experience say about the validity of testing?
- In paragraph 3, Morse notes that some parents have filed lawsuits alleging that the high-stakes tests violate children's civil rights. What do you think?
- Argue for or against using standardized tests to measure what students have learned.

Beyond the Classroom: Write a letter to the editor of the *Boston Globe* to convince Paul Cellucci either to take the standardized test he has so far refused to take or to hold his ground and not take it. Be sure to give reasons for your stand.

How I Learned to Read and Write
FREDERICK DOUGLASS

Born a slave to a slave woman and her white master, Frederick Douglass ran away to the North, where he fought vigorously for African-American rights after the Civil War. For 16 years, he edited an influential African-American newspaper, and he also earned an international reputation as a reformer, an orator, and a writer. In this excerpt from his first autobiography, Douglass describes his struggle to learn to read and write, a struggle that led to "the pathway from slavery to freedom."

Preview.   Most of us who have been through school take for granted the ability to read and write. Consider for a moment what it would be like if you could not do these things by listing 10 problems you would encounter if you lacked these basic literacy skills.

Vocabulary.   If any of the following words from the selection are unfamiliar to you, study their meanings before reading.

commenced (1) began
ell (1) about 45 inches
revelation (1) something that is discovered
to wit (1) namely
stratagems (2) schemes or tricks
depravity (2) state of evil
chattel (3) a piece of property, an object owned by someone
emancipation (6) act of setting free
unabated (7) with undiminished force; unrelieved
abolitionists (8) people who wanted to eliminate slavery
treacherous (8) lying, untrustworthy

Very soon after I went to live with Mr. and Mrs. Auld, she very kindly commenced to teach me the A, B, C. After I had learned this, she assisted me in learning to spell words of three or four letters. Just at this point of my progress, Mr. Auld found out what was going on, and at once forbade Mrs. Auld to instruct me further, telling her, among other things, that it was unlawful, as well as unsafe, to teach a slave to read. To use his own words, further, he said, "If you give a nigger an inch, he will take an ell. A nigger should know nothing but to obey his master—to do as he is told to do. Learning would *spoil* the best nigger in the world. Now," said he, "if you teach that nigger (speaking of myself) how to read, there would be no keeping him. It would forever unfit him to be a slave. He would at once become unmanageable, and of no value to his master. As to himself, it could do him no good, but a great deal of harm. It would make him discontented and unhappy." These words sank deep into my heart, stirred up sentiments within that lay slumbering, and called into existence an entirely new train of thought. It was a new and special revelation, explaining dark and mysterious things, with which my youthful understanding had struggled, but struggled in vain. I now understood what had been to me a most perplexing difficulty—to wit, the white man's power to enslave the black man. It was a grand achievement, and I prized it highly. From that moment, I understood the pathway from slavery to freedom. It was just what I wanted, and I got it at a time when I the least expected it. Whilst I was saddened by the thought of losing the aid of my kind mistress, I was gladdened by the invaluable instruction which, by the merest accident, I had gained from my master. Though conscious of the difficulty of learning without a teacher, I set out with high hope, and a fixed purpose, at whatever cost of trouble, to learn how to read. The very decided manner with which he spoke, and strove to impress his wife with the evil consequences of giving me instruction, served to convince me that he was deeply sensible of the truths he was uttering. It gave me the best assurance that I might rely with the utmost confidence on the results which, he said, would flow from teaching me to read. What he most dreaded, that I most desired. What he most loved, that I most hated. That which to him was a great evil, to be carefully shunned, was to me a great good, to be diligently sought; and the argument which he so warmly urged, against my learning to read, only served to inspire me with a desire and determination to learn. In learning to read, I owe almost as much to the bitter opposition of my master, as to the kindly aid of my mistress. I acknowledge the benefit of both. . . .

2   I lived in Master Hugh's family about seven years. During this time, I succeeded in learning to read and write. In accomplishing this, I was compelled to resort to various stratagems. I had no regular teacher. My mistress, who had kindly commenced to instruct me had, in compliance with the advice and direction of her husband, not only ceased to instruct, but had set her face against my being instructed by any one else. It is due, however, to my mistress to say of her, that she did not adopt this course of treatment immediately. She at first lacked the depravity indispensable to shutting me up in mental darkness. It was at least necessary for her to have some training in the exercise of irresponsible power, to make her equal to the task of treating me as though I were a brute.

3   My mistress was, as I have said, a kind and tender-hearted woman; and in the simplicity of her soul she commenced, when I first went to live with her, to treat me as she supposed one human being ought to treat another. In entering upon the duties of a slaveholder, she did not seem to perceive that I sustained to her the relation of a mere chattel, and that for her to treat me as a human being was not only wrong, but dangerously so. Slavery proved as injurious to her as it did to me. When I went there, she was a pious, warm, and tender-hearted woman. There was no sorrow or suffering for which she had not a tear. She had bread for the hungry, clothes for the naked, and comfort for every mourner that came within her reach. Slavery soon proved its ability to

divest her of these heavenly qualities. Under its influence, the tender heart became stone, and the lamblike disposition gave way to one of tiger-like fierceness. The first step in her downward course was in her ceasing to instruct me.
She now commenced to practise her husband's precepts. She finally became
even more violent in her opposition than her husband himself. She was not satisfied with simply doing as well as he had commanded; she seemed anxious to
do better. Nothing seemed to make her more angry than to see me with a newspaper. She seemed to think that here lay the danger. I have had her rush at me
with a face made all up of fury, and snatch from me a newspaper, in a manner
that fully revealed her apprehension. She was an apt woman; and a little experience soon demonstrated, to her satisfaction, that education and slavery were
incompatible with each other.

4   From this time I was most narrowly watched. If I was in a separate room
any considerable length of time, I was sure to be suspected of having a book,
and was at once called to give an account of myself. All this, however, was too
late. The first step had been taken. Mistress, in teaching me the alphabet, had
given me the *inch,* and no precaution could prevent me from taking the *ell.*

5   The plan which I adopted, and the one by which I was most successful,
was that of making friends of all the little white boys whom I met in the street.
As many of these as I could, I converted into teachers. With their kindly aid,
obtained at different times and in different places, I finally succeeded in learning to read. When I was sent on errands, I always took my book with me, and
by going one part of my errand quickly, I found time to get a lesson before my
return. I used also to carry bread with me, enough of which was always in the
house, and to which I was always welcome; for I was much better off in this
regard than many of the poor white children in our neighborhood. This bread
I used to bestow upon the hungry little urchins, who, in return, would give me
that more valuable bread of knowledge. I am strongly tempted to give the
names of two or three of those little boys, as a testimonial of the gratitude and
affection I bear them; but prudence forbids;—not that it would injure me, but
it might embarrass them; for it is almost an unpardonable offence to teach
slaves to read in this Christian country. It is enough to say of the dear little fellows, that they lived on Philpot Street, very near Durgin and Bailey's yard. I
used to talk this matter of slavery over with them. I would sometimes say to
them, I wished I could be as free as they would be when they got to be men.
"You will be free as soon as you are twenty-one, *but I am a slave for life!* Have
not I as good a right to be free as you have?" These words used to trouble
them; they would express for me the liveliest sympathy, and console me with
the hope that something would occur by which I might be free.

6   I was now about twelve years old, and the thought of being *a slave for
life* began to bear heavily upon my heart. Just about this time, I got hold of a
book entitled "The Columbian Orator." Every opportunity I got, I used to read
this book. Among much of other interesting matter, I found in it a dialogue between a master and his slave. The slave was represented as having run away

from his master three times. The dialogue represented the conversation which took place between them, when the slave was retaken the third time. In this dialogue, the whole argument in behalf of slavery was brought forward by the master, all of which was disposed of by the slave. The slave was made to say some very smart as well as impressive things in reply to his master—things which had the desired though unexpected effect; for the conversation resulted in the voluntary emancipation of the slave on the part of the master.

7   In the same book, I met with one of Sheridan's mighty speeches on and in behalf of Catholic emancipation. These were choice documents to me. I read them over and over again with unabated interest. They gave tongue to interesting thoughts of my own soul, which had frequently flashed through my mind, and died away for want of utterance. The moral which I gained from the dialogue was the power of truth over the conscience of even a slave-holder. What I got from Sheridan was a bold denunciation of slavery, and a powerful vindication of human rights. The reading of these documents enabled me to utter my thoughts, and to meet the arguments brought forward to sustain slavery; but while they relieved me of one difficulty, they brought on another even more painful than the one of which I was relieved. The more I read, the more I was led to abhor and detest my enslavers. I could regard them in no other light than a band of successful robbers, who had left their homes, and gone to Africa, and stolen us from our homes, and in a strange land reduced us to slavery. I loathed them as being the meanest as well as the most wicked of men. As I read and contemplated the subject, behold! that very discontentment which Master Hugh had predicted would follow my learning to read had already come, to torment and sting my soul to unutterable anguish. As I writhed under it, I would at times feel that learning to read had been a curse rather than a blessing. It had given me a view of my wretched condition, without the remedy. It opened my eyes to the horrible pit, but to no ladder upon which to get out. In moments of agony, I envied my fellow-slaves for their stupidity. I have often wished myself a beast. I preferred the condition of the meanest reptile to my own. Any thing, no matter what, to get rid of thinking! It was this everlasting thinking of my condition that tormented me. There was no getting rid of it. It was pressed upon me by every object within sight or hearing, animate or inanimate. The silver trump of freedom had roused my soul to eternal wakefulness. Freedom now appeared, to disappear no more forever. It was heard in every sound, and seen in every thing. It was ever present to torment me with a sense of my wretched condition. I saw nothing without seeing it, I heard nothing without hearing it, and felt nothing without feeling it. It looked from every star, it smiled in every calm, breathed in every wind, and moved in every storm.

8   I often found myself regretting my own existence, and wishing myself dead; and but for the hope of being free, I have no doubt but that I should have killed myself, or done something for which I should have been killed. While in this state of mind, I was eager to hear any one speak of slavery. I was a ready listener. Every little while, I could hear something about the abolitionists. It

was some time before I found what the word meant. It was always used in such connections as to make it an interesting word to me. If a slave ran away and succeeded in getting clear, or if a slave killed his master, set fire to a barn, or did any thing very wrong in the mind of a slaveholder, it was spoken of as the fruit of *abolition*. Hearing the word in this connection very often, I set about learning what it meant. The dictionary afforded me little or no help. I found it was "the act of abolishing"; but then I did not know what was to be abolished. Here I was perplexed. I did not dare to ask any one about its meaning, for I was satisfied that it was something they wanted me to know very little about. After a patient waiting, I got one of our city papers, containing an account of the number of petitions from the north, praying for the abolition of slavery in the District of Columbia, and of the slave trade between the States. From this time I understood the words *abolition* and *abolitionist,* and always drew near when that word was spoken, expecting to hear something of importance to myself and fellow-slaves. The light broke in upon me by degrees. I went one day down on the wharf of Mr. Waters; and seeing two Irishmen unloading a scow of stone, I went, unasked, and helped them. When we had finished, one of them came to me and asked, "Are ye a slave for life?" I told him that I was. The good Irishman seemed to be deeply affected by the statement. He said to the other that it was a pity so fine a little fellow as myself should be a slave for life. He said it was a shame to hold me. They both advised me to run away to the north; that I should find friends there, and that I should be free. I pretended not to be interested in what they said, and treated them as if I did not understand them; for I feared they might be treacherous. White men have been known to encourage slaves to escape, and then, to get the reward, catch them and return them to their masters. I was afraid that these seemingly good men might use me so; but I nevertheless remembered their advice, and from that time I resolved to run away. I looked forward to a time at which it would be safe for me to escape. I was too young to think of doing so immediately; besides, I wished to learn how to write, as I might have occasion to write my own pass. I consoled myself with the hope that I should one day find a good chance. Meanwhile, I would learn to write.

9   The idea as to how I might learn to write was suggested to me by being in Durgin and Bailey's ship-yard, and frequently seeing the ship carpenters, after hewing, and getting a piece of timber ready for use, write on the timber the name of that part of the ship for which it was intended. When a piece of timber was intended for the larboard side, it would be marked thus—"L." When a piece was for the starboard side, it would be marked thus—"S." A piece for the larboard side forward, would be marked thus—"L. F." When a piece was for starboard side forward, it would be marked thus—"S. F." For larboard aft, it would be marked thus—"L. A." For starboard aft, it would be marked thus—"S. A." I soon learned the names of these letters, and for what they were intended when placed upon a piece of timber in the ship-yard. I immediately

commenced copying them, and in a short time was able to make the four let-ters named. After that, when I met with any boy who I knew could write, I would tell him I could write as well as he. The next word would be, "I don't believe you. Let me see you try it." I would then make the letters which I had been so fortunate as to learn, and ask him to beat that. In this way I got a good many lessons in writing, which it is quite possible I should never have gotten in any other way. During this time, my copy-book was the board fence, brick wall, and pavement; my pen and ink was a lump of chalk. With these, I learned mainly how to write. I then commenced and continued copying the Italics in Webster's Spelling Book, until I could make them all without looking on the book. By this time, my little Master Thomas had gone to school, and learned how to write, and had written over a number of copy-books. These had been brought home, and shown to some of our near neighbors, and then laid aside. My mistress used to go to class meeting at the Wilk Street meeting-house every Monday afternoon, and leave me to take care of the house. When left thus, I used to spend this time writing in the spaces left in Master Thomas's copy-book, copying what he had written. I continued to do this until I could write a hand very similar to that of Master Thomas. Thus, after a long, tedious effort for years, I finally succeeded in learning how to write.

Understanding Content

1. Why did Mr. Auld forbid his wife to teach Douglass how to spell? That is, why did he consider it "unsafe"?
2. How did Douglass react to Mr. Auld's refusal to allow him to learn to read?
3. Explain how Douglass taught himself to read.
4. How did reading *The Columbian Orator* and Sheridan's speeches on Catholic emancipation affect Douglass? Why was he affected that way?
5. Why did Douglass feel for a time that learning to read was a curse?
6. Why did Douglass want to learn to write before escaping?

Considering Structure and Technique

1. In your own words, write out the thesis of "How I Learned to Read and Write." In which paragraph is the thesis best expressed?
2. For what audience do you think Douglass wrote the autobiography from which "How I Learned to Read and Write" is taken?
3. In what kind of order are the details arranged?
4. "How I Learned to Read and Write" was written well over a hundred years ago. In what ways does Douglass's language seem dated to you? Cite specific examples of dated language. Does the dated language affect your enjoyment of the selection? Explain.

Exploring Ideas

1. Why does Douglass call reading "the pathway from slavery to freedom" (paragraph 1)?
2. Why does her exposure to slavery change Mrs. Auld's behavior? That is, why was slavery "injurious to her" (paragraph 3)?
3. Using the information in the selection for clues, describe the kind of person Douglass was. Do you consider him a hero and role model? Explain.
4. After reading "How I Learned to Read and Write," do you want to read the autobiography from which it is taken? Why or why not?
5. In paragraph 3, Douglass says that "slavery soon proved its ability to divest" Mrs. Auld of her "heavenly qualities." Explain what you think Douglass means and how it is that Mrs. Auld lost her "heavenly qualities."

Writing Workshop: Using Commas with Interrupters

A word, phrase, or clause that interrupts the flow of a sentence without changing its basic meaning is considered an **interrupter** and should be set off with commas. The following examples of this comma rule come from "How I Learned to Read and Write." (The interrupters are underlined as a study aid.)

1. Set off a single-word interrupter.

   To use his own words, <u>further,</u> he said, "If you give a nigger an inch, he will take an ell. Paragraph 1

   <u>Thus,</u> after a long, tedious effort for years, I finally succeeded in learning how to write. Paragraph 9

   The above examples show that *transitions* are often interrupters.

2. Set off phrases that are interrupters.

   Any thing, <u>no matter what,</u> to get rid of thinking! Paragraph 7

3. Set off clauses that are interrupters.

   My mistress was, <u>as I have said,</u> a kind and tender-hearted woman. . . . Paragraph 3

Writing Workshop Activity

Review readings in this book, magazines or newspapers, to find four examples of commas used to set off interrupters.

Language Notes for Multilingual and Other Writers

A **gerund** is an *-ing* verb form that functions as a noun. Because it functions as a noun, a gerund can act as a subject, as the object of a verb, as the object of a preposition, or as a complement. The following sentences from "How I Learned to Read and Write" illustrate these functions.

gerund functioning as the subject: The <u>reading</u> of these documents enabled me to utter my thoughts. . . . Paragraph 7

gerund functioning as the object of a verb: I immediately commenced <u>copying</u> them, and in a short time was able to make the four letters named. Paragraph 9

gerund functioning as the object of a preposition: The plan which I adopted, and the one by which I was most successful, was that of <u>making</u> friends of all the little white boys whom I met in the street. Paragraph 5

gerund functioning as a complement: It was this everlasting <u>thinking</u> of my condition that tormented me. Paragraph 7

From Reading to Writing

In Your Journal: Explain how much reading and writing you do and what kind or reading and writing they are.

With Some Classmates: Although the United States no longer allows slavery, we do allow a number of other social ills to persist: homelessness, poverty, discrimination, and so forth. Describe a social problem we allow to exist, explain why we do not work harder to eliminate the problem, and go on to suggest a possible solution.

In an Essay

- Tell about a time you learned something that had a profound effect on you. Explain what you learned as well as how you learned it.
- Douglass tells about teaching himself to read and write. Tell about a time you taught yourself something. Explain the reason you wanted to learn and how you taught yourself.

- Think about how you are affected by your own reading and writing skills and explain how these skills have helped you and/or how they have hurt you.
- Douglass says that he was motivated to learn because of Mr. Auld's negative comments about teaching slaves to read. Tell about a time someone's comments or behavior motivated you to strive for a goal.

Beyond the Writing Class: Do some research and write a report on slavery in the United States suitable for an international student who knows little about this aspect of American history. Include any information you think will help the student understand the period of slavery—perhaps how long slavery was practiced, the number of slaves in this country, how the slaves were procured, how a slave could become free, an explanation of abolitionists, the Underground Railroad, and so on.

I Just Wanna Be Average
MIKE ROSE

Mike Rose is a writer, English teacher, and critic of the American education system who has won awards from the National Council of Teachers of English, the National Academy of Education, and the John Simon Guggenheim Memorial Foundation. In the following selection, excerpted from *Lives on the Boundary* (1989), Rose considers the problems with tracking, vocational education, and remedial classes. As someone who was tracked into vocational and remedial classes, Rose has first-hand knowledge of his subject.

Preview. In high school, one of Rose's classmates expressed his aspiration this way: "I just wanna be average." What does it mean to be an average student? Is being average positive or negative? How are average students perceived by teachers and classmates?

Vocabulary. If any of the following words from the selection are unfamiliar to you, study their meanings before reading.

spate (1) large number
crow and preen (7) brag
doily (8) a lace table covering
miscellany (8) variety
metronomic (8) rhythmic
tenuous (9) insubstantial
Horace's Companion (10) a book about education in the United States
somnambulant (11) sleep-walking
rough-hewn (13) crudely formed
apocryphal (13) false
restive (14) restless
laryngectomize (14) to remove the larynx
platitudinous melee (14) a mix of overused expressions
pedagogy (19) teaching theory
finessing (19) maneuvering
rejoin (25) respond
opine (25) to offer an opinion
incipient (25) beginning
extrinsic (27) external
intrinsic (27) internal
venal (27) corrupt
spectroscopic (27) a measure of electromagnetic radiation

Entrance to school brings with it forms and releases and assessments. Mercy relied on a series of tests, mostly the Stanford-Binet, for placement, and somehow the results of my tests got confused with those of another student named Rose. The other Rose apparently didn't do very well, for I was placed in the vocational track, a euphemism for the bottom level. Neither I nor my parents realized what this meant. We had no sense that Business Math, Typing. and English-Level D were dead ends. The current spate of reports on the schools criticizes parents for not involving themselves in the education of their children. But how would someone like Tommy Rose, with his two years of Italian schooling, know what to ask? And what sort of pressure could an exhausted waitress apply? The error went undetected, and I remained in the vocational track for two years. What a place.

2   My homeroom was supervised by Brother Dill, a troubled and unstable man who also taught freshman English. When his class drifted away from him, which was often, his voice would rise in paranoid accusations, and occasionally he would lose control and shake or smack us. I hadn't been there two months when one of his brisk, face-turning slaps had my glasses sliding down the aisle. Physical education was also pretty harsh. Our teacher was a stubby ex-lineman who had played old-time pro ball in the Midwest. He routinely had us grabbing our ankles to receive his stinging paddle across our butts. He did that, he said, to make men of us. "Rose," he bellowed on our first encounter; me standing geeky in line in my baggy shorts. "'Rose'? What the hell kind of name is that?"

3   "Italian, sir," I squeaked.

4   "Italian! Ho. Rose, do you know the sound a bag of shit makes when it hits the wall?"

5   "No, sir."

6   "Wop!"

7   Sophomore English was taught by Mr. Mitropetros. He was a large, bejeweled man who managed the parking lot at the Shrine Auditorium. He would crow and preen and list for us the stars he's brushed against. We'd ask questions and glance knowingly and snicker, and all that fueled the poor guy to brag some more. Parking cars was his night job. He had little training in English, so his lesson plan for his day work had us reading the district's required text, *Julius Caesar*, aloud for the semester. We'd finish the play way before the twenty weeks was up, so he'd have us switch parts again and again and start again: Dave Snyder, the fastest guy at Mercy, muscling through Caesar to the breathless squeals of Calpurnia, as interpreted by Steve Fusco, a surfer who owned the school's most envied paneled wagon. Week ten and Dave and Steve would take on new roles, as would we all, and render a water-logged Cassius and a Brutus that are beyond my powers of description.

8   Spanish I—taken in the second year—fell into the hands of a new recruit. Mr. Montez was a tiny man, slight, five foot six at the most, soft-spoken and delicate. Spanish was a particularly rowdy class, and Mr. Montez was as prepared for it as a doily maker at a hammer throw. He would tap his pencil to a

room in which Steve Fusco was propelling spitballs from his heavy lips, in which Mike Dweetz was taunting Billy Hawk, a half-Indian, half-Spanish, reed-thin, quietly explosive boy. The vocational track at Our Lady of Mercy mixed kids traveling in from South L.A. with South Bay surfers and a few Slavs and Chicanos from the harbors of San Pedro. This was a dangerous miscellany: surfers and hodads and South-Central blacks all ablaze to the metronomic tapping of Hector Montez's pencil.

9   One day Billy lost it. Out of the corner of my eye I saw him strike out with his right arm and catch Dweetz across the neck. Quick as a spasm, Dweetz was out of his seat, scattering desks, cracking Billy on the side of the head, right behind the eye. Snyder and Fusco and others broke it up, but the room felt hot and close and naked. Mr. Montez's tenuous authority was finally ripped to shreds, and I think everyone felt a little strange about that. The charade was over, and when it came down to it, I don't think any of the kids really wanted it to end this way. They had pushed and pushed and bullied their way into a freedom that both scared and embarrassed them.

10   Students will float to the mark you set. I and the others in the vocational classes were bobbing in pretty shallow water. Vocational education has aimed at increasing the economic opportunities of students who do not do well in our schools. Some serious programs succeed in doing that, and through exceptional teachers—like Mr. Gross in *Horace's Compromise*—students learn to develop hypotheses and troubleshoot, reason through a problem, and communicate effectively—the true job skills. The vocational track, however, is most often a place for those who are just not making it, a dumping ground for the disaffected. There were a few teachers who worked hard at education; young Brother Slattery, for example, combined a stern voice with weekly quizzes to try to pass along to us a skeletal outline of world history. But mostly the teachers had no idea of how to engage the imaginations of us kids who were scuttling along at the bottom of the pond.

11   And the teachers would have needed some inventiveness, for none of us was groomed for the classroom. It wasn't just that I didn't know things—didn't know how to simplify algebraic fractions, couldn't identify different kinds of clauses, bungled Spanish translations—but that I had developed various faulty and inadequate ways of doing algebra and making sense of Spanish. Worse yet, the years of defensive tuning out in elementary school had given me a way to escape quickly while seeming at least half alert. During my time in Voc. Ed., I developed further into a mediocre student and a somnambulant problem solver, and that affected the subjects I did have the wherewithal to handle: I detested Shakespeare; I got bored with history. My attention flitted here and there. I fooled around in class and read my books indifferently—the intellectual equivalent of playing with your food. I did what I had to do to get by, and I did it with half a mind.

12   But I did learn things about people and eventually came into my own socially. I liked the guys in Voc. Ed. Growing up where I did, I understood and admired physical prowess, and there was an abundance of muscle here. There

was Dave Snyder, a sprinter and halfback of true quality. Dave's ability and his quick wit gave him a natural appeal, and he was welcome in any clique, though he always kept a little independent. He enjoyed acting the fool and could care less about studies, but he possessed a certain maturity and never caused the faculty much trouble. It was a testament to his independence that he included me among his friends—I eventually went out for track, but I was no jock. Owing to the Latin alphabet and a dearth of *R*s and *S*s, Snyder sat behind Rose, and we started exchanging one-liners and became friends.

13   There was Ted Richard, a much-touted Little League pitcher. He was chunky and had a baby face and came to Our Lady of Mercy as a seasoned street fighter. Ted was quick to laugh and he had a loud, jolly laugh, but when he got angry he'd smile a little smile, the kind that simply raises the corner of the mouth a quarter of an inch. For those who knew, it was an eerie signal. Those who didn't found themselves in big trouble, for Ted was very quick. He loved to carry on what we would come to call philosophical discussions: What is courage? Does God exist? He also loved words, enjoyed picking up big ones like *salubrious* and *equivocal* and using them in our conversations—laughing at himself as the word hit a chuckhole rolling off his tongue. Ted didn't do all that well in school—baseball and parties and testing the courage he'd speculated about took up his time. His textbooks were *Argosy* and *Field and Stream*, whatever newspapers he'd find on the bus stop—from the *Daily Worker* to pornography—conversations with uncles or hobos or businessmen he'd meet in a coffee shop, *The Old Man and the Sea*. With hindsight, I can see that Ted was developing into one of those rough-hewn intellectuals whose sources are a mix of the learned and the apocryphal, whose discussions are both assured and sad.

14   And then there was Ken Harvey. Ken was good-looking in a puffy way and had a full and oily ducktail and was a car enthusiast . . . a hodad. One day in religion class, he said the sentence that turned out to be one of the most memorable of the hundreds of thousands I heard in those Voc. Ed. years. We were talking about the parable of the talents, about achievement, working hard, doing the best you can do, blah-blah-blah, when the teacher called on the restive Ken Harvey for an opinion. Ken thought about it, but just for a second, and said (with studied, minimal affect), "I just wanna be average." That woke me up. Average? Who wants to be average? Then the athletes chimed in with the clichés that make you want to laryngectomize them, and the exchange became a platitudinous melee. At the time, I thought Ken's assertion was stupid, and I wrote him off. But his sentence has stayed with me all these years, and I think I am finally coming to understand it.

15   Ken Harvey was gasping for air. School can be a tremendously disorienting place. No matter how bad the school, you're going to encounter notions that don't fit with the assumptions and beliefs that you grew up with—maybe you'll hear these dissonant notions from teachers, maybe from the other students, and maybe you'll read them. You'll also be thrown in with all kinds of kids from all kinds of backgrounds, and that can be unsettling—this is especially true in places of rich ethnic and linguistic mix, like the L.A. basin. You'll see a handful of students far excel you in courses that sound exotic and that are only in the curriculum of the elite: French, physics, trigonometry. And all this is happening while you're trying to shape an identity, your body is changing, and your emotions are running wild. If you're a working-class kid in the vocational track, the options you'll have to deal with will be constrained in certain ways: you're defined by your school as "slow"; you're placed in a curriculum that isn't designed to liberate you but to occupy you, or, if you're lucky, train you, though the training is for work the society does not esteem; other students are picking up the cues from your school and your curriculum and interacting with you in particular ways. If you're a kid like Ted Richard, you turn your back on all this and let your mind roam where it may. But youngsters like Ted are rare. What Ken and so many others do is protect themselves from such suffocating madness by taking on with a vengeance the identity implied in the vocational track. Reject the confusion and frustration by openly defining yourself as the Common Joe. Champion the average. Rely on your own good sense. Fuck this bullshit. Bullshit, of course, is everything you—and the others—fear is beyond you: books, essays, tests, academic scrambling, complexity, scientific reasoning, philosophical inquiry.

16   The tragedy is that you have to twist the knife in your own gray matter to make this defense work. You'll have to shut down, have to reject intellectual stimuli or diffuse them with sarcasm, have to cultivate stupidity, have to convert boredom from a malady into a way of confronting the world. Keep your vocabulary simple, act stoned when you're not or act more stoned than you are, flaunt ignorance, materialize your dreams. It is a powerful and effective defense—it neutralizes the insult and the frustration of being a vocational kid and, when perfected, it drives teachers up the wall, a delightful secondary effect. But like all strong magic, it exacts a price.

17   My own deliverance from the Voc. Ed. world began with sophomore biology. Every student, college prep to vocational, had to take biology, and unlike the other courses, the same person taught all sections. When teaching the vocational group, Brother Clint probably slowed down a bit or omitted a little of the fundamental biochemistry, but he used the same book and more or less the same syllabus across the board. If one class got tough, he could get tougher. He was young and powerful and very handsome, and looks and physical strength were high currency. No one gave him any trouble.

18   I was pretty bad at the dissecting table, but the lectures and the textbook were interesting: plastic overlays that, with each turned page, peeled away skin, then veins and muscle, then organs, down to the very bones that Brother Clint, pointer in hand, would tap out on our hanging skeleton. Dave Snyder was in big trouble, for the study of life—versus the living of it—was sticking in his craw. We worked out a code for our multiple-choice exams. He'd poke me in the back: once for the answer under *A*, twice for *B*, and so on; and when he'd hit the right one, I'd look up at the ceiling as though I were lost in

thought. Poke: cytoplasm. Poke, poke: methane. Poke, poke, poke: William Harvey. Poke, poke, poke, poke: islets of Langerhans. This didn't work out perfectly, but Dave passed the course, and I mastered the dreamy look of a guy on a record jacket. And something else happened. Brother Clint puzzled over this Voc. Ed. kid who was racking up 98s and 99s on his tests. He checked the school's records and discovered the error. He recommended that I begin my junior year in the College Prep program. According to all I've read since, such a shift, as one report put it, is virtually impossible. Kids at that level rarely cross tracks. The telling thing is how chancy both my placement into and exit from Voc. Ed. was; neither I nor my parent had anything to do with it. I lived in one world during spring semester, and when I came back to school in the fall, I was living in another.

19   Switching to College Prep was a mixed blessing. I was an erratic student. I was undisciplined. And I hadn't caught onto the rules of the game: why work hard in a class that didn't grab my fancy? I was also hopelessly behind in math. Chemistry was hard; toying with my chemistry set years before hadn't prepared me for the chemist's equations. Fortunately, the priest who taught both chemistry and second-year algebra was also the school's athletic director. Membership on the track team covered me; I knew I wouldn't get lower than a C. U. S. history was taught pretty well, and I did okay. But civics was taken over by a football coach who had trouble reading the textbook aloud—and reading aloud was the centerpiece of his pedagogy. College Prep at Mercy was certainly an improvement over the vocational program—at least it carried some status—but the social science curriculum was weak, and the mathematics and physical sciences were simply beyond me. I had a miserable quantitative background and ended up copying some assignments and finessing the rest as best I could. Let me try to explain how it feels to see again and again material you should once have learned but didn't.

20   You are given a problem. It requires you to simplify algebraic fractions or to multiply expressions containing square roots. You know this is pretty basic material because you've seen it for years. Once a teacher took some time with you, and you learned how to carry out these operations. Simple versions, anyway. But that was a year or two or more in the past, and these are more complex versions, and now you're not sure. And this, you keep telling yourself, is ninth- or even eighth-grade stuff.

21   Next it's a word problem. This is also old hat. The basic elements are as familiar as story characters: trains speeding so many miles per hour or shadows of buildings angling so many degrees. Maybe you know enough, have sat through enough explanations, to be able to begin setting up the problem: "If one train is going this fast . . ." or "This shadow is really one line of a triangle. . ." Then: "Let's see . . ." "How did Jones do this?" "Hmmmm." "No." "No, that won't work." Your attention wavers. You wonder about other things: a football game, a dance, that cute new checker at the market. You try to focus on the problem again. You scribble on paper for a while, but the

tension wins out and your attention flits elsewhere. You crumple the paper and begin daydreaming to ease the frustration.

22   The particulars will vary, but in essence this is what a number of students go through, especially those in so-called remedial classes. They open their text-books and see once again the familiar and impenetrable formulas and diagrams and terms that have stumped them for years. There is no excitement here. *No* excitement. Regardless of what the teacher says, this is not a new challenge. There is, rather, embarrassment and frustration and, not surprisingly, some anger in being reminded once again of long-standing inadequacies. No wonder so many students finally attribute their difficulties to something inborn, organic: "That part of my brain just doesn't work." Given the troubling histories many of these students have, it's miraculous that any of them can lift the shroud of hopelessness sufficiently to make deliverance from these classes possible. . . .

23   Jack MacFarland couldn't have come into my life at a better time. My fa-ther was dead; and I had logged up too many years of scholastic indifference. Mr. MacFarland had a master's degree from Columbia and decided, at twenty-six, to find a little school and teach his heart out. He never took any creden-tialing courses, couldn't bear to, he said, so he had to find employment in a private system. He ended up at Our Lady of Mercy teaching five sections of senior English. He was a beatnik who was born too late. His teeth were stained, he tucked his sorry tie in between the third and fourth buttons of his shirt, and his pants were chronically wrinkled. At first, we couldn't believe this guy, thought he slept in his car. But within no time, he had us so startled with work that we didn't much worry about where he slept or if he slept at all. We wrote three or four essays a month. We read a book every two to three weeks, start-ing with the *Iliad* and ending up with Hemingway. He gave us a quiz on the reading every other day. He brought a prep school curriculum to Mercy High.

24   MacFarland's lectures were crafted, and as he delivered them he would pace the room jiggling a piece of chalk in his cupped hand, using it to scribble on the board the names of all the writers and philosophers and plays and nov-els he was weaving into his discussion. He asked questions often, raised every-thing from Zeno's paradox to the repeated last line of Frost's "Stopping by Woods on a Snowy Evening." He slowly and carefully built up our knowledge of Western intellectual history—with facts, with connections, with specula-tions. We learned about Greek philosophy, about Dante, the Elizabethan world view, the Age of Reason, existentialism. He analyzed poems with us, had us reading sections from John Ciardi's *How Does a Poem Mean?*, making a po-tentially difficult book accessible with his own explanations. We gave oral re-ports on poems Ciardi didn't cover. We imitated the styles of Conrad, Hemingway, and *Time* magazine. We wrote and talked, wrote and talked. The man immersed us in language.

25   Even MacFarland's barbs were literary. If Jim Fitzsimmons, hung over and irritable, tried to smart-ass him, he'd rejoin with a flourish that would spark the indomitable Skip Madison—who'd lost his front teeth in a hapless

tackle—to flick his tongue through the gap and opine, "good chop," drawing out the single "o" in stinging indictment. Jack MacFarland, this tobacco-stained intellectual, brandished linguistic weapons of a kind I hadn't encountered before. Here was this *egghead*, for God's sake, keeping some pretty difficult people in line. And from what I heard, Mike Dweetz and Steve Fusco and all the notorious Voc. Ed. crowd settled down as well when MacFarland took the podium. Though a lot of guys groused in the schoolyard, it just seemed that giving trouble to this particular teacher was a silly thing to do. Tomfoolery, not to mention assault, had no place in the world he was trying to create for us, and instinctively everyone knew that. If nothing else, we all recognized MacFarland's considerable intelligence and respected the hours he put into his work. It came to this: the troublemaker would look foolish rather than daring. Even Jim Fitzsimmons was reading *On the Road* and turning his incipient alcoholism to literary ends.

26   There were some lives that were already beyond Jack MacFarland's ministrations, but mine was not. I started reading again as I hadn't since elementary school. I would go into our gloomy little bedroom or sit at the dinner table while, on the television, Danny McShane was paralyzing Mr. Moto with the atomic drop, and work slowly back through *Heart of Darkness,* trying to catch the words in Conrad's sentences. I certainly was not MacFarland's best student; most of the other guys in College Prep, even my fellow slackers, had better backgrounds than I did. But I worked very hard, for MacFarland had hooked me. He tapped my old interest in reading and creating stories. He gave me a way to feel special by using my mind. And he provided a role model that wasn't shaped on physical prowess alone, and something inside me that I wasn't quite aware of responded to that. Jack MacFarland established a literacy club, to borrow a phrase of Frank Smith's, and invited me—invited all of us—to join.

27   There's been a great deal of research and speculation suggesting that the acknowledgment of school performance with extrinsic rewards—smiling faces, stars, numbers, grades—diminishes the intrinsic satisfaction children experience by engaging in reading or writing or problem solving. While it's certainly true that we've created an educational system that encourages our best and brightest to become cynical grade collectors and, in general, have developed an obsession with evaluation and assessment, I must tell you that venal though it may have been, I loved getting good grades from MacFarland. I know how subjective grades can be, but they came tucked in the back of essays like bits of scientific data, some sort of spectroscopic readout that said, objectively and publicly, that I had made something of value. I suppose I'd been mediocre for too long and enjoyed a public redefinition. And I suppose the workings of my mind, such as they were, had been private for too long. My linguistic play moved into the world; . . . these papers with their circled red B-pluses and A-minuses linked my mind to something outside it. I carried them around like a club emblem.

28   One day in the December of my senior year, Mr. MacFarland asked me where I was going to go to college. I hadn't thought much about it. Many of the students I teach today spent their last year in high school with a physics text in one hand and the Stanford catalog in the other, but I wasn't even aware of what "entrance requirements" were. My folks would say that they wanted me to go to college and be a doctor, but I don't know how seriously I ever took that; it seemed a sweet thing to say, a bit of supportive family chatter, like telling a gangly daughter she's graceful. The reality of higher education wasn't in my scheme of things: no one in the family had gone to college; only two of my uncles had completed high school. I figured I'd get a night job and go to the local junior college because I knew that Snyder and Company were going there to play ball. But I hadn't even prepared for that. When I finally said, "I don't know," MacFarland looked down at me—I was seated in his office—and said, "Listen, you can write."

29   My grades stank. I had A's in biology and a handful of B's in a few English and social science classes. All the rest were C's—or worse. MacFarland said I would do well in his class and laid down the law about doing well in the others. Still, the record for my first three years wouldn't have been acceptable to any four-year school. To nobody's surprise, I was turned down flat by USC and UCLA. But Jack MacFarland was on the case. He had received his bachelor's degree from Loyola University, so he made calls to old professors and talked to somebody in admissions and wrote me a strong letter. Loyola finally accepted me as a probationary student. I would be on trial for the first year, and if I did okay, I would be granted regular status. MacFarland also intervened to get me a loan, for I could never have afforded a private college without it. Four more years of religion classes and four more years of boys at one school, girls at another. But at least I was going to college. Amazing.

Understanding Content

1. Explain the intent of the vocational education track. Did the vocational track at Our Lady of Mercy fulfill that intent? Explain.
2. Why does Rose say that school "can be a tremendously disorienting place"?
3. How are students in vocational tracks constrained by their placement in these tracks?
4. What does Rose's placement in the vocational track and later move to the college prep track say about the educational system?
5. What kind of student was Rose while he was in the vocational track? What kind of teacher was Jack McFarland?

Considering Structure and Technique

1. Rose uses descriptive details throughout the selection. For example, in paragraph 2, he describes his teacher as "a stubby ex-lineman." In

paragraph 9 he says that Dweetz moved "quick as a spasm," and "the room felt hot and close and naked." Cite four other descriptions that you find particularly effective. Why do you like them? What do they contribute to the piece?

2. In paragraphs 12–14, Rose tells about three of this classmates: Dave, Ted, and Ken. Why does he single out these three for special mention?
3. How does Rose use examples in the selection?
4. Rose uses a great deal of informal language. For example, in paragraph 9, he says, "One day Billy lost it." However, his word choice is often formal, as well. For example, in paragraph 14, he refers to an "exchange that became a platitudinous melee." Then there are times, as in paragraph 15, that he is profane. How does this wide range of diction affect the piece?

Exploring Ideas

1. What does Rose mean when he says, "Students will float to the mark you set"?
2. "I Just Wanna Be Average" is an excerpt from Rose's book, *Lives on the Boundary*. Based on what you know from the excerpt, what do you think the book title means?
3. Do you think that the objections Rose has to "so-called remedial classes" in high school also hold true for remedial classes in college? A number of four-year colleges have eliminated remedial classes. Do you think that is a good idea? Explain your views.
4. What do you think would have happened to Rose if Jack MacFarland had not entered his life?
5. In paragraph 9, Rose refers to "the rules of the game." What rules does he mean? Give two or three of them.

Writing Workshop: Using a Quotation from the Piece as Its Title

The title "I Just Wanna Be Average" comes from the text of the selection; it is taken from paragraph 14 and underscores how significant Rose finds this comment by his high school classmate. Using a line from your writing as its title can be effective when the line stimulates interest, reflects the writing's spirit, or conveys part of the writing's message.

Writing Workshop Activity

Select an essay you wrote earlier this term and retitle it with a quotation from that essay. (As an alternative, retitle an essay from this book with a quotation.) Which title do you like better, the original or the quotation? Why?

Language Notes for Multilingual and Other Writers

"I Just Wanna Be Average" includes a number of pejorative terms for various people. Because these terms can be offensive, avoid them if you are not 100 percent sure of the effect they could have.

1. A *geek* is a carnival performer who performs disgusting acts, such as biting the heads off chickens. The term is often used as an unflattering reference to a person who doesn't fit well into a group.

   . . . me standing <u>geeky</u> in line in my baggy shorts. Paragraph 2

2. *Wop* is a pejorative term for an Italian.

   "<u>Wop</u>!" Paragraph 6

3. *Hodad* is a put-down term that surfers use for non-surfers.

   This was a dangerous miscellany: surfers and <u>hodads</u> and South-Central blacks all ablaze to the metronomic tapping of Hector Montez's pencil. Paragraph 8

4. An *egghead* is an unflattering term for a smart person or intellectual.

   Here was this <u>*egghead,*</u> for God's sake, keeping some pretty difficult people in line. Paragraph 25

5. A *slacker* is an unflattering term because it means "a lazy person."

   . . . most of the other guys in College Prep, even my fellow <u>slackers,</u> had better backgrounds than I did. Paragraph 26

From Reading to Writing

In Your Journal: Tell about the best or worst experience you had in school. Also explain how you have been affected by that experience.

With Some Classmates: Explain how school affects students' self-esteem, illustrating your points with examples from your experience and observation.

In an Essay

- In paragraph 15, Rose gives several reasons that "school can be a tremendously disorienting place." Tell about a time school was a disorienting place for you. Also explain why it was disorienting and how you were affected by the disorientation.

- Tell about a time you or someone you know "float[ed] to the mark [some-one] set" (paragraph 10).
- In paragraph 27, Rose gives his view of grades. Explain any similarities and differences between your view of grades and Rose's as well as how grades have affected you.
- Suggest one change that would improve education in the United States and argue for the adoption of that change.

Beyond the Classroom: Research the advantages and disadvantages of tracking by checking the library or Internet and interviewing teachers and administrators. Then write a paper that summarizes its chief advantages and disadvantages.

CHAPTER 10

THE POWER OF LANGUAGE: INFLUENCE OR CONSEQUENCE?

"You have it easily in your power to increase the sum total of this world's happiness now. How? By giving a few words of sincere appreciation to someone who is lonely or discouraged. Perhaps you will forget tomorrow the kind words you say today, but the recipient may cherish them over a lifetime."

Dale Carnegie

"A word after a word after a word is power."

Margaret Atwood

"Language is magic; it makes things appear and disappear."

Nicole Brossard

"Slang is a language that rolls up its sleeves, spits on its hands, and goes to work."

Carl Sandburg

Coming to an Awareness of Language
MALCOLM X

Civil rights and Black Muslim leader Malcolm X (1925–1965), whose life is chronicled in Spike Lee's 1992 movie *Malcolm X,* was imprisoned for burglary at the age of 21. In jail, he encountered the teachings of Black Muslim leader Elijah Muhammad and embraced them. Although a powerful speaker, Malcolm X had not always been good with words. As the following excerpt from his *The Autobiography of Malcolm X* (1964) reveals, he studied hard to improve his language skills.

Preview.   Open a dictionary at random to any page and count the words you do not know. Would you like to learn these words and be able to use them? If so, how do you think you could go about learning them?

Vocabulary.   If any of the following words from the selection are unfamiliar to you, study their meanings before reading.

hustling (1)   slang for making money by doing something illegal
Elijah Muhammad (1897-1975) (1)   leader of the Black Muslims 1935-1975
stir (3)   slang for prison
hype (3)   trick
articulate (8)   characterized by clear, expressive language
functional (8)   capable of operating
emulate (10)   imitate
inevitable (17)   unavoidable

I've never been one for inaction. Everything I've ever felt strongly about, I've done something about. I guess that's why, unable to do anything else, I soon began writing to people I had known in the hustling world such as Sammy the Pimp, John Hughes, the gambling house owner, the thief Jumpsteady, and several dope peddlers. I wrote them all about Allah and Islam and Mr. Elijah Muhammad. I had no idea where most of them lived. I addressed their letters in care of the Harlem or Roxbury bars and clubs where I'd known them.

2   I never got a single reply. The average hustler and criminal was too uneducated to write a letter. I have known many slick sharp-looking hustlers, who would have you think they had an interest in Wall Street; privately, they would get someone to read a letter if they received one. Besides, neither would I have replied to anyone writing me something as wild as "the white man is the devil."

3   What certainly went on the Harlem and Roxbury wires was that Detroit Red was going crazy in stir, or else he was trying some hype to shake up the warden's office.

4   During the years that I stayed in the Norfolk Prison Colony, never did any official directly say anything to me about those letters, although, of course, they all passed through the prison censorship. I'm sure, however, they monitored what I wrote to add to the files which every state and federal prison keeps on the conversion of Negro inmates by the teachings of Mr. Elijah Muhammad.

5   But at that time, I felt that the real reason was that the white man knew that he was the devil.

6   Later on, I even wrote to the Mayor of Boston, to the Governor of Massachusetts, and to Harry S. Truman. They never answered; they probably never even saw my letters. I hand-scratched to them how the white man's society was responsible for the black man's condition in this wilderness of North America.

7   It was because of my letters that I happened to stumble upon starting to acquire some kind of a homemade education.

8   I became increasingly frustrated at not being able to express what I wanted to convey in letters that I wrote, especially those to Mr. Elijah Muhammad. In the street, I had been the most articulate hustler out there—I had commanded attention when I said something. But now, trying to write simple English, I not only wasn't articulate, I wasn't even functional. How would I sound writing in slang, the way I would *say* it, something such as, "Look, daddy, let me pull your coat about a cat. Elijah Muhammad—"

9   Many who today hear me somewhere in person, or on television, or those who read something I've said, will think I went to school far beyond the eighth grade. This impression is due entirely to my prison studies.

10   It had really begun back in the Charlestown Prison, when Bimbi* made me feel envy for his stock of knowledge. Bimbi had always taken charge of any conversation he was in, and I had tried to emulate him. But every book I picked up had few sentences which didn't contain anywhere from one to nearly all of the words that might as well have been in Chinese. When I just skipped those words, of course, I really ended up with little idea of what the book said. So I had come to the Norfolk Prison Colony still going through only book-reading motions. Pretty soon, I would have quit even these motions, unless I had received the motivation that I did.

11   I saw that the best thing I could do was get hold of a dictionary—to study, to learn some words. I was lucky enough to reason also that I should try to improve my penmanship. It was sad. I couldn't even write in a straight line. It was both ideas together that moved me to request a dictionary along with some tablets and pencils from the Norfolk Prison Colony school.

12   I spent two days just riffling uncertainly through the dictionary's pages. I'd never realized so many words existed! I didn't know *which* words I needed to learn. Finally, just to start some kind of action, I began copying.

13   In my slow, painstaking, ragged handwriting, I copied into my tablet everything printed on that first page, down to the punctuation marks.

*Another inmate.

14   I believe it took me a day. Then, aloud, I read back, to myself, everything I'd written on the tablet. Over and over, aloud, to myself, I read my own hand-writing.

15   I woke up the next morning, thinking about those words—immensely proud to realize that not only had I written so much at one time, but I'd written words that I never knew were in the world. Moreover, with a little effort, I also could remember what many of these words meant. I reviewed the words whose meanings I didn't remember. Funny thing, from the dictionary's first page right now, that "aardvark" springs to mind. The dictionary had a picture of it, a long-tailed, long-eared, burrowing African mammal, which lives off ter-mites caught by sticking out its tongue as an anteater does for ants.

16   I was so fascinated that I went on—I copied the dictionary's next page. And the same experience came when I studied that. With every succeeding page, I also learned of people and places and events from history. Actually the dictionary is like a miniature encyclopedia. Finally the dictionary's A section had filled a whole tablet—and I went on into the B's. That was the way I started copying what eventually became the entire dictionary. It went a lot faster after so much practice helped me pick up handwriting speed. Between what I wrote in my tablet, and writing letters, during the rest of my time in prison I would guess I wrote a million words.

17   I suppose it was inevitable that as my word-base broadened, I could for the first time pick up a book and read and now begin to understand what the book was saying. Anyone who has read a great deal can imagine the new world that opened. Let me tell you something: from then until I left that prison, in every free moment I had, if I was not reading in the library, I was reading on my bunk. You couldn't have gotten me out of books with a wedge. Between Mr. Muhammad's teachings, my correspondence, my visitors . . . and my reading of books, months passed without my even thinking about being imprisoned. In fact, up to then, I never had been so truly free in my life.

Understanding Content

1. Why did Malcolm X begin writing letters in prison?
2. Why did Malcolm X get no response to his letters?
3. Why did Malcolm X begin studying in prison?
4. In paragraph 10, Malcolm X says that he was "going through only book-reading motions." What does he mean? How does he solve the problem?

Considering Structure and Technique

1. Paragraphs 5 and 7 are each only one sentence. Is that a problem? Why are these paragraphs so brief?
2. How are the details in "Coming to an Awareness of Language" orga-nized?

3. One way to achieve transition between paragraphs is to repeat words or forms of words. (See p. 36 for more on this point.) How is this technique used to achieve transition between paragraphs 9 and 10? Between paragraphs 11 and 12? Between paragraphs 12 and 13? Between paragraphs 16 and 17?

Exploring Ideas

1. Malcolm X distinguishes between being "articulate" and being "functional" with language. Explain that distinction. Do you think it is an important one? Why or why not?
2. In paragraph 8, Malcolm X asks how he would sound writing his letters in slang. Answer that question.
3. What do you think of the way Malcolm X went about improving his vocabulary? Would this technique work for you? Explain.
4. In the last paragraph, Malcolm X says that after he began reading, he became truly free. Explain how he could be free while he was in prison.

Writing Workshop: Using Commas with Clauses Introduced by Who *and* Which

The words *who* and *which* often introduce **clauses** (word groups with both subjects and verbs). If the clause is necessary for identifying who is referred to, then do not use commas.

Anyone <u>who has read a great deal</u> can imagine the new world that opened. Paragraph 17 [The underlined clause introduced by *who* is necessary for identifying which "anyone" can imagine, so no commas are used before and after the clause.]

I'm sure, however, they monitored what I wrote to add to the files <u>which every state and federal prison keeps on the conversion of Negro inmates by the teachings of Mr. Elijah Muhammad.</u> Paragraph 4 [The underlined clause introduced by *which* is necessary to identify which files are kept, so no comma is used before the clause.]

If the clause is not necessary for identifying something, then commas are used.

I have known many slick sharplooking hustlers, <u>who would have you think they had an interest in Wall Street.</u> . . . Paragraph 2 [The underlined clause introduced by *who* is not necessary to identify who is being referred to so a comma is used before the clause.]

The dictionary had a picture of it, a long-tailed, long-eared, burrowing African mammal, <u>which lives off termites caught by sticking out its tongue as an anteater does for ants</u>. Paragraph 15 [The clause introduced by *which* is not necessary for identifying the mammal, so a comma is used before the clause.]

Writing Workshop Activity

Compose four sentences with clauses beginning with *who* and four sentences with clauses beginning with *which*. Be sure to place commas appropriately if the clauses are not necessary for identification.

Language Notes for Multilingual and Other Writers

The **past progressive tense** allows a writer to show continuous action in the past, that is, action that was ongoing. To form the past progressive, use *was* or *were* (depending on whether the subject is singular or plural) with the present participle. A good example of the past progressive tense (underlined as a study aid) appears in this sentence from "Coming to an Awareness of Language":

What certainly went on the Harlem and Roxbury wires was that Detroit Red <u>was going</u> crazy in stir, or else he <u>was trying</u> some hype to shake up the warden's office. Paragraph 3

From Reading to Writing

In Your Journal: "Coming to an Awareness of Language" is an excerpt from *The Autobiography of Malcolm X.* Would you like to read the full book? Explain why or why not.

With Some Classmates: Read "Reading for Success" on page 404. Then write a one- to two-page dialogue between Malcolm X and Richard Rodriguez. The topic of the dialogue should be the importance of reading and language skills.

In an Essay

- Malcolm X worked hard to overcome his language limitations. Tell about a handicap, limitation, or deficiency that you have overcome. Explain what motivated you, how you solved the problem, and what effects overcoming the problem has had on you.
- Evaluate your own language skills and explain how those skills have hurt or helped you over the years.

- Malcolm X was largely self-taught. Tell about a time you taught yourself to do something. Focus on your motivation and the process you followed to teach yourself.
- In the last paragraph, Malcolm X says that even though he was in prison, he felt free. Write your own definition of freedom, concentrating on what makes you feel free and why it makes you feel that way.

Beyond the Writing Class: Research ways people can improve their vocabularies. Then write a set of instructions for students who want to improve their vocabularies.

Today's Kids Are, Like, Killing the English Language. Yeah, Right.

KIRK JOHNSON

Kirk Johnson is a reporter on the metropolitan desk of the *New York Times*. In the following piece, which first appeared in that newspaper in 1998, Johnson examines three expressions common among today's youth: "duh," "yeah right," and "like."

Preview.   Kirk Johnson is not surprised that "duh," yeah right," and "like" are commonly used by young people, for he believes the expressions are understandable outgrowths of the information age. But just how common are they? Record the number of times you hear or use these expressions in one afternoon or evening.

Vocabulary.   If any of the following words from the essay are unfamiliar to you, study their meanings before reading.

maligned (1)   injured
brahmins (1)   intellectual or social snobs
stolid (2)   unemotional
hyperbole (3)   exaggeration
archaic (4)   obsolete, outdated
Manichean (4)   the doctrine of conflict between opposites, such as light and dark
supple (5)   flexible
savvy (7)   knowing
caustic (7)   sharp
incisive (7)   penetrating
esthetic (11)   artistic
yin and yang (11)   in Chinese philosophy, the opposing forces of positive and negative
antithesis (11)   direct opposite
overwrought (11)   worked up
inert (12)   motionless
semiotics (14)   pertaining to signs or symbols
pubescence (14)   puberty
self-deprecation (17)   diminishing one's own value
paradox (21)   a seeming contradiction
binary code (21)   computer notation based on 0 and 1

As a father of two pre-teen boys, I have in the last year or so become a huge fan of the word "duh." This is a word much maligned by educators, linguistic brahmins and purists, but they are all quite wrong.

2   Duh has elegance. Duh has shades of meaning, even sophistication. Duh and its perfectly paired linguistic partner, "yeah right," are the ideal terms to usher in the millennium and the information age, and to highlight the differences from the stolid old 20th century.

3   Even my sons might stop me at this point and quash my hyperbole with a quickly dispensed, "Yeah, right, Dad." But hear me out: I have become convinced that duh and yeah right have arisen to fill a void in the language because the world has changed. Fewer questions these days can effectively be answered with yes or no, while at the same time, a tidal surge of hype and mindless blather threatens to overwhelm old-fashioned conversation. Duh and yeah right are the cure.

4   Good old yes and no were fine for their time—the archaic, black and white era of late industrialism that I was born into in the 1950's. The yes-or-no combo was hard and fast and most of all simple: It belonged to the Manichean red-or-dead mentality of the cold war, to manufacturing, to "Father Knows Best" and "It's a Wonderful Life."

5   The information-age future that my 11-year-old twins own is more complicated than yes or no. It's more subtle and supple, more loaded with content and hype and media manipulation than my childhood—or any adult's, living or dead—ever was.

6   And duh, whatever else it may be, is drenched with content. Between them, duh and yeah-right are capable of dividing all language and thought into an exquisitely differentiated universe. Every statement and every question can be positioned on a gray scale of understatement or overstatement, stupidity or insightfulness, information saturation or yawning emptiness.

7   And in an era when plain speech has become endangered by the pressures of political correctness, duh and yeah right are matchless tools of savvy, winking sarcasm and skepticism: caustic without being confrontational, incisive without being quite specific.

8   With duh, you can convey a response, throw in a whole basket full of auxiliary commentary about the question or the statement you're responding to, and insult the speaker all at once! As in this hypothetical exchange:

9   *Parent: "Good morning, son, it's a beautiful day."*

10   *Eleven-year-old boy: "Duh."*

11   And there is a kind of esthetic balance as well. Yeah-right is the yin of duh's yang, the antithesis to duh's emphatic thesis. Where duh is assertive and edgy, a perfect tool for undercutting mindless understatement or insulting repetition, yeah right is laid back, a surfer's cool kind of response to anything overweight or oversold.

12   New York, for example, is duh territory, while Los Angeles is yeah-right. Television commercials can be rendered harmless and inert by simply

saying, "yeah, right," upon their conclusion. Local television news reports are helped out with a sprinkling of well-placed duhs, at moments of stunning obviousness. And almost any politician's speech cries out for heaping helpings of both at various moments.

13   Adolescent terms like "like," by contrast, scare me to death. While I have become convinced through observation and personal experimentation that just about any adult of even modest intelligence can figure out how to use duh and yeah right properly, like is different. Like is hard. Like is, like, dangerous.

14   Marcel Danesi, a professor of linguistics and semiotics at the University of Toronto who has studied the language of youth and who coined the term "pubilect" to describe the dialect of pubescence, said he believes like is in fact altering the structure of the English language, making it more fluid in construction, more like Italian or some other Romance language than good old hard-and-fast Anglo-Saxon. Insert like in the middle of a sentence, he said, and a statement can be turned into a question, a question into an exclamation, an exclamation into a quiet meditation.

15   Consider these hypothetical expressions: "If you're having broccoli for dinner, Mr. Johnson, I'm, like, out of here!" and "I was, like, no way!" and, perhaps most startling, "He was, like, duh!"

16   In the broccoli case, like softens the sentence. It's less harsh and confrontational than saying flatly that the serving of an unpalatable vegetable would require a fleeing of the premises.

17   In the second instance, like functions as a kind of a verbal quotation mark, an announcement that what follows, "no way," is to be heard differently. The quote itself can then be loaded up with any variety. The quote itself can then be loaded up with any variety of intonation—irony, sarcasm, even self-deprecation—all depending on the delivery.

18   In the third example—"He was, like, duh!"—like becomes a crucial helping verb for duh, a verbal springboard. (Try saying the sentence without like and it becomes almost incomprensible.)

19   But like and duh and yeah right, aside from their purely linguistic virtues, are also in many ways the perfect words to convey the sense of reflected reality that is part of the age we live in. Image manipulation, superficiality, and shallow media culture are, for better or worse, the backdrop of adolescent life.

20   Adults of the yes-or-no era could perhaps grow up firm in their knowledge of what things "are," but in the Age of Duh, with images reflected back from every angle at every waking moment, kids swim in a sea of what things are "like." Distinguishing what is from what merely seems to be is a required skill of an 11-year-old today; like reflects modern life, and duh and yeah right are the tools with which such a life can be negotiated and mastered.

21   But there is a concealed paradox in the Age of Duh. The information overload on which it is based is built around the computer, and the computer is, of course, built around—that's right—the good old yes-or-no binary code: Billions of microcircuits all blinking on or off, black or white, current in or current out. Those computers were designed by minds schooled and steeped in the world of yes or no, and perhaps it is not too much of a stretch to imagine my sons' generation, shaped by the broader view of duh, finding another path: binary code with attitude. Besides, most computers I know already seem to have an attitude. Incorporating a little duh would at least give them a sense of humor.

Understanding Content

1. Why has Johnson become a fan of "duh" and "yeah right"?
2. Why are "yes" and "no" less serviceable today than they were in the 1950s?
3. Explain the difference between "duh" and "yeah right."
4. How does use of "like" reflect the context of modern life?

Considering Structure and Technique

1. In paragraph 4, Johnson characterizes the 1950s with references to politics (the cold war), a television show (*Father Knows Best*), and a movie (*It's a Wonderful Life*). Do you think these references effectively describe the decade? Why or why not?
2. Johnson chooses words carefully for precision and vividness. Notice, for example, "yawning emptiness" (paragraph 6), "matchless tools of savvy, winking sarcasm" (paragraph 7), and "moments of stunning obviousness" (paragraph 12). Cite three other examples of precise, vivid language. Why is this language so effective?
3. **Tone** refers to the writer's attitude toward the subject. For example, a writer's tone can be serious, sarcastic, angry, playful, intimate, flip, and so forth. How would you describe Johnson's tone?
4. How does Johnson make a smooth shift from his discussion of "duh" and "yeah right" to his discussion of "like"?

Exploring Ideas

1. What do you think Johnson means when he says that "plain speech has become endangered by the pressure of political correctness"?
2. Do you agree with Johnson's view about "duh" and "yeah right"? Why or why not?
3. Johnson never specifically states why the use of "like" scares him. Using evidence in the essay, try to determine why that word scares him.
4. Many people become annoyed by young people's use of "like." Why do you think that is?

Writing Workshop: Using Hypothetical Examples

A **hypothetical example** is one devised from what *could* happen, rather than what actually *did* or *does* happen. Johnson uses two hypothetical examples of speech, in paragraphs 9–10 and 15. These examples did not occur exactly as they are written, but are effective because they are plausible—they *could have occurred*. A hypothetical example must seem as if it could reasonably occur, or readers will not accept it as valid support.

Writing Workshop Activity

Write a hypothetical example to illustrate one of these statements:

- Sometimes it is better to be lucky than to be smart.
- Things are not always what they seem to be.
- Television influences our view of the world.

Language Notes for Multilingual and Other Writers

The **active voice** is used to emphasize the performer of an action, which appears as the subject of the sentence. The **passive voice** is used to emphasize the receiver of an action which appears as the subject.

> *active voice:* The child <u>hit</u> the ball. (The primary focus is on the child, who performed the action.)

> *passive voice:* The ball <u>was hit</u> by the child. (The primary focus is on the receiver of the action, which is the ball.)

Passive voice is usually used when the performer of the action is unknown or unimportant or when the author does not want to indicate who performed the action. Here are some examples of passive voice from "Today's Kids . . . ."

1. I <u>have become</u> convinced that duh and yeah right have arisen to fill a void in the language . . . Paragraph 3

2. . . . that I <u>was born</u> into in the 1950's . . . Paragraph 4

3. And duh, whatever else it may be, <u>is drenched</u> with content. Paragraph 6

4. Television commercials <u>can be rendered</u> harmless and inert by simply saying, "yeah, right," upon their conclusion. Paragraph 12

5. Local television news reports <u>are helped out</u> with a sprinkling of well-placed duhs, at moments of stunning obviousness. Paragraph 12

6. Those computers <u>were designed</u> by minds schooled and steeped in the world of yes or no . . . Paragraph 21

From Reading to Writing

In Your Journal: How often do you use "duh," "like," and "yeah right"? In what contexts are these expressions appropriate? In what contexts are they inappropriate?

With Some Classmates: Kirk Johnson says that "duh" and "yeah right" are understandable results of the information age. Discuss one or more other effects of the information age.

In an Essay

- In paragraph 4, Johnson describes the 1950s by referring to a political event (the cold war), a television show (*Father Knows Best*), and a movie (*It's a Wonderful Life*). Select a decade you have lived through and name one or more events, movies, fads, and so on that help define or describe it. You can draw on the media, trends, books, political events, economic events, inventions, discoveries, or anything else you think is appropriate. Be sure to explain why aspects of the decade you choose to define or describe the decade so well.
- Select a common expression (slang or otherwise) and, like Johnson, evaluate either its linguistic strengths or its linguistic weaknesses.
- In paragraph 19, Johnson says that "duh," "yeah right," and "like" "convey the sense of reflected reality that is part of the age we live in." Explain to what extent we live in an age of reflected reality, and cite examples to illustrate your view.

Beyond the Writing Class: Johnson says we must separate reality from "what merely seems to be." Research virtual reality and report on one or more of its more significant applications. (See also "Stepping through a Computer Screen, Disabled Veterans Savor Freedom" on p. 238.)

Mother Tongue
AMY TAN

Amy Tan has been a language development consultant to programs serving developmentally disabled children and a freelance business writer. Her first work of fiction was the best-selling *The Joy Luck Club* (1989). It was followed by the best-selling *The Kitchen God's Wife* (1992), and *100 Secret Senses* (1999). In addition, she has written stories and children's books. "Mother Tongue" originally appeared in *The Threepenny Review* in 1990.

Preview. For Amy Tan, the influences of her immigrant mother's "broken" English were both positive and negative. At first ashamed of her mother's English, Tan came to embrace it and use it as only a writer can. To appreciate the reaction to the imperfect English Tan's mother spoke, assume that two people are applying for a job as a bookkeeper. One was born in this country and speaks unaccented, "perfect" English. The other was born in another country and speaks heavily accented, "broken" English. The second applicant is a better bookkeeper than the first applicant. Who do you think is likely to get the job? Why?

Vocabulary. If any of the following words from the essay are unfamiliar to you, study their meanings before reading.

evoke (2)   call up
wrought (3)   worked or shaped
transcribed (5)   wrote out
belies (7)   proves false
Forbes (7)   a magazine dealing with financial issues
Wall Street Week (7)   a television show on PBS devoted to financial matters

I am not a scholar of English or literature. I cannot give you much more than opinions on the English language and its variations in this country or others.
2   I am a writer. And by that definition, I am someone who has always loved language. I am fascinated by language in daily life. I spend a great deal of my time thinking about the power of language—the way it can evoke an emotion, a visual image, a complex idea, or a simple truth. Language is the tool of my trade. And I use them all—all the Englishes I grew up with.
3   Recently, I was made keenly aware of the different Englishes I do use. I was giving a talk to a large group of people, the same talk I had already given to half a dozen other groups. The nature of the talk was about my writing, my life, and my book *The Joy Luck Club*. The talk was going along well enough

until I remembered one major difference that made the whole talk sound wrong. My mother was in the room. And it was perhaps the first time she had heard me give a lengthy speech, using the kind of English I have never used with her. I was saying things like, "The intersection of memory upon imagination" and "There is an aspect of my fiction that relates to thus-and-thus"—a speech filled with carefully wrought grammatical phrases, burdened, it suddenly seemed to me, with nominalized forms, past perfect tenses, conditional phrases, all the forms of standard English that I had learned in school and through books, the forms of English I did not use at home with my mother.

4   Just last week, I was walking down the street with my mother, and I again found myself conscious of the English I was using, the English I do use with her. We were talking about the price of new and used furniture and I heard myself saying this: "Not waste money that way." My husband was with us as well, and he didn't notice any switch in my English. And then I realized why. It's because over the twenty years we've been together I've often used that same kind of English with him, and sometimes he even uses it with me. It has become our language of intimacy, a different sort of English that relates to family talk, the language I grew up with.

5   So you'll have some idea of what this family talk I heard sounds like, I'll quote what my mother said during a recent conversation which I videotaped and then transcribed. During this conversation, my mother was talking about a political gangster in Shanghai who had the same last name as her family's, Du, and how the gangster in his early years wanted to be adopted by her family, which was rich by comparison. Later, the gangster became more powerful, far richer than my mother's family, and one day showed up at my mother's wedding to pay his respects. Here's what she said in part:

6   "Du Yusong having business like fruit stand. Like off the street kind. he is Du like Du Zong—but not Tsung-ming Island people. The local people call putong, the river east side, he belong to that side local people. That man want to ask Du Zong father take him in like become own family. Du Zong father wasn't look down on him, but didn't take seriously, until that man big like become a mafia. Now important person, very hard to inviting him. Chinese way, came only to show respect, don't stay for dinner. Respect for making big celebration, he shows up. Mean gives lots of respect. Chinese custom. Chinese social life that way. If too important won't have to stay too long. He come to my wedding. I didn't see, I heard it. I gone to boy's side, they have YMCA dinner, Chinese age I was nineteen."

7   You should know that my mother's expressive command of English belies how much she actually understands. She reads the *Forbes* report, listens to *Wall Street Week,* converses daily with her stockbroker, reads all of Shirley MacLaine's books with ease—all kinds of things I can't begin to understand. Yet some of my friends tell me they understand 50 percent of what my mother says. Some say they understand 80 to 90 percent. Some say they understand none of it, as if she were speaking pure Chinese. But to me, my mother's English is perfectly clear, perfectly natural. It's my mother tongue. Her language, as I hear it,

is vivid, direct, full of observation and imagery. That was the language that helped shape the way I saw things, expressed things, made sense of the world.

8   Lately, I've been giving more thought to the kind of English my mother speaks. Like others, I have described it to people as "broken" or "fractured" English. But I wince when I say that. It has always bothered me that I can think of no way to describe it other than "broken," as if it were damaged and needed to be fixed, as if it lacked a certain wholeness and soundness. I've heard other terms used, "limited English," for example. But they seem just as bad, as if everything is limited, including people's perceptions of the limited English speaker.

9   I know this for a fact, because when I was growing up, my mother's "limited" English limited *my* perception of her. I was ashamed of her English. I believed that her English reflected the quality of what she had to say. That is, because she expressed them imperfectly her thoughts were imperfect. And I had plenty of empirical evidence to support me: the fact that people in department stores, at banks, and at restaurants did not take her seriously, did not give her good service, pretended not to understand her, or even acted as if they did not hear her.

10   My mother has long realized the limitations of her English as well. When I was fifteen, she used to have me call people on the phone to pretend I was she. In this guise, I was forced to ask for information or even to complain and yell at people who had been rude to her. One time it was a call to her stockbroker in New York. She had cashed out her small portfolio and it just so happened we were going to go to New York the next week, our very first trip outside California. I had to get on the phone and say in an adolescent voice that was not very convincing, "This is Mrs. Tan."

11   And my mother was standing in the back whispering loudly, "Why he don't send me check, already two weeks late. So mad he lie to me, losing my money."

12   And then I said in perfect English, "Yes, I'm getting rather concerned. You had agreed to send the check two weeks ago, but it hasn't arrived."

13   Then she began to talk more loudly. "What he want, I come to New York tell him front of his boss, you cheating me?" And I was trying to calm her down, make her be quiet, while telling the stockbroker, "I can't tolerate anymore excuses. If I don't receive the check immediately, I am going to have to speak to your manager when I'm in New York next week." And sure enough, the following week there we were in front of this astonished stockbroker, and I was sitting there red-faced and quiet, and my mother, the real Mrs. Tan, was shouting at his boss in her impeccable broken English.

14   We used a similar routine just five days ago, for a situation that was far less humorous. My mother had gone to the hospital for an appointment, to find out about a benign brain tumor a CAT scan had revealed a month ago. She said she had spoken very good English, her best English, no mistakes. Still, she said, the hospital did not apologize when they said they had lost the CAT

scan and she had come for nothing. She said they did not seem to have any sympathy when she told them she was anxious to know the exact diagnosis, since her husband and son had both died of brain tumors. She said they would not give her any more information until the next time and she would have to make another appointment for that. So she said she would not leave until the doctor called her daughter. She wouldn't budge. And when the doctor finally called her daughter, me, who spoke in perfect English—lo and behold—we had assurances the CAT scan would be found, promises that a conference call on Monday would be held, and apologies for any suffering my mother had gone through for a most regrettable mistake.

15   I think my mother's English almost had an effect on limiting my possibilities in life as well. Sociologists and linguists probably will tell you that a person's developing language skills are more influenced by peers. But I do think that the language spoken in the family, especially in immigrant families which are more insular, plays a large role in shaping the language of the child. And I believe that it affected my results on achievement tests, IQ tests, and the SAT. While my English skills were never judged as poor, compared to math, English could not be considered my strong suit. In grade school I did moderately well, getting perhaps B's, sometimes B-pluses, in English and scoring perhaps in the sixtieth or seventieth percentile on achievement tests. But those scores were not good enough to override the opinion that my true abilities lay in math and science, because in those areas I achieved A's and scored in the ninetieth percentile or higher.

16   This was understandable. Math is precise; there is only one correct answer. Whereas, for me at least, the answers on English tests were always a judgment call, a matter of opinion and personal experience. Those tests were constructed around items like fill-in-the-blank sentence completion, such as, "Even though Tom was _____ , Mary thought he was _____ ." And the correct answer always seemed to be the most bland combinations of thoughts, for example, "Even though Tom was shy, Mary thought he was charming," with the grammatical structure "even though" limiting the correct answer to some sort of semantic opposites, so you wouldn't get answers like, "Even though Tom was foolish, Mary thought he was ridiculous." Well, according to my mother, there were very few limitations as to what Tom could have been and what Mary might have thought of him. So I never did well on tests like that.

17   The same was true with word analogies, pairs of words in which you were supposed to find some sort of logical, semantic relationship—for example, "Sunset is to nightfall as _____ is to _____ ." And here you would be presented with a list of four possible pairs, one of which showed the same kind of relationship: red is to stoplight, bus is to arrival, chills is to fever, yawn is to boring. Well, I could never think that way. I knew what the tests were asking, but I could not block out of my mind the images already created by the first pair, "sunset is to nightfall"—and I would see a burst of colors against a

darkening sky, the moon rising, the lowering of a curtain of starts. And all the other pairs of words—red, bus, stoplight, boring—just threw up a mass of confusing images, making it impossible for me to sort out something as logical as saying: "A sunset precedes nightfall" is the same as "a chill precedes a fever." The only way I would have gotten that answer right would have been to imagine an associative situation, for example, my being disobedient and staying out past sunset, catching a chill at night, which turns into feverish pneumonia as punishment, which indeed did happen to me.

18   I have been thinking about all this lately, about my mother's English, about achievement tests. Because lately I've been asked, as a writer, why there are not more Asian Americans represented in American literature. Why are there few Asian Americans enrolled in creative writing programs? Why do so many Chinese students go into engineering? Well, these are broad sociological questions I can't begin to answer. But I have noticed in surveys—in fact, just last week—that Asian students, as a whole, always do significantly better on math achievement tests than in English. And this makes me think that there are other Asian-American students whose English spoken in the home might also be described as "broken" or "limited." And perhaps they also have teachers who are steering them away from writing and into math and science, which is what happened to me.

19   Fortunately, I happen to be rebellious in nature and enjoy the challenge of disproving assumptions made about me. I became an English major my first year In college, after being enrolled as pre-med. I started writing nonfiction as a freelancer the week after I was told by my former boss that writing was my worst skill and I should hone my talents toward account management.

20   But it wasn't until 1985 that I finally began to write fiction. And at first I wrote using what I thought to be wittily crafted sentences, sentences that would finally prove I had mastery over the English language. Here's an example from the first draft of a story that later made its way into *The Joy Luck Club*, but without this line: "That was my mental quandary in its nascent state." A terrible line, which I can barely pronounce.

21   Fortunately, for reasons I won't get into today, I later decided I should envision a reader for the stories I would write. And the reader I decided upon was my mother, because these were stories about mothers. So with this reader—in mind—and in fact she did read my early drafts—I began to write stories using all the Englishes I grew up with: the English I spoke to my mother, which for lack of a better term might be described as "simple"; the English she used with me, which for lack of a better term might be described as "broken"; my translation of her Chinese, which could certainly be described as "watered down"; and what I imagined to be her translation of her Chinese if she could speak in perfect English, her internal language, and for that I sought to preserve the essence, but neither an English nor a Chinese structure. I wanted to capture what language ability tests can never reveal: her intent, her passion, her imagery, the rhythms of her speech and the nature of her thoughts.

22   Apart from what any critic had to say about my writing, I knew I had succeeded where it counted when my mother finished reading my book and gave me her verdict: "So easy to read."

Understanding Content

1. What effects did the "limited" English of Amy Tan's mother have on the mother? On the daughter?
2. Why did Amy Tan's mother require her daughter to impersonate her on the telephone?
3. Tan suggests a possible explanation for the fact that Asian Americans do better in math than English. What is that explanation?
4. Why did Tan become a writer?
5. What principles of effective writing did Tan learn from her mother?

Considering Structure and Technique

1. The title of the essay includes some word play. What is it?
2. Sometimes writers use **topic sentences** to let the reader know what a paragraph is about (see p. 38). Which paragraphs begin with topic sentences? Do these topic sentences assist you as a reader? Explain.
3. In paragraph 6, Tan reproduces her mother's English. Why do you think she does this?
4. An **anecdote** is a brief story (see p. 209). Which paragraphs include anecdotes? What do those anecdotes contribute?
5. Why does Tan place quotation marks around the words "broken" and "limited" when they appear before *English*?

Exploring Ideas

1. What do you think Tan means when she refers to one variety of English she uses with her husband as "our language of intimacy . . . that relates to family talk, the language I grew up with" (paragraph 4)?
2. What does the essay suggest about how our speech affects the way we are viewed by others?
3. What do you think the essay says about the American system of education?
4. Do you agree with Tan that "'That was my mental quandary in its nascent state'" (paragraph 20) is a terrible line? Why or why not?

Writing Workshop: Considering Audience

In paragraph 3, Tan says, "Recently, I was made keenly aware of the different Englishes I do use." The truth is that we all use more than one variety of language, and the one we use at any given time depends upon who our reader or listener is, that is, upon our **audience**. For writers, audience is particularly important because the characteristics of our readers influence the kinds of words we use, the number of details we include, and the kinds of details we include. To appreciate the influence of audience, imagine yourself writing a letter to your best friend and asking for a $100 loan. Now imagine yourself writing the letter to your wealthy aunt, whom you have not seen for ten years. Think about how differently those letters would be written because of the different audiences. Effective writers keep a clear sense of audience in mind when they compose. As Amy Tan says in paragraph 21, "Fortunately, . . . I later decided I should envision a reader for the stories I would write."

Writing Workshop Activity

Form a group with two classmates and assume you are trying to raise money for your local food bank by sending letters requesting a $25 donation. One of you should write a letter to a good friend requesting a donation; this friend is a poor student with little extra money. One of you should write to a local business person who has money for charitable contributions but who gets many requests for donations. One of you should write to a person who believes the homeless get what they deserve. After writing your letters, compare them for word choice, kinds of details, and number of details. Report similarities and differences to the class with explanations of how audience affects each letter.

Language Notes for Multilingual and Other Writers

The forms of do *(do, did, does)* can be either action verbs or helping verbs. This fact is illustrated in "Mother Tongue."

1. As action verbs, these forms show activity, process, movement, or thought.

   So I never <u>did</u> well on tests like that. Paragraph 16

2. As a helping verb, these forms can provide emphasis or appear with *not* or *never* to convey a negative.

   emphasis: Recently I was made keenly aware of the different Englishes I <u>do</u> use. Paragraph 3

   negative: . . . he <u>didn't</u> notice any switch in my English. Paragraph 4

From Reading to Writing

In Your Journal: Amy Tan sometimes felt limited and embarrassed by her mother's speech. Does anything in your immediate family embarrass or limit you? Respond in one or two pages.

With Some Classmates: In her last three paragraphs, Tan says something about the qualities of effective writing. Summarize the characteristics of good writing that she refers to, and then write your own definition of good writing. Finally, attach a piece of writing—one of yours or a professional author's—that illustrates some or all of the characteristics you and Tan mention.

In an Essay

- The English spoken by Amy Tan's mother had a profound effect on the author. Pick one characteristic of one of your parents, and explain how that characteristic affects or affected you.
- Even if no one in your family speaks English as a second language, you (like Tan) still use "different Englishes." For example, you probably speak one way in the classroom, another way at home, another way with your friends, and so forth. Compare and contrast two or more of the different Englishes that you use and explain how each variety is suited to its audience.
- Reread paragraphs 8 through 12 and then explain whether or not people who do not use standard English (the variety of English taught in school) speak "broken" or "limited" English. Be sure to explain why you believe as you do. Also, go on to explain whether people who do not use standard English are at a disadvantage.
- Paragraphs 15 through 17 tell something of Tan's experience with math and English in school. Pick one of these subjects and tell of your experiences—positive or negative.
- If you speak more than one language, tell about any difficulties you experienced learning and using your second language. Have any of your experiences been similar to Tan's? If you do not speak a second language, interview someone who does and then write the essay.

Beyond the Writing Class: What point does Amy Tan make about standardized tests such as IQ tests and the SAT? Locate three or four articles on standardized tests, achievement tests, and and/or IQ tests. Summarize the authors' main points and indicate whether these authors agree or disagree with Tan. Your essay should be suitable for an education class.

For the Love of Language
GEOFFREY COWLEY

Geoffrey Cowley is a senior editor for *Newsweek*. "For the Love of Language" first appeared in a fall/winter, 2000 special edition of that magazine that focused on child development. In the piece, he reports on the social and biological forces that cause children to learn their native languages.

Preview. "For the Love of Language" describes the process by which children learn language, a process that is remarkable, if not miraculous. Test your knowledge of this process by identifying which of the following statements is true. (The right answer is in the selection.)

1. Babies begin learning language in the womb.
2. Children begin naming things when they are almost a year old.
3. The first six months of life are the most crucial for language development.

Vocabulary. If any of the following words from the selection are unfamiliar to you, study their meanings before reading.

cochlear (1)   a part of the ear
trimester (3)   a three-month period
parse (4)   to break into grammatical units
hybrids (4)   mixes
discrete (4)   separate
speaking in tongues (5)   a reference to incomprehensible speech, literally a
    form of prayer
blather (5)   chatter
analogous (5)   similar to
innate (6)   inborn, internal
mimicry (7)   imitation
syntax (7)   sentence structure
cognitive (8)   intellectual, of the mind
operant conditioning (8)   influencing behavior with rewards and
    punishments
propensity (10)   tendency
congenital (10)   occurring at birth
culpable (10)   responsible

Age is an advantage if you're trying to learn geometry or swing dancing. But language is different. Consider Paige Arbeiter. She was a 2-pound 7-ounce preemie when she earned the nickname "Little Houdini" six years ago. A day and a half after delivery, she pulled the tube off her face to breathe on her own. And she dazzled her intensive-care nurses by inching across her incubator to bang a tiny foot out the door. When Paige went home after six weeks, her parents noticed that loud noises didn't faze her. Their pediatrician told them repeatedly not to worry, but when Paige was 10 months old they took her to New York's Long Island Jewish Speech and Hearing Center for tests. The verdict: she was nearly deaf in both ears. "Most people we told said, 'Oh, you caught it so early, she'll be just fine'," her mom recalls. "But we learned we'd missed a very important period in her speech and language development." Thanks to a cochlear implant and speech therapy, the spunky 6-year-old now proudly counts to 10. But her overall proficiency remains that of a toddler.

2   Language is one of the most awesome tasks the human mind performs, and babies are uniquely poised to master it. They map meanings onto words while still sporting diapers, and they tackle grammatical analysis before learning to wield a fork. By the age of 3, most kids are generating sentences they've never heard spoken—and using them to alter the contents of other people's minds. Unfortunately, language doesn't always emerge without a hitch. As experts learn more about how kids learn to talk, they're also learning to spot disorders that can undermine the process. Impaired hearing is just one of them.

3   The journey to language begins in the womb. During the third trimester of pregnancy, many mothers notice that their babies kick and wiggle in response to music or loud noises. The sound of speech may draw a less spirited reaction, but there is little question that fetuses hear it. Researchers at New York's Columbia Presbyterian Medical Center have found that fetuses' heart rates drop predictably when their mothers speak a simple phrase ("Hello, baby"). And French scientists have gone a step further, showing that a fetus who's been hearing the same sound repeated ("babi, babi") will react to a sudden reversal of its elements ("biba, biba"). Within 96 hours of birth, babies distinguish their mother tongue from a foreign language, sucking more vigorously when they hear it spoken.

4   How does a child start to parse this river of sound into meaningful units? Simple conditioning is part of the story. Anyone bombarded by a particular language hears certain sound combinations more often than others, and babies are quick to home in on the most probable combinations. In one revealing study, a team led by University of Wisconsin psychologist Jenny Saffran familiarized 8-month-old infants with three-syllable nonsense words such as "bidaku" and "padoti" by playing them in random order on a voice synthesizer. Then the researchers reshuffled the syllables and tested the kids again. The babies easily distinguished bidaku and padoti not only from other nonwords like "dadobi" but also from hybrids like "kupado," a sequence they would have heard on the training tape whenever "bida-KU" bumped up against "PADO-ti." Long before they could attach meanings to words, these kids were processing them as discrete units—saying, in effect, "Call me 'pretty' or call me 'baby.' Just don't call me 'ty-ba.'"

5   Conversing with a child of this age, you'd never guess she harbored such thoughts. Most kids are content to coo and scream for the first six months, but during the second half of the first year, they take up speaking in tongues. They'll go on endlessly about "ma-ma-da-da" without the slightest indication that they know what they're talking about. But psychologists Roberta Michnick Golinkoff and Kathy Hirsh-Pasek observe in their new book, "How Babies Talk," such blather is a step on the road to articulate speech. "Babbling is analogous to putting a puzzle together over and over," they write. "Just as children learn a good deal about how puzzle pieces differ in small but significant ways, so do babies learn how to manipulate the pieces of sound that make up the puzzle of language." It's not just the syllables that make babbling so speechlike. It's the dead-on rhythms and the patterns of intonation. In one French study, laymen listening to recorded statements by babblers from various countries picked out the future Francophones with near-perfect accuracy.

6   Within months of their 1st birthday, most kids start attaching names to things. And whether they're learning Swahili or Swedish, they go about it in much the same way. Instead of proceeding by trial and error—unsure whether "doggie" refers to a part of a dog, to one dog in particular, or to anything with four legs—children start with a set of innate biases. They assume that labels refer to wholes instead of parts (the creature, not the tail) and to classes instead of items (all dogs, not one dog). They also figure that one name is for any class of object (if it's a dog, it's not a cow). These assumptions are not always valid—there's only one Lassie, after all, and any dog qualifies as a mammal—but they enable kids to catalog new words with breathtaking efficiency. A typical child is socking away a dozen words a day by 18 months, and may command 2,000 of them by the age of 2.

7   This is when things get interesting. A chimp with a signboard can learn to associate symbols with particular objects and actions, but toddlers do much more than that. Having acquired their words through mimicry, they start combining them—according to abstract rules that no one has taught them—to express their thoughts and feelings. Their first sentences may be crude utterances such as "Gonna cry!" or "Uppy me!" But between 24 and 30 months, kids who have never heard of a syntax usually start marrying noun phrases to verb phrases to explain who did what to whom. If they happen to speak English, they know that "man bites dog" and "dog bites man" tell different stories, despite their identical words.

8   Some scholars have argued that kids learn to form sentences just as they learn to perceive word boundaries—by listening for statistical regularities in other people's speech. Grammatical analysis doesn't require specialized cognitive software, they say; it boils down to operant conditioning. According to this argument, a baby who encounters the sentences "the boy likes apples" and "the boy likes oranges" 50 times each will learn that the words "the," "boy" and "likes" are tightly correlated in certain circumstances, whereas apples and oranges show up only 50 percent of the time. As the baby encounters more

sentences, the web of associations expands, providing more templates for original utterances.

9   But recent studies suggest there is much more to the story—that children actively seek out abstract grammatical rules. In one clever experiment, researchers led by New York University psychologist Gary Marcus presented 7-month-old infants with a language problem that couldn't be solved by operant conditioning alone. First the children spent two minutes listening to a series of three-word "sentences" such as "ga-ti-ga" and "li-na-li." The "words" varied from one sentence to the next, but the syntax didn't: any word appearing in the first position also appeared in the third. After familiarizing the children with these samples, the researchers played a different set of sentences—some obeying the A-B-A rule ("wo-fe-wo"), and some violating it ("wo-fe-fe"). The babies had never heard any of these new utterances, yet their attention patterns suggested that "wo-fe-wo" sounded familiar while the "nongrammatical" A-B-B sequences surprised them. The implication that the kids weren't merely seeking out association among "words" they'd already heard. They were spontaneously extracting the principles governing word order in general.

10   The language instinct runs so deep that even severely retarded children usually learn to talk. But this unique human propensity isn't foolproof. Any number of congenital or early-life problems—autism, hearing defects, brain lesions, social isolation—can derail language development. And an estimated 3 percent to 7 percent of children suffer from a selective, unexplained difficulty known as specific language impairment, or SLI. These kids exhibit normal hearing and intelligence, and have no other known handicaps. Yet they're late to talk, and even after they start, their facility and comprehension lag. They may say things like "I eating ice," even in grade school, and many go on to experience reading difficulties. Studies suggest the problem runs in families, but no one has identified culpable genes.

11   Unfortunately, there is no widely accepted treatment for SLI. Experts are even divided on the nature of the problem. Some suspect it's an auditory-processing disorder, in which the brain fails to distinguish properly among the brief blasts of sounds that encode language. In separate studies, neuroscientist Paula Tallal of Rutgers University and communication specialist Beverly Wright of Northwestern University have found that SLI children are less adept than their peers at picking out brief tones amid other sounds of similar frequency. Both of these researchers believe that auditory-training programs, in which children hear exaggerated versions over and over, can ease SLI by heightening phonological awareness.

12   Other experts believe SLI is at root a grammatical disorder, and their findings are equally compelling. Working with MIT cognitive scientist Kenneth Wexler, Mabel Rice of the University of Kansas has shown repeatedly that affected children, though aware of grammatical categories, share problems with certain verb forms. Most English speakers learn by the age of 3 to mark

regular verbs with "s" in the third person ("he walks"). SLI kids tend to stick with the infinitive, saying "he walk" and "she play." And auditory-processing problems are an unlikely explanation, because the same children effortlessly add "s" to nouns to form plurals. It's possible that SLI is a varied syndrome and that different researchers are charting different manifestations. But in assessing both auditory and grammatical deficits in SLI kids, researchers led by Oxford University psychologist Dorothy Bishop have found the grammatical ones far more pervasive. "It seems as if we need to look beyond auditory processing," they conclude in a preliminary report.

13   SLI may never be preventable. By contrast, the more serious language problems facing little Paige Arbeiter can often be prevented today. If a newborn's hearing impairment is diagnosed and treated within six months, says Dr. Lynn Spivak of Long Island Jewish Medical Center, the child usually develops normal speech and language on schedule. But because the critical period for language development is so brief, any delay can have major consequences. Though Paige now thrills her parents by saying words like "butterfly," she may never have an intuitive feel for syntax. When she strings words together, the results tend toward "Go outside, Paige Mommy!" Thanks in part to the 1999 Newborn and Infant Hearing Screening and Intervention Act, 34 states now offer the $25 test for all babies before they leave the hospital. It's a small price to pay for so vast a wonder as language.

Understanding Content

1. What evidence suggests that even before they are born, babies begin learning language?
2. What role does conditioning play in language learning?
3. When it comes to learning words, what can a human child do that a chimpanzee cannot?
4. Explain what specific language impairment is.

Considering Structure and Technique

1. What approach does Cowley take to the introduction? Is that approach effective? Explain.
2. In the first sentence of paragraph 5, Cowley uses the pronoun *she*. Why? What do you think of the use of the feminine pronoun here?
3. In some cases, Cowley cites both the findings and procedures of psychological experiments, yet he could have just given the findings. What is gained by also explaining the procedures?
4. To what extent is process analysis (the explanation of how something is done; see p. 354) part of "For the Love of Language"?

Exploring Ideas

1. In paragraph 2, Cowley says that "language is one of the most awesome tasks the human mind performs." What makes the task so awesome?
2. In paragraph 3, Cowley refers to "the journey to language." Is this metaphor (comparison) appropriate? Explain.
3. Paige's pediatrician wrongly told her parents not to worry about her failure to respond to sound. Should the doctor be punished in some way? Explain.
4. On the basis of what you learned in the selection about biological and sociological forces that influence language development, what recommendation would you make to expectant parents and parents of newborns?

Writing Workshop: Using a Question and Answer as a Topic Sentence

A **topic sentence** is a signpost because it tells the reader what a paragraph is about. (See p. 38.) For example, paragraph 3 opens with this sentence to indicate that the focus of the paragraph is on language development before birth: "The journey to language begins in the womb." In paragraph 4, a different approach is used; Cowley includes a question and answer to note the paragraph's focus: "How does a child start to parse this river of sound? Simple conditioning is part of the story." The question and answer indicate that the paragraph will focus on the role of conditioning in language development.

An occasional question-and-answer format can work well, but use it sparingly. Using too many questions and answers can give writing a clumsy feel.

Writing Workshop Activity

Select a paragraph in "For the Love of Language" and write a question and answer that provides the paragraph's focus.

Language Notes for Multilingual and Other Writers

The **present perfect tense** is formed with *have* or *has* and the past participle, like this:

I have grown.	She has explained.	They have complained.
You have eaten.	The child has slept.	The cars have stopped.
He has explained.	We have traveled.	

The present perfect tense can be used to show action that began in the past and continues to have an effect in the present. This use of the present perfect tense is illustrated in "For the Love of Language." (The present perfect tense forms are underlined as a study aid.)

1. Researchers at New York's Columbia Presbyterian Medical Center <u>have found</u> that fetuses' heart rates drop predicatably when their mothers speak a simple phrase ("Hello, baby"). Paragraph 3
2. And French scientists <u>have gone</u> a step further. . . . Paragraph 3
3. . . . kids who <u>have</u> never <u>heard</u> of a syntax usually start marrying noun phrases to verb phrases to explain who did what to whom. Paragraph 7
4. . . . Mabel Rice of the University of Kansas <u>has shown</u> repeatedly that affected children . . . share problems with certain verb forms. Paragraph 12

From Reading to Writing

In Your Journal: How important is research in language learning and language development? Do you think the government should fund additional studies? Why or why not?

With Some Classmates: Write a script for a televised public service announcement to be broadcast in states that do not perform hearing screening tests on newborns in hospitals. The announcement should urge parents to get their infants' hearing tested.

In an Essay

- "For the Love of Language" makes clear that the early months of an infant's life are critical to language development. Similarly, an increasing body of evidence demonstrates the importance of a child's first year in other areas of development. What do you think the importance of this year suggests about how we should approach child care in this country?
- Cowley explains part of the process by which language is learned. Select something you know (sign language, distance running, gardening, rock climbing, jewelry-making, and so forth) and explain how to perform the process so someone can learn to do it.
- Argue for or against passage of the Newborn and Infant Hearing Screening Intervention Act in all states.

Beyond the Writing Class: Research on the Internet or in your library how parents can help their children learn language, and write up your findings in a way new parents would find helpful.

Classrooms of Babel

CONNIE LESLIE, WITH DANIEL GLICK
AND JEANNE GORDON

With increasing numbers of foreign-born students in American classrooms, schools must face the challenge of educating students who speak many different languages. In "Classrooms of Babel," which first appeared in 1991 in *Newsweek,* the authors describe some of the ways schools are meeting the challenge.

Preview. "Classrooms of Babel" points out some of the challenges that arise when nonnative speakers of English are in classes taught in English. If you are a nonnative speaker of English, write a page or two in your journal explaining what it is like to be in English-speaking classrooms. If you are a native speaker of English, explain what you think it is like for nonnative speakers of English in American schools.

Vocabulary.   If any of the following words from the essay are unfamiliar to you, study their meanings before reading.

PS 217 (1)   Public School 217 (in New York, schools are given numbers)
Urdu (1)   a language spoken in India and Pakistan
proficiency (4)   competence
bilingual (5)   able to speak two languages
Tagalog (6)   a language spoken in the Philippines
euphemism (8)   a mild expression that is substituted for an offensive one

For picture day at New York's PS 217, a neighborhood elementary school in Brooklyn, the notice to parents was translated into five languages. That was a nice gesture, but insufficient: more than 40 percent of the children are immigrants whose families speak any one of 26 languages, ranging from Armenian to Urdu.

2   At the Leroy D. Feinberg Elementary School in Miami, a science teacher starts a lesson by holding up an ice cube and asking, "Is it hot?" The point here is vocabulary. Only after the students who come from homes where English is not spoken learn the very basics will they move on to the question of just what an ice cube might be.

3   The first grade at Magnolia Elementary School in Lanham, Md., is a study in cooperation. A Korean boy who has been in the United States for almost a year quizzes two mainland Chinese girls who arrived 10 days ago. Nearby a Colombian named Julio is learning to read with the help of an American-born boy.

4   In small towns and big cities, children with names like Oswaldo, Suong, Boris or Ngam are swelling the rolls in U.S. public schools, sitting side by side with Dick and Jane. Immigration in the 1980s brought an estimated 9 million foreign-born people to the United Stares, slightly more than the great wave of 8.8 million immigrants that came between 1901 and 1910. As a consequence, at least 2 million children or 5 percent of the total kindergarten-through-12th-grade population have limited proficiency in English, according to a conservative estimate from the U.S. Department of Education. In seven states including Colorado, New Mexico, New York and Texas, 25 percent or more of the students are not native-English speakers. And all but a handful of states have at least 1,000 foreign-born youngsters. As a result, says Eugene Garcia, of the University of California, Santa Cruz, "there is no education topic of greater importance today."

5   How to teach in a Tower of Babel? Since a 1974 Supreme Court decision, immigrant children have had the right to special help in public schools. But how much? And what kind? Many districts have responded by expanding the bilingual-education programs they've been using for the past two decades. In these classes, students are taught subjects like social studies, science and math in their native language on the theory that children must develop a foundation in their mother tongue before they can learn academic subjects in a new language. Proponents say that even with bilingual education it takes between four and seven years for a nonnative to reach national norms on standardized tests of most subject material.

6   In most schools, it's not economically feasible to hire bilingual teachers unless there are 20 or more students who speak the same language m the same grade. Even then, there aren't many math, chemistry or biology teachers who can handle Vietnamese or Tagalog. In addition, critics like author and former Newton, Mass., teacher Rosalie Pedalino Porter argue that the typical bilingual programs for Spanish speakers used over the last two decades haven't worked. The clearest indication of the failure, she charges, is the high dropout rate for Hispanic children—35.8 percent compared with 14.9 percent for blacks and 12.7 percent for whites.

7   Bilingual classes aren't an option in a classroom where a dozen languages are spoken. In schools such as Elsik High in Houston and New York's PS 217, all immigrant children are mixed in ESL (English as a second language) classes on their grade level. ESL teachers give all instruction in English; their special training helps them work with kids who start out not knowing a single word. Some students remain in ESL classes for three or four years. Others move into regular classes but return to an ESL room for remedial periods.

8   Still other schools such as Houston's Hearne Elementary School use the "total immersion" method. With 104 of Hearne's 970 students speaking one of 23 languages, principal Judith Miller has encouraged all of her teachers to take ESL training so that immigrant youngsters can remain in classes with their native-English-speaking peers. "The limited-English children are able to interact with their peers better and learn social skills. They also seem much hap-

pier," says Miller. Opponents see total immersion as a euphemism for "the good old days" when non-English-speaking students sank or swam in mainstream America without special treatment.

9   **Nurturing Atmosphere.** Some schools have found that immigrant parents can be a great resource, either as volunteers or hired aides When members of New York's PS 217 Parents Association noticed that non-English-speaking families rarely made any connection with the school, they won a $10,000 grant and hired five mothers of immigrant students as outreach workers. One day each week, these women, who speak Urdu, Chinese, Russian, Haitian-Creole or Spanish, do everything from acting as interpreters at parent-teacher conferences to helping families find city services.

10   California is experimenting with "newcomer" schools that act as a one-year stopover for foreign-born children before they move on to a neighborhood school. These centers mix children of all ages in a given classroom and offer comprehensive services such as immunizations and other health care. Bellagio Road Newcomer School for grades four through eight is one of two such schools in Los Angeles. While most classrooms are Spanish bilingual, other students are taught in English. Teaching assistants who speak a variety of languages help out with translating. Principal Juliette Thompson says the aim is to provide a nurturing atmosphere for a year while the children, many of whom carry psychological scars from living in war-torn countries like El Salvador, learn some fundamentals of English. The newcomer schools seem to be working well, but they don't reach many kids. "Unfortunately," says Laurie Olsen, a project director for an advocacy group, California Tomorrow, "the real norm is far less optimistic than what you see happening in the newcomer schools."

11   A method borrowed from Canada recognizes that the problem is not one-sided. Called "two-way immersion," the program requires students to learn subject matter in both languages. Classes in the voluntary enrichment program encourage mixed groups of native speakers and English speakers to acquire new vocabulary. Public schools like PS 84 in Manhattan also use two-way immersion to attract upper-middle-class parents. Lawyer Holly Hartstone and her husband, a doctor, enrolled their 9-year-old son Adam in PS 84, where nine of the school's 25 classes are involved in voluntary Spanish two-way immersion. When Adam grows up, his parents expect that he'll live in a global community and need more than one language. These programs are catching on around the country. Two-way immersion in Japanese, which began three years ago in a Eugene, Ore., elementary school has spread to Portland, Anchorage and Detroit. And the French program at Sunset Elementary School in Coral Gables, Fla., recently received a grant from the French government.

12   **Young Yankees.** Being a stranger in a strange land is never easy. "All the English-speaking kids should learn a foreign language. Then they'd know how hard it is for us sometimes," says 17-year-old Sufyan Kabba, a Maryland high-school junior, who left Sierra Leone last year. But here they are, part of the nation's future, young Yankees who in the end must rely on the special strength of children: adaptability.

Understanding Content

1. Explain how bilingual education works. What are the chief difficulties with bilingual education?
2. Explain how ESL classes approach the challenge of teaching students who are nonnative speakers of English.
3. Explain how "total immersion" works. What is "two-way immersion"?
4. What are "newcomer schools"? What do they offer that other programs do not?

Considering Structure and Technique

1. Paragraphs 1 through 3 open the essay with three specific examples. What purpose do these examples serve?
2. Paragraph 4 includes some statistics. What do these statistics contribute to the essay?
3. In addition to the examples in paragraphs 1 through 3, the essay includes many other examples. Which paragraphs contain examples? What purpose do these examples serve?
4. Paragraph 5 includes a number of questions. What purpose do these questions serve?

Exploring Ideas

1. Explain the reference to the Tower of Babel in the title and in paragraph 5. Do you think the reference is appropriate? Why or why not?
2. The authors claim that opponents of total immersion see it "as a euphemism for 'the good old days' when non-English-speaking students sank or swam in mainstream America without special treatment" (paragraph 8). Do you think the comparison of total immersion to the "good old days" is a good one? Do you agree that allowing immigrant students to sink or swim is a good idea? Explain your views.
3. Of the approaches described in the essay, which one do you think is best? Why?
4. Where does the last sentence of the essay place responsibility for learning English and other subjects? Do you agree? Explain.

Writing Workshop: Paragraphing

In general, writers begin a new paragraph each time they begin a new idea. Sometimes, however, writers use paragraphs to set things off or break things up. That is, a writer might divide a discussion that could be one paragraph into more than one paragraph to set something off for emphasis. For example, paragraphs 1 through 3 all illustrate how schools are affected by the influx of immigrant students. These paragraphs could be combined into one. However, to emphasize the illustrations, each example is set off in its own paragraph.

Paragraphs 5 and 6 show how a writer can use paragraphs to break up a long discussion and give the reader's eyes a rest. Both paragraphs discuss bilingual education programs and, therefore, could be combined. However, the resulting paragraph would be very long and hard on the reader. Dividing the discussion into two paragraphs offers the reader a less taxing presentation.

Writing Workshop Activity

Find a piece of writing that runs five or more paragraphs, either in this text or one of your other textbooks. Identify the reason for each body paragraph: to begin a new idea, to break up a long discussion, or to provide emphasis.

Language Notes for Multilingual and Other Writers

Several idiomatic expressions appear in "Classrooms of Babel."

1. *A handful* refers to a small amount (only a small amount fits in a person's hand).

   And all but <u>a handful</u> of states have at least 1,000 foreign-born youngsters. Paragraph 4

2. *The good old days* refers to a previous time, generally remembered as better than the present. To *sink or swim* means to succeed or fail without any help. It refers to throwing someone who cannot swim into the water to learn to swim unassisted or face drowning.

   Opponents see total immersion as a euphemism for <u>"the good old days"</u> when non-English speaking students <u>sank or swam</u> in mainstream America without special treatment. Paragraph 8

3. *Catching on* means increasing in popularity.

   These programs are <u>catching on</u> around the country. Paragraph 11

From Reading to Writing

In Your Journal: In a page or so, explain what you think foreign-born students can contribute to American classrooms. Consider language, culture, experiences, and customs when you respond.

With Some Classmates: Each group member should interview a student who speaks English as a second language and get answers to the following questions:

a. Have you encountered any problems in the classroom? If so, what are they?
b. Have you been able to solve any problems you encountered? If so, how? If not, why not?
c. What support has the school provided you? The teachers? Other students? Has that support been sufficient?
d. What else can be done to provide you with support?

Using the answers to the above questions and any other information you learn, explain what it is like for multilingual students at your school. Then go on to assess whether or not the students get sufficient support and what else, if anything, should be done.

In an Essay

- Write a description of all the approaches for teaching immigrant children explained in "Classrooms of Babel." Evaluate their strengths and weaknesses and determine which approach is the best. Be sure to explain why that approach is the best.
- Describe what you think would be a good program for dealing with immigrant children in public schools. You can draw on the best features of the programs discussed in "Classrooms of Babel," along with your own ideas. Explain the benefits of your program. Also, if there would be any obstacles to implementing your program, such as cost, mention those obstacles and suggest how they might be overcome.
- In paragraph 12, the authors quote Sufyan Kabba, who states that English-speaking students should learn a foreign language. Agree or disagree with Kabba, citing specific reasons for your view.

Beyond the Writing Class: Many colleges actively work to bring in students from other countries because the diversity they provide enriches campus life. Check with your campus admissions office, office of student affairs, or multicultural student division to learn how much of your student population is from other countries. If your campus enjoys the diversity that comes from having many foreign-born students, write an article for your campus newspaper that discusses the benefits of your rich multicultural population. If your campus does not enjoy that diversity, write an article arguing that your school should do more to recruit students from other countries.

Doublespeak
WILLIAM LUTZ

English professor William Lutz has degrees in both English and law. An expert on language, he has devoted much of his career to writing about the dangers of misleading language. Lutz has been the editor of *Quarterly Review of Doublespeak,* and he has written or cowritten dozens of articles and books, including *Doublespeak: From Revenue Enhancement to Terminal Living* (1989), from which the following selection is taken.

Preview. William Lutz defines *doublespeak,* the use of language to deceive and to alter our perception of reality. Here are some examples of doublespeak from the selection. See if you can determine their meaning.

- "diagnostic misadventure of a high magnitude"
- "incontinent ordnance"
- "initiates a career alternative enhancement program"

Vocabulary. If any of the following words from the selection are unfamiliar to you, study their meanings before reading.

taboo (4) something forbidden or restricted
deprivation (6) loss
at variance (6) different from
incontinent (7) unrestrained
pretentious (9) showy, pompous
esoteric (9) understood by only a particular few
profundity (9) depth
constituted (11) composed, made
cynicism (19) distrust of people's motives

There are no potholes in the streets of Tucson, Arizona, just "pavement deficiencies." The Reagan Administration didn't propose any new taxes, just "revenue enhancement" through new "user's fees." Those aren't bums on the street, just "non-goal oriented members of society." There are no more poor people, just "fiscal underachievers." There was no robbery of an automatic teller machine, just an "unauthorized withdrawal." The patient didn't die because of medical malpractice, it was just a "diagnostic misadventure of a high magnitude." The U.S Army doesn't kill the enemy anymore, it just "services the target." And the doublespeak goes on.

2   Doublespeak is language that pretends to communicate but really doesn't. It is language that makes the bad seem good, the negative appear positive,

the unpleasant appear attractive or at least tolerable. Doublespeak is language that avoids or shifts responsibility, language that is at variance with its real or purported meaning. It is language that conceals or prevents thought; rather than extending thought, doublespeak limits it. . . .

How to Spot Doublespeak

3   How can you spot doublespeak? Most of the time you will recognize doublespeak when you see or hear it. But, if you have any doubts, you can identify doublespeak just by answering these questions: Who is saying what to whom, under what conditions and circumstances, with what intent, and with what results? Answering these questions will usually help you identify as doublespeak language that appears to be legitimate or that at first glance doesn't even appear to be doublespeak.

First Kind of Doublespeak

4   There are at least four kinds of doublespeak. The first is the euphemism, an inoffensive or positive word or phrase used to avoid a harsh, unpleasant, or distasteful reality. But a euphemism can also be a tactful word or phrase which avoids directly mentioning a painful reality, or it can be an expression used out of concern for the feelings of someone else, or to avoid directly discussing a topic subject to a social or cultural taboo.

5   When you use a euphemism because of your sensitivity for someone's feelings or out of concern for a recognized social or cultural taboo, it is not doublespeak. For example, you express your condolences that someone has "passed away" because you do not want to say to a grieving person, "I'm sorry your father is dead." When you use the euphemism "passed away," no one is misled. Moreover, the euphemism functions here not just to protect the feelings of another person, but to communicate also your concern for that person's feelings during a period of mourning. When you excuse yourself to go to the "restroom," or you mention that someone is "sleeping with" or "involved with" someone else, you do not mislead anyone about your meaning, but you do respect the social taboos about discussing bodily functions and sex in direct terms. You also indicate your sensitivity to the feelings of your audience, which is usually considered a mark of courtesy and good manners.

6   However, when a euphemism is used to mislead or deceive, it becomes doublespeak. For example, in 1984 the U.S. State Department announced that it would no longer use the word "killing" in its annual report on the status of human rights in countries around the world. Instead, it would use the phrase "unlawful or arbitrary deprivation of life," which the department claimed was more accurate. Its real purpose for using this phrase was simply to avoid discussing the embarrassing situation of government-sanctioned killings in countries that are supported by the United States and have been certified by the United States as respecting the human rights of their citizens. This use of a

euphemism constitutes doublespeak, since it is designed to mislead, to cover up the unpleasant. Its real intent is at variance with its apparent intent. It is language designed to alter our perception of reality.

7   The Pentagon, too, avoids discussing unpleasant realities when it refers to bombs and artillery shells that fall on civilian targets as "incontinent ordnance." And in 1977 the Pentagon tried to slip funding for the neutron bomb unnoticed into an appropriations bill by calling it a "radiation enhancement device."

Second Kind of Doublespeak

8   A second kind of doublespeak is jargon, the specialized language of a trade, profession, or similar group, such as that used by doctors, lawyers, engineers, educators, or car mechanics. Jargon can serve an important and useful function. Within a group, jargon functions as a kind of verbal shorthand that allows members of the group to communicate with each other clearly, efficiently, and quickly. Indeed, it is a mark of membership in the group to be able to use and understand the group's jargon.

9   But jargon, like the euphemism, can also he doublespeak. It can be—and often is—pretentious, obscure, and esoteric terminology used to give an air of profundity, authority, and prestige to speakers and their subject matter. Jargon as doublespeak often makes the simple appear complex, the ordinary profound, the obvious insightful. In this sense it is used not to express but impress. With such doublespeak, the act of smelling something becomes "organoleptic analysis," glass becomes "fused silicate," a crack in a metal support beam becomes a "discontinuity," conservative economic policies become "distributionally conservative notions."

10   Lawyers, for example, speak of an "involuntary conversion" of property when discussing the loss or destruction of property through theft, accident, or condemnation. If your house burns down or your car is stolen, you have suffered an involuntary conversion of your property. When used by lawyers in a legal situation, such jargon is a legitimate use of language, since lawyers can be expected to understand the term.

11   However, when a member of a specialized group uses its jargon to communicate with a person outside the group, and uses it knowing that the nonmember does not understand such language, then there is doublespeak. For example, on May 9, 1978, a National Airlines 727 airplane crashed while attempting to land at the Pensacola, Florida airport. Three of the fifty-two passengers aboard the airplane were killed. As a result of the crash, National made an after-tax insurance benefit of $1.7 million, or an extra 18¢ a share dividend for its stockholders. Now National Airlines had two problems: It did not want to talk about one of its airplanes crashing, and it had to account for the $1.7 million when it issued its annual report to its stockholders. National solved the problem by inserting a footnote in its annual report which explained that the $1.7 million income was due to "the involuntary conversion of a 727."

National thus acknowledged the crash of its airplane and the subsequent profit it made from the crash, without once mentioning the accident or the deaths. However, because airline officials knew that most stockholders in the company, and indeed most of the general public, were not familiar with legal jargon, the use of such jargon constituted doublespeak.

Third Kind of Doublespeak

12   A third kind of doublespeak is gobbledygook or bureaucratese. Basically, such doublespeak is simply a matter of piling on words, of overwhelming the audience with words, the bigger the words and the longer the sentences the better. Alan Greenspan, then chair of President Nixon's Council of Economic Advisors, was quoted in *The Philadelphia Inquirer* in 1974 as having testified before a Senate committee that "It is a tricky problem to find the particular calibration in timing that would be appropriate to stem the acceleration in risk premiums created by falling incomes without prematurely aborting the decline in the inflation-generated risk premiums."

13   Nor has Mr. Greenspan's language changed since then. Speaking to the meeting of the Economic Club of New York in 1988, Mr. Greenspan, now Federal Reserve chair, said, "I guess I should warn you, if I turn out to be particularly clear, you've probably misunderstood what I've said." Mr. Greenspan's doublespeak doesn't seem to have held back his career.

14   Sometimes gobbledygook may sound impressive, but when the quote is later examined in print it doesn't even make sense. During the 1988 presidential campaign, vice-presidential candidate Senator Dan Quayle explained the need for a strategic-defense initiative by saying, "Why wouldn't an enhanced deterrent, a more stable peace, a better prospect to denying the ones who enter conflict in the first place to have a reduction of offensive systems and an introduction to defense capability? I believe this is the route the country will eventually go."

15   The investigation into the Challenger disaster in 1986 revealed the doublespeak of gobbledygook and bureaucratese used by too many involved in the shuttle program. When Jesse Moore, NASA's associate administrator, was asked if the performance the shuttle program had improved with each launch or if it had remained the same, he answered, "I think our performance in terms of the liftoff performance and in terms of the orbital performance, we knew more about the envelope we were operating under, and we have been pretty accurately staying in that. And so I would say the performance has not by design drastically improved. I think we have been able to characterize the performance more as a function of our launch experience as opposed to it improving as a function of time." While this language may appear to be jargon, a close look will reveal that it is really just gobbledygook laced with jargon. But you really have to wonder if Mr. Moore had any idea what he was saying.

Fourth Kind of Doublespeak

16   The fourth kind of doublespeak is inflated language that is designed to make the ordinary seem extraordinary; to make everyday things seem impressive; to give an air of importance to people, situations, or things that would not normally be considered important; to make the simple seem complex. Often this kind of doublespeak isn't hard to spot, and it is usually pretty funny. While car mechanics may be called "automotive internists," elevator operators members of the "vertical transportation corps," used cars "pre-owned" or "experienced cars," and black-and-white television sets described as having "non-multicolor capability," you really aren't misled all that much by such language.

17   However, you may have trouble figuring out that, when Chrysler "initiates a career alternative enhancement program," it is really laying off five thousand workers; or that "negative patient care outcome" means the patient died; or that "rapid oxidation" means a fire in a nuclear power plant.

18   The doublespeak of inflated language can have serious consequences. In Pentagon doublespeak, "pre-emptive counterattack" means that American troops attacked first; "engaged the enemy on all sides" means American troops were ambushed; "backloading of augmentation personnel" means a retreat by American troops. In the doublespeak of the military, the 1983 invasion of Grenada was conducted not by the U.S. Army, Navy, Air Force, and Marines, but by the "Caribbean Peace Keeping Forces." But then, according to the Pentagon, it wasn't an invasion, it was a "predawn vertical insertion." . . .

The Dangers of Doublespeak

19   These . . . examples of doublespeak should make it clear that doublespeak is not the product of carelessness or sloppy thinking. Indeed, most doublespeak is the product of clear thinking and is carefully designed and constructed to appear to communicate when in fact it doesn't. It is language designed not to lead but mislead. It is language designed to distort reality and corrupt thought. . . . When a fire in a nuclear reactor building is called "rapid oxidation," an explosion in a nuclear power plant is called an "energetic disassembly," the illegal overthrow of a legitimate government is termed "destabilizing a government," and lies are seen as "inoperative statements," we are hearing doublespeak that attempts to avoid responsibility and make the bad seem good, the negative appear positive, something unpleasant appear attractive; and which seems to communicate but doesn't. It is language designed to alter our perception of reality and corrupt our thinking. Such language does not provide us with the tools we need to develop, advance, and preserve our culture and our civilization. Such language breeds suspicion, cynicism, distrust, and, ultimately, hostility.

Understanding Content

1. In your own words, write out a definition of *doublespeak*. Define each of the four kinds of doublespeak.
2. When is a euphemism *not* doublespeak?
3. When is jargon a form of doublespeak?
4. Why does Lutz consider doublespeak dangerous?

Considering Structure and Technique

1. How does Lutz use examples to support his points? Are the examples effective? Explain why or why not.
2. Many of Lutz's examples of doublespeak come from Alan Greenspan, the Reagan administration, the U.S army, the U.S. State Department, the Pentagon, and NASA. What can you conclude from the fact that so much doublespeak comes from such sources?
3. How does Lutz use contrast to help support his points? Is the contrast effective? Explain.
4. Lutz introduces each category of doublespeak in his classification with a topic sentence. (See p. 38 on topic sentences.) What are those topic sentences?

Exploring Ideas

1. Is there any overlap among Lutz's four categories of doublespeak? That is, could some of the same examples of doublespeak appear in more than one category? Explain.
2. Find two examples of doublespeak in a newspaper or magazine. Note what kind of doublespeak each example is.
3. Do you think high school English teachers should include lessons on recognizing doublespeak? Why or why not?
4. In his novel *1984,* which is about a totalitarian state, George Orwell devises a language called *newspeak* to control thought through language. The term *doublespeak* was coined with *newspeak* in mind. Explain why *doublespeak* is an appropriate term.

Writing Workshop: Classifying

Classifying is grouping to show the different types of something. For example, Lutz classifies the different kinds of doublespeak (euphemism, jargon, gobbledygook, and inflated language). Sometimes writers classify to inform their readers, as when a writer classifies the different kinds of computers to make the reader more knowledgeable about options that are available for purchase. Other times, writers classify in order to fully convince the reader of something, as Lutz writes to convince the reader that all doublespeak is dangerous.

When you classify, you can indicate you are doing so in a thesis, such as this one:

There are at least four kinds of doublespeak. Paragraph 4

You can also use topic sentences to introduce each category (grouping), such as these topic sentences that Lutz uses:

The first is the euphemism . . . . Paragraph 4

A second kind of doublespeak is jargon. . . . Paragraph 8

A third kind of kind of doublespeak is gobbledygook or bureaucratese. Paragraph 12

The fourth kind of doublespeak is inflated language that is designed to make the ordinary seem extraordinary. . . . Paragraph 16

Writing Workshop Activity

Pick a topic for classification from the list below.

1. ways to study for an exam
2. ways to deal with rude people
3. ways to end a relationship
4. ways to lose weight
5. ways to make friends
6. ways to write an essay

Decide what groupings should appear in the classification; then write a list of the characteristics for each grouping.

Language Notes for Multilingual and Other Writers

The **coordinating conjunctions** (*and, but, or, nor, for, so, yet*) most often join elements *within* a sentence, like this: We can eat in the dining hall, at the pizza place, <u>or</u> in my dorm room. In informal or semiformal writing, you will see these words *beginning* sentences, as in these examples from "Doublespeak":

<u>And</u> the doublespeak goes on. Paragraph 1

<u>But</u> jargon, like the euphemism, can also be doublespeak. Paragraph 9

<u>Nor</u> has Mr. Greenspan's language changed since then. Paragraph 13

You should, however, avoid starting sentences with coordinating conjunctions in most formal academic and business writing.

From Reading to Writing

In Your Journal: After reading "Doublespeak," do you think your reading and writing behaviors will change in any way? Explain.

With Some Classmates: Evaluate to what extent doublespeak is used in the academic community. You can consider such things as college catalogues, press releases, written and spoken teacher and student comments, statements made by administrators, and letters and promotional material mailed to students. Cite examples to support your view and draw a conclusion about language use and its effects in the academic environment.

In an Essay

- Lutz says that jargon is used to impress. Discuss one or more other things that people do to impress others. Cite examples and explain whether or not these practices are harmful.
- Select one advertisement or two related advertisements and explain how the language aims to mislead consumers and influence their buying behavior.
- Like Lutz, classify a particular kind of language: the language of students, the language of teachers, the language of sportscasters, the language of musicians, the language of teenagers, and so forth.

Beyond the Writing Class: Look up a recent political speech and analyze the language for examples of doublespeak. Explain how the doublespeak influences people who read or hear the speech.

Talk in the Intimate Relationship: His and Hers

DEBORAH TANNEN

Linguistics professor Deborah Tannen has extensively researched communication between the sexes. She has reported her findings on television, including the *Today* show, in newspapers, and in popular books. "Talk in the Intimate Relationship" is taken from one of those books, *That's Not What I Meant* (1986).

Preview. Some of Tannen's research, reported in the selection, is an effort to explain the friction between men and women that results from communication breakdowns. What about you? Do you find it difficult or easy to communicate with members of the opposite sex? Explain.

Vocabulary. If any of the following words from the selection are unfamiliar to you, study their meanings before reading.

incongruent (3) showing disagreement or lack of correspondence
attuned (4) sympathetic
deferential (5) respectful or courteous, as if to a superior
rife (6) frequent; widespread
adamantly (18) unyielding; inflexibly
plausible (21) believable
abashed (24) embarrassed; showing loss of self-confidence
catatonia (24) a mental illness marked by lack of movement and speech
quintessentially (25) purest in form
divergent (30) extending in different directions

Male-female conversation is cross-cultural communication. Culture is simply a network of habits and patterns gleaned from past experience, and women and men have different past experiences. From the time they're born, they're treated differently, talked to differently, and talk differently as a result. Boys and girls grow up in different worlds, even if they grow up in the same house. And as adults they travel in different worlds, reinforcing patterns established in childhood. These cultural differences include different expectations about the role of talk in relationships and how it fulfills that role. . . .

2   **He Said/She Said: His and Her Conversational Styles.** Everyone knows that as a relationship becomes long-term, its terms change. But women and men often differ in how they expect them to change. Many women feel, "After

all this time, you should know what I want without my telling you." Many men feel, "After all this time, we should be able to tell each other what we want."

3   These incongruent expectations capture one of the key differences between men and women. . . . Communication is always a matter of balancing conflicting needs for involvement and independence. Though everyone has both these needs, women often have a relatively greater need for involvement, and men a relatively greater need for independence. Being understood without saying what you mean gives a payoff in involvement, and that is why women value it so highly.

4   If you want to be understood without saying what you mean explicitly in words, you must convey meaning somewhere else—in how words are spoken, or by metamessages. Thus it stands to reason that women are often more attuned than men to the metamessages of talk. When women surmise meaning in this way, it seems mysterious to men, who call it "women's intuition" (if they think it's right) or "reading things in" (if they think it's wrong). Indeed, it could be wrong, since metamessages are not on record. And even if it is right, there is still the question of scale: How significant are the metamessages that are there?

5   . . . Metamessages are a form of indirectness. Women are more likely to be indirect, and to try to reach agreement by negotiation. Another way to understand this preference is that negotiation allows a display of solidarity, which women prefer to the display of power (even though . . . the aim may be the same—getting what you want). Unfortunately, power and solidarity are bought with the same currency: Ways of talking intended to create solidarity have the simultaneous effect of framing power differences. When they think they're being nice, women often end up appearing deferential and unsure of themselves or of what they want.

6   When styles differ, misunderstandings are always rife. As their differing styles create misunderstandings, women and men try to clear them up by talking things out. These pitfalls are compounded in talks between men and women because they have different ways of going about talking things out, and different assumptions about the significance of going about it.

7   The rest of this [discussion] illustrates these differences, explains their origins in children's patterns of play, and shows the effects when women and men talk to each other in the context of intimate relationships in our culture.

8   **Women Listen for Metamessages.** Sylvia and Harry celebrated their fiftieth wedding anniversary at a mountain resort. Some of the guests were at the resort for the whole weekend, others just for the evening of the celebration: a cocktail party followed by a sitdown dinner. The manager of the dining room approached Sylvia during dinner. "Since there's so much food tonight," he said, "and the hotel prepared a fancy dessert and everyone already ate at the cocktail party anyway, how about cutting and serving the anniversary cake at lunch tomorrow?" Sylvia asked the advice of the others at her table. All the

men agreed: "Sure, that makes sense. Save the cake for tomorrow." All the women disagreed: "No, the party is tonight. Serve the cake tonight." The men were focusing on the message: the cake as food. The women were thinking of the metamessage: Serving a special cake frames an occasion as a celebration.

9　Why are women more attuned to metamessages? Because they are more focused on involvement, that is, on relationships among people, and it is through metamessages that relationships among people are established and maintained. If you want to take the temperature and check the vital signs of a relationship, the barometers to check are its metamessages: what is said and how.

10　Everyone can see; these signals, but whether or not we pay attention to them is another matter—a matter of being sensitized. Once you are sensitized, you can't roll your antennae back in; they're stuck in the extended position.

11　When interpreting meaning, it is possible to pick up signals that weren't intentionally sent out, like an innocent flock of birds on a radar screen. The birds are there—and the signals women pick up are there—but they may not mean what the interpreter thinks they mean. For example, Maryellen looks at Larry and asks, "What's wrong?" because his brow is furrowed. Since he was only thinking about lunch, her expression of concern makes him feel under scrutiny.

12　The difference in focus on messages and metamessages can give men and women different points of view on almost any comment. Harriet complains to Morton, "Why don't you ask me how my day was?" He replies, "If you have something to tell me, tell me. Why do you have to be invited?" The reason is that she wants the metamessage of interest: evidence that he cares how her day was, regardless of whether or not she has something to tell.

13　A lot of trouble is caused between women and men by, of all things, pronouns. Women often feel hurt when their partners use "I" or "me" in a situation in which they would use "we" or "us." When Morton announces, "I think I'll go for a walk," Harriet feels specifically uninvited, though Morton later claims she would have been welcome to join him. She felt locked out by his use of "I" and his omission of an invitation: "Would you like to come?" Metamessages can be seen in what is not said as well as what is said.

14　It's difficult to straighten out such misunderstandings because each one feels convinced of the logic of his or her position and the illogic—or irresponsibility—of the other's. Harriet knows that she always asks Morton how his day was, and that she'd never announce, "I'm going for a walk," without inviting him to join her. If he talks differently to her, it must be that he feels differently. But Morton wouldn't feel unloved if Harriet didn't ask about his day, and he would feel free to ask, "Can I come along?," if she announced she was taking a walk. So he can't believe she is justified in feeling responses he knows he wouldn't have.

15　**Messages and Metamessages in Talk between . . . Grown Ups?** These processes are dramatized with chilling yet absurdly amusing authenticity in

Jules Feiffer's play *Grown Ups*. To get a closer look at what happens when men and women focus on different levels of talk in talking things out, let's look at what happens in this play.

16   Jake criticizes Louise for not responding when their daughter, Edie, called her. His comment leads to a fight even though they're both aware that this one incident is not in itself important.

17   JAKE: Look, I don't care if it's important or not, when a kid calls its mother the mother should answer.
        LOUISE: Now I'm a bad mother.
        JAKE: I didn't say that.
        LOUISE: It's in your stare.
        JAKE: Is that another thing you know? My stare?

Louise ignores Jake's message—the question of whether or not she responded when Edie called—and goes for the metamessage: his implication that she's a bad mother, which Jake insistently disclaims. When Louise explains the signals she's reacting to, Jake not only discounts them but is angered at being held accountable not for what he said but for how he looked—his stare.

18   As the play goes on, Jake and Louise replay and intensify these patterns:

        LOUISE: If I'm such a terrible mother, do you want a divorce?
        JAKE: I do not think you're a terrible mother and no, thank you, I do not want a divorce. Why is it that whenever I bring up any difference between us you ask me if I want a divorce?

The more he denies any meaning beyond the message, the more she blows it up, the more adamantly he denies it, and so on:

        JAKE: I have brought up one thing that you do with Edie that I don't think you notice that I have noticed for some time but which I have deliberately not brought up before because I had hoped you would notice it for yourself and stop doing it and also—frankly, baby, I have to say this—I knew if I brought it up we'd get into exactly the kind of circular argument we're in right now. And I wanted to avoid it. But I haven't and we're in it, so now, with your permission, I'd like to talk about it.
        LOUISE: You don't see how that puts me down?
        JAKE: What?
        LOUISE: If you think I'm so stupid why do you go on living with me?
        JAKE: *Dammit! Why can't anything ever be simple around here?!*

It can't be simple because Louise and Jake are responding to different levels of communication. As in Bateson's example of the dual-control electric blanket with crossed wires, each one intensifies the energy going to a different aspect of the problem. Jake tries to clarify his point by overelaborating it, which gives Louise further evidence that he's condescending to her, making it even less likely that she will address his point rather than his condescension.

19   What pushes Jake and Louise beyond anger to rage is their different perspectives on metamessages. His refusal to admit that his statements have implications and overtones denies her authority over her own feelings. Her attempts to interpret what he didn't say and put the metamessage into the message makes him feel she's putting words into his mouth—denying his authority over his own meaning.

20   The same thing happens when Louise tells Jake that he is being manipulated by Edie:

> LOUISE: Why don't you ever make her come to see you? Why do you always go to her?
> JAKE: You want me to play power games with a nine year old? I want her to know I'm interested in her. Someone around here has to show interest in her.
> LOUISE: You love her more than I do.
> JAKE: I didn't say that.
> LOUISE: Yes, you did.
> JAKE: You don't know how to listen. You have never learned how to listen. It's as if listening to you is a foreign language.

Again, Louise responds to his implication—this time, that he loves Edie more because he runs when she calls. And yet again, Jake cries literal meaning, denying he meant any more than he said.

21   Throughout their argument, the point to Louise is her feelings—Jake makes her feel put down—but to him the point is her actions—that she doesn't always respond when Edie calls:

> LOUISE: You talk about what I do to Edie, what do you think you do to me?
> JAKE: This is not the time to go into what we do to each other.

Since she will talk only about the metamessage, and he will talk only about the message, neither can get satisfaction from their talk, and they end up where they started—only angrier:

> JAKE: That's not the point!
> LOUISE: It's *my* point.
> JAKE: It's hopeless!
> LOUISE: Then get a divorce.

American conventional wisdom (and many of our parents and English teach-ers) tell us that meaning is conveyed by words, so men be literal about words are supported by conventional wisdom. They may not simply deny but actually miss the cues that are sent by how words are spoken. If they sense something about it, they may nonetheless discount what they sense. After all, it wasn't said. Sometimes that's a dodge—a plausible defense rather than a gut feeling. But sometimes it is a sincere conviction. Women are also likely to doubt the re-ality of what they sense. If they don't doubt it in their guts, they nonetheless may lack the arguments to support their position and thus are reduced to re-peating, "You said it. You did so." Knowing that metamessages are a real and fundamental part of communication makes it easier to understand and justify what they feel.

22   **"Talk to Me."** An article in a popular newspaper reports that one of the five most common complaints of wives about their husbands is "He doesn't lis-ten to me anymore." Another is "He doesn't talk to me anymore." Political scientist Andrew Hacker noted that lack of communication, while high on women's lists of reasons for divorce, is much less often mentioned by men. Since couples are parties to the same conversations, why are women more dis-satisfied with them than men? Because what they expect is different, as well as what they see as the significance of talk itself.

23   First, let's consider the complaint "He doesn't talk to me."

24   **The Strong Silent Type.** One of the most common stereotypes of Ameri-can men is the strong silent type. Jack Kroll, writing about Henry Fonda on the occasion of his death, used the phrases "quiet power," "abashed silences," "combustible catatonia," and "sense of power held in check." He explained that Fonda's goal was not to let anyone see "the wheels go around," not to let the "machinery" show. According to Kroll, the resulting silence was effective on stage but devastating to Fonda's family.

25   The image of a silent father is common and is often the model for the lover or husband. But what attracts us can become flypaper to which we are unhappily stuck. Many women find the strong silent type to be a lure as a lover but a lug as a husband. Nancy Schoenberger begins a poem with the lines "It was your silence that hooked me, so like my father's." Adrienne Rich refers in a poem to the "husband who is frustratingly mute." Despite the initial attrac-tion of such quintessentially male silence, it may begin to feel, to a woman in a long-term relationship, like a brick wall against which she is banging her head.

26   In addition to these images of male and female behavior—both the result and the cause of them—are differences in how women and men view the role of talk in relationships as well as how talk accomplishes its purpose. These dif-ferences have their roots in the settings in which men and women learn to have conversations among their peers growing up.

27   **Growing up Male and Female.** Children whose parents have foreign accents don't speak with accents. They learn to talk like their peers. Little girls and little boys learn how to have conversations as they learn how to pronounce words: from their playmates. Between the ages of five and fifteen, when children are learning to have conversations, they play mostly with friends of their own sex. So it's not surprising that they learn different ways of having and using conversations.

28   Anthropologists Daniel Maltz and Ruth Borker point out that boys and girls socialize differently. Little girls tend to play in small groups or, even more common, in pairs. Their social life usually centers around a best friend, and friendships are made, maintained, and broken by talk–especially "secrets." If a little girl tells her friend's secret to another little girl, she may find herself with a new best friend. The secrets themselves may or may not be important, but the fact of telling them is all-important. It's hard for newcomers to get into these tight groups, but anyone who is admitted is treated as an equal. Girls like to play cooperatively; if they can't cooperate, the group breaks up.

29   Little boys tend to play in larger groups, often outdoors, and they spend more time doing things than talking. It's easy for boys to get into the group, but not everyone is accepted as an equal. Once in the group, boys must jockey for their status in it. One of the most important ways they do this is through talk: verbal display such as telling stories and jokes, challenging and sidetracking the verbal displays of other boys, and withstanding other boys' challenges in order to maintain their own story—and status. Their talk, is often competitive talk about who is best at what.

30   **From Children to Grown Ups.** Feiffer's play is ironically named *Grown Ups* because adult men and women struggling to communicate sound like children: "You said so!" "I did not!" The reason is that when they grow up, women and men keep the divergent attitudes and habits they have learned as children—which they don't recognize as attitudes and habits but simply take for granted as ways of talking.

31   Women want their partners to be a new and improved version of a best friend. This gives them a soft spot for men who tell them secrets. As Jack Nicholson once advised a guy in a movie: "Tell her about your troubled childhood—that always gets 'em." Men expect to *do* things together and don't feel anything is missing if they don't have heart-to-heart talks all the time.

32   If they do have heart-to-heart talks, the meaning of those talks may be opposite for men and women. To many women, the relationship is working as long as they can talk things out. To many men, the relationship isn't working out if they have to keep working it over. If she keeps trying to get talks going to save the relationship, and he keeps trying to avoid them because he sees them as weakening it, then each one's efforts to preserve the relationship appear to the other as reckless endangerment.

Understanding Content

1. In your own, words, write out the thesis of "Talk in the Intimate Relationship."
2. Why does Tannen say that men and women are from different cultures?
3. Tannen says that men and women have different expectations for talk. What are those different expectations?
4. What are "metamessages"? Why are women more attuned to them than men?
5. According to Tannen, how do their different styles of talking affect communication between men and women?
6. According to Tannen, why do men and women communicate differently?

Considering Structure and Technique

1. How do paragraphs 1 through 7 function in the selection? You may have found these paragraphs more difficult to read than the rest of the selection. Why are they more difficult?
2. What purpose do the examples in paragraphs 8 through 11 serve? The ones in paragraphs 15 through 21? The ones in paragraph 24?
3. Where does cause-and-effect analysis appear in the selection? (See p. 31 on cause-and-effect analysis.)
4. For what purpose and to what audience do you think Tannen is writing?

Exploring Ideas

1. In two or three sentences, write out some advice for a couple on the eve of their wedding, advice that will help them communicate more effectively. Your advice should reflect something you learned from "Talk in the Intimate Relationship."
2. In general, how do you think the communication style of women affects them in the workplace?
3. What did you learn from the essay that you might be able to use in life? How will you use that information?
4. Would we be better off if women tried harder to communicate the way men do, or if men tried harder to communicate the way women do? Explain.

Writing Workshop: Using Examples of Varying Length

Examples help readers understand a point and help writers prove that something is true. (Examples are also discussed on pp. 31 and 329.) As "Talk in the Intimate Relationship" reveals, examples can be long, short, or of moderate length. To appreciate this fact, notice that a long example appears in paragraphs 15 through 21; short examples appear in paragraphs 12 and 24; examples of moderate length appear in paragraphs 8 and 13.

Workshop Activity

What do you think determines the length of an effective example? Give illustrations from the selection.

Language Notes for Multilingual and Other Writers

In declarative sentences, the subject (S) usually comes before the verb (V). This is called **normal word order,** and it looks like this:

    S   V

<u>Women</u> <u>are</u> more attuned to metamessages.

In questions, the verb usually comes before the subject. This is called **inverted word order,** and it looks like these examples from "Talk in the Intimate Relationship":

      V   S

Why <u>are</u> <u>women</u> more attuned to metamessages? Paragraph 9

             V   S

How significant <u>are</u> <u>the</u> <u>metamessages</u> that are there? Paragraph 4

When the verb includes a helping verb the inverted order is slightly different. The helping verb (HV) appears first, then the subject, then the main verb (MV). Here are some examples:

    HV   S   MV

"<u>Would</u> <u>you</u> <u>like</u> to come?" Paragraph 13

    HV S MV

"<u>Can</u> <u>I</u> <u>come</u> along?" Paragraph 14

From Reading to Writing

In Your Journal: How much of what Tannen says is confirmed by your own experience? Cite instances that either bear out or contradict any of the points she makes.

With Some Classmates: Tannen says that women are more attuned to metamessages than men. With one or two classmates cite examples from your own experience and observation that show that Tannen is right (or wrong).

In an Essay

- Like Tannen, select two groups of people and contrast their communication styles. For example, you could contrast the communication styles of parents and teenagers, doctors and patients, teachers and students, or Northerners and Southerners. Use examples to illustrate the different styles, and if possible, explain why the groups communicate the way they do.

- In paragraph 6, Tannen says that the different communication styles of men and women lead to frequent misunderstandings. Tell about a time when your communication style differed from someone else's, causing a misunderstanding. Explain how the communication styles differed.
- In paragraph 1, Tannen says that boys and girls grow up in different worlds. Agree or disagree with her, citing specific evidence to support your view.
- If you are from a different country, describe the ways in which communication styles in your country differ from those in the United States. Have the differences created any problems for you? As an alternative, explain any differences between the communication styles of men and women in your native country.

Beyond the Writing Class: Observe the communication styles of men and women in the classroom. Take note of any similarities and differences that you observe. Then write an essay that explains the implications of your discoveries and Tannen's findings for the teaching profession. For example, if you discover that female teachers are more likely to call on male students who sit in the back, then you can note that teachers must be careful to keep class participation evenly distributed.

⇒⇒ CONNECTING THE READINGS

1. A **literacy narrative** tells about a positive or negative experience a person has had with reading or writing, either in or out of the classroom. "Coming to an Awareness of Language" (p. 440), "Learning to Write" (p. 388), "How I Learned to Read and Write" (p. 418), "Reading for Success" (p. 404), and "Mother Tongue" (p. 452) are literacy narratives. Write a literacy narrative of your own.

2. Consider "I Just Wanna Be Average" (p. 427), "Classrooms of Babel" (p. 467), and "Reading for Success" (p. 404), along with your own experience and ideas and then discuss the best strategies for educating immigrant students who do not speak English very well.

3. "In Praise of the F Word" (p. 393), "I Just Wanna Be Average" (p. 427), and "Is That Your Final Answer" (p. 412), all deal with the problem of underprepared students. Evaluate the solutions described in each of these pieces and then argue for one of them or a different one that you propose.

4. "Doublespeak" (p. 473) and "The Truth about Our Little White Lies" (p. 10) both discuss forms of dishonesty. How common are these forms of dishonesty, and how are they different or the same? What do they say about American society?

5. In "Today's Kids . . ." (p. 446) and "Doublespeak" (p. 473), some forces that shape language are noted. In addition, the media influence language usage. Advertising slogans such as Nike's "Just Do It" are seen on T-shirts and billboards. Political "sound bites" such as "I didn't inhale" and "Read my lips, no new taxes" are repeated on the news and make their way into everyday speech. Television shows and movies make their contributions as well. Remember Clint Eastwood's, "Go ahead; make my day"? Discuss one or more media influences on language. If you like, you can limit yourself to one element of language, such as vocabulary, or one aspect of the media, such as advertisements.

6. Select any problem raised in any reading in this book and discuss whether our schools have helped create the problem, to what extent our schools are helping to solve the problem, and/or how our schools can help solve the problem.

PART 6

Viewpoints in Transition: Responding to Multiple Essays

In part 6 you will read three essays on each of two topics: bio-engineered food and stem cell research. Each group of three essays gives multiple perspectives on the topic, so after reading all three selections, you will have an overview of thinking on the issue at hand. You can then bring your reflections to bear on the writing tasks given after the third selection.

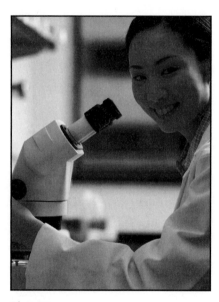

SuperStock

PhotoDisc

CHAPTER 11

BIOENGINEERED FOOD: MANNA FROM HEAVEN OR FRANKENFOOD?

"When tillage begins, other arts follow. The farmers therefore are the founders of human civilization."

Daniel Webster

"Love and business and family and religion and art and patriotism are nothing but shadows of words when a man's starving."

Maxim Gorky

"Technology made large populations possible; large populations now make technology indispensable."

Joseph Wood Krutch

"Training is everything. The peach was once a bitter almond; cauliflower is nothing but cabbage with a college education."

Mark Twain

Grains of Hope
J. MADELEINE NASH

Senior correspondent for *Time* magazine, J. Madeleine Nash specializes in science writing. She has written a number of cover stories for *Time* and received a number of awards for her writing on physics, cancer, and evolution. "Grains of Hope" first appeared in *Time* in July 2000.

Preview. Nash looks at genetically modified crops and their ability to feed starving populations—if people can agree on their safety. To appreciate the magnitude of the task of feeding the people of the world, consider that currently the world's population is over 6 billion and that figure will double before too long.

Vocabulary. If any of the following words from the selection are unfamiliar to you, study their meaning before reading.

gruel (2)   a thin porridge or cereal
formidable (4)   inspiring awe or wonder
transgenic (7)   across species
biosphere (8)   living things together with their environment
arable (11)   fit for or cultivatable by plowing
quiver (11)   the container for arrows
encumbered (16)   hampered, impaired
proprietary (16)   exclusive
affluent (16)   wealthy
hyperbole (18)   exaggeration
allergens (18)   substances that cause allergies
contaminants (19)   things that infect
fodder (20)   food
entomologist (21)   one who studies insects
encroachment (21)   attack, infringement
per se (22)   as such
ludicrous (28)   laughable
intrinsically (30)   in itself
inimical (30)   harmful
genomes (31)   sets of chromosomes with their genes

At first, the grains of rice that Ingo Potrykus sifted through his fingers did not seem at all special, but that was because they were still encased in their dark, crinkly husks. Once those drab coverings were stripped away and the interiors polished to a glossy sheen, Potrykus and his colleagues would behold the seeds' golden secret. At their core, these grains were not pearly white, as ordinary rice is, but a very pale yellow—courtesy of beta-carotene, the nutrient that serves as a building block for vitamin A.

2   Potrykus was elated. For more than a decade he had dreamed of creating such a rice: a golden rice that would improve the lives of millions of the poorest people in the world. He'd visualized peasant farmers wading into paddies to set out the tender seedlings and winnowing the grain at harvest time in handwoven baskets. He'd pictured small children consuming the golden gruel their mothers would make, knowing that it would sharpen their eyesight and strengthen their resistance to infectious diseases.

3   And he saw his rice as the first modest start of a new green revolution, in which ancient food crops would acquire all manner of useful properties: bananas that wouldn't rot on the way to market; corn that could supply its own fertilizer; wheat that could thrive in drought-ridden soil.

4   But imagining a golden rice, Potrykus soon found, was one thing and bringing one into existence quite another. Year after year, he and his colleagues ran into one unexpected obstacle after another, beginning with the finicky growing habits of the rice they transplanted to a greenhouse near the foothills of the Swiss Alps. When success finally came, in the spring of 1999, Potrykus was 65 and about to retire as a full professor at the Swiss Federal Institute of Technology in Zurich. At that point, he tackled an even more formidable challenge.

5   Having created golden rice, Potrykus wanted to make sure it reached those for whom it was intended: malnourished children of the developing world. And that, he knew, was not likely to be easy. Why? Because in addition to a full complement of genes from *Oryza sativa*—the Latin name for the most commonly consumed species of rice—the golden grains also contained snippets of DNA borrowed from bacteria and daffodils. It was what some would call Frankenfood, a product of genetic engineering. As such, it was entangled in a web of hopes and fears and political baggage, not to mention a fistful of iron-clad patents.

6   For about a year now—ever since Potrykus and his chief collaborator, Peter Beyer of the University of Freiburg in Germany, announced their achievement—their golden grain has illuminated an increasingly polarized public debate. At issue is the question of what genetically engineered crops represent. Are they, as their proponents argue, a technological leap forward that will bestow incalculable benefits on the world and its people? Or do they represent a perilous step down a slippery slope that will lead to ecological and agricultural ruin? Is genetic engineering just a more efficient way to do the business of conventional crossbreeding? Or does the ability to mix the genes of any species— even plants and animals—give man more power than he should have?

7   The debate erupted the moment genetically engineered crops made their commercial debut in the mid-1990s, and it has escalated ever since. First to launch major protests against biotechnology were European environmentalists

and consumer-advocacy groups. They were soon followed by their U.S. counterparts, who made a big splash at last fall's World Trade Organization meeting in Seattle and last week launched an offensive designed to target one company after another. . . . Over the coming months, charges that transgenic crops pose grave dangers will be raised in petitions, editorials, mass mailings and protest marches. As a result, golden rice, despite its humanitarian intent, will probably be subjected to the same kind of hostile scrutiny that has already led to curbs on the commercialization of these crops in Britain, Germany, Switzerland and Brazil.

8   The hostility is understandable. Most of the genetically engineered crops introduced so far represent minor variations on the same two themes: resistance to insect pests and to herbicides used to control the growth of weeds. And they are often marketed by large, multinational corporations that produce and sell the very agricultural chemicals farmers are spraying on their fields. So while many farmers have embraced such crops as Monsanto's Roundup Ready soybeans, with their genetically engineered resistance to Monsanto's Roundup-brand herbicide, that let them spray weed killer without harming crops, consumers have come to regard such things with mounting suspicion. Why resort to a strange new technology that might harm the biosphere, they ask, when the benefits of doing so seem small?

9   Indeed, the benefits have seemed small—until golden rice came along to suggest otherwise. Golden rice is clearly not the moral equivalent of Roundup Ready beans. Quite the contrary, it is an example—the first compelling example—of a genetically engineered crop that may benefit not just the farmers who grow it but also the consumers who eat it. In this case, the consumers include at least a million children who die every year because they are weakened by vitamin-A deficiency and an additional 350,000 who go blind.

10   No wonder the biotech industry sees golden rice as a powerful ally in its struggle to win public acceptance. No wonder its critics see it as a cynical ploy. And no wonder so many of those concerned about the twin evils of poverty and hunger look at golden rice and see reflected in it their own passionate conviction that genetically engineered crops can be made to serve the greater public good—that in fact such crops have a critical role to play in feeding a world that is about to add to its present population of 6 billion. As former President Jimmy Carter put it, "Responsible biotechnology is not the enemy; starvation is."

11   Indeed, by the year 2020, the demand for grain, both for human consumption and for animal feed, is projected to go up by nearly half, while the amount of arable land available to satisfy that demand will not only grow much more slowly but also, in some areas, will probably dwindle. Add to that the need to conserve overstressed water resources and reduce the use of polluting chemicals, and the enormity of the challenge becomes apparent. In order to meet it, believes Gordon Conway, the agricultural ecologist who heads the Rockefeller Foundation, 21st century farmers will have to draw on every arrow in their agricultural quiver, including genetic engineering. And contrary to

public perception, he says, those who have the least to lose and the most to gain are not well-fed Americans and Europeans but the hollow-bellied citizens of the developing world.

Going for the Gold

12   It was in the late 1980s, after he became a full professor of plant science at the Swiss Federal Institute of Technology, that Ingo Potrykus started to think about using genetic engineering to improve the nutritional qualities of rice. He knew that of some 3 billion people who depend on rice as their major staple, around 10% risk some degree of vitamin-A deficiency and the health problems that result. The reason, some alleged, was an overreliance on rice ushered in by the green revolution. Whatever its cause, the result was distressing: these people were so poor that they ate a few bowls of rice a day and almost nothing more.

13   The problem interested Potrykus for a number of reasons. For starters, he was attracted by the scientific challenge of transferring not just a single gene, as many had already done, but a group of genes that represented a key part of a biochemical pathway. He was also motivated by complex emotions, among them empathy. Potrykus knew more than most what it meant not to have enough to eat. As a child growing up in war-ravaged Germany, he and his brothers were often so desperately hungry that they ate what they could steal.

14   Around 1990, Potrykus hooked up with Gary Toenniessen, director of food security for the Rockefeller Foundation. Toenniessen had identified the lack of beta-carotene in polished rice grains as an appropriate target for gene scientists like Potrykus to tackle because it lay beyond the ability of traditional plant breeding to address. For while rice, like other green plants, contains light-trapping beta-carotene in its external tissues, no plant in the entire *Oryza genus*—as far as anyone knew—produced beta-carotene in its endosperm (the starchy interior part of the rice grain that is all most people eat).

15   It was at a Rockefeller-sponsored meeting that Potrykus met the University of Freiburg's Peter Beyer, an expert on the beta-carotene pathway in daffodils. By combining their expertise, the two scientists figured, they might be able to remedy this unfortunate oversight in nature. So in 1993, with some $100,000 in seed money from the Rockefeller Foundation, Potrykus and Beyer launched what turned into a seven-year, $2.6 million project, backed also by the Swiss government and the European Union. "I was in a privileged situation," reflects Potrykus, "because I was able to operate without industrial support. Only in that situation can you think of giving away your work free."

16   That indeed is what Potrykus announced he and Beyer planned to do. The two scientists soon discovered, however, that giving away golden rice was not going to be as easy as they thought. The genes they transferred and the bacteria they used to transfer those genes were all encumbered by patents and proprietary rights. Three months ago, the two scientists struck a deal with

AstraZeneca, which is based in London and holds an exclusive license to one of the genes Potrykus and Beyer used to create golden rice. In exchange for commercial marketing rights in the U.S. and other affluent markets, AstraZeneca agreed to lend its financial muscle and legal expertise to the cause of putting the seeds into the hands of poor farmers at no charge.

17   No sooner had the deal been made than the critics of agricultural biotechnology erupted. "A rip-off of the public trust," grumbled the Rural Advancement Foundation International, an advocacy group based in Winnipeg, Canada. "Asian farmers get (unproved) genetically modified rice, and AstraZeneca gets the 'gold.'" Potrykus was dismayed by such negative reaction. "It would be irresponsible," he exclaimed, "not to say immoral, *not* to use biotechnology to try to solve this problem!" But such expressions of good intentions would not be enough to allay his opponents' fears.

Weighing the Perils

18   Beneath the hyperbolic talk of Frankenfoods and Superweeds, even proponents of agricultural biotechnology agree, lie a number of real concerns. To begin with, all foods, including the transgenic foods created through genetic engineering, are potential sources of allergens. That's because the transferred genes contain instructions for making proteins, and not all proteins are equal. Some—those in peanuts, for example—are well known for causing allergic reactions. To many, the possibility that golden rice might cause such a problem seems farfetched, but it nonetheless needs to be considered.

19   Then there is the problem of "genetic pollution," as opponents of biotechnology term it. Pollen grains from such wind-pollinated plants as corn and canola, for instance, are carried far and wide. To farmers, this mainly poses a nuisance. Transgenic canola grown in one field, for example, can very easily pollinate nontransgenic plants grown in the next. Indeed this is the reason behind the furor that recently erupted in Europe when it was discovered that canola seeds from Canada—unwittingly planted by farmers in England, France, Germany and Sweden—contained transgenic contaminants.

20   The continuing flap over Bt corn and cotton—now grown not only in the U.S. but also in Argentina and China—has provided more fodder for debate. Bt stands for a common soil bacteria, *Bacillus thuringiensis,* different strains of which produce toxins that target specific insects. By transferring to corn and cotton the bacterial gene responsible for making this toxin, Monsanto and other companies have produced crops that are resistant to the European corn borer and the cotton bollworm. An immediate concern, raised by a number of ecologists, is whether or not widespread planting of these crops will spur the development of resistance to Bt among crop pests. That would be unfortunate, they point out, because Bt is a safe and effective natural insecticide that is popular with organic farmers.

21   Even more worrisome are ecological concerns. In 1999 Cornell University entomologist John Losey performed a provocative, "seat-of-the-pants"

laboratory experiment. He dusted Bt corn pollen on plants populated by monarch-butterfly caterpillars. Many of the caterpillars died. Could what happened in Losey's laboratory happen in cornfields across the Midwest? Were these lovely butterflies, already under pressure owing to human encroachment on their Mexican wintering grounds, about to face a new threat from high-tech farmers in the north?

22   The upshot: despite studies pro and con—and countless save-the-monarch protests acted out by children dressed in butterfly costumes—a conclusive answer to this question has yet to come. Losey himself is not yet convinced that Bt corn poses a grave danger to North America's monarch-butterfly population, but he does think the issue deserves attention. And others agree. "I'm not anti biotechnology per se," says biologist Rebecca Goldberg, a senior scientist with the Environmental Defense Fund, "but I would like to have a tougher regulatory regime. These crops should be subject to more careful screening before they are released."

23   Are there more potential pitfalls? There are. Among other things, there is the possibility that as transgenes in pollen drift, they will fertilize wild plants, and weeds will emerge that are hardier and even more difficult to control. No one knows how common the exchange of genes between domestic plants and their wild relatives really is, but Margaret Mellon, director of the Union of Concerned Scientists' agriculture and biotechnology program, is certainly not alone in thinking that it's high time we find out. Says she: "People should be responding to these concerns with experiments, not assurances."

24   And that is beginning to happen, although—contrary to expectations—the reports coming in are not necessarily that scary. For three years now, University of Arizona entomologist Bruce Tabashnik has been monitoring fields of Bt cotton that farmers have planted in his state. And in this instance at least, he says, "the environmental risks seem minimal, and the benefits seem great." First of all, cotton is self-pollinated, so that the spread of the Bt gene is of less concern. And because the Bt gene is so effective, he notes, Arizona farmers have reduced their use of chemical insecticides 75%. So far, the pink bollworm population has not rebounded, indicating that the feared resistance to Bt has not yet developed.

Assessing the Promise

Are the critics of agricultural biotechnology right? Is biotech's promise nothing more than overblown corporate hype? The papaya growers in Hawaii's Puna district clamor to disagree. In 1992 a wildfire epidemic of papaya ringspot virus threatened to destroy the state's papaya industry; by 1994, nearly half the state's papaya acreage had been infected, their owners forced to seek outside employment. But the help arrived, in the form of a virus-resistant transgenic papaya developed by Cornell University plant pathologist Dennis Gonsalves.

26   In 1995 a team of scientists set up a field trial of two transgenic lines— UH SunUP and UH Rainbow—and by 1996, the verdict had been rendered. As

everyone could see, the nontransgenic plants in the field trial were a stunted mess, and the transgenic plants were healthy. In 1998, after negotiations with four patent holders, the papaya growers switched en masse to the transgenic seeds and reclaimed their orchards. "Consumer acceptance has been great," reports Rusty Perry, who runs a papaya farm near Puna. "We've found that customers are more concerned with how the fruits look and taste than with whether they are transgenic or not."

27   Viral diseases, along with insect infestations, are a major cause of crop loss in Africa, observes Kenyan plant scientist Florence Wambugu. African sweet-potato fields, for example, yield only 2.4 tons per acre, vs. more than double that in the rest of the world. Soon Wambugu hopes to start raising those yields by introducing a transgenic sweet potato that is resistant to the feathery mottle virus. There really is no other option, explains Wambugu, who currently directs the International Service for the Acquisition of Agri-biotech Applications in Nairobi. "You can't control the virus in the field, and you can't breed in resistance through conventional means."

28   To Wambugu, the flap in the U.S. and Europe over genetically engineered crops seems almost ludicrous. In Africa, she notes, nearly half the fruit and vegetable harvest is lost because it rots on the way to market. "If we had a transgenic banana that ripened more slowly," she says, "we could have 40% more bananas than now." Wambugu also dreams of getting access to herbicide-resistant crops. Says she: "We could liberate so many people if our crops were resistant to herbicides that we could then spray on the surrounding weeds. Weeding enslaves Africans; it keeps children from school."

29   In Wambugu's view, there are more benefits to be derived from agricultural biotechnology in Africa than practically anywhere else on the planet—and this may be so. Among the genetic-engineering projects funded by the Rockefeller Foundation is one aimed at controlling striga, a weed that parasitizes the roots of African corn plants. At present there is little farmers can do about striga infestation, so tightly intertwined are the weed's roots with the roots of the corn plants it targets. But scientists have come to understand the source of the problem: corn roots exude chemicals that attract striga. So it may prove possible to identify the genes that are responsible and turn them off.

30   The widespread perception that agricultural biotechnology is intrinsically inimical to the environment perplexes the Rockefeller Foundation's Conway, who views genetic engineering as an important tool for achieving what he has termed a "doubly green revolution." If the technology can marshal a plant's natural defenses against weeds and viruses, if it can induce crops to flourish with minimal application of chemical fertilizers, if it can make dryland agriculture more productive without straining local water supplies, then what's wrong with it?

31   Of course, these particular breakthroughs have not happened yet. But as the genomes of major crops are ever more finely mapped, and as the tools for transferring genes become ever more precise, the possibility for tinkering with

complex biochemical pathways can be expected to expand rapidly. As Potrykus sees it, there is no question that agricultural biotechnology can be harnessed for the good of humankind. The only question is whether there is the collective will to do so. And the answer may well emerge as the people of the world weigh the future of golden rice.

Biotechnology in Agriculture
BIOTECHNOLOGY INDUSTRY ORGANIZATION

The Biotechnology Industry Organization is a trade association for organizations, businesses, and industry groups that supports many forms of biotechnology, including bioengineered food. Thus, you probably can guess the point of view of the following piece (February 2000) taken from its website.

Preview. Although the world's population continues to grow aggressively, many countries are unable to grow enough food to support their population. The Biotechnology Industry Organization believes bioengineered food can solve that problem with minimal risk.

Vocabulary. If any of the following words from the selection are unfamiliar to you, study their meanings before reading.

toxic (8)   deadly
infestation (10)   a harmful invasion or swarm
microorganism (14)   a living thing that can be seen only with a microscope
formulations (15)   formulas or preparations
prevalent (16)   common or widespread
herbicides (17)   agents that destroy plants or stop their growth
biotoxins (21)   naturally occurring poisons
allergens (25)   substances that cause allergies

Biotechnology uses advanced plant breeding techniques to introduce beneficial traits to the crops we grow for food and fiber.

2   Farmers and plant breeders have labored for centuries to improve the crops that produce our food. Traditional breeding methods include selecting and sowing the seeds from plants with beneficial characteristics, such as higher yield, better nutrition and resistance to disease. By breeding plants with these good characteristics, plant breeders combined the genetics of those plants, long before the science of genetics was understood.

3   The tools of biotechnology allow plant breeders to select genes that produce beneficial traits and move them from one plant to another. The process is far more precise and selective than traditional breeding.

4   Biotechnology also removes the technical obstacles to moving genetic traits between plants and other organisms. This opens up a world of genetic traits to benefit food production in a number of ways.

Helping to Feed the World through Biotechnology

5   In 1900, the global population was approximately 1.6 billion. Now, at the beginning of a new century, this number has surged to 6.0 billion, and the United Nations estimates that the global population will reach 10 billion by 2030. Today, 70 percent of the people on the planet grow what they eat. By 2025, the U.N. estimates that half will live in cities and need to be fed through market channels. Some estimates indicate that world food production will have to double on existing land over the next 30 years if it is to keep pace with anticipated population growth.

6   While the United States and other developed nations produce surpluses of staples like rice, corn and other grains, many countries are not self-sufficient. Often, this is because of climate or other environmental limitations that make it difficult to grow conventional crop plants. Biotechnology may make it possible to "customize" the genetic makeup of crop plants so they can grow in exceptionally dry or wet, hot or cold climates. This could make self-sustaining agriculture a reality for people in areas of the world that aren't currently able to feed their population.

7   Increased crop yield, greater flexibility in growing environments, less use of chemical pesticides and improved nutritional content make agricultural biotechnology, quite literally, the future of the world's food supply.

Environmental Benefits

8   Beyond biotechnology's agricultural and economic benefits, the industry offers great promise in increasing crop yields without greater reliance on traditional chemical pesticides. For example, proteins that are toxic only to certain insects, and harmless to all other animals and people, are produced by the Bacillus thuringiensis, or Bt, bacterium, an organism that occurs naturally in soil. By transplanting the genes that produce those proteins into crop plants, we can make the plant toxic to pests that normally feed on it. This makes it possible to reduce our reliance on chemical pesticides.

9   Other agricultural biotechnology products, like modified pulp trees for use in paper production, will allow manufacturers to use less water and other natural resources, and to produce less waste from the production stream, while producing higher-quality materials.

Building on Centuries of Science

10   Traditional agriculture has relied for centuries on crossbreeding and hybridization to improve the quality and yield of crops and to overcome natural obstacles such as plant viruses and pest infestations. Crossbreeding and hybridization involve the controlled breeding of plants and animals with desirable traits (or that lack undesirable characteristics) to produce offspring that have the best traits of the parent organisms.

11   In today's world, virtually every plant and animal grown commercially for food or other applications is a product of crossbreeding and/or hybridization. Unfortunately, these processes are often costly, time consuming, inefficient and subject to significant practical limitations. For example, producing corn with natural resistance to certain insects could take dozens of generations of traditional crossbreeding, if it is possible at all.

12   In addition, some of the other methods for controlling challenges to a plant's survival (i.e., insects, plant diseases, viruses and weeds) can currently be addressed only through the use of chemical pesticides that may harm the environment.

13   But there is another way. We can, for example, take the gene responsible for creating the substance that makes the bacteria toxic specifically to the insect and transfer it to a plant. The plant's cells take up the new genetic information as their own and produce the protein, which protects the plant from the insect without the help of externally applied pesticides.

Biopesticides

14   Several biopesticides are in use today. Biopesticide products are based on natural agents such as microorganisms and fatty acid compounds. They are toxic to targeted pests (such as the European corn borer) and do not harm humans, animals, fish, birds and beneficial insects. In addition, because biopesticides act in unique ways, they can control pest populations that have developed resistance to conventional pesticides.

15   One of the most common microorganisms used in biologically based pesticides is the Bacillus thuringiensis, or Bt, bacterium. Several of the proteins produced by the Bt bacteria are lethal to individual species of insects. By using Bt bacteria in pesticide formulations, target insects can be eliminated without relying on chemically based pesticides.

16   It is also possible to use pheromones in pest control. Pheromones are naturally occurring substances that insects produce to attract mates. In pest control, pheromones are used to attract insects away from crop plants. In recent years, for example, pheromone-based traps were used to control fruit fly infestations in California. The European corn borer, one of the most prevalent pests, costs the United States $1.2 billion in crop damage each year.

Herbicide Tolerance

17   Planting conditions good for crops will also sustain unwanted weeds that can reduce crop yield. To prevent this, herbicides are sprayed on crops. Often, herbicides must be applied several times during the growing cycle, at great expense to the farmer and possible harm to the environment.

18   Using biotechnology, it is possible to make crop plants tolerant of specific herbicides. When the herbicide is sprayed, it will kill the weeds but have no effect on the crop plants. This lets farmers reduce the number of times herbicides

have to be applied and reduces the cost of producing crops and damage to the environment.

Natural Resistance to Pests and Viruses

19 We can, today, transplant the genetic information that makes a given bacterium—such as the Bt bacterium—lethal only to a specific insect (but not to humans or animals) into plants on which that insect feeds. The plant that once was a food source for the insect now kills it. This process, which has no effect whatsoever on humans or other species, means that it becomes less necessary to spray crops with chemical pesticides to control infestations.

20 A number of products are in development that will control insects as well as conventional insecticides, thereby reducing the use of chemical products.

21 Bt technology is used to develop and specially formulate a line of biotoxin and fatty acid–based products for field testing in the poultry and livestock industries.

How Agricultural Biotech Is Regulated

22 Since combining specific genes from donor and host plants does not alter the basic nature of the host plant, the result of genetic modification is predictable and can be carefully controlled. As with any new variety of food, the developers test extensively for safety, quality and other factors.

23 U.S. regulatory policy for biotechnology products was put into place in 1986 with the publication by the White House Office of Science and Technology Policy of the "Coordinated Framework." This framework builds on the work of international expert bodies (such as the Organization for Economic Cooperation and Development [OECD] and the U.S. National Academy of Sciences). The responsibilities of regulatory agencies are clarified, linked to the laws they administer, and coordinated with other agencies that have potentially overlapping responsibilities.

24 The Food and Drug Administration (FDA) is responsible for approving the safety of all foods and new food ingredients. In addition, all producers are required to ensure the safety and quality of anything they introduce into the food supply.

25 The FDA requires strict premarket testing and regulatory oversight of genetic modifications that significantly alter the nutritional value of the host food, use genetic material from outside the traditional food supply or use known allergens.

26 The FDA also requires labeling of any genetically modified food product that significantly alters the host food's nutritional value or uses material from a known allergen. For example, any product that used a gene from a peanut, which is a potential allergen, would be subject to testing and labeling requirements. The FDA also has the authority to order unsafe products off the market.

27   The U.S. Department of Agriculture (USDA) and the Environmental Protection Agency (EPA) impose safety requirements and/or performance standards on the development of pesticides, herbicides and genetically enhanced test crops. USDA regulates to ensure that new crop varieties improved through biotechnology are at least as safe as those produced through traditional breeding programs. Rigorous assessments are conducted of material concerning the derivation of the new varieties and their performance under contained and controlled field trials. Each field trial is subjected to review for site specific safeguards. This extensive regulatory oversight has resulted in more than 5,000 field trials and commercial plantings on over 20,000 test and commercial plots in the United States alone over the past 13 years. The results of all these trials have been fully in accordance with expectations.

28   The EPA also coordinates with USDA and FDA, using its own statutes to regulate the growing of plants with pest-protection characteristics. The EPA sets allowable food residue tolerance levels for any novel compounds that might be used.

Pandora's Pantry

JON R. LUOMA

Jon R. Luoma is a contributing editor to the *New York Science Times* and *Audubon*. He has written several books, including *The Hidden Forest: The Biography of an Ecosystem* (1999). "Pandora's Pantry," which originally appeared in *Mother Jones* (January-February 2000), presents some of the arguments against bioengineered food.

Preview. Luoma describes the FDA's attitude toward bioengineered food as "wait-and-see." What do you think that means?

Vocabulary. If any of the following words from the essay are unfamiliar to you, study their meanings before reading.

discerning (1)   discriminating
moratorium (2)   time out
toxicity (11)   having the property of being poisonous or harmful
debilitating (16)   weakening and harmful
genome (19)   a chromosome with its genes
nascent (22)   beginning
sanguine (22)   hopeful
verbatim (22)   word-for-word
laissez-faire (29)   a policy of noninterference
quell (30)   subdue
juggernaut (34)   a force that crushes everything in its path

Trudy Burgess stands beside an orange-and-black bus parked in downtown Invercargill, New Zealand, urging residents to think before they eat. As people pass the eye-catching vehicle on this October day, Burgess warns them of a potential danger they probably faced over breakfast: food from plants that have been genetically altered. "The reality is that 60 percent of all processed foods are at risk," Burgess explains to a local reporter. "We want people to be more discerning when they are shopping."

2   Burgess and other activists also want to keep genetically engineered (GE) foods off the market while the New Zealand government studies the health and environmental effects of taking genes from one species and inserting them into another. So far, more than 91,000 New Zealanders have signed a petition calling for a moratorium on genetically engineered foods imported from the United States. Throughout Europe and Asia, a growing number of scientists, elected officials, and activists have sounded the alarm over bioengineered agriculture. Japan, the largest importer of American crops, is now considering

"Companies are manipulating the food supply in ways never before possible. People need to know that some of these foods could turn out to be unhealthy to eat or harmful to the environment."

13   Gene-altered crops may endanger human health in several ways. New crops could produce unexpected allergens, or chemicals that can interfere with enzymes or hormones in the body. (Disruption of hormones in a pregnant woman's body can be profoundly damaging to her offspring.) One of the most disturbing prospects is that engineered proteins from living things that humans have never consumed will end up in supermarket foods, and that some could trigger heretofore unknown health effects.

14   Some of the earliest attempts at modified foods indicate just how risky genetic tampering can be. Seed company Pioneer Hi-Bred developed a soybean containing DNA from Brazil nuts that boosted levels of the amino acid methionine, making the beans more nutritious as animal feed. Many observers were quick to endorse the new bean. "Because Brazil nuts and methionine are known to be safe," the *Washington Post* declared in 1992, "the new soybean variety might not require formal FDA approval." As it happens, the *Post's* optimism was unfounded. The company later realized that people allergic to Brazil nuts might also be allergic to the beans—some of which would have inevitably found their way into soy-based products for human consumption. In 1996, Pioneer withdrew the product.

15   Not every company has acted so quickly. Scientists are still questioning whether gene-altered bacteria used to make the dietary supplement L-tryptophan caused deadly consequences. L-tryptophan is an essential amino acid that occurs naturally in such foods as turkey and milk. It plays a crucial role in the production of the brain chemicals serotonin and melatonin, and consumers have used it as a dietary supplement to treat depression, sleep disorders, and a variety of other physical and psychological ailments. In the past, manufacturers produced it by extracting it from bacteria. But in the 1980s, a Japanese company, Showa Denko K.K., developed a method to boost production of the chemical: It inserted new genes into the bacteria, inducing them to make greater amounts of L-tryptophan.

16   In 1989, shortly after the product hit the shelves, more than 1,500 Americans became afflicted with a mysterious ailment dubbed Eosinophilia-Myalgia Syndrome, a debilitating disorder that can cause severe muscle pain, heart problems, memory defects, and paralysis. Thirty-seven people died during the outbreak. Nearly all the victims had been taking Showa Denko's L-tryptophan, which was found to contain potent traces of toxic compounds. Scientific studies were unable to prove conclusively what generated the toxins. But scientists in the United States and Canada have published analyses indicating that the genetic engineering may have boosted the concentrations of L-tryptophan produced by the bacteria, causing molecules of the compound to bond, thus producing the toxins.

17   Beyond human health concerns, genetic engineering poses potential threats to the environment. One of the biotech industry's goals is to develop

crops that are resistant to herbicides. That, in turn, would enable farmers to saturate their fields with potent herbicides, killing all the weeds but allowing the crop to survive; for the seed makers, this could lead to greater demand for their own herbicides. Monsanto, in fact, has already developed corn and soybeans that are highly resistant to its commercially successful herbicide, Roundup. After 2002, the company plans to introduce "Roundup Ready" wheat. But there's a catch: Many scientists fear that the wheat will hybridize with—and pass its herbicide tolerance to—a closely related weed called goat grass. The resulting hybrid could become what the EDF's Goldburg calls a "superweed," invulnerable even to an herbicide as powerful as Roundup.

18   Other genetically engineered crops might also cause unintended damage to ecosystems. Last year, scientists from Cornell University reported in the journal *Nature* that pollen from Bt-laced corn could escape from farm fields, settle on nearby milkweed plants, and kill the larvae of beneficial insects, such as monarch butterflies, that feed on milkweed. Though the biotech industry's leading trade group dismissed the report, the Union of Concerned Scientists and four leading environmental groups called on the EPA to restrict the planting of Bt corn and study the product's effects.

19   All of this—the threat to monarchs, the potentially allergenic Hi-Bred soybeans, the illness and death linked to tainted L-tryptophan—comes as no surprise to Dr. Richard Lacey. A professor of medical microbiology at the University of Leeds and an expert on food safety, Lacey predicted the malady that descended on Britain in the mid-1990s and came to be called "mad cow disease." "Recombinant DNA technology is an inherently risky method for producing new foods," insists Lacey. "Its risks are in large part due to the complexity and interdependency of the parts of a living system, including its DNA. Wedging foreign genetic material in an essentially random manner into an organism's genome necessarily causes some degree of disruption, and the disruption could be multifaceted."

20   The danger, adds Lacey, lies in how little we know. "It is impossible to predict what specific problems could result in the case of any particular genetically engineered organism," he says.

21   Given the potential risks—and the warnings from respected scientists—how did genetically engineered crops find their way onto farms, and then into supermarkets, with such ease? A review of the federal policymaking process, supported by testimony and documents from a lawsuit against the FDA, suggests that the political influence of the biotech industry effectively silenced government regulators charged with safeguarding the public.

22   The hands-off approach to regulation began during the Bush administration, which was eager to foster a nascent biotech industry with the potential to generate corporate profits and foreign trade. On May 21, 1992, only days before the FDA issued its permissive policy on GE foods, a top administration official weighed in. James B. MacRae Jr., assistant administrator of the Office of Management and Budget, sent a memo to White House counsel C. Boyden Gray suggesting that the policy "should avoid emphasizing obligatory FDA re-

view and oversight," and instead allow the industry to regulate itself "with informal FDA consultation only if significant safety or nutritional concerns arise." MacRae also suggested that the FDA policy "should state that newer techniques actually may produce safer foods." (The budget bureaucrat's sanguine prediction appeared, verbatim, in the final document.)

23   But the FDA did more than yield to political pressure—it also ignored the concerns of its own experts. According to internal memos and computer files uncovered during a lawsuit brought against the agency in 1998 by two public interest groups, the Alliance for Bio-Integrity and the International Center for Technology Assessment, some of the government's own scientists disagreed with its developing policy.

24   In 1992, the year the policy was issued, Dr. Louis J. Pribyl of the FDA's Microbiology Group warned in an internal memo of "a profound difference between the types of unexpected effects from traditional breeding and genetic engineering." Dr. Linda Kahl, an FDA compliance officer, concurred that plant breeding and genetic engineering are different processes, adding that "according to the technical experts in the agency, they lead to different risks."

25   In a letter written the previous October, James Maryanski, manager of the FDA's biotechnology working group, acknowledged that some scientists felt strongly that more testing was needed. "As I know you are aware," he wrote to Canadian counterparts working on a policy of their own, "there are a number of specific issues for which a scientific consensus does not exist currently, especially the need for specific toxicology tests."

26   And that December, Dr. Mitchell J. Smith, head of the Department of Health and Human Services Biological and Organic Chemistry Section, drafted a memo to the FDA urging regulators not to repeat the errors of the past: "Just because the agency failed to evaluate 'new substances' introduced by conventional breeding," Smith wrote, "gives it no reason to continue to do so now with new biotechnology."

27   But when the FDA was confronted in court with evidence of such internal opposition, the agency responded by suggesting that the comments were only from low-level employees. "The FDA has not denied in court that their scientists made those statements," says attorney Steven Druker, who directs the Iowa-based Alliance for Bio-Integrity. "They're now claiming that those were the views of a handful of 'low-level employees,' which is a misrepresentation."

28   Other testimony offered in the lawsuit indicates that some government experts had been questioning the safety of GE foods all along. Biologist Regal testified that while attending a 1988 conference in Maryland he spoke with several FDA scientists concerned about biotech crops. "I was shocked to learn the extent of uncertainty" over the safety of GE foods, he recalled. "Government scientist after scientist acknowledged there was no way to assure the safety of genetically engineered foods. Several expressed the idea that, in order to take this important step of progress, society was going to have to bear an unavoidable measure of risk."

29   Some observers expected that the Clinton administration would adopt a harder line against genetically modified foods, especially since Vice President Al Gore had taken a keen interest in the subject well before the 1992 election. In the early 1980s, then-Senator Gore had chaired a congressional subcommittee that criticized the government for inadequately assessing the risks of biotech organisms; he had again criticized the biotech industry in a 1991 law journal article. But under Clinton, the FDA has stuck to its laissez-faire policy, and the administration itself has taken up biotech promotion with gusto, leaning heavily on foreign governments to accept genetically engineered foods created by U.S. biotech giants. In 1998, for instance, the administration threatened to withdraw from a proposed trade pact if New Zealand required labeling of gene-altered foods.

30   This heavy-handed approach has failed to quell growing public suspicion of biotech products, both at home and abroad. Last August two major Japanese breweries, the Kirin Brewery Company and Sapporo Breweries, announced that they would not use gene-altered corn in their beer, and the Gerber and H. J. Heinz baby-food makers have also rejected modified ingredients. Whole Foods Market, the nations largest natural foods chain, requires suppliers of its house brands to certify that their products contain no genetically modified substances, and requests the same of all other suppliers. And soybean exporter Archer Daniels Midland has instituted a two-tiered price system, offering farmers 18 cents extra per bushel of traditional soybeans because it is having trouble selling modified soybeans overseas.

31   Public outcry has forced Congress to consider regulation. After more than 500,000 people signed a petition demanding tougher controls for gene-altered foods, a bipartisan group of 20 representatives introduced legislation in November that would require labeling of genetically engineered products. A parallel Senate bill is in development at this writing.

32   For its part, the FDA says it is already doing enough to protect the public. "We do feel that the current regulatory scheme is adequate," an FDA spokesperson told *Mother Jones*. That sentiment is echoed by Dr. Nega Beru, a consumer-safety officer in the agency's regulatory policy branch. Asked how the FDA can maintain a policy that these foods are "generally recognized as safe" when a large number of well-credentialed scientists say they do not recognize them as such, Beru responded, "We're not aware of any information that shows that these foods possess any unique health concerns, and we're not aware that these foods are any different than foods produced by traditional methods." In short, the philosophic underpinnings of the 1992 policy on GE foods still prevail.

33   Still, the FDA's spokesperson said the agency is in "listening mode," pointing to public meetings that it had planned for late 1999 in Washington, Chicago, and Oakland. The meetings, she said, were for "anyone who is interested to tell us about any new science or about ways we can better inform the public about these products." Afterward, she added, the FDA would review the comments "over some unspecified period of time."

34   Given its wait-and-see attitude—and its close ties to the industry—the FDA appears unlikely to use its authority to slow the biotech juggernaut without additional pressure from the public or Congress. "They've been holding hearings like this for 15 years," says Regal. "They spend a lot of money holding meetings, listen and take lots of notes, maybe even invite a few scientists in to be the conscience of the republic. Then nothing changes."

⇒ FROM READING TO WRITING

Drawing on One Essay

1. *"Grains of Hope."* Summarize "Grains of Hope" for someone who knows little about genetically engineered crops. Your purpose is to give that person a sense of the debate surrounding the issue of bioengineered food. (See p. 14 on summaries.)
2. *"Grains of Hope."* Agree or disagree with Ingo Potrykus's statement in paragraph 17: "It would be irresponsible, not to say immoral, *not* to use biotechnology to try to solve [the problem of hunger]."
3. *"Biotechnology in Agriculture."* Summarize the ways the federal government regulates and monitors biotechnology in the United States. Explain whether you are confident that federal agencies are adequately regulating bioengineered food.
4. *"Pandora's Box."* The Food and Drug Administration accepts public comment on matters before it. With that in mind, write a letter to the agency to voice your opinion, concerns, questions, and recommendations regarding bioengineered food.

Drawing on Two or Three Essays

5. Summarize the chief benefits and potential drawbacks of genetically engineered food and evaluate whether the benefits outweigh the drawbacks.
6. Currently, the Food and Drug Administration does not require companies to label genetically altered food as bioengineered unless the food differs significantly from its conventional counterpart. Agree or disagree with this policy.
7. Write a letter to one of your representatives or senators to express your support for or objection to bioengineered food.
8. The world population is over 6 billion and predicted to double in 50 years. Should we pursue bioengineered food as a way to feed this increasing population, which includes millions who are malnourished or starving? If not, what alternative do you suggest?

CHAPTER 12

STEM CELL RESEARCH: EXPERIMENTATION OR EXPLOITATION?

"There is no cure for birth and death save to enjoy the interval."

George Santayana

"Science without religion is lame; religion without science is blind."

Albert Einstein

"Science has nothing to be ashamed of, even in the ruins of Nagasaki."

Jacob Bronowski

"Nature is usually wrong."

James Whistler

God and Science
ARTHUR ALLEN

Arthur Allen is a staff writer for the *Washington Post,* the newspaper in which "God and Science" appeared October 15, 2000. The article presents some of the arguments on both sides of a controversial issue: using stem cells harvested from embryos for medical research. As you read, think about whether Allen gives a balanced overview.

Preview. Should scientists be permitted to engage in research that uses cells from aborted embryos—if their research holds hope for curing a number of terrible diseases? That is the issue explored in "God and Science." Why do you think the piece is titled as it is?

Vocabulary. If any of the following words from the selection are unfamiliar to you, study their meanings before reading.

spawned (1) brought forth
pirouette (3) a ballet move
replicate (3) copy exactly
template (5) a model
toxins (5) harmful or poisonous substances
regenerate (5) renew
linear (6) in a straight line
eugenic (7) related to controlling human mating to produce offspring with
  particular traits
NIH (8) National Institutes of Health
in vitro (9) occurring outside the body
genome (19) a chromosome and its genes
lucrative (19) profitable
bespeaks (21) indicates
reclusive (21) withdrawn from society
tenuous (30) insubstantial
quandary (31) dilemma
caricature (36) cartoonish takeoff
straw man (36) a weak opposition
fatalistic (36) believing that things are predetermined and that people are
  powerless
abate (39) decrease
brogue (40) accent
logistically (44) referring to the details of an operation

For all the emotion it has spawned, the stem cell issue has only been with us really since November 1998, when two teams of scientists, one at the University of Wisconsin, the other at Johns Hopkins University, announced they had cultured human cells that might have the power to become any cell or tissue in the body.

2   The stem cells derived by John Gearhart's group at Johns Hopkins actually came not from embryos, but from the primitive sex organs of aborted Baltimore fetuses. The fetuses were about two months old and resembled shrimp. The Wisconsin group grew its stem cells from 14 embryos donated anonymously by patients who had undergone fertility treatments at the University of Wisconsin Hospital in Madison.

3   The cells grown in the two labs were not exactly like any cells growing inside us. In the body, the inner cell mass of the embryo is an emerging life, a ballerina folded into herself before she begins to leap and pirouette. The cells these scientists extracted seem to replicate forever without fundamentally changing—as long as they are fed the proper mix of chemicals.

4   After more than a year, in which his original cells divided more than 300 times, Wisconsin researcher James Thomson finally froze the original batches "because we were tired of working on weekends." Before they were frozen, he had noticed that if the stem cells' diet was altered, or the colonies grew too dense, they spontaneously began to differentiate into blood cells, pulsating cardiac muscle, spiky neurons. It would clearly take a lot of work to understand and control those changes, let alone to make a pancreas. But the potential was enormous.

5   To scientists, they are "immortalized" cells, because they have the potential to become any kind of cell. They could also be used to create a powerful new biological tool—a template for testing new drugs and toxins and studying the biochemical pathways of the healthy and the sick. The cells might provide an alternative to some animal testing. And most importantly, someday, they could be used to build tissues that would regenerate Parkinsonian brains and rotting livers and decaying hips.

6   "It had always been thought that the stages of an organism were linear—once you leave one phase, it's gone forever. That once you have the misfortune of suffering a stroke, or a brain disease, you're in the wrong phase, it's too bad," says Harvard neurobiologist Evan Snyder. "It turns out that development is going on throughout your life. The stem cells don't disappear. You can pull them out, put them in a dish, grow them, put them back. Maybe there will be situations where we don't need to do organ transplants. We can rebuild organs from scratch, so to speak, with cells in a dish."

7   Within weeks of publishing their data, Thomson and Gearhart were swept up in a frenzied debate. To get to his laboratory, Gearhart, an earnest Midwesterner, sometimes had to pass hostile antiabortion protesters. At one point he and his 11-year-old daughter were driving down the street near his office and she turned to him with a shocked look. "My name is on those signs,"

Gearhart recalls her saying. Somebody was holding up a banner that read, "Gearhart and Johns Hopkins, Nazi Partners in Eugenic Experimentation."

8   While Thomson and Gearhart went forward in their work with funding from Geron Corp., the federal government proceeded cautiously. In 1996, back when few people knew anything about the potential of embryonic stem cells, Rep. Jay Dickey (R-Ark.), with Doerflinger's assistance, had successfully introduced an amendment to an appropriations bill prohibiting the NIH from funding scientific work "in which human embryos are damaged or destroyed."

9   But Thomson and Gearhart had changed the picture, and NIH, which opposed the Dickey amendment from the beginning and now saw an opportunity for major research advances, decided, essentially, to do an end run around the restriction. It got a legal opinion from the Department of Health and Human Services stating that while the amendment prohibited NIH from funding research that created or destroyed human embryos, NIH could fund research on cells from embryos that had been destroyed by someone else. The ruling formed the basis of the guidelines published Aug. 23 for embryonic stem cell research. To make sure in vitro fertilization patients weren't pressured into donating embryos, the guidelines stated that the fertility specialist who harvested the embryo couldn't be the same person who destroyed it to remove its cells. The parents of the embryo had to give informed consent, and the embryo had to be treated "respectfully."

10   But if NIH was trying to tread gingerly on the feelings of those who opposed the destruction of embryos, it failed spectacularly. Of the more than 50,000 people who responded to NIH's call for comment on last December's draft of the guidelines, more than three-quarters opposed them. Many of them called the NIH scientists baby killers and Nazi doctors. "The people who want to dissect a human embryo are the same people who want to pull a baby out of the mother's womb feet first and puncture the head and suck the brains out," says Dickey. "There's no difference in the two philosophies."

11   Doerflinger, writing on behalf of the bishops conference, asked acidly how it was possible to treat an embryo with respect while killing it, and how you could get informed consent from the people who agreed to have it killed. As for the NIH's end run around Dickey, Doerflinger says "it's like saying you won't pay to have someone kill me, but will experiment on my heart right after watching someone else rip it out of my body. Either way I'm dead . . ."

12   Among the patients who wrote in to oppose the guidelines was Chris Currie, a 37-year-old diabetic who, like Sam Melton, could benefit dramatically from stem cell research. But, he said, he would reject any cure or treatment that came from embryos. "I'm the one who has to think, 'What might this embryo have grown up to be? Would it have been someone who laughed and loved, married and had kids—all the things I've done? . . . How does God see this? What judgment will be laid upon me if I do this?' You can't so easily punt on those questions when you're the one who's directly benefiting."

13   The emotion and venom startled NIH, although it had been down this road before. Since 1993, it had funded research using cells from aborted fe-

tuses and faced intermittent attacks from abortion opponents. But fetal tissue was a different issue. The fetuses used in the work of about 300 NIH-funded researchers across the country, many of them brain scientists, had been aborted by women freely; NIH and these researchers had nothing to do with that choice.

14   But human embryos? Until about 20 years ago they existed only inside a woman's reproductive system. Technology made it possible to grow them in petri dishes, and today 330 fertility clinics in the United States do so. Typically they retrieve and fertilize 15 eggs from each woman who comes to them for treatment, but usually implant fewer than a third of those fertilized eggs. The remaining embryos die or are destroyed, or are donated, or put in storage. Fertility experts say at least 100,000 of these eggs are in storage in America.

15   The embryo put in deep freeze consists of about 100 cells, and each of these cells contains all the information needed to start a unique genetic existence. Each embryo is a potential life—very potential, but much more than abstract. Yet it's hard to work up empathy for these frigid particles, smaller than the tiniest hailstone. They are human, but are they humans? At the other end of the spectrum, brown-eyed Sam Melton, his blood sugar rising and falling with dizzying irregularity, is not in the least bit abstract. He's altogether more personable than the embryos. So are the 1.5 million individual Parkinson's patients who might gain from stem cell research, the 300,000 burn victims and potentially millions of others.

16   After testifying before Specter's subcommittee in January 1999, Doug Melton sat back and watched the whole debate with a mixture of impatience and disgust. To him, embryonic stem cell research carried a moral imperative that went beyond his family's experience. He saw no substantial excuse not to begin.

17   "In a few years they may be able to make embryos from blood cells. Does that make blood donation an abortion? Is masturbating half an abortion? I'm not a zealous nut who's sure this is the only way to cure the disease, but like all parents of diabetic children, I think it's our nation's obligation to use the enormous resources we have to pursue ways of making lives better."

18   From the beginning NIH intended to push forward. "You'll notice we invited comments on the guidelines—we didn't invite comments on whether we would fund the research," says Lana Skirboll, director of science policy at NIH. Still, "the length of time this has taken is a reflection of the care we've given the issue."

19   But Melton had begun to conclude that NIH, long the chief supporter and funder of biomedical research in the United States, wasn't going to move fast enough on this front for him. The politics and bureaucratic necessities were bogging things down, and who knew for how long. Meanwhile, the private sector was moving in on NIH's turf. With the Human Genome Project to map out the human genetic code, private companies were ready and eager to compete with the federal government and pay for exotic research that held out the promise of lucrative new drugs and therapies. Stem cell research was a hot

new arena for biotech companies. And so, while much of the scientific community was waiting to see whether the NIH would fund embryonic stem cell research, Doug Melton was making other calculations.

20   On a Thursday morning in spring, Melton is standing in the auditorium on the secluded campus of the Howard Hughes Medical Institute in Chevy Chase, preparing to address 40 people who have nothing to do with the federal government but have lots of money to devote to cutting-edge medical research.

21   Everything about the institute bespeaks power and wealth: The rooms are high-ceilinged, almost cathedral-like; the furniture hand-crafted wood, very expensive; the carpets are deep and soothing; the glassed-in courtyard crawling with feathery vines and potted palms. In the institute's foyer is a full-size oil painting of Howard Hughes, the reclusive billionaire who created the institute, in his pilot's suit.

22   Melton is no stranger here. In addition to being chairman of Harvard's department of molecular and cellular biology, Melton since 1994 has been one of the 300 top U.S. biomedical researchers on whom the Hughes Institute lavishes ample, opened-ended funding, allowing Melton to devote his life to the single-minded pursuit of the pancreatic beta cell. Once a year, Hughes asks its fundees to come to Chevy Chase and explain their research, their plans. To fulfill that request Doug Melton has flown in from Boston.

23   As an introduction to Melton's talk, Thomas Cech, a Nobel laureate and the director at Hughes, makes a slight joke. He says that the first time he met Doug he thought to himself; "He's too nice to be at Harvard." Everyone laughs. Melton does seem awfully gentle and plain-spoken as he lays out his plan of attack on the pancreas-making problem.

24   So far, he tells the group, he has been able to direct the creation of generic pancreatic cells from the embryonic stem cells of mice. But he has been unable to get the specialized pancreatic cells that make insulin. After such cells are created, the next logical step would be to devise a way to transplant the cells into diabetic mice without generating an adverse immune-system reaction. There are many steps ahead, many challenges, and that's why, Melton says, he wants to take the next step, and start using human cells—embryonic stem cells, to be precise.

25   "I used to hold the view that we should wait until we cured diabetes in the mouse," he concludes. "But I guess I changed my view because I'm getting older and life is short."

26   The questions from this audience, which includes some top scientists as well as administrators and clerical staff, are polite and to the point. Technical issues are raised. Questions are asked about the origins of diabetes and its sharp increase in the United States in recent years. This is not a religious crowd, or a politics-saddled NIH review committee. This is a group that supports Melton's research and understands that, as much as it may sound like pie-in-the-sky material to the lay person, most scientists believe it is likely that someday Melton will succeed.

27   As Andrew McMahon, a British scientist at Harvard who does similar work with kidneys, puts it: "It's not only reasonable, it's inevitable that this problem will be solved."

28   In fact, scientists are beginning to use stem cells to cure diseases. Osiris Pharmaceuticals in Baltimore has begun clinical trials using connective tissue stem cells to rebuild human muscle. Scientists in Colorado have had some success using stem cells from aborted human fetuses to treat Parkinson's.

29   The key part of Melton's visit to Hughes comes after his talk, over lunch at the institute cafeteria with Cech and James Gavin, a diabetes expert. Melton is hoping that the Hughes Institute, born of Hughes's antigovernment paranoia, can help him bypass the government's reluctance to fund controversial research. The symbolism is not lost on him.

30   The three men talk about NIH's stem cell dilemma and about other difficulties that the lobbying against this research is causing. The Hughes Institute would like to help him obtain the stem cells and understands the issues involved. "An agency like NIH is vulnerable to political tides and under obligation to try and reflect some sense of a national consensus on an issue of this type," says Gavin. "It will always be in a somewhat tenuous position with respect to an issue like stem cells. It's not that the private sector feels no obligation to consider ethical issues. But what the private sector can do is come to a decision after due diligence, and proceed with a sense of its own mission."

31   That said, the institute can't help Melton out of his current quandary. At present, the sole American source of embryonic stem cells is the University of Wisconsin, which has set up a corporation that offers academic researchers access to James Thomson's cells. More than 100 researchers have expressed interest in the cells—they cost $5,000 up front for a starter kit. But the contract sent to Melton for use of the cells comes with two unusual clauses. One states that Geron Corp., which funded the research on stem cells at both Wisconsin and Johns Hopkins, holds the rights to any discovery arising from work with Thomson's cells; the other, a generic bailout clause, says that the university's foundation can at any time order Melton within 90 days to destroy the stem cells and any experiments he's done with them.

32   Harvard won't go along with these terms. Neither, it turns out, will the Hughes Institute. Melton leaves Hughes feeling disappointed. As he heads back toward his son and his lab in Boston he examines his other, limited, options. Melton knows that a group in Australia has created its own immortal embryonic stem cell lines. British and Israeli researchers are also trying to develop the cells. Given that Congress and NIH are not moving ahead swiftly on the issue, that could leave Melton with what he calls "the extreme possibility." By which he means he would take his family and, in the name of science and his diabetic son, "move out of the country."

33   The Clinton administration has tried to create a consensus on stem cell research, but it seems to have changed few minds. Beginning early last year, the 18-member National Bioethics Advisory Commission (NBAC) held 10 stem

cell meetings around the country and compiled 3,000 pages of testimony from clerics and philosophers, scientists and doctors, lawyers and sociologists. A committee of the American Association for the Advancement of Science pondered stem cells at length, as did an NIH advisory board.

34   None of the stem cell panels contained a single member strongly opposed to embryo research, so to critics, their decisions seemed to be foregone. "The basic function of these panels seems to be articulate reasons for what the people who appointed them already wanted to do," Richard Doerflinger said not long after NBAC issued its report saying stem cell research should go forward.

35   And so the battle shifted to Congress, where legislation both to allow and to prohibit federally funded stem cell work has been introduced. About 90 patient groups that wanted embryonic stem cell research to go forward joined last spring to create CURE—Coalition for Urgent Research, which enlisted scientists and high-profile patients like Christopher Reeve and Parkinson's sufferer Michael J. Fox to argue their case. In response, a smaller collection of clergy and doctors opposed to embryonic stem cell research formed Do No Harm.

36   The names—CURE vs. Do No Harm—provide a catchy, but caricatured summation of the conflict. It is surely hype to claim that stem cells will bring cures, because no one can, with certainty, predict the outcome of such basic research. And the effort to block stem cell research at times appears to be a straw man for the abortion debate. But the two names do reflect a more basic cultural difference—between an interventionist, technical approach and an inevitably fatalistic, religious worldview.

37   In the Senate, Arlen Specter and Tom Harkin (D-Iowa) have introduced legislation that would allow NIH-backed scientists not only to use embryonic stem cells, but to derive them from IVF embryos. In the House, Carolyn Maloney (D-N.Y.) and Constance Morella (R-Md.) have introduced a resolution supporting the NIH guidelines and are using it to muster resistance to a new Dickey-led push to legislate an outright ban on embryonic research. After doing head counts on the bill, the House leadership apparently has decided not to allow Dickey or anyone else to add anti–stem-cell-research language to the appropriations bill that provides funding for NIH.

38   "There seems to be a gentleman's agreement that [the appropriations bills] won't be touched," a frustrated Doerflinger said after hearing of the decision this summer. Now, everything rests on the election. Republican presidential nominee George W. Bush opposes the NIH guidelines and could override them if elected. Even if Democratic nominee Al Gore becomes president, Republicans could try a legislative attack on the research—but it's unlikely they'll have the votes, opponents acknowledge.

39   On the sidelines, many cell biologists have come to hope that Congress will do nothing. They believe that if NIH research were to get started and produce some therapeutic successes, social fears would abate, as they did years

ago over organ transplants. "Transplantation is a taboo in our society until it works," says Ronald McKay, a leading NIH stem cell researcher.

40   McKay, whose Scottish origins are evident in his brogue, doesn't scoff at the public's queasiness about stem cell research. After appearing recently on a BBC program about stem cells with Doerflinger, McKay asked a few relatives back in London what they thought of it. They told him his work sounded "spooky"—the "yuck factor" at work.

41   "The Catholic position is probably closer to that of the public than ours," McKay concedes. "I have colleagues who say that with some easy genetic engineering we could make humans without a forebrain. And grow that. For harvesting organs. I find that spooky. And yet these colleagues say, 'Ron, what's the problem? That wouldn't be a person.'"

42   McKay, for his part, wishes that NIH had forced the stem cell issue instead of issuing guidelines that tried, and failed, to please everyone. He believes, as do Specter and Harkin, that federally funded scientists should be permitted to derive stem cells from embryos, as well as use them. Limiting work done in the public arena, McKay believes, will simply drive it into private firms that are under no obligation to release information about their experiments.

43   "America spends $15 billion a year on biomedical research," McKay says, looking out his fifth-floor window over a growing thicket of buildings on the NIH campus. "It's one of the greatest things about America. If you put basic data in private hands, you're going to change the nature of biology, and of life."

44   As it is, some scientists won't be seeking NIH funding even if Congress doesn't intervene to shut down the research. The NIH guidelines are too narrow and restrictive, they say, too politically correct and logistically impractical. They'd rather go to the private sector. Johns Hopkins's John Gearhart, already funded by Geron Corp., says patient groups are lining up to support his research with private money. "They're all interested. Millions of people could benefit from this," he says.

45   Geron Corp., which created a minor scandal by successfully filing a patent in Europe for human cloning and also controls the patents in the United States for genes that apparently enable cells to divide forever, is one of a handful of companies moving ahead with stem cell efforts. When Thomas Okarma, the company's chief scientist, gave a talk at an AAAS meeting this spring, many scientists could be seen madly scribbling notes.

46   "This is exactly why we need public-funded research," says a senior NIH official, who asked not to be named. "None of what he's talking about has been published." And that, the official says, can hurt both science and the public.

47   One chilly evening, McKay walks into a Chevy Chase condominium where 26 gray-haired people, most of them in their fifties, are waiting for him to address their Parkinson's support group. Parkinson's patients lack

dopamine-producing neurons, a type of brain cell involved in movement, among other things. Parkinson's is a progressive disease, and many of those here tonight are early Parkinson's patients—they've got symptoms like shaking hands and depression and fatigue and disrupted sleep. But they're baby boomers, a generation accustomed to getting what it wants, and they aren't too sick to be squeaky wheels. Research on Parkinson's is well funded, and it has reached the stage where new effective therapies might be available in five years.

48   "We're near," says Perry Cohen, a health policy consultant who has Parkinson's and helped organize the support group. "Parkinson's has a good chance of getting a product out the door."

49   As the evening goes on and their medication wears off, some people begin to tremble. Others don't seem to move at all. McKay searches for the simple terms to explain what he's doing, what he can realistically offer these people whose suffering is, after all, what allows him to do his research. "It's like we can grow these cells in our garden," he says. "You don't have to have Parkinson's to think that's pretty cool. But if you do have Parkinson's, it's quite interesting. We can make unlimited numbers of the cells that you're missing."

50   Rusty Glazer, a fit-looking 56-year-old who retired from the General Accounting Office this year because stiffness and gastrointestinal problems were bothering him at work, is weighing his own thoughts about stem cell transplants out loud. "Do you have any ethical issues with working with these cells?" he asks.

51   "Of course," McKay says. He clasps his hands and tips his head down in thought. "Look at it this way—I'm interested in how the brain works. And if that was my only motivation, maybe that wouldn't be enough of a reason to work with these cells. There are ethical questions. But there is brain disease, isn't there? So there are competing ethical questions here."

52   And around the room, a lot of people nod in agreement.

53   Richard Doerflinger, of course, does not agree. For him, the ethical imperative is to find alternatives to embryo research. So now he is hunkering down to convince Congress that adult stem cells are the right way to go. He is waiting to see what happens in the presidential election. And he recognizes that eventually this might have to end up in the courts.

54   "The lawyers I've asked are still scratching their heads about who has standing to sue," Doerflinger says. "The embryo can't. Members of Congress can't." But Doerflinger is determined to find someone who can.

55   For Doug Melton, back home in suburban Boston, the ethics of the matter come down to a little boy who, as we talk, has been dribbling a ball around the parlor and suddenly returns to the dining room and crawls into his mothers arms. "I need a cookie, Mom. I'm low," he says, meaning that his blood sugar has suddenly dropped, which can happen throughout the day with diabetics.

56   "I'm low, too," sister Emma says. "Can I have another cookie?" Everyone laughs.

57   Just to be sure, though, Gail does another pinprick test on Sam. And damned if the boy isn't telling the truth. During a half-hour conversation his blood sugar has plunged from 97 to 41—there's too much insulin and not enough glucose circulating in his blood.

58   "He's getting an insulin reaction," Gail says and sends Emma off quickly to get Sam's glucose tablets. "Did you play a lot of soccer today?" she asks her son. Sam nods and sits very still.

59   Gail strokes her son's forehead. Everyone holds his or her breath for a moment. "That's about 20 points away from a coma," Doug Melton says quietly. "If we had done nothing . . ."

60   The next day Melton is back in his lab at Harvard. A co-worker brings him a slide with cells she cultured from a 15-day-old mouse fetus. Under the microscope lies an archipelago of insulin-producing pancreatic beta cells, just what they've been trying to create. To be sure, these cells come from a rodent, and many steps lie ahead. But there's something about the view under the slide that's energizing.

61   The cells are stained deep blue. Somehow it seems a hopeful color.

Embryos under the Knife
LORI B. ANDREWS

Lori B. Andrews is a professor at Chicago-Kent College of Law and the director of the Institute for Science, Law, and Technology. The author of six books, Andrews wrote "Embryos under the Knife" to appear on the Internet site *Salon* in August 2000.

Preview. "Therapeutic cloning" is the creation of an embryo clone of a person in order to use the stem cells from the embryo to treat the person's illness. What do you think of this idea?

Vocabulary. If any of the following words from the essay are unfamiliar to you, study their meanings before reading.

in vitro (1)   outside the body
ectopic (1)   occurring somewhere other than in the uterus, as in the fallopian tubes
cede (2)   surrender
surrogate (5)   substitute
inexorably (5)   unrelenting
quadriplegic (7)   paralyzed in the arms and legs
articulating (10)   speaking
cavalier (10)   unconcerned
fodder (10)   feed
toxic (14)   harmful or poisonous
trove (17)   valuable collection
burgeoning (20)   blooming
touts (20)   praises
veritable (20)   actual
cadavers (28)   dead bodies

When Maureen Kass entered the in vitro fertilization program at a Long Island hospital, she took fertility drugs to increase the number of eggs she produced. Using a long needle guided by ultrasound, her doctor removed her eggs and fertilized them in a plastic dish with her husband's sperm. In eight attempts, she became pregnant twice. The first one ended in a miscarriage; the other resulted in an ectopic pregnancy that had to be surgically removed. Already the Kasses had spent nearly $75,000 on their fertility treatments, but still no baby.

2   On the ninth attempt, Maureen's doctors removed 16 eggs. Nine were fertilized—too many to be safely implanted into Maureen. So five embryos

were frozen for later use. Like most IVF clinics, the hospital insisted that the couple sign an advance directive regarding the fate of the frozen embryos in case the Kasses no longer wished to use them. The choices were to terminate the embryos, donate them to another couple, or cede them to research. The Kasses chose research.

3   Now their private decision is at the heart of a public controversy. In the next few months, Congress will decide whether a ban on research that destroys embryos should be lifted altogether. At fertility clinics across the country, over 150,000 human embryos lie suspended in liquid nitrogen tanks resembling three-foot-tall thermoses. Scientists and biotech companies want access to these embryos, not to create a baby for an infertile couple, but to use the embryos' stem cells to produce medical treatments. These primitive cells can grow into every type of tissue, including nerves, bones and muscles. But turning human embryos into biological factories raises enormous ethical concerns, converting potential people into products and launching us on a slippery slope toward genetic enhancement and the cloning of human beings.

4   I've spent the last 20 years studying the ever-growing monster of reproductive technology and have followed the debate about embryo research with increasing alarm. What seems to be a simple issue of medical progress—Can we save lives with tissue that would never otherwise be used?—has the potential to turn into a sci-fi nightmare that many would not imagine possible.

5   Each step along the way, from sperm donation to in vitro fertilization to surrogate mothers to embryo research, we have gradually yet inexorably moved closer and closer toward engineering human life to fulfill individual desire. The compelling tales of infertile couples moved us to endorse creating the potential test-tube babies. And the hopeful pleas of the sick and injured are making us consider the idea of medical research on the leftover embryos. Now a British panel of doctors has suggested that their government allow cloned embryos for research purposes.

6   This week, Great Britain's chief medical officer, Liam Donaldson, urged Parliament to allow doctors to begin "therapeutic cloning." This involves creating an embryo that is a clone of the patient and using that embryo as the source of stem cells, which would guarantee that the resulting tissue is not rejected. Yet perfecting a technique to clone human embryos would pave the way for any such embryo to actually be implanted in a woman to create a living, breathing human clone.

7   Stakes are high on both sides. At congressional hearings last April, the former Man of Steel, Christopher Reeve, urged the use of embryo stem cells on spinal cord injury victims. Reeve, rendered quadriplegic after a fall from a horse, is confined to a wheelchair which he directs with his breath (a hard breath turns it right, a soft one, left). To speak, he must wait for his respirator to swish air over his vocal chords.

8   "Why has the use of discarded embryos for research become such an issue?" Reeve asked. "Is it more ethical for a woman to donate unused embryos

that will never become human beings, or let them be tossed away as so much garbage when they could help save thousands of lives?"

9   But critics of embryo research hold no truck with such rhetoric. David Prentice, an embryologist at Indiana State University, likens Reeve's argument "to the one in Nazi Germany saying we're going to have these Jews killed, so why not experiment on them?"

10   A little inflammatory? Perhaps, but Prentice is articulating the concerns of many who are dismayed by the headlong rush towards embryo stem cell research and what it signals about medicine's increasingly cavalier attitude toward human life. Since removal of the cells destroys the embryo itself, some women have also voiced their concern that embryos will become nothing more than research fodder.

11   "It's not like I left a toenail cell at the clinic," says Risa York, an in vitro fertilization patient with seven frozen embryos. "Each embryo is a potential child. We have to be very careful—and respectful—about how we make decisions about them."

12   Despite such dissenting views, embryo research now seems inevitable. This month, the National Institutes of Health (NIH) plans to give the go-ahead for embryo stem cell research—a slap in the face to legislators who believe that it violates an existing federal law banning research which destroys embryos. NIH claims to have found a loophole: federally funded researchers will not remove the cells themselves (which would terminate the embryos), but will perform research on cells that have already been removed.

13   Douglas Johnson, legislative director of the National Right to Life Committee, responds bluntly: "If we had a law that barred research in which porpoises were killed, no one would entertain for five seconds that a federal agency could arrange for someone else to kill the porpoises and then proceed to use them in research."

14   The upcoming congressional bill, sponsored by Sen. Arlen Specter, R-Pa., will allow federally funded embryo stem cell research on leftover in vitro embryos, like the ones the Kasses stored at the Long Island clinic. This bill, which has overwhelming support due to the compelling testimony of patients like Reeve, would lead to massive experiments on embryos by researchers at the NIH and at university labs and medical centers that receive federal funding. Already, on the NIH Web site, every institute has posted a plan for what it will do if it can use embryo stem cells. The Heart, Blood and Lung Institute wants to repair failing hearts and grow new heart chambers. General Medical Sciences wants to develop artificial skin. Even Environmental Sciences wants to get into the act, proposing to use embryo stem cells to test "the toxic effects of biologicals, chemicals and drugs."

15   Yet if this sounds like an issue that will divide pro-lifers with their strict life-is-sacred values against liberal humanists with their let's-control-fate-through-science convictions, think again. While staunch pro-lifers, such as Sen. Gordon Smith, R-Ore., have embraced the research because of its potential

medical benefit, some pro-choice Protestant groups are lobbying against the bill.

16   Protestant theologian Gilbert Meilander of Valparaiso University in Indiana argues that while abortion is justified because of the claims of the pregnant women, "there is no such direct conflict of lives involved in embryo research." The 8.5 million member United Methodist Church opposes embryo stem cell research on the grounds that it turns human life into a commercial product.

17   A far-fetched fear? Not for the West Coast infertility clinic director who recently called me for advice about the unclaimed embryos in his care. Recognizing that human embryos are now a treasure trove of potential medical cures, he queried: "We have lots of embryos that couples haven't asked about for a while. Can we sell them to a biotech company?"

18   But imagine the heartache of the couple who comes back to the clinic a few years later to get pregnant only to learn that their future child has been turned into a kidney. Even couples like the Kasses, who checked off "research" on the forms, might have expected that the clinic would be doing the sort of research that was most important to the couple—infertility research. They might be appalled by the idea that their embryo was converted into a set of nerve cells that was for sale to the highest bidder.

19   And what if the couple now disagree on the fate of the embryo? After their ninth attempt at in vitro fertilization failed, Maureen and Steve Kass divorced. She then wanted to use her frozen embryos to create a child, but Steve disagreed. After five years of litigation, the highest New York court decreed that the fate of the embryo was governed by the form the couple had initially filled out, saying leftover embryos could be used for research. Although Mrs. Kass desperately wants a baby from the embryos created with her eggs, those embryos are now fodder for research.

20   What's perhaps more disturbing is that there's no guarantee that embryo stem cells will be used to cure serious diseases. Indeed, biotech companies can make more money by offering to use them for the burgeoning market of "enhancement" medicine. Where cardiac patients might need new heart cells to repair a damaged chamber, athletes may use these same cells to increase stamina. Geron Corp., which holds the exclusive U.S. license on embryo stem cell technology, touts the artificial skin it is developing as a treatment not just for burn victims but for people with sun damage and other age-related conditions. Indeed, 70-year-old Specter let slip his real interest in embryonic stem cells when he referred to them as "a veritable fountain of youth."

21   "You could use embryo stem cells for genetic engineering and enhancement," says Prentice, who predicts that doctors will say: "If you want to be a marathon runner, we'll fix that for you."

22   Across the world, government policymakers are eyeing the United States to see how the laws around embryo research will develop. Many countries have national bans on embryo research that forbid even privately funded companies like Geron from undertaking such work. A member of the French Par-

liament is concerned that medical products made from human embryo cells will become so routine that Europeans will inadvertently use them, despite their own laws. He advocates an "ethical" label, like the European labels that indicate which foods are genetically engineered and which clothes were not made with child labor, to give people a choice not to partake of the products of human embryos.

23   Specter is trying to head off criticism by including two restrictions in his bill. The proposed law bans the *creation* of embryos for research (relying only on "excess" embryos from infertility clinics) and forbids the implantation of cloned embryos to create humans. But neither limit is likely to last. As Dr. Edmund Pellegrino of Georgetown University, a Roman Catholic physician and ethicist, puts it: "How is it possible to separate 'spare' embryos from embryos intentionally produced as stem cell sources? The temptation to make 'spares' is obvious."

24   And eventually, even the bright line against cloning whole humans will grow blurry. Specter's cosponsor on the bill, Sen. Tom Harkin, D-Iowa, has already gone on record as favoring human cloning. When President Clinton previously urged Congress to ban cloning, Harkin said there should be no limits to scientific research. He told Clinton, "Take your ranks alongside Pope Paul V who in 1616 tried to stop Galileo."

25   Does opposing embryo stem cell research really mean throwing in one's towel with the Pope Pauls of history? Or is there something to be said for restraining the technologies that control life?

26   Ironically, despite charges that this ban will block promising medical research, it may be having just the opposite effect. The legal restrictions on embryo stem cell research (including flat-out bans on embryo research in eight states—Florida, Maine, Massachusetts, Michigan, Minnesota, North Dakota, Pennsylvania, and Rhode Island) have sent scientists scurrying to find other body cells with similar properties. Over the past year, a series of scientific breakthroughs occurred that challenged the traditional idea that adult cells were permanently wedded to their specialized roles in the body.

27   "Everyone thought that adult cells had gone past the point of no return," says geneticist Eugene Pergament of Northwestern School of Medicine. "But now we know that, from a genetic perspective, any cell with a nucleus can be made into a stem cell."

28   In research on mice, Italian and Canadian scientists found that adult stem cells from the brain can shed their identities and reinvent themselves as blood cells. Researchers at the University of Toronto discovered retinal stem cells in adults that could be used to regenerate damaged eyes. Pancreatic stem cells—including those taken from cadavers—can be persuaded to create insulin-producing cells. And, just this week, researchers announced that adult stem cells from bone marrow can create nerve cells to potentially treat Alzheimer's, Parkinson's, or spinal cord injuries.

29   The latest findings suggest that adult stem cells have a development repertoire close to that of embryo stem cells. They retain their potential after long-term culture, and can be frozen for later use. If adult stem cells live up to their potential, there may be less reason to disturb those souls-on-ice in infertility clinics.

30   "The issue is bigger than the fate of some embryos," says Risa York. "It's possible to be pro-choice and still respect human embryos as life." She worries that commercializing embryos—seeing them as just the raw material for medical products—is a trend that could diminish us all. Yet in an era when reproductive medicine is changing faster than a baby grows, York's vision may soon seem quaintly antiquated.

Helping People Requires
Making Hard Decisions
PAUL ROOT WOLPE

Paul Root Wolpe is on the faculty at the Center for Bioethics, department of psychiatry and department of sociology, at the University of Pennsylvania. "Helping People Requires Making Hard Decisions" first appeared in the *Philadelphia Inquirer* in September 2000. In the selection, Wolpe recognizes the benefits of stem cell research and calls for ethical guidelines that will allow the research to proceed.

Preview.   Wolpe believes we need to allow stem cell research to go forward—within certain ethical guidelines—because it holds promise for alleviating human suffering. He calls this posture a compromise. In what way do you predict it is a compromise?

Vocabulary.   If any of the following words from the selection are unfamiliar to you, study their meanings before reading.

undifferentiated (2)   lacking specific identity
sinew (2)   connective tissue
advocacy (6)   embracing a cause, helping
transgenic (9)   across species
blastocysts (9)   cells in a developing embryo
scrutiny (11)   close examination
alleviate (12)   lessen
valiant (12)   brave

Experiments are under way, or soon will be, on growing new brain tissue for people with Parkinson's disease, new pancreatic cells for diabetics, new tissue for damaged hearts—replacement parts for organs and tissues that are failing, injured or malfunctioning.

2   What makes these advances possible? The new field of embryonic stem-cell technology. These are the undifferentiated cells in a developing embryo that will eventually grow into human organs, skin, bone, sinew—all the tissues of our body. Scientists have isolated those cells and are learning how to control their growth. The implications for relief of suffering and disease are tremendous.

3   As with many such breakthroughs, however, there is a catch. The most reliable source of these cells today are frozen human embryos and aborted fetuses.

4   The National Institutes of Health, which has banned the use of federal funds for embryo research in general, has just released a set of controversial guidelines that will allow federally funded researchers to do stem-cell research under carefully monitored conditions. For example, the stem cells must be derived from embryos that are "in excess of clinical need" (that is, are going to be discarded anyway), and donors must be informed and consent to the research use of their embryos. Some see the guidelines as a reasonable compromise, while others see them as an end-run around the ban on embryo research.

5   **Opposition:** George W. Bush opposes the guidelines and has said he would block the NIH plan through executive order if elected. A group of conservative lawmakers, led by Sen. Sam Brownback, R-Kan., and Rep. Jay Dickey, R-Ariz., have vowed to block the changes.

6   On the other hand, a coalition of more than 25 patient advocacy groups, including the Juvenile Diabetes Foundation, the National Health Council, the American Association for Cancer Research and the Christopher Reeve Paralysis Foundation, praised the NIH guidelines as a major step in the treatment of disabling diseases. The Clinton administration and Al Gore also are strong supporters.

7   The stem-cell controversy is only one example of the moral dilemmas that will face us as we gain the power to grow organs, replace genes, even mix species. We are becoming the craftsmen of our own bodies in ways never dreamed of by our forebears. We may find old ways of looking at these issues lacking.

8   Some argue, for example, that we should not destroy any cell or tissues (like the fertilized egg, or embryo) with the power to develop into human beings. Once, that was a fairly clear proposition. An embryo was an embryo, and it lived only in a woman's womb.

9   Now we can create parts of embryos, potential embryos, transgenic embryos, blastocysts and fetal tissue and cloned transgenic embryonic cells—which we can then freeze, store, split, reunite and then plant in a womb. Every cell in your body today is a potential human being if we use cloning technology. The old definitions are no longer applicable; simple discussions of "potential human beings" no longer fit scientific reality.

10   The answer is not to throw up our hands or to suggest that there can be no morality in the new biotechnologies. On the contrary, what is needed is a renewed ethical inquiry, an attempt to craft a modern scientific morality that retains our basic ethical principles in the bewildering world of cellular genetics.

11   The NIH guidelines are an admirable attempt to do just that. They clearly affirm that embryos are more than convenient tissues, that the creation of an embryo may never be a casual or calculated act, and that only those embryos already slated for destruction may be used—and then, as few as possible. They encourage stem-cell research in federally approved programs, open to the scrutiny of the public, rather than in private biotech companies with no public oversight or accountability.

12   Is the compromise perfect? Probably not. But it is an attempt to negotiate the tough new moral world of biotechnology, to protect reproduction and the moral status of the embryo while allowing important research that will ultimately alleviate grave human suffering. In our imperfect immoral world, it seems to me a valiant and admirable stance.

FROM READING TO WRITING

Drawing on One Essay

1. *"God and Science."* Summarize the views on both sides of the stem cell issue. Then explain whether the debate is best framed as God vs. science, being sure to explain your view.
2. *"God and Science."* In paragraph 14, Allen notes that sometimes eggs not used for fertilization die, are put in storage, or are destroyed. What do you think should be done with these eggs? Why?
3. *"Embryos under the Knife."* Summarize Andrews's arguments against stem cell research and note which are the most compelling.
4. *"Embryos under the Knife."* Agree or disagree with the court ruling mentioned in paragraph 19.
5. *"Helping People Requires Making Hard Decisions."* In paragraph 10, Wolpe says that we need "to craft a modern scientific morality that retains our basic ethical principles in the bewildering world of cellular genetics." Do you think the NIH guidelines he mentions in paragraph 11 accomplish this? Explain.

Drawing on Two or Three Essays

6. In paragraph 7 of "God and Science," Allen notes that a protestor's sign refers to stem cell researchers as partners in Nazi eugenic experiments. If necessary, research what Nazi eugenic experiments were. Then explain whether the comparison is fair and accurate.
7. Write a letter to the National Bioethics Advisory Committee giving your views on guidelines for the procurement and use of embryos for research. Consider whether a woman should be told her embryos might be used for research, whether private companies can pay women for embryos, whether women can become pregnant in order to donate embryos, and anything else you think is significant.
8. The stem cell research debate involves conflicting ethical issues. Explain what they are and how they conflict. If you can think of a resolution or suitable compromise, discuss it.
9. Research the early controversy surrounding organ transplants, and explain the similarities and differences between that controversy and the one surrounding stem cell research.

ACKNOWLEDGMENTS

Allen, Arthur: "God and Science," from *The Washington Post*. © 2000 by Arthur Allen. Reprinted by permission of the author.

Alvarez, Julia: "Hold the Mayonnaise," from *The New York Times Magazine*. © 1992 by Julia Alvarez. Reprinted by permission of Susan Bergholz Literary Services, New York. All rights reserved.

Andrews, Lori B.: "Embryos Under the Knife," from *Salon.com*. Reprinted with permission.

Angelou, Maya: "Graduation," from *I Know Why the Caged Bird Sings* by Maya Angelou. © 1969 & 1997 by Maya Angelou. Used by permission of Random House, Inc.

Baker, Russell: "Learning to Write," from *Growing Up* by Russell Baker. © 1982 by Russell Baker. Reprinted by permission of Don Congdon Associates, Inc.

Biotechnology Industry Organization: "Biotechnology in Agriculture," from the *Editors' and Reporters' Guide to Biotechnology, Bio 2000*, February 2000, http://www.bio.org/aboutbio/guide2000/guide_agriculture.html. © 2000 by Biotechnology Industry Organization. Reprinted by permission.

Chan, Sucheng: "You're Short Besides!" from *Making Waves: an Anthology of Writings by and about Asian American Women* edited by Yen Mei Wong, Diane. © 1989 by Asian Women United of California. Reprinted by permission of the author.

Cisneros, Sandra: "Only Daughter," from *Glamour*. © 1990 by Sandra Cisneros. Reprinted by permission of Susan Bergholz Literary Services, New York. All rights reserved.

Cole, Diane: "Don't Just Stand There," from *A World of Difference*, Special Supplement to *The New York Times*, April 1989. © 1989 Diane Cole. Reprinted by permission of the author.

Cowley, Geoffrey: "For the Love of Language," from *Newsweek* Fall/Winter 2000 Special Edition. © 2000 by Newsweek, Inc. All rights reserved. Reprinted by permission.

Daum, Meghan: "Virtual Love." This article originally appeared in *The New Yorker Magazine*, August 1997. © 1997 by Meghan Daum. Reprinted by permission of the author.

Dertouzos, Michael L.: "The Future of Computing," from *Scientific American* August 1999. Reprinted with permission. © 2000 by Scientific American. All rights reserved.

Dillard, Annie: "The Chase," from *An American Childhood* by Annie Dillard. © 1987 Harper & Row. Reprinted by permission of HarperCollins Publishers, Inc.

Douglass, Frederick: "How I Learned to Read and Write," from the *Life And Times of Frederick Douglass*, 1882.

Gage, Nicholas: "The Teacher Who Changed My Life," from *Parade*. Reprinted with permission of Parade, © 1989.

Gunnerson, Ronnie: "Parents Also Have Rights," from *Newsweek,* March 2, 1987. © 1987 by Ronnie Gunnerson. Reprinted by permission of the author.

Healy, Melissa: "Fighting to Fill the Values Gap," from the *Los Angeles Times,* 25 May 1986. Reprinted by permission.

Henderson, George: "Race in America," from National Forum: The *Phi Kappa Phi Journal.* © 2000 by George Henderson. Reprinted by permission of the publishers.

Hirschfelder, Arlene B.: "It Is Time to Stop Playing Indians," from the *Los Angeles Times,* November 25, 1987. © 1987 by Arlene Hirschfelder. Reprinted by permission of the author.

Johnson, Kirk: "Today's Kids Are, Like, Killing the English Language. Yeah, Right," from *The New York Times*. Reprinted by permission.

Kingsolver, Barbara: "Stone Soup," from *High Tide in Tucson.* © 1995 by Barbara Kingsolver. Reprinted by permission of the author.

Kleinfield, N. R.: "Stepping Through a Computer Screen, Disabled Veterans Savor Freedom," from *The New York Times,* 12 March 1995. Reprinted by permission.

Kluger, Jeffrey: "Can We Stay Young Forever?" originally from *Time,* November 18, 1996. © 1996 Time Inc. Reprinted by permission of Time, Inc. Reprinted with permission from the April 1997 Reader's Digest.

Lemonick, Michael D.: "Will Tiny Robots Build Diamonds One Atom at a Time?" from *Time Digital,* September 2000. © 2000 Time Inc. Reprinted by permission.

Leo, John: "Anti-Male Bias Increasingly Pervades Our Culture." Reprinted by permission of the author and *JewishWorldReview.com* at http://www.jewishworldreview.com.

Leslie, Connie with Daniel Glick and Jeanne Gordon: "Classrooms of Babel," from *Newsweek,* February 11, 1991. © 1991 by Newsweek, Inc. All rights reserved. Reprinted by permission.

Lewin, Tamar: "Growing Up, Growing Apart," from *The New York Times,* Section 1 page 1, June 25, 2000. Reprinted by permission.

Liu, Sophronia: "So Tsi-fai," originally from *Hurricane Alice,* Fall 1986. © 1986 by Sophronia Liu. Reprinted by permission of the author.

Luooma, Jon R.: "Pandora's Pantry," from *Mother Jones*. Reprinted by permission of The Foundation for National Progress.

Lutz, William: "Doublespeak," from *Doublespeak—From Revenue Enhancement to Terminal Living* by William Lutz. ©1989 Blonde Bear, Inc., a division of Harper & Row. Reprinted by permission of HarperCollins Publishers, Inc.

Malcolm X. and Alex Haley, "Coming to an Awareness of Language." Excerpt from *The Autobiography of Malcolm X* by Malcolm X and Alex Haley. © 1964 by Alex Haley and Malcolm X. © 1964 by Alex Haley and Betty Shabazz. Used by permission of Random House, Inc.

McKenna, George: "The Transmission of Hope," from the *Altantic Monthly,* May. 2000. © 2000 by George McKenna. Reprinted by permission of The Atlantic Monthly and the author.

Meier, Daniel: "One Man's Kids," from *The New York Times Magazine*. Reprinted by permission.

Miller, Bruce H.: "Life Is Measured by Grade-Point Averages," from the *San Jose Mercury News,* April 1982. Reprinted by permission of The San Jose Mercury News.

Morese, Jodie: "Is That Your Final Answer?" from *Time*. © 1999 Time Inc. Reprinted by permission.

Nash, Madeleine J.: "Grains of Hope," from *Time*. © 1996 Time Inc. Reprinted by permission.

Neal, Patsy: "My Grandmother, the Bag Lady," from *Newsweek*, February 11, 1985. ©1985 by Patsy Neal. Reprinted by permission of the author.

Noda, Kesaya E.: "Growing Up Asian in America" from *Making Waves: An Anthology of Writings by and about Asian American Women* edited by Yen Mei Wong, Diane. © 1989 by Asian Women United of California. Reprinted by permission of the author, Kesaya E. Noda.

Peterson, Karen S.: "The truth about our little white lies," from *USA TODAY*, July 26, 1983. © 1983, *USA TODAY*. Reprinted with permission.

Peyser, Marc and Donatella Lorch: "High School Controversial," from *Newsweek*, March 20, 2000. © 2000 by Newsweek, Inc. All rights reserved. Reprinted by permission.

Quealey, Nora: "Truck Assembly Line Worker," included in *Alone in a Crowd: Women Tell Their Stories* by Jane Reith Schroedel. Reprinted by permission of Temple University Press. © 1985 by Temple University. All rights reserved.

Rodriguez, Richard: "Complexion," from *The Hunger of Memory* by Richard Rodriguez. © 1982 by Richard Rodriguez. Reprinted by permission of Georges Borchardt, Inc., for the author.

Rodriguez, Richard: "The Achievement of Desire," from *The Hunger of Memory* by Richard Rodriguez. © 1982 by Richard Rodriguez. Reprinted by permission of Georges Borchardt, Inc., for the author.

Rose, Mike: "I Just Wanna Be Average." Reprinted with the permission of The Free Press, a Division of Simon & Schuster, Inc., from *Lives on the Boundary: The Struggles and Achievements of America's Underprepared* by Mike Rose. © 1989 by Mike Rose.

Rosenblatt, Roger: "Screams from Somewhere Else," from *Time*. © 1996 Time Inc. Reprinted by permission.

Sandroff, Ronnie: "Invasion of the Body Snatchers: Fetal Rights vs. Mothers' Rights." This article originally appeared in *Vogue*, October 1988. © 1988 by Ronnie Sandroff. Reprinted by permission of the author.

Santiago, Roberto: "Black and Latino." from *Boricuas: Influential Puerto Rican Writings—An Anthology* by Roberto Santiago. © 1989 by Roberto Santiago. Reprinted by permission of the author.

Sheehy, Gail: "Predictable Crises of Adulthood," from *Passages* by Gail Sheehy. © 1974, 1976 by Gail Sheehy. Used by permission of Dutton, a division of Penguin-Putnam Inc.

Sherry, Mary: "In Praise of the F Word," from *Newsweek*, May 6, 1991. © 1991 by Mary Sherry. Reprinted by permission of the author.

Siegel, Charles: "A New Declaration of Independence," from *Utne Reader*. Reprinted by permission of Northbrae Book and Utne Reader.

Stangl, Juthica: "India: A Widow's Devastating Choice," from *Ms.* © 1984 by Juthica Stangl. Reprinted by permission of the author.

Staples, Brent: "Just Walk on By: A Black Man Ponders His Power to Alter Public Space," from *Ms.* © 1986 by Brent Staples. Reprinted by permission of the author.

Steffan, Joseph: "Honor Bound," from *Honor Bound* by Joseph Steffan. © 1992 by Joseph Steffan. Used by permission of Villard Books, a division of Random House, Inc.

Tan, Amy: "Mother Tongue." © 1990 by Amy Tan. First appeared in *The Threepenny Review*. Reprinted by permission of the author and the Sandra Dijkstra Literacy Agency.

Tannen, Deborah: "Talk in the Intimate Relationship" from *That's Not What I Meant*. © 1986 by Deborah Tannen. Reprinted by permission of HarperCollins Publishers, Inc./ William Morrow.

Walker, Alice: "Beauty: When the Other Dancer Is the Self," from *In Search of Our Mothers' Gardens: Womanist Prose* by Alice Walker. © 1983 by Alice Walker, reprinted by permission of Harcourt, Inc.

Wallerstein, Judith and Sandra Blakeslee: "On the Brow of the Hill," from *Second Chances: Men, Women, and Children a Decade After Divorce.* © 1989 by Judith Wallerstein and Sandra Blakeslee. Reprinted by permission of Ticknor & Fields/Houghton Mifflin Co. All rights reserved.

White, E.B.: "Once More to the Lake," from *One Man's Meat*, text copyright by E. B. White. © 1941 by E. B. White. Reprinted by permission of Tilbury House Publishers, Gardiner, Maine.

Wolpe, Paul R.: "Trying to Retain Basic Principles in Fast-moving World of Genetics," from *The Philadelphia Inquirer.* © 2000 by Paul R. Wolpe. Reprinted by permission of the author.

Zabludoff, Marc: "Fear and Longing." © 1998 by Marc Zabludoff. Reprinted with permission of *Discover Magazine.*

INDEX

541